INTRODUCTION TO
Comparative
Politics

INTRODUCTION TO
Comparative Politics

*Challenges of Conflict and
Change in a New Era*

Fourth Edition

John D. Nagle

Syracuse University

Nelson-Hall Publishers/Chicago

Project Editor: Dorothy Anderson
Cover Painting: *Untitled*, by Katherine Steichen Rosing

Library of Congress Cataloging-in-Publication Data

Nagle, John D. (John David)
  Introduction to comparative politics : challenges of conflict and change in a new era / John D. Nagle. — 4th ed.
    p. cm.
  Includes bibliographical references (p.   ) and index.
  ISBN 0-8304-1408-8
  1. Comparative government. I. Title.
JF51.N34   1995
320.3—dc20   94-25615
                                                                        CIP

Manufactured in the United States of America

10   9   8   7   6   5   4   3   2   1

 The paper used in this book meets the minimum requirements of American National Standard for Information Sciences—Permanence of Paper for Printed Library Materials, ANSI Z39.48-1984.

Contents

ESSAY: THINKING ABOUT POST–COLD WAR POLITICS IN THE LIBERAL DEMOCRACIES

ESSAY: MANAGING CONFLICT AND CHANGE IN POST-COMMUNISM

ESSAY: FINALLY EXITING THE THIRD WORLD?

Preface to the Fourth Edition

Preparing this new edition has been a demanding challenge, quite different from the earlier editions. With the end of the Cold War, the collapse of European communism, the breakup of the Soviet Union, the end of the apartheid regime in South Africa, the unification of Germany, the expansion of the European Union, and a series of "earthquake" elections in Japan, Italy, France, and Canada, the comparative study of governments around the world must now focus on the politics of great change, rather than the normal politics of first, second, or third worlds. The classic or traditional Cold War patterns of performance are now in transition from a relatively known politics to a new and uncertain politics of managing great transformations of new kinds, without a road map or a patented "success formula." I have tried to convey the sense of this new era, to describe the kinds of challenges and conflicts that are reshaping political life for so many nations today, without pretense of predictive power or certainty of outcomes.

In this task, I have been aided by the advice and knowledge of many colleagues, including Ron McDonald, Steve Koff, John Agnew, Lou Kriesberg, Al Mazur, John Hodgson, Lily Ling, Mark Rupert, Reinhard Kühnl, Wilfried von Bredow, Hans See, Frank Deppe, Bernd Löwe, Peter Schultze, Claus Leggewie, Rainer Rilling, Eizens Silins, Ting Gong, Feng Chen, Jin Min Chung, Jin Young Kim, Jongwoo Han, Bing Hu, Alfredo Robles, Sankaran Krishna, Gautam Basu, Bhavna Dave, Lemmu Baissa, Geraldine Forbes, Skip Greenblatt, Mab Huang, Stefan Elkins, Tomas Kosma, Ferenc Zsigo, Katalin Fabian, Martina Klisperova, Viera Farkasova, Sona Hermochova, Jonathan Bach, Mara Ustinova, Andrei Zdravomyslov, Andrei Korneyev, Valery Tishkov, and Isidor Wallimann. Special thanks to Alison Mahr for her research on the data of the tables for this edition. Their ideas and commentary have been most helpful to my own thinking and interpretations, for which I bear responsibility, while they remain blameless.

1

Learning from Comparison—
Today More Than Ever

In some ways, the past several years have been a severe challenge for the field of comparative politics. The fast-moving events in Eastern Europe and the former Soviet Union and Yugoslavia have forced comparative scholars to rewrite and revise their treatments of the classic Communist political systems and gave birth to a new category of description, "post-communism," which says something about what has just collapsed but nothing about what is now in its place. More recently, in the liberal democracies, major political earthquakes have shaken the long-established party systems of Italy, France, Japan, and Canada, and have created a kind of unstable new array of political forces, parties, and movements. And in South Africa, India, Mexico, Korea, Taiwan, and Brazil, there are clear breakthroughs which are in the process of overturning the Cold War political order, creating a climate of both optimistic hope and worried anxiety about the turmoil of transition.

All of these events have given rise to the realization, now an expectation, that the world of nations has entered into a new era of major political transformation, which requires special attention to the key role of a "politics of managing great transitions." Comparative scholars (like myself) who have written texts in the previous era of relative stability of system-types (liberal democracies of the First World, communist systems of the Second World, and mostly authoritarian regimes of the Third World), must now rethink what are the most important features of a post–Cold War world of major transitions.

But this new era of great change has at the same time been a wonderful breath of fresh air for our work and has emancipated our thinking from old assumptions and "wisdoms" which, on further reflection, were often time bound to a particular era now past. As in the past, comparative politics has been given a new impulse for creativity by new events which demand a fresh analysis and a fresh framework for analysis. That is the spirit which I have attempted to bring to this introductory text, with the hope that it will arouse and inform the interest of students in the larger and yet ever-closer world of

1

nations. Even in the United States, with its self-image of uniqueness among nations, citizens and leaders are looking at other nations' ideas (especially Canada's and the Netherlands') of how to provide decent health care for their citizens, at other ways (especially in Japan and Germany) of building government-industry cooperation for research, development, and trade. Without a doubt the future of the United States and its citizens will be more closely tied to the outcomes of the major changes now underway in all regions of the globe than in previous eras, and I would encourage Americans to learn about the historic events unfolding now in Russia, South Africa, China, Nigeria, Japan, India, and Mexico, so that they may better understand the stake that Americans have in a peaceful, democratic, humane, and just politics in other nations, as well as their own.

Signs of a New Era for Comparison of Nations

What are the signs of this new era, and what role does comparative analysis have to play in understanding its meaning?

First and foremost, the whole system of Cold War divisions of the global community into blocs of nations and system-types has crumbled. The end of European communism has meant the end of communism as a clearly distinct political system-type in contemporary politics. Even though China remains a Communist system in theory, its economic reformism prophesies an end to this regime-type in the not-too-distant future. With the end of classic communism, however, the ties that bound the Western democracies together have grown weaker, and the commonalities of the Cold War, which helped define the community of liberal democracies, have given way to new pressures and new demands for major changes in party systems, in political life, and in policy agendas. And in the developing nations, the end of the Cold War has raised new challenges to ruling elites and to their record of authoritarian rulership and corrupt practices.

In the post-Communist systems, political life (and therefore political conflict) is engaged in several simultaneous great transformations to establish new governing institutions and new political processes, to marketize and privatize economic activity and find a place in the international finance and trading systems, and often to establish a new or reestablish an old national identity.

In the affluent liberal democracies, increasingly mobile capital investment in low-wage regions, challenges from new trading powers, and unfavorable demographic trends have produced a financial crisis of the welfare state, growing structural unemployment, and new regional, racial, and anti-immigrant strains in the social fabric. Old established leaderships and parties are seen as ineffectual and lacking in a vision for this new era, giving rise to a search for new parties or political leaders as diverse as Ross Perot in the

United States, the Northern Leagues in Italy, and younger, reformist, anti-corruption leaders like Tsutomo Hata and Morihiro Hosokawa who defected from the long-dominant Liberal Democratic party in Japan.

In those areas formerly designated as the Third World (neither affluent liberal democracies nor Communist), this period also is characterized by increased challenges to established elites by younger leaders, by new rising middle classes, by nonmilitary political parties and groups, and often by dissatisfied ethnic, religious, regional, or language groups. But the now-recognized qualitative differentiation among these nations and regions calls for some new descriptions of regions or particular cases in this period of great change. The common experiences of historical colonial domination and post-independence neocolonial dependency have been significantly and differently modified over the past thirty to forty years, and this variety is reflected in the type of challenge each regime faces.

As happened earlier in this century, the end of an era has been accompanied by the birth of new nations, or would-be nations. At the end of World War I, for example, there were several new nations born as democracies in Eastern Europe with the dismembering of the Austro-Hungarian Empire and parts of the Russian Empire. After the end of World War II, the decolonization era created nearly one hundred new nation-states from the British, French, Dutch, Spanish, United States, and later the Portuguese colonial domains. Now, in the most recent period, the breakup of the Soviet Union, Yugoslavia, Czechoslovakia, and Ethiopia has created over twenty new internationally recognized nation-states. Many other ethnic groups in South Asia, Africa, Central and Southwest Asia, the Caucasus, and Canada (Quebec) are also pushing for greater independence and perhaps nation-state status. We are in a third period in this century of a "birth of nations," in which new states are struggling to define their political systems and to maintain their new status.

In this new era of increasing globalization of finance, trade, and production, the comparison of nations must also come to terms with the challenge to the nation-state as the primary object of study. For some purposes, the nation-state has become too integrated in the global economy to be a fully sovereign, independent community which can be compared to other nation-states. The rise of economic regionalism, as in the European Community (since November of 1993 now officially the European Union), the North American Free Trade Agreement (NAFTA), the Association of South East Asian Nations (ASEAN), and perhaps eventually the Commonwealth of Independent States (CIS), calls for much greater attention to the international economic ties of nation-states (though it seems that there is as yet no correspondingly viable and dynamic political regionalism). At the same time, for other purposes, the nation-state has become too large, too bureaucratic, and too strong for some subnational groups, who fear the loss of their identity in

3

the homogenization of a national culture. Especially in periods of economic dislocation, fiscal crisis, and questioning of borders generally, the nation-state in the current era is vulnerable to autonomy movements, separatist demands, and ethnic liberation struggles. Comparative studies must deal with the question of whether the modern nation-state has become too overloaded and too overbearing for the variety of group-specific demands placed upon it, particularly in a "time of troubles."

Each of these developments taken separately would warrant major shifts in emphasis in the comparison of nations. Taken together, they demand a new framework, one which can still utilize the benefits of the comparative method but which frames the classic questions of the field anew.

A Defense of Comparative Analysis

The field of comparative analysis, particularly that area dealing with communist systems, has come under critical scrutiny in recent years for its failure to predict the sudden collapse of communism in Europe and the Soviet Union in 1989–91. This criticism is both accurate and at the same time useful if it reminds us of the limits not just of comparative analysis but of all fields of political inquiry, which are unable to predict short-term unusual events or upheavals with any reliability. On the other hand, if this criticism is meant to deny the usefulness of comparing nations or if this is meant to discourage the whole enterprise of comparative politics, then this implication is mistaken and should be rejected.

In fact, comparative studies of the European and Soviet Communist regimes throughout the 1980s did detail the decline in economic vitality of these regimes. Other studies demonstrated the growth of popular dissatisfaction, even among elites, with the old political system. The Gorbachev program was correctly seen as a major effort to address the deficiencies of the Soviet economy and to reform the Soviet political system in a major way. Most comparativists correctly saw *perestroika* and *glasnost* not as mere propaganda or as minor tinkering but rather as a major reform initiated from above by Gorbachev and his leadership team. Likewise, studies of the Chinese Communist reform project of Deng Xiaoping were correct in characterizing this process as a major change in that economic system, with wide-ranging consequences for the political regime's long-term maintenance. Careful study of the Soviet and Chinese communist reform projects of Michael Gorbachev and Deng Xiaoping brought out the forces that were pushing each regime to greater efforts to change their systems' performance. What could not be predicted was the point in time when major reform, and the instability which it produced, would go beyond reform within the existing political structures, when it would topple the existing structures.

In fact, comparative analysis as a whole did its job rather well, informing an interested citizenry and responsible political leaders about the longer-term trend of events, the implications of these reform movements, and both the difficulties they were meant to address and the new contradictions they would themselves introduce. It would have been exceptional and unrealistic to have expected that comparative analysis, or any other form of analysis, would have predicted, say in 1985 or even 1988, the dramatic turn of events from the summer of 1989 through the dissolution of the Soviet Union in December of 1991. Such powers of political prophesy, if they truly existed, would of course command greater attention and even greater monetary compensation that even the best minds now receive.

Another challenge to the project of comparing nations is, as mentioned above, the questioning of the nation-state as the proper, or at least the dominant, focus of interest of comparative analysis (Ross and Trachte, 1990). With the increasing globalization of economic activity, most particularly finance, commerce, and production, but also international migration of both professional and unskilled labor, the nation-state seems incomplete and less than adequate as a focal point for data collection and case analysis. Regionalism would seem to require a more transnational and multilevel form of analysis. And on the other hand, the recent rise of subnational forces, often related to ethnic, linguistic, religious, or regional minorities, may remind us that the nation-state is an aggregation which can mask very significant variations and inner conflicts.

In response, I would emphasize that there is of course no inherent reason why comparative analysis cannot be applied to regions and regional politics (where this exists) and to subnational groupings (whether geographically distinct or not). But at the same time, I would argue that the era of the nation-state, for better or worse, is by no means over; rather, it has become now the universal goal of virtually all peoples around the world. In some parts of South-Eastern Europe, the former Soviet Union, Central Asia, Africa, South Asia, and the Middle East, the formation of the nation-state as a political entity has not yet taken root or is at an early stage of development. And despite the growth of regional economic markets, of which the European Union (EU) is the most advanced, this has nowhere yet produced a regional political entity able to compete with or displace the nation-state for loyalty, identity, and political decision making. Whoever has any doubt about this proposition can look to the role of the European Union in the Balkan wars of the early 1990s. In its first major test in the post–Cold War era, the European Union failed miserably to formulate any coherent foreign or military policy on the civil wars in former Yugoslavia. National political differences among Germany, France, and Britain prevented any European initiative from emerging, and EU leaders were totally incapable of forging any "European policy" in the absence of a natural coincidence of nation-state perspectives. Nothing has yet replaced the nation-state as the largest effective political

5

aggregate. The nation-state remains today the largest aggregation of individuals for which political citizenship has palpable meaning.

In these circumstances, comparative analysis of nations and their political systems still supercedes analysis of both subnational and supranational units in importance, because that is the level at which the most important political decisions are made and implemented and to which most citizens direct their political behavior. At the same time, comparative politics must constantly review this situation, because as global economic integration continues, political life will over the long term be raised to the supranational level. Likewise, with the long-term weakening of the coherence of national economies, subnational or local political competition for benefits within the global economy will also increase.

In a more positive light, comparative politics has several advantages relative to other fields of political inquiry, such as American politics, international relations, and political theory. First of all, comparative politics is both empirical and theoretical. Comparative scholars must be skilled in practical research methods for studying different systems (empirical research, which can include language skills, living experience in another culture, and long-standing interaction with international scholars). Comparative scholars also utilize theory building, both inductive and deductive, as a basic component of their work. Inductive theory building comes from recognition of patterns and correlations from extensive empirical research in a wide variety of settings. This leads to general propositions, which then form hypotheses that can be tested through additional empirical work. Deductive theory building comes from the assembly of a small number of core theoretical assumptions from which testable hypotheses can be derived and confirmed or disconfirmed through empirical research. In practice, comparative research has been a synthesis of both inductive and deductive approaches, working in a dialectical pattern of competition over time. By comparison, American politics, by its inherent focus on one case, the United States, is very rich in empirical description but relatively weak in theory building. International relations, due in part to the dominance of the realist theoretical model and the struggle over that model at very abstract theoretical levels, has often in the last two decades become terribly abstract, with little empirical base and quite weak in practical research. Political theory is of course oriented heavily to theory and has only limited connections to any specific real-world research agenda.

Comparative politics, over the postwar period, has developed and offered "modernization theory" as its synthesis from theory and research practice. The debate over "modernization theory," beginning in the 1960s and continuing today (over issues of Eurocentric bias, for example), have given impulses for further research and the development of alternative theories (dependency theory, for example), which in turn have generated revisions and defenses from proponents of modernization theory.

In this process of combined inductive/deductive theory building and building a cumulative record of practical research, comparative politics has, I believe, identified and tried to deal with several major questions of human development, each of which will recur throughout this text in various contexts. First and foremost, is there one singular path of political development or are there several, each worthy in some way of qualifying as "development"? Does the Western path stand as the future for all other societies, or is history open enough to permit plural forms of political modernization? The answers to this question can be found only by making an ideological leap of principled faith or by serious attention to the actual evolution of many different political systems, which is the embodiment of the comparative method. The agenda of comparative research on this mega-question defines the limits of our predictive capacity in our study of long-term political system development.

A second key issue raised by comparative politics is the question of whether political development occurs by stages, each stage succeeding an earlier stage that has outlived its utility and each to be transcended later by a still more developed stage. Are there such clearly defined stages, or are there far more continuities, which make definitions of "stages" arbitrary and misleading? Are there possibilities of "skipping" stages, of some nations catching up with the most developed without going through each and every presumed "intermediate" stage? Is there still in the modern era the possibility of "regression" or "decline" among national political systems, so that, as in the case of some ancient empires and prosperous city-states, once-attained levels of competent governance may be lost and the political system fall into long-term decay? Is there a "final" stage, beyond which no general improvement can be made, because this is the perhaps rather boring "end to history?" The work of comparative politics on this mega-question has important implications for the extent of human control over or manipulation of political development, conversely for the limits of great reform or directed transformation.

Finally, comparative political analysis has built up a valuable storehouse of information on a series of important issues in the development of political systems. Comparative politics, more than any other field of political inquiry, has come to grips with the relationship between economic development and democratization. Does economic modernization have to come first, to be followed by democratic transformation? Can the two processes take place simultaneously or even reinforce each other? At what point does democratization become necessary for further development? The different paths taken by Korea, India, China, and Russia provide good examples from which other nations may draw important lessons by careful comparison of results. Comparative politics has also studied the processes of reform and revolution, their causes and effects. Does the failure or blockage of reform lead to revolution? What are the requisites for revolutionary change, and what are the longer-term effects of revolution? How do reform and revolution lead to both change and eventual conservative reaction? These issues are as relevant today in post-Communist East Europe and the former Soviet Union as in France after 1789, Russia after 1917, or Mexico after 1910. Comparative politics has studied the policy processes and outcomes of different nations, in particular, fields such as industry, education, health care, housing, and social security. Comparisons of the policy process in the Western democracies, in the classic Communist systems, and in Latin American nations have become part of the research agenda of the field of comparative politics. What can one Western democracy learn from the health care policies of other democracies? What is the range of economic development policies that have worked for the East Asian nations?

This is, of course, not everything, but it is an impressive array of issues that, especially in the current era of great transformations, are important for both citizens and political decision-makers. This text will attempt to involve students in thinking for themselves about these issues and how their outcomes affect the future of our country, in the admittedly idealistic belief that an informed and involved citizenry is the crucial foundation for the American democracy.

Competing Value Systems, Political Choice, and System Performance

In comparing political systems, we will be faced with how different regimes make political choices as to what will be top priorities for allocation of resources and what will be lower priorities or neglected areas. In making these choices, regimes try to legitimate their allocations according to some values or to some coherent set of values (value systems, often labeled ideologies), and their opponents dissent (insofar as audible dissent is possible) according to some different set of values (dissent on strictly technical issues aside). These value systems or ideologies are in basic contradiction to each other and produce competing ideas about what problems are most important and how to allocate resources through government action and inaction. In any political system, and in any policy area, values and value systems will be utilized by competing interest groups to justify their policies and actions.

Historically, in the Western tradition at least, we can identify three basic ideologies that in the modern era continue to shape political discourse: conservatism, liberalism, and socialism. Each of these grand perspectives offers a coherent world view or *Weltanschauung,* a set of values or priorities for human society, and its own image of the good society. Each has demonstrated its capacity to motivate citizens, to legitimate or to challenge regimes, to inspire new beginnings for nations. Each ideology leaves out or minimizes values other than its own and is therefore incomplete as a description of what human beings desire or how they relate to society; each, pushed to its own extreme or utopian end, contains the seeds of dystopia and catastrophe.

No matter what some ideologues may claim, there exist several contradictory value systems rather than one, because the human condition itself is full of contradictions. If there were in fact one unified ideology that could capture the essence of the human condition, then it would by now have become apparent, and alternative competing ideologies would have died out. The most basic contradictions of the human condition are related to three key quandries:

1. Human beings are mortal, and they know it. They feel at various times a need to identify a larger spiritual meaning to this earthly existence.
2. Human beings are individuals. Each person is consciously separate from the collectivity and seeks freedom to develop his or her own personality, at times in discord with current community norms.
3. Human beings are social. They choose to live together, they feel a need for social interaction, and they care about the kind of society they live in.

There may be a fourth quandry, which is just now reaching levels of popular consciousness, namely, that the human species lives in a complex ecological system with all other species, and that this system can be threatened by human activity. It remains to be seen whether this quandry is subsumable under one or more competing value systems, or whether environmentalism represents a new qualitative dilemma of the human condition not reducible to other ideologies.

It may well be that conservatism, liberalism, and socialism draw their respective strengths (and weaknesses) from their ability to articulate one (but not all) of these conditions that define the human experience. It means that until and unless these key quandries somehow disappear, a single value system will be unable to address the needs and desires of all people regardless of stage of life, economic situation, or cultural background.

"Conservatism" refers here to the classic and generic wisdom of an Edmund Burke, a Gustav le Bon, a Joseph le Maistre (or perhaps a Confucius from a non-Western setting). The conservative values the stability of tradition, the proper or natural ordering of society and social relations, the spiritual and religious meaning of human existence, and loyalty to one's land and people (cf. McClelland, 1970). In Western feudal society, this meant upholding the true faith of the country, accepting one's natural place in the social hierarchy, and defending one's homeland and people against outsiders. The conservative value system is cautious about human nature and individual rationality. It rests upon the assumption of limited possibilities for most and the acceptance of an inevitable hierarchy in human society. It sees spiritual faith as offering fulfillment and consolation for the sufferings and tragedies of earthly existence. It finds value in a moral order for the soul. The individual needs a transcendent identity as a member of the larger tradition, whether religious, ethnic, kinship, linguistic, cultural, or national, which survives beyond any lifetime. The watchwords of conservatism are: *faith, tradition, country*. Conservatism is the politics of *human identity*.

"Liberalism" as used here is the principled belief in the individual, in his or her rationality, and in the liberty to choose one's own path to self-improvement. Liberalism in the Western tradition is identified with the thinking of Adam Smith, John Locke, Emanuel Kant, and John Stuart Mill. Liberalism is optimistic about the individual, who has common sense and can reason for her- or himself. Liberalism values the freeing of human reason from constraints, including religion, tradition, or government, in favor of enterprise and innovation, which are seen as the engines of progress for humankind. Efficiency in the economy depends on the freeing up of individual opportunity. It is up to the individual to make his or her own way, to succeed or fail, and to decide on the meaning of life. For liberalism, the individual comes before society, self-interest before the collective welfare, and personal choice before community norms. The watchwords of liberalism are: *liberty, reason, individualism*. Liberalism embraces the politics of *individual freedom*.

"Socialism" covers a broad tradition including Robert Owen, Charles Fourier, Pierre Joseph Proudhon, and Karl Marx (see Laidler, 1968). Socialism places its priorities on ideas of social justice, which means a society committed to meeting the basic human needs of the whole population. Socialism seeks some greater degree of social equality, enough to achieve what would be widely recognized as fairness or equity, and it promotes solidarity among groups to achieve solutions to problems. Socialism argues for a social responsibility for the material well-being (welfare) of the poor and disadvantaged as more important than the maximum opportunity for individual wealth. Socialism emphasizes basic economic security rather than unlimited economic risk taking. It puts the common good above the rights of self-centered individualism. Socialism reminds us that no man (or woman) is an island, that each individual depends on the larger society, and that solidarity among people is what holds the good society together. The watchwords of socialism are: *equality, security, solidarity*. Socialism demands a politics of *social justice*.

Most people, at different times, feel the values of each of these great ideological traditions, even if they do not label them as conservative, liberal, or socialist. Especially in the United States, many ideas that we connect with American conservatism are in fact classic liberalism in the European context, and many ideas we associate with American liberalism would be called social democratic or socialist in Europe.

So, for example, many people who do not go to church or belong to any religious group and do not think of themselves as especially religious, feel the need for a spiritual interpretation of life at times of family tragedy or in times of personal danger (war, natural disaster). As people age, they often find that they have developed a sense of tradition about their neighborhood, town, favorite sports team, or nation, and they feel offended by changes, innovations, even "improvements" that wipe away the familiar, the comfortable, the "natural" elements of their earlier years. On the other hand, even many quite "liberal" or "socially progressive" citizens feel annoyed at government bureaucracy when they face it themselves or at paying higher taxes even for worthwhile programs. And who does not at some time, very often in youth, feel the need to do something different, something adventurous, that he or she hasn't done before, to break out of the mold of conformity, and to express his or her individuality. Who, finally, is not at some time affected by personal encounters with the homeless and the down-and-out amidst our affluence, or even by television coverage of the social tragedy of plant closings that devastate communities. Who at times does not feel that there is too much unfairness in our society, that ordinary people don't get a fair break, that those at the top get away with breaking the law. Do these different feelings and the values that they reflect mean that people are simply confused or can't get their values straight? Perhaps to an ideologue that would be one answer; people should choose one clear and coherent ideology and stick to it no matter what happens. But fortunately that is a minority opinion not shared by most people, who have a sense that life is contradictory, that sometimes we identify with a value strongly for certain circumstances but not for others, and not blindly for all cases. Most people are not ideologues, because they recognize the contradictory complexity of the human condition, which calls for hard choices among competing values in varying circumstances.

Each of the three great value systems contains elements that are in conflict with the other two, and none can encompass all the value priorities of human society. In trying to increase the attention and resources given to any one value, a political system will increase the contradictions with other values. Only ideologues would claim that one value system can meet all human needs, without sacrifice and without internal contradiction. For example, if a political system tries to improve its performance in economic growth by promoting greater material rewards for business entrepreneurship (a liberal economic value), it will decrease its commitment to the goals of social equality and solidarity, at least in the short term. In this age of global corporations, whose activities go far beyond the nation-state, greater freedom of business activity may conflict with conservative values of loyalty to country and one's own people. If a political system tries to crack down on crime, to

11

improve the quality of life in neighborhoods, in schools, and for families, it comes into conflict with aspects of personal liberty such as rights of privacy, freedom of movement, presumption of innocence, or the right to own a handgun or semi-automatic rifle. Massive spending for police, courts, and prisons also comes into conflict with spending priorities favoring education, health care, and day-care for children. If the political system tries to increase equality, for example, to redistribute income more evenly through progressive taxation or closing tax loopholes for the rich, conflicts will develop both with conservative distaste for a leveling of social classes and with liberal support for clear market incentives needed to promote individual effort and economic efficiency.

Many issues produce conflicts within as well as between value systems. Population control policies in many developing nations especially are seen as desirable by some conservatives, some liberals, and some socialists for purposes of the survival and strength of the nation, for providing greater individual opportunities through smaller families, and for maintaining basic human welfare. On the other hand, these same measures may be opposed by other conservatives (for contradicting religious values against family planning), liberals (for restricting personal choice through government power), and socialists (for discriminating against the poor as a class, while the rich have as many children as they want). Much depends on how an issue is defined and how a policy to deal with that issue is to be carried out. The point remains that politics in all systems face conflicting values and will have to make policy decisions that prefer some values over others. Politics therefore involves trade-offs among competing choices; different systems develop their own pattern of policy priorities that reflect the trade-offs their regimes support.

Trade-offs abound between environment and economic growth, between government regulation and the private marketplace, between community standards of decency and artistic/commercial freedoms. They ensure that politics is never simple and that most solutions to existing problems involve some "side-effect" costs (foreseen or surprising) or new problems caused by the "solution." Partial coalitions of value systems are possible and often determine the broad outline of political preferences in a given nation during a given political era. In schematic terms, which are always muddled in actual practice, liberals and socialists, both of whom hold humanist, secular values, may combine against conservatives on issues of separation of church and state and against the imposition of religious doctrine on citizens. On the other hand, conservatives and liberals may combine against socialists on the need for greater social inequality as either an economic incentive or as the natural state of affairs. Finally, conservatives and socialists may agree (though for different reasons) on the need for social limits to materialist greed and individual egoism, a stance that contradicts liberal values.

These struggles over value priorities in practical politics may be productive

12

or destructive of political development. Conflicts among competing goals may give rise to new syntheses in which progress may be made on several value positions but new conflicts arise out of the new higher level synthesis. For example, the new (Keynesian) welfare state programs that developed out of the Great Depression of the 1930s in the Western democracies certainly provided a higher level of both social equity and economic growth for several decades after World War II, and few would want to return to pre-Depression conditions. Yet the new bureaucratism of the welfare state and government intervention into economic life and the life of every family have also produced new conflicts and problems peculiar to this higher synthesis. Thus, the struggle of values may bring progress but no once-and-for-all equilibrium, harmony, or balance. On the other hand, value conflict may, in some societies, result in a failure to find new syntheses and may harden competing positions into sterile combat, resulting in short-term ideological victories that guarantee long-term failure. An ideological regime that tries to permanently ignore competing values and their (partial) validity deprives itself of the dynamic for system learning. Openness of political debate (this was Gorbachev's idea of *glasnost*) and civility in political struggle may facilitate a higher learning curve for the system, but there are no guarantees. In the United States, one of the world's most stable democracies, the elimination of slavery as a legal institution could not be settled without a bloody civil war. Unpredictability is what makes politics so interesting and makes glib extrapolations of current trends or "success" formulas unconvincing.

At various times, liberals and socialists have pronounced conservatism dead (one need only recall the "god is dead" slogans of the 1960s), socialists or communists have relegated liberalism to the "trashbin of history" (during the Great Depression, for example), and most recently, liberals and conservatives have claimed that socialism is now an idea with no future. A more realistic perspective recognizes that no historic value system is without lasting attraction, because each speaks to certain deeply felt human desires and needs. Likewise, a broad comparative perspective, which is the view of this text, also must recognize that no one value system by itself provides a complete and adequate understanding of the individual and of society, that each is subject to continuing challenge. Moreover, in a complex dialectical process, each value system in fact needs the others for its own further evolution, since in isolation each becomes sterile dogma.

Each value system has undergone periods of questioning and has shown a capacity to adapt to historical experience and changing socioeconomic and political structures (Rejai, 1984). Classic conservatism and the Roman Catholic church's political conservatism, at least in the West, have overcome earlier opposition to political democracy; in good measure this is a lesson drawn from their collaboration with fascism in the 1920s and 1930s. In the United States, conservative thinking has generally repudiated its earlier support for racial segregation and its ideas of a natural racial hierarchy. Western liberalism has also learned from the class and women's struggles in the nineteenth and early twentieth centuries for equal citizenship rights for all citizens. Today, liberalism could not conceive of excluding any group from full citizenship status on the basis of either property requirements or gender disqualification. And (Western) liberalism, from the challenges of the Great Depression, has modified its position on the role of the state in economic matters, generally becoming more agreeable to expanded regulatory and social service activity. Socialism was modernized in the nineteenth century through the works of Proudhon, Owens, and Marx. What had been, in the feudal period, a predominantly agrarian and craft guild socialism hostile to modern urban industrial development now welcomed modern science and industry as a new opportunity for fulfilling socialist goals. Socialism may now also be learning from the collapse of communism and the negative features of Western welfare statism, as well as from the "new social movements" for peace, environment, and women, which may produce a renewed socialist agenda compatible with post-industrial, environmental, and global market requirements.

This description of conservative, liberal, and socialist value systems and their evolving competition has centered on the Western experience and has not attempted to include the social and political value systems associated with Confucianism, Buddhism, Hinduism, and Islam. Nor does it touch on the political thinking of the Arab historian Ibn Khaldun (1332–1406), the Indian nonviolence theorist Mohandas K. (Mahatma) Gandhi (1869–1948), the Three Principles of the People theory of Sun Yat-sen (1867–1925), the popular socialist thought of Cuban Jose Marti (1853–1895) or the African socialism of Leopold Senghor (1906–) and Julius Nyerere (1922–) (see Sigmund, 1967). Non-Western and non-European value systems may contain different emphases or syntheses of the values expressed in Western conservative, liberal, and socialist thought, but the contradictions of competing values cannot be avoided in any system. The predominantly conservative cast of Confucian thought on proper government, morals, and ethics is at odds with the values of individualism and equality. Sun Yat-sen attempted to combine nationalism, democracy, and socialism into his theoretical framework, thereby tolerating internal contradictions within his overall system. Much of modern non-Western political theory has been heavily influenced, either in acceptance and assmiliation or rejection, by Western thought, and this has produced new variant and hybrid theories.

Three Worlds of Managing Great Transitions

Political systems do not rethink their overall priorities in a major way very frequently; too much conflict is involved in basic reworkings of political system priorities. Therefore, different political systems contain characteristic and defining mixtures (syndromes) of value preferences that have evolved from past political struggles. These mixtures are not immutable; they have changed over time, and they can evolve further still. Right now we are in an era of great change in virtually all regions of the world. The previously popularized division of political system-types into Three Worlds—the affluent liberal democracies, the communist party-states, and the mostly authoritarian developing nations—was an intellectual child of the Cold War, which placed a high premium on identifying ideological friends, foes, and possible converts. This scheme has eroded considerably with the collapse of European communism and the economic dynamism of the East Asian NICs (Newly Industrialized Countries). Yet the great political transformations now begun are hardly consolidated, and we are now witness to a period of extraordinary openness in many nations as to what will be the character of the political systems in the post–Cold War era of the New World Order. Indeed, some scholars (cf. Huntington, 1993, and Jowitt, 1993) are already convinced that this period will be not only quite open but also marked by new and not-so-new great conflicts and disorders, implying that comparative researchers should be cautious about their prognostications of political development.

We know a lot more about where different political systems undergoing great change are coming from than where they will ultimately (in the longer term of a generation or so) stabilize themselves. And since even in great transformations there is some considerable degree of continuity in popular attitudes, behavior patterns, and political leadership, it makes some sense to deal with the politics of great transitions according to the different pretransition situations, which were more stable and which characterized nation-state regimes for one or more generations in the postwar period.

A comparative analysis of political systems that concentrates on the "politics of great change" can still benefit from a basic division into three worlds: (1) the politics of post-communism, of exiting from classic Communist regimes; (2) the politics of post-industrialism, of exiting from the classic welfare state democracy; and (3) the politics of developmentalism, of exiting from the Cold War Third World.

In each case, it is necessary to have some basic understanding of what each system created in the postwar period, what were its priorities and symptomatic trade-offs, its achievements and failures, so that we can understand better what has triggered the current major transitions, which are quite different for post-Communist Russia or Hungary, post-industrial Britain or Italy, and post-Third World Korea or Taiwan, to name some examples.

For each "world of transition," the historical and theoretical underpinnings of the political system-type are outlined, with particular stress on the reasons for the erosion of the political formula that defined Western democracies, communist systems, and Third World authoritarianism for most of the postwar period. Special attention is given also to the type of political struggle that marks the transition from the political formula of the Cold War era to the search for a new political formula not yet consolidated or, in some cases, not yet conceived.

For each "world of transition," we then focus on actual regime performance in several main areas, including: (1) economic growth; (2) social inequality; (3) personal liberty; and (4) quality of life. Each chapter deals with one performance area, detailing how the political system is attempting to come to grips with basic changes in that area (for example economic growth), and how changes in one area impact on other performance areas (for example social inequality or quality of life).

Economic development as a performance area includes basic industrialization and urbanization and also, now, de-industrialization and global economic diversification. It includes measures of per capita gross domestic product (and, more recently, purchasing power parity), standards of education, housing, health care, and social service programs. Although the necessity and even the desirability of high growth rates has been increasingly debated in the West, economic development remains a key area of system performance, for without development, even the most free, unpolluted, and egalitarian society confines its people to a physically hard and immobile life. There is little questioning of the desirability of growth among the poor nations of the world.

Social equality concerns the distribution of income and wealth, social inequalities of class and minorities in education, elite recruitment, and the legal system. Special attention is given to gender inequalities and the record of each system-type in dealing with these inequalities, especially now during this period of great transition. Equality in its many forms, equality of both opportunity and result, has become a political rallying point with particular strength in the postwar years (cf. Bell, 1974), and it is now clear that, in addition to growth, social equity (fairness) is a very important area of system performance. Even systems with good records of aggregate growth that fail to provide for some minimal level of social justice may find themselves skating on thin ice.

Personal liberty is a third area of system performance to be evaluated for each "world of transition." Freedom of speech and of the press, the right to vote in free and fair elections, freedom of religion and travel, the right to organize into unions and other interest groups, and the right to a fair trial are all included under the category of personal liberty. Personal freedom, as has often been pointed out, does not feed or clothe people, and it may not contribute to social equality either, but it is still a valued goal of millions in both rich and poor nations, perhaps most so when it is threatened or lost. Personal liberty is an especially important area to watch during periods of great political struggle and disorder, when many people may be tempted by a strong leader who seems to offer order and an end to insecurity.

The fourth area of system performance is titled "quality of life." Here we include, and attempt to measure, crime and criminal justice, the quality of family life, environmental issues, chronic unemployment and underemployment of human skills, and signs of social alienation such as drug and alcohol abuse. How free we are, and how free we are to enjoy material prosperity, can be severely limited by violent street crime and professional crime, family breakup, social marginalization of certain groups, and of course by environmental decay in the larger society. Many quality-of-life items listed here, once perhaps taken for granted or not seen as political issues, have in the last two decades become part of the political agenda of more and more nations, including the poorer developing nations.

Some Basic Points

As the following chapters present material on the "politics of great transitions" and on the changing performance mixtures of each political system-type, keep in mind the following (arguable) propositions, which are the most important "lessons" of this text:

1. Each type of political system has its own special pattern (mixture or syndrome) of performance priorities and nonpriorities. While there is considerable variation within each system, especially now in an era of greater openness and transition, the most basic differences in performance "mix" are those that exist between system-types.
2. No political system is able to maximize all performance areas at the same time. Each has its own special strengths and weaknesses that are peculiar to its own political mixture or political formula. Performance failures in certain areas are not just mistakes in policy or abuses by particular leaders but are part of an overall "package deal" of the entire system.
3. As a corollary to the above, contradictions exist within all political systems that create basic performance patterns of success and failure. Trade-offs among performance priorities must be expected of any system. The "normal" pattern of system trade-offs or contradictions may be taken as one definition of the system itself. Development of the system to a higher level may take care of some problems but will also create new contradictions. This is especially important to watch in periods of great change, when earlier patterns of "normal" system performance are decaying and new patterns are only beginning to emerge.
4. Political systems are not equal in overall balance of performance successes and deficiencies. It matters a lot whether one lives in an affluent liberal democracy, a Communist/post-Communist regime, or a developing authoritarian system. The types of great changes now underway are so important because they have the potential to affect the daily lives of untold millions of individuals in both positive and tragic ways.

17

2

From the Liberal Welfare State
to a Post-Industrial Democracy

The post–World War II era of the welfare state democracy, which marked a period of extraordinary social peace, growth, and political stability in the liberal democratic systems of Western Europe, North America, and Japan, is coming to an end. To understand why the politics of the Cold War welfare state are now undergoing profound strain that will lead to a qualitatively different political formula or perhaps varied formulas for this grouping of economically affluent and democratic societies, we must first appreciate how difficult the birth of liberal democracy has been among the world's societies and how much time and conflict was involved in the emergence of both the theory and practice of liberal democracy. We will examine the historic changes in political thinking that built the intellectual basis for a free citizenry and an elected government responsible to the people. We will look at the different and difficult paths to liberal democracy in Sweden, Germany, and Japan, noting the variations and commonalities in this drawn-out evolutionary struggle. And we will highlight the roles of that institutional centerpiece of liberal democracy, the freely elected and effective parliament.

Liberal Democracy—Theory and Practical History

The emergence of liberal democracy as a new type of political system in Western Europe and North America (later in Japan) is inextricably bound up with the capitalist/industrial revolution and the passing of feudalism in those areas. It should not be surprising that theories of liberal democracy have borrowed heavily from the concepts of economic liberalism (classic capitalism).

The early theorists of liberal democracy (more likely to have been called republicanism) were proposing a radical, even revolutionary break with the political theory that described and supported the feudalist monarchies. Feudalism rested on rule by an aristocratic class (or estate) of titled landowners (barons, dukes, earls, counts, and such) capped by a royal family that provided the monarch (king or queen). The monarch was typically though not always assumed to rule by "divine right." In other words, God (always either Catholic or Protestant) had chosen this royal family and its heirs to rule over the nation, and the work of the monarchy was also the will of God. The royal family in turn supported (established) a state religion that was to be regarded as the only true religion of the land. Before the Reformation in the sixteenth century, this religion was Roman Catholicism throughout Western Europe. After the Reformation it became Anglicanism in England and Lutheranism in Prussia and Scandinavia. The state church, for its part, was almost without exception a staunch support for the monarchy, preaching obedience not only to the monarch but also to his or her helpers, the local lords of the manor. In feudal society each person was born into a station in life, a social caste (an estate), and there was little one could do to change that status. People were socialized from birth into accepting as divine fate their station in life. One could be a very good peasant, but to hope to be advanced into the aristocracy or allowed to marry an aristocrat was insanity. On the other hand, even the most miserable lord would not be demoted to commoner or peasant.

The feudal system began to be challenged with the rise of a new class, which was an extension of the town burgher estate in the Middle Ages. This new class was the modern business or entrepreneurial middle class, which represented a new form of production, the factory system, and a new form of distribution, the free market system. As the economic power of this new bourgeoisie grew, new theories of government that reflected the changing social order also surfaced. One of the forerunners of these theories is the *Leviathan* by Thomas Hobbes. Hobbes wrote in the England of the seventeenth century, actually somewhat in advance of industrial capitalism, but in the midst of the challenge to the English monarchy posed by Oliver Cromwell and his New Model Army. Hobbes, perceiving that "divine right" doctrines were coming unstuck, attempted to justify the monarchy (and the absolute authority of the state) on other grounds, namely egoistic self-interest. Assuming that mankind is by nature egoistic but rational, Hobbes argued that people come together to found a civil society based not on the word of God but on a social contract that reflects their individual self-interest. To achieve their selfish ends, people agree (covenant) to give up certain natural rights (and retain others) in return for the state's (monarch's in Hobbes's day) assurance that all citizens will do the same, or be punished if they do not. The innovations in Hobbesian theory lie in the notions that: (1) the social order is a human, not a divine, construct; (2) that the egoistic self-interest of each adds up to the best social result; and (3) that one of the chief roles of the state is to guarantee the enforcement of contracts (covenants). Although Hobbes intended his *Leviathan* as a new rationale to support absolutist monarchy, his line of reasoning foreshadowed many features of later theorists of representative government. John Locke, for example, bases his call for republican government on the rational self-interest of the citizen; Locke's theory of the social contract is also a secular, or nonreligious, image, implying a separation of church and state and tolerance for religious pluralism. The secularization of politics, i.e., the removal of a state-supported religion, is one of the radical departures of liberal democratic thought from the feudal system.

Other early theorists of liberal democracy stressed in different ways the notion of competing interests as the foundation of political life and of a desirable social order. Montesquieu emphasized, for example, the separation of governmental powers into executive, legislative, and judicial branches. This checking and balancing of various branches of government has found much more favor in the American experience than in the European, but is not without its influence on continental parliamentary systems as well, particularly in the notion of an independent judiciary and nonpartisan civil service. Madison, in the *Federalist Papers*, asserts the need for a balanced contention of factions within society to avoid tyranny, one of the chief worries of the American founding fathers. No one faction of citizens should be permitted to gain a position from which it could subdue and suppress other factions. Competition of factional (special) interests in the political arena will balance out to the best result for the society as a whole. Let us note here that when Hobbes, Locke, Montesquieu, and Madison defend the social contract of the citizenry or the rights of the citizen to elect representatives to government, they took for granted that this citizenry would include only male property owners of some substance. *No one* among these early theorists of liberal democracy advocated or envisaged voting rights (the franchise) for the nonpropertied, for factory and farm workers, for women, and certainly not for slaves. The term "bourgeois democracy" describes rather precisely and objectively the limited extent of political participation intended by these proponents of early capitalist democracy; the bourgeoisie and its ideologists were fighting not for universal suffrage but for their own class rights. Only Jean Jacques Rousseau, among these early democratic theorists, stressed social equality as a presumption of the new proposed democratic system.

These early theories, then, with the exception of that of Rousseau, are in broad agreement with the economic theories of early capitalism, especially the Manchester School liberalism of writers like Adam Smith. Smith, in his classic *Wealth of Nations*, describes capitalist society as a competition of each against all, with egoistic self-interest the motivation for behavior. Through an "invisible hand" of the marketplace, however, the aggregation of individual self-interests ends up to be the optimal social outcome as well, Smith postulates. The laws of supply and (effective money) demand would assure production of those goods and services needed by the population, and competition among entrepreneurs would serve both to keep profit levels in bounds and to encourage new and more efficient production methods. In the governmental realm, Smith's main point was to call for limited government, one that could guarantee the sanctity of contracts and maintain law and order and a stable currency, but little else. As with Locke, Madison, and Montesquieu, one of the main goals of government as Smith saw it was the negative one of avoiding tyranny, especially the return to the absolute monarchy of feudalism. Certainly Smith did not want government messing around with the "invisible hand" of the marketplace. The affairs of the economy were best left to the judgment of entrepreneurs and consumers; two of the characteristics of liberal democracy in capitalist economies have historically been the basic separation of political rights and property rights, and the reluctance of government to infringe on the rights of property.

Once again, let us for the record make clear that while Adam Smith and others of his persuasion thought of capitalism as a progressive advance over feudalist production, the fruits of this progress were not destined for the working class. In fact, with the introduction of the factory assembly line under capitalism, Smith has the following rather pessimistic prediction for the modern industrial worker:

> The understandings of the greater part of men are necessarily formed by their ordinary employments. The man whose whole life is spent in performing a few simple operations . . . has no occasion to exert his understanding. . . . He generally becomes as stupid and ignorant as it is possible for a human to become. . . . His dexterity at his own particular trade seems in this manner to be acquired at the expense of his intellectual, social and martial virtues. But in every improved and civilised society, this is the state into which the labouring poor, that is, the great body of the people, must necessarily fall. (Quoted in Tucker, 1972:287)

Fortunately, theories of liberal democracy have become remarkably more progressive during the nineteenth and twentieth centuries, in the course of the political struggles that the initial rigid ideology and harsh practice of laissez-faire capitalism generated. The liberal welfare state of the post-Depression, post–World War II era has been able to synthesize into modern liberal democratic practice many of the goals of socialism, while on the other hand bowing also to the still-strong ideals of conservatism. Whereas in 1900 the state's control of economic resources through taxation amounted to only 2 to 3 percent of gross national product (GNP), by the 1980s this control had grown to somewhere between 30 and 45 percent in all the liberal democracies (Deutsch, 1987). As Heidenheimer, Heclo and Adams (1990) have argued, from the point of view of either strict capitalist economic reasoning or pure liberal ideology, welfare state democracy should be impossible. "It fails to satisfy socialist criteria for production organized around social needs rather than profit motives. In fact every Western welfare state is highly ambiguous about how social needs are actually to be defined and who defines them. Yet the welfare state also fails to satisfy conservative [that is, capitalist] criteria for maximizing individual liberty. It does not leave people, as Milton Friedman put it, 'free to choose,' and it neither fully accepts nor rejects market mechanisms. In terms of ideological clarity, the welfare state is incoherent'' (1990:368).

But this has been a strength, not a weakness. Western liberal democracy has shown great adaptability to changed circumstances and has been able to take on new goals and practices to maintain its popular legitimacy. In Europe, the influence of democratic socialism expressed through labor unions and socialist, social democratic, and labor parties has given the European welfare state a stronger "social market" outlook, while maintaining some degree of conservative class-consciousness and traditional attachments to national and religious norms from pre-industrial times. In Japan, on the other hand, one might argue that the traditionally conservative order is still the strongest element in the political culture there, despite the gradual expansion of Western liberal influences, with only minor concessions to socialist ideals. Even many of the social welfare elements of the Japanese political system have a conservative nationalist and corporatist character. The United States, by comparison, lacks a true conservative feudal past, and has the weakest socialist tradition in labor and political organizing. As Louis Hartz (1955) pointed out some time ago, the United States is dominated by liberal thinking, and most of our political debates are grounded in liberal assumptions.

Patterns of Liberal Democratic Development

It is difficult to pinpoint the first beginnings of liberal democracy. Some of the Italian and Greek city-states, and especially the merchant capitalist center of Venice, possessed many of the institutions and procedures that we associate with liberal democracy today. Iceland is considered by many experts to have had the first and longest lived effective parliament. But the transformation of the British monarchy into a parliamentary democracy is surely one of the first and steadiest examples of the birth of liberal democracy. Britain was also the first nation to begin the industrialization process, and in Britain industrialization was more gradual and drawn out than in later industrializing countries. Most observers have related Britain's slow pace of capitalist development to its evolutionary political transformation. Characteristic of the British experience was the partial, step-by-step advancement of the powers and rights of Parliament against the Crown. As early as 1265 the so-called Simons Parliament had assembled in revolt against King Henry III. In a series of confrontations, reforms, and sometimes rebellions (the Glorious Revolution of 1688), Parliament established its right to assemble on a regular basis and to control the administration of the king's government. Gradually Parliament and later the House of Commons (the lower chamber) within Parliament supplanted the monarchy entirely as the basis for establishing a government. As the scope of powers of the House of Commons increased, so also did the electoral base from which it was elected and to whom the Members of Parliament (MPs) were responsible. The fact that this movement was gradual did not mean that it was always peaceful or that the privileged aristocracy or royal family gave way with grace and of their own volition.

The great Reform Act of 1832, which eliminated the practice of "rotten boroughs" (districts where seats in Parliament could literally be bought and sold) and established an expanded electorate of property owners who paid a certain uniform minimum level of property taxes, was passed by the Commons but was twice rejected by the House of Lords, until riots in the streets convinced the Lords to pass the bill on a third go-round. With the process of expanding suffrage to new social strata (the working class and finally women) came legal recognition of trade unions, the right to strike, and explicit protection of freedoms of speech, press, and assembly. Workers' political parties, despite some rough going initially, pushed their way into the party system.

We may forget that in the liberal democracies even today the struggle for the effective right to vote is not ancient history but either recent history or current politics. Women's suffrage in the United States, Germany, Sweden, and a number of other nations dates back only to the end of World War I. In Switzerland, one of the most stable and the most prosperous liberal democracy, women still cannot vote in certain cantons (states), although they can vote in national elections. In the United States, the de facto right to vote for southern black citizens began only with enforcements of the 1965 Voting Rights Act, which began to counter the violence and chicanery used to disfranchise black citizens in the South. Even now, residence and prior registration regulations in the United States serve to effectively *disenfranchise* millions of American citizens, and voter turnout in the United States compares poorly with levels of voting participation in most other Western democracies.

In other areas as well, there remains some unfinished business with regard to many of the liberties associated with liberal democratic theory. In West Germany, there is still religious instruction in the public schools, and parents in most areas must send their children to either the local Catholic or Protestant school; unless a citizen formally renounces his or her religion, a 10 percent tax surcharge is levied on his or her income tax by the government and given over to the church. Secularization of the political system, in other words, has not yet been completed in educational and tax affairs.

In France the government-owned television networks are notoriously progovernment in their news coverage, and though this lessened somewhat under former president Valery Giscard d'Estaing it was still far from the position of TV news coverage in most other liberal democracies. In West Germany, since an antiradical law (*Radikalenerlass*) took effect in 1972, there have been political firings or nonhirings of suspected or admitted radicals in the civil service, which includes all teachers and railway, postal, public

23

transit, and public communications employees, as well as employees in all national, state, and local government offices. This virtual ban on practicing one's vocation (*Berufsverbot*) without having committed any crime whatsoever would be labelled a political purge if it took place in a communist country. The condition of liberal democracy still has room for improvement, even by its own standards.

Stable Development of Liberal Democracy: Sweden

In some countries, this developmental process was relatively steady, and while not necessarily peaceful, was not reversed in any major aspect for any significant period of time. There were, in other words, no major retrogressions. Once unions were legally recognized, their legal status was not revoked. Once enfranchised, workers or women were not later denied the right to vote. Press freedoms, subject to serious infringement in both England and the United States at the start of the nineteenth century, were constantly broadened, and while there were some relapses (mostly in wartime), never was there any serious or successful attempt to establish a controlled press. In this group of nations, which includes Great Britain, the United States, Canada, Australia, New Zealand, the Netherlands, Belgium, Norway, Denmark, Switzerland, Iceland, and Ireland (since its independence in 1922), stability of the democratic system has been highest. Even during periods of acute crisis (war, depression, acute political strife), the system has remained essentially intact. Belgium, the Netherlands, Norway, and Denmark did, of course, have fascist occupation regimes forced upon them after being conquered by Hitler's *Wehrmacht* in World War II. To be sure, during both world wars liberal democracies did impose more narrow limits on certain liberties, and some opponents of the war (Socialist leader Eugene V. Debs, for example) and some ethnic groups (e.g., the Japanese-Americans in World War II) were ill-treated and denied basic rights. And yet even these serious infringements, regrettable and probably unjustified and unnecessary even under duress of war, did not, in this group of democratic nations, threaten the basic evolution of the system.

One example of democratic development worth discussing at length is the Swedish system. In its broad outlines, the Swedish pattern of democratic development is certainly more typical of a successful system-transformation than that of the United States. Indeed, as will become clearer in the next chapters, the United States is an atypical case of political development, one that in many respects is unlikely and unsuited to serve as a model for emulation or export. In particular, the United States lacked the struggle of democratic forces with a feudal aristocracy, which was present in nearly all other cases of smooth (or nonsmooth) evolution of a modern democracy, and for which Sweden is a good illustration (see Giddens, 1973). While there are many similarities between the British and Swedish patterns, the Swedish example is presented for two reasons: first, its unfamiliarity to American students; and second, its multiparty system, which is a good point of comparison with the Anglo-American two-party systems, both because it is a stable multiparty system and because it has an array of parties that is typical of European democratic systems generally.

Like the British Parliament, the Swedish *Riksdag* has its roots in the early history of the Swedish monarchy. As Adams (1970) has noted, the kings of medieval Sweden were elected by a body called the *Riksmöte*, probably the first instance of national popular participation in an election. Acquisition of the throne by election instead of birthright clearly hindered the development of an absolutist monarchy. After 1371, the monarch was further limited by his oath of office and by a detailed feudal version of a policy platform (*Handfästing*), which the nobility exacted from the new king. Over the next two centuries, many kings were removed from office on grounds of breach of oath. The first *Riksdag* was convened in 1435, following a peasant uprising against the Danish monarchy, which then dominated Sweden as well as Norway and Finland (then the eastern province of Sweden). As Adams convincingly argues, the *Riksdag*, initially an emergency assembly convened by the Swedish Crown to deal with a particular crisis but kept in existence because of a plentiful supply of crises in the latter part of the sixteenth century, gradually became a regular fixture of the legal-political system, holding sessions every three years as required by a 1660 law. Four estates—the nobility, clergy, burghers, and peasantry—were represented in the *Riksdag*.

This should not give an impression of an inevitable or uncontested rise of the Swedish parliament to dominance. Even in the most gradual and eventually most successful cases of parliament building, there were defeats and temporary setbacks. Nils Herlitz (1939) has outlined the major constitutional struggles between *Riksdag* and Crown since the assertion of an independent and unified Swedish nation-state under Gustav Vasa, elected King Gustav I by the *Riksdag* in 1523. At least twice the monarchy was able through various devices to reverse the progress toward a parliamentary system. In 1682 King Karl XI succeeded in uniting the clergy, burgher, and peasant estates behind him to impose an absolutist monarchy over the nobility. This was again overturned in 1719 after the death of Karl XII, when the *Riksdag* proclaimed an ''Era of Liberty'' and adopted a constitution limiting monarchial powers. As both Adams (1970) and Hancock (1972) agree, the initial experience with parliamentary ascendancy was not especially impressive. Two parliamentary groupings, the aristocratic and militarist Hats, said to have been in the pay of Louis XV of France, and the commoner-based and fiscally conservative Caps, said to have been bribed by the Russian tsar, were not really organized political parties but preparty foreign-policy factions, whose control of the *Riksdag* paved the way for the bloodless antiparliamentary coup (1772) by King Gustav III, which restored again the king's absolute right to veto legislation. Following the annexation of Finland by the Russian empire in 1808–9, a formal constitution was adopted, confirming the division of the *Riksdag* into four estates. It was not until the 1860s that the *Riksdag* was restructured as a bicameral legislature (more in line with other European parliaments), with an upper house indirectly elected but with a limited franchise based on property qualifications. At this point (see Verney, 1957; Rustow, 1955) the overwhelming majority of the population (about 80 percent) were still not permitted to vote, and the system was still dominated by the king and land-owning nobility.

It took still another fifty years of keen struggle before the expansion of the franchise covered all adult males (1907–9) and finally females as well (1919–21). But by the early 1920s, the principles of parliamentary responsibility and parliamentary government had made their final breakthrough. Now the monarch was no longer the chief executive, but was forced to nominate as prime minister the leader of the majority (whether single-party or coalition) in the *Riksdag*. The cabinet under the prime minister now assumed in practice the daily control over the administration of government.

Hancock (1972:20–32) describes this period from 1870 to 1920 as one of fundamental economic, social, and party system development, which accompanied the ascendancy of liberal democracy. During this period the industrialization of the Swedish economy transformed the workforce from overwhelmingly agrarian to increasingly urban industrial. Those employed in agriculture declined from 72 percent of the economically active population to 44 percent, while those engaged in industry and commerce rose from 20 to 50 percent. The system of isolated villages and farms producing food and handicrafts for immediate family consumption and local trade was giving way to commercial agriculture, factory production, and a money exchange economy. Modern rail transport and communications were especially important to Sweden in overcoming the isolating effects of terrain and climate to facilitate the growth of national export markets, although it also led to the appearance of cyclical economic crises associated with capitalist development. This in turn led to growing worker-owner conflict and to emigration, mainly to North America, for over a million Swedes during the nineteenth century. This period produced advances in a national education system and the spread of literacy skills to all classes; the growth of trade unionism (the feudal guild system had been abolished in 1842) as the mainstay of the new Socialist movement; the partial emancipation of women in the areas of education and of property holding and divorce rights; and the proliferation of new religious, temperance, student, and consumer cooperative groups associated with the new social order. As the old economic and social order declined, new political parties representing the working and business classes began to challenge the political order, which was still dominated by the aristocracy and challenged until then only by farmer interest groups. Brogan and Verney (1968:50) describe the

Swedish party system that developed in this period as quite appropriate to its traditions:

> Broadly speaking, the four main social groups in Sweden—wage earners, salaried employees, farmers, and businessmen—are represented in the legislature by the four main parties—the Social Democrats, Liberals, Center (formerly the Agrarians), and Conservatives. . . . It is doubtless no accident that a people accustomed for centuries to being divided into four estates of the realm should after a generation or two of social and political transition (1865–1905) find a need for four political parties, each tending to depend on the support of one of the main social groups into which twentieth-century Sweden is divided. The age of individualism and of liberalism was short-lived. Sweden passed very quickly from a condition of semifeudalism to one of semisocialism.

The Swedish system of proportional representation, whereby a party's number of seats in the *Riksdag* (since 1971 a unicameral parliament) is determined by its percentage of the popular vote, has probably contributed to the maintenance, if not to the original appearance, of the multiparty system.

Only the party of the industrial working class, the Social Democrats, represented a clearly novel addition to the traditional estate system. The Communist party broke away from the Social Democrats in 1917, the year of the Bolshevik revolution, to form a second workers' party, but has remained a minor fixture of the party system (though of occasional importance both as support and competition on the left for the Social Democrats). The Social Democrats, on the other hand, have remained the largest single party since 1914, and governed, either alone or in coalition with another party, from 1933 until 1976, with only one short break of three months in 1936. Just when it seemed to some observers that Sweden, alone among the liberal democracies, was developing into "something of a one-party system on a national scale" (Adams, 1970:157) after forty-three years of Social Democratic-led government, the three-party coalition of Liberals, Conservatives, and Agrarians finally succeeded in getting together (there are real differences of both interests and philosophy among them) and securing a narrow majority in the 1976 *Riksdag* elections. The Swedish case is sure evidence that neither a multiparty system nor proportional representation by themselves lead to political instability, any more than two-party systems or majority district electoral mechanisms produce political stability.

It should be emphasized that despite the existence since the 1920s of five parties, the popular conception of the Swedish party system has developed over the years into one of loose bipolarity, with the three bourgeois parties (Conservative, Liberal, and Agrarians) pitted against the workers' parties. "Bourgeois bloc" and "workers' bloc" characterize other multiparty systems in a useful manner as well and undercut some of the seeming differences between two-party and multiparty models. In fact, given the continued existence

27

in Parliament of the British Liberals (getting 10 to 15 percent of the vote but only a handful of seats) and the German FDP (Liberals) in the *Bundestag* (5 to 10 percent of the vote and seats), only the United States among the liberal democracies has evolved a strict two-party system. In this sense the United States' experience is atypical within the general pattern.

A key element in the successful evolution and stability of the Swedish liberal democracy was the behavior of major parties and social classes at vital junctures of the political transformation in the late feudal or postfeudal period (see Giddens, 1973). On the one hand was the willingness of conservative elements of the old aristocracy and later of the industrialist class to give way and even to lend support and legitimation to basic sociopolitical reforms and not to resort to violence or abandon the parliament as the locus of struggle. Thus the Conservative party, unlike its namesake in Germany, supported the extension of the franchise in 1907–9 and the establishment of parliamentary government in 1919–21. Conservatives have learned to live with the extensive welfare state programs introduced over the years by Social Democratic governments and now would claim only to desire to administer such programs less bureaucratically, more efficiently, and perhaps with lower costs. At the same time, this tolerance on the right was in part facilitated by the reformist rather than revolutionary/radical approach of the working class unions and party organizations. From the early leadership of Branding through Hansson and Erlander to Palme, the Social Democratic leadership has committed itself to gradual change through strictly parliamentary means, concentrating on partial reforms within the capitalist economy rather than the radical transformation to a planned socialist economy. One exception to this general rule occurred in the Socialist pressure for change throughout Europe at the end of World War II. The Swedish Social Democrats put forward a twenty-seven-point program critical of capitalism and aiming at transformation of at least certain aspects of it but without denying basic rights of private ownership. Even this more radical proposal was dropped in 1948 after a heated campaign against it by the three bourgeois parties.

The break with Marxist theory occurred even earlier in Sweden than in socialist movements in France, Germany, or Italy and enabled the party to both expand its electoral appeal to members of the white-collar middle class and to form coalitions at times with the Liberal and Agrarian parties. The development of the Swedish welfare state has been the result of much more of a consensus policy, and even when a coalition of nonsocialist parties finally managed to displace the Social Democrats and form a new government in 1976, it proceeded to cut back on the rate of increase in social expenditures, but maintained the integrity of the system as a whole. And after the Social Democrats regained control of the government in 1982, they continued the cautious reforms in spending restraint begun by their political rivals. In general, through the slow-growth 1980s, both the Social Democrats and the opposition have recognized the need for consolidation of existing programs. They have not initiated new programs, but also they have not attacked previous basic commitments. Elections in September of 1991 again gave four nonsocialist parties a majority in the Swedish parliament, and further gradual erosion of Sweden's generous social programs is expected. Swedish democracy exemplifies the gradual shift in political consensus that evolves with changing circumstances, but that never threatens the basic stability of the democratic system and the broad ability of all major parties to work with each other even while offering limited alternatives in election competition. One should note and appreciate how rare this combination is within the global family of nations.

Interrupted Democratic Development: Germany

Another group of contemporary liberal democracies has experienced a far more checkered pattern of development, marked by major upheavals and reversals. In France, Germany, Italy, and Japan (as well as in Greece, Spain, Portugal, and Finland), the movement toward democracy or the democratic system itself has been overwhelmed by the forces of reaction, and for a time democracy has been replaced by dictatorship, generally fascist in nature.

To better appreciate some of the factors related to a pattern of interrupted democratic development, we may take the example of Germany. To be sure, Germany is not necessarily typical in its pattern of interrupted or unstable democratization, and its experienced setbacks cannot necessarily serve as an explanation for French, Japanese, and Italian reversals of liberal democracy in their histories. Although there are similarities, it is perhaps understandable that the cases of deviation from the pattern of steady democratic growth form an even less homogeneous group experience than the original pattern itself.

One problem affecting German political development (the German Question) was that of establishing the modern German nation-state. The Germanic clan or tribal culture appears in recorded history before the birth of Christ in the struggle with the Roman Empire. The warrior tribes were the main bulwark against the Romans; the decline of Rome was associated with the migration of these Teutonic tribes throughout Europe (and even into North Africa). Toward the end of the fifth century the Frankish tribes under Clovis conquered Roman Gaul and united the territories of much of present-day France and West Germany. By the year 800, the German-Frankish chieftain Charlemagne (or Karl der Grosse) controlled an empire including France, Germany, Austria, Spain, and Italy and was crowned Emperor of the Holy Roman Empire of the Germanic nation by the pope. Soon after Charlemagne's death, however, his empire was split among his grandsons; the Holy Roman Empire included most of Germany, Austria, the Netherlands, Belgium, and Switzerland. Although geographically impressive, the empire was a loosely

29

organized and shifting set of kingdoms, principalities, and city-states, dominated for most of its history by the Austrian house of Hapsburg (1273–1806), which provided the emperor. As such, effective government for most Germanic peoples was the *Landsherr* (or local monarch) and its feudal diet (*Landstand*). Only in the free cities of the Hanseatic League did the rise of the burgher class of merchant capitalism produce for a time a trend toward political liberalism, with personal liberty and civil rights for all citizens. But these Hansa cities were cut off from influencing the states of the empire as a whole by their autonomy. In the fifteenth century they were for the most part attacked and incorporated into the monarchial territories. The French historian Vermeil (1969:56) suggests that "this enforced intergradation in the territorial order cost the German people its political education. Little by little the proud and independent burghers were humbled. Had circumstances permitted, they might have made of Germany a great modern democracy."

The Reformation, while uniting Germans in some ways, served to divide them in other ways, almost always to the detriment of the peasants and townspeople and to the benefit of the provincial aristocracy. Martin Luther, who gave Germany a uniform written language, left behind a conglomeration of states with new religious cleavages between Protestants and Catholics. Lutheranism, potentially populist and democratic in tone, became a tool of the nobility and the aristocratic authorities (*Obrigkeiten*). As rebellious peasants challenged not only the Catholic church but the aristocracy itself, demanding abolition of serfdom, lower taxes, and elected parsons, Martin Luther turned against the masses, preaching hellfire and damnation for these "murderers and robbers who must be stabbed, smashed or strangled, and should be killed as mad dogs" (quoted in Heidenheimer, 1971:6). In the end, Lutheranism became institutionalized as an aid to monarchy, a rigid dogma supporting the established feudal order and forsaking the plight of the lower estates (classes). By the end of the Thirty Years War (1618–48), the states of Germany were still divided, still dominated by the Austrian emperor, materially exhausted and falling behind economic developments in France, England, and the Netherlands.

In the eighteenth century, however, a German state of the northeast, Prussia, under the reign of Frederick the Great, built a well-drilled army and an efficient centralized bureaucracy, both staffed by sons of the landowning aristocracy (*Junkers*). It expanded its territory to the east, mostly at the expense of the Poles and Lithuanians, and in the nineteenth century was preparing to challenge both France and Austria for the role of unifier of a modern German nation-state.

The old Holy Roman Empire (the first German Reich), often cited by historians as neither holy, nor Roman, nor much of an empire, was finally to fall victim to the Napoleonic Wars of 1790–1815. During the period 1805–15,

Napoleon had forced the establishment of a Confederation of the Rhine, giving some major liberal reform impetus to the states of southwest Germany in particular. When the French revolutionary armies were defeated in 1814–15, with Prussia as one of the victorious coalition partners against Napoleon, the Holy Roman Empire was not resurrected. Instead, a Germanic confederation of some thirty-eight states, both large (Hessia, Bavaria, Saxony) and small (Saxe-Coburg-Gotha, Lauenburg) was established, with no effective national political system yet in sight. The Austrian emperor assumed nominal executive control, but the Diet of the confederation required a unanimous vote before any decision could be taken. This doctrine of absolute state's rights made the confederation a rigid monument to the privilege of the local nobility, which is of course what it was meant to be as part of the post-Napoleonic restoration of the feudal order. In Baden, Bavaria, Wurttemberg, and Hesse-Darmstadt, however, the local monarchs had granted constitutions providing for essential civil liberties, Christian equality, and equality before the law for all citizens. Bicameral legislatures (*Landtag*) with an upper house reserved for the nobility and a lower house for the burgher class exercised some power of the purse, but without achieving any dramatic breakthrough to effective parliamentary democracy, even at the state level.

A customs-union (*Zollverein*) did facilitate freer trade within the confederation, and there was some modernization of agriculture and in the 1840s the introduction on a significant scale of machine production and the building of a national road network and postal service. Still, Germany lagged far behind France and England in industrial development at midcentury.

A first attempt at unification came with the revolution of 1848. In the wake of popular uprisings in Paris, Berlin, and Vienna that for a time had the ruling Prussian and Austrian aristocracies off balance and unable to do much about the course of events, a parliament was convened in the commercial city of Frankfurt/Main to draw up a national constitution. Composed mainly of educated and professional men, the Frankfurt Assembly produced a constitutional charter, after much haggling and many diversions, calling for a constitutionally bound monarchy and a bicameral parliament, one chamber representing the states and the other, the national electorate, able to challenge the executive's administration of government. The charter called for separation of church from state and education, free enterprise, and individual liberties.

But the Frankfurt Assembly lacked an armed force to back its liberal ideals, and it never had the solid popular support of the citizenry. By the time it got around to offering the crown of a united but liberal republican Germany to the king of Prussia, the reactionary nobility had recovered their confidence, and the Assembly was dispersed by Austrian and Prussian troops. The liberal bourgeois revolution had failed to unite Germany; even in its failure at Frankfurt, as Krieger (1972) has rightly noted, the German idea of liberty was a compromise between monarchy and republican principles. It was not conceivable that Germany could be unified and attain at least quasi-parliamentary government except by playing off the crown against the local aristocracy. The people, it would seem, were not deemed capable of supporting the burden of sovereignty, even at the height of German liberalism.

The defeat of 1848 had a long-lasting effect on the politics of the German bourgeoisie. Observers from a variety of perspectives have remarked on the particular corporate authoritarianism of the German industrialist class, its acceptance of economic liberalism, of free enterprise and the most rational profit-seeking, without any commitment to political liberalism (liberal democracy) as was the case in England, Sweden, the Netherlands, and the United States. By the time of the unification of the nation under Bismarck's leadership in 1871, the older generation of intellectual liberal leaders had given way to a new generation of industrial capitalists concerned if at all with politics, then with unity, order and stability. Already by the 1860s, "the middle classes still maintained connections with the older liberal ideals, but the pursuit of economic interests was already strong enough to shift the primary focus of political concern from liberal parliamentarianism to liberal nationalism" (Krieger, 1972:405). The German bourgeoisie, having failed to unite the country under the banner of liberal democracy, now turned in a different direction. They were ready to accept national unity under conservative aristocratic domination if it meant economic growth, strong state protection from the workers' movement, and, increasingly, protection against an effective popular democracy. Vermeil writes that the German capitalist class now "saw in the (Kaiser's) Reich ruled under Prussian hegemony nothing but a guarantee of economic progress, and in national unity nothing but the essential condition for certain bureaucratic and military achievements" (1969:199). This pattern of support for the political system on purely materialistic grounds meant that in times of economic crisis, loyalty to the system would be extremely problematic. While this was not responsible for the downfall of the Kaiser's empire, it was later to play a key role in the undoing of the Weimar democracy.

The modern German state is in large measure the result of Bismarck's political genius. In a series of confrontations with Austria (1866) and France (1870–71) engineered by Bismarck, Prussia's armies defeated its major rivals for domination in Germany. In 1871 King Wilhelm accepted the imperial crown of the new German empire, but Bismarck, his chief minister, was wise enough to endow the new system with at least the trappings of a constitutional and preparliamentary system; real power rested with the crown, the military, and the bureaucracy, all staffed by the landed nobility. The constitution set up a national parliament, with a lower house (*Reichstag*) elected on the basis of universal male suffrage, progressive for its time. A multiparty system quickly emerged, and considerable press freedom was permitted. This popularly elected *Reichstag* was kept from effective power, however, by the sole jurisdiction of the emperor over foreign and military affairs and by the Kaiser's power to appoint the chancellor, who was head of governmental administration.

There was also a second chamber, the *Bundesrat*, with delegates representing the states of the empire and dominated by Prussia, which alone held seventeen of the fifty-eight votes. This more compliant upper house with considerable responsibility for both legislation and administration further weakened the position of the *Reichstag*. Finally, much domestic legislation and administration of matters most directly affecting the average citizen was left to the individual states. In the state of Prussia, for example, the state legislature was still elected according to feudal estate, with the nobility, a tiny minority of the population, electing one-third of the delegates, the burghers one-third, and the great majority of workers and peasants also one-third.

For the next twenty years, Bismarck, the so-called Iron Chancellor, was quite successful at keeping the *Reichstag* factions at bay through a never-ending series of shifting coalitions, confrontations and concessions (somewhat simplistically, a strategy of divide and rule). For example, in his battle with the rising working-class Social Democratic party (SPD), Bismarck first attempted outright suppression under the anti-Socialist law (1881–90). During this period, the party was banned, union organization was severely constrained, and party and union militants were arrested or exiled. When Bismarck realized after a decade of police suppression that the workers' movement would not fade away under pressure but was in fact growing stronger, he reversed gears, dropped the police suppression, and initiated a series of far-reaching social insurance programs, the first of their kind in the West, to take the wind out of the SPD's sails and to cement the loyalty of the working class to the state.

As a point of contrast with the Swedish and American experiences, both national unification and the early foundations of a welfare program were associated in Germany with the authoritarian government of the Kaiser, not with achievements of liberal democracy or its parliamentary machinery.

The party system of the *Reichstag* reflected the class and religious cleavages of the society. The Conservatives (and smaller Reich party) represented the landed aristocracy; the National Liberals, the nationalist and increasingly conservative industrialists; the Catholic Center party, the religious Catholic minority; the Progressives, the still liberally oriented elements of the intelligentsia and bourgeoisie; and the Social Democrats, the urban working class. Recruitment of party leaders mirrored these divisions in class and religion, with little integration of interests across class lines. Still, this multiclass-based party system was also present in Sweden, without the same negative effects on liberal democracy. Factors other than multipartism were more important in the failures of democratization in Germany, especially the orientation of the modern business class, one of the growing social influences in the era of industrial expansion, toward liberal democracy and its realization.

As the Social Democrats grew stronger and the economic position of the aristocratic Junkers declined, the nationalistic industrialist class gradually threw in its lot with the old order to stave off the advent of both democracy and socialism, which were increasingly equated with each other. It may be said that the German bourgeoisie, having failed to achieve a liberal parliamentary system in 1848 before the rise of the organized labor movement in the last quarter of the century, came to actively oppose liberal democracy, which it now associated not with the rise of capitalism but with the rise of socialism.

In the United States, of course, the birth of liberal democracy preceded both industrialization and the union movement. In Sweden it would appear that it was the relative moderation of the aristocracy that made the difference. While we can point to certain factors, such as Sweden's earlier achievement of national unity, its religious homogeneity, and in particular its only marginal involvement in the power struggles of central Europe in the nineteenth century, that aided Sweden's democratic transformation, it must also be recognized that for Sweden, as for Germany, industrialization came at the same time as the crucial push for democratization, with the same possibility of opposition to democracy by the business class. Here we must, with Vermeil (1969), recognize some essential differences among capitalist classes across national borders between generations, differences that make the relationship between the development of capitalism and business class support for liberal democracy a contingent one rather than an automatic one. We shall return to this crucial point later, when we consider the prospects for liberal democracy in those nations yet to achieve an industrial revolution.

By the outbreak of World War I, the *Reichstag* still remained a deeply divided preparliament, unable to effectively check or balance the Kaiser and his ministers, though none of the chancellors after the forced resignation of Bismarck in 1890 possessed his political talents.

The *Reichstag* still had not established itself as the basis for forming a government or for passing final judgment on policy and legislative matters. This breakthrough was only to come with the defeat of the Kaiser's armies in the course of war; in November of 1918, with the war lost and the populace "bled white," unrest began to spread throughout the land. The German High Seas Fleet mutinied, and workers began to occupy some major factories. The Kaiser abdicated and fled the country, leaving the prodemocratic forces to sign the humiliating Versailles Treaty and to try to pull the shattered country together. Although the young Weimar democracy survived early attempts at both socialist revolution and reactionary coups d'etat, it was clearly a system born under less than auspicious circumstances. Nevertheless, the Weimar Republic was the first full-blown system of liberal democracy to be established in Germany, with a universal adult franchise, abolition of many privileges of the aristocracy in the state governments, and with a majority in the *Reichstag* clearly the basis for forming a government and enacting legislation. As the German political historian Karl-Dietrich Bracher (1970) has pointed out, it was by no means the case that Weimar democracy was doomed from the start. Even with the disadvantages of an army general staff clearly disloyal to the republic and a bureaucracy and judiciary packed with reactionary and aristocratic elements also of dubious loyalty, it took the wrenching experience of the Great Depression to propel the Nazi party (National Socialist German Workers party) under Hitler from less than 3 percent of the vote in 1928 to 37 percent by 1932, and then a coalition of the Nazis with the party of wealthy landowners and big business, Hugenberg's National Conservatives and the Catholic antidemocratic schemer von Papen, to finally overwhelm the young democracy.

It was the Protestant middle and upper classes that in troubled times, ever fearful of socialist revolution, had turned toward order and stability, this time in the form of fascist dictatorship. Lipset (1963) has documented the flight of middle-class voters from the liberal German Democratic party, the German Moderates, and the German Middle-Class party to the Nazis and to a lesser extent to the Nationalist Conservatives. More recent evidence from Hamilton (1983) has shown, however, that Nazi support was highest in the most wealthy Protestant upper-class districts. Already in 1931 a formal alliance of Nazis and Nationalist Conservatives illustrated which groups would eventually overthrow the Republic. Even the relatively conservative historian Golo Mann (1968:400–401) could not deny the collaboration of the capitalist class in the building of fascism:

> The majority (of conservatives), under the party leader Hugenberg, entered into an alliance with the National Socialists whom they copied though showing a little more restraint; they talked of the "November criminals", of the "outrage of Versailles", of the treachery and inefficiency of democracy and the rest. Hugenberg was a rich man, the owner of an enormous publishing and newspaper business. . . . The concentration of all enemies of the Republic on the right was called the Harzburg Front after the spa where the whole gang, industrialists, generals, bankers, and party leaders met in 1931. What they had in common was hostility to the Republic.

With the naming of Hitler as chancellor, the disintegration of democratic institutions began, and at a pace and with a ferocity unequalled by the fascist regimes in Italy, France, and Japan. Within a matter of months, opposition parties were banned, starting with the Communists (KPD); opposition newspapers were shut down and nonoppositional media subjected to increasing censorship; civil rights of political, ethnic, and religious minority groups were first abused and then totally suppressed, leading ultimately to the establishment of concentration camps for the extermination of Communists, Jews, and Gypsies;

labor unions were abolished and replaced with a bogus labor front (DAF) that openly favored business over workers' interests; the economy, which remained in private hands, was reoriented toward military production; in foreign affairs, an aggressive nationalism and lust for conquest characterized the new regime (see Bracher, 1970; Neumann, 1942). Schweitzer (1964) sees the Nazi regime, at least prior to the wartime mobilization, as a sort of four-way coalition including the Nazi party, the secret police, the generals, and big business, who agreed on the goals of "military and economic rearmament, the suppression of trade unions, and the invigoration of capitalist institutions" (504). The coalition consensus on higher profit for big business resulted in a sharp decline of wages and salaries as a percentage of national income, whereas income from property, entrepreneurial activity, and corporate profits rose from 30.4 to 39.2 percent between 1932 and 1939 (Knauerhase, 1972:129).

Only total defeat in World War II brought the system down. It is only since 1949 that a liberal democracy, reimplanted by the Western occupation forces in the Federal Republic, has grown and prospered and has over time come to be identified with political and economic success. Since 1949 the *Bundestag*, the lower house, has been an effective parliament, the party system gradually transformed itself into a two-and-a-half party system (Social Democrats, Christian Democrats, and the smaller Free Democrats) through a stepwise decline to insignificance of the radical left (Communists) and radical right (neo-Nazis). A temporary re-emergence of the radical right, the NPD, to between 5 and 10 percent of the vote during the recession of 1965–66 was associated with the same lingering dynamic of economic crisis and authoritarian attitudes (Nagle, 1970) that posed a fatal threat to Weimar. But in the 1974–75 recession, much worse and longer than the one a decade earlier, no such right radical (or left radical) movement emerged, and it may be that a new generation of Germans of all social classes have now positively identified themselves with liberal democracy for better or for worse, in good times and not-so-good times. In the 1980s, the rise of the environmentalist Greens as a new party in the *Bundestag* has affirmed the opportunity for the "new social movements" to enter the political arena, as well as the commitment of the Greens to compete within the parliamentary system. In the latter 1980s, the new right-extremist Republican (REP) party was able to garner some votes in state and local elections using antiforeigner (especially anti-Turkish) themes and assertive nationalist rhetoric, and some observers (Ely, 1989; Leggewie, 1990) have seen in this a general decline in the capacity of the main established parties to integrate new issues and younger generations into the political mainstream. With the inevitable disruptions now accompanying German unification, the rise of nationalist fervor in neighboring Eastern Europe, and the additional challenge of integrating 16 million citizens of East Germany into Western liberal democracy, Germany will face a new test of the postwar democratic political culture.

Some Special Comments on Japanese Democracy

Japan's democracy, constructed after World War II with the oversight of the United States occupation authorities from 1945 to 1952, has been the major example of liberal democracy in a non-Western culture. For several decades, little attention was paid to Japanese democracy as a variant of liberal democracy, although the formalities of liberal democracy, including a multiparty system, regular competitive elections to the Diet or parliament, and the formation of cabinets from the leadership of the majority Liberal Democratic party (LDP) were clearly present. Most descriptions of the Japanese system noted the long-term dominance (some would say monopoly) of the conservative LDP in national politics, the stability of the system, and the close cooperation between business and government in economic policy making. The minor roles of organized labor and the opposition Japan Socialist party have been noted in passing, along with the splintered nature of the opposition, which includes also the Communist party, the Democratic Socialist party, and the Komeito (Clean Government party). In the 1980s, however, as Japan's economic strength grew to superpower proportions, many observers (cf. for example Reischauer, 1988; Prestowitz, 1988; Kennedy, 1987) have investigated the Japanese democratic experience and have compared the "Japanese model" to other great nations, to see how Japanese politics worked to make the economy so strong. Many observers have concluded that Japanese democracy is quite different from the other affluent liberal democracies, and there is still much to be learned about just how this very important system is developing. Although there is much about Japanese politics that is still rather unclear to Western and even Japanese political analysts, there are some points that set Japan off from the norm of liberal democracies.

First and foremost, since the reestablishment of Japanese self-government in 1952, there has never been a major change in government. The LDP, which came into existence as the result of a merger in 1955 between two conservative parties (Liberals and Democrats), has won every election and has not yet been seriously challenged for national power. There has never been a government led by a left-of-center or labor-based party. In the other reconstructed democracies, Germany and France, there has been at least one major change in national government, including a shift from center-right to center-left (or back again), and in Italy at least there has been extensive participation in national governing by the Socialists and in regional governing by the Communists. Japan has had a single conservative party in charge for more than forty years.

Second, Japanese politics has been and still is conducted much more behind closed doors, within the six major factions of the LDP and within the bureaucratic structures of government. Major policy decisions and choices of the prime minister, as well as of lesser officers, are negotiated in the smoke-filled rooms of the factions of the LDP. Inter-factional politics is more

37

determining of policy and office-holding than is electoral politics, and is largely out of public view. As Robert Scalapino and Junnosuke Masumi noted nearly thirty years ago, Japan is "an open society made up of closed components" (1962:153), and this is reflected in the effectively closed nature of politics, despite its formally open institutions. Citizens are more or less limited to reactions to the effects of policies and leaders rather than participating in issue formulation or candidate selection. This contrasts sharply with the greater citizen and voter involvement in policy debate and candidate choice in most of the other liberal democracies, especially since the 1960s.

Third, the role of big business money in Japanese politics, in particular in the LDP but also in other parties on occasion, is extraordinary, pervasive, and dominant, despite numerous financial scandals and even convictions of leading Japanese politicians. In 1972, Prime Minister Tanaka was caught up in a financial scandal that forced him to resign his office. He was formally charged in 1976 and convicted in 1983, but appealed his conviction to higher courts. Throughout this period he remained the leader of the largest LDP faction, a kingpin in Japanese politics, and only his declining health after 1985 forced him out of active politics. In another scandal, the Recruit Company was revealed in 1988 to have given expensive gifts and stock shares to leading members of the LDP and government ministries. Again there were resignations, of Prime Minister Takeshita and three other ministers, but the system of "money politics" was left untouched. A new political insider-trading stock scandal in 1991 brought this comment from Shigezo Hayasaka, one-time aide to Prime Minister Tanaka, "This is an insider society. It is not unusual for us to share this kind of information with friends. . . . Even to my eyes, it's not a matter of right or wrong, or morals, but differences in our two cultures. Put more frankly, Japan is a society of insider dealings." (*New York Times*, Feb. 2, 1991, p.35)

Fourth, since World War II, Japan, unlike Germany, has not engaged in much soul-searching about its militarist and imperialist past. While the Germans went through several stages of "overcoming the past," of admitting past crimes and built-up prejudices, as a necessary step to building a more tolerant and democratic political culture, in Japan virtually nothing of a similar nature has been undertaken. Quite the opposite. Japanese textbooks approved by the education ministry gloss over the brutalities of Japanese military aggression in Korea and China, and as recently as the latter 1980s a cabinet minister asserted that Japan's military occupation of China was proper and even "defensive" against threats from the Western industrial powers. Yet in 1987 Prime Minister Nakasone said it was time to "close the books on the postwar period," and he visited the Yasukuni Shrine to honor Japan's war dead. To many, it appeared that Japan had not yet repudiated its past actions, nor come to terms with the underlying causes of past aggressions against its neighbors and suppression of domestic dissent.

Only after several more years of scandal and the most serious financial crisis in Japanese postwar history did the ruling LDP lose its majority in the July 1993 elections. Led by Tsutomo Hata and Morihiro Hosokawa, defectors from the LDP reform wing, a seven-party coalition formed the first non-LDP government in thirty-eight years and set out on a moderate reform course that promised honesty, a reformed elections system, and greater attention to consumer interests. The new prime minister, Hosokawa, also for the first time straightforwardly apologized for Japan's past aggression against its neighbors. This change of government represented a potential further democratization of the Japanese political system.

Taken together, this means that while Japan has been extraordinarily successful economically and very stable politically, its democratic institutions have yet to be really tested. They remain more formal than functional and have not been put to use to the same degree as in other Western democracies. Despite a postwar overlay of Western liberalism and the formal politics of liberalism, Japan in many ways remains a traditionally conservative polity, in which "creative conservatism" (Pempel, 1982) has remained effectively dominant. Japanese political culture, like Japanese society, is still much more group-oriented than individual-oriented. This long tradition of Japanese citizen loyalty to the group's expectations and norms contrasts with the Western liberal tradition of individualism and individual political action. On the other hand, the younger generations do show more support for individualistic values, and less for traditional values (Ike, 1973), so that there has been some evolution within Japanese political culture over the postwar period. What is not yet known is what political difference this evolution would make in a period of greater social or economic stress than Japan has experienced for several decades.

Parliament—Centerpiece of Liberal Democracy

Certain institutions may characterize a political system-type. Liberal democracy has long been identified with the development of a national parliament or legislature that is the focal point of political debate and broad policy making. As the centerpiece of liberal democracy, the parliament serves as a forum for contending interests, factions, or parties. It is the assemblage of openly elected representatives of the citizenry. Early struggles of bourgeois democracy, as cited previously, were histories of the emergence of a politically effective and competitively elected parliament (in England the House of Commons, in Germany the *Reichstag*, in Sweden the *Riksdag*, and in the United States the Congress).

In the twentieth century, many other political institutions have developed within the industrial democracies of the West to challenge or transcend the important roles of the parliament. A consolidated two-party or multiparty system has at times seemed to signal a decline of parliament in favor of effective policy making within the party organizations, especially during periods of one-party dominance, as in the forty-year period of government by the Social Democrats in Sweden, or the long period of Republican dominance in the United States after the Civil War, or during the Adenauer era of the 1950s and early 1960s in West Germany. In these periods, the party organization seemed to dominate the parliament as the focal point for political decision making.

The executive branch of government has also challenged the central role of parliament, especially in crisis or wartime situations and under inspired or forceful leadership. President Roosevelt during the Great Depression and World War II, Winston Churchill as the British wartime prime minister, President de Gaulle in the first decade of the Fifth French Republic, and Chancellor Adenauer in West Germany overshadowed both their own parties and the parliament, certainly in popular attention and political initiative. In the latter 1960s, under both President Johnson and President Nixon, it was feared that an "imperial presidency" was developing in the United States, able to conduct government affairs in virtual disregard for Congress and through a creeping takeover of Congress's legislative functions.

Finally, the growth of government bureaucracy, necessary for administration of the vast array of welfare and regulatory programs and for expanded peacetime military establishments and state-run industries, has appeared to place much political decision making beyond the reach of any elected government body. In some systems, notably the French Fourth Republic (1945–58) and the postwar Italian democracy, both noted for frequent turnover in coalition governments, the higher civil service was viewed as a source of political continuity. In Britain also, the top echelons of the civil service provided a continuing expertise and administrative experience for state-run industries that outlasted any particular Labor or Conservative government and that was of growing importance as a center of decision making.

All of these perceptions have some validity, and they describe some of the basic additions to parliamentary democracy over the past century and a half. Yet the Congress, the *Bundestag*, the House of Commons, and the *Riksdag* have always rebounded from periods of weakness and responded to challenges from particular parties, prime ministers, and presidents, and even from bureaucracy. Other political systems, both communist and Third World, may have an effective party organization, or a strong executive, or a stabilizing civil service. But it is the historic birth of an elected parliament and its continued vitality that mark liberal democracy as a political system-type. Conversely, the demise of liberal democracy, as in Germany in the 1930s, Italy in the 1920s, or the postwar Czechoslovakian Republic in 1948, has been marked by the demise of an effective parliament. Juan Linz (1990), a noted scholar of comparative politics, has concluded that presidentialism, which gives a central role to the national executive, is less conducive to stable liberal democracy than are parliamentary systems, and is part of the problem facing democratic development in Latin America.

The democratic parliament tends to be an institution of moderation and partial reforms generally incapable of leading any radical social change, whether revolutionary or counterrevolutionary. In this sense, also, parliament has been the instrument of "moderate" parties from the conservative right to the social democratic left, those parties whose goals could be achieved by incremental reforms within the existing capitalist system. The parliament of liberal democracy is in many ways the ideal institution for avoiding basic social change. Its openness assures that competing social interests will try to counteract any policy movement that might adversely affect their own interests. Moreover, those interests that benefit most from the status quo are generally the best positioned to press their case and are free to use their considerable financial resources to influence both legislators and voters. The necessity for periodic re-election of representatives biases parliament against programs calling for short-term (or long-term) sacrifice in order to achieve longer-term goals. Even a reform-minded party with a parliamentary majority must try to avoid drastic shifts in policy that would, in the short run, lead to economic disruption and social disorder, which would lead either to some loss of electoral support or to a military coup. The politics of broad consensus building are preferred to the politics of class polarization. Successful parties and leaders in parliamentary systems are typically, though not always, those who occupy the middle ground, not those who advocate controversial programs. Politics tends to chase after short-run public favor, at the expense of either constant programmatic action or political education. Social and economic planning is hindered by parliamentary democracy, though not entirely ruled out. This is, we would posit, one of the functions of the institution: to discourage notions of social and economic planning, which might develop the capability for a transition to socialism.

Governing parties cannot risk carrying out radical social policies if they wish to remain in office and maintain the liberal democratic system. Parliamentary democracy limits its scope of "normal" policy choices to those that do not question the existing social order, but that try to amend it through partial measures. Parliament is not an institution designed for political mobilization of have-not groups in the society; rather it is best suited to diminish, but not eliminate, the impact of lower-class demands and to increase the likelihood of stalemate or watering-down of radical proposals. Parliaments as institutions have not always survived periods of severe economic and social crisis; there are limits to the containment of both lower-class demands for basic change and bourgeois support for fascist suppression of militant worker organizations. By the same logic of moderation, parliament has limited impact in shaping its own political environment. Almost by definition, it cannot take decisive action to resolve impending class violence, revolutionary upsurge, civil war, or fascist coup. But within the postwar period of growth and increasing prosperity in the developed capitalist nations, parliament plays a central moderating and consensus-building role in the liberal democracies.

Achievements and Erosion of the Cold War Welfare State

The liberal welfare democracy of the post–World War II era was in great measure a practical, nonpurist response to the sufferings of so many citizens during the Great Depression and the two world wars in the first half of this century. In a wide-ranging consensus across conservative, Christian democratic, liberal, social democratic, and socialist parties, postwar politics sought to prevent the return of the economic and social insecurity that had profoundly marked earlier generations. Whether under the conservative government of Konrad Adenauer in West Germany or the socialist government of Tage Erlander in Sweden, government interventions into economic and social life were initiated and expanded until by the 1970s between one-third to two-thirds of the nation's total economic activity (gross domestic product, or GDP) was in some fashion passing through government hands. Despite warnings from hard-line economic liberals that this situation would lead to catastrophe and economic ruin, political leaders from virtually all points of the spectrum supported this general trend, and most arguments turned on technical questions of efficiency and actual implementation. The longer this trend continued without breakdown or catastrophe, the more the basic assumptions of the welfare state became the normal situation and the general expectations of both political leaders and broad majorities of the citizenry. For two generations, the success of the welfare state democracy seemed unquestionable, as described in more detail in the following chapters. Broad prosperity, extending deep into the working class itself, became the natural state of affairs. Workers in the Western democracies began to consider themselves middle class, and sharp class conflicts faded noticeably.

The achievements of this historic class compromise, this package of trade-offs, or new political economy (to use a bit of jargon), were extraordinary and were in large measure responsible for the triumph of the Western democracies over communism in the Cold War. It is understandable that many citizens in these democracies are anxious and fearful that this success formula is now eroding. The postwar economic recovery reached new historic highs in consumer affluence, and recessions did not spiral downward into new depressions. Concerted government action to counteract economic downturns became a standard feature of Western democratic politics. Basic, even generous, state-sponsored security programs were developed to ameliorate the hazards of life and the risks of market economies, such as severe illness, disablement, old age, unemployment, and poverty-level income. Without a doubt these programs worked to improve the lives of countless millions. Combined with relatively large-scale military spending as part of the Western alliance's commitment to safeguarding the peace, this became a Cold War era of peace, prosperity, and social security for the great majority.

In the area of personal liberty, the postwar democracies became by far the most tolerant and protective of human rights, both in those countries like the United States and Great Britain, the most stable and long-lived of the democracies, and in Germany, Japan, Italy, and France, which had to be reconstructed as democracies after World War II. Postwar Germany had become by the 1970s a kind of *Modell Deutschland*, a leading economic power in Europe, a good citizen within the European Community and NATO, and a tolerant and humane democratic culture. Why, then, should the welfare state democracy have eroded, and why is it now in a process of great change to something still unclear but qualitatively different?

Erosion and Its Consequences

The gradual erosion of the liberal welfare state has various roots, and the signs of decay have been increasing since at least the early 1970s. Many critiques of the welfare state have rested on moralistic grounds, arguing that government intrusion and government paternalism have sapped the spirit of individual effort and responsibility. Welfarism has been cited endless times as the root cause of moral degeneration and a dependency syndrome. Such attacks go back to the earliest days of public efforts to provide relief from economic disaster, health crises, and social problems. While they no doubt have some element of truth, they do not explain why it is only now that the welfare state democracies are in such trouble and need to find some new political formula. Often, when basic political change becomes necessary, economic reasons are the most fundamental, and this is arguably also the case for the welfare state. Within the Western democracies, the financial situation has been deteriorating, and this deterioration accelerated in the late 1980s. The total package of welfare state services and programs in virtually all of the liberal democracies was in fiscal crisis by the early 1990s. While high-level corruption, bureaucratic mismanagement, and low-level fraud were often cited as causes of this crisis, the more basic problems lay elsewhere.

First, and perhaps foremost, economic growth in the liberal democracies has slowed down since the 1970s. The reasons are not entirely understood, but the effects are clear. With slower growth, the raising of tax revenues to pay for social services has become more difficult and onerous, while the demand for social services has increased. In fact, with slower growth has come higher unemployment—structural unemployment—which means that a smaller percentage of the work-age population is paying into social security programs of all types and a larger percentage is drawing upon these same security budgets, for example, for unemployment, family support, and food stamps.

Second, partly as a result of affluence and peace, the populations of the liberal democracies have aged considerably. Birth rates have fallen as people have chosen to have smaller families, and the percentages of senior citizens continues to grow rapidly. This has a double impact on social expenditures, since a smaller proportion of the population is working (and paying into social security programs) and a larger portion is in retirement (and drawing their benefits from these programs).

Third, in the vital area of health care, government spending has increased rapidly in virtually all of the democracies. This is also in part related to the aging of the population, since the elderly are greater consumers of health care services. At the same time, modern medical technology and professional long-term care have made it possible to prolong life but at an alarming increase in costs, both to private and public budgets.

All of the above have created a situation of high government spending for a wide array of social services, which adds to the cost of production for business and industry in the liberal democracies. These costs, which include formal wages and salaries of workers, engineers, managers, and corporate executives as well as social benefits, must now compete in a much more global economic order. Modern communications, lower transportation costs, and the development of worldwide financial networks have made it possible for increasing business investment in low-wage, low-social-benefit nations (Mexico, Philippines, Pakistan, and now Eastern Europe, too). German workers, British managers, United States engineers, and French farmers are finding that they are in price/wage competition with people in poorer circumstances than themselves and that the modern corporation is increasingly transnational in outlook, free to invest its capital where it can derive the greatest profit from production. High private wages and salaries, increases in life expectancy and access to health care, and generous social benefits in the affluent liberal democracies, success of the postwar welfare state systems, are now sources of capital and job migration overseas, which further undermine the viability of welfare state democracy, the political success formula of the postwar era. The result has been growing structural deficits in the liberal democracies and the search for a new type of politics that criticizes the welfare state, its tax burdens, and its inability to provide for enough growth to balance its budgets.

The sum effect of these strains on the fiscal (budgetary) health of the postwar welfare state has been a gradual demoralization of the citizenry and political leaders alike about the politics of their nations. Conservative attempts in the 1980s by Prime Minister Margaret Thatcher in Great Britain and President Ronald Reagan in the United States to regain economic dynamism through wide-ranging deregulation and privatization programs did not solve the long-term structural crisis, although they certainly did launch the first clear break in the postwar consensus. In the early 1990s, most government leaders of the liberal democracies, from Francois Mitterrand of France to Giulio Andreotti of Italy to John Major of Britain to Kiichi Miyazawa of Japan and even Helmut Kohl of Germany, suffered severe losses in citizen confidence, and many leading political parties, including the Liberal Democratic party in Japan and both the Christian Democrats and the Socialists in Italy, were regarded as deeply corrupted by long years in office and temptations for self-enrichment. Of course, there had been earlier periods of economic crisis, as, for example, during the oil price shocks of the 1970s, and earlier rounds of political scandal and corruption, too, but in the wake of the Cold War and with the decline in prospects for continuing the welfare state with its generous benefits and social guarantees, a sense of sullen disillusion (the German term is *Verdrossenheit*) with politics as usual has set in, and there are now clear signs that in some of the liberal democracies, the old order is breaking up, and a transition to a new politics, not yet quite clear and nowhere consolidated, has begun. The signs are diverse and impact the established parties and leaders in a variety of settings, but they portend a basic change in the life of the liberal democracies.

In the United States, the 1992 elections ousted President George Bush, the acclaimed leader of the 1991 Desert Storm victories in the Gulf war, from office and ended twelve years of Republican administration. Bill Clinton was elected on a platform of ''change'' as a ''new type of Democrat,'' representing a new generation of leadership. But the most startling phenomenon of 1992 was the emergence of billionaire Ross Perot as the antipolitician, the outsider who challenged the establishment and, despite some flaky campaign moves, won 19 percent of the vote.

In France, the elections of 1993 ousted the Socialist government, which had governed for most of the previous twelve years, and so diminished the Socialist vote that Michel Rocard, a long-time Socialist strategist and former premier, called for a conference to reinvent the Socialist left through some sort of ''big bang'' that would both destroy the old politics of French socialism and give birth to a new Socialist agenda. But not many French citizens expect the new center-right government to do anything too wonderful either. The urge to kick out the incumbents was not matched by a new and convincing political vision from either Giscard d'Estaing's Republicans or Jacques Chirac's neo-Gaullists.

In Italy, 1993 witnessed a flood of corruption scandals among leading political and business figures who had been mainstays of Italian political life for decades. Regional and local elections confirmed that an earthquake in public opinion was taking place. In the wealthier North, the right-wing regional populist Northern League of Umberto Bossi, long regarded as a

45

political quack, became the strongest party. In the center region of Italy, the Democratic Party of the Left (the renamed communists) became the leading party. The Socialist party of Bettino Craxi (under investigation for corruption) was almost wiped out. The Christian Democrats retained some strength in the poorest southern region, where their connections with the local elites and the mafia seem to have survived. But nationally, the Christian Democrats, the governing party for over forty-six years, ceased to exist (the remnants are now the Popular party).

In the March 1994 national elections, the biggest winner was billionaire media entrepreneur Silvio Berlusconi and his Forza Italia (Go Italy), confirming again the potential for new Perot-type populism.

In Japan, a series of corruption scandals involving leading figures of the ruling Liberal Democratic party and the public disgust with the old men of the LDP running politics-as-usual in the midst of Japan's most serious economic slowdown since the war, led to the resignation of Miyazawa's government and the partial splintering of the LDP, with some younger reformists forming their own parties. In the elections of July 1993, the LDP lost its majority in the parliament after thirty-eight years in power, and seven opposition parties formed a new governing coalition under Hosokawa, the new prime minister.

In Germany, a climate of *Politikverdrossenheit* (sullen disillusion with politics) has resulted from rising unemployment, cutbacks in social programs for the first time in Germany's postwar history, and a series of scandals that have led to resignations from government, business, and labor leaders. Meanwhile, the flood of ethnic Germans from Eastern Europe, economic migrants, and political refugees since 1989 has met with a rising tide of right-extremist antiforeigner violence (and also with mass candlelight marches against hate and violence), which the government has been unwilling or unable to contain. Polls show a loss of confidence in the established parties, and it is not clear what new alternative politics may emerge from this.

For the young adults of the liberal democracies in particular, the general expectation for the first time since World War II is that they will not do as well economically as their parents (Riding, 1993). In particular, they are disillusioned with politics—both government and opposition—and are the most alienated from the usual political formula of the postwar era. This is a critical sign that the political socialization process that was for two generations after World War II so successful in the liberal democracies has now eroded badly and is unconvincing for those now forming their basic attitudes toward the political system.

Robert Leicht, a leading editorialist for the liberal German magazine *die Zeit,* has commented on the need for fundamental rethinking of what left, right, and liberal mean in the post-1989 world, and he has challenged conservatives, liberals, and socialists to remain true to their core values but, at the same time, reinvent their politics.

At the latest, the watershed of 1989 with its consequences forces everyone, from right to left, to rethinking, to revision. None of the old patented answers can be mechanically repeated. But the visions, the old core values have not lost their meaning; quite the contrary: we have them to thank after all for this transformation. Time and prelude to a clarifying struggle. Or, to say it with a verse from T. S. Elliot: "Time for you and time for me / and time yet for a hundred indecisions and for a hundred visions and revisions." (Leicht, 1993:3; my translation from the German)

In this new era of great transitions, the consensus politics of the liberal welfare state is giving way to a much more open competition for a new political formula that can mobilize new enthusiasm and offer a convincing vision of a better future. This period is bound to contain some bitter conflicts and, as Antonio Gramsci once said about the end of an era, "morbid symptoms," but it is also an exciting period of new possibilities and innovation, which an open, pluralistic, democratic system should be able to handle. The present task of liberal democracy as a system is to facilitate this transition through reinvigorating the democratic political culture and rebuilding public confidence that democratic government does work. Without knowing what the new political formula of post-industrial, post–Cold War democracy will look like (although there are some hints), we will focus in the following chapters on the tough job of reworking political priorities and policy trade-offs in this transitional era.

3

Affluent Consumerism—
Now in Danger?

The pattern of performance trade-offs of the Western democracies in the Cold War era was to a very great extent based on successful economic growth policies that provided an underpinning (a foundation) for policies in the areas of social equality, personal liberty, and even quality of life, were more socially generous to the poor, were able to accommodate the emancipation and greater personal liberty of women, and of ethnic, religious, and other minorities, and could even afford to address at least some of the new environmental issues of affluent consumer societies. The loss of economic growth dynamism in the West, beginning in the 1970s, has, however, put this package (or political economy) into doubt, giving rise to new insecurity among both citizens and political elites about the future and new challenges to the old consensus politics and the parties that represented the "old formula." But before we can address the politics of great change of the current period, we must understand the nature of the "old formula" and its achievements, for they were in many respects the reason for the victory of the West over the communist challenge of the Cold War.

The Political Economy of Western Democratic Prosperity

The economies of the Western democracies have undergone significant transformation since the early phases of industrialization in the nineteenth century, which have pushed them ever further from the idealized laissez-faire model of Adam Smith. According to Smith and other theorists of capitalism, the state's role should be minimal in economic life, and there should be few regulations or limitations on the rights of private property. Each individual, whether business owner or laborer, should face the market conditions independently and alone. This early purist ideal was, however, gradually modified to embrace a much-expanded economic role for a democratically elected government and various forms of cooperation among leaders of large

48

organizations representing government, business, and labor. Especially after the traumatic experiences of the Great Depression and World War II, democratic governments pledged to their citizens a new effort, called the New Deal/Fair Deal in the United States, and in Germany the "social market economy," to manage economic growth of the nation-state so that all citizens would benefit and could have greater assurance in their material standard of living. (Note: I will generally refer to West Germany from 1949–90 and unified Germany since 1990 simply as Germany. Where a comparison between the old West Germany and the former East Germany is necessary, or where a clarification is required, I will make this distinction.) This package of modifications, the result of a century of democratic political struggle, is often called the neoliberal model, which has been the dominant consensus of the post–World War II era, embracing both moderate conservative parties of the right and moderate socialist parties of the left. This compromise between strict economic liberalism and the social consensus of democratic politics created a period of widespread postwar prosperity for the great majority of citizens.

This increasing economic prosperity, outlined in this chapter, began to stagnate in the 1970s, and in the last years of the Cold War era new political challengers began to undermine the "normal" politics of the postwar era of mass prosperity. Presently, the neoliberal consensus of the Western democracies, in the era of post–Cold War transformation, is severely eroded, although its broad features are still largely intact. It is under attack from several directions; a search for a new consensus, or new alternatives, marks the politics of the 1990s in virtually all liberal democracies.

To understand this current period of greater uncertainty and the politics of change from the neoliberal model of economic policy, we must first look at the developments that first gave rise to the neoliberal economic growth model and those developments that are now undermining its foundations.

Key Aspects of the Postwar Formula

One trend in the development of capitalism in the industrial era was the growing complexity of corporations and the accompanying concentration of economic power among the largest enterprises. The business enterprise progressed through several stages in the past century, including (1) growth of professional management, (2) growth of more impersonal stock ownership, (3) widening of a firm's market, both nationally and internationally, and (4) widening of product array, both through internal diversification and corporate merger.

In industry and in agriculture, small and middle-sized family-owned and family-operated businesses lost out to a much smaller number of large and more complex corporations. The local family firm was superseded by the nationally based corporation, which in turn has been progressively integrated into the multinational conglomerate, largely self-financing and with increasing operations abroad for resources, manufacturing, and marketing. Large multinationals such as Exxon, General Motors, Thyssen, Unilever, and Nippon Steel have annual sales that exceed the total annual production (GNP) of most nations. From one sector of the economy to another, sales and profits have been concentrated in the hands of perhaps three or four giants. Rather than a multitude of small enterprises fiercely competing to survive under the "invisible hand" of the market, a monopoly capitalism tended toward collusion and price setting as the rational way for the largest corporations to maximize and stabilize profits and sales. Smaller firms were still subject to a market they could not control, however, and their profit margins were correspondingly the lowest. (In the United States profits have been negative for the smallest businesses since the end of World War II.)

A second trend was the growth of government and its role in maintaining economic prosperity. The Great Depression of the 1930s ended the orthodoxy of an unregulated market capitalism. Through a combination of new economic theory, trial and error, and wartime government intervention in the economy, the liberal democracies assumed a new and growing responsibility, widely recognized as legitimate, for limited intervention in the marketplace. The whole point of Keynesian economics, developed in the Depression era, was to moderate the excesses of capitalist development, and especially to avoid another Great Depression. Since the free market clearly could not guarantee this, Western governments undertook means to regulate the economy, to ensure that economic slowdowns, a normal part of the business cycle, did not spiral into catastrophe, or that economic booms did not overheat and then suddenly burst. Four main aspects of governmental activity can be identified with the new "Keynesian" orthodoxy: (1) regulation of economic activity, (2) welfare spending, (3) military spending, and (4) government employment.

Regulatory activities of banking and finance operations, stock exchanges, labor-management relations, and general marketing practices were designed to prevent the recurrence of unsound stock speculation and banking practices and class violence that marked Western capitalism prior to 1929. Monitoring the economy closely, government attempted to provide a climate of both investor and consumer confidence for stable but moderate growth.

Welfare spending, apart from its humanitarian goals, served as a major support for consumer spending among the elderly, the jobless, the sick and disabled, and the retired and thus provided support for business activity. During the Depression, consumer spending dried up as joblessness increased, adding to the downturn in production and employment. Welfare spending became an avenue for maintaining consumer demand even in, or especially in, the event of recession.

Large-scale military spending in the Cold War years was an additional means of governmental support for business activity. Military contracts provided a considerable source of sales and profits for many of the largest corporations, especially in the United States (President Eisenhower warned, in 1960, of a growing "military-industrial complex"). Government military spending in the liberal democracies did not return to prewar peacetime levels and served as an element in an overall "Keynesian" strategy.

In the liberal democracies, government also became a sort of "employer of last resort" in two ways. Government (nonmilitary) bureaucracy increased markedly with the growth in welfare programs and regulatory bodies, producing a large increase in civil service employment. In Britain and Italy especially, many bankrupt or unprofitable businesses in automaking, steel, and shipbuilding were "saved" through nationalization, primarily to maintain employment levels. In the United States, where nationalization was ideologically unacceptable, the federal government nevertheless provided billions to the railroads, to Lockheed International, and to the Chrysler Corporation, and for essentially the same reasons.

Taken together, this political intervention into the capitalist economy significantly moved the economy from its early laissez-faire principles. By the 1980s, liberal democratic governments were regulating and redistributing resources at very substantial levels of total Gross Domestic Product (GDP). Tax revenues were now between 30 and 50 percent of GDP, and virtually every field of economic activity was extensively regulated and monitored. In the German model, which is often cited as one of the most successful of the Western economies, only about half of GDP is produced according to strict market rules, and more than 40 percent of all prices are directly or indirectly determined through government action (Schmid, 1990:28). Especially in the agricultural sector, government subsidies and regulation of crop plantings and marketing mechanisms is far from the unfettered free market model throughout the European Union, the United States, and Japan. In Japan, the most dynamic success story of the postwar period, the close collaboration between government and industry, the planning for development of new sectors of the economy, and the protection given to domestic markets and products by government, industry, and labor were not exactly what free traders and free marketeers idealized. Yet the evolutionary development of the modern welfare state and heavily regulated economy were the main features of the most successful growth period of modern times, and became established features of all of the liberal democracies. The modern welfare-state democracy assumed the role of managing the economy, though not directly planning production for the economy as a whole.

Economic Slowdown and New Challenges

Beginning in the 1970s, the economic growth of most Western democracies began to slow down noticeably (Japan's slowdown was delayed until the late 1980s). In the 1970s, the oil-price shocks of OPEC added to this slowdown, creating a decade of stagflation, combining higher inflation with slow growth, or stagnation, and higher unemployment. The growth of the state bureaucracy and state intervention in the economy, which required higher taxation to meet the expanded role of government, also began to produce a political backlash. The antitax revolt of Mogens Gilstrup's Progress party in Denmark in 1973 was an early sign of this, but did not then signal any basic change in the overall political landscape. In the 1980s, new conservative leaders like Margaret Thatcher in Great Britain and Ronald Reagan in the United States proposed programs to dismantle large parts of the regulatory and welfare state bureaucracy in order to restore free market conditions. Prime Minister Thatcher's conservative government of the 1980s privatized many state-owned industries (such as British Petroleum, British Telecommunications, Jaguar, British Airways, British Gas, and British Steel) as well as most public housing, and she broke the power of the British trade unions, while giving the financial world in London freer rein. The newly privatized industries generally improved their performance, with sharp reductions in jobs. Yet, after more than a decade in office, Mrs. Thatcher ran into stiff opposition in her bid to replace the popular National Health Service and to place a regressive poll tax on every citizen, and she was ousted from office by her own Conservative party, which viewed her ultimately as too ideological. President Reagan, in two terms in office, was able to lower tax rates for the wealthy and disconnect government regulatory supervision, especially in banking, in the belief that this would spur greater investment, increase economic growth, and balance the budget.

This supply-side economics, however, while increasing growth rates in the 1980s, did not reduce the deficit; rather, it produced record deficits while permitting the mismanagement and looting of the savings and loan industry by crooks and quick-profit speculators. In addition, President Reagan could not transfer his personal popularity to the Republican party, and during the 1980s, a Republican president faced a solidly Democratic Congress. On the European continent, on the other hand, the conservative Christian Democratic government of Helmut Kohl, while promising a real change (*Wende*) in its 1982 election victory, in practice continued the social market economy consensus. At the end of the 1980s, Thatcherism and Reaganomics had demonstrated the popularity of an antigovernment, antitax, and antibureaucratic new conservatism, but at the same time, these first serious attempts to dismantle the welfare state had also shown the resiliency and still-strong popular support for the wide range of security programs and social services provided by big government. Most citizens certainly wanted to pay less for government, and they wanted to be free from government bureaucracy, but they still demanded as many and better services and protections from their government. In the last analysis, neither the British nor the U.S. economy was significantly improved overall by Thatcherism or Reaganomics, although corporations and financial institutions were freed from much regulation and legal restriction. However, these regimes showed that it was now politically possible to break with the postwar consensus through a program of wide-ranging deregulation, privatization, and tax reductions. They demonstrated the strategic weakness of organized labor and encouraged political free-marketeers to return to a politics of class conflict and greater social inequality.

In the early 1990s, however, new, nonestablished parties and movements have emerged in many liberal democracies to challenge the political landscape and channel the growing discontent of the public with the economic performance of their leaders. In the United States, the Ross Perot phenomenon in the 1992 election was a sign of growing frustration of a large part of the body politic with both major parties. Ross Perot represented a kind of new national populism that sought to break the old Keynesian consensus, using many of the same slogans as Reagan or Thatcher but from outside the established party framework. In Northern Italy, the sudden popularity of Umberto Bossi and his anti-Rome, anti-immigrant, and anticorruption Lombardi League (now the Northern League), as well as the discrediting of the long-ruling but surely corrupted Christian Democratic party, was a sign of the impending reshaping of Italian politics. The 1994 victory of the Italian media magnate Silvio Berlusconi and his Perot-style Forza Italia (Go Italy!) ''vote'' confirmed this trend. In the Canadian national elections of 1993 the nativist populist Reform party made a strong showing, especially in the western provinces, while the Quebec Bloc gave proof of the new separatist and Francophone-nativist political strength in Quebec. The long-ruling Conservative party of Brian Mulroney and Kim Campbell was decimated in those same Canadian elections, winning only two seats in the new parliament, while the Liberals gained an absolute majority of seats without a majority showing in the popular vote. In the French elections of 1993, it was the long-ruling Socialist party of Francois Mitterrand that was badly defeated, while the Gaullists and Republicans gained an overwhelming majority of parliamentary seats without an especially strong popular mandate. The voters in many of the liberal democracies have repudiated the incumbent government, whether conservative or socialist, but without much enthusiasm for the other established parties. In France and Germany, the rise of discontent over the perceived failures of the old formulas for growth and the perceived corruption of the old party leaders has given new space for nationalist-populist parties on the far right, namely, Jean Marie le Pen's National Front in France and Franz Schönhuber's Republicans in Germany. While not nearly as successful as the efforts of Bossi or Perot, these movements are also signs of the weakening support for the postwar version of ''normal politics.'' While these new movements do not yet have government power, and their messages are often both crude and largely negative, their power comes from the inability of the long-established parties and their leaders to continue the economic growth formula of the postwar period. Although, as we shall see, the liberal democracies are still very rich societies, the strong economic growth that provided widespread consumer prosperity and public funds for a wide range of services has given way to new insecurities and a search for a new package of political trade-offs (a new political economy). In the early 1990s, right-wing nationalist-populist movements and parties have made some impact with their antiforeigner, antigovernment, anti-elite, anticorruption,and antibureaucratic themes, which put the blame on targeted groups or established elites or the old political consensus.

Affluence in the Liberal Democracies

Probably the most basic and most outstanding feature of the advanced liberal democracies is economic wealth. A quantitative comparison between the liberal democracies and the developing world is astounding and even shocking to those who have not seen it before. The per capita GNP (Gross National Product) of Sweden was twenty times that of the Philippines, eleven times that of Colombia, nineteen times that of Egypt, fifty times that of Burma, thirty-four times that of Pakistan, twenty-six times that of Kenya, fifteen times that of Ghana. The general ratio in per capita income between the rich, developed nations and the poor, developing nations by the 1970s was roughly 20 to 1 according to economist Rosenstein-Rodan (1972). This did not take into account that there are middle-class people in the rich nations living well above their countries' averages and that the poorest strata in the poor nations live below their national averages, so that between a middle-class Swede and a Philippine peasant, the income gap was actually on the order of 100 to 1.

As startling as the huge gap in income is the fact that it is a relatively recent historical phenomenon. Rosenstein-Rodan estimates that in the early nineteenth century, the nations of Western Europe and North America, already the wealthier nations, had per capita income levels only twice those of the poorer nations. In the meanwhile, the rich lands/poor lands gap grew tenfold, from 2 to 1 to 20 to 1. Western democracies, by the 1970s, had all reached the level of mass consumer societies. With some relative differences, of course, within this community of nations, family ownership of large consumer durables such as an automobile, television, radio, refrigerator, and a mixed variety of other appliances had been realized for a substantial proportion, and sometimes overwhelming majorities, of the population. These material outputs of advanced capitalism were generally accessible to average members of the blue-collar working class and white-collar employee class as well as to higher social strata of professionals and business owners, and in quantity/proliferation unheard of in the most prosperous periods of the pre-Great Depression years.

Within the community of the affluent nations are some basic features worth special note. One is that the American standard of living, measured in gross national product (GNP) per capita, was surpassed by the 1970s in both Sweden and Switzerland (see table 3.1). The differences between American

Table 3.1   Selected Indicators of Affluence

	Switzerland	Germany	United States	United Kingdom	Sweden	France	Japan
GNP/capita (1990)	$32,250	22,360	21,810	16,080	23,780	19,590	25,840
GDP purchasing power equivalent (1991)	$21,700	W: 19,200	22,470	15,900	17,200	18,300	19,000
TVs/1,000 (1990)	407	570	815	435	474	406	620
Radios/1,000 (1990)	855	899	2,123	1,146	888	896	907
Autos/1,000 (1989)	479	526	748	449	462	494	455

Sources: CIA, *The World Factbook 1992;* UNDP, *Human Development Report, 1993;* OECD, *Economic Survey of the United States, 1991–92.*

GNP/capita and GNP/capita in West Germany, Holland, Denmark, and Norway were also minor by the mid-1970s and fluctuated with changes in the exchange rate of the dollar against the various European currencies. The most rapid growth of GNP/capita has been achieved, however, by the Japanese, who by the late 1980s had even surpassed the United States in GNP/capita ranking. There is considerable debate among social scientists on the validity of GNP figures as a measure of economic well-being. In part, the volatility of currency exchange rates since the collapse of the Bretton-Wood system in 1971 has made it clear that the mechanical translation of Japanese yen or German marks into dollars at one moment, or even averaged for one year, lacks substance when trying to compare material living standards between nations. For example, if in one year the dollar loses 30 percent of its value versus the value of the Japanese yen, does that really mean that U.S. living standards have dropped by 30 percent relative to Japanese standards? Economists have now developed measures of purchasing power equivalent (PPE), which try to compare the purchasing power of consumers for a given "market basket" of goods. This method, however, also has its limitations, in trying to compare different cultural tastes and quality preferences. Whose cultural tastes decide what constitutes a standard market basket, for example? GNP also leaves out the "hidden economy," or illegal and black market sectors, of each system, and this may vary considerably by country. On the other hand, do we want to add in the value of illegal drug sales, prostitution, and weapon smuggling to the Gross National Product, as a measure of our economic well-being? Figures given here for GNP/capita and PPE/capita should not therefore be taken as unquestioned or absolutely valid measures, but rather as initial and tentative bases for further comparison and analysis of specific fields of performance, such as occupation, education, health, housing, and social welfare.

The growth of the rich/poor gap between the world's nations is one of the most basic changes of the last century and a half and is related to two straightforward factors. First, the nations of Western Europe and North America (plus Japan) were the first to experience industrialization under capitalism, and the productivity increases of an industrial economy increased the differentials between rich and poor nations. Second, the political-economic-military imperialism practiced by the industrial economies in the underdeveloped societies widened differentials between rich and poor nations.

Analysis of the second factor will have to wait until our discussion of political systems in the less developed nations. For now it is enough to establish correlates of industrial growth in the leading capitalist nations in the historically quite modest time span of one hundred fifty years. Table 3.2 presents a variety of aggregate data that describe some broad demographic features of the liberal democracies. The liberal democracies were the first to successfully industrialize their economies, the way in which things are produced. In all the liberal democracies, 20 to 34 percent of the male workforce is employed in the manufacturing/mining sectors of the economy. As industrialization has advanced since the turn of the century, this percentage stabilized and then in the last two decades declined. Since the early 1900s, the sector of the workforce with the most rapid growth has been the nonmanual or white-collar employee sector, which includes office personnel, most government workers, sales and distribution personnel, managerial/supervisory, and professional/ technical employees. With the decline of older industrial areas and the displacement of new industrial investment overseas, the workforce of the liberal democracies has more and more been concentrated in the broad "services" sector. Since the Second World War, the category of professional/ technical employee has grown most noticeably within the nonmanual occupations, reflecting the increasing importance of specialized training and technical expertise in the functioning of government, corporate, and educational complexes.

Between 10 and 25 percent of the employed male workforce now hold positions characterized chiefly by a higher education. Whereas 75 to 85

Table 3.2 Occupational Structure and Residence, 1991

	Switzerland	Germany	United States	United Kingdom	Sweden	France	Japan
Population (in millions):	6.8	79.9	252.5	57.6	8.6	57.0	124.0
Percent of workforce in (1989–91):							
Industry:	30	30	26	20	28	20	34
Agriculture:	6	4	3	2	7	7	7
Services:	64	66	71	78	69	73	59
Urban population (Percent)	60	85	75	89	84	74	77

Source: UNDP, *Human Development Report*, 1993.

percent of the population were engaged in agriculture in these nations in the early 1800s, now less than one-tenth are still active in farming. In the most highly industrialized nations (Britain, West Germany, the United States) the figure is less than 4 percent. While there are still sizeable agricultural populations in Japan, Italy, and France, with holdovers from the peasantry of feudalism and the small farmer (smallholder) of early capitalism, agriculture has on the whole been modernized along commercial-industrial lines, most conspicuously in the United States, where the Jeffersonian ideal of the independent yeoman tiller of the soil has become an endangered species, and farming is dominated by huge agro-corporations. It is not only in the urban economy but also and perhaps as vitally in agricultural production that the economies of the liberal democracies have been transformed over the last century and a half.

This growth of industrial society in the Western democracies also was associated with the growth of cities, and it was in the cities that the concentrated educational, cultural, and material wealth of society was located, as well as the basis of political power. The cities were desirable places to live and work and were magnets for migrants from both the countryside and from other countries. Many of the wealthy democracies welcomed millions of immigrants to work in their factories and urban services. Germany actively recruited 4 million foreign workers from Turkey, Yugoslavia, and southern Europe; France welcomed foreign laborers from its former colonies of Algeria, Morocco, Tunisia, and West Africa; Britain permitted millions of its former colonial subjects to resettle and envigorate the British economy in medical practice, shop-keeping, and factory work. But in the last stages of the Cold War, with stagnation or slow growth, the industrial sector was in sharp decline, and high-wage, high-benefit manufacturing jobs were eliminated in large numbers as corporate investment in new manufacturing moved to low-wage and low-benefit nations. Now, even when there is positive economic growth after a recessionary low, the unemployment rate has not gone down much (see chapter 6 on joblessness), and the jobs lost in steel, automobile, chemical, or consumer durables industries have not been regained.

With this development, the economic well-being of the large industrial cities, from Cleveland, Chicago, and Detroit in the United States, to Manchester and Liverpool in Britain, to Essen and Dortmund in Germany, and to industrial Paris and Metz in France, was undermined, leading to increased ghettoization, urban decay, and flight of the middle class to suburban bastions. The urban centers have lost the economic vitality of the postwar prosperity years. Some restructuring, as in Pittsburgh and Manchester, has revived center-city areas on a much reduced scale, but large numbers of industrial middle-class families have seen their retirement and their children's future increasingly threatened. In the United States, the signs of urban decay and disorder are perhaps most pronounced, and the new poverty of the inner cities is most dramatic. But many of the same signs are now apparent in the other Western democracies.

57

From Elite to Mass Education

All of the items that will be discussed below are interrelated with the economic achievements of the postwar democracies. There is no intent to imply any one-way causality from economic growth to educational, health, housing, or welfare fields. Such descriptions oversimplify a complex pattern of mutual reinforcement and organic interdependence. The particular historic development of the industrial democracies exhibits a pattern of interrelationship among these elements that is now in the process of erosion, if not crisis, that is part of the great change underway.

In the West, literacy was already fairly widespread at the point of industrial takeoff. Gutenberg's invention of movable type for printing in the fifteenth century represented a technological revolution for literacy skills far in advance of industrial capitalism. But as Western societies urbanized, more and more members of the middle and lower classes were drawn into an expanded, national educational system. In the city, in the factory, and in the store the modern worker or employee had to be able to read, write, and reckon. Replacement of the local subsistence or village barter economy with the mass-market, currency-based exchange system required attainment of new skills on a mass scale, at least for males. Literacy in Britain in the early 1800s may have been around 30 percent; by 1841–45 literacy reached nearly 70 percent among adult males and among females about 50 percent; by 1920 literacy rates were over 90 percent for all the Western industrial powers except Italy. Near-universal literacy was reached before World War II.

In the postwar era, the expansion of the educational system and of educational opportunities occurred at the secondary (high school, gymnasium, lycee, grammar school) level and in higher education (college, university, higher technical institute). In the European school systems of the early 1950s, pupils were generally channeled at an early age (ten to eleven) into either college preparatory secondary schools or general education and technical vocational schools. Overwhelmingly, the children of upper-middle-class, well-educated parents filled the prestigious college prep schools, while the sons and daughters of farmers, workers, and white-collar employees ended up in the secondary schools that led only to vocational or technical skill schools at best. This process is known as "class channeling" and tends, of course, to make upward mobility much more difficult for children of lower social origins. Perhaps only 2 to 5 percent of college-age young people actually attended a college or university in the early 1950s, and they were overwhelmingly from higher social backgrounds. Class channeling makes clear at a very tender age who are the winners, the upwardly mobile, and who the losers, the underclass of the society. In Germany, the student cultures of the *Hauptschule* (general education), *Realschule* (technical/vocational), and *Gymnasium* (college-track) are social worlds apart. In the first there is a sense of harsh but realistic

58

adjustment to a lesser future (or tough talk and rebelliousness); in the last there are pride, self-esteem, and wide horizons, coupled with better manners and respectful treatment from teachers. British sociologist Frank Parkin (1971:64) gives a good summary of the impact of class channeling on ambitions among English schoolchildren:

> The evidence suggests that from a fairly early age low status members are *taught* to narrow their social horizons. The selection of "appropriate" reference groups is then likely to follow as the children become adult. By this time they will have received reasonable training in the art of not "seeing" the privileged for purposes of comparison.

In the United States, on the other hand, with the exception of a relatively small number of elite prep schools such as Exeter, Groton, and Choate for the offspring of the rich, there has historically been little class channeling within secondary schools (this statement will be amended somewhat in the following chapter). Secondary education in the United States has been comprehensive, meaning that generally all who attend the public schools go through the same institutions. Here again, the lack of a feudal past made the American experience unique and, in this case, progressive. Heidenheimer, Heclo, and Adams (1990:43–46) have outlined the political struggles in Britain, Germany, and Sweden in changing over from a class channeling to a comprehensive secondary school system.

In Sweden (and Norway) Social Democratic governments in power for decades were able to complete the transformation and thus to raise opportunities of higher education for working-class children as well as to expand them markedly for middle-class children. In Sweden, the proportion of university students of working-class origins rose from 8 percent in 1947 to 16 percent by 1963, with the upward trend expected to continue (Parkin, 1971:111). In Britain, after some modest beginnings in the 1950s, the Labour government of

Table 3.3   Education Spending as Percent of GNP

	Switzerland	Germany	United States	United Kingdom	Sweden	France	Japan
1975	5.1	5.1	7.4[a]	6.6	7.3	5.2	5.5
1980	5.0	4.7	6.7[a]	5.6	9.0	5.0	5.8
1985	4.8	4.5	5.0	4.9	7.7	5.8	5.0
1989	4.8	4.1	5.3	4.7[b]	7.8[c]	5.5[c]	4.7[b]

Source: *UNESCO Statistical Yearbook*, 1990, 1991, 1992.
a. includes private expenditures on education
b. 1988
c. 1990

Harold Wilson was able, in the 1964–70 period, to put into motion a stronger trend toward ''comprehensivization'' in the secondary schools. Despite some rearguard delaying actions by the succeeding Conservative government (with Margaret Thatcher as minister of education), the number of comprehensive high schools rose steadily from 262 in 1965 to 1,835 by 1973, enrolling nearly half of all secondary school students (as opposed to less than 10 percent in 1965). By 1980, most British grammar schools had changed to the comprehensive system, encompassing 85 to 90 percent of students. Even in the face of Conservative delaying tactics, comprehensive reform over twenty-five years had transformed and broadened the social base of high school education.

In Germany, attempts to create comprehensive schools under the SPD-FDP social-liberal government of Willy Brandt (1969–74) failed rather miserably, even in their final, extremely watered-down format. Rigid opposition from the Christian Democrats, secondary school teachers, and middle-class parents, coupled with the SPD's recent and still-tenuous leadership in national government, led in 1974 to the tacit admission by Brandt's successor, Helmut Schmidt, that plans for educational reform of the secondary school system were being abandoned. The brief momentum for comprehensivization in the 1960s had failed to achieve a decisive breakthrough, and the percentage of German students in comprehensive secondary schools was still only 2 percent by 1980.

The Japanese secondary school system is a mixture of comprehensive and channeling systems. Japanese students generally go on to complete their high school degree, with only a 6 percent dropout rate (compared to nearly 30 percent for the United States (Heidenheimer et al., 1990:42). Most students go to local high schools in their districts, but students are channeled into those schools on the basis of rigorous exams. Japanese high schools are therefore highly ranked, with highest status going to those with the most stringent entrance requirements, which in turn gives their graduates the best university-track opportunities. By all accounts, the better high schools are a very stressful environment for Japanese students, with university life much more relaxed. The Japanese system retains a clear hierarchy of selection and higher standards for entrance into the best high schools, while maintaining a formally common school system.

The comprehensive secondary school reforms of the 1960s and 1970s succeeded most dramatically in Norway and Sweden, where, as both Parkin (1971) and Tomasson (1965) point out, strong social democratic parties were in power for decades. But comprehensivization also gradually won out in Britain. Despite some Conservative resistance, the momentum of earlier Labour initiatives continued. On the other hand, in the United States, where comprehensive school systems have been long established, concerns about the quality of education and functional illiteracy among high-school graduates have led to demands for higher standards or parent-based choice of high school.

In the area of higher (post-secondary) education, the total number of places in colleges, universities, and higher technical institutes expanded remarkably in the postwar period, especially in the 1960s and 1970s (see table 3.4). Higher education has grown from a small elitist recruitment filter to a mass institution in all the liberal democracies. The United States led the way, with Sweden, Germany, France, and Japan following somewhat slower growth curves in total enrollments, and Britain trailing noticeably behind. On the other hand, with this tremendous growth in university systems has come pressure on faculty, facilities, and student housing that by the 1980s were causing serious rethinking about the commitment to increasing enrollments. The slower economic growth of the 1970s and 1980s has made the connection between a university degree and placement in the job market more problematic in almost all the liberal democracies. Japan, with its continued strong economic growth and close connection between university professional training and government or corporate career, has remained an exception. But in the United States, Germany, France, and Italy, a college degree is more loosely tied to job placement now than in the 1960s, with resultant tensions between commitments to mass higher education and the harsher realities of a more stringent market for professional careers. Growing numbers of young college degreeholders were not able to find employment in their fields, especially in education and government professional service in the 1980s, producing a backup or long waiting list in numerous fields. Restrictions on student enrollments in specific fields have been introduced in Sweden and Germany. French attempts to limit or cut back overall enrollments or to tie them specifically to job market

Table 3.4   Enrollments in Higher Education, 1960–1990

	Switzerland	Germany	United States	United Kingdom	Sweden	France	Japan
Percentage of age group enrolled in higher education:							
1960	5	6	32	9	9	7	10
1970	10	13	49	14	21	20	17
1980	21	27	56	20	37	25	31
1990	28	33[a]	75	25[a]	33	40	31[a]
Students per 100,000 population:							
1970	821	830	4,148	1,084	1,756	1,581	1,744
1980	1,347	2,395	5,311	1,468	2,062	2,318	2,065
1990	2,118	2,810[a]	5,608	2,063[a]	2,281	3,026	2,184[a]

Source: *UNESCO Statistical Yearbook*, 1974, 1985, 1990, 1991, 1992.
a. 1989

openings have produced large-scale student protests, however, that have so far forced the government to back down.

More Correlates: Health and Health Care

One of the most significant changes in the course of the industrial development in the West since the early 1800s has been the increase in life expectancy. In late feudal Europe, average life expectancy was generally between thirty and thirty-five years for males and thirty-five to forty years for females. Infant mortality rates were extremely high, so that even with high birthrates, population growth was minimal. Even then, life expectancy was somewhat higher in Europe than in Mexico, India, and China. As table 3.5 clearly shows, in the cases of England and Sweden the advent of industrialism has been associated with a dramatic doubling of life expectancy.

Part of this revolution in longevity can be attributed to increases in economic resources available through the preindustrial merchant capitalist or early factory system economy, which improved basic nutrition, clothing, and shelter for the general population. Economic historian T. S. Ashton (1948:4–5, 64) attributes the decline in death rates in England, and especially infant death rates, to the introduction of cheap cotton underwear and lye soap. These increased personal hygiene possibilities for great numbers of people, reducing the risk of infection, a common cause of early death. Ashton notes also the improvement in nutrition through the introduction of the potato from the New World and through the availability of wheat instead of inferior grains such as rye and barley for daily consumption. Use of brick walls and slate roofs instead of timber and thatch also reduced the incidence of disease-carrying pests in the home, which had been another source of mortal danger to infants in feudal agrarian society. Although by all accounts working-class housing in the early urban manufacturing centers left much to be desired, Ashton argues that "larger towns were paved, drained, and supplied with running water; . . . and more attention was paid to such things as the disposal of refuse and the proper

Table 3.5   Average Life Expectancy

	Sweden			England and Wales	
	Male	**Female**		**Male**	**Female**
1755–76	33.2	35.7			
1816–40	39.5	43.6	1841	40.2	42.2
1901–10	54.6	57.0	1901–10	48.5	52.4
1936–40	64.3	66.9	1937	60.2	64.4
1988	74.2	80.2	1987–88	72.4	78.1

Sources: *Encyclopaedia Britannica*, 1953 ed., vol. 7, p. 114; *UN Statistical Yearbook*, 1987; HMSO Central Statistical Service, *Annual Abstract of Statistics*, 1991.

burial of the dead" (1948:5). All of these factors, hardly associated yet with advanced technology or even industrialism per se, had reduced the death rate by nearly half between 1740 and 1820 in Britain, creating a growing population with far more children surviving infancy.

It is important to note that quite in advance of "modern medicine" and miracle drugs produced by advanced technology, these relatively simple and straightforward additions to nutrition, clothing, hygiene, and housing possibilities had already done much to improve life expectancy. Health care includes not only what a professional health service system can deliver, but also (perhaps even more fundamentally) basic necessities that are available to the populace, from the highest to the lowest social strata. In the West, the provision of these basics preceded the development of national medical systems, either private or socialized, able to provide modern medical technology for health care. This is doubly important, for in the Third World the process has been at least partially reversed. Medical technology is relatively easy to export, and the training of a corps of competent doctors and paramedical personnel is within the reach of even fairly poor nations. What is lacking in the Third World is access by the poorest classes to adequate amounts of the basics of nutrition, housing, clothing, and sanitation. Until these are available, the power of medical technology is limited (see chapter 13).

The progress and breakthroughs of modern science included the field of medicine. As society became more urban, more interdependent, less locally self-sufficient, the role of national medical organizations and public health authorities expanded. The variety of approaches to providing access to professional medical care has been considerable, although all the Western industrial nations have participated in the trend toward some form of comprehensive health system that could loosely be called socialized medicine. Heidenheimer et al. (1975:9) have provided a useful sketch of Western European experience in establishing public health services:

1. Conservative monarchs introduce a national hospital plan to maintain the health of soldiers and ex-soldiers and then extend the services to the general population (Sweden, eighteenth and nineteenth centuries).
2. Conservative politicians introduce public health insurance programs in an attempt to deprive rising socialist parties of an appealing issue (Germany, 1883).
3. Liberal parties introduce health insurance partly in an attempt to keep organized skilled workers from defecting to either conservative or labor parties (Britain, 1911).
4. Social democratic governments take the lead in transforming health systems partially financed through public sources into comprehensive, integrated public systems that supply almost all the health care in the country (Britain, 1948; Sweden, 1970s).

The United States has been the notable laggard in this field. Extreme opposition from the powerful American Medical Association (AMA) and private insurance companies has prevented the establishment of any comprehensive national health insurance program. Public health expenditures, which stood at 0.4 percent of U.S. GNP in 1913, stood at 0.7 percent in 1932 and were still less than 1 percent by 1964 (Heidenheimer et al., 1975:18). For veterans, a special case, socialized medicine has been a reality for some time in the United States. More recently, the aged under Medicare and the poor under Medicaid have received at least basic coverage. The majority of Americans purchase some medical insurance coverage from private insurance carriers, and a significant percentage (20 to 25 percent in recent estimates) are uninsured and depend on personal finances for purchases of medical care.

Only in the 1990s, with the election of President Clinton, has development of a comprehensive national health care system become a high policy priority in the United States, primarily because of the exploding costs of health insurance premiums and total health care costs (cf. table 3.6) and the fear of losing job-related health care coverage by an increasing number of citizens.

Some relatively significant differences exist in the medical emphases of the various systems in the liberal democracies. The British National Health Service (NHS), as Odin Anderson (1972) has shown, has emphasized the role of the general practitioner (GP) physician. The United States has the highest proportions of surgeons (and specialists generally), and Sweden has poured prodigious resources into its hospital centers. It should be added that, in the 1970s, each of these three health systems showed some ability to adapt and re-evaluate its priorities. Under the Labour government of Harold Wilson in

Table 3.6   Health Care Indicators

	Switzerland	Germany	United States	United Kingdom	Sweden	France	Japan
Life expectancy (1991)	79.1	75.8	75.7	76.5	77.8	77.8	79.2
Population per physician (1984–89)	696	380	419	700	387	320	663
Infant mortality/ 1,000 births (1990)	7	9	10	9	6	8	5
Total health costs as percent of GDP (1990)*	7.7	8.1	12.4	6.2	8.7	8.9	6.5
Total health costs as percent of GDP (1980)*	7.2	7.9	9.2	5.8	9.5	7.4	6.6

Sources: *Statistical Abstract of the United States,* 1989, 1992; *UN Statistical Yearbook*, 1990–91; UNDP, *Human Development Report*, 1993.
*preliminary estimates

the 1970s, the Health Ministry has built up the number and role of local health centers. Hospital-centered care, the most expensive format of health care services, has now been somewhat de-emphasized by the Swedish government in favor of more decentralized health centers. And in the United States, repeated criticisms of large-scale unnecessary surgery performed by a surplus of surgeons has led medical schools once again to emphasize training of doctors in primary medical care fields (internal medicine and pediatrics).

Despite the differences in types of coverage and modes of health-care delivery, the liberal democracies have all, with the single exception of the United States, committed themselves to universal national health care for all citizens. Despite long years of AMA propaganda in the United States about the evils of socialized medicine, it is in fact the United States that lags somewhat behind most other liberal democracies in health-care indicators, while at the same time spending the largest percentage of GNP (12.4 percent in 1990) on health-care services. The increase in health-care costs has affected all the liberal democracies in the 1980s, however, and cost containment for physician payments, new medical technologies, and long-term elder care has become a major issue. Attempts in Britain by the Thatcher government, however, to undermine the National Health Service through either switching to an insurance-based system or complete privatization have been opposed by substantial to overwhelming majorities (Heidenheimer et al., 1990:93). With the continued aging of the population in the 1990s, each health-care system will face additional ethical and economic issues of health-care distribution and perhaps rationing. Indeed, as table 3.7 indicates, the growth in the percentage of the elderly population, clearly a positive outcome of the peace and prosperity of the Cold War era, nevertheless poses a poignant problem in the current transitional era of crisis in government budgets generally and public health care expenditures in particular.

More Correlates: Housing

Decent housing and a healthy home environment are important elements in the daily welfare of every person. Any discussion of housing conditions in the contemporary liberal democracies should be set in the perspective of how dramatically current circumstances diverge from those of early capitalism or late feudalism. Most observers agree that the housing conditions of the early working class were terrible. T. S. Ashton, a scholarly celebrant of capitalism, nevertheless admits the decline in urban housing standards in England of the early 1800s:

> After 1793 the import of timber from the Baltic was restricted and the price of labour of bricklayers and carpenters went up. . . . This meant that if dwellings were to be let at rents which the workers could afford to pay they had to be

65

Table 3.7   Age Structure: Population Aged 65 and Older as a Percentage of
Total Population

	1950	1970	1990
Switzerland	9.6	11.4	14.9
West Germany	9.4	13.2	15
United States	11.5	9.8	12.3
United Kingdom	10.9	13.2	15.7
France	11.2	12.9	13.7
Sweden	10.3	13.7	18
Japan	4.9	7.1	11.9

Sources: 1950: B.R. Mitchell (1981), *European Historical Statistics 1750–1975* (London: Macmillan);
(1982), *International Historical Statistics: Africa and Asia* (London: Macmillan); (1983), *International
Historical Statistics: The Americas and Australasia* (London: Macmillan).
1970: OECD, 1988.
1990: World Bank, *World Development Report*, 1992.

> smaller and less durable than those of the eighties (1780s: J.N.). The rows of
> ill-built, back-to-back houses, into which the rapidly growing population of the
> towns was pressed, were largely the product of wartime conditions [i.e., the
> Napoleonic wars]. (1948:160)

In some early manufacturing towns such as Manchester and Liverpool, which
had large numbers of poor working-class Irish, 10 to 15 percent of the
population were living in cellars. Cellars of those times were dark, dank,
filthy places, the poorest of housing.

The young Friedrich Engels gave this stirring eyewitness account of the
working-class district of Manchester in the year 1842:

> Everywhere half or wholly ruined buildings, some of them actually uninhabited,
> which means a great deal here; rarely a wooden or stone floor to be seen in the
> houses, almost uniformly broken, ill-fitting windows and doors, and a state of
> filth! Everywhere heaps of debris, refuse, and offal, standing pools for gutters,
> and a stench which would alone make it impossible for a human being in any
> degree civilised to live in such a district. . . . Passing along a rough bank, among
> stakes and washing lines, one penetrates into this chaos of small, one-storied,
> one-roomed huts, in most of which there is no artificial floor; kitchen, living and
> sleeping-room all in one. In one such a hole, scarcely five feet long by six
> broad, I found two beds—and such bedsteads and beds!—which, with a staircase
> and chimney-place, exactly filled the room. In several others I found absolutely
> nothing, while the door stood open, and the inhabitants leaned against it.
> Everywhere before the doors refuse and offal; that any sort of pavement lay
> underneath could not be seen but only felt, here and there, with the feet. This
> whole collection of cattle-sheds for human beings was surrounded on two sides
> by houses and a factory, and on the third by the river, and besides the narrow

stair up the bank, a narrow doorway led out into another almost equally ill-built, ill-kept labyrinth of dwellings.

Enough! The whole side of the Irk is built in this way, a planless, knotted chaos of houses, more or less on the verge of uninhabitableness, whose unclean interiors fully correspond with their filthy external surroundings. And how could the people be clean with no proper opportunity for satisfying the most natural and ordinary wants? Privies are so rare here that they are either filled up every day, or are too remote for most of the inhabitants to use. How can people wash when they have only the dirty Irk water at hand, while pumps and water pipes can be found in decent parts of the city alone? . . .

Such is the Old Town of Manchester, and on re-reading my description, I am forced to admit that instead of being exaggerated, it is far from black enough to convey a true impression of the filth, ruin, and uninhabitableness, the defiance of all considerations of cleanliness, ventilation, and health which characterise the construction of this single district, containing at least twenty to thirty thousand inhabitants. And such a district exists in the heart of the second city of England, the first manufacturing city of the world. (Reprinted in Tucker, 1972:432–34)

This description by Engels, we should note, attests to poor housing conditions well after the end of the Napoleonic Wars, which Ashton cited as the cause of bad housing conditions for workers earlier in the century. Certainly over the next century housing conditions gradually improved for the population, including the working class.

In both Europe and Japan, but not in the United States, tremendous losses in urban housing during World War II created drastic shortages in the early postwar years, which had to be made up before advances beyond the prewar level could be achieved. In most major German and Japanese cities, over 80 percent of prewar housing had been either destroyed or heavily damaged. In France, Britain, and Italy, war damage was less extensive, but shortages resulting from low levels of construction during the Great Depression and near zero levels during the war still called for major housing programs. In the United States as well, inexpensive Veteran's Administration and Federal Housing Authority loans fueled an unprecedented housing boom. However, the balance of public-to-private housing construction has varied considerably in each country. In Europe, the prewar political reluctance to get government involved in housing construction to any significant degree gave way first to the necessity for making up for wartime losses, then to the increased demands for housing created by a growing percentage of elderly citizens (no longer living with their children) and by the postwar baby boom (Heidenheimer, 1975). In Britain, Sweden, France, Germany, and the Netherlands, among others, public and quasi-public (largely nonprofit, government regulated) housing-starts in the early 1970s still constituted between one-third (Germany) to two-thirds (Sweden, France) of all new housing. In the 1980s, however, most of the governments of Western Europe cut back on their direct and indirect financing of housing. In Britain, the percent of new housing directly financed by government had dropped from 48.6 percent in 1970 to only 15.3 percent by 1985; in France, the share of new housing built by nonprofit agencies fell from 32.2 percent in 1970 to 17.3 percent in 1984. In Sweden and in the Netherlands, however, nonprofit agency new housing construction remained at high levels (55.1 and 35.7 percent respectively by mid-decade). And in Japan, which rebuilt most of its housing stock after the war with government loans, though using private builders, the trend since the 1960s has been towards more, not less government financing of housing (Heidenheimer et al., 1990:103–4).

Again, the experience of the United States is the anomaly, where opposition to major government efforts has kept public housing to less than 1 percent of total housing. This is, of course, partly explained by the lesser need for an immediate massive postwar program of housing construction in the United States, untouched by war damage. It is also partly explained by the ideological reluctance of both major American political parties to oppose private construction firms, real estate interests, apartment owners, and private banks in financing and building public housing on more than a minimal scale. In Europe, Labour, Socialist, and Communist parties have from both ideological heritage and the lessons of practical politics backed low-cost public housing, or public housing in general, against the interests of the capitalist housing marketplace. Parties of the working class have backed the notion of decent housing as a basic right of the individual that should be protected through government. Even Conservative, Gaullist, and Christian Democratic governments find it easier to keep public housing programs going than to face stiff opposition by curtailing them drastically. Finally, it must be recognized that in the United States public housing (as with many aspects of welfare) continues to be identified with a black racial minority long the object of discrimination and hostility. In American society, as in no other Western democracy, this association has stigmatized the very concept of "welfare" and confounded efforts to create public housing programs that would benefit not only blacks but other lower income groups as well.

With whatever mixture of public and private construction and financing the liberal democracies built or rebuilt decent housing for their populations after World War II, the basic outcome was that, by the 1970s, citizens of these nations had come to expect a historically very high standard for housing comforts for themselves and their families. By the 1980s, however, despite continuing (mostly slow) growth of the economy, a new housing crunch was emerging. In many urban areas, affordable housing for low-income families was not sufficient to meet demand. At the bottom of the social ladder, new homeless populations, different from the earlier alcoholics and addicts, began to emerge as part of the new urban landscape. In Germany, for example, where homelessness was virtually unheard of in the 1960s and 1970s, suddenly homelessness (*Obdachlosigkeit*) became a social issue.

In part, the decline in low-cost housing construction is due to the decline in public funding in an era of budget crises in nearly all the liberal democracies; in part, it is another symptom of an increasingly two-track economy, with much new apartment and home construction aimed at the affluent upper-middle class and very little devoted to the newly poor or working poor. In housing, as in so many other areas at the end of the Cold War, the new class divisions of Western democracy are becoming sharper and more visible.

Financing the Welfare State

In addition to education, health care, and housing, we can identify other government programs that can be subsumed under the general heading of welfare. A 1964 study by the U.S. Department of Health, Education, and Welfare (HEW) lists five categories of welfare benefits: (1) old age, invalidism, death; (2) health care; (3) work disability compensation; (4) unemployment compensation; and (5) family allowances. The HEW study omits housing as an area of welfare concern, perhaps because system commitment to public housing in the United States has been so weak. By the 1960s, all of the Western democracies had developed some programs or coverage in all of the five areas, with the exception of the United States, which had no programs in the category of family allowances (Groth, 1971:162–63). In the late 1960s, the Nixon Administration proposed a Family Assistance Plan (FAP), which would have provided uniform assistance to needy families with children. Heidenheimer et al. (1975:204–5, 218–19) described the defeat of the FAP proposal by an alliance of liberals, who complained that too little was being offered, and conservatives, who wanted to kill the proposal outright. Support from the White House also faded in the course of the struggle over welfare reform, and the proposal was lost. However, a Supplementary Security Income (SSI) program to be administered by the existing Social Security Administration was passed, though it was limited to the categories of the elderly, blind, and disabled poor. The food stamp program was greatly expanded, with provisions for a uniform minimum income level for family participation. Heidenheimer et al. (1975:219) reported that by 1975 "the food stamp program covered more persons (including working family heads) than the original highly controversial FAP proposal, cost as much, and offered benefits at least as large."

The welfare state in the advanced capitalist nations has been in the process of development for nearly a century. Its first major or large-scale origins can be found in Bismarck's social insurance programs for health, the aged, and disabled of the 1880s. The purpose of these programs, as mentioned earlier, was to blunt the appeal of the rising socialist movement in the Kaiser's Germany. Most observers (see Groth, 1971:158; Heidenheimer et al., 1975: 194–95) ascribe the first passage of an unemployment insurance program under the British Liberal government in 1911 to an attempt to win over the workers from the growing Labour party. Once again, the basic motivations were not altruism or humanitarianism (although these were of course widely advertised), but a political response to the perceived threat of socialism and a recognition of the determination of a growing and militant industrial working class. Even so, the breadth of the coverage and the benefit levels of social programs before the Great Depression were quite modest. This was a pre-Keynesian era of economic thinking in the West, and government welfare outlays were not generally viewed as an integral part of government action that would maintain (or even raise) consumer spending, vital to a healthy economy. Thus these early welfare programs did little to avert or alleviate the downward spiral of unemployment and suffering of the Depression era. Even the reforms of the 1930s by the New Deal and other Depression-era governments in the West were insufficient to spark an economic recovery. Most observers agree that only the massive defense spending for the military of World War II provided the impetus for a return to prosperity.

It was only in the post–World War II period that the commitment of the liberal democracies to significant welfare spending levels on a variety of programs gained a political consensus and became a fiscal reality. Quantitative comparisons of government outputs in the welfare field are likely to be complex and often controversial, depending on definitions of what gets included or excluded as welfare spending. Fortunately, there are some figures available that give rough impressions of the extent of welfare spending within nations over time and of the variation among nations by political system-type. Table 3.8 documents the upward trend of social spending as a percentage of gross domestic product (GDP) since World War II. In all cases there has been a significant rise, but with some equally important differences in levels and rates of growth. Some leaders in welfare spending in the early 1950s, Germany and France, have remained relative leaders. Some nations, the United States, Japan, and Switzerland, have remained pinch-penny laggards, despite rises in spending levels as a percentage of GDP. Sweden, now popularized as the prototype of the welfare state, occupied only a middling position twenty-five years ago and became only gradually a welfare leader. The Dutch, relative laggards in 1950, experienced in the 1960s an explosion of welfare reform, which by 1980 placed them among the big spenders of the liberal democratic community.

Occasionally the "creeping socialism" or welfarism feared by conservatives not only creeps but also gallops. It is not necessarily the case that certain nations, by virtue of some unchangeable "individualist" or "collectivist" political culture, are destined to remain at the low or high end of the spectrum

Table 3.8   Social Security Expenditures and Tax Revenues as Percent of GDP, 1960–1990

	Social Security Costs				Tax Revenues		
	1960	**1970**	**1980**	**1990**	**1970**	**1980**	**1990**
Switzerland	5.7	6.3	12.7	13.4	23.8	30.8	31.7
Germany	12	13.1	16.6	15.3	32.9	38.2	37.7
United States	5	7.9	10.9	10.8*	29.2	29.5	29.9
United Kingdom	6.8	8.7	11.7	12.2	36.9	35.3	36.7
Sweden	8	11.1	17.6	19.7	40	49.1	56.9
France	13.5	17	19.2	21.4	35.1	41.7	43.7
Japan	3.8	4.6	10.1	11.5	19.7	25.4	31.3
Netherlands	n/a	17.4	25.9	26.3	37.6	45.8	45.2

Source: OECD, *Historical Statistics*, 1960–90, 1960–81.
*1989

of welfare spending among the liberal democracies. In fact, comparative studies of levels of welfare spending have found relatively few correlates of welfare spending that would explain the differences within the liberal democracies (see Wilensky, 1975; Heidenheimer et al., 1975; Pryor, 1968; Groth, 1971; Jackman, 1975).

More important than the still-considerable differences that currently exist among the rich democracies of the West was the cleavage globally between the rich and poor nations. In a survey of sixty-four nations for the year 1966, Wilensky (1975:19) found that the top quartile of nations in terms of per capita GNP spent an average of 13.8 percent of that GNP on social security programs, whereas the two bottom quartiles spent only 4.0 percent and 2.5 percent respectively. All nations in the top quartile were liberal democracies, including the United States, Sweden, Switzerland, Germany, France, Britain, and the Netherlands. In the second richest quartile of nations, the level of welfare spending averaged 10.1 percent of GNP for all sixteen nations, but this aggregate of semirich countries was a mixed bag of communist, liberal democratic, and developing nations. For the five developed liberal democracies in this quartile (Japan, Italy, Austria, Ireland, Israel), average welfare spending was 12.8 percent of GNP; for the seven richest and most industrialized communist nations (USSR, Czechoslovakia, East Germany, Hungary, Poland, Bulgaria, Romania) the average was 11.5 percent of GNP; but for the four developing nations (Venezuela, Spain, Greece, Trinidad-Tobago), the average fell to 5.9 percent, much closer to the general averages for the poorer nations of the bottom thirty-two nations in the study. In other words, on a global scale, there were two categories of nations that qualitatively lead in levels of welfare spending: the developed liberal democracies and the industrial communist nations (for further discussion of welfare spending in the communist countries, see chapter 8).

In comparative perspective, welfare spending reaches the highest levels on a global scale among the developed nations, both democratic and communist. While it is problematic to speculate on what levels of welfare spending would be found in a contemporary industrial fascist system, Groth (1971:171–74) notes that the fascist regime in Italy and the Nazi regime in Germany "spent less [on welfare] in proportion to national income than their predecessors" (p. 173). This was, in part, consistent with the fascist tendency to extoll "survival of the fittest" notions, which relegate the weak and poor to continued oppression or extinction by the strong. But Groth also remarks: "The relative niggardliness of fascism and nazism was rooted not only in the social philosophy of its leaders but in the social and economic conservatism of many of their backers, allies and supporters" (p. 174).

If we concentrate only on differences in levels of spending for welfare within the community of liberal democracies, there are two explanations that scholars in this area have uncovered. The first is that the earlier welfare programs were instituted (Heidenheimer et al., 1975:189), the higher the current levels of spending are for those programs. The basic reasoning is that once initiated and established, administrative "incrementalism" tends to widen the base of coverage and raise the levels of support over time (i.e., "creeping socialism" or the "foot in the door" notion). Typically, coverage is initially extended to limited and less well-off portions of the population (the poor, aged, blind, disabled) and broadened stepwise into comprehensive plans for most or all citizens. Because of the prosperity of the postwar era, and especially in the inflation-prone years of the latter 1960s and 1970s, there has been a tendency to link benefits to current living standards and living costs. This has been done by raising benefit levels to a more contemporary living standard and by linking benefits to rates of inflation, assuring increased spending in proportion to inflation rates. This has also acted as a considerable drain on the funding for social security systems. In the United States and West Germany, two of the most powerful capitalist economies, the financing of social security had become an acute problem by the mid-seventies, with major new taxation required to refinance the system.

A second factor has been related in some studies (Pryor, 1968) to levels of welfare spending—the proportion of aged people in the society. The proportion of the population over the age of sixty-five has grown considerably because of increased life expectancy and declining birthrates since the inception of social security programs in all the liberal democracies. Pryor's data (1968:466) indicate that in the late 1950s, over 60 percent of welfare expenditures went to the aged in one form or another in the United States, Germany, and Austria. Thus a rise in the proportion of the elderly has a major impact on levels of welfare spending.

Beyond this, there is little that can be definitively said about the reasons for the relative positions of the liberal democracies in welfare spending. The work of scholars such as Jackman, Wilensky, Heidenheimer, and Pryor has refuted many myths about the supposed effects on welfare spending of "individualist" versus "collectivist" ethics, military spending versus welfare spending, or centralized versus decentralized political systems. Wilensky (1975:113–19) is particularly effective in knocking down fallacious arguments about the harmful effects of welfare spending on democracy itself, while not ignoring the real possibilities of middle-class taxpayer revolts against welfare.

The conservative offensive of the 1980s against welfarism and welfare costs has had the effect of limiting new program initiatives and the growth of costs, but has not changed these systems more than marginally. Most observers have viewed this period as one of consolidation rather than radical change, and public opinion continues to support a broad role for the welfare state (Heidenheimer et al., 1990:366–68). On the other hand, the continuing fiscal crisis of several liberal democracies (Sweden, the United States, Italy), the slower growth of recent years, and the continuing aging of the population has raised new challenges to the welfare state consensus.

The general level of government debt, which in the mid-1970s was still manageable in most of the liberal democracies (cf. table 3.9) and even included surpluses in Germany, Japan, and Sweden, has deteriorated over the last two decades in almost all cases. With slower growth bringing in lower tax revenues and higher outlays for health care and jobless benefits, government finances have structurally slipped into the deficit category. Currently, all of the liberal democracies face significant national debt, and interest charges consume an increasing portion of government budgets. This debt trap, in turn, puts pressure on all categories of government spending, and the welfare spending services are especially vulnerable. These challenges to the liberal democratic social welfare state have now intensified, with the fiscal crisis of the state, and

Table 3.9   General Government Net Debt

	Percent of GDP			
	Liabilities (+) or assets (−)			
	1974	**1979**	**1989**	**1992**
West Germany	− 4.7	11.5	22.5	22.7
United States	21.7	19.1	30.4	37.9
United Kingdom	59.9	47.8	30.4	35.6
Sweden	− 30.1	− 19.8	− 5.4	3.4
France	8.1	13.8	24.8	28.8
Japan	− 5.3	14.9	14.7	6.1

Source: OECD, *Economic Outlook*, Dec. 1992.

the slow erosion of organized labor as a political force in Western Europe and North America. The social democratic ideas which gave rise to welfarism are on the defensive and are still searching for sources of reinvigoration and new direction; yet, while the democratic welfare state is eroding, it has been accepted as a basic institution even by most conservative parties, such as the Gaullists in France, the Christian Democrats in Germany and Italy, and the mainstream Conservatives in Britain. After two generations of building the postwar welfare state, the politics of post–Cold War change will probably produce gradual reform and the growth of experimentation, rather than wholesale scrapping or reversion to pre-Depression economic ideology.

4

Social Equality—
An Eroding Commitment

The liberal democracies made a social contract with their citizens in the aftermath of the Great Depression of the 1930s. In short, it was that government, in cooperation with business and labor, would establish a range of programs and policies that would reduce the most extreme disparities that had fueled class conflict under a laissez faire or classical liberal market. This was a difficult task for societies that still had fundamentally capitalist market economies, but in the period of postwar recovery and then prosperity, national governments were able to constrain, regulate, or adjust market outcomes in order to achieve more equal or equitable outcomes without unduly raising anxieties among the economic elites. This commitment to greater social equity was a necessary element in the East-West confrontation with communism, which claimed that capitalism exploited the working class mercilessly. Only a "capitalism with a human face" could defuse the class antagonisms that communists had been able to politically exploit in the Depression years. A stable democratic front against communism required some heightened concern over the degree of inequality between rich and poor, capitalists and workers, and among ethnic, religious, and gender groups in the population.

But in the last two decades, economic globalization of production and distribution, made possible by communications, transportation, and financial revolutions, began to undermine this commitment. National governments were unwilling to constrain capital investment from going overseas, and national corporations had no particular commitment to maintaining good jobs at good wages in Detroit, or Düsseldorf, or Milan, when workers in Taiwan, Mexico, Philippines, or Pakistan could perform similar work for one-tenth the wages. In recent years, the debate over the North American Free Trade Agreement (NAFTA) in the United States and the widening of the European Community (now the European Union, or EU) to include lower-wage nations of Southern Europe, and perhaps also some of the low-wage nations of postcommunist East Europe, has just begun to politicize these issues, but the

75

internationalization of corporate investment to low-wage areas continues to destroy good-paying manufacturing jobs in the Western democracies, while bringing good returns for stockholders in the West. The result has been the birth of new inequality, a new class division between winners and losers of modernization (*Modernisierungsgewinner* and *Modernisierungsverlierer* in German analysis), and both new affluence and new poverty of the de-industrialization of the West. The trade-off of the Cold War compromise is disappearing, and the trend toward greater inequality is now part of the current transitional period.

In this chapter the distribution of wealth and income, justice, health/education/welfare, political elite recruitment, and the situation of minorities and women in the liberal democracies are discussed under the heading of *inequality*. Under the general umbrella of quality of life (see chapter 6), such problems as crime, drugs/alcoholism, pornography, divorce rates, social isolation, unemployment, and pollution are discussed. In part, this is clearly an artificial division, since the ill effects of crime, drugs, alcoholism, pollution, joblessness, and even the loss of family values fall more heavily on the poor, the urban working class, and the minorities than on the wealthy, suburban, dominant strata. To be sure, drug addiction and alcoholism are also problems of the well-to-do and especially of their offspring, but the upper-middle-class youth addict in all probability avoids the criminal justice system and gets first-rate treatment and understanding for his or her addiction along with repeated chances to pursue a promising career pattern. Pollution and crime can threaten virtually any neighborhood or community, but the more affluent residents have the resources to run away to newer, safer, cleaner areas, taking their resources with them and even further hindering the ability of their ex-neighborhood to meet the threat of crime or pollution. Still, there are at least some limits to the ability of those in higher social strata to escape the problems that typify modern capitalism and quality-of-life issues. The division is probably valid as a relative distinction, certainly not as an absolute one.

Inequality: How Much and Is It Changing?

The liberal notion of equality that developed in the writings of Locke, Montesquieu, Madison, and Jefferson was specifically limited to the legal-administrative sphere of society. Its radical, even revolutionary, character lay in its opposition to the legally sanctioned privileges of the aristocracy and the church, which were privileges of birth and state-sponsored religious dogma rather than of achievement or free choice. As one author put it recently:

> The classic liberal concept of equality implies equality before the law, where there are no legally designated differences in status, reward, or privilege without regard to performance. Specifically, it originated as a middle-class concept that

entailed opposition to aristocratic privilege, promotion of individual liberties against perceived governmental oppression, and promotion of the rules that the same legal standards are applicable to all males. In its more advanced manifestations, liberal equality entailed such political goals as extension of the suffrage. Equality in this sense is not concerned with differences in opportunity that are the result of differences in the distribution of social and economic resources. (Mayer, 1977:136)

Even this statement probably gives too much credit to classic liberalism, since, as described in chapter 2, liberalism was quite content to limit the suffrage to male property holders. It was primarily the not-always-peaceful agitation of the labor movement and later the women's suffrage movement that forced the gradual step-by-step expansion of voting rights. Still, it is clear that classic liberalism raises no objections against gross inequalities of wealth, income, education, housing, and health care as long as these disparities are not fixed by law. In fact, classic liberalism has been most consistent in its objections to any political efforts to ameliorate social inequality. Economist Gaston Rimlinger (1971:305–31) shows that at best, classic liberalism is compatible with some forms of social security financed by wage-earners themselves, as long as they *do not decrease levels of income or wealth inequality,* but attempt only to better manage the scarce market resources of individual citizens.

The feudal order, which liberalism opposed, contained some rather elaborate tradition-based reciprocal obligations between lord and peasant, which included not only a paternalistic *noblesse oblige* on the part of the aristocracy, but in many cases detailed arrangements for the provision of protection and welfare of the masses in cases of armed attack, drought, plague, and other calamities. In its period of ascendancy, therefore, liberalism sought to break down notions of class (social) obligations, paternalistic or otherwise. Classic liberal theory, supported by the doctrines of Parson Malthus and of Social Darwinism, in fact opposed even those elements of social welfare that were patently nonredistributive:

The liberal capitalist civilization that emerged in the late eighteenth century rejected the traditional protectionism of the old social order. It denied the poor man's claim to a right to protection by society; it discarded the concept of paternal responsibility of the rich for the poor. In the liberal industry state, every man was to be free to pursue his fortune and was to be responsible for his success or failure. (Rimlinger, 1971:35)

Liberal theory, a forerunner of liberal democracy in the West, fought against claims of social obligation and social justice. It is in the area of social inequalities that liberal democracies have been most reluctant to act, and their actions are most likely to be half-hearted.

The Wealth-and-Income Gap

We can start most reasonably with a discussion of disparities in income and wealth that characterize the Western democracies. Economist Martin Schnitzer expresses the importance of wealth distribution as a key to understanding disparities in other areas quite nicely, as well as the problem that wealth inequality raises for the meritocratic claim of democracy:

> Although wealth in itself is not a bad thing, there is certainly a conflict between the way in which it is concentrated in the hands of a few and the American belief in equality of opportunity. With wealth goes economic power and prestige. The wealthy can afford to send their children to the best schools and provide them with the right contacts in employment. Inheritances also compound inequality through generations. Those who are wealthy can finance their own or others' campaigns for political office and thus successfully obtain political power. In no country is this more pronounced than the United States. The wealthy can hire expensive and successful lawyers to widen the scope of legitimate tax avoidance for themselves and also to resolve in their favor any legal conflicts with the less wealthy. (1974:43)

Although Schnitzer's evaluations are limited here to the United States, his remarks are applicable with some modifications to the liberal democracies in general. The effects of wealth disparity go beyond the ability to "buy" various benefits; rather they constitute together the basis for the continuation (although at a high level of overall development and economic well-being) of a class-divided society.

First of all, however, we should establish some definitions of wealth and income and then try to measure the actual extent of inequality that exists currently in a number of liberal democracies. By wealth we mean the sum total of all assets owned by individuals (or families). This includes land, buildings, factories, stocks and bonds, homes, jewels, every imaginable kind of commodity, as well as cash on hand. By income we mean reported individual (or family) earnings in a single year. These include income from work such as wages and salaries, and income from wealth, such as interest, capital gains, dividends, and rents. Despite some rather complex issues of reporting accuracy, valuation, and cross-national units of measurement for income and wealth in various societies (see Schnitzer, 1974, and Cromwell, 1977, for some cogent explanations), we can make some reasonably accurate calculations and comparisons among the liberal democracies in this area.

Two tools frequently used by economists to summarize the degree of inequality in the wealth or income (or any other commodity) distribution are the Lorenz curve and the Gini ratio. In figure 4.1, a solid line represents the Lorenz curve for an entirely equalized distribution of income (which exists in no country and serves only as a polar extreme). This straight line indicates

Figure 4.1: The Lorenz curve and Gini ratio.

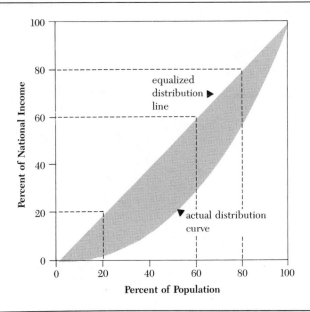

that any given percentage of the population receives the same percentage of the national income. The ''lowest'' 20 percent gets 20 percent, the ''top'' 20 percent gets 20 percent, the bottom 60 percent gets 60 percent, and so on. The dotted line indicates an hypothesized Lorenz curve for an income distribution in which the bottom 20 percent on the income ladder receives only 5 percent of national income, the top 20 percent receives 40 percent, and the bottom 60 percent gets 30 percent of national income. In this hypothesized example, the shaded area between the actual Lorenz curve and the completely equalized Lorenz curve (actually a forty-five degree angle straight line) represents the amount of inequality in the system. This area of inequality can be expressed as a ratio to the maximum theoretically possible amount of inequality and is called the Gini ratio. The greater the Gini ratio, which runs from a minimum of zero to a maximum of unity, the greater the inequality of income distribution. Figure 4.2 illustrates the distribution of income, wealth, and income-producing wealth in the liberal democracies. With some variations across nations, the distribution of household income has a Gini ratio of .30 to .50, while the distribution of household wealth typically has a Gini ratio of between .70 and .80. We may divide all family wealth into two categories, one covering family social security and pension savings for retirement, the family home, and personal belongings, and a second covering income-producing capital, such

Figure 4.2: Illustration of postwar income and wealth distribution in the United States.

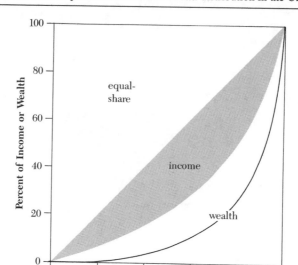

as stocks, bonds, real estate, and business investment capital. In the liberal democracies, family wealth for personal and retirement use has a Gini ratio of between .60 and .70, whereas investment capital is the most unequally distributed, with a Gini ratio of .80 or more. In France, for example, income distribution had a Gini ratio of about .50, compared to a Gini ratio of .70 for family noninvestment wealth, and a Gini ratio of .86 for income-producing investment capital (Kessler and Masson, 1987:166). In general, the inequality of investment capital is greatest, double the inequality in income distribution.

As the welfare state developed, tax systems worked some change on the pretax distribution of household income. In general, income tax systems have had some degree of progressivity, which means that higher income households pay higher tax rates, thus reducing somewhat the after-tax income inequality. The difference between before-tax and after-tax situations is one benchmark of the general level of commitment of the welfare state to social equality.

In the case of Sweden, the tax system, including national and local income taxes and contributions to the national old-age pension program, were structured so as to reduce income inequality considerably. The Gini ratio in 1970 decreased from .36 on pretax income to .26 on after-tax income. The bottom 40 percent of Swedish income earners received only 15.3 percent of pretax income, but 20.4 percent of after-tax income. The top 5 percent of income earners in Sweden accounted for 17.1 percent of pretax income, but only 10.8 percent of after-tax income (Schnitzer, 1974:85–86). In Britain and Germany also there was some smaller reduction in income inequality as a result of national tax structures.

In the United States, on the other hand, there was virtually no reduction of levels of income disparity from government tax policy. This may seem rather surprising in view of loud cries of anguish among the well-to-do of confiscatory or punitive tax rates. Such protests come more reasonably from middle-income families.

How was it possible that a progressive income tax rate of 14 percent to a maximum rate of 70 percent (prior to 1981) failed to achieve *any* measurable degree of income redistribution? The reasons were both clear and have been well documented in any number of studies of U. S. tax laws. United States tax laws, unlike those in Sweden or even Britain and Germany, had massive tax loopholes that lower considerably the tax rates actually paid by the wealthy. In particular, capital gains (on sale of assets held six months or more) were taxed at only half the rate applied to wages and salaries; also, interest on state and local bonds is entirely tax-free. In both areas, the average citizen did not have sufficient capital to benefit from these tax loopholes. Only those who already held wealth could benefit from these tax provisions that permit income from wealth to be taxed not at all or less than income from work. Philip Stern (1973:94) noted that for those fortunate citizens with annual incomes of over $1 million, all tax loopholes added together provide an average *savings* in taxes (tax avoidance) of $720,490 yearly and reduce the effective rate of

Table 4.1   Gini Index for Income Distribution in the Liberal Democracies

	DPI* Gini		Household Gini		Percent of Household Income Going to		
					Top 10 Percent	Bottom 40 Percent	
Switzerland	—	—	0.30	(1978)	29.8	16.9	(1982)
United States	0.35	(1986)	0.34	(1980)	25.0	15.7	(1985)
Sweden	0.28	(1987)	0.32	(1981)	20.8	21.2	(1981)
United Kingdom	0.33	(1986)	0.32	(1979)	23.3	17.3	(1979)
West Germany	—	—	0.30	(1978)	23.4	19.5	(1984)
France	—	—	0.35	(1975)	25.5	18.4	(1979)
Netherlands	0.27	(1987)	0.27	(1981)	23.0	20.1	(1983)
Japan	—	—	0.28	(1979)	22.4	21.9	(1979)
Australia	0.34	(1985)	0.40	(1975–76)	25.8	15.5	(1985)

Sources: World Bank, *World Development Report*, 1991, 1992; Denny Braun, *The Rich Get Richer* (Chicago: Nelson-Hall, 1991), p.75; Timothy M. Smeeding, "Income Inequality in Rich Countries During the 1980's," *The Luxembourg Income Study*, 1993.
*disposable personal income

taxation to about half the official rate. Estimates of losses in tax revenue range from a low of $36 billion to a high of $97 billion for the year 1971. As both Stern and Schnitzer concluded, the effect is that the progressivity of the income tax is reduced, and at the very top of the income scale some $2 billion of tax welfare was doled out to the three thousand richest American families. This was, for comparison, equal to the total amount spent by the federal government in 1971 to provide food stamps for the needy (Schnitzer, 1974: 47). If welfare for the rich balances welfare for the poor, it should not be surprising if the degree of income inequality remains unchanged. Those in the middle tended to be the greatest tax losers.

Partly in response to problems of tax evasion and tax resistance, and partly due to the ideological offensive of economic liberalism in the 1980s, tax codes have been reformed in most of the liberal democracies, with the effect of lowering the top tax rates, reducing the complexity of the tax system (at least relatively), and reducing the number of tax loopholes. While tax revolts such as Proposition 13 in California or Mogen Glistrup's Progress party in Denmark remained relatively localized and ephemeral political movements, their appearance also pushed the welfare state, whether governed by staunch conservatives like Margaret Thatcher in Britain or socialists like Francois Mitterrand in France and Ingvar Carlsson in Sweden, to move in the direction of reducing the direct tax burden on all taxpayer classes. A greater share of the total tax burden was shifted to indirect consumption taxes, which tend to have a greater impact on lower and middle income groups. These changes have made the total taxation system less progressive; less governmental redistribution of income to lower income groups was the general trend of the 1980s.

Despite the introduction since the turn of the century of nominally (officially) quite progressive income tax laws in all of the liberal democracies and the expansion in the post-World War II era of total levels of taxation (of all kinds), there are some notable differences in the effects, if any, of taxation on the levels of income inequality. In Sweden, in fact, a progressive and strictly enforced tax system does produce significant equalization in the distribution of income. In France (and Italy) massive tax fraud by the rich is tolerated by the government, which thereby increases the burden of taxation on the average income earner. In the United States, and to some degree in Britain and Germany, tax loopholes offer what amounts to tax welfare for the rich, which again shifts the burden of taxation to middle-income groups.

Recent research from the Luxemburg Income Study, which compared income distribution changes among six Western democracies in the 1980s, and which included income distribution both before and after government taxation and transfer programs, found that the general trend was toward greater inequality of family earnings in four of the six nations, but most sharply in the United States and Great Britain. Government taxation and transfer policies continued to reduce inequality considerably in Sweden and the Netherlands, but were much less effective in the United States and Great Britain. "While all governments, including the U.S., are generally redistributive in terms of reducing market-driven income inequality, the level and trend in this effectiveness differ widely by nation. In the U.S., government redistribution policy grew weaker in the 1980s, reinforcing widening the top to bottom spread in the market income distribution" (Smeeding and Coder, 1993:10). Smeeding and Coder estimate further that this trend has continued into the 1990s, and generally the trend toward greater inequality in income has become a feature of the post–Cold War period of economic transition, with some variation among the liberal democracies in terms of the political elite's motivation to tolerate increasingly greater rich-poor divisions within a democratic society.

With respect to wealth, by almost any standard, there is a great degree of concentration of assets, especially investment capital assets, in the hands of a very small minority of the population. How extreme this concentration is can be judged from figures on the percentage of national wealth controlled by the top 1 percent, top 5 percent, and top 20 percent of the population (see table 4.2). In all the liberal democracies, the upper classes hold almost all productive income-producing assets, so that the bottom 80 percent of the population owns less than 20 percent. In the United States, the bottom quarter of the population owns zero assets as a group, since their debts cancel out their assets; the poorest 8 percent in fact have negative wealth, since they owe more than they own.

The concentration of income-producing wealth is very high throughout the liberal democracies. The richest 1 percent in the United States in 1983 (Wolff and Marley, 1989:809) owned 74 percent of all corporate stock (Gini ratio = .89), owned 70 percent of all financial securities (Gini ratio = .75), owned 97 percent of trust fund equity (Gini ratio = .93), owned 63 percent of

Table 4.2 Distribution of Wealth in Selected Liberal Democracies

	Percentage of wealth held in:				
Population	**United States (1983)**	**Britain (1975)**	**France (1977)**	**Germany (1973)**	**Sweden (1975)**
top 1%	36	23	19	28	16
top 5%	58	47	45	—	35
top 20%	82	82	81	—	65
Gini ratio	.81	.82	.78	—	—

Sources: E. Wolff and M. Marley, "Long-term Trends in U.S. Wealth Inequality," in R. Lipsy and H. Tice (eds.), *The Measurement of Savings, Investment and Wealth* (1988), p. 806; A. Fouquet and D. Strauss-Kahn, "Size Distribution of Personal Wealth in France (1977)," *Review of Income of Wealth 30*, 4 (1984):408; E. Wolff (ed.), *International Comparisons of the Distribution of Household Wealth* (1987), p. 153.

unincorporated business equity (Gini ratio = .79), and owned 55 percent of all non-owner-occupied real estate (Gini ratio = .75). In France, in 1977 (Kessler and Marley, 1987:170), the richest 10 percent owned 80 percent of all investment real estate, 73 percent of all stocks, shares, and bonds, and 72 percent of all business equity. In Sweden in the mid-1970s the richest 0.3 percent of all households controlled half the value of all listed corporate stock shares (Spant, 1987:63). In spite of the growth in numbers of citizens who own some shares of stock, the development of "populist capitalism" in terms of broad deconcentration of income-producing wealth has yet to appear. Socialist critic Michael Harrington argued, "The top 1 percent of the wealth holders own 62 percent of all publicly held stock; the top 5 percent have 86 percent, the top 20 percent have 97 percent. So much for our stockholder democracy" (1976:277). With this concentration in the holdings of stocks, bonds, income property, and business equity, it is not surprising that over half of all income derived from wealth, in the form of interest, rents, dividends, and business profits, goes to the top 1 percent on the income scale and close to 100 percent goes to the top 10 percent on the income scale (Schnitzer, 1974: 197).

Granted that there still exists an enormous concentration of wealth in the liberal democracies, and lesser but quite formidable concentrations of income as well, isn't there a trend toward greater equality? Some have argued that as the modern welfare state has emerged in the Western democracies, distribution of income and wealth has become gradually more egalitarian, although few, given the data above, would argue that we have reached any sort of egalitarian state of affairs as yet. Economist Simon Kuznets (1950) theorized several decades ago that as traditional agrarian societies begin to industrialize, the degree of income inequality rises initially (in the era of robber baron capitalism) and then tends to decline as the industrial society matures. Daniel Bell boldly claimed that "a sticky fact of Western society over the past two hundred years has been the steady decrease in income disparity among persons" (cited by Harrington, 1976:276).

Much research indicates, however, that rather than any steady trend over such a long timeframe, there have been several periods of change in the degree of income and wealth disparity in those nations that are now liberal democracies (Williamson and Lindert, 1976; Brown, 1988:321–22). In the United States and Britain, for example, it appears that there was a strong trend in the nineteenth century towards greater income inequality, which lasted in the United States up to the beginning of World War I, and which peaked earlier in Britain. In the 1920s, the level of inequality in income may have reached a highwater mark and peaked at a very high plateau. This was followed by a significant levelling process, which was related to both the Great Depression and then to the wartime mobilization. After World War II, this gradual trend continued into the 1960s, much of it attributable to the strength of organized labor and labor-based parties in the prosperous postwar growth period. In Britain, a 1975 royal commission report showed a decline in the before-tax income of the richest 1 percent from 17 percent of national income in 1938–39 to 11 percent in 1949–50, and down to 6 percent by 1972–73 (Harrington, 1975:270).

The trend of wealth distribution was clearly in the direction of deconcentration from the 1920s to the 1970s in Britain, the United States, Sweden, and perhaps France (Wolff and Marley, 1987:9–11; Brown, 1988: 390–93). The share of wealth in England and Wales held by the top 1 percent declined from 61 percent in 1923 to 32 percent in 1972, and went down to 23 percent (in the United Kingdom) by 1980. In the United States, the share of wealth controlled by the top one-half of 1 percent declined from just over 30 percent in the 1920s to about 20 percent in the 1970s (Smith, 1987:81). And in Sweden, the decline for the top 1 percent was from 50 percent of all wealth in 1920 to about 20 percent by 1975 (Spant, 1987:60).

This historic trend was reversed by the 1980s, however. In a major study of wealth distribution commissioned by the Joint Economic Committee of the U.S. Congress, the degree of wealth concentration was found to have increased between 1963 and 1983. In 1963, the richest 0.5 percent controlled 25.4 percent of national assets, and this had increased to 35.1 percent by 1983. The richest 10 percent owned 65.1 percent of wealth in 1963; this had increased to 71.7 percent by 1983 (Kloby, 1987:7; also Wolff and Marley, 1989:814). Roland Spant (1987:70) also reports that in Sweden "the long trend towards less inequality now seems to be broken, and the richest groups' share of total wealth was probably higher in 1983 than in 1975." It seems clear that the *current trend* in the liberal democracies, in both income and wealth distribution, is *towards greater inequality* at the beginning of the 1990s, and has probably been so for more than a decade.

Much data compiled over the past two decades indicate that beginning in the 1960s, and accelerating in the 1980s, the current trend in income distribution has been towards greater inequality. Analyses by Parkin (1971: 120) on Norway and Britain, by Henle (1972) on the United States, and by Schnitzer (1974:112) on Germany indicate that the gradual equalization trend began to be reversed in the 1960s. Between 1979 and 1987 in the United States, the Reagan years, family income for the poorest fifth of the population declined by 6.1 percent, while for the top fifth it increased by 11.1 percent (*New York Times*, March 23, 1989:1). In Britain under the Thatcher government, the top 20 percent on the income scale increased their share from 38 percent in 1979 to 42 percent in 1987, while the bottom 20 percent saw their share shrink from 7 to 6 percent (*le Monde selection*, August 16–22, 1990:9). Even in countries with a strong social security network and continuing aggregate growth, such as the Federal Republic of Germany, the 1980s produced visible signs of a growing inequality. Homelessness, begging, and the erosion of older industrial communities and neighborhoods were now associated with the new supply-side economic policies of the period, and these problems were growing at the same time that the economies were generally growing, and many people were leading very affluent lifestyles. In Germany, the term *Zweidrittelgesellschaft* (two-thirds society) came to symbolize the new inequality in which the top two-thirds of society was doing okay, and at the top quite well, but the bottom one-third was losing ground and without good prospects for the future. The post-industrial society seemed to have less equality associated with it—many losers from the modernization process (*Modernisierungsverlierer*), as well as winners, with an increasing gap between them.

It may be that the Great Depression, which ruined many of the rich, and World War II, which quickly produced full employment and higher wartime wages in a scarce labor market, produced a shift towards greater equality in several of the liberal democracies between 1929 and 1945 (Harrington, 1976: 277; Schnitzer, 1974:57; Williamson and Lindert, 1976:73–77). The progressive taxation systems to finance the modern welfare-state democracy after World War II, especially in nations with strong social democratic and labor parties, made an impact that may have lasted through the period of postwar recovery and industrial growth into the early 1960s. It would appear that despite the significant rise of living standards for the population as a whole, this general movement came to a halt and was then reversed by the latter 1970s and most clearly by the 1980s.

Capitalist market economies, even in a modern welfare-state democracy, seem to have a strong tendency towards increasing inequality in wealth, which requires strong and sustained political pressure to counteract on a nationwide basis. Governments in the liberal democracies have to be specifically and strongly committed to greater equality in the face of normal market pressures if any movement towards greater equality is to be expected. A policy of "benign neglect" is very likely to produce even greater inequality through the workings of the capitalist market.

The New Poverty in the Liberal Democracies

One of the achievements of the postwar liberal democracies was the significant and relatively durable reduction of material poverty, by historic standards, to quite low levels. Yet, in the 1980s, signs of a "new poverty" appeared in nearly all the liberal democracies. The most overt signs were an increase in visible homelessness in the large urban areas. Many homeless, especially in rural areas, remain quite "invisible" to the political system. But in much more systematic fashion, research from the Luxemburg Income Study (LIP) of several Western democracies in the 1980s found that, even after redistributive taxation and transfer programs of government are included, poverty levels were generally increasing in four (United States, Australia, Germany, and

Sweden) of the seven nations studied and was decreasing in only two (Netherlands and Canada), while stagnant in France (Smeeding, 1992). Moreover, in the United States particularly, poverty among children was rising rapidly, from 14.7 percent in 1979 to over 20 percent by 1986, a clear result of the Reagan revolution, which weakened what was already the weakest antipoverty income security system among the liberal democracies in the study. By comparison, child poverty rates in Sweden were less than 2 percent, in France less than 5 percent, and in Canada and Australia about 9 percent in the mid-1980s. Even in Great Britain under the Thatcher government, child poverty rates were still only 7.4 percent in 1986. Smeeding concludes in his policy recommendation that "every other nation studied outperforms the United States in this arena. We need to begin to make poverty a priority in this country, starting especially with poor children, where we tolerate a level of disadvantage unknown to any other major advanced country on earth" (1992:35).

Yet, if the economic stagnation and rising unemployment rates in the European Union in the 1990s are any indication, even in those democracies more dedicated to antipoverty efforts it will be difficult to avoid the general trend to greater poverty rates generally, since the financial basis for income security support systems has been weakened and continues to weaken. This may, of course, only mean that government effort needs to be even greater and more focussed on the near-poor and working poor, and that the political struggle to retain income security programs will be sharper as the Cold War political consensus further erodes.

Educational Inequality: Money versus Merit

We began this discussion of inequality in the liberal democracies with a quote from Martin Schnitzer on the ways in which money can be transformed into occupational, educational, and political privilege. In this section we will detail some of the disparities in life opportunities due to inequalities of wealth. It must be emphasized at the start, however, that for the overwhelming majority of the well-to-do, young and old alike, wealth is inherited, not self-made. The rags-to-riches dream of America especially and to some extent of all capitalist societies has indeed been fulfilled for some in each generation, yet all the data we have on the wealthy in *every* liberal democracy indicate that the wealthy were born into wealth. The advantages that money confers are thus unearned by these individuals, which contradicts both the norm of equality of opportunity and the standard of merit achievement.

One area of conferred privilege is education. We have already recounted the "class channeling" system of many European school systems (chapter 3). Parkin's study shows that only small minorities of university students in Britain (25 percent), Norway (25 percent), Sweden (16 percent), Denmark (10 percent), France (8 percent), Austria (8 percent), the Netherlands (5 percent), and Germany (5 percent) were of working-class backgrounds at the beginning of the 1960s. In Britain, with a larger-than-average proportion of working-class university students, only 2 percent of all working-class children got as far as the university versus 20 percent of all middle-class children (Heidenheimer et al., 1975:131). Even these figures underestimate the disparity of educational opportunities, since the definition of middle-class is a relatively broad one and includes some fairly modest positions. With the tremendous growth of the higher education system in the 1960s and 1970s, some greater upward educational mobility was also provided for working class children, for minorities, and for women. In Britain, the percentage of university students from working-class families increased by 1969 to 21 percent; in Germany the enrollment from worker backgrounds reached 15 percent by the late 1970s. In the European democracies the number of female university students rose from about one-third of all university students in 1960 to over 40 percent by 1980. Only in Japan, where the university system also plays a more visibly decisive role in sharply stratifying career opportunities, do women still represent only about one-fourth of students (Heidenheimer et al., 1990:48–49).

The expansion of the higher education system in the 1960s and 1970s in many if not all of the liberal democracies undoubtedly gave many individuals greater opportunities both in education and in career choices, yet the expansion of college-level education has not and cannot by itself produce greater equality. The reasons are many. In the first place, those best able to take advantage of the increases in college and university enrollment were the sons and daughters of the middle class, regardless of merit or innate ability. A study by David Cohen (1972, cited by Harrington, 1976:273) showed that of U.S. high school seniors in the bottom 20 percent according to IQ scores and whose families were in the bottom 20 percent on the income scale, only 10 percent went to some sort of college. Of those seniors in the bottom 20 percent in IQ scores but whose parents were in the wealthiest 20 percent, 40 percent went on to college. In the European school systems there exist elite private secondary schools that provide quality university-track preparation for the offspring of the affluent.

Even in the United States, where most middle-class children are likely to go to public schools, the wealth related property-tax system of public school financing provides similar disparities in quality of education between middle-class and working-class districts. James Coons, in a study of public schools in Ohio, which does more state funding of its schools than most states, concluded: "In Ohio a child's public education is dependent for its quality upon the private wealth of its district. It is as simple as that" (1970: 80; cited in Heidenheimer et al., 1975:132). This has been compounded in the United States by the racial factor, so that poorer schools, especially in the inner cities, also tended to have overwhelmingly black enrollments.

As the number of colleges and universities has increased, moreover, the quality of the college or university has become increasingly more important than just the fact of college attendance. Studies by Coleman et al. (1966), Little and Westergaard (1964), and Jencks (1972) have indicated the strong influence of social class background in affecting the quality of education received. Wilensky expressed surprise that any sociologist should by now have failed to perceive the inability of even universal college education "to effect by itself a major redistribution of income or a revolution in equality" (1975:4). Wilensky noted that in California, community colleges turn out graduates for such occupations as bank clerks, chefs, technicians, and lower-level white collar positions; the state colleges and universities provided the economy with middle-level personnel in teaching, commerce, industry, and government. Graduates of the elite campuses (Berkeley, Stanford) were overwhelmingly programmed for higher professional and executive posts. In the 1980s, a new problem of stagnant economies intensified the competition for good occupational placements among university graduates. As the number of new professional jobs in the 1980s has fallen below the now-raised levels of graduates in many European democracies, the universities have become for many a holding bin from which employment perspectives seem rather dim. It is common to find taxi drivers in Rome or Naples with doctoral degrees, or sales personnel in Frankfurt or Hamburg shops with education degrees. In Germany, the number of graduates seeking teaching positions at all levels has exceeded available places, resulting in a long list of aspirants with little or no hope of finding professional teaching employment. In some fields, a restrictive entrance ceiling (called *numerus clausus*) has attempted to match graduates to available employment opportunities, but this has meant an even greater social filtering of the top aspirants for fields like medicine. Many German students find themselves studying in fields of secondary interest, and they tend to extend their studies rather than enter the unpromising job market. In this sense the university becomes the "waiting room" (*Wartezimmer*) of society, frustrating to students, faculty, and university administrators alike. While educational expansion in the 1960s and 1970s created higher expectations and greater access to the requisite higher education, it has since the 1980s run up against the barrier of a constrained job market, giving rise to a new inequality, both of social class and of generation. For a career at the top or elite levels of the occupational ladder, the quality education required is still very much class related; that is, recruitment to top jobs through the higher educational system, even in its much-expanded form, is largely a self-recruitment process from within the top strata. British sociologist Anthony Giddens, in a comparative study of several Western democracies, summarized the situation.

> In the capitalist societies, the educational qualifications associated with recruitment to elite groupings will tend to be very much those associated with a background of material privilege. What influences elite recruitment is not that the aspirant

recruit possesses a degree in physics or engineering, but that the degree is conferred at Oxford or Harvard; and, whatever the variability which may exist in degree of "closure" of elite recruitment between different societies, it is everywhere true that ownership of wealth and property continues to play a fundamental part in facilitating access to the sort of educational process which influences entry to elite positions. (1973:263–64)

Fitness to Rule: Inequality in Elite Recruitment

Elite recruitments include top jobs in industry, commerce, the high-paid, high-status professions, the military, judiciary/civil service, and elective government. Comparative studies on the background of elites in the liberal democracies agree on the tremendous overrepresentation of the upper and upper-middle class in all of these different elite groupings.

A variety of analyses has shown the extent of overrepresentation of higher occupations, higher social origins, and higher educational attainment among members of both elective and nonelective elites in the liberal democracies. In one of the best syntheses of research findings, Robert Putnam (1976:ch. 3) estimated that in the United States, Britain, Italy, and Germany, only 1 to 3 percent of national legislators had had manual occupations, while 60 to 65 percent of the working population were in the manual job category. This might be expected, since it could well be that the skills necessary for legislation are not those necessary for manual occupations. Yet if one looks at the social origins of legislators (see table 4.3), Putnam found, as have other researchers, that there was no equality of opportunity for those of lower-class origins to rise to political elite status.

As has been pointed out in cross-national elite comparisons by Nagle (1977), Miliband (1969), and Bottomore (1966), the United States political elite has been considerably more closed to the working class than in nations like Britain or Italy, where strong socialist, labor, or Communist parties have afforded citizens from humbler backgrounds at least some opportunities for

Table 4.3 Social Origins of National Legislators (Percentage figures)

	United States	Canada	United Kingdom	France	Italy	West Germany
Higher managerial/ Professional	73[a] (44)[b]	81	46 (58)	56	48 (28)	42 (35)
Manual working class/Farmer	11 (18)	12	15 (22)	9	11 (36)	17 (30)

Source: Adapted from Blondel, 1973: 160–62, and Putnam, 1976: 23.
a. estimates from Blondel.
b. estimates from Putnam.

advancement through politics. The United States never developed a working-class party. Thus, despite a much-advertised "log cabin" myth of American political leadership, there has never been at any time during the history of the Republic any significant recruitment from the lower social strata. The American Congress, the cabinet, and governorships have been dominated, with little alteration from industrialization, immigration, boom, or depression, by businessmen and professionals, overwhelmingly lawyers (Nagle, 1977; Matthews, 1954).

In Germany, on the other hand, the Social Democratic party (SPD) and, during the Weimar period from 1919 to 1933, the Communist party (KPD) sent considerable numbers of deputies to the *Reichstag* who were not only from humble origins but from working-class occupations. As the SPD grew in strength from 1871 to 1912 in the Kaiser's Germany, the share of deputies from blue- and white-collar occupations increased considerably (table 4.4). The direct representation of industrialists and nontitled landowners peaked at the height of industrialization about the turn of the century and the share of seats held by the aristocracy declined gradually. The German "Revolution of 1918" dramatically increased the direct presence of worker/employee types in the *Reichstag*, and the KPD deputy faction, especially after the proletarianization of the party in the 1920s, was made up almost entirely of young radicalized workers. As prosperity returned to postwar Germany in the 1950s, however, recruitment of workers, blue collar and white collar, became less and less common, and by the 1960s recruitment came overwhelmingly from higher occupational strata.

Despite the political turmoil that has marked much of German history in the last century, other nations of the West have shown a roughly similar pattern. With the impact of industrialization the political role of the aristocracy has been weakened, though with some considerable variation in time lag from country to country. Nontitled representatives from the new business class and even more from the upper echelons of management, civil service, and the professions have become attractive candidates from conservative, Christian Democrat, and liberal parties. Most of the early working-class parties, including the German SPD, the British Labour party, the French Socialists, and the Swedish Social Democrats, which once sent mostly workers to parliament at the beginning of the century, have, ever since achieving some national power, and especially in the period of post–World War II prosperity, nominated more and more of their candidates from higher occupational strata. Through this process of *embourgeoisement*, British Labourite MPs, for example, who were 80 to 100 percent workers between 1900 and 1920, were only 30 to 40 percent workers between 1955 and 1975. It would appear that the phenomenon of Eurocommunism, by which the Italian, French, and Spanish (in post-Franco Spain) Communist parties attempted to make themselves acceptable governing parties in the Western democracies, also brought a decline in the recruitment

Table 4.4   Occupations of Reichstag/Bundestag Deputies, 1871–1983

	1871	1893	1912	1919	1932	1949	1961	1972	1983
Worker/Employee	0	6	15	30	37	49	13	15	19
Landowner/Business Owner	15	31	19	14	17	14	19	8	13
Manager/ Professional	37	30	46	49	41	32	63	72	65
Aristocracy	42	25	14	(a)	—	—	—	—	—
Other	6	8	6	7	5	5	5	5	3

Source: John D. Nagle, *System and Succession: The Social Bases of Political Elite Recruitment* (Austin: University of Texas Press, 1977), pp. 128–29. Reprinted by permission of the publisher.
a. After the fall of the Kaiser in 1918, the small percentages of deputies with titles were included under their nontitled occupations.

of worker deputies from these parties (Putnam, 1976:179). The transformation was most notable in the Italian Communist party, which has had both the will and the opportunity to practice the strategy of Eurocommunism in a liberal democratic setting.

Administrative, nonelective elites tended to be at least as unrepresentative as elected political elites, and in some cases significantly more so (table 4.5). In Britain, Germany, and France, where the senior civil service enjoys great prestige and power, recruitment has been quite class-selective, and the social composition of this elite has been more biased in favor of the upper classes than the elective political elite. Evidence from Guy Peters (1978:92–93) on the social origins of senior civil servants in several other democracies, while not strictly comparable because of shifting definitions and different years of sampling, confirms the general picture. Percentages of administrative elites from working-class origins have been relatively low in Switzerland (15 percent in 1969), France (17 percent from 1953–1968), the Netherlands (15 percent in 1973), Canada (13.2 percent in 1957), and, surprisingly, very low in early postwar Denmark (4.3 percent in 1945) and Sweden (3.0 percent in 1949). Peters attributed much of the upper strata over-representation to the inequalities in higher education, which "despite attempts to make post-secondary education more available . . . still remains a sanctuary of the upper and middle classes" (p. 94). In those countries like the United States and more recently Sweden, that have comprehensive secondary school education and much-expanded higher educational opportunities, a somewhat higher proportion of the administrative elite might be expected to come from working-class origins, but even here, there are noneducationally based social biases at work in the elite levels of the bureaucracy:

> Like all organizations, they tend to replicate themselves, and there is a strong tendency to recruit people who are like those already in the positions. This type

of organizational bias is perhaps especially strong during the personal interviews generally required for appointments to upper-echelon positions. (Peters, 1978: 94–95)

There is sufficient evidence to state that it is not only the university degree but also the degree at the right (most prestigious) university that has granted entrance into the top administrative elite. Miliband (1969), Bottomore (1966), and Peters (1978) have demonstrated the preponderance of Oxford and Cambridge (the Oxbridge connection) graduates who constituted two-thirds of all top British administrators, and the dominance of Paris university graduates, who made up three-fourths of entrants to the elite Ecole Nationale d'Administration. In Japan nearly 80 percent of the senior civil service graduated from Tokyo Imperial University (Kubota, 1969). In the United States the senior civil service as a whole does not have the same prestige, and there has been no elite university connection comparable to that in France or Britain; only in the high-status U.S. Foreign Service did Ivy League school graduates tend to dominate.

By all accounts, this class bias in nonelective elites held for judicial and military elites as well, with some minor differences (see Miliband, 1969: 61–62, and Bottomore, 1966). For example, recruitment to the American military leadership has been from "the upper-middle rather than truly higher or definitely lower classes. Only a very small percentage of these are of working-class origins" (Mills, 1956:192). This compares with a somewhat

Table 4.5   Occupational Backgrounds of Government Ministers, 1945–1981 (Percentage)

Country	1*	2*	3*	4*	5*	6*
United States	3	42	29	13	7	—
Canada	4	50	16	19	4	1
Sweden	—	25	10	25	15	1
United Kingdom	5	33	20	15	10	6
West Germany	—	34	18	21	9	4
France	3	46	15	20	6	1
Italy	1	25	16	27	1	4
Japan	2	31	21	28	—	—
Australia	7	34	24	8	22	3
Switzerland	—	67	—	12	4	—

Source: Adapted from Jean Blondel, *Government Ministers in the Contemporary World* (London: Sage, 1985), pp. 277–79.

*Occupational Code:
  1. army
  2. lawyers and civil servants
  3. business management and white collar
  4. engineers and teachers
  5. farmers and manual workers
  6. party or trade union

more exclusive and still aristocratically-tinged basis of advancement into the British, German, and French top officer corps.

In the area of economic elites, which includes business owners, corporate executives, and leading professionals, the picture of class dominance has been even stronger. Westergaard (1965:89), Giddens (1973:170–71, 181–82), and Parkin (1971) have emphasized that studies of social mobility in the liberal democracies have found that "virtually all movement, whether upward or downward, inter- or intragenerational, across the nonmanual/ manual division, is 'short-range' " (Giddens, 1973:181). Miller (1960) reported that generally less than 5 percent of sons of manual workers make "the big leap," a long-range upward move, to higher business circles and top professions. A high figure of 8 percent was reported for the United States, giving credence to the notion of greater fluidity of class lines in American society, although Giddens (1973:170) reported that long-range mobility from working class to elite positions seemed to be generally higher in Japan as well as the United States compared with most European societies. Studies in Germany, Japan, Britain, Canada, and the United States show that generally three-quarters of current business and professional elites came from upper- and upper-middle-class backgrounds, while less than 10 percent were from working-class homes. One could always find success stories of self-made men and women, but these have been statistically infrequent. Recent studies in the United States indicate that a child whose father is in the bottom 5 percent of the income scale has only 1 chance in 20 of rising to the top 20 percent of the income scale, but has a 2 in 5 chance of staying poor or near poor. A child whose father is in the top 5 percent, on the other hand, has a 42 percent chance of staying in the top 20 percent and only 1 chance in 200 of winding up in the bottom 20 percent. While many children will do better or worse than their parents, "the best predictor of how well you'll do is still how well your parents did" (Nasar, 1992).

While all elites, with the minor exception of union leaders, in contemporary capitalist society have been quite unrepresentative of the general population along class lines, a general rule of thumb suggested by Putnam (1976:24–25) is that elected political elites are somewhat less unrepresentative than administrative elites and that economic elites are least representative of all. It would appear further that with respect to political elites, the trend since World War II has been toward greater inequality in the social basis of recruitment in several democracies, including Germany and Britain. Indeed, in Germany, the return to economic prosperity and the institutionalization of the Bonn democracy was matched step for step by the progressive closing out of the working class from political elite recruitment, by Social Democrats as well as by Christian Democrats.

The High Cost of Justice: Inequality before the Law

One area of equality is supported with some enthusiasm by liberal theory and widely held to be compatible with both capitalism and liberal democracy. This is equality of the individual before the law, the notion that due process of law, the administration of justice, and the enforcement of criminal statutes and government regulations should be impartial, blind to the social origins and circumstances of the individual. Yet even here it is all too evident that wealth has been able to transform itself into influence in the legal system, to provide a class-biased administration of the law in favor of the rich.

In all the liberal democracies, the overwhelming proportion of those persons actually arrested for crimes, those convicted of criminal behavior, and those serving time in prison are of lower social origins, poorly educated and from largely unskilled and semiskilled occupations. There is, in fact, relatively little official recording of crime by the well-to-do. Is it simply that criminal behavior is relatively infrequent among the upper classes? American criminologist Edwin Sutherland (1974) answered that the bias of the criminal justice system assures that most police effort goes toward fighting, however efficiently or inefficiently, crimes committed by lower-class individuals, that criminal prosecutions are more likely against blue-collar transgressions of law, and that jail sentences are much more likely and longer for the lower-class convicted. Sutherland coined the phrase "white-collar crime" to cover the range of illegal activities engaged in by people of high social status, whether prosecuted by the criminal justice system or not. He estimated from his case-by-case survey of white-collar criminality in the United States that such crimes as falsified company balance sheets, security fraud, real estate fraud, fraudulent bank security transfers, insurance fraud, tax fraud, and price-fixing cost the citizenry much more than even the most spectacular bank robberies, burglaries, or hijackings, yet they seldom, *even when discovered*, lead to penalties as severe as those for blue-collar crimes. Sutherland's landmark study of seventy large corporations and their unlawful practices involving over one thousand legal or administrative decisions against them led him to the following conclusions:

> The upper class has greater influence in moulding the criminal law and its administration than does the lower class. The privileged position of white-collar criminals before the law results to a slight extent from bribery and political pressures, principally from the respect in which they are held and without special effort on their part. The most powerful group in medieval society secured relative immunity by "benefit of clergy," and now our most powerful groups secure relative immunity by "benefit of business or profession." (1974: 43)

Donald Cressey, a research colleague of Sutherland who helped to advance the study of white-collar crime and develop a sociological theory of criminal justice, gave this conclusion:

> White-collar crimes—crimes committed by persons of respectability and high social status in the course of their occupations—also are extremely widespread, but an index of their frequency is not found in police reports. Prosecution for this kind of crime frequently is avoided because of the political or financial importance of the parties concerned . . . or because of the difficulty in securing evidence sufficient for prosecution, particularly in the areas of crimes by corporations. (1974:40)

This inequality before the law for corporate criminals is all the more glaring since opinion polls show that the public regards white-collar and executive crime as serious offenses, more serious even than many "blue-collar" crimes such as burglary and robbery (Clinard and Yeager, 1980:5–9). German political scientist Hans See (1990:190–91) has given estimates of the cost of economic crime (*Wirtschaftskriminalität*) in Germany of between 48 and 130 billion D-Mark for 1982 (about $20–50 billion), but found that relatively few resources are committed to combatting this executive/elite criminality. Most estimates of the costs to the public of corporate crime show that it is far greater than that of street crime; for example, one case of illegal corporate price-fixing among plumbing fixture manufacturing businesses cost consumers over $100 million, whereas the largest sum netted from a robbery was only $4 million, involving a Lufthansa warehouse in New York City in 1978. Yet, Clinard and Yeager, at the end of their recent study of corporate crime, concluded:

> The corporate executive runs little risk of a criminal conviction or prison sentence for his illegal actions on behalf of the corporation. Complex legal and social features, as well as bias within the system, operate in such a manner that corporate officers are largely insulated from the consequences of their socially harmful actions. . . . (1980:297)

The authors added that corporate criminals, even when caught and convicted, are often welcomed back into top positions in the business community and do not lose their social standing, nor do they consider their actions "criminal," but rather just part of the corporate necessities of doing business.

According to Cressey (1974) and Gurr et al. (1975) business fraud was on the increase in Western Europe and the United States in the postwar era, but was not accurately reflected in official statistics, which indicated only the tip of the iceberg. There are differing opinions as to the cause of criminality generally (see Gordon, 1977:ch. 6; Quinney, 1970) as well as of criminality among the upper classes, who do not suffer from economic deprivation, social discrimination, or any apparent mental pathology. But among the specialists who have studied white-collar criminality, there seems to be a broad consensus that the application of criminal statutes, prosecution of offenders, and punishment of the guilty is markedly biased in favor of those from the top levels of society. Gilbert Geis's (1967) close analysis of the 1961 antitrust case against General Electric and Westinghouse and Bacon and Mays's (1970) and Schafer's (1976) analyses of differential treatment by social class of criminality agree on the class bias of the criminal justice system.

There is rather firm evidence from studies in Sweden, Norway, Finland, the United States, and England that with respect to juvenile delinquency as well social class is a deciding factor as to whether delinquent behavior is subject to criminal prosecution or is treated as a private (noncriminal) matter: "The kinds of offenses that middle-class youngsters commit may be similar to those lower-class children commit, i.e., damage to property, petty theft, etc., but they tend, in the main, to be dealt with not as crimes, but as childish indiscipline" (Bacon and Mays, 1970:133).

Those in high public office, even when caught with hand deep in the public till, are seldom criminally prosecuted and even less often jailed if prosecuted. Spiro Agnew, former vice-president of the United States under Nixon, was never required to serve any jail sentence for his crimes of bribery and extortion. Former Prime Minister Tanaka of Japan, who was tried and convicted in the multi-million-dollar Lockheed bribery scandal from the 1970s, did not serve any prison sentence and until a later heart attack continued to be a top political leader in the governing LDP, because his wealth and political clout permit the endless delay of "justice." The same is true of the Italian defense ministry officials, including two ministers of defense bribed by Lockheed who have not been charged to date with anything. While there are of course some spectacular cases of court convictions of the rich and powerful (Ivan Boesky, Billy Sol Estes of a former era), these are rare exceptions.

One of the symptoms of the erosion of the success formula of the liberal democracies in the 1980s and 1990s has been the rise in high-level corruption and executive-level criminality. In the United States, the Reagan administration permitted the looting of the savings and loan industry (cf. esp. Pizzo, Fricker and Muolo, 1991), which cost the taxpayers (as of fall 1993) over $200 billion. A few of the most visible culprits (George Keating of the failed Lincoln Savings and Loan and Edward McBirney of the failed Sunbelt Savings Association) were tried, convicted, and sentenced to jail terms. But the executives from the leading law firms and accounting firms who made fortunes from their services to the S&Ls and whose legal and auditing malfeasance allowed the plundering of the S&Ls to continue, have made out-of-court settlements that pay some restitution but avoid any personal penalties that might come from criminal indictments and public trial. For example, the country's second largest accounting firm, Ernst and Young, repaid $400 million in order to prevent legal action against its executives, and the second largest law firm, Kaye, Scholer, Fierman, Hayes and Handler, paid $41 million in its out-of-court settlement for its role in the S&L scandal. The legal firm of Jones Day agreed to repay $51 million for its role in the failure of Keating's Lincoln Savings, which cost U.S. taxpayers $2.5 billion (see Nagle, 1992).

In Japan, a series of scandals (for example, the Recruit affair) involving multimillion dollar bribes to top political leaders of the long-ruling Liberal Democratic party—including Shin Kanamaru, perhaps the most powerful party leader—played a major role in the 1993 defeat of the LDP and the establishment of the first non-LDP government since the 1950s. The corrupt use of finance sector funds in Japanese politics has been known for decades, but has seldom resulted in criminal prosecution for bribery, extortion, or graft.

In Italy, the criminal corruption of the governing Christian Democratic party and its minor coalition partner, the Socialist party, became a leading issue in Italian politics in the 1980s. Extortion for government contracts, bribery of public officials, and theft of public funds was deeply entrenched in the Italian system, along with close ties between the Christian Democrats and the Italian mafia, especially in Sicily and Naples. For decades, however, political corruption went unpunished, while brave prosecutors and judges who tried to pursue high-level criminality were often assassinated by the mafia. The inability of Italian justice to pursue elite crime was a major factor in the 1993 collapse of the Christian Democratic party in local elections and its decision to disband as a party.

What these recent cases (and many more could be added, from Germany's Flick influence-buying practice, the Cardinal Marcinkus/Vatican Bank scandal, and the British government role in the BCCI affair) demonstrate is the continuing bias of justice in the affluent liberal democracies, the relative immunity of the powerful from prosecution, and the corruption of justice through financial power. The citizen backlash against high-level corruption in countries like Japan and Italy gives some hope for reform in the 1990s, but the structural barriers to the achievement of equal justice are formidable without strong democratic oversight and regulation of elite-level financial practices, now required on both a national and international scale.

Some Special Inequalities: Women's Emancipation

Inequality of opportunity in the liberal democracies extends, of course, to groups other than social classes, most notably to women and to certain ethnic, racial, religious, and regional groups. The case of American blacks is both a clear and, despite the indisputable gains of the civil rights movement, continuing example of severe racial inequality. Inequality based on religious background can be demonstrated for Roman Catholics in Northern Ireland (see Putnam, 1976). But for purposes of cross-national comparisons on the widest basis, we will concentrate here on the patterns of inequality for women in the liberal democracies, since women constitute approximately half the population in each country and since many, though by no means all, of the factors limiting the emancipation of women are similar in nature if not strength.

The field of politics has been dominated by men since the founding of parliamentary systems in the eighteenth and nineteenth centuries. Women were one of the last groups in the population to achieve the voting franchise, in most cases about 1920 (though in Switzerland not until 1971). Up to the 1970s, only token numbers of women were in political office, either in the national parliament or in cabinet positions, and in "women-related" offices such as the family ministry. In some cases, such as Germany, the representation of women in the *Bundestag* had even declined from the late 1940s to the 1970s. Beginning in the 1970s, however, women's movements and political organizations promoting women's issues have begun to transform the composition of the political class in the liberal democracies (with the notable exception of Japan). The levels of women's representation in democratic parliaments (see table 4.6) has grown sharply, but with several notable variations. In the Scandinavian countries, the increase has been most pronounced, and has included cabinet positions as well (Means, 1976:382). In the 1980s, the Norwegian parliament had 35 percent female deputies, and the government of Prime Minister Gro Harlem Brundtland included eight women in the cabinet of eighteen. In the continental European systems, the increase has gone beyond token levels in Germany, Italy, the Netherlands, and Switzerland, but has not yet begun to approach levels where female cabinet candidates, normally recruited from the ranks of parliament, are appointed to more than a few token ministries. In Germany, the Greens party has committed itself to gender equality among its own officeholders, and has shamed the established parties into giving some greater opportunities to women. France lags somewhat behind other European community nations, partially because it has the weakest women's and environmentalist movements, which have generally been advocates of gender equality in political recruitment. Most retarded in this trend are the United States, Britain, and Japan. While women gained mayoral and state legislative offices with greater frequency in the United States in the 1980s, this has yet to have an impact on the national level. In Britain as well, the era of Mrs. Thatcher has not yet had any larger impact for women in political life at the national level. In Japan, despite the example of Takeo Doi as leader of the opposition Japan Socialist party in the 1980s, women remain almost invisible in Japanese political life.

Data on occupational roles filled by women are mixed, but not much more encouraging. In the professions and higher management, women are still a small minority. Time-series data presented by Bernard (1971) and

Table 4.6   Women Decision Makers in Government

	Parliamentary seats occupied by women (%)		Year of women's suffrage	Executive offices; economic, political and legal affairs (%)	Social affairs (%)	All ministries (%)	Ministerial level (%)
	1975	1991		1987	1987	1987	1987
Switzerland	8	14	1971	3	—	3	13
Germany	6	20	1919	5	30	8	12
United States	4	6	1920	12	12	12	6
United Kingdom	4	6	1918*	4	21	8	8
France	2	6	1944	3	25	10	0
Sweden	21	38	1921	9	8	9	18
Japan	1	2	1945	0	0	0	0
Italy	4	13	1945	0	17	3	5
Netherlands	9	21	1919	10	5	8	6
Norway	16	36	1913	19	25	20	33

Source: UN, *The World's Women: Trends and Statistics, 1970–1990.*
*For women over 30 years of age; 1928 for full voting equality with men (over 21; now 18 for both)

Iglitzin and Ross (1976) indicated that in several of the liberal democracies, notably the United States and Germany, there was even some worsening of the economic position of women between 1950 and 1970. In the United States, for example, 11.4 percent of natural scientists in 1950 were women, but by 1967 only 8 percent were women. This decline accompanied a rapid growth in the 1960s of the demand for and pay scale of scientists. Likewise, in 1950 more than half of elementary school principals were women, but this figure declined dramatically by 1970 to less than one in five (Mandel, 1975:125–26). This decline occurred in a period of improving status and pay scale for public school administrators and teachers. An insultingly low 1.4 percent of U.S. high school principals in 1970 were women. Bernard, among others, has hypothesized that when occupational roles gain in status and salary, women will be squeezed out by men, whereas women will be permitted to fill jobs of primarily low or declining position on the job hierarchy.

From the 1960s to the 1990s, the women's movement has had a considerable impact in the field of employment. In the higher-status positions, women have made gains in the numbers and percentages of doctors, lawyers, scientists, engineers, and managerial personnel in virtually all of the liberal democracies (see table 4.7 for data on the United States). At the same time, it must be noted that women still tend to be clustered at the lower end of each professional category, while at the very top levels of professional, executive, and administrative power, men still predominate. Aburdene and Naisbitt (1992:61) report that in 1991, from a list of the top 6,502 corporate officers (vice president and above) of the Fortune 500 companies, only 175 were women (less than 3 percent). Still, this is an increase from the 1960s figure of less than one-half of 1 percent. In terms of educational opportunities in the professions, women in the liberal democracies have also made significant gains (table 4.8), more rapidly in nations such as Sweden, less rapidly in Japan and Switzerland.

Table 4.7   U.S. Women in High-Status Occupations, 1960–1992
(Women as percentage of all persons in occupation)

	(percent women in each profession)		
	1960	1983	1992
Doctors	7	16	20
Lawyers	4	15	21
College faculty	22	36	41
Natural scientists	20	21	27
Engineers	0[a]	6	9
All managerial	14	32	42

Sources: *Statistical Abstract of the United States*, 1968, 1993.
a. Less than 0.5 percent

Table 4.8   Enrollment of Women in Higher Education

	As percent of total enrollment		As percent of students in the natural sciences		As percent of students in engineering		As percent of students in math and computers		As percent of students in commercial and business administration	
	1970	1990	1970	1990	1970	1990	1980	1990	1980	1990
Switzerland	23	35	16	27	2	4	19	15	14	25
Germany[a]	27	41	19	31	2	7	29	23	37	43
United States[b]	36	51	20	38	2	13	37	39	42	49
United Kingdom	39	48	22	40	2	12	25	26	30	46
France[c]	45	53	33	31	—	19	24	—	60	49
Sweden[d]	42	54	23	44	6	20	23[e]	22	37	51
Japan[a]	28	39	13	16	1	4	20	21	—	—

Sources: *Unesco Statistical Yearbook*, 1970, 1971, 1974, 1975, 1984, 1992

a. Germany and Japan are for 1970, 1980 and 1989

b. 1970 figures are from 1971; 1980 figures are for graduates at the third level; 1990 figures are for graduates at the third level in 1985.

c. France is for 1967, 1982 and 1990

d. Sweden is for 1970, 1979 and 1990

e. 1981

Note: For Japan, the figures for commercial and business administration are not broken out. They are included in the category for social and behavioral sciences.

In terms of income inequality between full-time employed women and men, there is still much room for improvement in the liberal democracies. Among the most progressive is Sweden, with ratios ranging from 72 to 93 percent by economic sector of employment. Among the most backward are the United States and Great Britain, with ratios ranging from 46 to 65 percent. Especially disappointing in these two nations is the recognition that in banking and insurance, two modern service sectors where job growth has been high, the female/male earnings ratios have not been generally higher than other, declining sectors. This is not an encouraging sign for the future. If we compare the trend in women's wages as a percent of men's wages (in all nonagricultural occupations) over the past two decades, the trend has been gradually upward, with some nations, like Australia and France (as well as Sweden) quite a bit ahead of the United States, Great Britain, and especially Japan. A lot of progress has been made, but in the most laggard of the liberal democracies, there is a long way to go before gender equality in the workplace is reached.

No assessment of women's emancipation in the liberal democracies would be complete without noting the emerging poverty among women and children in single-parent female-headed households. Research by Sylvia Ann Hewlett (1986) indicated that particularly in the United States, the rise of divorce rates and the move into the job market by large numbers of women with small children has led to the growth of poverty for children and for mothers with small children. Hewlett pointed out that after divorce, the material standard of living of ex-husbands rose by an average of 42 percent, but declined for the ex-wives and children by 73 percent. Further, two-thirds of custodial mothers received no child support from the father, and legal authorities were notoriously ineffective in enforcing court-ordered child support.

Maternity leave and day-care facilities in the United States are less available and less generously supported than in the European democracies. In the 1980s, the Reagan Administration cut back federal support for day-care and nutrition programs. Public support for day care actually fell by some 25

Table 4.9   Female Wages as a Percent of Male Wages, 1990–1991

Switzerland	68
Germany	74
United States	59
United Kingdom	67
Sweden	89
France	88
Japan	51

Source: UNDP, *Human Development Report*, 1993.

percent from 1980–86. The result was that 77 percent of those below the poverty line in the United States are women and children. While similar tendencies are also visible in the European democracies (and in post-Communist East Europe and Russia, see chapter 9), they are less pronounced, and government efforts in Western Europe to aid needy mothers and children have generally been stronger.

5

Liberty—Historic Gains Need to Be Defended

Liberty is taken here in the classic sense of freedom from arbitrary coercion for the individual. Although individual liberty has never been realized in the absolute, certainly there is a tremendous range of system tolerance for individual behaviors across the span of history and nations. Democratic liberty is fairly easy to define in its essence: the right to dissent against authority and the right to be different—to choose among real choices. There's nothing very tricky about liberty as a concept; it's the practice of liberty that is so difficult. Whenever one dissents from authority, it's likely to cost something.

By living in society, we agree not to do certain things, such as commit murder, loot, or attack our fellow citizens. These are deprivations of liberty that savages and wild animals possess. But we are better off, we think, living in society under these limitations (Hobbes). If we kill, pillage, or commit arson, the authorities (i.e., the state) are empowered to (try to) catch and punish us. There are many laws and regulations that we are supposed to follow, and if we do not, we may be penalized. Our liberty is always circumscribed by law. Every individual's liberty is limited by the rights, and mere existence, of others in society. However, the ability of the liberal democracies to tolerate dissent within quite broad limits, and in many cases to make public facilities and monies available for expressions of opposition groups, is certainly a quality that is admired by citizens of nations where such individual freedom does not exist.

On the other hand, lest we forget the real world of liberal democracy, two things should be noted. One is that the resources for exercising liberty are not equally distributed (see chapter 4). Mr. H. L. Hunt, a now-deceased billionaire, could (and did) buy up a string of newspapers (over one hundred) to bring his views to society. Only the rights of purchasing power in a market economy gave him the possibility of converting wealth into political influence.

While it is true that a person is free to use his or her personal (even if limited) resources to be heard, to try to organize with others of similar opinion for the purpose of convincing opponents and more likely the great apathetic majority to support some position, it is not true that dissent does not cost something beyond the few dollars put into it. A person's opinions, if they are known to and unpopular with an employer, could cost that person a job, or a promotion, or maybe just a raise. Indeed, while most people in the liberal democracies (or perhaps in most nonrevolutionary societies) are not dissidents and most are not union, feminist, or gay rights activists, studies of public opinion in the liberal democracies (Stouffer, 1954; Nagle, 1970) have shown that strong pluralities or majorities would in fact deny rights of free speech and assembly to many unpopular minority groups. This makes the record of the liberal democracies all the more impressive, since in many areas suppression of civil liberties for certain minority groups has been politically popular. Here the independent judiciary, a check on the executive and legislative functions of government, has been particularly important, especially in the United States, in protecting and expanding the rights of blacks, women, workers, atheists, radicals, and homosexuals, to name a few, to a level more comparable with those of nondissident or nonminority groups.

It is not an easy thing to defend the liberty of someone or some group that you disagree with, perhaps very strongly, especially when you have majority sentiment on your side. Yet, as Rosa Luxemburg pointed out long ago, democracy is the practical right to be in the minority and not be suppressed. Dr. Martin Niemoller, the German Protestant theologian, after the experience of the Nazi Third Reich, made an astute observation on the costs of the failure to defend the liberty of the other person. When the Nazis first suppressed the Communists, Niemoller hesitated to voice opposition, because he was not a Communist and opposed the Communists. When they began rounding up Socialists, he hesitated again, because he was not a Socialist and opposed Socialism. When they persecuted the Jews, he hesitated again. But when the Nazis came after him, the pattern of social and political suppression of dissent had already been established, in part through his earlier silence.

A Global Survey of Personal Liberty

The development of individual liberty, even if limited both in extent and by social class initially, has, in the West, been closely associated with the evolution of liberal democracy as a political system. Liberal democracy in turn has been generally more loosely associated with the development of capitalism in the West, in Europe, in North America, and in European-offspring nations such as Australia and New Zealand. In the pre-1945 period, however, advanced capitalism was also associated with fascism and authoritarianism in countries like Germany, Italy, France, and Japan; in these countries liberal democratic systems were restored only by external force after their complete defeat in the last world conflict.

Since 1945, as in no previous era, we can associate the achievement of wide personal liberties with all the advanced capitalist systems, which serve at the same time as the boundary of the stable liberal democracies. Democratic capitalism, even with the remaining issues of voting rights for women in Switzerland and the purges of radicals from public service jobs in West Germany, has become virtually coterminous with guaranteed protection of a wide variety of political and civil liberties.

Freedom House, a conservative American think-tank, issues periodic reports on the status of both political and civil liberties in every nation. Each country is subjectively ranked on a scale of 1 (greatest protection of liberty) to 7 (greatest restriction on liberty), so that different degrees of effective personal liberty are recognized.

While these judgments are of course debatable for individual nations, and are admittedly measured by *current Western standards*, they nevertheless can be useful for illustrating our point about the global extent of liberty and its post–World War II association with Western advanced capitalism. This connection is a result of two polarizing trends: (1) the strengthening and expansion of personal liberty in the Western democracies, and (2) the lower level of personal liberty in several other regions where either Communist, military, or other one-party regimes were in power.

We have added also the scaled rankings on human rights developed by Charles Humana, which run from 0 to 100, with higher rankings associated with greater protection of human rights. Table 5.1 gives the Freedom House rankings for selected liberal democracies for both the mid-1970s and for the most recent years, as well as the Humana scale for the most recent period. What is most noteworthy is the consistently high ranking for all of the liberal democracies on both scales, with minor differences. If we compare these results with the rankings given later (in tables 10.1 and 15.1 for the Communist/ post-Communist and developing nations), the consistency of liberal democratic achievements in this area is striking. Other types of political systems may sometimes hold fairly free elections and may sometimes allow freedom of speech or freedom of religious practice, but the long-term and durable support for personal liberty is much more problematic. The liberal democracies have had their failings, as will be amply noted below, but they, better than other political system-types, have provided the opportunities for improving their own records.

The World War II defeat of European and Japanese fascism has solidified the advanced capitalist nations into a more homogeneous grouping of political systems. The postwar decolonization in the Third World meant formal independence for nearly a hundred "new" nations. But Western hopes for the adoption of Western-type political systems, with the same priority attached to personal liberty, have not been realized. Communist revolutions in Eastern Europe, Asia, Africa, and Cuba produced systems with sharply divergent

Table 5.1   Indicators of Liberty in the Liberal Democracies

	Political Rights (scale of 1 to 7)		Civil Rights (scale of 1 to 7)		Human Rights Rating (%)
	1977	1992	1977	1992	1991
United States	1	1	1	1	90
United Kingdom	1	1*	1	2*	93
Switzerland	1	1	1	1	96
Germany	1	1	2	2	98
France	1	1	2	2	94
Sweden	1	1	1	1	98
Italy	2	1	2	2	90
Japan	2	1	1	2	82

Sources: Freedom House, *Freedom in the World: Political Rights and Civil Liberties* (New York: Freedom House, 1993), pp. 620–21; Raymond Gastil, *Freedom in the World: Political Rights and Civil Liberties 1978* (New York: Freedom House, 1978) pp. 10–13; Charles Humana, *World Human Rights Guide* (New York: Oxford Univ. Press, 1992), pp. xvii–xix
*Excluding Northern Ireland
Note: The political rights and civil liberties indices are on a scale of 1 to 7, with 1 representing the most free and 7 the least free category. The Human Rights Rating is a percentage.

views of personal liberty (as well as other matters). Personal liberty, as defined and practiced in the wealthy capitalist world, has simply not been as attractive or as practical as might have been expected. Freedom House spokesman Raymond Gastil, in a rather discouraging world survey of personal liberty, comments that "in ranking countries in terms of civil and political rights we do not mean to imply that these rights exhaust the definition of a good or desirable political system. Some free states may be less desirable to live in than some unfree states, especially where the unfree state provides a more adequate standard of living or a more challenging future" (1976:12).

Personal liberty, as a goal, is in competition not only with economic development but also with the goals of social equality and quality of life. People may favor greater social equality at the expense of lesser personal liberty; they may favor a greater effort in fighting crime (a quality of life item) at the expense of personal liberty. The choice comprises a complex, many faceted array of values. And it is not always the case that the sacrifice of one goal guarantees progress toward another goal.

With the democratic and nationalist revolutions in Eastern Europe in 1989–90, the collapse of the former Soviet Union in 1991, and the seeming spread of democracy in Latin America, the Philippines, Korea, Pakistan, and parts of Africa in the latter 1980s, it appears that human liberty has indeed gained ground around the world, with the liberal democracies of the West as models. Yet a closer examination of the struggle for personal liberty in the Western democracies reveals how long and protracted has been the effort to reach the current level, and how personal liberty even in the most advanced democracies often conflicts with other values and interests; even in the 1990s, the struggle is not over.

Developments in Liberty since 1945: The United States

The early 1950s in the United States were the heyday of McCarthyism and red-hunting. Members of the Communist party were arrested and sent to jail under the Smith Act for allegedly plotting to overthrow the government. Radicals, Socialists, and even progressive liberals were purged from the AFL and CIO union leaderships, from the civil service, from colleges and public school, from the entertainment world, and from television, radio, and press establishments. Not only did these people (including people like Pete Seeger, Zero Mostel, and Will Geer), convicted of no crime whatsoever, lose their jobs, but they were also blacklisted so could not find new ones. The era of the fifties, of the "silent generation," was one of heavy-handed treatment of dissidents to the left of anti-Communist liberalism.

Those purged and blacklisted served, of course, as a warning to others who might be tempted to express similar opinions. In legal parlance this is called a "chilling effect" on free speech, but this phrase does not adequately express the human suffering and injustices of the "red scare" purges of the period, which went far beyond the tragicomic anticommunist crusade of Senator Joe McCarthy (see Wolfe, 1973). In the 1950s, when a singer in the United States expressed opinions or sang songs deemed radical or socialist, he or she was blacklisted in the industry.

In the 1950s, throughout the South and much of the rest of the United States, blacks were denied basic rights through racial exclusion enforced either by legal statute or by Ku Klux Klan terror. Blacks were denied access to housing in certain neighborhoods; and public services, including schools, garbage collection, street maintenance, and police protection, were basically neglected in black ghettoes by an all-white government. The black American was definitely discriminated against in his or her own country with the open support of federal, state, and local governments. If you were born before 1965, you were alive when a black citizen might be murdered for attempting to register to vote in Mississippi; when a black was not allowed to take an empty seat in the front of a public bus in Montgomery because that seat was reserved for whites only; when a black person could not get lunch counter service at a southern Woolworth's, where only whites were served. The degradation of the black American was a systematic part of American life, as American as apple pie. It was not occasional, or accidental, or a "misunderstanding."

Through the 1950s and 1960s, however, pressure for change built up. The civil rights movement, through the NAACP (National Association for the

Advancement of Colored People), made some progress in the courts against school desegregation. Yet, despite the 1954 Supreme Court ruling that all segregated school systems must integrate "with all deliberate speed," a decade later little actual compliance with the law had taken place. Both in the South and elsewhere white school and local authorities had defied the law with impunity. By the early 1960s, more militant civil rights groups such as CORE (Congress of Racial Equality), SNCC (Student Nonviolent Coordinating Committee), and Martin Luther King, Jr.'s SCLC (Southern Christian Leadership Conference) had begun to push the civil rights cause through the tactics of economic boycott, sit-ins, mass marches, and demonstrations. A strategy including large-scale but nonviolent civil disobedience was introduced to attempt to force federal government attention to the issues of equal rights for black citizens. In Mississippi in June 1964, three civil rights workers who were trying to aid the registration of black voters were brutally murdered by Ku Klux Klan members with the connivance of local law enforcement. The murders of James Chaney, Michael Schwerner, and Andrew Goodman was an important case, which goaded the federal government to action against Klan terror and suppression of black voting rights. It should be noted that Schwerner and Chaney were white and that even more brutal murders of black citizens had been ignored or left to white southern justice. Eventually those guilty of the murders were brought to trial under federal law and convicted of abusing the civil rights of the victims. It is important to note that, at the time of this writing, the state of Mississippi still has not charged anyone with murder in this case. In several other cases of murders of civil rights workers, southern justice authorities have also refused to actively pursue indictments (Smothers, 1989:7). Apparently even today justice in such cases is not to be expected.

One could reasonably mark the point at which white government authorities began to respond positively to civil rights with the Watts riot of 1965. By 1968, urban black rioting was becoming unprofitable for at least some segments of the white business class, and it was at this point that real if partial advances in civil rights came to *de facto* realization. One corporate executive summed up the rationale for action on civil rights:

> Since the Detroit and Newark riots in 1967, a closer identity has sprung up between the needs of the ghetto economy and the needs of the normal economy. The riots now reach beyond the black or "grey" areas of the cities and threaten the entire American economy. Curfews and enforced closings of businesses undermine downtown real estate values. Riots now mean massive losses of profits, millions of forfeited wages, and cancelled conventions for entire cities. (Quoted in Wolfe, 1973:46)

The real enforcement of and compliance with the 1964 Civil Rights Act and the 1965 Voting Rights Act marked the beginning of the end of officially sanctioned racial discrimination, although it is clear that even today some discrimination in schooling, housing access, and especially jobs still exists through entrenched resistance from local school boards, real estate agencies, unions, and businesses. Yet the fact remains that on a variety of fronts, progress has been made. Herbert Gans (1973:136–37) argues that the ghetto rebellions were responsible for the temporary upsurge in government and business programs to alleviate the effects of racism. This is also part of the American (and European) heritage of liberal democracy, going back to the bitter and violent union struggles of the period from the mid-nineteenth century through the Great Depression years. The gains in civil liberties have been won in hard struggle against those who dominate in the economy and in government. They are the result of contradictions in the society that boil up at certain points and must be addressed and resolved, at least partially or for the short run.

In the late sixties, the escalation of American intervention in Vietnam and the corresponding growth of the antiwar movement at home brought with it a widening of civil rights in other respects. In the earliest antiwar protests, marchers in demonstrations were often attacked by supporters of government war policy while police stood by and watched, often later arresting only the antiwar demonstrators (see Parenti, 1974, ch. 8). Sometimes police would themselves "rough up" protesters. Public officials who freely granted march or parade permits to prowar groups such as the Veterans of Foreign Wars or the American Legion refused the same to antiwar groups. All manner of chicanery was employed to keep antiwar candidates or antiwar propositions off the ballot in local, state, and federal elections; petition signatures would mysteriously "disappear" after being handed in to election officials, or some "irregularity" would be manufactured to invalidate the petitions. Eventually, however, the antiwar movement became too strong, too widespread, and too militant to be stopped, short of the murderous type of force that was only briefly and tragically applied in 1970 at Kent State and Jackson State.

But there was another reason for the acceptance of civil protest as a legitimate form of dissent against the war policy, and that was the split within the established political leadership itself. United States intervention in Vietnam was a bloody and costly disaster from start to finish; it was wrong from a multitude of perspectives. Gradually, established public officials already holding high office and long a part of the national political scene, figures like Eugene McCarthy, George McGovern, Robert Kennedy, and Ted Kennedy gave their support to the movement, making it more difficult to discount or denounce it as extremist or Communist-inspired or treasonous. Civil rights leaders such as Martin Luther King, Jr., Coretta King, Stokely Carmichael, and Dick Gregory added their voices and joined at least partially the civil rights and antiwar efforts. Some relatively progressive unionists like Leonard Woodcock of the UAW, the independent electrical workers (UE), and some AFL-CIO chiefs who defied George Meany's hawkish stand on the war lent working-class support. The system grudgingly conceded greater opportunities for voicing opposition—marching, petitioning, running candidates, and speaking on radio and television. By the early 1970s, the right to publicly voice dissent was being practiced by millions with far less fear or probability of reprisal, but again it was a gain made through struggle.

The machinery of liberal democracy was not the unbiased, neutral, "conversion process" pictured in theory; it never was and never will be, so long as it is run by people who themselves have a strong interest in the outcomes produced by democracy. The increases in individual liberty have usually, though not always, been accompanied by bitter confrontations, often including individually targeted violence, rioting, and even rebellion. From the revelations of Watergate and the post-mortem dissection of the Vietnam issue, we now know that the United States government, including the CIA, FBI, IRS, and a host of state and local agencies, engaged in a wide variety of illegal and unconstitutional acts directed against civil rights, antiwar, and leftist organizations. Not only President Nixon engaged in and encouraged such practices as telephone taps, FBI and CIA burglaries, and IRS tax intimidation. The FBI had a long-standing program of counterintelligence (COINTELPRO) and disruption, threats, and break-ins directed against groups such as the Socialist Workers party that FBI Director Hoover considered "subversive." Hoover also considered Martin Luther King, Jr. subversive and had anonymous threatening letters sent to King suggesting suicide as the only way out. Violent repression of the Black Panther party is a matter of record (Wolfe, 1973). The murder of Black Panther leaders Mark Clark and Fred Hampton in their beds by Chicago police in December of 1969, officially an "accident" for which no one has been convicted, must be seen as part of the known and now exposed overall program of repression against the Black Panthers.

The results of pressure for greater personal liberty have not been reversed, even in the conservative political era of the 1980s. New conservative leaders like Newt Gingrich or Jack Kemp do not advocate a return to racial segregation or the suppression of blacks' voting rights. The greater personal liberty afforded to gays and women, while opposed by many conservative and ultra-conservative political and religious fundamentalist organizations, was not directly attacked by the recent conservative administration. Even the older generation of conservative political leaders like Ronald Reagan and Barry Goldwater, who opposed federal desegregation measures and civil rights legislation, no longer fought for a reversal of these historic measures.

This is not meant to imply that the struggle for the maintenance of personal liberty is over or that there will be no threats to personal liberties in the United States in the future. Indeed, the AIDS epidemic has in recent years raised the possibility of a political backlash against the gay community. It may be tempting for some political leaders to use public fears of the disease to mobilize public support for suppression of civil rights for homosexuals. Still, up to now, public health officials have in general resisted this trend and have insisted on treating AIDS as a public health problem and not as a weapon against gays. This is a remarkable change in the public health field from just a generation ago, when homosexuality was treated as a disease.

Alan Wolfe has done an excellent job of describing the types and extents of repression in liberal democracy and of relating this repression to the interests of the economic and political system:

> The history of liberalism has been a struggle between those who controlled the society and found the tenets of a limited liberal state perfectly to their liking and those who wished to share in the blessings of liberal society but were not allowed to do so (or were permitted to do so only after a struggle) because they had no base of private property from which to act. For this reason, many of the victories of liberal society were won through the martyrdom of groups that were not liberal. The IWW, for example, a syndicalist and socialist organization, did more to establish the right to speak freely on a street corner than any other group in American history. . . . When people choose to remain powerless, they refuse to claim the benefits of liberal society for themselves. But what happens when oppression is no longer accepted, when the demands are made? Then the fundamental contradiction of liberal society asserts itself. Liberalism can work only by being restrictive, particularly to those in power. Each attempt to extend the principles of liberalism to a powerless group has been convulsive. (1973: 229)

Wolfe rightly notes that gains made through struggle are important gains, though they did not change the fundamental nature of the social order. Herbert Gans (1973:136–37) fears the backlash effects of attempts to achieve progress in civil rights or social welfare through disruptive activities, while admitting the short-term victories connected with convulsive confrontation. The record shows, however, that violence, intimidation, and disruption are practiced by the authorities in liberal democracy against dissident groups who try to participate in the political system in order to both improve their economic situation and challenge existing policies.

It is comforting to think that progress toward greater individual liberty could be made through entirely peaceful means; that would eliminate the unpleasantness and personal risk to which those in the forefront of unionist, civil rights, and antiwar movements have historically been exposed. Many early union leaders, socialists, and black activists were shot or lynched; they never lived to enjoy the rights for which they fought. Many personal accounts of early struggles for workers' rights attest to the reluctance of most to get involved for fear of reprisal. *The Autobiography of Mother Jones* (1925), the story of an early union organizer, recounts the repeated attempts to travel the road of entirely peaceful organization, electoral participation, and court cases to get the system to work by its professed ideals. The struggle for personal liberty however has seldom been an entirely peaceful process, and generally the political system has responded only at the point at which protests were becoming dysfunctional (that often means too expensive) for established elite interests. The real wonder is that in the face of spreading protests, liberal democracies have generally expanded personal liberty rather than escalating repression, as is the norm in most other systems.

Germany: Liberty in a Reconstructed Democracy

The greatest postwar gains in personal liberty in the industrialized capitalist nations have been made in Germany, Italy, Japan, and France, where the defeated fascist regimes were replaced by reconstructed parliamentary systems. In 1949, after four years of government by the Allied occupation authorities, the Federal Republic of Germany (*Bundesrepublik*) held its first elections for a new parliament (*Bundestag*). Many parties ranging from the far right to the Communist party of Germany on the left were permitted to compete in the elections, and only the Nazi party was outlawed from reorganizing. Under the new federal government, freedoms of press, assembly, speech, party competition, union organization, fair trial, religious practice, and emigration, all suppressed between 1933 and 1945 by the Nazi regime, were restored and supported by the internal political system (as opposed to the Allied occupation command). Despite some restrictions and retrogressions to be discussed below, the German democracy has since 1949 provided the same general level of protection of personal liberty that characterizes the more stable liberal democracies, such as Britain and the United States. Germany's expansion of personal liberty continues to dwarf all other trends and (together with that of Japan, Italy, and France) represents the most significant development in personal liberty in the industrial world, and perhaps in the entire world, since World War II.

The first years of the *Bundesrepublik* coincided with the heightened East-West tensions of the Cold War. Germany was integrated into the anti-Communist alliance forged by the United States. While McCarthyism was rampant in the United States, in Germany, too, Communists, leftists, and left liberals were purged from positions of leadership in the unions, the schools, and the media. The Communist party of Germany was outlawed in 1956, and many of its leaders were persecuted for presumed disloyalty to the constitution (Basic Law). The era of Chancellor Adenauer's leadership in the 1950s and early 1960s was one in which dissent and nonconformity, in life-styles as well as politics, were discouraged, sometimes through the power of government. A turning point in this trend toward authoritarian conformity came in 1962, when Adenauer's defense minister, Franz Josef Strauss, seized the offices of *Der Spiegel*, a left-liberal news magazine, after the publication of a story

114

critical of the preparedness of Germany's armed forces. The editor and five assistants were arrested. Strauss even had the *Spiegel* reporter, Conrad Ahlers, arrested in Spain, where he was vacationing. Had Strauss's actions been allowed to stand, freedom of the press would have been dealt a major blow. But, amidst national and international protest, Strauss was forced to back down and to resign from the cabinet, although he remained head of the powerful Bavarian Christian Social Union (CSU). The Spiegel Affair, rather than resulting in a defeat for press freedom, served to encourage investigative reporting and lively criticism of government policies.

Through the 1960s, the exercise of personal and political liberty increasingly and openly challenged not only the CDU-dominated governments of chancellors Adenauer and Erhard, but also the perceived lack of effective choice among the three parties (Christian Democrats, Free Democrats, and Social Democrats) represented in the *Bundestag*. From the radical right, the National Democratic party (NPD) denounced the institutions of liberal democracy as responsible for the "moral decline" of German society and advocated a nationalist and reunited Germany similar to the Germany of 1939. Founded in 1964, a tiny remnant of earlier right-wing groups, the NPD suddenly won 7 to 10 percent of the vote in several state-level elections in 1966–68. This was a period of mild recession and the so-called grand coalition government of the two largest parties, the Christian Democrats and Social Democrats (see Nagle, 1970). Many feared that the NPD, like the Nazi party of the Weimar Republic, would build voter support on popular fears and prejudices (against foreign workers and foreign influences and against communists, Jews, and homosexuals) and on an appeal to nationalist and militarist sentiment. Some advocated a legal ban on the NPD to forestall this possibility, citing the experience of Weimar. However, the NPD strongly professed its loyalty to the Basic Law and had committed few overt acts of violence. Indeed, in the 1969 election campaign, NPD speakers often had to be protected against anti-NPD demonstrators. In many localities, pressure from major parties, unions, and businesses was used to deny access to meeting halls for NPD gatherings, and NPD election posters were torn down and destroyed much more frequently than those of the major parties. The governing CDU-SPD coalition ultimately resisted the temptation to outlaw the NPD, and the right-radicals received only 4.3 percent of the national election vote, failing to get any seats in the *Bundestag*. By the 1970s the National Democratic party had shrivelled to insignificance.

The New Left, often termed the Extra-Parliamentary Opposition (APO), also challenged the social and foreign policies of the CDU-SPD grand coalition. Inspired in part by philosopher Herbert Marcuse, and led in part by Rudi Dutschke, a student of Marcuse, the APO attacked the government's support for United States intervention in Vietnam and the close relationship with the Shah of Iran. They called for democratization of economic life, for student participation in university government, and for sexual emancipation from middle-class conventions. One demonstration protesting an official visit to Germany by the Shah in 1967 resulted in the shooting of one student by police. In some respects, the demonstrations by the APO in the latter 1960s, like the Spiegel Affair of the early 1960s, served to widen the scope of practical personal liberty in that after some initial violent confrontations, police and local government officials gradually accepted nonviolent street demonstrations as a normal part of democratic political life, and police reactions became more restrained. The New Left, which was quite hopeful that far-reaching change might be possible in the 1960s, was largely disillusioned by the inability of SPD Chancellor Willy Brandt (1969–74) to carry out even a modest educational restructuring and industrial reform (*Mitbestimmung*). Promises and plans for student participation in university governance were largely abandoned in the more conservative atmosphere of the latter 1970s.

West German politics in the 1970s was one of mixed gains and setbacks for personal liberty. On the one hand the government had become obsessed with maintaining security for public officials in the era of Baader-Meinhof kidnappings and murders of political leaders, judges, and businessmen. Barbed wire around government ministries, armored car patrols, and machine-gun sentries have produced a palpable feeling of uneasiness, particularly in the capital city of Bonn. The Baader-Meinhof terrorism may have partially succeeded in one of its goals, namely that of goading the government into treating all citizens as potential security risks.

As has been stated elsewhere, this attitude was reflected in the administration of a 1972 decree prohibiting "radicals" from public employment at any level. Since school teachers, university professors, railroad engineers, bus drivers, telephone and telegraph personnel, employees at the several state-owned iron and coal facilities, plus all members of the federal, state, and local civil service were part of governmental employment, "radicals" could be barred from a good number of jobs, which essentially barred them from practicing their professions (*Berufsverbot*). In applying for public employment, an applicant had to pass a loyalty test. Standards varied from state to state, and from year to year, depending on the political climate. Teachers in particular were denied jobs for simply belonging to leftist organizations or for legally demonstrating against the Vietnam War. The loyalty hearing brought forth stories from professional "informants" or personal enemies, and they certainly had a chilling effect on critical social analysis in the schools.

On the positive side, new citizen coalitions (*Bürgerinitiativen*) emerged that promoted a wide series of issues on which the main parties did not offer much choice. Environmentalist and antinuclear groups (led by the BBU, the Federal League of Environmental Citizen Initiatives) forced questions of nuclear reactor safety, reactor siting, energy planning, and especially nuclear waste disposal onto the political agenda through actions ranging from court suits and public hearings to mass demonstrations and civil disobedience. In the 1980s, the new Green party began to contest elections directly, with modest success. The Greens held about 8 percent of *Bundestag* seats after the 1987 national elections and represented a variety of "new social movements," including peace activists, environmentalists, and feminists, at both the federal level and in most states (Länder). Although split into several factions, the Greens were pioneers of a "new politics" which favored more direct and active citizen participation in governing. After initial attempts to vilify the Greens as either Communist or know-nothing, the main parties, especially the SPD, started to rethink their positions and called for more public dialogue on nuclear power. These were signs that increasing numbers of Germans perceived liberty as going beyond voting once in four years and were willing to participate in politics beyond the organization of the major parties.

German political culture continued to change in the 1980s, with the generational succession of younger Germans and their search for a new identity (Honolka, 1987). This study showed a more tolerant, more democratic, less nationalist trend in German culture, and a desire for more active participation in political life. But in the latter 1980s, the far-right Republican Party tried, with some success, to mobilize a backlash vote with new national-populist slogans that promised a renewed nationalist pride and sought to profit from anti-foreigner sentiment among some segments and locales in German society. With the unification of Germany, and with the influx of peoples from Eastern Europe into Germany seeking jobs, housing, and economic opportunities, the new Germany will be tested in its commitment to personal liberty for the variety of ethnic groups that now are living and working there. The trend of the postwar evolution in Germany has been towards a multicultural society, embracing peoples of many different cultural and ethnic backgrounds; Germany had become a land open to immigrants from other parts of Europe, from Turkey and Yugoslavia, southern Italy and Greece. Yet German citizenship is still defined in a manner that equates "being a German" with German ethnic background, in contrast to the United States' multicultural approach. An important issue for Germany in the 1990s will be its treatment of ethnic minorities that wish to continue to live and work in Germany. In late September of 1991, riots broke out in several cities in both eastern and western Germany, with neo-fascist youth gangs beating up Vietnamese, Africans, Romanians, and other foreigners who were seeking asylum in Germany. The living quarters of these foreigners were burned, and they were driven out of these localities. The rise of antiforeigner violence has now become a major test of German commitment to build a multicultural society and to protect the rights of ethnic minorities living and working in Germany.

The rapid absorption of East Germany by West Germany within one year of the Wall's opening in November 1989 also opened new issues of liberty and justice for the German legal and administrative systems. In the rapid restructuring of the former East Germany, tens of thousands of professors, teachers, and administrators are being fired from their jobs and essentially closed out of their careers not because of any crime they committed, but because they were communists. This wholesale purge (called *Abwicklung*, or "winding up"), especially in academia and the schools, is a bad foundation for building a presumably more tolerant and open society in eastern Germany. The coldness of the dismissals and the lack of opportunity for defending oneself is at odds with democratic legal traditions of due process, openness, and evidence. In the universities, this purge goes against all notions of academic free expression and pluralism. In the fall of 1991, trials were begun against four former East German soldiers charged with the murder of an East German who tried to flee to the West in early 1989. Other former East German leaders, including Erich Honecker and spy chief Markus Wolf, have also been charged with murder and treason. These people are being charged with acts which were not crimes under East German law, to which they were loyal, and while East Germany was recognized as an independent state. The shootings of fleeing East Germans at the Berlin Wall were reprehensible and deserving of condemnation and of admission of guilt. But the precedent of bringing legal charges against both leaders and ordinary soldiers may set a pattern of revenge-seeking which does not bode well for protection of due process in a united Germany.

The Expansion of Personal Liberty: A Highwater Mark of Performance

The stretching of liberty to its current bounds in liberal democracy has been a turbulent process. And this is the second lesson that needs to be stressed. In the postwar era, the practice of dissent has been broadened in all the Western democracies; those in positions of power have made concessions rather than continue or escalate a repressive strategy. This was by no means the only possibility and is in fact a relatively rare turn of events in the last century in world political developments.

Even in the advanced industrial nations, there is the alternative of fascism compatible with capitalist economics and at times suitable to the business class. If those who dominate the present order are not willing to make concessions as a necessary price for maintaining the essentials of the economic and social hierarchy intact, they may well opt for a more aggressively repressive system. One might argue that this is what whites (the propertied class) in Rhodesia (Zimbabwe) and South Africa chose to do in building apartheid-type systems. And it is instructive to note that these white settler groups are the offspring of British and Dutch political cultures, which in Europe have relatively unblemished records of steady democratic development.

In general, in the aftermath of World War II, the fascist alternative has been in disrepute in the industrial West, and despite some occasional stirrings on the neofascist right (the NPD) in Germany, the National Front in Britain, the MSI in Italy, the Poujadists in France, and perhaps elements of the Wallaceite AIP in the United States), it is still correct to say that the broad postwar consensus against fascism remains intact. The military defeat of the fascist alternative in Germany, Japan, Italy, and France, at least for the prolonged period of economic growth during the Cold War decreased the ability of the "haves" to overtly coerce or threaten the "have nots" or to silence dissent; compromise and concession become more likely. At the present time, individual liberty is at a highwater mark in the community of Western democracies. Never before has it been so true that individual liberty is a correlate of liberal democracy in advanced capitalism.

However, it would be well to note that, with high unemployment and sluggish growth in most of the liberal democracies in the early 1990s, right-extremist youth gangs and neofascist thugs were engaging in increasingly more violent attacks on foreign workers and new immigrants in Germany, France, Italy, Britain, and the United States. In the attack on a refugee hostel in Rostock, Germany, in 1992, the local police and law authorities were negligent in their duty to protect refugees and foreign laborers against violence. The interior minister of the new conservative government in France, Charles Pasqua, has been pandering to the anti-immigrant fever, and has announced his goal of "zero immigration," tougher requirements for work permits, and greater police surveillance of foreigners (Darnton, 1993).

In the post–Cold War era of difficult long-term economic transformation, the liberal democratic governments will be challenged to uphold the basic human rights of resident noncitizens and other ethnic minorities, even when there is significant antiforeigner and anti-immigrant sentiment among the voters which might be coopted by antiforeigner and anti-immigrant policies. In general, in the current period of tougher choices for the liberal democracies, the gains in personal liberty will need to be defended against populist backlash, which seeks to find visible scapegoats and easy answers for the problems of this uncertain era.

6

Quality of Life—
The Disillusionment of Modernity

For the liberal democracies of the Cold War era, strong and affluent economies, protection of personal liberty, and at least modest commitments to social equity were all part of the success formula. It was widely assumed that if these aspects of the neo-liberal package of policy priorities were met, then many of the other aspects of social life would also show positive developments. If the mass unemployment of the Great Depression era could be eliminated, and people could feel more secure as productive members of society, then many social ills could be reduced. It was widely assumed, for example, that strong economies and decent jobs for the great majority of families would reduce crime, would strengthen family and community life, and would eliminate social dispair and alienation. Yet, to the dismay of many, these prosperous and free societies in the Cold War era experienced an escalation of crime, rampant drug and alcohol abuse, record rates of family breakup, disastrous social alienation and community decay, and an array of environmental problems that we group together here under the "quality of life" performance area.

Even in a relatively prosperous and free society, problems of crime, drug addiction, alcoholism, family disintegration, alienation, unemployment, and pollution may severely hamper or even negate the enjoyment of both formal liberty and material affluence. Some of the keenest observers of Western societies, such as Erich Fromm (1955), David Reisman et al. (1950), Herbert Marcuse (1967), and Daniel Bell (1974, 1976) have argued from a variety of political perspectives and psychological, economic, and cultural approaches that the worship or fetishism of material goods is itself at the root of a "cultural crisis of modern liberal capitalism." The theme of "having more, but enjoying it less" has been voiced often, usually in loose terms, so that it is somewhat difficult to know just what should be examined under the heading "quality of life." There is disagreement as well on the causes and cures (if any) for the various problems most often subsumed under this heading.

Pope John Paul II has consistently criticized the erosion of moral values under the influence of capitalist materialism. In his *Centesimus Annus* (1991) and in his visits to various Western democracies, he has called for a rebirth of Christian morality and its application to social problems to build human dignity. Pope John Paul II declared that:

> Development must not be understood solely in economic terms, but in a way that is fully human. It is not only a question of raising all peoples to the level currently enjoyed by the richest countries, but rather of building up a more decent life through united labor, of concretely enhancing every individual's dignity and creativity. (John Paul II, 1991:12)

From the perspective of Catholic doctrine, the Pope views many of the social ills of the affluent liberal democracies as signs of the spiritual dead-end of the consumerist mentality:

> A striking example of artificial consumption contrary to the health and dignity of the human person, and certainly not easy to control, is the use of drugs. Widespread drug use is a sign of a serious malfunction in the social system; it also implies a materialistic and in a certain sense destructive "reading" of human needs. In this way the innovative capacity of a free economy is brought to a one-sided and inadequate conclusion. Drugs, as well as pornography and other forms of consumerism which exploit the frailty of the weak, tend to fill the resulting spiritual void. (1991:15)

Others contend that industrial society is to blame and that a return to nature and the countryside, either to small farm or communal life, is the answer. The communes founded in the 1960s and early 1970s by young Americans were symptomatic of these attitudes. Despite the demise of most such experiments after a few years, the longing for a more human-scale, less competitive, less bureaucratic life, is still evident not only in the United States but in Germany, Sweden, and Britain as well.

Others argue that these problems are inherent in modern, urban, mobile societies in general, and that we must simply learn to live with and perhaps adjust to them if we want to continue to enjoy the material benefits of our complex and highly productive economy. This advice may sound either hard-hearted or tough-minded, depending on one's values, but it does often provide an antidote to the scaremongering prevalent in many discussions of the problems of modern industria. Some would question whether frequent divorce is a social ill at all and would argue that drug experimentation is a mind-expanding and creative new freedom, indeed a question of personal freedom (for a good discussion, see Bakalar and Grinspoon, 1984), that pollution is much exaggerated and not a serious danger, and that unemployment no longer means severe material deprivation. Hardly anyone contends that

121

violent crime is good for us, but some (Bell, 1953) have seen nonviolent and "victimless" crimes (such as gambling, prostitution, and graft) as quite functional or even necessary and discount apparent recent crime waves as statistical illusions. In this section we will contend with these divergent viewpoints as we present data on crime, family breakdown, unemployment, pollution, and alienation and loss of community in the midst of material wealth. We can scarcely hope to come to any fine judgments as to the sources of all these phenomena of modern liberal democratic societies. Our main purpose is to gain a better idea of the magnitude and trends in each of these areas.

Crime and Nonrehabilitation: The Dark at the End of the Tunnel

Any cross-national comparison of crime in contemporary societies runs into problems of definitions and statistics. Crimes may be differently defined and laws differently enforced in various nations, especially in decentralized legal systems like that of the United States or West Germany. Laws change over time, and the enforcement of laws also changes. We know that crime statistics, that is, crimes reported to the authorities, are only a fraction of total crimes actually committed. Homicides are well reported, but many burglaries and thefts, and perhaps most corporate crimes, go undetected or unreported. The underreporting of rape is attributable to social pressures on the victim and the perception that involvement with the authorities will bring further agony and little chance of justice. Many thefts, burglaries, and assaults never come before the criminal justice system for a variety of reasons, but primarily because of a belief that the police will not catch the thief or assailant and that if they do, the courts will not punish (or rehabilitate) the offender or protect the victim from further harm. Gurr (1977:16–17) estimated that official crime statistics in Britain and the United States underestimate the total volume of criminal behavior by ratios from 2:1 to 10:1. Surveys of crime victimization for the general population reveal these discrepancies between official and actual criminality. Gurr argued, however, that reported crime statistics do correspond to relative frequency of criminal behavior and that they can thus be used, with caution, to tell us about trends in the incidence of crime.

In a most careful long-term analysis of crime in the cities of London, Stockholm, Sydney (Australia) and Calcutta from the early 1800s to the present, Gurr, Grabosky, and Hula (1977) noted a common pattern for the more developed Western societies, a pattern from which Calcutta deviates sharply. They found a dramatic rise in criminality, both violent and nonviolent, in the West since the Great Depression, with the greatest increases occurring in the latter 1960s and early 1970s. The upward trend for white-collar crime began during the Depression itself and continued to accelerate through the post-World War II era. The rate for known white-collar crimes increased in

London by 700 percent between 1945 and 1970 and in Stockholm also by 700 percent between the late 1920s and the early 1970s (1977:635–36).

In the field of violent crime, London experienced a tripling of the murder rate between 1950 and 1970 and Stockholm had a 500 percent increase in assaults from the 1940s to the 1970s. In Sydney, the rise in violent crime was somewhat more delayed, but in the 1960s there was a 40 percent jump in homicides and serious assaults and a staggering 800 percent leap in armed robbery. Robbery, that most common of crimes, was up by 3,000 percent in London between the 1930s and the early 1970s and by 600 percent in Stockholm over the same general period. Sydney again experienced a somewhat delayed rise in "common crime," with a doubling of larceny and a tripling of burglary from just 1960 to 1970. Gurr and his associates found these data generally in line with trends in reported crime from France, England and Wales, the United States, and with specific studies for a number of cities such as Boston and Chicago (pp. 646–47).

More startling than the massively documented and publicly perceived growth of criminality of all types in the post-Depression West was the reversal this represented vis-à-vis the declining crime rate for Western societies overall from the early 1800s to the 1920s. According to Gurr, the low point of criminality in Western societies was probably reached in the 1920s, ending a century of sometimes erratic but nevertheless considerable declines in reported criminal behavior in London, Stockholm, Sydney, Boston, Chicago, and Buffalo. It would appear that after bottoming out in the immediate pre-Depression years, the rate of criminal behavior began to climb again in the developed West, slowly at first, but with a sharp acceleration in the 1960s during a period of unprecedented affluence (figure 6.1).

This increase in crime and criminal violence now in some areas effectively limits the freedom of many, especially women and the elderly, who fear to go outside their homes after dark or even during daytime. Vandalism of both private and public property, seemingly senseless brutality in the neighborhood and increasingly in the schools, massive shoplifting, and repeated armed robbery against local merchants have created a climate of fear and despair, a tangible if not easily quantifiable loss of community morale. In the 1980s, in the United States, there was a leveling off or slight decline in crime rates, which is generally attributed to a leveling off or decline in the proportion of young adult males in the population. In Germany, on the other hand, Interior Minister Friedrich Zimmerman reported (*The Week in Germany*, Feb. 24, 1988) a strong rise in criminality from 1.9 million cases in 1966 to 4.4 million in 1986 and saw no end to this current trend. Nevertheless, crime rates remain at a new and higher plateau in most of the liberal democracies at a time not of economic depression or collapse but during the period of the greatest economic affluence in their histories.

There is still some significant variation to this general trend: the United

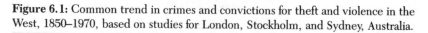

Figure 6.1: Common trend in crimes and convictions for theft and violence in the West, 1850–1970, based on studies for London, Stockholm, and Sydney, Australia.

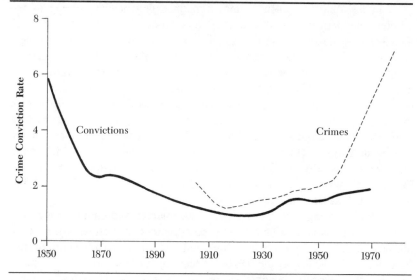

Source: Adapted from T. Gurr, P. Grabosky, and R. Hula, *The Politics of Crime and Conflict* (Beverly Hills, Calif.: Sage, 1977), pp. 60–61.

States seems to have experienced the sharpest rise in crime, with less marked trends in most of the continental European democracies. In violent crime categories, the United States is at the top of the list; in 1990, homicide rates in the United States were four times higher than in England, and about ten times higher than in Japan. Japan seems to be the least affected by crime among the affluent democracies. Although Japan's criminal underworld organizations (the yakuza) are well known and feared, they are a fairly minor feature of Japanese daily life and the larger society. Gang warfare does erupt sometimes (Erlanger, 1990:1), and there are an estimated 86,000 yakuza in Japanese crime syndicates, but this number declined in the 1980s.

An additional negative feature of the new criminality is the recognition, now widespread, that the criminal justice system does little to actually rehabilitate, or reform those criminals who are apprehended. Rather, prisons often harden criminal behavior patterns, and when prisoners are released at the end of their sentences, they are quite likely to commit further crimes. This pattern of repeat criminality, called "recidivism," means that in the United States, about 60–70 percent of convicted criminals will commit more crimes (and be caught) within three years after release from prison (*New York Times*, April 3, 1989, p. 11). One general factor that seems to decrease criminal behavior on

124

the part of released convicts is the aging process. With increasing age, especially for males, the likelihood of further crime declines, but this is hardly a success for the prison system, which in 1990 incarcerated 755,000 people in the United States (*New York Times*, Oct. 8, 1990, p. 8), as compared to 133,000 in 1945 and 210,000 in 1965. This includes federal and state prisons only, not city and county jails, which in 1990 held an additional 340,000 inmates as compared to 86,000 in 1950. The United States is somewhat unusual among the liberal democracies in terms of the prisoner population per capita. While the number of prisoners has grown in other liberal democracies in the postwar period as well, the growth in numbers, both in absolute figures and per capita, has been much more modest. In England and Wales, for example, the inmate population numbered 21,000 in 1951 and grew to 43,000 by 1981; in Germany, the inmate population hovered around 48,000 in the 1960s.

In a comparative study of prison incarceration rates in the liberal democracies, German criminologist Hans Joachim Schneider (1980:64) estimates that by the mid-1970s, rates of incarceration in the United States had surpassed 200 per 100,000 population, as compared to about 200 for Canada, 100 for England and Wales, 60 for Germany, 50 for Norway, and only 25 for the Netherlands. By 1990, the U.S. incarceration rate had surpassed 426 per 100,000 population (*New York Times*, Jan. 7, 1991, p. 14), making the United States the world leader in this unhappy category, surpassing South Africa (333) and the Soviet Union (268). The United States is here a rather clear deviant among the Western democracies in terms of the size of its prison population. This is all the more discouraging since this rise in crime to a new plateau and incarceration to all-time highs has occurred in a period of widespread affluence and greater personal liberty.

Table 6.1   Crime Rates and Prisoner Population in Liberal Democracies (per 100,000)

	Murders		Rapes		Drug Crimes		Prisoners
	1980	1990	1980	1990	1980	1990	1980–86
Switzerland	2.3	3.2	6.1	6.3	205	280	54
Germany	4.4	3.9	11.2	8.2	101	165	77
United States	10	9.4	36.0	41.2	—	—	426
England and Wales	1.6	2.3	2.5	6.7	10	20	77
Sweden	4.7	7.0	10.6	16.4	746	326	—
France	3.9	4.5	3.5	8.1	20	100	40
Japan	1.4	1.0	2.2	1.3	2	18	45[b]

Sources: Interpol, *International Crime Statistics*, 1979–80, 1985, 1991; UNDP, *Human Development Report*, 1992, 1993.
a. 1983
b. 1980–85

Explanations for the post-Depression rise in crime are varied, but not too varied to be summarized briefly. Radical criminologist Richard Quinney (1969, 1970, 1977) and economist David Gordon (1977) have argued that crime is endemic to a class-divided capitalist order, that criminality is partly functional to the system at levels of corporate price fixing, political bribery and corruption, even tax evasion, and is partially a sign of class conflict at levels of common street crime, especially in poor working-class districts. German political scientist Hans See (1990) sees executive-level criminality and economic crime in corporate and other elite groupings as a basic and unavoidable component of the profit-seeking capitalist mechanism. The development of capitalist relationships, the use of the capitalist logic of accumulation, even the economic success of the system produces more such criminality, not less. The success yardstick of capitalism undermines all competing social, ethical, and moral standards of behavior, and at the same time produces growing opportunities for economic crimes to achieve success. Gurr (1977) argued from the viewpoint of a political scientist that the goals and interests of political elites are also important factors in determining how public order will be maintained. In the face of rising crime rates and public responsiveness to "law and order" slogans throughout the West,

> the elite and governmental response has been relatively tolerant. At least two plausible explanations come to mind. One is paralyzing lack of agreement among interested parties about the most effective policies to follow. Second, elites and officials are in fact relatively little concerned about these kinds of crime because their costs—unlike the cost of civil strife—are sustained mainly by the ordinary citizens, who are most likely to be assaulted and who bear, directly and indirectly, most of the costs of personal and commercial theft. (1977:683–84)

Sociologist Daniel Bell (1974, 1976), psychologist Erich Fromm (1955), and political analyst Richard Goodwin (1974), among a host of others, have criticized the hedonist individualism and fetishism of commodities and things (cars, clothes, houses, swimming pools, country clubs—Veblen's conspicuous consumption) that increasingly characterize the social spirit of Western capitalism. The breakdown of the Protestant (and Jewish) ethic of work and frugality, and of the Catholic ethic of social obligation and family values generally, has given way to the ascendancy of possessive individualism as the modern capitalist expression of freedom. For the well-to-do corporate executive and the poor urban working-class youth alike, the objects of success are material possession (and their flaunting), and the means employed to get them are secondary and purely utilitarian considerations. Since law enforcement is lax or nonexistent against corporate crime and ineffectual against common crime, illegal means are, from an economic viewpoint, increasingly popular.

Still another view emphasizes elements of the urban environment in encouraging deviant or antisocial behavior, of which crime is one subset. Gurr (1977) and Nettler (1974) pointed to cultural heterogeneity, overcrowding, anonymity, and intergroup friction as factors of Western urban civilization that might explain increases in crime and strife. Cultural heterogeneity and the mobility/anonymity of urban society promote the decay of normative standards and greater possibilities of deviant behavior, while urban population densities and close group contact provide fuel for aggressive behavior. Gurr (1977) argued that social scale and cultural heterogeneity, taken together with the economic imperatives of system and the goals and interests of political elites, provide the important elements that condition the extent and treatment of public and social disorder.

Observers like Gurr, Bell, Fromm, and Goodwin are not optimistic about the future of Western democracy in fighting criminality. Bell sees this as a cultural crisis of capitalism, a historic disjunction between the still-successful world of productive capacity and the new hedonism of consumption. The liberal dream of rehabilitation of criminals seems now a utopian failure, and there is little hope that prisons in any Western society can reassimilate most inmates into productive life. On the other hand, a return to the brutalizing punishment of criminals common two centuries ago is politically unrealistic and would probably escalate criminal disorder into civil rebellion in several countries, as Gurr suggests (1977:767).

The Family in Uncertain Transition

The family is the basic building block of most civilizations. People the world over, at very different levels of economic development and facing a variety of problems and possibilities, when asked what they aspire to in life, include a happy and healthy family life. Pollster Hadley Cantril (1965) in his twelve-nation cross-national comparison of the patterns of human concerns, concluded that "in nearly all the countries studied, the major hopes and aspirations are those involved in maintaining and improving a decent, healthy family life" (1965:35). Yet modern Western society in many ways disrupts or erodes traditional family structures and roles, without replacing them with some functional alternatives. The extended family, with several generations living under the same roof, first gave way to the nuclear family, encompassing only the parents and their minor children. The elderly grandparents and widowed aunts and uncles live apart and increasingly in communities (or ghettoes) of the aged. More women have gone out to seek employment in recent years in most liberal democracies, methods of birth control and abortion have become widely available, and birth rates have fallen steadily, in many countries to below zero population growth (ZPG) levels. Economic rationality, maximizing of personal income, pursuing a satisfying and lucrative career, and freedom to

127

"do your own thing" or "be your own person" militate against having and even more against personally raising children. The result is that, given competent birth control techniques, the average family size has been getting smaller.

These trends are more advanced in the United States, Sweden, and Germany, less so in Japan, where the traditional family order and modern industrialism seem to coexist. Of course, what is economically most rational for each individual, namely, abstaining from child rearing entirely, is ultimately suicidal for the society at large. The possibility that the population of (West) Germany might shrink from 65 million to 22 million by the year 2070 (*The Times*, London, April 27, 1979, p. 7), with an increasing percentage of aged and an increasing burden on a dwindling younger generation, reveals one of the many contradictions of modern industria. The rise of the self-interested individual implies the decline of the collective (or social) sense of belonging and obligation necessary to keep societies, communities, and ultimately families together.

It is apparent that today there is simply not the same effort made to save troubled marriages as there was a generation ago, nor does the presence of small children in the family delay or prevent a family breakdown. In the early postwar years, it was common, especially among middle-class families in the United States, West Germany, and Britain, to keep a marriage together "for the sake of the children," or simply to avoid the greater social ostracism that divorce brought. The children of such troubled marriages did not always benefit from socially imposed pressures against divorce, but there should be no pretense that children of divorced parents are today beneficiaries of better home care and greater parental guidance and affection. There is no need to exaggerate the extent to which the traditional bonds of marriage and family life have declined in the West, and there is no good reason to idealize a golden past of family life, either (see Sussman, 1972, for typical argumentation that divorce is a healthy sign of personal problem solving and searching for a newer life-style). Divorce rates throughout the liberal democracies are on the rise and have been since the late 1950s (table 6.2).

In a comprehensive study of divorce and the law in several societies over long periods of time, Max Rheinstein (1972) points out that while formal divorce rates were low throughout the West in the nineteenth century, informal divorce through abandonment or migration was common among the lower classes. We cannot be sure that family breakup is at an historic peak for Western civilization. We can be sure that there has been a significant increase in marriage breakups since the 1950s throughout the Western democracies generally.

After a flurry of broken wartime marriages in 1946–47 in the United States, Britain, Germany, and France, divorce rates fell off dramatically and remained low through the fifties. This began to change in the late fifties and

Table 6.2   Divorce Rates per 1,000 Population

	1965	1970	1975	1980	1985	1990
United States	2.46	3.45	4.75	5.19	4.95	4.70
Sweden	1.24	1.61	3.14	2.39	2.37	2.26
Germany	0.99	1.26	1.73	1.56	2.10	1.94
United Kingdom	0.78	1.18	2.43	2.99	3.08	2.88
Japan	0.79	0.94	1.07	1.21	1.38	1.27
France	0.71	0.79	1.16	1.71	1.95	1.87
Canada	0.46	1.37	2.23	2.59	2.46	3.08*
Switzerland	0.85	1.02	1.39	1.71	1.76	1.96

Source: U.N., *Demographic Yearbook*, 1982, 1983, 1989, 1991.
*1989
Note: The UN *Demographic Yearbook* does not specify whether the figure for Germany is for the old
Laender or the entire country. However, the divorce rate for East Germany in 1989 was 3.01 and the rate
for West Germany was 2.04.

early sixties. Divorce rates have been on the rise ever since, with some clear
differences in magnitude among the liberal democracies. Catholic societies
such as France, Italy, Switzerland, and West Germany, which is half Catholic,
and traditionalist Japan, are still well below the divorce levels presently
experienced in the United States, Sweden (and Scandinavia generally), and
Britain. It must be noted, however, that in Catholic societies, the official
divorce statistics underestimate the rate of actual family breakup very considerably.
In Italy the number of "unofficial" divorces made liberalization of the
divorce laws a national issue in the 1970s. By the mid-seventies, divorce rates
in the United States, Sweden, and Britain had reached all-time highs, surpassing
even the immediate post–World War II divorce splurge.

In Scandinavia and the United States, between one-third and one-half of
all marriages end in divorce. Rheinstein (1972:307–13) and Sussman (1972)
attributed the increase in divorce in the West to the breakthrough in the 1960s
of the ethic of "individualist liberalism." Rheinstein concluded that changes
in the legal statutes on divorce are not causes but symptoms of this new ethic,
which was related in turn to: (1) changes brought about by the industrialization
of the economy; (2) the new economic position of women; (3) the declining
relevance of religion; and (4) greater individual geographic mobility.

An indicator of the decline of the more traditional two-parent family is
the rise in the percentage of births to unmarried women over the past thirty
years in all of the Western democracies, again with the notable exception of
Japan. In Sweden today, the majority of births are to unmarried women, while
in the United States, France, and Great Britain, over one-quarter of births are
to unmarried women. While many of these unmarried women do live on a
long-term stable basis with their partners and provide two-parent family

settings for their children, this trend also coincides with the rise of the female-headed one-parent family, with all of the economic problems associated with one-parent families, past and present (see also chapter 4 on inequality of women). There is now a wide pluralism of family arrangements common to most liberal democracies, but there is little reason to think that the troubled transition of family life has found a satisfactory new solution.

Mass Unemployment: Return of a "Solved" Problem

Even as per capita GNP continues to rise to unprecedented levels in the liberal democracies, at the bottom of the socioeconomic ladder, a growing mass of chronically unemployed and underemployed workers has emerged since the 1970s. Mass unemployment, one of the classic symptoms of a boom/bust capitalism from its inception through the Great Depression, had seemed on the way to a satisfactory, though not complete, resolution through the postwar triumph of Keynesian economic policies and active government intervention in the marketplace economy. Through a series of fiscal and monetary policies designed to spur capital investment, promote job creation by private industry, government welfare, other spending to keep consumer demand high, direct job creation by the government as employer of last resort, and government nationalization and subsidization of bankrupt industries, a "mixed" capitalist system would be able to keep unemployment levels down. Additionally, much-expanded unemployment and welfare benefits would change unemployment from a personal and family catastrophe to an unpleasant but much more manageable situation for those few who still faced joblessness.

For over a quarter of a century, this optimism seemed to be justified. With the partial exception of the United States, where unemployment remained qualitatively higher, the Western democracies, after the reconstruction of the war-shattered economies of Germany, France, Italy, and Japan, all enjoyed high growth rates and low, even miniscule, unemployment levels by the 1960s. In Germany, the *Wirtschaftswunder* brought domestic unemployment to less than 1 percent and attracted over 4 million foreign workers (*Gastarbeiter*) from Spain, Italy, Greece, Turkey, and Yugoslavia to Germany, mostly for menial or factory work that Germans were no longer willing to perform. The European Common Market countries together attracted over 8 million foreign workers. In Japan, the larger companies in the postwar prosperity virtually guaranteed lifetime employment (tenure) to their workers after an initial trial period, so that even in less favorable times a firm did not lay off workers to cut costs. In progressive Sweden (see Schnitzer, 1970) government reserve investment funds and extensive and effective job retraining and job placement at government expense added to the array of tools available in the liberal democracies, and also succeeded in reducing unemployment to just 1 percent by the 1960s. In Italy and Britain, governments followed a policy of extensive nationalization of financially troubled industries and government subsidy to preserve jobs. In Italy also the Christian Democrats made government an employer of last resort for millions through its patronage system. Even in the United States, with chronic high unemployment especially among blacks and with greater ideological blinders against national planning for full employment (nationalization, or direct job creation by government), unemployment was forced down below the 4 percent mark between 1966 and 1969. This was, of course, related to massive military spending on the Vietnam War and the drafting of hundreds of thousands of young men into the armed forces.

The price for keeping unemployment low in the post–World War II liberal democracies was a modest inflationary trend. The Keynesian approach to steering or guiding the economy called basically for a reversal of the disastrous balanced budget policies followed by both conservative (Herbert Hoover in the United States) and social democratic (Hermann Müller in Weimar Germany) governments during the Great Depression era. But frequent pump-priming through deliberate deficit spending would very likely also create a general upward drift of prices and a climate of inflation as the norm. While this bothered Conservative and Christian Democratic parties somewhat, by the 1960s even Republicans in the United States (although not the Goldwater wing), Conservatives in England, Christian Democrats in West Germany, and Gaullists in France had grudgingly accepted the basic notions of Keynesianism as the new orthodoxy. In the perceived political choice between modest inflation and the danger of severe recession or even depression, parties from moderate Conservative to Social Democratic seemed to share a consensus in favor of keeping unemployment down. While the business cycle had not been eliminated, there was confidence that it could be "damped down" or kept within acceptable bounds.

Then came the OPEC oil embargo of 1973, the quadrupling of oil prices, and the recession of 1974–75 throughout the non-Communist world. This was the most serious recession since the Great Depression and was different from previous recessions in several aspects. First, the recession hit virtually all of the liberal democracies simultaneously (with the partial exception of Sweden). Previously, recessions in the developed West, as in the United States in 1957–58 and Germany in 1966–67, had been more isolated occurrences; still-healthy economies could help bring the afflicted (most frequently Britain and Italy) out of their most difficult times through loans, imports, and investments. Now the economies of the industrial West were, more or less, in lock step, and there was much wrangling and paralyzing disagreement over who should or could afford to help whom out of the recession. After nearly three decades of growth and freer trade among the nations of the West, there is now a serious danger of protectionist trade conflict, a breakdown on international currency exchange policies, and a loss of undisputed American leadership in Western affairs generally.

Second, unemployment rose to postwar highs in the 1974–75 recession, not only in the United States, but also in Germany, France, Britain, and the Netherlands, where in the 1960s joblessness had been at very low levels. Figures from Sweden indicate that a determined and progressive social democracy was able to avoid the general trend of unemployment (though at the cost of severe inflation), while the figures for Japan illustrate the effectiveness of conservative but benevolent paternalism of large Japanese corporations in minimizing official joblessness.

Third, the 1974–75 recession introduced a new phenomenon into the lexicon of Western economists—"stagflation." Generally speaking, mainstream economists had seen inflation and unemployment as trade-offs, so that recessionary high unemployment should have damped down inflationary pressures in both wage and price areas. The mid-1970s recession, however, combined both high unemployment and high (not modest) inflation rates. Inflation for the years 1974 through 1977 averaged 18.8 percent in Italy, 17.6 percent in Britain, 12.3 percent in Japan, 10.9 percent in France, 8.8 percent in Canada, 7.6 percent in the United States, and a comparatively mild 4.9 percent in Germany. And while inflation remained high, the "recovery" years 1976 and 1977 did not reduce unemployment to prerecession levels throughout the liberal democracies generally. The worldwide recession of 1981–82 pushed unemployment figures to even higher levels than those experienced in the mid-1970s recession. In many of the liberal democracies, the jobless rate passed 10 percent, and in Great Britain, Ireland, and Belgium, it reached closer to 15 percent by late 1982. These are levels comparable to the first (but not worst) years of the Great Depression, and even in the economic recovery of the 1980s unemployment rates did not decline to levels of the pre-1973 period. Each new business upturn since the mid-1970s seems to have had less strength, and each downturn has thrown larger numbers of people out of work. The optimism of two decades, of *Wirtschaftswunder*, the Great Society, and *Il boom*, of confident Keynesianism, had been shattered.

The liberal democracies have tried a variety of strategies to deal with the consequences of "stagflation," with mixed results (Heidenheimer et al., 1990:172–82). Policy choices between unemployment and inflation were more difficult to manage than in the 1950s and 1960s. In some of the smaller European nations with social democratic governments, such as Sweden, emphasis was placed on maintaining full employment, even at the cost of higher inflation, and this was done with steady cooperation between strong union and strong business interests, a governing process that has been termed democratic corporatism. In nations with conservative regimes, such as Britain and the United States, unemployment was allowed to climb to much higher levels, in an effort to dampen inflation. In West Germany, after a change in government from the Social-Democratic-led coalition to the Christian-Democratic-led coalition in 1982, government policy put greater emphasis on controlling

Table 6.3 Percentage of Births to Unmarried Women in Liberal Democracies

	1960	1970	1980	1989
Germany	6	6	8	11
United States	5	11	18	27
United Kingdom	5	8	12	27
France	6	7	11	28
Sweden	11	18	40	52
Japan	1	1	1	1

Source: *Statistical Abstract of the United States*, 1992.

inflation, and allowed unemployment to balloon to more than 2 million in a sharp departure from the very low levels maintained since the 1950s. Only in Japan, of the larger nations, has a more traditional corporatist government, in close collaboration with strong business groups, been able to keep both unemployment and inflation relatively low. In Japan, both labor and the socialist left are weak, and have not played a major role in economic policy formulation. As noted by Heidenheimer (1990:173), the Japanese case is hard to classify, and illustrates again the unique traits of Japanese politics among the liberal democracies. By the late 1980s, although growth had returned and inflation was down from the levels of the previous decade, joblessness remained at relatively higher levels. In Germany, the strongest economy in Europe, unemployment remained at the 2 million level through the decade, giving rise to the concept of the two-thirds (*Zweidrittelgesellschaft*) society, where aggregate growth does not trickle down to the bottom third, but does benefit the top two thirds of the population. Those at the bottom in the ongoing economic restructuring process are the "modernization losers" (*Modernisierungsverlierer*), who face bleak prospects in the job markets of the 1990s.

A report by experts of the Organization for Economic Cooperation and Development (OECD), which regularly tracks and advises on economic policy in the rich liberal democracies, warned that in the 1990s, economic growth was not producing more jobs (i.e., *jobless growth*); their forecast for European Union was 17 million unemployed or about 12 percent for 1994. The United States, with its more flexible job market, was able to produce relatively more new jobs, but many of these were poorly paid and without a future, increasing the numbers of "working poor." In Japan, on the other hand, the OECD report noted the growth of "hidden unemployment" in Japanese firms that was beginning to be translated into real unemployment as firms sought to cut labor costs, despite a long tradition of guaranteed employment. These developments were seen as a threat to social peace and a cause of growing economic "protectionism" by political leaders (Daniels, 1993).

Although the liberal welfare state has continued to shoulder responsibility for managing the economy so as to keep unemployment or its economic consequences tolerable, this has become increasingly difficult in nearly all of the liberal democracies. It now appears that mass joblessness in the 1990s may be a regular feature of these wealthy societies, a feature that once seemed destined to disappear.

Some comments on the official jobless statistics are necessary to interpret the real extent of the human problem of being unemployed or underemployed. In Italy, official joblessness is only the tip of the iceberg, due to the creation of literally millions of do-nothing slots in an already-bloated government civil service and in the nationalized industries. These positions are unproductive (parasitic) from any economic point of view, and their wages and salaries are really surrogates for unemployment or welfare payments. In Germany, in addition to the unemployed workers, there are also many more workers on short-time, that is, workers who had full-time jobs but are now forced to work only part-time. In the United States, the official unemployment rate does not count workers who are too discouraged about job prospects to be actively looking for work, workers who are involuntarily working part-time, and the working poor, those who are working full-time but are earning incomes below the poverty level. David Gordon (1977:70–75) estimates that even the lowest, most conservative estimates of total underemployment in the United States in 1975 would come to 17 percent, or double the official jobless rate. Moreover, unemployment in the liberal democracies is not evenly spread among all social groups, but is much higher among young workers, women, and some ethnic/racial minorities. Official black unemployment in the United States is double white unemployment, and youth unemployment (for ages fifteen to twenty-four) is also about twice the overall rate.

As for the human meaning of unemployment or underemployment, any number of studies show the high correlation between joblessness or marginal employment and almost every other social ill, from poverty to trouble with the law to drug abuse and alcoholism to family disintegration and mental disease. And while no one can seriously relate unemployment in the liberal democracies to the threat of starvation anymore, it is by no means clear that the subjective loss of self-worth and alienation is any less damaging. As many theorists of relative deprivation have pointed out, the welfare poor and unemployed "on the dole," whether in the black ghettoes of Watts, Hough, and Harlem, in the poor Irish and working-class districts of Liverpool, Manchester, and London, or the shantytowns around Rome and Naples, do not compare themselves to the sidewalk-dwellers of Calcutta or Frantz Fanon's "wretched of the earth" in the poorest nations. They do not necessarily feel fortunate by comparison with the lowest of the low, especially when they live in close proximity to the luxury townhouses and apartments, shops, entertainment spots, and restaurants of the rich. Capitalism as an economic system has often been characterized as

Table 6.4   Unemployment in Liberal Democracies, 1965–92

	1965	1970	1975	1980	1985	1992
United States	4.5	4.9	8.5	7.2	7.2	7.5
Sweden	1.1	1.4	1.4	2.0	2.8	4.9
Former West Germany	0.6	0.7	4.7	3.4	7.4	6.6
United Kingdom	1.6	2.7	4.5	7.0	13.2	9.8
Japan	0.8	1.2	1.9	2.0	2.6	2.2
France	1.4	1.7	2.4	6.3	10.3	10.4
Canada	3.9	5.9	6.9	7.5	10.5	11.3

Sources: U.N., *Statistical Yearbook*, 1983–84; *Statistical Abstract of the United States*, 1987; Economist Intelligence Unit, *Country Reports for the Third Quarter*, 1993.

"creative destruction," a process of constantly remaking the productive system through the abandonment of older practices and the adoption of new. In the liberal democracies, the process of abandonment of older "smokestack" industries for newer computer, communications, and information sectors has destroyed millions of good-paying, skilled, blue-collar jobs and has required whole communities and regions to retool and restructure or perish. Many new jobs have also been created for those with the new skills and located in the new growth cities and regions. On balance, however, this process has left many in the working class and even the middle class with little chance for reaching the material standard of living, job security, or sense of a stable community their parents had. In declining neighborhoods, cities, and regions, joblessness is much more than just an economic statistic. It is loss of hope, and the new youth bitterness sporadically emerges as seemingly anomic violence, for example as riots at soccer matches in Britain and Italy, as ethnic conflict in New York, Birmingham, and Lyons, or as gang violence in Naples, Berlin, or Los Angeles. People, especially young people, who have lost hope and have no future do not simply disappear from the face of the earth, or agree to live out their desperation quietly. Their marginalization creates a violent potential that can be directed against diverse targets in situations of opportunity, when authority momentarily slackens or retreats. These bursts of social anger are quite systemic, and they have become a major social problem for the liberal democracies.

Pollution: The Solvable Problem

Pollution has been included in the catalog of quality-of-life issues because of the attention it has drawn over the last decade and because of the wide array of literature that almost monotonously tells us of some new poison or pollutant that may threaten our well-being. While air, water, nuclear waste, and even noise pollution are indeed social problems and political issues worth discussing,

135

the message of this subsection is, in brief, that pollution is one of the more manageable ills of the affluent democracies. In the field of pollution politics, as British social analyst Barbara Ward puts it:

> There is an optimistic school for which its opponents coined the phrase "techno-fixers"; there is a pessimistic school whom the techno-fixers tend to dismiss as "doom-sayers." In between lie as many nuances, differences of emphasis, and varying priorities as can be observed in the battle of ideologies. But the broad distinction between hope and despair sets the direction of the debate. (1976:69)

While optimism is called for as far as the developed nations are concerned, pessimism may be more appropriate for the poorer nations. In fact, pollution may be an issue in the affluent West in some measure because we have already attained material abundance and can afford to spend more energy, time, money, and skills on environmental quality.

First of all, pollution is hardly a new phenomenon or limited to the most industrialized nations. Air pollution in Mexico City, on a good day, runs ten times the permissible health limit established for cities of the United States. Cynthia Enloe (1975, ch. 4) emphasized that caring about the environment is for most of the world's nations a luxury issue. Both air and water pollution in Calcutta, São Paulo, and Lagos are at harmful levels daily, without becoming a political priority. When we talk of polluted air and water, stench, and deafening noise, we should be aware that these are found in their worst form in the cities and slum-cities of the poorest societies (see Ward, 1976, part 4, and ch. 16).

It is probable that the worst cases of local pollution in the Western nations are already in the past. Engels's description, cited earlier, of working-class Manchester in the mid-nineteenth century left little doubt of the intolerable degree of filth, stench, fouled water and air, and unabated factory noise that characterized daily life in working-class districts. John A. Loraine (1972), in his thoughtful balance sheet of pollution of different varieties, pointed out that London and Nottingham suffered from air pollution as early as the thirteenth century due to the burning of soft coal (with high sulphur content) for domestic heating. (Calcutta develops a similar but much intensified pollution from the burning of animal dung for domestic heating.) London's air pollution problems were increased tremendously during the industrial revolution. The first recorded killer smog occurred in London in 1873, when a dense, immobile mass of polluted air hanging over the city killed approximately one thousand people. Other bad bouts of air pollution were recorded in London in 1880, 1882, 1891, and 1892 and in Glasgow in 1909, where Dr. Harold Antoine De Voeux first coined the term "smog" (smoke and fog). Photochemical smog began to appear over Los Angeles in the 1940s. Occurrences of heavy air pollution combined with a thermal inversion (where a layer of cold air sits on a layer of warmer air, trapping air pollutants) killed sixty people on the River Meuse in Belgium in 1931 and killed twenty people and hospitalized hundreds more in the small industrial town of Donora, Pennsylvania, in October of 1948. The worst case on record, however, occurred in London in December of 1952, when a thermal inversion plus a week-long smog killed approximately four thousand people.

Pollution disasters have continued to occur, of course. In Japan in the early 1970s, four separate court cases brought to public attention and politicized the disastrous effects of industrial pollution, which resulted in over one hundred deaths and nearly two thousand injuries from mercury poisoning ("Minimata disease"), cadmium poisoning, and petrochemical air pollution (Enloe, 1975:321–32). In 1976 in Seveso, Italy, an entire village was abandoned and sealed off after an explosion in a chemical plant, which poisoned the air, ground, and water for miles around. The wreck of the supertanker *Torrey Canyon* in 1967 in the English Channel fouled fishing grounds and beaches with more than 30,000 tons of crude oil. Eleven years later the breakup of another supertanker, the *Amoco Cadiz*, carrying 220,000 tons of crude oil, destroyed many miles of French coast for fishing and resort industries. In 1989, the *Exxon Valdiz* accident spilled thousands of tons of crude oil into Alaska's Prince William Sound, fouling shoreline and destroying wildlife for miles. It seems likely that as long as industrial production facilities and urban lifestyles require large amounts of fossil energy fuels and petrochemical products, these environmental "accidents" will occur with some regularity, as an expectable byproduct of the economic growth mechanism. And even though it is probably true that urban air pollution levels are lower now than at the peak of the industrialization drive in the late 1800s or even the first half of the twentieth century, the fact that more people now live in urban areas combined with the fact that an increasing percentage of the population is over sixty-five (and more susceptible to respiratory ailments) could mean that more people are harmed by these lower pollution levels. In any case, reductions in current air pollution could produce a meaningful improvement in well-being.

Yet there is good evidence that since the belated and in most cases forced recognition of the pollution problem by governments in the United States, Japan, Sweden, and to some lesser extent Britain, effective steps have been taken in several areas that have already had some significant (i.e., measurable) effects in reducing pollution and guarding against pollution. In *Death of Tomorrow* (1972), John Loraine singled out the three main sources of air pollution as industry, motor cars, and domestic fuel consumption. The mix of villains differs by country and by locality in each country. In the United States, the decline in the use of coal for both home heating and industry has meant that automobile use has risen in importance as a source of air pollution. Government-mandated controls on the amount of lead permissible in gasoline in the United States and other Western nations, as well as requirements for

137

emission controls on new cars, have been making a dent in measured levels of air pollution in such cities as New York and Los Angeles.

Barry Commoner (1987), in a summary of the progress made in environmental pollution control, cited several hopeful signs. For example, from 1975 to 1985 in the United States, lead emissions dropped by 86 percent, sulfur dioxide emissions by 19 percent, and carbon monoxide emissions by 14 percent. Similarly, Japanese sulphur dioxide emissions decreased by 77 percent between 1970 and 1985 as a result of vigorous governmental action (United Nations, 1989:58). In the area of air pollution, therefore, Commoner argued that recent history teaches us that progress is possible given governmental, technical, and social effort. On the other hand, in the area of water pollution, only one-fifth of some four hundred river testing locations showed improvement in water quality between 1974 and 1981. In the area of toxic chemical pollution, the banning of the agricultural pesticide DDT reduced the levels of DDT in human body fat by 79 percent between 1970 and 1983. In other words, increased awareness of environmental issues and hazards in selected areas has produced, in a fairly short time span, notable changes. In other areas, such as toxic chemical production, waste disposal, and radiation exposure, little overall progress, and some regression, has taken place. Commoner predicted a long struggle, but took some satisfaction in the growth of political movements such as the Greens, who now hold seats in parliaments and/or regional and local governments in Germany, Switzerland, and Italy, and who are linking environmental decisions to basic questions of the economics of production technology. While Commoner emphasized the tremendous changes that must occur to safeguard the environment for human society, this is one area where the liberal democracies, because of their tremendous social wealth and their high level of opportunity for political dissent, may be better able to cope than in most other quality-of-life issues.

Signs of Alienation and Loss of Community Morale

Other aspects of liberal democratic society are just as much signs of decay and sickness as crime, family breakup, and unemployment. In the post-World War II period, drug addiction has grown to qualitatively new levels throughout the West. While drug addiction is most severe in the United States (with Sweden apparently a close second) with an estimated 150,000 to 600,000 heroin addicts alone, there are large and relatively open addict communities in Stockholm, Berlin, and Amsterdam as well as in New York, Washington, and San Francisco. In the years from 1960 to 1980, drug usage took a "great leap forward" in the West. Drug arrests in the United States, despite some trend toward decriminalization and police nonenforcement in some localities, increased from 31,000 in 1960 to 230,000 by 1969. Drug arrests of persons under eighteen climbed from less than 2,000 to nearly 60,000 in the same period

(Wald and Nutt, 1972:27). In some black ghettos hard-drug addiction is a mass phenomenon. Holahan (1972:288) estimated that between 8 and 12 percent of all black males aged fifteen to thirty-four in Washington, D.C., were drug addicts. In Britain, where drug addiction has never reached anything like American or Swedish proportions, the number of officially registered heroin addicts climbed from a mere 62 in 1958 to 2,240 by 1968, and cocaine addicts from 25 to 564 (May, 1972:349). Stockholm had an addict population of some 10,000. The highest addict death rate from overdose, however, was found in Germany and especially in (West) Berlin.

The German Addiction Center in Hamburg reported in 1981 that there were an estimated 300,000 to 600,000 addicts to some drug, of which 50,000 to 70,000 were heroin addicts. Some trends in addiction included drug (and alcohol) use at earlier ages, more women involved in illegal drug use, and greater usage of two or more drugs at the same time. Forty percent of addicts in Germany were under twenty-one years of age (*The Week in Germany*, March 20, 1981).

Alcohol abuse remains the most common form of dependency and the most dangerous in terms of deaths caused. It is estimated that there are about 11 million alcohol-dependent people in the United States, while in Germany the estimate is 1.2 to 2.8 million. Alcohol abuse in Germany is responsible for sixteen times more fatalities than drug abuse, and approximately 90,000 people become alcoholics each year.

Modern chemistry has created some new hallucinogenic drugs, such as LSD and more recently PCP, that can be manufactured with relative ease in small garage or home workshop laboratories. These new drugs have added a new dimension of faddishness to the recent rise in addiction. More important, however, has been the change in the composite picture of the addict in the affluent liberal democracies. Nils Bejerot, in his wide-ranging study of drug addiction in different countries, summarized the situation about 1950 as follows:

> Until about twenty years ago dependence on sedative and stimulant drugs was a phenomenon largely confined in economically advanced countries to two relatively well-defined groups. In most countries there was a group of addicts drawn from the upper and professional classes, including a substantial group from medical or allied occupations, who had ready access to narcotics and stimulant drugs prone to cause dependence. In some countries, and the U.S.A. in particular, there was a much larger addiction problem closely associated with poverty and underprivilege. (1970:v)

Given this profile in the early postwar years, one might have expected for drug addiction "a decline in parallel with the eradication of poverty and disease and the improvement of living conditions," Bejerot suggested. What emerged in the 1960s and 1970s, however, was a new population of drug users from fifteen to twenty-five years old and from all social classes—the well-to-do, the middle class, and the working class, as well as the poorest in society. Drug addiction and drug usage have grown to be symptomatic characteristics of the sickness of society in general, not just the deviant behavior of the ghetto poor or a few upper-class medical practitioners. Drug addiction today in the West reflects not just despair of bitter poverty but a wide-ranging sense of alienation of the middle-class user from society. Illegal drug trafficking in the 1980s became a giant economic network. In the United States, its sales volume was estimated at $100 billion to $150 billion, which made it larger than the automobile industry in economic power and which enabled it to influence various elements of law enforcement, courts, and banking to suit its needs. Swiss sociologist Jean Ziegler (1990) has presented strong evidence that drug traffickers have been able to corrupt the Swiss banking system to launder their profits, and that the legal authorities are unable or unwilling to prevent this use of the banking system. It is perhaps to be expected that when such large amounts of money are controlled by criminal cartels, those organizations generally will be able to corrupt any authorities that stand in their way. This recognition has produced serious proposals for legalization of most drugs so that the large profits can be eliminated from organized crime, and the corrupting influence diminished. Legalization would be an admission of policy defeat in terms of the basic causes of drug-taking and drug addiction: it is a policy of cutting losses and trying to stem the worst effects of the drug problem.

Drug usage is of course not confined to heroin, cocaine, LSD, PCP, etc. Millions of men and women seek to forget their anxieties, relax their tensions, produce pleasant sensations, or simply get through the day by the use and abuse of legally obtainable uppers and downers, stimulants and tranquilizers, and of course alcohol.

To many observers of the liberal democratic societies, the average citizen has been losing his or her sense of social or community belonging and has felt incapable of personally getting involved to solve problems of crime, drugs, delinquency, pornography, and loneliness. The world was shocked in 1964 when in New York City Kitty Genovese was stabbed to death by a street assailant while some twenty-nine people witnessed the slaying in progress and did nothing to help the victim. No one came running, no one shouted out a window for help, no one called the police. No one wanted to get involved, each hoped only to escape harm or inconvenience by remaining isolated from the immediate tragedy. Escapism, whether by the abandonment of the cities or troubled neighborhoods by the well-to-do or the middle class, or through drugs, alcoholism (and family abandonment?), through noninvolvement behind bolted doors, or through extreme subordination of self to any number of cults is a sign of the times, an abandonment of community effort or at times a grotesque attempt to find a collective existence. It is a recognition, explicit and implicit, of the decline of local control over events that affect the quality of life in the immediate environment.

Into the Post–Cold War Era

This chapter has presented several areas of citizen concern in the affluent liberal democracies. Of the issues of criminality, family breakup, pollution, unemployment, and personal alienation, there are signs of improvement only in the area of pollution (mainly of air and water). This is because pollution is at least in part manageable as a technical problem and does not directly involve social, class, or interpersonal relations. Liberal democracies have been much more able to deal with technical and aggregate economic issues than with questions of either social equality or social morale. By the end of the 1980s, while the Western democracies were at the highwater mark in material affluence and personal liberty, they were also experiencing severe signs of erosion of community and social morale. The rise in crime, drug addiction, homelessness, and corruption at all levels of society, seemed to indicate a general decline in the socialization capacity of these societies. The great socializing institutions of the neoliberal political economy, such as church, trade unions, businesses, schools, neighborhoods, and families have weakened. In their place, for many of the young, have come peer groups, such as inner-city gangs, sports fan clubs, new youth cults and sects, or nothing at all. Whether these new peer socialization groups can function in ways that produce some new sense of community and family morale remains to be seen. A cultural transition is still in process, with little certainty about the prospects for improving the quality of life in these rich, free, yet troubled societies.

In the 1980s, even before the end of the Cold War, new political movements and parties were challenging the established political leaders, whether conservative, liberal, or social democratic, over the perceived failures in the quality-of-life performance area. The decline of urban life, the erosion of family life, the rise of crime and especially violent crime, and the alienation of a growing portion of youth in the liberal democracies have raised the political priorities in this area. In an era of economic transition and lowered material expectations for many, the politics of this quality-of-life area may become much more important. The question is whether the politics of cities, crime, family, and youth alienation are dealt with through a new populist demagoguery that seeks scapegoats and simple answers, or whether the liberal democracies will be able, more deliberately and less emotionally, to experiment with new strategies. It is just possible that now, with less public money available and with less faith in the old party politics of government programs, citizen-based coalitions, using new combinations of conservative, liberal, and socialist values, may be able to develop more effective answers to these issues.

ESSAY: THINKING ABOUT POST–COLD WAR POLITICS IN THE LIBERAL DEMOCRACIES

What we have suggested in these chapters is that the old neoliberal consensus is eroding, though still largely in place. The primary reason for this erosion is the rise in overall costs of the welfare state, combined with the internationalization of capital investment. Of the partners in the old government-business-labor consensus, business has had the greatest motivation and opportunity to opt out, and it has increasingly done so. In the international trading and finance system, there are no democratic controls on capital and no role for democratic politics to defend labor interests. Labor, less mobile than capital and finance, has had the least motivation to opt out of the old postwar formula and has been fighting a defensive action to keep the old consensus together. This strategy is now more visibly a losing response after the collapse of communism and the increased opportunities for investment in low-wage, low-benefit nations. Government, whether conservative (Reagan and Thatcher) or social democratic (Mitterrand and Gonzalez), has increasingly sided with the more powerful and dynamic business leadership, although still trying to portray itself as mediator and conciliator of social interests. In the aftermath of the East-West conflict, the governments of liberal democracies will continue to satisfy the more dynamic sectors of business, who can take their investment out of the country to more favorable settings. Unless and until some new labor-based coalition can invent a sufficiently strong counterbalance, requiring a new social compromise with the force of democratic law, the liberal democratic state will favor big business and disfavor labor.

This new imbalance in a democratic polity will not go unchallenged. The rise of new national-populist movements of various stripes (the Reform party in Canada, Ross Perot in the United States, Umberto Bossi's Northern Leagues in Italy, Franz Schönhuber's Republikaner in Germany, and Jean Marie le Pen's National Front in France) is the first and easiest reaction. It represents the dangers in this transition of a new nationalism, backlash against immigration and immigrants, antiforeigner violence, economic protectionism, and autarchy. Recent elections and the debates over NAFTA and Maastricht show the strength of the new national-populist challenge, now generally at about 15 to 20 percent of electorate.

On the left of the spectrum, signs of a new agenda are just beginning to emerge, with increased conciliation between the old left (labor-based parties and trade unions) and the new social movements (environmentalists, feminists, alternative life-styles, multicultural advocates). In Germany, the ongoing dialogue between Social Democrats and Greens shows both the potential and the difficulties of a new red-green alliance. The outlines of a new politics on the left must still be refined, but they include a broader coalition of all working people, less reliance on government support and government bureaucracies, greater direct citizen participation through more decentralized organization, and most of all, international solidarity with broadly labor-based movements in all parts of the world. It is clear that labor-based coalitions must compete with the power of international business on an international level in order to reestablish credibility for a new political compromise, both internationally and in national politics.

In terms of our four performance areas, the current period of transition continues toward lower material expectations (but still quite high in cross-national comparison) from economic development. As a new trade-off for more modest standards of living, citizens might well demand greater attention and achievements in the quality of life factors, such as crime fighting, more security for family life, and improved community morale. The current trend toward greater inequality could lead to new class divisions and bitterness if it continues, requiring more government attention to redistribution programs or, on the other hand, less government attention to poverty and the poor. Likewise, in the personal liberty area, slow growth or jobless growth may lead to less tolerance toward ethnic minorities, immigrants, and cultural pluralism, or it may lead to a renewed struggle for civic tolerance and mutual support among ethnic, religious, regional, and other groups.

The political landscape is shifting, and only the ongoing struggle of individuals and groups and of leaders and citizens, and the invention of new political alternatives, will determine what the new consensus, if any, will look like in any detail. Liberal democracy provides many opportunities for established interest groups and political parties to slow down the pace of change; the balancing of parliamentary and executive power with the addition of judicial restraint and, in many cases, the further division of government between national, state, and local levels provide safeguards against wholesale abandonment of long-established commitments to social welfare systems. More likely is a continuation of the now-clear process of returning to basic conservative, liberal, and socialist values and then applying them to the new circumstances. The great probability is that the heritage of stable and successful democracy in the long postwar peace will contain this uncertain struggle within the bounds of democracy itself. The postwar democracies are stronger than they were in the interwar 1920s and 1930s, and they have built up a lot of political legitimacy. The democracies must use this time for political rethinking productively to renew citizens' confidence and to rebuild popular optimism in the future of liberal democracy.

7

The Rise and Fall of
Communism—Challenges
for Post-Communism

The twentieth century began without a single Communist political system in place, and it is just possible that it will end without any classic communist systems still in power. But this century has been deeply marked by the rise and fall of communism as a major political system-type, which at its greatest expanse encompassed some sixteen nations with about one-third of the world's population. Until the 1989–90 collapse of communism in Eastern Europe, no Communist system once in place had ever been overthrown or reformed into a democratic system. Communism for several generations had built a reputation for system stability, by whatever means, and therefore the rapid success of the anti-Communist popular movements of 1989–90, followed by the collapse of the Soviet Union less than two years later, was an historic turning point in the understanding of these systems and their temporary nature. How is it that such a fearsome system, which seemed so powerful throughout the Cold War, disappeared so meekly and quickly? And what now comes after the sudden fall of communism?

Communism now appears to be a transitory stage in political evolution, a system that over time decays and generates internal dynamics of transition to some other type of political order, a transition that may be generically labelled post-communism. In the mid-1990s, we now see, after the first few years of post-communism in Europe, the variety of interim results of the struggle to define the new post-Communist political system. In some countries—particularly Hungary, Poland, and the Czech Republic—two rounds of democratic elections have now been held, and the major institutions of liberal democracy seem to be functioning. In some other countries, particularly in the former Soviet Union and the former Yugoslavia, post-communism has meant civil war and the rise of authoritarian nationalist regimes, which, while no longer Communist, are certainly not liberal democracies, even though national leaders like Tudjman in Croatia or Milosevic in Serbia may have been elected in some fashion. And in the republics of the former Soviet Union, there is great political instability and basic conflict over the shape of the political system, with the anomaly that most leaders of almost all the former Soviet republics are ex-Communists, including Yeltsin of Russia, Kravchuk of Ukraine, Shevardnadze of Georgia, Brazauskas of Lithuania, and Nazarbayev of Kazakhstan. The political struggles in these nations, as well as the expected power struggles to come after the death of top leader Deng Xiaoping in China, or Kim Il-sung in North Korea (who died in July of 1994), or the political retirement under whatever circumstances of Fidel Castro in Cuba, are open to a variety of outcomes, although some nations have a much higher level of uncertainty than others.

Post-communism as a concept says nothing about the nature of the newly emerging systems, only that they are emerging from a relatively long period of Communist rulership. In that sense, the weight of the communist past still is clearly an important factor for interpreting the possible course of the post-Communist transitions. Much of our analysis in the following chapters is devoted to understanding the "classic" Communist systems, how they emerged, how they performed, and why they went into irreversible decline as political systems. This analysis of what "has been" may tell us something about what "may be" in the future, although with each passing year, the reemergence of pre-Communist traditions and issues, and the influence of specifically post-Communist personalities, parties, and movements, will weigh more heavily in the balance.

Theoretical Origins

Modern theories of socialism and communism were developed chiefly in the nineteenth century after the ultimate failure of the French Revolution and the final defeat of the Napoleonic armies in 1814–15. This period, from 1815 to 1914, was one of relative peace and industrialization in Europe. Economic developments such as the expansion of the free market system, first in England and France, later in Germany and northern Italy, were changing the social and political anatomy of Western Europe as well as of the United States and Japan. But the benefits brought by increased production, new inventions, and greater personal liberty had to be balanced against the costs of miserable living and working conditions for the new urban working class and against the constant specter of unemployment. The rise of industrial capitalism, celebrated by liberal economic and political thought, looked very different from the perspective of working-class Manchester. Modern socialism has developed in response to the spread of modern capitalism, and especially to the capitalist form of industrialization. As with ancient and feudal notions of socialism, modern socialism represented the politics of social justice, now applied to urban industrial society. The type of socialism we will be describing here might also be called industrial socialism.

The suffering of the working class in nineteenth-century capitalism stood in sharp contrast to the opulent wealth of a handful of plutocrats (the captains of industry) such as Thyssen and Krupp, Morgan and Vanderbilt. Those who criticized the suffering and inequities associated with capitalism were not always socialists. Some were aristocrats or religious thinkers hoping for a return to (or the salvation of) agrarian feudalism and monarchy. The socialists constituted a group of critics who wanted to build a more just society fundamentally different from capitalism, without returning to feudal monarchy. Among those socialist (or Communist—the terms were at that time interchangeable) theorists there was considerable disagreement over the strategy for bringing about the transition from capitalism to socialism. Marx emphasized, though granting some possible exceptions, the revolutionary overthrow of capitalism and the bourgeois state by a mass uprising of the urban working class, the proletariat. English industrialist Robert Owen and his followers, on the other hand, set up socialist communities (New Lenark, New Harmony) in England and the United States to act as models for the rest of society. The Frenchman Pierre Proudhon emphasized a decentralized syndicalist system based on a workers' takeover of the factories. The Russian nobleman Mikhail Bakunin sought to bring an end to capitalism through terrorism and assassination of high government officials. His new socialist society was cast in an anarchist image, that is, having no formal government, but rather direct self-government by the people.

Socialist thinkers disagreed also in their basic attitudes about technology and urban industrialism. Marx believed that the new technology of capitalism was a revolutionary breakthrough for mankind and that it offered the possibility for eliminating poverty, disease, and ignorance throughout the world if only it could be applied justly and rationally through socialism. Agrarian socialists (often called populists) believed that the new industrial technology and the crime-ridden, crowded, dirty cities being spawned by it were the root of the evils of capitalism. They hoped to reverse urbanization and industrialization, to revive the communal (that is, socialist) spirit of the villages and small towns. The Owenites favored using industrial innovations, but on a more decentralized small-town or small-city basis, to avoid pollution and overcrowding.

There was consensus perhaps only on the idea that this new society would be more just, and therefore more egalitarian, than capitalism. This may sound like very little to agree on, yet the immorality and unfairness of capitalism appeared so great that this made (and in the developing nations is still making) the concept of socialism a powerful and motivating force for a more just society. It is today quite likely that those pressing for greater social justice will call themselves socialists. And on the other side of the fence, the wealthy and privileged in most societies are also the most dependably antisocialist, the most opposed to any form or element of socialism. Only in a few

147

countries, most notably the United States, do leading proponents of greater social justice still disclaim all forms of socialism and consider themselves liberals.

Marxist Socialism

Of all the theories of socialism that arose in the last century, certainly those of Karl Marx had the greatest impact. In Marx's own time, there was no one predominant theory of socialism; Proudhon, Owen, and Bakunin probably had greater followings than did Marx. Yet the popular identification of socialism with Marxism is a historic development that for some time overshadowed the socialist thought of Marx's competitors.

Marx (1818–83) never lived to see socialism, of any type, in operation in any country. Most of his writings dealt with the workings of capitalism and the reasons for the predicted overthrow of capitalism. They do not give a detailed blueprint for the operation of a socialist society. Marx said that the proletariat itself would have to work out the details. In the *Communist Manifesto*, Marx and Engels did outline some general policies that would start society down the road to socialism once the bourgeoisie had been overthrown:

1. Abolition of property in land and application of all rents of lands to public purposes.
2. A heavy progressive or graduated income tax.
3. Abolition of all right of inheritance.
4. Confiscation of the property of all emigrants and rebels.
5. Centralization of credit in the hands of the State, by means of a national bank with State capital and an exclusive monopoly.
6. Centralization of the means of communication and transport in the hands of the State.
7. Extension of factories and instruments of production owned by the State; the bringing into cultivation of waste-lands, and the improvement of the soil generally in accordance with a common plan.
8. Equal liability of all to labour. Establishment of industrial armies, especially for agriculture.
9. Combination of agriculture with manufacturing industries; gradual abolition of the distinction between town and country, by a more equable distribution of the population over the country.
10. Free education for all children in public schools. Abolition of children's factory labour in its present form. Combination of education with industrial production, &c., &c. (Tucker, 1978:490)

Radical as these proposals were for their time, Marx related them to the transitional phase of the "dictatorship of the proletariat," before full communism is achieved. Only in the era of full communism would humanity apply the general ethic of "from each according to his abilities, to each according to his

148

needs.'' Eventually humankind would reach a fully classless society, with no one born into great wealth or stultifying poverty, a society that would have overcome exploitation of workers, racial or ethnic groups, and women. Production would be socially planned; the means of production (factories, farms, offices) would be collectively owned rather than in private hands. Marx believed that under full communism, government bureaucracy, including police and military, would "wither away" as citizen associations took over the tasks of social administration. In such a society all would participate in governing, not just a few "professionals." In short, there would be no full-time politicians, bureaucrats, or generals; all these roles would be performed by ordinary citizens on a short-term or rotating basis.

Although Marx spoke in the *Manifesto* of a "dictatorship of the proletariat" and hoped for a revolutionary overthrow of capitalism, his vision of the new society of the future was described as follows:

> In place of the old bourgeois society, with its classes and class antagonisms, we shall have an association, in which the free development of each is the condition for the free development of all. (Tucker, 1978:491)

Marx also spoke of the communist party—but his idea of that party and its role in politics and in relation to the working class:

> The Communists do not form a separate party opposed to other working-class parties. They have no interests separate and apart from those of the proletariat as a whole. They do not set up any sectarian principles of their own, by which to shape and mould the proletarian movement. (Tucker, 1978:483)

Although Marx's own ideas also changed in later years, the ideas of the 1848 *Manifesto* should be kept in mind when we discuss Lenin's revisions of Marxism to Russian revolutionary organizing.

Evolutionary Socialism

Marx was disappointed in his hopes for socialist revolution in Europe. He had never considered the possibility of a socialist revolution succeeding in one country, but had hoped that a socialist revolution, following the pattern of the French Revolution of 1789, would sweep across national boundaries, becoming an international workers' uprising. Underestimating the forces of nationalism, he had helped to found the Workingman's International to promote socialism throughout Europe and to build international working-class solidarity. By 1895, when Engels died, it was becoming clear that predictions of revolution would not be fulfilled. To be sure, workers were rebelling against poor wages and working conditions by building union organizations against formidable odds. But the union movement and the socialist parties that it supported were for the most part not revolutionary. Gradually, though not without a good deal of violence, unions and working-class parties received recognition and were able to push through partial reforms on child and female labor, voting rights for working men, factory safety, hours and wages, and union bargaining rights. Daily life for the urban worker and his or her family at the turn of the century was still no bed of roses, but it did seem as though the working class could begin to share the benefits of industrialization by working and struggling within the capitalist system. From this perspective, one branch of socialist thought, generally called social democracy, extensively revised Marx's ideas and eventually abandoned Marxism.

In general, wherever real democratic opportunities have been available for socialists, socialist movements have overwhelmingly opted to participate in electoral politics and to pursue a democratic socialist path. The choice, it must be stressed, was not theirs alone; the ruling classes, both the aristocracy and the bourgeoisie, had the primary choice and power to decide whether they would permit democracy to expand, and permit socialists to freely contest for governmental power (see chapter 2).

Eduard Bernstein, a close friend of Engels and a prominent publicist for the German Social Democratic party (SPD) until the 1930s, advanced a major critique of Marx, which argued that: (1) capitalism was not about to explode from its own internal contradictions; (2) a workers' revolution had become very difficult, if not impossible, because of advances in military technology (especially the machine gun and breech-loaded cannon); and (3) a gradual democratization of the political and economic system could create a more just society (socialism) without revolution. The key to this "evolutionary socialism" was education of workers, promotion of the union movement, and support for workers' parties. Socialism would come through ballots rather than bullets. Social democrats and laborites would be the loyal opposition, which would someday become the governing party, playing by the rules of the system itself. Of course, this meant giving up notions of international working class solidarity when it clashed with the "national interest" or with the spirit of nationalism in electoral politics.

The great test of the social democratic movement (organized as the Second International) came in 1914 at the outbreak of World War I. It was clear that the war would be a disaster for the working class. They would die by the thousands (eventually by the millions) in the front lines, while industrialists and aristocrats amassed war profits and directed the battlefield slaughter from safe vantage points. The question for the socialist and labor movements in Germany, Britain, France, Russia, Italy, Austria, and later the United States was whether to unite (via the Second International) to oppose the war in the name of the international working class or to individually support the war policies of their own nations in order to prove their nationalist loyalty. In nearly every case, the revisionist social democrats voted with liberals and conservatives to support the war. One of the few exceptions was the American Socialist party, which refused in 1917 to abandon its opposition to American participation in the war, an action for which socialist leader Eugene V. Debs was jailed. Lenin's Bolsheviks in Russia also opposed the war and were subsequently denounced as traitors and as German agents. A minority of socialists who opposed or came to oppose the war formed the beginnings of the communist parties of Western Europe. Rosa Luxemburg and Karl Liebknecht, for example, split off from the Majority Social Democrats in Germany to form the Spartacus League, which in 1919 became the German Communist party. Indeed, World War I marks the historic split in the international socialist movement into social democrats and revolutionary communists. This split has continued, with moderate Social Democrats like Willy Brandt, François Mitterrand, Felipe Gonzalez, Golda Meir, and Olof Palme as representatives of the Second International and the heritage of evolutionary socialism. The communist parties, on the other hand, joined together in the Third International under the tutelage of the Bolsheviks and became associated with the theories of Lenin as well as Marx (hence the title Marxist-Leninist).

Leninism

Lenin also noted the diminished revolutionary possibilities in the more developed West and even remarked on the growing prospects of a "labor aristocracy," a relatively well-to-do segment of workers, in these nations. But Lenin explained this as a result of imperialism, whereby the developed West between 1875 and 1914 had divided up the non-Western world into colonial empires and spheres of influence.

Through the exploitation of cheap native labor and resources, Western capital was able to find new sources of profit, allowing it to make concessions to the working class in the developed metropolises of Europe and North America. This decreased the revolutionary tendencies in these most advanced nations, so that, contrary to Marx's expectations, the proletariat was becoming less radicalized. Lenin argued that the locus of revolution had been displaced from the developed West to the less-developed nations now dominated by Western imperialism and its corporate multinationals. As the non-Western peoples were forcibly integrated into the world capitalist system and subjected to patterns of development dictated by the Western multinationals, they would organize to defend themselves and liberate their countries from imperialism, both political and economic. Lenin predicted that wars of national liberation would erupt to deprive Western capitalism of its sources of profits, and that these revolutions in the underdeveloped world would then lead to the re-emergence of the class struggle and working-class revolution in the West. Lenin, of course, was working and planning for a revolution in Russia (the weak link in the chain of international finance capitalism), but always with the hope that this would be the spark to ignite a revolution in Europe (especially Germany). A socialist Europe could then aid, on equitable terms, in the industrial development of Russia. Like Marx, Lenin did not envisage building socialism in Russia, but considered international-scale revolution a necessity.

Preparing for revolution in tsarist Russia, or in the underdeveloped nations generally, would require a different type of organization from that of Western social democratic parties. In tsarist Russia there existed no freedom of speech, no free elections, no rights of union organization; instead there were extensive secret police spying and torture and violent suppression of dissent. There was little room for an open, public, democratic socialist movement to operate. The conditions to which Bernstein was responding in Western Europe (even in the Kaiser's Germany) simply did not exist in most of the underdeveloped world. Lenin saw the need for a vanguard party of a new type, a tightly organized, disciplined cadre of professional revolutionaries, dedicated to the revolution above all. The Leninist party member would be willing to suffer deprivation, jail, and worse over long periods when revolution seemed hopeless, so that when the conditions for revolt appeared, the chance would not be missed. The rebellious workers (and perhaps even peasants) would have a coherent, even paramilitary, leadership, able to topple the old order. Without a vanguard party, the revolutionary upsurge may be delayed or diverted, giving the old order time to regroup or (as frequently happened and still happens) call for outside help.

Lenin's vanguard party would have to be as professional and as capable in the use of force as its opposition if the revolution were to succeed. The Leninist party would be governed according to a set of rules called democratic centralism, which provided for: (1) election of party leaders by the membership, (2) regular reports by leaders to members, (3) open debate of issues before deciding on a policy line, and (4) strict obedience to leadership and policy decisions.

This "party of a new type" model ran into heavy criticism within the European socialist movement. The objections to Lenin's theory of the vanguard party were twofold. First, social democrats like Yuri Martov and Eduard Bernstein argued that a socialist revolution in still-underdeveloped nations like Russia in the early 1900s was wildly premature. These countries first had to go through the capitalist stage, which was still in its infancy. Each stage of development as outlined by Marx is necessary and cannot be skipped. Lenin was accused of being a modern Jacobin, trying to push for revolution where the social conditions were not yet ripe. In such a case, as with the Jacobins of the French Revolution, the revolution would have to resort to terror to maintain power, and even then it would fail, as had Robespierre's regime. This could lead to a degeneration of the revolution into a military dictatorship (Napoleon) or it could end with the restoration of the *ancien regime* (as in

France in 1815), all at tremendous cost in human suffering and discredit to the original ideals of the revolution.

A second objection was raised by Rosa Luxemburg and those more sympathetic to revolutionary socialism. Luxemburg was concerned that Lenin's vanguard party would continue in power as a new ruling class after the old order had been overthrown. Marx had originally foreseen a spontaneous workers' revolution that would be quickly victorious and would produce not a new governing elite, but rather a governing majority, the proletariat. Luxemburg feared that Lenin's professional cadre of revolution-makers would not disband after leading the revolution, but would provide a new undemocratic and dangerous obstacle to building socialism. Leninism, at its very beginnings, was unacceptable to many socialists, both democratic parliamentary and revolutionary. They rightly saw two major deviations from original Marxism which would misshape any regime that might come to power under the Leninist political formula. The first was the historical backwardness of economic and cultural development in Russia, which Marxists saw as a necessary basis for a socialist transition to communism. The second was the great likelihood that the vanguard Leninist party would become a new dictatorial ruling class. The same party of professional revolutionaries, which Lenin correctly saw as capable of winning the revolutionary struggle in a nondemocratic political environment, would not simply give up its newly acquired power, but would become a new and powerful elite, ruling over the working class.

The Russian Revolution—First and Alone

The first political system to call itself socialist was established by the 1917 October Revolution in Russia. The autocratic tsarist system had been challenged by revolutionary upheavals before World War I, in 1905–1906, but had managed with the help of the army to survive for another decade. At the beginning of World War I, in fact, it seemed that an upsurge in nationalistic patriotism would restore some measure of popular support for Tsar Nicholas II. However, the fortunes of war quickly eroded this early optimism when Russian losses at the front mounted to disastrous proportions. Meanwhile, the tsar's corrupt and inept government lost whatever public confidence it had held, and the economy became both overloaded by the war effort and shattered by the loss of industrial facilities to the advancing German armies. In February of 1917, popular unrest in the capital city of Petrograd came to the boiling point. One day, an international women's day march, a demonstration of steel workers from the huge Putilov works, and food riots combined to overwhelm the local tsarist authority. Rather than firing on the masses, most soldiers joined the demonstrators, and in a few days the tsar had lost control of the effective use of coercion. But as Nicholas II abdicated, national political power was split. The Provisional Government composed of conservatives, liberals, and some agrarian reformers took control of the civil bureaucracy and national ministries. Local revolutionary councils (soviets) of workers, peasants, and soldiers sprang up, as in 1905, to challenge the legitimacy of the Provisional Government. In the following months, a power struggle developed between the more moderate Provisional Government and the revolutionary soviets. Lenin's Bolsheviks and other revolutionary groups were constantly increasing their influence. The Provisional Government made several mistakes during this period that showed it was out of touch with mass sentiment. In particular, it kept Russia in the war, although it was clear that it could not stop the German advance. It refused also to expropriate and redistribute the vast landholdings of the nobility and the Russian Orthodox church, although it was clear that peasants were already taking matters into their own hands, whether the government approved or not. By late fall, Lenin and Trotsky had finalized plans for an armed uprising to topple the Provisional Government. On October 25, 1917, armed units of Red Guards took over the major banks, telegraph offices, rail stations, and ministries and stormed the Winter Palace in Petrograd. A coalition Bolshevik-Left Socialist Revolutionary government was proclaimed, and when the Russian troops at the front signalled their support, the overthrow of the Provisional Government was complete.

The Bolsheviks had promised "Bread, Land, and Peace." In their first months in office, they expropriated the holdings of the church, the nobility, and big industrialists without compensation and legalized the redistribution of land to the peasantry. After several months of debating the war and peace issue, Lenin's government signed a peace treaty with Germany at Brest-Litovsk. Under the terms of the treaty, Russia surrendered huge chunks of former Russian territory to the Germans. The Left Socialist Revolutionaries, who favored continuing the war against Germany, unleashed a wave of terror against supporters of the treaty, assassinating several top Bolsheviks and the German ambassador and shooting Lenin in the head. The Western allies of wartime Russia used the separate peace as an excuse to invade Soviet Russia with expeditionary armies and to finance a comeback by the reactionary tsarist elements (the White armies). American forces occupied Murmansk in the North, British troops took control of the Baku oil fields, and Japanese armies marched into Siberia. Germany still controlled much of European Russia. At its low point in 1918, the Bolshevik government controlled only about one-seventh of the territory of the old Russian Empire.

Lenin had hoped that revolution in Russia would ignite revolution in Europe (especially Germany), and there were indeed uprisings in Germany and Hungary in 1918–19 in the aftermath of the defeat of the Central Powers in World War I. Revolutionary councils were set up in Berlin and Munich, many of the large factories in the Ruhr were taken over by workers, and a Soviet Republic was established for several months in Hungary. Ironically, however, but in keeping with revisionist thinking, the majority Social Democrats in Germany used the reactionary military command of the kaiser (who had fled the country) to suppress the socialist revolution, and revolutionary leaders like Rosa Luxemburg and Karl Liebknecht were assassinated by right-wing paramilitary death squads.

This policy sealed the fate of the 1918 socialist uprising in Germany and left Soviet Russia alone and encircled by hostile capitalist powers. Against these apparently long odds, the Bolsheviks won the civil war of 1918–21. Trotsky became a self-taught military genius, built the Red Army to a strength of 5 million men, and along with other Bolsheviks defeated the White armies and forced the British, Americans, and Japanese to withdraw. The White terror was more than answered by the Red terror of the Cheka (forerunner of the People's Commisariat for Internal Affairs, the NKVD). And the Bolsheviks had considerable popular support, primarily from the small but concentrated industrial working class but also from the poor peasantry. Western support of the most reactionary and anti-Semitic opponents of the Bolsheviks only increased tacit or active support for Lenin's government among Russian Jews, for example, as the lesser evil.

By early 1921, the Bolsheviks faced a situation unanticipated by Marx, Lenin, or Bernstein. A socialist revolution had succeeded in a backward underdeveloped country, a huge multiethnic collection of peoples. But the revolution had failed in Europe. Soviet Russia was alone and isolated, the target of total economic blockade by the West. On the other hand, although the Bolsheviks had indeed used terror to maintain themselves in power, the revolution had not lost its base of popular support, nor had it degenerated into military dictatorship.

What would be the future course of a socialist revolution in this predominantly peasant society? Through most of the 1920s the Bolshevik party debated this issue. The New Economic Policy (NEP) adopted in 1921 made major concessions to the more entrepreneurial peasantry (the kulaks) and to businessmen in retail trade. This was initially a program of reconstruction designed to bring the war-ruined economy back to its prewar levels of output, which it did by 1926–27. But it was becoming apparent that the NEP could be continued only by further concessions to the kulaks and that industrialization would be slowed considerably if this course were taken. Still, there was a significant faction of the party that favored doing just this in order to maintain the good will of the peasantry (including the kulaks). Another faction proposed rapid industrialization and collectivization of agriculture, with both agriculture and industry centrally managed through five-year plans. This would mean austere consumer levels for many years and forcible expropriation of kulak lands, but it was seen as a necessary economic prerequisite to building Russian socialism and defending it against a hostile foreign environment.

This industrialization debate was intensified and complicated by the death of Lenin after a series of paralyzing strokes in January of 1924. The major factions and leaders, notably Trotsky, Stalin, Zinoviev, and Kamenev, fought not only over policy alternatives but also over leadership succession. Originally Stalin had favored a continued NEP, which he labelled "Socialism in One Country." Trotsky had favored the "New Course" program of rapid industrialization. In an economic crisis that arose in 1927–28 after Stalin's faction had defeated Trotsky politically, Stalin reversed himself and adopted many of the "New Course" ideas, but in extreme form. He then put into effect, in 1928, the first Five-Year Plan for industrialization, collectivization, and urbanization at levels far more ambitious than had originally been proposed. This evoked massive resistance from the kulaks in the countryside and their bloody suppression and liquidation by the Red Army.

The rupture of the worker-peasant alliance was followed in the 1930s by Stalin's purges of other (real and imagined) opponents in the party, government, and military, and even of the secret police (NKVD) itself. Massive labor camps were set up to accommodate millions of Stalin's victims, who labored in the mines, lumber camps, and construction projects run by the NKVD camp administration (GULAG). Alexander Solzhenitsyn has eloquently described the horrors of the Stalinist forced labor system.

Yet, with all of its terrors and paranoia, Stalin's regime pushed Russia's economic development ahead at an impressive, even unprecedented, rate. The combination of "terror and progress" (Moore, 1966) did produce a decisive break with the agrarian peasant society and the Soviet Union was irreversibly on its way to becoming an industrial giant. Despite the purges, despite the economic deprivation in consumer goods and the forced savings for industrial investment, and despite the even greater human sacrifices and economic losses during World War II inflicted by Hitler's Wehrmacht, the USSR by the early 1950s had emerged as an industrialized economic and military power.

The Stalinist model in the Soviet Union that developed out of Leninism became the original model of classic communism. It was, in most respects, very far from the expectations of Marx, and it fulfilled the dire predictions of democratic socialists like Bernstein and Martov and revolutionary socialists like Luxemburg. Yet despite its many failings, it also had some significant successes, in industrialization and in military victories, that cemented the regime's hold on power and made the Leninist political formula and the Soviet model attractive for revolutionary leaders in other economically less developed and politically nondemocratic societies.

The Chinese Revolution and the Two-Line Struggle

In the Chinese Communist party, the long period of civil war struggle against Chiang Kai-shek's Nationalists before the CCP victory in 1949 was quite different from the relatively quick initial success of Lenin's Bolsheviks in 1917. In the course of the struggle, the CCP developed a special tradition of periodic self-criticism and rectification (behavior change) campaigns within the party organization, and it developed a pattern of factional argument and debate inside the party leadership. After the CCP came to power in China, this intraparty factionalism (sometimes referred to as the two-line struggle) continued, mostly between the allies of Mao Zedong and the allies of Deng Xiaoping. Mr. Deng was most interested in economic modernization to make China strong, and he was less interested in following ideological dogma if that hindered growth and industrialization. He was an economic pragmatist, who said that the "it doesn't matter if a cat is white or black, as long as it catches mice." The Maoists were by contrast more interested in upholding the egalitarian and class struggle principles of communism, even when this interfered with economic modernization. Mao, looking at the Soviet experience and the emergence in the USSR of a new *nomenklatura* ruling class, launched several campaigns to avoid the Soviet pattern and to keep revolutionary motivation high. The Great Leap Forward of the late 1950s and the Great Proletarian Cultural Revolution of the latter 1960s came at those points when Mao and his faction were in ascendance. But Mao, despite his own glorification as the Great Helmsman, did not eliminate his factional foes (as Stalin had done). Deng Xiaoping and his clique made several comebacks, notably in the early 1960s, and then again after Mao's death in 1976, and turned the CCP's attention back to making economic progress. Even through the reform period, beginning in 1978 and extending through the 1980s, observers have noted the continuing intraparty conflicts over political ideology versus economic reform, with the proponents of wide-ranging marketization and privatization winning more and more victories, interspersed with short periods of partial retreat.

The Chinese case is perhaps qualitatively different from almost all other ruling communist parties, because within the CCP genuine policy debate and factional leadership struggle over policy were intermittantly possible, with important consequences for the whole policy line of the regime. In China, too, the CCP could learn in the 1960s and 1970s from an alternative success model of economic development, namely from the East Asian authoritarian developmentalist regimes of Taiwan, South Korea, and Singapore. In the Chinese case, a ruling Communist party showed a greater learning capacity, at least for economic reform, than was possible in European or Soviet communism. Whether this greater learning capacity of the CCP will outlive Deng Xiaoping, and whether it can be eventually extended to political reform, are unanswered questions. The bloody crackdown on the democracy movement in Tienanmen Square of June 1989 has given one answer, which is that unlike the European and Soviet communist elites of 1989–91, the Chinese leadership was still quite willing to use deadly force to maintain its monopoly of political power.

Expansion and Polycentrism

Following the defeat of fascism in World War II at the hands of the war-time alliance between the Soviet Union and the Western democracies there emerged several new communist systems. Between 1945 and 1950 communist parties came to power in Poland, Romania, Bulgaria, Hungary, Yugoslavia, Albania, Czechoslovakia, East Germany, North Korea, China, and North Vietnam.

In Eastern Europe, the Soviet Army of occupation in several cases imposed a communist regime as the postwar political system. Although there is disagreement as to the internal strength of local communist movements, it is generally agreed that in Poland, Romania, and East Germany, the local communist parties came to power largely through the aid of an occupation force, the Red Army. In several places, however, local communist parties developed mass popular followings of their own and were able, after the end of World War II, either to directly assume control of the government (as in Yugoslavia and Albania) or to defeat their opponents in a more protracted revolutionary war (as in Vietnam and China). In China, Mao's People's Liberation Army defeated Chiang Kai-shek's American-supported Nationalist armies, and in North Vietnam, Ho Chi Minh's Viet Minh were able to overcome French attempts to recolonize Indochina.

A third pattern includes Czechoslovakia, Hungary, and Bulgaria. In these countries, local communist parties had widespread popular support and built impressive records of resistance to both reactionary aristocracies and fascism. Yet the presence or near-presence of the Soviet Red Army clearly assisted these parties in defeating and eliminating the local opposition to the establishment of a communist system.

After 1960, several communist systems emerged in Latin America, Asia, and Africa, making the geographical scope of communism worldwide. In the 1960s, Cuba, under the leadership of Fidel Castro, turned to the Soviet Union initially for military aid against American intervention (the CIA-sponsored Bay of Pigs invasion), then for economic aid to counteract the United States-organized economic blockade.

In the 1970s, after the failure of American intervention in Vietnam, Cambodia, and Laos, the puppet governments of those countries were overthrown by indigenous Communist movements, resulting in a reunited Vietnam and Khmer Rouge and Pathet Lao governments. In Africa, more than a decade of guerrilla warfare and the overthrow of the Salazar-Caetano dictatorship in Portugal led to the withdrawal of Portuguese colonial forces in 1974, leaving the Front for the Liberation of Mozambique (FRELIMO) to form the first independence government in Mozambique. In the wake of the Portuguese departure from Angola, divisions among three major contenders for power led to a brief civil war with considerable outside intervention by the United States, Zaire, South Africa, the Soviet Union, and Cuba. With Soviet-Cuban aid, the Marxist Popular Movement for the Liberation of Angola (MPLA) of Augostinho Neto gained control of the central government over the CIA and the Zaire-backed National Front for the Liberation of Angola (FNLA) and the South African-backed National Union for the Total Independence of Angola (UNITA) although fighting has continued to devastate that country.

The post–World War II expansion of communist systems to all continents meant several things. First and foremost, it led to the phenomenon of "polycentrism," or multiple independent centers of Communist politics and "models" of communism (see Bertsch and Ganschow, 1976).

First to challenge Soviet claims to sole leadership of the Communist movement was Tito's Yugoslav League of Communists. In 1948 Tito's regime refused to integrate Yugoslavia into the military and economic bloc being promoted by Stalin. Although originally fashioned along Soviet lines, Yugoslav communism over the years developed its own quite distinctive program, which included a private noncollective agriculture, decentralized management of industry through factory-elected worker councils, liberalized travel and trade policies, and nonalignment in foreign policy.

Next to challenge Soviet authority within the Communist world were the Chinese Communists. The Sino-Soviet split developed gradually during the 1950s, in large part out of Chinese disapproval of destalinization in the USSR, launched in 1956 by Nikita Khrushchev. To Mao this meant betrayal of world revolution (through detente with the West) and the restoration of capitalism in the Soviet Union. China's split with the USSR grew to such proportions that, at least in terms of foreign policy, Peking in the 1970s sought alliances with other governments, parties, and movements primarily on the basis of anti-Soviet orientations. Only in the latter 1980s did the Chinese leadership moderate its criticism of Moscow and show some interest in dispute resolution.

Within this Sino-Soviet split, several ruling Communist parties showed their independence by remaining neutral. Cuba, Romania, North Korea, and North Vietnam for a long time refused to take sides in the debate and tried to cultivate friendly relations with both sides. Cuban collaboration with the Soviets to aid the MPLA in Angola and the Mengistu regime in Ethiopia, however, led to Chinese denunciation of Castro and Cuban communism. China also chose to side with the Khmer Rouge in their border conflict with Vietnam, thus pushing Vietnam into clearer alliance with the USSR. And Albania, Peking's long-time ideological ally, split with China and steered its own independent and very isolated course.

Finally, from Western Europe's major communist parties came the challenge of Eurocommunism (an explicit break from Moscow's policy line), continued and extensive criticism of the Soviet system, and firm commitments to parliamentary democracy as the only path to socialism in countries like Italy, France, and Spain.

159

On the other hand, the Soviet Union protected its dominance on several occasions by intervening directly with military forces (Berlin, 1953; Hungary, 1956; Czechoslovakia, 1968) in Eastern Europe. Even in this region, however, the Soviet Union has had to accept Romania's independent course as well as the maverick Yugoslav system. The birth of the independent trade union Solidarity in Poland in 1980 was an expression of both rejection by Poland of the Soviet model and, originally, support for a "Polish model," a decentralized, democratic, and self-managing economic and political system. The emergence of Solidarity, already in 1980–81 gave proof of the growing internal challenge to existing Communist systems, especially those in Eastern Europe that were imposed from outside by the Soviet Union.

Polycentrism meant not only criticism of the Soviet system from within the Communist world and open debate over the correct model for building socialism among both ruling and nonruling Communist parties, but also, as demonstrated in the border clashes between Vietnam and Cambodia, China and the Soviet Union, and China and Vietnam, armed confrontation between Communist states. In retrospect, the expansion of communism was at the same time a process of increasing differentiation from the Soviet model and from Soviet leadership.

The Vanguard Party—Centerpiece of Communist Systems

The characteristic institution of Communist systems has been the Leninist vanguard party. The roles of the Leninist party in Communist political systems include: (1) making the revolution, (2) suppressing political opposition, and (3) modernizing economic and social structures. As predicted in Lenin's theories, the vanguard party was capable of leading a socialist revolution to victory in armed conflict.

Once in power, the vanguard party has not relinquished state power or allowed political competition but has consolidated and become the only organized political force in the society. As Lenin's critics had said, the vanguard party has opted for suppression of political dissent in the name of defending the revolution.

In most Communist systems (with the partial exception of Yugoslavia's market socialism), the vanguard party in power has served as the key for mobilizing and organizing the society for industrialization. With major productive facilities in the hands of the state, the party has directed the planning of the economy, sometimes with greater centralization, sometimes with less, but with a thoroughness and directedness that sets communist industrialization apart from that of other developing nations.

Not all Leninist parties have played all three major roles, nor have they played them in the same fashion. In Cuba, still something of an anomaly, revolution was made without a Communist party in the lead, and the Cuban

Communist party that was built only several years later has been somewhat of an unknown in the Cuban system. In Yugoslavia, the party largely abdicated its central planning of the economy in the 1950s while still suppressing dissent, though with relative mildness. In China, the approach to economic development has varied considerably, depending on whether Maoist or anti-Maoist factions in the party were in charge. And in Czechoslovakia, in 1968, the Czech Communist party abandoned press censorship and suppression of dissent before a Soviet-led invasion overthrew and dismantled the Prague Spring.

It was possible, therefore, for Leninist parties to deviate from the fulfillment of certain typical roles. Reform and restructuring programs in the People's Republic of China under the post-Mao Deng leadership and in the Soviet Union under the Gorbachev leadership indicate that the ruling Leninist parties have been capable of significant changes, including reductions, in the economic and political roles of the party, as the result of lessons learned from past experience and experimentation both at home and in other Communist systems. And yet, the ruling party has been the most identifiable feature of communist systems as diverse as those of the USSR, China, and Yugoslavia. It has remained the center of political decision-making and the arbiter of future development, even in those cases where it has chosen to abdicate certain roles.

Politics of traditional Communist systems have been centered, therefore, not in the formal offices of government, such as the prime minister and his cabinet, nor in the parliament, for these offices were subordinate to decisions made within the party. Individuals who held important government positions were not unimportant, however, for usually they are also important leaders in the party. But some of the most important political leaders, such as Leonid Brezhnev or Mao Zedong, held no government position for many years, but were responsible for top-level party organizations. Authoritative policy decisions and considerations of alternatives originated within the Politburo of the party and were sometimes referred also to the next-lower level of the Central Committee. The Secretariat, which was responsible for staffing party organizations with full-time party workers (cadre), was a particularly important focal point of political power, since power over personnel appointments to the party and state *nomenklatura*, the list of important administrative posts, implied considerable ability to manipulate policy decisions.

Politics in the Leninist vanguard party were typically closed to individuals and groups outside the party. The logic of closed decision making, of general impenetrability, was typical of classic communist politics. For purposes of leading armed revolution in backward and undemocratic systems, a closed and even clandestine political style may be a crucial advantage. Antithetic to parliamentary democracy, which invites dissent through openness, the vanguard party discouraged dissent through opaqueness of the system. And in the party's role as organizer and mobilizer for development, especially in the earliest phases of industrialization, the closed nature of decision making facilitated long-range planning requiring consumer austerity. If these choices had been publicly debated, if they had been more able to be influenced by public opinion, they would have been more difficult to make.

This closed and monopolized decision-making process within the Leninist party increasingly became a hindrance to further evolution of the system. It blocked honest and innovative criticism and feedback, from loyal socialists as well as from opponents of socialism. It led to falsification of data, avoidance of problem recognition, and severe limitations on acceptable solutions to failures in system performance. This was sometimes recognized by communist leaders and parties themselves. Mao had called for "a hundred flowers" of criticism of the regime in China in the 1950s, the Prague Spring reform communists had allowed a free press in 1968, and Mikhail Gorbachev had launched his *glasnost* or openness campaign in 1985 as the first major step toward reforming the Soviet system. For these efforts to succeed, however, would require a major restructuring of the entire political system, which would no longer be monopolized by the Leninist party, and would no longer be a (classic) Communist system.

Communism's Decline and the Meanings of Post-Communism

Communism arose in the twentieth century as a response to economic and social trauma of early capitalist modernization under nondemocratic regimes combined with the additional ravages of war. For a long time it appeared that Communist systems would be able to survive despite their obvious failings and undemocratic nature, since is was assumed that communist elites could and would use as much force as necessary to suppress any opposition. That was the assumed "totalitarian" nature of the regime. In that case, only foreign intervention or bloody armed uprisings could overthrow a totalitarian regime. But beginning in 1989 these assumptions have been turned on their head, and now the expectation is that Communist systems are temporary, that their failings lead over time to disillusionment among both citizens and significant portions of the political elite as well. Fortunately, the fall of communism in Eastern Europe in 1989–90 and the collapse of the Soviet Union in 1991 were far more peaceful than anyone could have imagined. The bloody experiences of Timisoara in Romania and Tienanmen Square in China in 1989, and the brutal civil–ethnonationalist wars in Yugoslavia after 1991 are proof that the crucial exit from communism could well have been different and could still be far less peaceful in the remaining communist systems. Nevertheless, the new expectation is that, in the foreseeable future, with greater or lesser speed and violence, Communist systems will become something other than traditional or classic Communist systems.

At what point do Communist systems become non-Communist, or at what point does post-communism begin? By our definition, the institutional centerpiece of classic communism was the ruling Leninist party. With the passage of time, the ruling party evolved from its original vanguard cadre of dedicated, ideologically committed professional revolutionaries into a bureaucratic managerial apparatus responsible for control of the economy and of virtually every sector of social life. The ruling party may have chosen to abandon certain tasks, or to allow some autonomy to other organizations. The Polish Communists made accommodations with the Catholic church, the Yugoslav Titoist regime permitted private agriculture and significant ethnic autonomy, and Deng's leadership has permitted widespread private market activity and free enterprise in China. Michail Gorbachev, under the slogans of *perestroika* and *glasnost*, ended party control over significant aspects of cultural, social, and economic life in the Soviet Union. Yet as long as the ruling party retained its political monopoly, these choices were still consistent with the traditional or classic Communist system and represented reforms and controlled evolution within the broad pattern of communism. British analyst Adam Westoby emphasized this evolutionary reform capacity of the Communist systems, which he characterized as "smart bureaucracies," capable of more change than many Western observers thought possible (Westoby, 1989, ch. 15). Westoby also noted the risks of reform communism, since reforms may awaken demands for change in the basic system, which is arguably what did happen in the Soviet Union under Gorbachev.

The boundary between system reform and system change may be blurred at times, but the key element will be the role of the Leninist party. In those systems where a Leninist party no longer retains its undemocratic hold on political power, the system is already non-Communist, and a post-Communist political transition is underway. Conversely, where the communist party retains its effective monopoly on political decision making, no matter how many economic or social reforms are introduced, the system is still recognizably a communist system. In 1994, therefore, the republics of the former Soviet Union are all post-Communist, despite the fact that in almost all republics ex-Communists and their ex-Communist party networks run the governments. In Lithuania, for example, the excommunist Democratic Party of Labor under long-time communist boss Algirdas Brasauskas was elected back into power in 1992, yet Lithuania is clearly not a Communist system any more. In Ukraine Leonid Kravchuk, an old Communist ideologue, was elected president in 1992 and governed until he was defeated in June 1994 by Leonid Kuchma, another ex-Communist. In the People's Republic of China, however, and in Vietnam, Laos, Cuba, and North Korea, Communist regimes still hold a monopoly on political power through undemocratic means.

There are some questionable cases where the boundary seems blurred. In Romania, the bloody overthrow of the communist tyrant Nicolai Ceausescu and his clan was followed by the dissolution of the old Communist party and a takeover by a National Salvation Front led by Ion Iliescu and many other former (reform-oriented) Communists. The military, which played a major role in the ouster of Ceausescu, has become a key factor in Romanian politics. Yet in two rounds of relatively free competitive elections, in 1990 and 1992, Iliescu and the National Salvation Front won a majority of seats in the parliament. The opposition parties argue that Romania is still a Communist system, that little has changed; they point to the use of mine workers to beat up students and other political protesters in Bucharest. Yet there is a lively opposition press, and opposition parties are able to operate, so that even in Romania the political system could best be described as post-Communist, even if not very democratic.

In Bulgaria, the ruling Communist party, having ousted its longtime leader Todor Zhivkov, renamed itself the Socialist party, embarked on a road of reform and democratization, and won the first free elections in June 1990, gaining a majority of seats in the parliament. In a second round of elections in 1992, the loosely organized Union of Democratic Forces (UDF) narrowly edged out the Socialists, and together with the Turkish minority party formed the first anti-Communist government. However, the UDF then began to fall apart, and the Bulgarian government in mid-1993 was replaced by a cabinet of nonparty ''experts'' supported by the Socialists and some ex-UDF deputies. Despite the continued political success of the ex-Communist Socialists in Bulgaria, however, it seems clear that here, too, the political system is in a post-Communist transition.

In Serbia, the Serbian Communist party, which reorganized itself as the Socialist party, and the ex-Communist leader Slobodan Milosevic, who had risen to popularity in Serbia on nationalist slogans, have maintained political control, while leading Serbia into a deadly war with Croatia and Bosnia and into isolation within the international community. Elections, most recently in 1992, pitted Milosevic against the Serbian-American Prime Minister Milan Panic, and Milosevic won. In the Serbian parliament, the Socialists remain the largest single party but do not have a clear majority and must govern in shifting coalitions. Opponents of Milosevic describe the Serbian regime as a communist regime. Despite what one may think of Milosevic and his policies, however, it seems more accurate to describe the political system of Serbia also as post-Communist. In Serbia, as in Bulgaria and Romania, it is unlikely that anything like classic communism could be revived, although a new nationalist authoritarianism may consolidate political power, and hopes of even imperfect democracy may be shattered.

In the first several years of post-Communist political transition, an initial phase of euphoria over the collapse of the old system has given way to much more complicated, often confusing, and conflict-laden politics. The opposition coalitions of 1989–90 in Eastern Europe were united only by anticommunism, the desire to replace the Communist government. Once that primary goal had been fulfilled, these broad coalitions immediately began to splinter into their component parts, at odds with each other over everything from policy and personnel. The early optimism that the new political systems would now become Western-style democracies, privatize their economies, and "join the West" has given way to more sober and, for some nations, pessimistic predictions. Some of the newly independent states of the former Soviet Union now seem to be headed towards a neo–Third World status. What can we say about this post-euphoria stage, which has mixed remnants of hope and excitement with new anxieties and bitterness?

It is important to keep in mind that several important advances were made in the early years of post-communism that have given democracy at least a chance in most parts of formerly Communist Europe. Most important is that, in most nations, the initial transfer of governmental power was peaceful, did not involve fighting, and did not involve the military directly in politics. Despite the attempted coup in Moscow in August 1991, the breakup of the Soviet Union was generally quite peaceful. Fighting in the Caucasus republics was not over the question of communism or the dissolution of the Soviet Union. In Hungary, the Communist party itself accelerated the transition to democracy in 1989–90; in East Germany, party leaders countermanded Erich Honecker's orders to use deadly force; in Czechoslovakia's "Velvet Revolution," the orthodox Communist party became paralyzed and largely watched events roll over it; in Poland, Solidarity negotiated a phased transfer of power with the communists. Broad "round-table" negotiations between the opposition and the communist regime kept the peace and moved the process quickly and decisively forward. Keeping the military out of politics is one achievement of the early years of transition, which so far has avoided the political dead-end of military interventionism so prevalent in other regions of the world, for example in Latin America, Africa, and parts of Asia as well. Only in Romania has the military played a key role in the post-Communist transition.

In most cases, generally free and fair elections have been held to decide on post-Communist governments. In some countries, two rounds of democratic national elections have been held. Despite much disillusionment among voters, this has begun to build up some practices of democratic election campaigning, of citizen-based interest group activity, of democratic constituency representation among legislators and government ministers. In short, at least some first steps have been taken to establish democratic traditions and practices. Nevertheless, these traditions are in many cases very weak, and already public sentiment has grown cynical about the gap between democratic rhetoric in election campaigns and the new leaders' actual behavior in office.

In those nations where the communist party had deeper roots and some remaining popular base of support, we should expect that the post-Communist

165

transition will have more elements or practices from the Communist period. As Adam Westoby has said:

> Criticism of Communist states which compares them abstractly with the West often fails to give proper weight to their different histories, including the popular experience of communism. . . . The Communist experience is not an accident or mistake from which societies can withdraw, and resume an alternative route of development. (1989:264)

This judgment applies most clearly to those systems where the Communist party made its own revolution and where it had built popular support upon a native socialist (or national populist) tradition.

Political Interpretations of Post-Communism

The new emerging politics of post-communism can be grouped into several broad interpretations, which in themselves represent images of the future political systems. One major interpretation, which was initially given much attention and media coverage in the West, is that liberal democracy is now being built on the ruins of European communism. Many leaders of the first post-Communist governments, such as Polish Prime Minister Tadeusz Mazowiecki from Solidarity and President Vaclav Havel in Czechoslovakia, expressed their wish to "join the West" by introducing the institutions and practices of Western democracy. They emphasized their nations' long-standing connections to the West, which had been interrupted during the Cold War by the division of Europe and which now would be renewed. Many educated professionals, and much of the urban middle class, see the future of their countries as a further extension or perhaps a rejoining of the "normal" development of liberalism (see chapter 2). To them, this represents the success formula for a "normal" society that has already proven itself. The word *normal* was used for the first few years of post-communism as an almost magical mantra that expressed the hope, or conviction, that Western democracies represented only good things, with no flaws worth mentioning. The problems of modern liberal democracy, such as crime, family breakup, or drugs, were often dismissed as old Communist propaganda. It may be ironic that many of the new "liberal" political leaders of Eastern Europe are aiming at a Western political success formula just at the point when this formula is breaking down in the Western democracies. Nevertheless, in the long-term struggle against communism by many liberal dissidents, the vision of Western democracy was held high as the desired alternative. This interpretation of post-communism supports a politics of liberal values, the politics of individual liberty.

A second major interpretation of post-communism, given less attention initially but now quite clearly and forcefully expressed, is that the collapse of communism has restored national independence (from Moscow, or from Belgrade, or from Prague) and has given new hope to ethnic nationalities that want to restore or expand their political sovereignty and territorial control to include all of their ethnic kin. Much of the initial resurgence of 1989–91 has been around themes of national liberation, national pride, and national intolerance. Bluntly stated, the decline of traditional communism in Europe has also released the emotions and inspirations of a kind of nationalism that flourished in the interwar period and in the previous century, and that has become obsolete in Western Europe since World War II. In the view of new nationalist leaders (some of whom are ex-Communists), tolerance and individual liberty are not the top priorities. Restoring or achieving old, sometimes centuries-old, goals of uniting all Romanians, all Hungarians, all Armenians, Serbs, or Albanians within territorial borders of the "true" homeland have top priority. Likewise, ethnic and religious minorities within the homeland are to be accorded minimal tolerance, and at best second-class citizenship. In this view, it is perfectly appropriate in Poland for Catholic doctrines to be required teaching in all schools. In ex-Soviet Georgia, one of the first acts of the elected nationalist government of President Zviad Gamsakhurdia was to eliminate the autonomy rights of the Ossetian minority. In Romania, at the end of 1990, the most popular newspaper in a newly freed press was the extremely nationalist *Vatra Romaneasca,* with a circulation of 600,000. Intolerance for the Hungarian minority and annexation of Moldova were its chief editorial issues. In Latvia and Estonia, nationalists have denied citizenship and property-owning rights to the large Russian-speaking minority, and some have openly called for expulsion of these minorities. The post-Communist ethnonationalist wars in former Yugoslavia, between Armenia and Azerbaijan, and in Tajikistan, Georgia, and Moldova have as their aim border changes, and if some borders can be changed by force, then other borders may be challenged. This interpretation of post-communism seeks to establish a national populist version of conservative politics, the politics of collective identity.

A still minor, and severely disadvantaged, interpretation of post-communism is that communism was a perversion and distortion of the humane goals of socialism, and that now there is a chance for a humane system that would combine political democracy and social justice. Many dissidents in the original Polish Solidarity, in the Czech and Slovak Charta 77, in the East German New Forum, and in the Soviet and Chinese dissident groups from the 1960s through the 1980s considered themselves Democratic Socialists. In the short term, the hopes of Jacek Kuron and Adam Michnik of Poland, Barbel Bohley in East Germany, Jiri Dienstbier in the Czech Republic, Boris Kagarlitsky and Roy Medvedev in Russia, Mihailo Mihailov in Yugoslavia, and Fang Lizhi in China have been bypassed by events, although these dissidents are still respected for their early and risky opposition to communism. The ideals of socialism have been blackened by their association with communism. Yet in many of these nations, socialism has deep roots that are beginning to reappear in support of new Democratic Socialist parties. The working class, its "official" trade unions discredited and facing economic disaster in many industries, has largely been a reactive rather than proactive force in post-communism. If the new liberal or nationalist regimes prove themselves to be not only anti-Communist but also antiworker, the politics of social justice may revive as a major contender in post-communism. In some parts of Eastern Europe, the pain of economic dislocation and nostalgia for the comfortable stability of the past have already given new socialist parties a short-term lift, returning ex-Communists to power in free elections in Lithuania in 1992, in Poland in 1993, and in Hungary in 1994. For the most part, however, these new socialist coalitions have not had time to develop a viable new vision for the future of their nations, and they are now stuck with managing the severe problems of economic transition.

Political Institutions of Post-Communism

With the demise of the ruling Leninist party, there has followed an institutional vacuum in post-communism. In the struggle for a post-Communist system, a competition between the elected parliament and the top executive post has developed in many nations. Freely elected and effective parliaments are the historic centerpiece of Western democracies. Yet, in many cases, the first elections to a free parliament resulted in a severely divided parliament, with no party able to put together a clear majority. In the Polish Sejm, after the 1991 elections, there were over twenty parties represented, none with over 12 percent of the vote. In other cases, parliaments have become bogged down, as can happen when conflicting constituent interests are freely expressed over plans for privatization, marketization, and reform of schools, health care, justice, and welfare programs. Nevertheless, the continued development of parliament as a key institution in post-communism is crucial for the viability of the liberal democratic interpretation of post-communism. Soviet analyst Alexander Mishkin (1990) described the evolution of the first competitively elected Congress of Peoples Deputies in 1989–90 as the key to the democratization process in the Soviet Union. A functioning parliamentary democracy, in this view, promotes tolerance and liberty, and gives some opportunity for both democratic socialism and moderate nationalism.

However, the pain of post-Communist transformation of the economy and society has also produced some popular support for a stronger and more decisive leadership than any parliament can provide. In many countries, there is a call for a strong, authoritarian leader who can get things done quickly and decisively, even if that means pushing democratic procedures aside. In Russia, following the breakup of the USSR, institutional feuding escalated between the elected president, Boris Yeltsin, and the elected Russian parliament, the

Supreme Soviet, with President Yeltsin relying more and more on decrees, and parliament becoming more obstructionist, until the bloody showdown of October 1993, when Yeltsin's soldiers burned out the barricaded parliament building, the Russian White House. Often, the feud was portrayed as a conflict between the reformer Yeltsin and the antireformist parliament. If the newly elected parliament and president fail to develop some working relationship, however, an authoritarian solution may be the outcome. If parliaments are overthrown or made into political puppets, whether by nationalist, ex-Communist, militarist, or reformist leaders, then no matter what economic transformations are undertaken, liberal democracy once again will be undermined. In that case, some new type of authoritarian strongman politics will be a dominant meaning of post-communism, at least for the current period.

8

Two Historic Transitions in Economic Development

The economies of nearly all the Communist and post-Communist societies are undergoing their second historic transition in this century in the search for a modern and prosperous economic model. In the first transition during the formative years of Communist rulership, these nations abandoned capitalist market economies and put in place a party-directed and state-managed system that controlled nearly all of the means of production. Now, in the second major restructuring, these systems, including both post-Communist Eastern Europe and the new nations of the former Soviet Union as well as the still-Communist People's Republic of China and Vietnam, are restoring some form of a capitalist market economy through various processes of marketization and privatization. Only the isolated Cuban and North Korean Communist regimes have, as of mid-1994, resisted this trend.

The first model of a Communist command economy was launched by the Soviet Union with its Five-Year Plan of 1928–32. Virtually the entire economy was state owned and state controlled. In that model, the Soviet central planning agency (GOSPLAN) set output quotas for factories, state and collective farms, and other state enterprises. Except for small "garden plots" left to collective farm families, all the productive means of the economy were subordinated to GOSPLAN, which set prices and wages, allocated basic investment, supplies, and personnel, and determined the rules for meeting production goals. In later Communist systems, the Soviet model was modified, and China and Yugoslavia in particular developed their own variants of Communist economies. There was also, after the death of Stalin in 1953, some limited reform of the original Soviet model, which however did not abandon its most basic features.

Currently, a second transition to some form of market economy is underway in almost all of these systems. The People's Republic of China was the first, in late 1978, to break with the basic principles of the command economy, as Deng Xiaoping introduced his "responsibility system" of reforms. The Chinese system gradually increased the scope of its reform program, so that by the early 1990s China's economy was primarily market-driven and commercialized, with few remnants of the old system. Vietnam's leaders, beginning in the latter 1980s, also decided to take a market reform path. In Eastern Europe and the states of the former Soviet Union, the collapse of the communist political regimes from 1989 to 1991 broke the barriers to a basic economic restructuring along capitalist market lines. Some nations, like Poland and the Czech Republic, opted for quick transitions, involving orthodox free market "shock therapy" in the Polish case and an innovative "coupon" privatization scheme in the Czech strategy. Hungary, which had experienced some limited marketization under the communist Kadar regime starting in 1968, has preferred a slower pace of reform and adjustment. In Russia, starting in January 1992, Yeltsin and his chief economist Yegor Gaidar imposed a price "shock therapy" to launch the structural reform of the economy, and privatization gained momentum the following year. In other states, such as Ukraine and Belarus, and in several of the Central Asian republics, reform has barely begun and the old structures of the command economy have continued to disintegrate. Nevertheless, with each passing year, it becomes less likely that the old system could be restored, even if the Communists or their successors were to return to power. In one way or another, some type of market economy is being developed, although it is likely that the process will be much longer than initially envisioned and will involve considerable political struggle along the way. (Only the former East German economy has good prospects for a quick restructuring, since it is being supported by massive transfers from western Germany of about $60 billion to $70 billion per year. Even in eastern Germany, with only 16 million people, the economic restructuring has been more painful and difficult than the early optimistic pronouncements of the Kohl government. How much more difficult and uncertain must be the reform process, therefore, in Russia with over 150 million people and much less aid, or Ukraine with over 50 million citizens?) In an entirely different category are those post-Communist nations like Croatia, Bosnia, Armenia, Azerbaijan, and Georgia, where interethnic warfare has ruined the prospects for the development of productive investment, trade, and business, and has instead inflicted the most cruel hardships on the people. Until these wars of the new nationalism, and in the case of Georgia, civil war as well, are settled, economic progress will remain a dream.

This chapter describes both the economic performance of the Communist centrally planned economies and the transitional economies of the current period. Data for many of the post-Communist economies are sketchy and quite subject to debate. This is inevitable in such a volatile period of change.

But these statistics are offered with some caution as the best estimates now available on the nature and effects of the coexisting processes of disintegration, marketization, and privatization in the early post-Communist period.

From the Soviet Model to Russian Market Reform

The first great task of the Soviet central planning system set by the party was to mobilize both human and natural resources for rapid industrialization of the economy. In this process, maximum investment was channeled into heavy industry (steel, iron, coal, electric power, machine-building, and defense industries) while investment in agriculture, consumer goods production (light industry), and housing construction were deliberately held down. Generally, a collectivized agriculture was used as a control mechanism to ensure sufficient foodstuffs at low state-set prices for the growing urban industrial work force.

This type of growth model has been termed *extensive growth*, relying on mobilization of previously underutilized labor and material resources. The central planning system paid much less attention to efficiency and technological innovation, and gave top priority to increasing bulk output, especially in key heavy industry sectors. The Soviet mobilization system was similar in some features to a wartime mobilization, in which the state takes over command of key resources and directs them to fulfilling not individual consumer demands but rather the overriding goals of victory for the nation as a whole. (The Germans utilized such a mobilization system in their "total war" effort in 1916–18 during World War I, and Trotsky and other Bolsheviks adopted some features of this for the Soviet command system.) This command system, however, was practiced not as an emergency wartime measure, but as a regular and continuing feature of the Soviet economy.

Until the death of Stalin in 1953, the Soviet and other East European economies were heavily committed to this extensive development phase of growth through mobilization of previously unemployed and underemployed resources. Canadian economist Alan Abouchar (1979:40–42) calculated that Soviet long-term growth rates (increase of gross national product per capita per year) averaged 4.7 percent over the period 1928–1975, even including the tremendous destruction of World War II. This growth record surpassed the long-term growth rate of all the major capitalist economies, including the United States (1.6 percent 1839 to 1962), Germany (1.7 percent 1871 to 1962), and Japan (2.2 percent 1879 to 1962). Even over the shorter period from 1950 to 1962 when Western capitalist economies were enjoying a postwar recovery from the Great Depression, Soviet per capita growth rates averaged 5.3 percent per year, compared with 3.3 percent for the United States, 2.3 percent for Great Britain, 4.9 percent for France, and 7.3 percent for West Germany, among the major Western systems.

American economist Robert Campbell, writing in the era of Soviet space successes (Sputnik) and rapid industrial expansion over three decades, considered the prospect that the Soviet GNP might overtake United States GNP. Despite inefficiencies and blatant examples of mismanagement, Campbell concluded: "In their concentration on industrialization as the major objective, Soviet planners have neglected other sectors and the relatively low rates of growth of these sectors temper the differential between the two countries in overall growth. Nevertheless, the Soviet gross national product has grown faster than ours in the past, and even if it slows down somewhat in the future, there will probably remain some differential in favor of the Russians" (1960: 195). In short, in the first postwar decades it was not clear that the Soviet model was doomed to failure, and, in fact, it had lifted the Soviet Union into the category of a major industrial power.

In Poland, Hungary, Bulgaria, and Romania, which were largely agrarian peasant societies before World War II, the Soviet model achieved a decisive industrial breakthrough. East Germany and Czechoslovakia were in the main already industrialized before the war, and the Soviet model brought additional industrialization, even overindustrialization. This process of extensive industrial growth depended on ever greater supplies of labor, materials, and energy, and was extraordinarily wasteful. In 1970, the developed Western democracies used 3.66 barrels of oil equivalents (boe's) for each $1,000 of GNP produced, whereas the industrial communist economies (of Eastern Europe and the USSR) required 10.02 boe's (United Nations, 1990:122). After the oil price shocks of the 1970s, the West was able by 1986 to reduce its energy inputs to 2.67 boe's per $1,000 of GNP, while the industrial communist nations remained at a much higher level (8.32 boe's), though they also reduced their energy inputs somewhat. In the 1980s, Soviet oil production peaked, new labor force entrants declined, and the environmental costs of industrial gigantomania were revealed; the old extensive growth model had reached its limits.

After Stalin's death Communist leaders paid increasing attention to expanded consumer production, welfare spending, improved housing, and more plentiful foodstuffs (especially meat). Khrushchev's economic program, a part of his "destalinization" effort, was an early but limited move in this direction in the 1950s and early 1960s. A set of reforms, most often associated with Soviet economist E. G. Liberman, were proposed to partially decentralize economic planning and to introduce some elements of marketing discipline and profit mechanisms at the enterprise level. These modest reforms were opposed, however, by party and state "conservatives" on grounds of both ideological and institutional self-interest and were introduced only in a diluted form, mainly in the textile sector. Premier Alexei Kosygin, in the latter 1960s and 1970s, tried to push similar reforms, but again without much success. The transition from a set of institutions and mechanisms aimed at *extensive* industrial growth to a system aimed at *intensive* consumer-oriented growth was inherently difficult for the Soviet system and for the East European nations and had not gotten very far up to the latter 1980s.

Attempts by East European systems to advance too far beyond the current Soviet model, as was the case in Czechoslovakia in 1968, and again in Poland in 1980–81, were vigorously opposed by Moscow conservatives, and the Czech liberal reforms were canceled after the Soviet-led invasion. In Hungary, however, where a New Economic Mechanism (NEM) was gradually and cautiously introduced over a long period under the leadership of Janos Kadar, market- and consumer-oriented reforms did go beyond the Soviet model, but with strict limitations for experimentation. Under the Gorbachev leadership after 1985, a new economic restructuring effort (*perestroika*) was launched to introduce greater incentives for "intensification" of production methods and greater reliance on market-type mechanisms. In 1987, small private businesses were permitted to organize, mainly in the service sector. An individual contracting system with collective farmers, begun several years earlier, has been expanded. A new law covering about 60 percent of all enterprises and giving more autonomy and responsibility for self-financing went into effect in January of 1988. These measures did produce a growing cooperative (private) sector with better consumer goods and services at much higher prices. And these reforms gradually undermined discipline of the old centrally planned economy. But there was also widespread popular and hard-line elite resistance against more far-reaching reforms to privatize the economy and to free prices and wages. By 1990, the early economic reforms of the original Gorbachev team were failing, food and other consumer goods were being increasingly diverted to the informal (free) markets, industrial production was falling, and a price-wage inflation spiral was accelerating. In the summer/fall of 1990, a "500 Day Plan" fashioned by more radical advisors around Stanislav Shatalin was developed, but resistance from Premier Ryzhkov and waffling by Gorbachev led to a policy stalemate. Although the Soviet economy muddled through the winter, by the middle of 1991 industrial production was falling rapidly, inflation was out of control, and there was virtually no central economic authority left in various republics and localities.

After the failed military coup by antireformists in August 1991 and the breakup of the Soviet Union into independent states, most of which were loosely associated in the Commonwealth of Independent States (CIS), the Russian government under President Boris Yeltsin, a hero of resistance to the August coup, launched an economic reform program engineered by a radical reform team headed by Yegor Gaidar. The first stage was freeing prices from government controls, which set off a wave of massive inflation, destroying most people's savings and the value of pensions for retired people. Privatization of large-scale industry did not follow immediately, but small businesses developed quickly, although they were often tied to protection schemes of various ethnic "mafia" groups. (The word *mafia* is used generically in Russia to denote organized crime and does not imply connections to the Italian mafia.) Collective agriculture was abolished, but settlement of the question of private ownership of land was delayed. Production in industry declined sharply as supply and distribution networks were disrupted, both by the breakup of the Soviet Union and by the price shock therapy. According to the London *Economist* estimates, industrial production dropped by 8 percent in 1991 and by nearly 19 percent in 1992; new fixed investment fell by 15 percent in 1991 and by a whopping 45 percent in 1992 (Economist Intelligence Unit, 1993). On the other hand, production seemed to have leveled off at about 70 percent of 1989 levels by late 1992, and in early 1993, there were some small signs of recovery in selected areas. Production of television sets, refrigerators, and washing machines rose modestly, whereas production of textiles, shoes, video recorders, and bikes continued to plummet. Because large-scale obsolete industry was still heavily subsidized by the government (under pressure by the parliament and the central bank in 1992–93), unemployment was still officially low (only 1 percent). But hidden unemployment, from unpaid leave, short-time work, and production stoppages, was estimated in the neighborhood of 12 million people. If large firms were forced to declare bankruptcy and close, unemployment would soar to 15 percent. The political conflict between President Yeltsin's government and the Russian parliament over the pace of reform and over the control of the privatization process led to Yeltsin's closing down of the parliament in September 1993, followed by an armed uprising of parliament militants in early October, which was quickly and bloodily suppressed by military units loyal to Yeltsin.

Although economic reform has produced significant change in the availability of goods in stores, and small-scale enterprise has grown rapidly, most people have lost ground so far, and a great deal of the new "bisnez" is closely connected to corruption and organized crime. There is a new class of wealthy Russian entrepreneurs, and new upscale German and French shops have moved into the once-dowdy GUM complex off Red Square in Moscow. Russia had a positive trade balance in the first half of 1993, exporting $9 billion more than it imported, but with the economic situation so volatile, much of the new wealth was transferred abroad (capital flight) to safe accounts in the West, and therefore was not productively invested in Russia.

In the first two years of Russian post-Communist transformation of the economy, more destruction than rebuilding has taken place, as overall production has fallen dramatically. Although President Yeltsin has often stated that the worst is now over and that economic rebirth will arrive soon, most citizens in Russia have grown cynical about all politicians in this new post-Communist era. On the other hand, this cynicism has so far been tied to a new political passivity rather than support for any antireform parties or personalities. For better or worse, Russians are focusing their attention on getting through this difficult and unsettling period and are less interested in the ideological framework of a new economic order.

Market Socialism in Yugoslavia

Experimentation with different variants of a socialist economy came from those Communist systems which arose from independently made revolutions, namely Yugoslavia and China. Initially, however, both of these nations were committed to the Soviet economic model, and in the first years after their revolutions, both Yugoslavia and China began relatively orthodox Soviet-style industrialization programs.

Tito's break with Stalin in 1948 did not immediately signal the emergence of the new Yugoslav model of "market socialism." But, beginning in the early 1950s, the Yugoslav League of Communists moved to implement, with some setbacks along the way, many of the market and profit-oriented reforms that have been blocked for so long in the Soviet Union. Yugoslav central planning was greatly weakened, agriculture remained in private hands, though redistributed from prewar ownership, and the prices of most goods and services were freed from both control and subsidy. The Yugoslav model developed its own unique emphasis on the role of workers' councils, which were directly elected at all larger enterprises and which were given increasing responsibility for overseeing the operations of individual factories with workers sharing in the enterprise's profits or losses. This process of developing a self-managing society was also extended to elected community social councils.

The Yugoslav leadership opened the economy to extensive trade with the West, permitted free emigration for its citizens, and allowed a good deal of small-scale free enterprise, particularly in tourist and service sectors. In larger self-managed factories, profit-making rather than quota-meeting governed the success or failure of the enterprise.

The Yugoslav economy, since the inception of "market socialism," was notable for its development of Western-style consumerism, especially among the more prosperous social groups and the more economically advanced regions (Slovenia and Croatia). Yugoslav manufacturers were also more competitive with Western quality standards, as they had to be to provide exports to the West, which enabled Yugoslavia to import Western consumer goods, pay for Western technology, and attract Western investment. A basic feature of the Yugoslav economic model was its partial integration into the international capitalist market, as opposed to the much greater "delinking" from the West experienced by the Soviet economy and other East European economies during the postwar period.

Yugoslav "market socialism" provided for: (1) greater worker participation in a decentralized economy; (2) greater availability of Western-style consumer goods; (3) greater room for private initiative and small business and agriculture;

and (4) more flexible market-oriented price and wage systems. The costs of these reforms are also fairly clear and are seen by most observers as inherent features of the Yugoslav experiment: (1) the return of mass unemployment, 10 to 15 percent generally; (2) chronic inflation tied to the inflationary environment of Western economies; and (3) a growing foreign debt burden related to the need for importing Western goods and technologies. (Poland experienced some of these same costs in the 1970s under the Western-financed industrial program of Edward Gierek, but without the benefit of internal Polish reforms that would have at least constituted a coherent system.)

One of the effects of Yugoslav decentralization was to revive nationalist rivalry in the six republics and two autonomous regions that made up the Yugoslav federation. In the north, Slovenia and Croatia did quite well economically, while Serbia, Bosnia, Montenegro, Macedonia, and the region of Kosovo were much poorer. Each republic gave priority to its own interests, and increasingly the Yugoslavian federal government became unable to manage the separatist ethnic forces that divergent levels of development only exacerbated. When free elections were held in 1990–91 in the various republics, the new nationalist leaders of the more well-to-do and Catholic republics of Slovenia and Croatia announced their intentions to "join the West" by seceding from the poorer republics, which set in motion the escalation of ethnic violence and armed conflict that engulfed much of Yugoslavia by the fall of 1991.

The fierce ethnic warfare that engulfed Bosnia-Herzegovina and much of Croatia, combined with the United Nations economic embargo applied to Serbia and Montenegro, has ruined the economy of Bosnia, crippled Serbia and Montenegro, and severely impacted Croatia. Only relatively prosperous Slovenia, ethnically homogeneous and well placed to trade with Italy and Austria, has come out of the breakup of Yugoslavia as an economic "winner." In the midst of civil war, which may yet spread to other areas of former Yugoslavia, new investment has dried up, production in many industries has ground to a halt, and the economics of looting and smuggling have taken root. Criminal gangs now control much goods traffic in the former Yugoslavia (excepting Slovenia), and brute force exacts its price from remaining economic activity.

The Yugoslav case, in the era of post-communism, illustrates another possible variant of transition, namely, from an inefficient economy that nevertheless provided relatively secure basics of life to a situation of violent conflict that ruins any prospects for successful economic development. The Yugoslav scenario is in this regard relevant to the circumstances in Armenia, Azerbaijan, Georgia, and partially to Moldova and the North Caucasus in Russia, where interethnic warfare and bandit violence have for the time being reduced the chances for economic rebirth to zero. Until ethnic warfare and civil violence are brought under control, the destroyed old economic order will be replaced primarily with the crude economics of plunder and extortion.

177

In these regions, post-communism has revealed its most negative potential and a prolonged period of disorder and despair.

The Chinese Transformation

Chinese communist development also began with an imitation of the Soviet model. Only in 1957, after Mao Zedong's split with the Khrushchev regime, did the Maoist faction of the Chinese leadership launch its Great Leap Forward, which marked several significant economic departures from Soviet practice. Mao, however, was opposed in his radical economic experiments by a strong "bureaucratic-technocratic" or "pragmatic" faction of the party, and Chinese economic development has experienced several shifts in direction, depending on which faction in the "two-line struggle" was dominant at the time. From 1949 to 1957, Chinese development followed a relatively orthodox Soviet model, with significant contributions of Soviet aid. This phase was followed by the radical Maoist development of huge peasant communes as the focal point for a rural-based strategy of both self-sufficiency and intermediate technology-industry. In contrast to the centralized, urban-based, heavy industry orientation of Soviet plans, Mao's model was decentralized to the peasant communes of about 20,000 people. These communes were elevated to an active, leading position in the Chinese economic plan of development, whereas the Soviet Union's collective and state farms had been passive, subdued elements in the Soviet industrialization drive.

After three years ("three lost years," according to Mao's opponents), and the failure of several aspects of the Great Leap Forward, the "pragmatic" faction associated with Liu Shaoqi and Deng Xiaoping regained control and reduced considerably the scope of the Maoist experiments. For the next several years, expertise, growth rates, and managerial efficiency were raised in priority. On the other hand, however, the Soviet economy, which had been denounced by Mao was no longer seen as an appropriate model to emulate. During this period, it appeared that Mao was gradually being eased into political retirement.

Then, in 1966, Mao began a political comeback with the aid of a mass campaign led by self-organized Red Guards and directed against bureaucratic and technocratic elites in government, economic management, universities, and even the party itself. At the cost of considerable economic and educational disruption, the Great Proletarian Cultural Revolution forced the leaders of the anti-Maoist faction from office and placed priority on correct "politics" (equality, anti-elitism, shaping a new culture) over practical economics (high growth rates, production efficiency, deference to expertise). The mass campaign of the Red Guards lasted for nearly three years, but the dominance of the radical party faction continued until Mao's death in 1976.

Immediately after Mao's death, a power struggle ensued, in which the so-called Gang of Four, including Mao's widow Jiang Qing, were defeated by a resurgent Deng Xiaoping and his associates. After 1976, this "pragmatic" faction reversed the policies of the Cultural Revolution and put forward a program of "four modernizations" (in agriculture, industry, national defense, and science and technology), which ambitiously aimed at making China a modern industrial power by the year 2000. Respect for higher education and formal training, hierarchy in management, priority to growth rates, and individual incentives, in short "economics in command," have been elevated to top importance, and Mao's economic ideas have been discarded.

Under Deng's leadership, the rural communes were broken up into small family farms, unleashing a burst of agricultural growth into the mid-1980s. This created a first historic success for the reform leadership, which then has expanded its project of marketization and, for all practical purposes, privatization. In a second phase in 1984, urban industry was forced to adapt to commercial market behavior, and urban private and cooperative enterprise were encouraged to develop. Internationally, China, which had isolated itself from the world trading system under Mao, re-entered the global marketplace to become a major exporter of textiles, household manufactures, and an increasingly complex array of goods. The reform Chinese leadership encouraged foreign capital, from Europe and the United States and Japan, to invest in Chinese joint ventures, under quite favorable terms. Investment by overseas Chinese was also permitted and has increased the economic ties to both Hong Kong (which will return to Chinese sovereignty in 1997) and to Taiwan (Republic of China). By the early 1990s China had become a dynamic major world trading nation, with a 1992 trade surplus of $10 billion with the United States and nearly $4 billion with Germany (*The Week in Germany*, Oct. 29, 1993).

The post-Mao leadership, since the introduction of the new "responsibility system" in December of 1978, has reported strong gains in both industrial and agricultural production. Western observers (see Hinton, 1983; Schell, 1984) have noted the rapid growth of small private businesses (restaurants, small hotels, services, transport) in the cities and the dismantling of commune agriculture in favor of family-centered, privatized, and mostly small-scale farming in the countryside. Under the new responsibility system, enterprising individuals and families have enjoyed considerable incomes unthinkable during Mao's time and have been able to purchase a wider array of consumer goods, which are also much more in evidence as a part of Chinese society. For those families with higher incomes, an affluent and even stylish standard of living has become a possibility. Chinese cities and villages now bustle with small- and middle-sized individual and family businesses, markets are better stocked with food, clothing, and consumer goods for sale at market prices, and China's enterprises, both state and private, have become much more tied into the world trading system. China, in relative terms, has gone through a mass consumer binge in the 1980s and 1990s that is unprecedented and that

179

contrasts sharply with the austerity, collectively organized production, and controlled equality of the Maoist period.

After several years of the "four modernizations" program, some difficulties have begun to emerge. The gains in production and the decentralization of economic decision-making have not produced enough jobs for China's growing population, and chronic unemployment has re-emerged as a social ill, especially among urban youth. Further, as Hinton (1983) has emphasized, the new pattern of small family farming has begun to show the classic side effects of overcultivation of small plots and overgrazing of pasture land. Pressure for short-term productivity on the land has neglected maintenance and improvement of agricultural infrastructure (dams, roads, irrigation systems, conservation programs). Despite some "readjustments" in the early 1980s, including cutbacks on purchases of Western technology projects, the party leadership remains committed to the basic outlines of the "four modernizations" programs.

According to World Bank estimates, China's economy, which had grown at a pace of 6.4 percent per year between 1965 and 1980, accelerated in the 1980s under the new "responsibility system" to an annual growth of 10.3 percent between 1980 and 1988 (World Bank, 1990:180). In the area of economic reform, the Deng four modernizations policies have had remarkable results, although they have not been tied to far-reaching political liberalization. Some Chinese and Western intellectuals have argued that this economic liberalization cannot continue without a basic political reform, but the June 1989 repression of the democracy movement in China has at least for the short term put an end to the modest political liberalization of the 1980s.

After the Tienanmen crackdown, some observers thought that the more ideological "conservatives" would regain political dominance and reverse the economic reform trend, but this did not happen. Instead, after a short period of retrenchment, Deng launched a new round of reforms, based on visits to the most dynamic southern provinces across the channel from Hong Kong, which have produced a new and volatile burst of growth in the early 1990s. Deng is committed to retaining the party's hold on power (he has said) for the sake of political stability. Yet the dynamism unleashed by his economic reforms is rapidly transforming China's economy into a far more diversified and complex mechanism, well imbedded in the world trading and financial system. This growth process has suffered from periodic bottlenecks (for example, in energy production needed for growth) and from episodes of speculation and inflation, but overall it has been so successful that there seems little chance of reversion to Maoist ideology. The Chinese Communist party has shown a great ability to learn from its past mistakes, and is guiding China toward a modern market system while still retaining a recognizably communist political regime. In this respect China's economic success has more in common with that of several other East Asian newly industrialized countries (NICs) such as Taiwan, South Korea, Singapore, and Hong Kong, which also successfully modernized their economies under authoritarian regimes (cf. chapter 13). Communist Vietnam is also pursuing its version of China's modernization strategy, with good initial results. If China should follow their example, then at some point authoritarian rule should give way to some form of democratization.

Diversity in Standards of Living

The Communist/post-Communist nations have been a diverse group in terms of their levels of economic development, and this has been reflected in the diverse levels of material well-being for the populace. In terms of GNP/capita, the East European nations such as Czechoslovakia and the former German Democratic Republic were fairly well-to-do nations on a global scale, while China, Vietnam, and North Korea were among the poor nations of the world.

In the 1980s, with the apparent stagnation and then decline of most Soviet-style economies, a wide-ranging academic and political debate about the estimates of standards of living, expressed in GNP per person, led to quite divergent figures. In the early post-Communist years of massive economic dislocation, rampant inflation, and expansion of the hidden (or second) economy, estimates also differ widely among sources, whereas national aggregate statistics, are likely to be misleading to some degree (see Rose, 1993). The figures for GNP per capita given in table 8.1 are only broad estimates, and reflect only gross levels of material standards of living.

Table 8.1   Indicators of Material Standards in Communist and
                   Post-Communist Nations

	USSR	Czecho-slovakia	Hungary	Yugo-slavia	Cuba	China	Vietnam
GNP/capita (1990)	3,430[a]	3,190	2,780	2,920[b]	2,000[b]	370	220[b]
Purchasing power parity (1990)	7,968[a]	7,300[e]	6,116	5,095[b]	2,200[e]	1,990	1,100[e]
TVs/1,000 (1990)	323[c]	412	410	197[c]	207	31	39
Radios/1,000 (1990)	685[c]	587	595	245[c]	345	184	108
Autos/1,000 (1985–89)	45[d]	200	169	131[c]	22	2	—

Source: UNDP, *Human Development Report*, 1991, 1992, 1993.
a. Russia
b. 1989
c. 1988–89
d. 1986–88
e. estimate
Note: Official Government data received by the responsible U.N. system agencies or other international organizations have been used wherever possible. The data in human development indicators, derived from many sources, inevitably covers a wide range of data reliability.

Since Khrushchev's first destalinization reforms of the late 1950s, the Soviet economy gradually paid more attention to producing consumer durables for its citizens. Khrushchev himself opposed production of private passenger cars, hoping to develop state rental-car agencies and avoid Western automobilization, but under Brezhnev and with the help of the Italian automaker Fiat, the Soviet (and other East European) industry began to turn out considerable numbers of Fiat-type Ladas. By the late 1980s, Soviet families had a widening array of consumer durables in their homes. Of all Soviet families, 99 percent had televisions, 92 percent had refrigerators, 40 percent had tape recorders, 70 percent had washing machines, 40 percent had vacuum cleaners, 65 percent had sewing machines, 14 percent had motorcycles, and 16 percent had an automobile (von Beyme, 1989: 199). While the percent of families with a car was low by comparison with most Western democracies, it had climbed from a mere 2 percent in 1970. Similarly, the percentages for the other consumer goods rose two- or three-fold during this period. Though the quality left much to be desired by international standards, the Soviet economy and other East European economies were evolving toward consumer-oriented production.

Noticeably lower on the scale of affluence was the Yugoslav economy, which was at a semi-industrialized or intermediate level. At the same time it was above the levels (per capita) of affluence reached by the Chinese system. Despite the undoubted growth in production in China since 1949, the Chinese economy was still concerned with producing the basic necessities for decent health, clothing, nutrition, and housing. Any diversion of human or material-technical resources to luxury goods production was firmly resisted by Mao, and much Chinese criticism of the East European and Soviet economies was aimed at their emulation of Western-style consumerism. Under the post-Mao leadership of Deng, however, consumerism has been encouraged, indicating a desire to move China's economy beyond the level of subsistence production.

Under the "four modernizations" reforms, Chinese citizens have been encouraged to "get rich," and Chinese markets both in the cities and in rural areas now provide an impressive array of consumer luxuries (stereos, video recorders, electronics) for those with money to buy them. In the countryside, wealthier peasants have gone on a binge of house-building, while public investments in schools and irrigation have been cut back.

The Communist development project made considerable progress in changing rural peasant societies into urban industrial complexes. The Soviet model's overconcentration on heavy industry was reflected in the proportion of the economy devoted to industry, as opposed to services (see table 8.2). Whereas the liberal democracies of the West have been gradually moving away from the old "smokestack industry" economies, the industrial Communist economies continued to neglect the service and consumer sector of development.

Overall, the first years of marketization and privatization under post-

Table 8.2   Sectoral Composition of Communist Economies (Percent)

Sector[a]	USSR[b]		Eastern Europe		China		For comparison: Developed market economies	
	1960	1987	1960	1987	1960	1987	1960	1987
Agriculture	21	20	23	12	38	34	6	3
Industry	52	46	55	61	42	46	30	23
Service	17	23	14	18	19	20	52	63

Source: United Nations, *Global Outlook 2000* (1990).
a. Other activities not included are mining, utilities, construction.
b. Years for USSR are 1970 and 1985.

communism, combined with the effects of political disarray and collapse of previously stable supply and distribution arrangements, have thrown the economies into sharp recession. The Economic Commission for Europe (Economist Intelligence Unit, 1993) estimates that industrial production fell by about 8 percent in Russia in 1991 and by a further 19 percent in 1992. Agricultural production also fell, but by lesser margins, about 4 and 8 percent for the same two years. In East Europe, Czechoslovak industry fell by nearly 25 percent in just 1991, followed by an additional 11 percent in 1992. At the same time, the freeing of prices from state control produced rapid inflation in prices of almost all consumer goods. In Russia (the worst case), inflation accelerated from only 6 percent in 1990 to about 2,500 percent in 1992 and continued in 1993 at very high levels. This led to an increasing reliance on Western hard currencies for transactions (U.S. dollars and German deutschmarks) in many restaurants, hotels, and small businesses. In Eastern Europe, the Czechoslovak (now Czech Republic and Slovakia) post-Communist regime was able to contain inflation to a peak of 60 percent in 1991 and reduce it to less than 10 percent by 1993. In Poland, heavy inflation began even before the first Solidarity government took office (59 percent in 1988), climbed to nearly 600 percent by 1990, and then was brought down to 60 percent in 1991. Hungary, which had been undergoing gradual marketization since 1968, and which continued a gradualist approach under the conservative MDF government of Josef Antall, was able to contain inflation to less than 35 percent at its peak.

In general, the transition to a market economy has been harder for the states of the former Soviet Union than for some of the East European post-Communist nations, perhaps because central planning had lasted for over sixty years in the USSR, whereas Eastern Europe had longer experience with market capitalism and less time under Communist central planning. The *Economist* (1993), which has produced some of the best efforts in tracking the progress of this transition, estimates that in Russia, gross domestic product

183

(GDP) per person fell from $5,516 to $4,325 in purchasing power parity from 1990 to 1992, or nearly 22 percent. For some other new states of the former USSR, the record was even worse: a drop of 31 percent in Estonia, 29 percent in Latvia, 33 percent in Lithuania, and in the war-torn and economically isolated Armenia and Georgia, a drop of about 50 percent.

While these shocks are severe and catastrophic in areas where ethnic warfare or civil war have broken out, there are also some signs of progress in the marketization and privatization process. In Prague and Budapest, commercial development is now quite advanced, currencies are stable, and the growth of new businesses has transformed the appearance and routines of these relatively prosperous cities. In Moscow and Riga (Latvia), the pace of big city life is now quicker, shops are more colorful, busy, and full of consumer goods, but many of these goods are from the West and few from domestic production. In smaller towns and rural areas, changes have been slower to arrive, and more of the old style still is evident. In some older industrial centers, one-industry cities where large factories have closed or radically reduced production and personnel, change has so far been equivalent to collapse and despair. Although there were predictions in 1992 and 1993 of imminent turnarounds and renewed growth, so far the light at the end of the tunnel has not yet appeared.

Heavy Investment in Education

One feature of the Communist systems (with the partial exception of China) was a heavy emphasis on education, both basic and advanced. On achieving power, Communist parties launched large-scale programs for adult literacy, expanded elementary school enrollments with the goal of including all school-age children, and later moved to expand secondary and higher education as institutions of mass education. This emphasis on education as a basic investment for development was demonstrated by high literacy rates achieved in Eastern Europe, high rates of school enrollment, and the high percentage of the gross national product spent on public education (see table 8.3). The Soviet Union, which has spent 7 to 8 percent of its GNP on education, and Cuba, which has spent 6 to 8 percent, were among the most generous in their budgeting for education, while the Chinese were relative laggards among the communist nations.

China's exception to this general pattern of heavy emphasis on education was especially pronounced during the period of the Cultural Revolution. The universities were almost closed down for several years and the Maoists were most suspicious, even hostile, toward higher education systems, perceiving them to be institutions for elitism. As in many other areas, Mao emphasized the priority of "politics" over "economics," which in education meant a stress on correct political thinking over technocratic expertise (i.e., the priority of being "red" over being "expert"). While fostering the expansion of

Table 8.3   Communism and Post-Communism: Educational Spending
and Literacy

	USSR	Czecho-slovakia	Hungary	Yugo-slavia	Cuba	China	Vietnam
Literacy percentage:							
1990 (est)	98[a]	97	97[b]	93	94	73	88
Percent of GNP spent on education:							
1975	7.6[c]	4.7	4.1	5.4	5.7[e]	1.8	—
1980	7.3[c]	4.0	4.7	4.7	7.2[e]	2.5	—
1985	7.0[c]	4.2	5.5	3.4	6.3[e]	2.6	—
1989	7.9[c]	4.7[d]	6.1	6.1[d]	6.7[e]	2.4	—

Sources: *Unesco Statistical Yearbook*, 1988, 1992; UNDP, *Human Development Report*, 1993.
a. 1989
b. 1980
c. as percent of net material product
d. 1990
e. as percent of global social product

primary education, the Maoist faction of the Chinese Communist party tried to integrate the school system into the lives of the peasants and workers. This meant that in the communes and factories, "barefoot teachers" or "worker teachers" ran the schools as part of their regular occupation, in many cases bypassing or uprooting more highly trained and technically competent teaching personnel. Chinese advances in nuclear technology and earth-orbiting satellites demonstrate that in certain top-priority cases, highly educated scientists and engineers were probably insulated from Mao's doctrines. But on the whole the Chinese commitment to expanding higher education, at least until recently, has been qualitatively different from, and less than, that of other communist systems. Only in the post-Mao period has China under Deng's leadership established a higher priority for education, especially higher education.

The expansion of higher education in the communist systems has increased opportunities for working-class children. In the Soviet Union, the polytechnical institutes founded in the 1920s and 1930s were filled by the sons and daughters of workers and peasants, while offspring of the out-of-favor bourgeoisie and nobility were denied college/university entrance. These restrictions were largely dropped in the 1930s, when entrance to higher education began to rest on merit examination scores (table 8.4). Khrushchev, as part of his destalinization campaign, attempted to improve educational opportunities for the collective farm family, but his reforms ran into a good deal of resistance and were passed only in watered-down form.

A second feature of higher education in the Communist nations was its emphasis on technical education as opposed to education in liberal arts or

Table 8.4   Communism and Post-Communism: Enrollments in Higher Education

	USSR	Czechoslovakia	Hungary	Yugoslavia	Cuba	China	Vietnam
	Percentage of Age Group in Higher Education						
1960	11	11	7	9	3[a]	—	1
1970	25	10	10	16	4	—	2[b]
1980	21	17	13	22	20	1	2
1990	23[c]	18	15	18	21	2	—
	Students per 100,000 Population						
1970	1,895	913	778	1,282	307	—	168[b]
1980	1,971	1,287	944	1,847	1,568	117	212
1990	1,820	1,215	970	1,374	2,304[d]	188	—

a. 1965
b. 1975
c. 1987
d. 1989
Source: *Unesco Statistical Yearbook*, 1982, 1986, 1992.

business administration. In part this reflected the planned linkage of education with economic development and the key role of science and technology in the modernization process.

Education under communism, given a basic loyalty to the system, was the path of upward mobility. In a system where no one could inherit and live off family wealth, educational attainment was all the more necessary for improving one's position. Lane (1971:508–9) has summarized the main features of Soviet education, which can be applied generally to communist systems:

> Education has become universal, ensuring widespread literacy, and Soviet education has emphasized technological competence. In all societies, education is a major determinant of the individual's life chances. This is particularly so in the USSR where the family has no legal rights over property. While Soviet education has attempted to bring down the barriers which barred deprived social and national groups from higher education, the cultural forces generated by family and parental occupation have asserted themselves. As in western societies, though perhaps to a lesser extent, professional strata pass on the advantages of their own education to their children thereby making them more educable, more worthy of "merit." . . . The main characteristics of Soviet education are its manifest connexion with economic and political institutions, and its emphasis on technological training and political socialisation. It is meritocratic, and now largely determines the life chances of the Soviet citizen.

In the first years of post-communism in Eastern Europe and the former Soviet Union, many young people have found it more advantageous to start small businesses or to get into the new market opportunities rather than continue their formal educations. Funding of schools and universities has plummeted, and teacher and faculty salaries are so low that most find additional income from either work in a second unofficial job or from social networks of barter and trade (cf. Rose, 1993). In some fields of science and engineering, but also in the humanities and social sciences, faculty are seeking to emigrate to the West or at least to work abroad for several years to make better salaries and support their families. New texts must be produced and new curricula implemented for studies in business, market economics, and finance. Old Communist texts are being discarded, but resources for replacements are scarce, and the basic infrastructure of education for the time being has a lower priority.

Health Care: Socialized Medicine

Next to education, provision of health care through a comprehensive system of socialized medical services has been a high priority of all Communist systems. The training of doctors and other medical personnel, the construction of hospitals and clinics, in short the entire public health system was financed and planned by the government. Medical education was free, as was education generally in the Communist nations. Physician services and hospital and sanatoria were free, although the patient may not have had much choice of physician. Generally speaking, there were several basic differences between socialized medicine in the Communist nations and Western health care or fee-for-service arrangements:

1. In the Communist nations, socialized medicine was introduced comprehensively and at an earlier stage of economic development than in the West, where it has been built up by piecemeal reforms.
2. Socialized medicine in Communist systems tended to emphasize preventive medicine as opposed to curative medicine; that is, more effort was placed on preventing illness than on dealing with the sickness after it appeared.
3. There was greater emphasis on medical care for children and the working-age population than on health care for the elderly, which is somewhat more emphasized in the West.

The commitment to basic health services available to all produced significant rises in life expectancy and declines in infant mortality in the Communist systems for a long time, until these systems began to stagnate in the 1970s and 1980s (table 8.5). The Soviet example, with the longest experience, has been summarized by Lawrence Mayer (1977) in his comparative study of industrial societies:

187

Table 8.5   Communism and Post-Communism: Health Care Indicators

	Russia	Czecho-slovakia	Hungary	Yugo-slavia	Cuba	China	Vietnam
Life expectancy (1989)							
Males	64.2	67.76	65.44	68.64[a]	72.66[b]	68[c]	63.66[f]
	42(1926)		55(1941)			35(1930)	
Females	74.5	75.29	73.79	74.48[a]	76.1[b]	70.9[c]	67.89[f]
	47(1926)		58(1941)			35(1930)	
Population per doctor (1984–89)	213	389	307	550[d]	530	1010	950
Infant mortality/ 1000 live births (1991)	22.7[e]	10.9	14	21.2	11.9	32.9	48.2

a. 1988–89
b. 1983–84
c. 1985–90
d. 1984
e. former USSR
f. 1979

Sources: UNDP, *Human Development Report*, 1992, 1993; UN, *Statistical Yearbook*, 1990–91; *Statistical Abstract of the United States*, 1992; James Sewell, *United States and World Development: Agenda for Action 1977* (New York: Praeger, 1977).

The system of medical care in the Soviet Union is formed around a network of polyclinics and is considered by many observers to be among the most effective in the world at giving basic medical services to the general population. Doctors, who are state employees, work together in these clinics to serve patients who are assigned to them with very little freedom of choice on either side. There are problems, such as the apparently shorter and less thorough training period and the fact that medications and facilities are not always the most modern ones. On the other hand, the Soviet Union is proud of the number of doctors (among the highest in the world in either absolute or relative terms) and of the fact that virtually everyone has access to a physician. Thus, while much of the freedom of choice is removed, the Soviet system seems to do well in its goal of providing basic medical services to virtually the entire population. (P. 361)

But in the 1980s, there was an increase in infant mortality in the Soviet Union, and Soviet medical technology was far below the level of the Western democracies. The Soviet Union also stopped providing statistics on life expectancy in 1972, a clear sign of unfavorable trends. The decline in life expectancy has been related to the difficulties of the Soviet economy in general, to the diversion of resources to military spending, and to the adverse health effects of widespread alcohol abuse (see chapter 11). This decline in life expectancy, from 69.3 years in 1969–70 to 67.7 in 1979–80 (von Beyme,

1989:202) was unusual for an industrial society, and differed from other Communist industrial societies (U.S. Department of Commerce, 1990:835–36), which had significantly higher life expectancies (72.8 years in East Germany, 71.7 in Czechoslovakia, 71.7 in Yugoslavia, 75.7 in Cuba, and 69.3 in China in 1989). Under Gorbachev's glasnost policies in the latter 1980s, Soviet authorities began again to release data on life expectancy in the Soviet Union, and to openly debate health-care issues such as alcoholism, poor sanitary conditions in Soviet hospitals, frequent abortions, drug abuse, and even AIDS. But with the decline of Russia's economy since 1990, health-care facilities have virtually been stripped of supplies, doctors have set up informal fee-for-service practices, and the public health care system is in disarray. As one sad example, during the bloody fighting in Moscow from October 3 to 5, 1993, radio broadcasts appealed to citizens to donate blood and medicines at a local hospital to help treat the wounded, since the hospital itself had no supplies. With the sudden poverty of the post-Communist state, public health services have virtually collapsed.

Once again the Chinese model provides the clear exception to the general pattern of communist health care systems. Maoism in the 1960s created for China a mixture of traditional medicine (including herbal medications and acupuncture) administered by thousands of "barefoot doctors" and "worker doctors" who were not full-time or professional physicians but talented peasants and workers with paramedical training. In three-month training sessions (usually two) these selected workers and peasants learned how to take care of most routine ailments in the communes and factories where they continued to work. Serious illness was referred to either the commune or the city hospital. Some foreign observers (Gaaster, 1972:137–38) praised the competence of these barefoot doctors.

Another aspect of China's health system was its use of mass campaigns in public hygiene, such as the "four-pest" campaign to kill flies, mosquitos, rats, and bedbugs (initially also sparrows). Visitors to the People's Republic often remarked on the cleanliness that separates China, a still poor society, from other poor (and not so poor) nations, where uncollected garbage, polluted water, stench, and vermin are a part of daily life for the average citizen. In the post-Mao period, however, the "barefoot doctor" system has been replaced, though rather unevenly, by a fee-for-service system between doctor and patient. It is not clear to what extent social health-care services are still available for those too poor to pay for individual physician care.

Problems and Achievements in Housing

Housing policy in the Communist nations aimed at providing every citizen with basic shelter at low, state-subsidized prices, and not much beyond this was achieved. Most observers agree that the Communist systems eliminated homelessness. However, housing quality and the availability of newer housing was a weak performance area in virtually all Communist systems, from the relatively wealthy to the very poorest. Average housing accommodations even in the more well-to-do Communist states of Eastern Europe were less spacious and had fewer amenities than in the liberal democracies of the West. Still, on a worldwide basis of comparison, the Communist nations did provide basic housing for their populations, and in countries like East Germany, Czechoslovakia, and even the USSR, housing standards did make some progress.

Some of the problems and shortcomings in the housing field can be attributed to the tremendous destruction suffered in World War II in Eastern Europe generally, but there was also great war damage in parts of Western Europe and in Japan. Two other factors were more basic to the lag in housing construction and in the quality of housing in the Communist nations. First, until Stalin's death in 1953, housing had a low priority in the centrally planned economies. With top priority given to heavy industry, investment in new housing was treated as a lower priority. The quality of both materials and trained personnel assigned to housing construction was also lower than in high-ranking industries. Thus, for a decade after the end of the war, these economies consciously let housing limp along as best it could, with all effort possible put into industrialization. A second factor was the large-scale urbanization that accompanied industrialization and that would have required great urban housing efforts just to keep the standards from falling. In the Soviet Union and Eastern Europe until the latter 1950s, the pace of urbanization related to the industrial revolution created a tremendous backlog of urban housing needs at the same time that investment in the housing sector was being deliberately held down. American political scientist Alexander Groth (1971:108–9) pointed out that in a comparison of Poland and Portugal in 1969, Poland had poorer housing statistics (and fewer private cars) despite its much higher levels of industry, education, and health care.

One measure of housing conditions used widely in Europe is total living space per person. Living space is measured in square meters (1 square meter is about 10 square feet) of floor space in state-owned apartments, private homes, or cooperative apartments, but does not include space taken up by kitchens, bathrooms, toilets, and halls. In the Soviet Union, 9 square meters per capita was established in 1922 as the minimum desirable norm. As of 1950, actual average living space per person was only 4.7 square meters, or about half the desirable minimum, and below what it had been in 1922. Construction efforts begun after Stalin's death raised the average to 8.2 square meters by 1975. But, as one critic has said, "Man cannot live on floor space alone" (Jacobs, 1975:74). And there was wide disparity in housing facilities between the more urban and industrial areas and the provincial villages and countryside. Thus, in 1971, of all public housing in Moscow, 100 percent had electricity, 99 percent had central heating, 99 percent had sewer connections,

99 percent had gas, 84 percent had bathtubs, 63 percent had hot water. In the predominantly rural Chuvash Autonomous Republic of the USSR, only a small percentage of housing units had bathtubs or showers, running water, or central heating. In these rural areas, most people still lived in one-story privately owned homes with few amenities, and even public housing standards in these regions were quite low. Most complaints related to frequent repairs needed, especially to roofs and to the overloading of hot water, gas, and sewer systems.

German political scientist Klaus von Beyme (1989:124) pointed out that even by 1987, nearly one-fifth of all Soviet apartments still lacked the normal qualities of a developed society. Nearly 17 percent lacked running water, 20 percent were without sewer connections, 25 percent did not have their own bath, and 37 percent did not have hot water. At the same time, survey results from the mid-1980s show that relative satisfaction with housing was greater than one might expect. In the rural areas, collective farm families were the most satisfied, having more spacious housing. But in a selection of big cities, too, 44 percent considered their housing situation as "good," as compared to 17 percent who considered it "bad" (ibid, 126). Even among the worst-off (mostly those in the oldest "communal" Kommunalka) boarding house arrangements, 37 percent said their situation was "bad," while 47 percent considered it "satisfactory" and 16 percent even found it "good." As in other performance areas, the Soviet system had fulfilled some basic expectations, though with low quality and much aggravation for its citizens.

On the brighter side for Soviet citizens (and for citizens in other Communist nations as well), the cost of housing was kept low. Because public housing was heavily subsidized by the government, an average family spent only 4 to 5 percent of its income for an apartment. Thus, in the 1970s it took a worker only 8 hours on the job to earn enough to pay the monthly rent in Moscow, as opposed to 55 hours for a worker in New York City, 53 hours in Munich, 62 hours in London, and 102 hours in Paris (Bush, 1975:56).

It is difficult to characterize the housing situation in China with any precision, since there are virtually no reliable statistics available. Two rather broad conclusions verifiable by visitors can be made, however. First and foremost, the Chinese Communist system in its first years in power produced a much more equitable distribution of housing than was true under the nationalist government that it replaced and eliminated the phenomenon of "homeless" or "roofless" people and families so prevalent in poor societies in the Third World. By all accounts housing was clean and orderly, a major factor in China's public health program and again a feature that distinguished China from most noncommunist Third World nations, even those with significantly higher levels of GNP per capita. Second, housing remained austere, lacking most of the amenities that are commonplace (and taken for granted) in the liberal democracies and in the more industrialized Communist countries of

Europe. Running water, indoor plumbing, even electrification were absent from the homes of the rural Chinese family, the great majority of the population. The Chinese system during its Maoist period, in housing as in so many other respects, showed both how much can be accomplished at low levels of economic development through political and social organization (social will-power) and what cannot be done without a major modernization of the way in which things are produced (industrialization). In the post-Mao period, the economic reforms of Deng Xiaoping's regime have privatized rural housing, and have abandoned centrally planned full employment that guaranteed some kind of housing for every family. This has led to the reemergence of shantytowns, squatter encampments, and street people in larger Chinese cities, beside train tracks and roads, on city outskirts, or in public places. But for those who have grown "rich" in China under the Deng reform program since 1978, new and more solidly middle-class houses have also been built.

Commitment to Social Welfare

Communist political systems had a strong commitment to social welfare programs, which included: elderly and invalid care, medical care and maternity benefits, work injury compensation, and income supplements to families with small children. Except in Yugoslavia's "market socialism," no programs existed for unemployment compensation, since central planning presumably eliminated mass unemployment. As in the liberal democracies, levels of welfare spending rose during the postwar years up to 1980, both in absolute figures and as a percentage of annual gross domestic product. As in the liberal democracies, there were some leaders and some laggards in welfare spending among the Communist systems. The most affluent industrial Communist states, Czechoslovakia, Hungary and East Germany, were among the high spenders on social welfare, while the Soviet Union was a relative laggard.

Alexander Groth summarized social welfare in the Communist political systems as follows:

Table 8.6   Social Welfare Expenditures as Percentage of GDP

	1960	1970	1980	1985–89
Soviet Union	10.2	11.9	14.1	13.7
Hungary	8.8	11.0	18.2	18.2
Czechoslovakia	15.4	18.0	18.9	18.4
Poland	8.9	10.7	15.7	11.5
Bulgaria	10.7	13.7	15.1	14.9
China	—	—	—	3.4*
Cuba	—	—	11.7	7.1*

*1984–89
Sources: ILO, *Cost of Social Security,* 1978–1980, 1981–1983; UNDP, *Human Development Report,* 1990.

Even though each of these systems subsumes a wide variety of levels of economic development, as between East Germany and North Vietnam, for example, or between Albania and Czechoslovakia, they all exhibit high welfare commitments. With the exception of the category of unemployment insurance (allegedly unnecessary in their planned, full-employment economies), all these states, excepting Red China with no general family allowance program, provide coverage under each of the remaining four categories of social insurance. Moreover, they do so with a generosity that apparently exceeds the contributions of many noncommunist regimes, whose wealth in terms of per capita GNP is considerably superior to theirs. (1971:164)

With the disruption of the post-Communist transition to market economies, state budgets for welfare programs have shrunk drastically, so that while many of these programs remain in place, the level of benefits (now including jobless benefits) is very low. An impoverished post-Communist state is beset by too many critical needs and in general has greatly diminished revenues from taxes. As Richard Rose (1993) has pointed out in a comparative study of how people are getting by in hard times in Bulgaria, Czechoslovakia, and Russia, individuals, families, and businesses (and one might add local governments) have, as one strategy, stopped paying taxes or fees to the state for a wide range of economic activities, legal, semi-legal and illegal. With the state faced with a revenue crisis, post-communism in its early years has brought broad abandonment of welfare commitments, with rising insecurity for individuals who rely on state pensions, disability benefits, or unemployment compensation. Unless healthy economic growth can be restored and stricter collection of tax revenues once again enforced, post-Communist political systems will not be able to provide any significant measure of social security for their citizens, in stark contrast to the recent Communist past.

Post-Communist Remarketization: Prospects and Problems

The performance for the East European and Soviet economies reached a peak in the 1970s; in those years, citizens of these Communist systems could depend on the economy to provide basic foodstuffs at stable and affordable prices, basic housing at very low cost, free health care, and good educational opportunities. Each year since the mid-1950s, the number of consumer items available had been increasing slowly, and the material standard of living had risen considerably. The Communist economic system provided basic, no-frills economic security for its citizens. This differentiated communism from the affluent liberal democracies, which provided a consumer paradise for most citizens, with some insecurity or economic risk as both an incentive and the price of progress. This also differentiated communism from most Third World systems, which did not provide basic economic security for most citizens, but at the same time supported a small minority in Western-style luxury (cf. chapters 12 and 13).

Quality of goods such as color televisions, refrigerators, and other consumer durables in the Communist economies was poor compared to what was available in the West, and waiting times for car purchases or new apartments were ridiculously long. Yet in extensive surveys of Soviet emigrants from the Soviet Union (Millar, 1987) as well as in surveys made possible under glasnost, citizens expressed relative satisfaction with many aspects of the Soviet economy, especially members of the generations that had experienced the grinding deprivation of the war and early postwar years. But among younger citizens, who increasingly knew about and longed for a real Western consumer life-style, this was not enough. And with the stagnation in economic growth that began in the 1970s and worsened in the 1980s, popular dissatisfaction with the Soviet-style command system mounted. Partial reforms were not sufficient to redress the failings of the old system nor to satisfy the new consumer expectations. With the Gorbachev *perestroika* initiatives came an ever-wider questioning and dismissal of the old system as a failure, and more radical calls for transformation to a free-market system like those in the West. With the collapse of Communist regimes in Eastern Europe and the election of non-Communist governments in both Eastern Europe and several republics of the Soviet Union, new programs were initiated to push this market transformation ahead. In some cases, most notably Poland, where the newly elected Solidarity government opted for a ''shock therapy'' approach, governments made rapid and enormous changes. In the Soviet Union, the collapse of Communist central authority after the failed August coup by antireform hardliners opened possibilities for more rapid economic reform. The bloody victory of President Yeltsin's government over the Russian parliament in October 1993 again gave his radical reform team new opportunities to push ahead on privatization and marketization. However, during the October fighting in Moscow, most citizens did not want to get involved; the reforms so far had produced more hardship than benefit, and most had become cynical about politics and politicians. In China, despite the June 1989 crackdown on the democracy movement, the Deng regime has continued its policy of market-oriented and export-oriented growth strategies, though with some retrenchment.

The era of communism's extensive growth project, or ''Communist industrialization,'' has come to an end in Europe and the Soviet Union. There is no going back to the old model, whatever political changes may occur in the next years, because the basic preconditions for the old way have disappeared. In China as well, this type of ''developmental communism'' (duRand, 1990) may be reaching its final stages.

Marketization has been the key to the reform or restructuring of the economies of Communist systems since the death of Stalin. The Liberman reforms of the 1960s, the Yugoslav ''market socialism'' since the 1960s, the

Hungarian New Economic Mechanism since 1968, and the Chinese "responsibility system" since 1978 are forerunners of the current drive to marketize these economies. Marketization will probably continue, possibly with setbacks and temporary reversals, and will continue to replace the remnants of the old system. Whether under non-Communists, reform socialists, Western-oriented liberals, or conservative nationalists, marketization will continue the long-term trend toward relinking and reintegrating these economies into the world trading system.

Marketization is a general or global concept that means many things to many people, and it is a political catch-all for economic aspirations in Communist and post-Communist societies. In terms of economic performance, it means some degree of privatization and some decrease in state intervention, enough to restore "the market" as the dominant disciplining force for economic development. This means ending state subsidies for goods and industries, freeing prices for consumer goods to rise to market levels, allowing inefficient firms to go bankrupt, permitting workers to be fired more freely, and subjecting domestic industries to more open competition from foreign producers. All this will undermine the basic economic security of the old system in favor of the shining hope of achieving a much more affluent consumer society.

This is the hope of both political leaders and most citizens, and there are some reasons for optimism. First and foremost, this historic economic transformation in Europe has the broad support, at least for the short term, of the populace, who are willing to experience some hardship if and so long as they believe there will be good results in the future. This is particularly the case if the government has the legitimacy to make hard decisions and have them enforced.

Second, the Communist societies have built up a good deal of human capital, skilled labor, and highly educated engineers and scientists, who form the human basis for economic renewal. This work force is relatively healthy and can afford some hardship without reaching desperation.

Third, the success of this market transformation is very important to the West, especially to the European Community nations of Western Europe, since it offers a tremendously expanded market for their goods and great future investment opportunities. Germany in particular, now unified, has a great stake in the success of the Eastern European economies.

Finally, the social market economies of the West provide a bright and shining model to emulate. As many economists in Eastern Europe now say, there is no more need or desire to "experiment" with new alternatives; the Western system has proved its superiority, and the goal is to emulate the West.

Yet, there is much that has been learned about the difficulties of making a successful transition to affluent Western-style market economies in Eastern Europe and the former Soviet Union over the first several years of post-Communist transition. Even the privileged case of East Germany, now formally reunited with prosperous West Germany, shows that the transition is much more painful, expensive, and longer-term than originally advertised. Western Germany has been transferring nearly $100 billion each year to restructure and integrate eastern Germany, yet by late 1993, this effort had not produced a sustained economic turnaround in eastern Germany. The other post-Communist nations of Eastern Europe and the former Soviet Union cannot possibly count on such generous aid, and their access to Western markets and capital investment is much more restricted. Despite some talk in 1990–91 of a new "Marshall Plan" for these post-Communist nations, nothing of the sort has actually materialized, and there is currently little prospect for any large-scale effort to aid this historic transition.

So far, the pain of economic transition has outweighed the benefits for most citizens, which accounts for some nostalgia for the social and material security of the old system. Yet even the return to government by former Communists (post-Communists?) in recent elections in Lithuania and Poland does not foretell any such return. Rather it is a protest against the painfulness of the transition, which will in one form or another continue.

Although marketization and privatization will continue, the results may be quite varied, and the chances of reaching a Western-style social market economy may be fading. The welfare state democracies themselves are undergoing some painful transitions, caused by a number of factors related externally to the globalization of investment and production and internally to the rising costs of the welfare state (cf. chapters 2 and 3). If the liberal democracies can no longer afford to maintain the affluent success formula of their postwar peak years (1960s and 1970s), how will it be possible for post-Communist Eastern Europe or Russia to copy this model? The dream of the first days of the revolutions of 1989–91 was to "join the West," which was proclaimed to be the "normal" modern society. Now it seems that this "West," this "norm," is itself eroding and is more visibly in crisis. It may be that post-communism will be forced to invent its own new model of economic development, which may be marketized and privatized, but may not look much like Sweden in the 1960s or West Germany in the 1970s. And the politics of this post-Communist market economy may also be quite different from the politics of liberal democracy.

With open borders and openness to Western trade, technology, and investment, some signs of a new economic dependency on the West in parts of Eastern Europe have emerged in the first several years of this transition. This syndrome of dependency (see chapters 12 and 13) is characteristic of some developing "Third World" nations and suggests that the new market-type economies will share some features of dependent development for some time. This would include dependency on foreign loans and credits and therefore submission to the discipline and austerity plans of the International Monetary Fund (IMF). It would include the loss ("brain drain") of highly skilled and motivated professionals and workers through migration to the West, where their skills would be much better rewarded, and where there is still much greater stability. Post-Communist "capital flight," the draining of domestic Russian or Polish or Romanian capital to safer banks and investments in the West, rather than being productively reinvested domestically, has already appeared. By one estimate, Russian "capital flight" to the West, mostly through illegal transfers, amounted to $26 billion by mid-1993 (Economist Intelligence Unit, 1993:45). Reliance on licensing of Western technologies for production and Western finance or investment to import new technologies are other aspects of dependent development now appearing in post-communism.

The post-Communist transition to market-type economies quickly destroyed previous linkages between regions of Eastern Europe and the former Soviet Union, disrupting long-established connections between suppliers, producers, and customers. The centrifugal forces of ethnic nationalism exacerbated the trend towards regional and even local delinking from trade and commerce. Still, the nations of Eastern Europe and the successor states of the former Soviet Union are gradually finding that they are collectively their own best markets and for many materials, the most efficient suppliers. Despite the many dislocations and interethnic suspicions, there are also forces that are encouraging the revival, on market terms, of regional trade and commerce. The Commonwealth of Independent States (CIS), which regrouped most of the ex-Soviet republics into a loose association, was quickly written off by many as without a future, but with the dawning of economic realities (e.g., Russia is willing to sell gas and oil to Ukraine, but Ukraine must be able to pay for it), the economic reintegration of many areas of the former Soviet Union under some political and economic formula is still quite possible. In 1993, a series of conferences hammered out some agreements on a new economic space for the CIS nations, which, as the romanticism of ethnic nationalism declines, may yet provide a practical economic basis for equitable and mutually beneficial regionalism.

These scenarios are only possibilities, and it is more likely that there will be other varieties of outcomes in post-communism. After all, these societies were quite diverse before the advent of communism, they had somewhat different experiences under communism, and they will almost certainly not all turn to one formula in post-communism. Now that the early illusions of quick success have faded, the hard struggle to reinvent a politics for economic growth has begun.

9

Social Equality—From State Egalitarianism to the New Inequalities

A major goal of communism, and one of its attractions in the twentieth century, was its commitment to building a classless society. A classless society would have much less inequality between social groups, by occupation, by ethnic or racial background, or between men and women. The Communist systems never achieved this goal, but they did reduce certain inequalities in income, wealth, and educational opportunity, and opened up considerable mobility for workers, peasants, and women. But there were privileges for communist elites, which clearly contradicted this principle of social equality. Yet the relative narrowing of incomes and living standards was one of the basic features of classic Communist regimes.

The post-Communist transition has reduced the commitment to social equality in favor of greater market (and nonmarket) incentives to make money and enjoy one's wealth. In all of the post-Communist societies, and in the dynamic market economy of Communist China (and Vietnam as well), inequalities between "winners" and "losers" are growing. This trend is one of the most visible and rapid changes in the first years of economic transition. The growth of new class divisions in post-communism is also one of the causes of bitterness and possible backlash against the economic reform process.

Marx foresaw the ultimate goal of communism not as an enforced equality, but rather as a classless solidarity in which the free development of each person was essential to the free development of the society. Under full communism the rallying cry would become "From each according to his abilities, to each according to his needs." This does not assume that all people have exactly the same needs or that the distribution of goods should be exactly equal. It assumes that people's needs are independent of the "market value" of the work they perform. Thus a factory worker's needs may be no less than a scientist's, even though the scientist's skills may be more scarce.

In the transition to communism, the Leninist one-party state generally had as its motto: "From each according to his abilities, to each according *to his work.*'' This recognized continuing material inequality based upon differences in the amount and quality of work contributed to society. Able-bodied persons with some exceptions (e.g., housewives) were expected to work in the economy. The Communist systems emphasized the worker's labor as the rationale for both personal and social progress.

After an initial revolutionary period of economic leveling, ruling communist parties changed their policies on the proper levels of social equality as they changed their priorities for economic and social development. Generally, Communist regimes permitted or introduced greater income and status inequality when they wanted to emphasize economic growth as a top priority. Growth and industrialization produced not only new inequalities but also contradictions to the ideological goal of an egalitarian society and popular resentment of those favored by the party's development policies. Communist cultures were marked by both encouragement of popular egalitarianism and the need to reverse egalitarian trends to stimulate economic growth. This tension between incentives for growth and popular concepts of social equity exists in all political systems, but because of the strong ideological commitment of communism to material equality, this was a particularly conflict-laden area in Communist systems—all the more so since the party-state took responsibility for the level of inequality in society.

With the freeing of prices and wages during the transition to market-type economies and quick development of both new market opportunities and widespread economic dislocations, post-Communist governments are retreating from earlier egalitarian commitments and allowing market forces to determine levels of wealth and poverty. Post-communism, for the foreseeable future, will be associated with rising new inequalities.

Income and Wealth Distribution

In terms of income distribution, the Communist countries were the most egalitarian. Yugoslavia's "market socialism" was less egalitarian in this respect than centrally planned East Germany, Czechoslovakia, Poland, and Hungary, but still more egalitarian than its Western capitalist neighbors (table 9.1). For example, the Gini ratio for family income in the 1970s was .24 in East Germany and .42 in West Germany (Cromwell, 1977). Remember that a Gini ratio of 0.0 would mean complete equality; a ratio of 1.0 would mean the greatest possible inequality. In a comparison of six liberal democracies and five Communist systems, E.S. Kirschen (1974:86) concluded that in wages and salaries (not counting income from property) there was 36 percent less inequality in the Communist systems.

While there are several reasons why income has been more evenly distributed under communism, one basic factor was the elimination of the private property wealth of the capitalist class. In the Communist nations,

Table 9.1   Communism: Income Distribution

	Gini Ratio	Percent of National Income Going to:	
		Top 10 Percent	Bottom 40 Percent
Soviet Union	.24–.30 (1979)[a]	—	
East Germany	.24 (1964)	16.9	26.3 (1970)
Czechoslovakia	.25 (1964)	17.4	27.4 (1964)
Bulgaria	—	18.8	26.6 (1962)
Poland	.26 (1964)	21.2	23.4 (1964)
Hungary	.27 (1969)	20.5	20.5 (1982)
Yugoslavia	.32 (1968)	22.9	18.7 (1978)

Sources: Howe, *United States and World Development,* 1975; World Bank, *World Development Report,* 1986; Vinocur and Ofer, 1987.
a. The Soviet estimates by Vinocur and Ofer (1987) are derived from interviews with 2,793 Soviet emigrants.

income from property was almost totally eliminated. There was no longer a tiny minority of the rich and superrich (the top 2 percent or so) that derived extremely high incomes from interest, dividends, rents, and capital gains. In Communist nations, almost all income came from work.

Kirschen's evidence indicated that even discounting income from property, in the post-Stalin era, wages and salaries were more equally distributed in Eastern Europe than in Western Europe. The debate over the appropriate level of wage and salary inequality was a central issue of Communist development. In many Communist nations, the debate passed through several stages and has followed changing regime priorities. In the earliest stages of the Russian Revolution (1918–21), income differentials were dramatically cut, and in some areas or industries wages were completely equalized. During the NEP period from 1921 to 1927, however, the party permitted a partial remarketization in agriculture and retail trade, which enabled some rich peasants (kulaks) and urban businessmen to make quite high incomes and at the same time left several million workers unemployed. This period represented a first retreat from the radical egalitarianism of the Revolution, and was brought to a sudden end by the launching of the First Five-Year Plan for forced-pace industrialization in 1928. With the rise of Stalin to power in the USSR and the drastic industrialization drive of the 1930s, the regime denounced "equality mongering" and introduced wage rates that provided material incentives for workers, managers, and engineers in top priority industries like steel, iron, and electricity, and great material disincentives for people working in consumer goods production and agriculture. Changes were made in inheritance and tax laws so that skilled workers and professionals could pass on their personal savings to their children. In the distribution of scarce goods like housing, appliances, and even food and drink, top managerial and administrative personnel were definitely favored, whereas previously they had been placed at the end of the waiting line (especially if they came from bourgeois social origins).

As a part of the destalinization campaign of the 1950s, this trend toward increasing wage inequality was again reversed. Through the post-Stalin period up to the 1970s there was a trend toward greater income equality, especially marked in the Soviet Union in comparison with the Stalinist period, less so in the other European Communist states, where the shifts in income policy were less pronounced (Parkin, 1971:144). This turn toward greater equality was implemented primarily along two paths: first, the establishment and then the raising of minimum wages for the poorest sector of the population, the collective farmers, and second, the lowering of wage differentials in specific industries, so that, for example, in the ferrous metal industry the ratio of highest-paid to lowest-paid worker fell from 3.6 to 1 to 2.6 to 1 from the 1950s to the late 1960s (Lane, 1971a:398).

English economist Peter Wiles (1975:25) estimated that the ratio of income between the top 10 percent (decile) of Soviet citizens and the bottom 10 percent grew from 3.82 in 1928 to 4.15 in 1934 at the end of the first Stalinist Five-Year Plan, to a peak of 7.24 in 1946, and then declined again to 4.4 in 1956 after Stalin's death, and to between 2.7 (1968) and 3.2 (1970) by the latter 1960s. Estimates of Soviet income inequality from interviews of 2,793 former Soviet citizens (Vinocur and Ofer, 1987) concluded that income in the USSR was more equally distributed than in the Western democracies, with stronger positions from the bottom 10 percent and bottom 20 percent of households in terms of national income shares. They also found that there had been no further equalizing during the 1970s. Under the Gorbachev reform proposals of the late 1980s, greater income inequality as an incentive to harder and more efficient work was seen as a necessary part of *perestroika*.

In the late 1980s, the rapid growth of semi-private cooperative businesses, and the spread of semi-legal and illegal "parallel markets" in the Soviet Union produced some very high incomes (by Soviet standards) for some enterprising souls. At the same time, large-scale unemployment has reappeared, and the decline in value of old-age and invalid pensions from inflation has produced greater economic distress at the bottom of the income scale. Squatter settlements of displaced people are beginning to appear in and around large cities, and a new underclass of the marginalized and homeless is being born. Both non-Communist and Communist governments in the early 1990s lacked the resources to support a social safety net for this new class of "losers" in the restructuring process. The phenomenon of marketization in Eastern Europe, whatever its pace and scope, means greater income inequalities, and this trend is likely to continue for some considerable time as economic restructuring erodes state-guaranteed income security, and market forces determine new "winners" and "losers" on a much wider scale of income and wealth disparity.

As Yugoslavia introduced a more liberal communism utilizing many market features, income differentials between highly qualified white-collar workers and unskilled blue-collar workers increased from 2.38 to 1 in 1954 to 3.33 to 1 by 1961 (Parkin, 1971:173). There is some evidence that the liberal Communist Dubcek regime, which introduced the 1968 Prague Spring (socialism with a human face), also planned to shift the income structure in favor of professionals and managerial personnel. Finally, although we have relatively little comprehensive data for China, Deng Xiaoping and his associates have discarded the radical egalitarianism of Maoism in favor of greater rewards for successful family farmers, businessmen, and the highly educated in professional, government, and managerial positions.

Much has been made in the West over the various advantages that party, state, and managerial elites enjoy in Communist societies. And it is true that the "new class," as Milovan Djilas (1957) termed it, benefited from privileged access to housing, shops, and special hospitals and spas. They often had at their service a state-owned car, telephones, and expense account travel and entertainment possibilities. Many received an extra month's salary each year and superior pension benefits. Yet, the conclusion of the British expert Mervyn Matthews in the 1970s was that "the Soviet elite, in 'capitalist' terms, if not in the context of Soviet society, is a poor elite. True, there are many ways of getting around the law and the possibilities of doing so appear to improve with social position. Some people do have two or more dwellings, a large boat, or an invaluable collection of eighteenth century porcelain. But spectacular American-style consumption and accumulation patterns are virtually unknown" (Matthews, 1975:133).

Matthews attributed the relative poverty of the Soviet elite to three factors: (1) the normative power of Marxism or communism; (2) strict controls on individual earnings; and (3) controls on property, which made it unlikely that anyone could accumulate (much less openly enjoy) great wealth. But a really powerful elite would be able to either change the laws or the system to allow for greater self-enrichment or to flout the laws by massive corruption of the court, tax, and finance authorities, as has been done for many years in Mexico.

The lesser inequality in income and wealth of the communist societies has rested on a mix of ideological, structural, and policy-making factors. With the passage of time in power, the idealist component eroded among Communist elites, giving rise to elite corruption, though at levels that were modest by Western or Third World standards. While first-generation Communist leaders like V. I. Lenin, Mao Zedong, Fidel Castro, or Ho Chi Minh did not use their power to enrich themselves and their families, second- and third-generation leaders, with less idealist commitment and more conventional desires, began to build up their material privileges. The worst case, and somewhat exceptional, was the megalomania of the Ceaucescu clan in Romania, which lived in luxury while enforcing severe austerity on the population. The relatively middle-class Wandlitz homes of East German leader Erich Honecker and his associates, the hunting lodges used by Communist functionaries in Poland, the spending sprees and corrupt dealings of Brezhnev's daughter Galina, or the corrupt business dealings of the children of Chinese communist leaders, while paling beside the fortunes amassed by Philippines dictator Ferdinand Marcos or Zairean dictator Joseph Mobutu, were nevertheless the target of broad public condemnation, and played an important role in the 1989–90 popular uprisings against these regimes. Part of this public furor came from the hypocrisy of these elites, who preached egalitarianism and social justice while permitting themselves relative comfort. Now that many of these elites have been ousted, post-Communist regimes must deal with the structural and policy sources of the Communist legacy of egalitarianism.

Educational Equality

In most Communist systems, where wealth or a secure position in the family business could not (with minor exceptions for owners of small farms and shops) be inherited, there was more emphasis on educational achievement for personal success. In the East European and Soviet systems, but not in China under Mao, this meant a strong role for education as a means of upward mobility and a more attractive career and life-style, though not necessarily high income. In the early years of these Communist systems, the educational system inherited from the old order was radically restructured. The old class channeling system, which had effectively deprived children of lower-class parents of chances of higher education, was abolished and replaced by a comprehensive school system, which was then expanded to include all school-age children. At first, admissions to higher education were deliberately tilted in favor of working-class and peasant children as a redress for past lack of opportunity and out of consideration for political loyalty. Gradually, entrance to institutions of higher education came to rest on merit entrance exams. As this happened, the percentages of students from lower-class and especially peasant origins began to decline, so that children of white-collar employees and professionals were overrepresented in institutions of higher learning. Table 9.2 illustrates, in the case of Poland, the dramatic rise in educational opportunities for working-class children between the Pilsudski dictatorship of the 1930s and the People's Republic of the early 1960s. As of the latter 1960s, Giddens (1973:236–37) reported that over half of all students in schools of higher education in Poland, Hungary, and Yugoslavia came from worker or peasant families. In the USSR about half of all students came from these

Table 9.2   Social Origins of Polish Students (Percentages)

Family Origin	1935–36	1960–61	1976–77
Manual workers	9.5	29.2	30.5
Peasants	5.0	18.5	11.9
Petty proprietors, craftsmen	12.0	4.6	
White-collar workers	38.0	46.5	54.1 (intelligentsia)
Upper class	35.5	1.2	3.5 (other classes)

Sources: A. Sarapata, in Szczepanski, 1966:46; Szczepanski, 1978:15.

backgrounds. This upward mobility represented a remarkable breakthrough for the lower classes and was one of the bases of working-class support for these systems. Communism gave many citizens chances that had been closed to them under the old order.

At the same time, most observers (Lane, 1976; Giddens, 1973; Parkin, 1971) noted that even given the relative equality compared to Western Europe, children of white-collar (nonmanual) family backgrounds were more prevalent in the universities, where they studied law, humanities, and the arts, while those from blue-collar families were more prevalent in the polytechnical, mining, railroad, and economics institutes. Thus blue-collar students more frequently went into applied fields in industry, whereas white-collar students tended toward the higher-status (though often poorly paid) professions.

Another area of concern for education equality is ethnic representation. The Soviet Union was a highly differentiated, multiracial and multiethnic society. Included in its 1970 census were some 129 million Russians, 41 million Ukrainians, 9 million Belorussians, 9 million Uzbeks, 6 million Tatars, 5 million Kazakhs, 4 million Azerbaidzhanies, 15 other nationalities with more than 1 million people each, and 103 smaller ethnic groups, each with under a quarter million members. In the late years of the tsarist regime, there was extreme inequality in education among the various nationalities, with almost universal illiteracy and no institutions of higher education among the Islamic peoples (Uzbek, Kazakh, Kirghiz, Tadzhik, Turkmen) of the Central Asian provinces. Public policy in the development of the USSR has aimed at bringing these groups into the mainstream of Soviet development in terms of both economic and educational equality. Vernon Aspaturian (1968) calculated an index of representation for different ethnic groups among students in institutions of higher education for 1927, 1956, and 1965 (see table 9.3). An index greater than 1.0 indicated overrepresentation of an ethnic group relative to its share in the population, and an index less than 1.0 indicated underrepresentation.

Aspaturian's data showed a trend toward ethnic parity in higher education, with the Central Asian nationalities making considerable gains, although

Jews, Georgians, Armenians, and Russians were still somewhat overrepresented. Lane (1976:94) noted that even though Jewish overrepresentation in higher education had fallen, the number of Jewish students rose from 51,600 in 1956 to 94,600 in 1965 as a result of the considerable expansion generally of college-level enrollments.

We might summarize the pattern of educational opportunities in Communist systems as being more open to working-class children and therefore more egalitarian, though there was still a long-term tendency for the intelligentsia to pass on through the family environment a greater "educability" to their children.

Equality in Elite Recruitment

Aside from income distribution and educational opportunities, social inequality appears in all societies in the selection of some people to positions of authority, whether in government, party offices, economic management, military leadership, or educational and cultural institutions. Communist systems of all varieties recruited a much larger share of their elites from the lower classes (workers and peasants) than the capitalist democracies. Even severe critics of these systems, such as Huntington and Brzezinski (1963) and Djilas (1957) recognized this basic fact. Djilas argued that even though the "new class" or party-state elites monopolizes political power and economic planning, it was not self-recruited from its own ranks:

Table 9.3   Ethnic Representation of Students in the USSR

Nationality	1927[a] Index	1959[b] Index	1965[c] Index	1959–65 Increase (thousands)	1959–65 Percent Increase
Russian	1.06	1.13	1.11	1,527	183
Ukrainian	.69	.75	.81	379	211
Uzbek	.11	.82	.83	65	213
Kazakh	.07	.94	1.06	48	218
Georgian	2.00	1.41	1.38	46	196
Kirgiz	.12	1.00	.80	10	149
Tadzhik	.08	.71	.57	11	157
Armenian	1.81	1.07	1.14	41	203
Turkmen	.21	.80	.80	10	174
Jewish	7.50	3.73	2.18	43	83
Tatar	.40	.75	.71	45	202

Source: Adapted from Aspaturian, 1968:177.
a. Total students = 168,000
b. Total students = 1,341,000
c. Total students = 3,866,000

The new class is actually being created from the lowest and broadest strata of the people, and is in constant motion. Although it is sociologically possible to prescribe who belongs to the new class, it is difficult to do so; for the new class melts into and spills over into the people, into the lower classes, and is constantly changing. (1957:61)

In other words, Communist elite recruitment was far more open to the lower classes than elite recruitment in the capitalist democracies, which, as Giddens (1973:240–41) pointed out, led to a different (and less pronounced) class structure within the Communist societies. This alone made it different from Western economic, social, and political elites, which were largely self-recruited from the upper strata of society.

Some of the most extensive information on the social background of various leadership groups in Communist systems comes from a study of legislative, administrative, party, managerial, and intellectual elites in Yugoslavia in the late 1960s. These data indicated that party and economic leadership was, relatively speaking, the most proletarian, with the administrative and especially the intelligentsia elites more likely to be recruited from nonworking-class social backgrounds. Among all the elite groupings, the peasantry was still considerably underrepresented.

One characteristic of communist political elites was that over time their educational levels have risen considerably. Among the original leaders of the Bolshevik party were people like Lenin, Zinoviev, and Trotsky, who had attended a university. But by the end of the civil war in 1921, the Bolshevik leadership had itself been proletarianized, and a majority of the Central Committee membership had only a primary- or secondary-school education. This situation remained until the launching of the great industrialization drive of the 1930s, when the politically loyal but poorly educated were replaced

Table 9.4   Social Origins of Yugoslav Elite (1968)

Figures are indices of representation among elites relative to proportion of the general population.[a]

Social Origin	Legislators	Administrators	Party Leaders	Economic Leaders	Intellectuals
Nonmanual worker	1.38	2.12	1.39	1.19	3.10
Manual worker	1.11	1.04	1.28	1.39	.92
Peasant	.69	.50	.56	.55	.20

Source: Based on Lane, 1971a:117.

a. An index greater than one indicates overrepresentation; an index less than one indicates underrepresentation.

Table 9.5   Educational Level of Soviet Central Committee Members, 1930, 1952, 1986

Education	1930 (percentage)	1952 (percentage)	1986 (percentage)
Primary/secondary	67	24	8
Technical institute	4	39	59
Military institute	—	5	11
Teacher/medical/law institutes	17	24	8
Party higher school	—	3	2
University	12	5	12

(many through the Great Purge) by younger cadres who were of proletarian origin and politically loyal to the system but also had some basic technical expertise to oversee the new industrial economy (table 9.5)

Since Stalin's death in 1953, this "expert trend" toward a managerial-technical elite, predominantly in applied fields, continued. The Chinese experience during Mao's time represented a contrast to the Soviet and Yugoslav patterns. Mao distrusted the "expert trend" and viewed this as a return to the "capitalist road" of development in Eastern Europe. In China, Mao struggled against Liu Shaoqi and Deng Xiaoping as Chinese advocates of a technocratic elite.

The communist industrialization project has generally required a more technically trained party and state elite, and some observers (Fischer, 1968; Hoffmann, 1982) have seen this trend as part of an evolution toward a technocratic-managerial elite, part of the so-called scientific-technological revolution of "developed socialism." The *nomenklatura,* or list of key positions to be filled by party loyalists, has been severely challenged by the upheavals of 1989–90, but much of this formerly communist technocratic and managerial elite was still in place, and a key issue was whether, under new noncommunist governments and economic restructuring, this holdover elite would be widely purged, or largely retained for its skills and experience in the emerging new market economies. In Poland, for example, one of the first post-Communist nations to privatize much of state industry under the Solidarity government of Tadeuz Mazowiecki, many of the new owners were the former Communist managers. This pattern has been repeated virtually everywhere in Eastern Europe and the former Soviet Union and has been termed "nomenklatura privatization," indicating that the main beneficiaries of the new economic order have been the managerial elites from the old Communist order. There has been much popular resentment against this outcome, but it was the prospect of becoming new business owners that convinced many "nomenklatura" managers to abandon communism for a new privatized market.

207

Women's Emancipation

The liberation of women has been one of the stated goals of communism since the days of Marx and Engels. Indeed, Marx and Engels considered the domination of men over women as the first form of class oppression, and they saw the liberation of women as a "bench mark" for the development of a humane and classless society in general. Lenin had specifically called for the employment of women in all phases of the economy and the liberation of women from household chores as necessary steps toward sexual equality. Unlike the theorists of capitalism or liberal democracy, the earliest advocates of communism explicitly supported women's liberation as an integral part of building a new society.

In the first years of nearly all Communist systems, most of the legal and semilegal (religious, traditional) barriers that oppressed women were officially removed. Marriage by consent, free divorce, abortion, equal rights of citizenship and personal property, equality before the law, equal pay for equal work were all passed into law or even written into the new constitutions. The crudest forms of commercial exploitation of women through concubinage, prostitution, and pornography were outlawed. Mass sexually oriented advertising and inane beauty contests were not found in Communist nations.

With the industrialization of the USSR came unparalleled occupational breakthroughs for women, which continued beyond the Stalinist industrialization drive and the war-time emergency. The percentage of higher professional positions held by women in the USSR rose from 28 percent in 1928 to 52 percent by the 1970s. Over 4.6 million Soviet women were employed as engineers, doctors, lawyers, teachers, economists, agronomists, and other professionals (Dodge, 1977:206), and 63 percent of all semiprofessional jobs (technicians, accounting, legal, medical personnel) were held by women (some 8 million). About 72 percent of all doctors, 69 percent of teachers, 64 percent of economists, 40 percent of agronomists, and 31 percent of engineers were women. By contrast, in tsarist Russia of 1913, only 10 percent of doctors were women. In the mid-1920s only 1 percent of engineers were women, although this had already risen to 13 percent by 1939 (Mandel, 1975:135). Soviet women broke through gender barriers in blue-collar occupations as well; 29 percent of construction workers, nearly 38 percent of railroad workers, and 17.3 percent of machine construction workers were women (Sacks, 1977:202). According to Mandel (1975:106) a third of all Soviet crane, derrick, and forklift operators were women, as were a majority of streetcar, bus, and subway train drivers. In 1926 less than one-eighth of typesetters were women; by 1959 nearly four out of five compositors were female.

The Soviet Union compared favorably not only with Western democracies in opening occupational and educational opportunities for women, but also with other Communist nations. In higher education, which was the key to entering professional occupations, women accounted for 49 percent of all students in the USSR, compared with 45.3 percent in Bulgaria, 44.5 percent in Hungary, 40 percent in Cuban colleges and 50 percent in Cuban universities, 42 percent in Poland, 40 percent in Yugoslavia, 38 percent in Czechoslovakia, 34 percent in East Germany, and 32 percent in Mongolia in the 1970s. In those fields of engineering and technology that in the West were almost exclusive male preserves, women made up 38.3 percent of student majors in the Soviet Union versus 28.5 percent in Cuba, 20 percent in Poland and China, 17 percent in Czechoslovakia, and only 8.6 percent in East Germany. In the People's Republic of China, the percentage of women in higher education overall rose from less than 20 percent in 1949 to about one-third by 1987 (Rai et al., 1992; Mandel, 1975:322).

Despite this undoubted advance toward emancipation of women in educational and occupational opportunities, especially in the USSR but to lesser degrees in all the Communist nations, there were still many areas where sex inequality (see Scott, 1974) continued to burden women. First, and perhaps most apparent, was the relative absence of women among the political elite. In the USSR in 1986, women represented only about 27 percent of party membership and held less than 3 percent of Central Committee seats and no Politburo positions. The picture in other Communist nations was little different, except for an occasional, one might say token, female cabinet or Politburo member, usually in a not very important ministry or party function. Second, even though women were better represented in the professions and in formerly "masculine" jobs generally, they were less in evidence as one went higher in each occupational hierarchy. Thus, while Soviet women made up nearly all the nursing personnel and seven of ten doctors, they accounted for a lesser 57 percent of heads of hospitals and head physicians and only 25 percent of neurosurgeons, the most prestigious and high-paying specialization. In education, 81 percent of primary- and secondary-school teachers were women in 1974–75, but only 31 percent of primary-school principals and 28 percent of secondary-school principals were women. It should be added that these figures had risen from 23 and 20 percent in 1960–1961, however (Dodge, 1977:218–22). Men still tended to get the better jobs even in those fields where women had for some time been active in large numbers. Third, Soviet working women, both professional and nonprofessional, carried a double burden of career and housekeeper. Soviet sociologists Leonid Gordon and E. Klopov (1975) pointed out that this inequality was related to the inequalities mentioned above: "Working women devote from 2 to 2.5 times more of their time to housework than do the men, therefore they have less opportunity for rest, raising their professional skills, and cultural levels—in general, less opportunity for their own development" (p.73).

Soviet authorities and other East European leaders in the 1980s openly recognized this inequality. In general, the system tried to deal with women's double burden through better daycare facilities for children, more labor-saving appliances, and better community laundering and shopping services. The system was much more reluctant to encourage men to change their attitudes. In the 1980s, Soviet women pressed for greater equality in job promotion, pay, and (especially) higher representation in the party leadership. The percentage of women among party membership rose from 23 to 27 percent from the 1970s to the 1980s, and nearly one-third of new members were women (Moses, 1986). For the first time since the early 1960s, a woman, Biryukova, was elevated to the Secretariat at the 27th Party Congress in 1986. Women's issues were voiced more openly, and women, both in and outside the party, articulated a series of demands that demonstrate, according to Moses (1986:401), "the evident ability of Soviet women as a group to shape the direction of public policy discussions and decisions in the USSR in the past decade." Issues such as health-care reform, family policy, divorce, and labor productivity became much more linked to solutions of women's problems in Soviet policy debates. However, with the collapse of Communist regimes in Eastern Europe in 1989–90 and the economic and ethnic turmoil in the entire region, women's issues have also been pushed into the background again.

In the first round of free elections in post-communism, the share of parliamentary seats held by women dropped sharply (see table 9.6). Of course, parliament under the old Communist system was a rubber stamp for party decisions, so the much higher percentages of women deputies did not indicate real political clout for women. Nevertheless, the first democratically elected post-Communist parliaments, which are legitimate institutions of

Table 9.6 Women's Parliamentary Representation in Eastern Europe and the USSR (percentage)

	1987	1990
Bulgaria	21	9
Czechoslovakia	30	6
Hungary	21	7
Poland		
Senate	—	6
Lower House	20	4
Romania	34	4
USSR		
Congress of Peoples' Deputies	—	16
Soviet Nationalities	31	14
Supreme Soviet	35	14

Source: UN, *The World's Women 1970–1990: Trends and Statistics.*

political influence, illustrate the relatively weak political power of women. In some ways, the concept of women's liberation or "feminism" is often associated with a discredited "women's emanicipation" under communism, and women's groups in post-communism have been on the defensive in the first years after the collapse of communism (Funk and Mueller, 1993). In Poland, the conservative Catholic church pressured the parliament (Sejm) to virtually outlaw abortion, and in most parts of Eastern Europe, women were being fired from jobs in greater percentages than men. The revival of religion as a new authoritative voice in post-communism has created traditionalist pressures for women to return to tending the home, cooking, and caring for husband and children, while leaving work careers and politics to men. But women's groups are beginning to fight back against the conservative pressures to maintain women's rights and to demand opportunities for women in post-communism on an equitable basis (Nadle, 1992).

Ethnic and National Inequality

The Leninist principles of working-class internationalism and the Soviet federal structures along national-republic lines were supposed to provide for the equality of different ethnic groups within the Soviet Union. However, the nondemocratic nature of the Soviet Union in its development up to the Gorbachev reform era did not build interethnic equality on a foundation of independent bargaining among legitimate or authentic representatives of the various ethnic/national communities which made up the Soviet Union. One consequence of the nondemocratic and centralist Soviet system was that many ethnic groups felt that their cultures were being degraded and their local resources exploited by a Russian-dominated elite in Moscow. While ethnic conflict was effectively suppressed for a long time under Soviet communist rule, and some indicators (neighborhood ethnic mixing, ethnic intermarriage) showed signs of ethnic and nationality coexistence and integration, once the Gorbachev reforms were taken seriously at the grassroots, both age-old and new ethnic grievances surfaced and began to boil over. Whether Armenians versus Azerbaijanis, Georgians versus Abkhazians or Ossetians, Moldavians versus Ukrainians and Turks, or Balts versus Russians, each ethnic minority felt that its history within the Soviet Union, and often within the Russian empire before that, had been one of unequal and discriminatory treatment, which could be resolved only by exiting from the USSR. Whatever the facts of economic or of cultural treatment, new nationalist leaders rose to prominence on themes of national pride and settlement of perceived economic grievances.

Beginning in 1990, virtually every republic in the Soviet Union declared its sovereignty, a so-called "parade of sovereignties" that has continued beyond the breakup of the Soviet Union at the end of 1991. The attempted military coup by antireform leaders in Moscow in August 1991 only accelerated the process of ethnic division and the rise of a new ethnonationalism. In many post-Communist states of the former Soviet Union and the former Yugoslavia, the struggle for political power is along ethnic lines, with new policies of economic and political inequalities bluntly stated and fiercely resisted, depending on one's ethnic loyalties.

With the collapse of communism and the breakup of the Soviet Union and Yugoslavia, especially, ethnic grievances in several new independent nations have reshaped politics around themes of new national identities, which would make members of the dominant ethnic group first-class citizens and members of minorities into second-class citizens or noncitizens with limited rights. In the political struggle over control of privatization and ownership of denationalized property, members of the dominant ethnic group would become the new propertied class, whereas minority groups would be generally excluded. New language laws require ethnic minorities in many new states to learn the new official language in order to keep their jobs or to apply for jobs, and new citizenship laws often exclude Russian and other minorities from citizenship and property rights. The rise of ethnic nationalism is now creating new inequalities to replace old inequalities and to settle old grievances.

With the hardships of economic dislocation and collapse of social services once provided by Communist regimes, ethnic scapegoating has also emerged as a feature of post-Communist politics. Anger over problems associated with unemployment, high prices, theft, smuggling, and prostitution are often placed on ethnic minorities, and the minority most often targeted in post-communism has been the Gypsies, or Roma. The Roma are spread throughout Europe but have no state or autonomous region of their own, and so they are virtually without protection from any government. Traditional stereotypes of Roma as unclean, dishonest, lazy, and criminal have made them convenient targets for popular frustrations. Roma have especially been persecuted in hard times, as they were by the fascist regimes of the 1920s and 1930s in East-Central Europe. Communist regimes had attempted to integrate the Roma people into the mainstream of society, providing steady jobs, housing, social welfare, and education (Kamm, 1993). In full employment, centrally planned economies, the Roma found some stable position within the larger society. This has now collapsed, and anti-Gypsy prejudices have escalated into skinhead, neofascist, and neighborhood attacks on the Roma. In the Czech Republic, otherwise noted for its peaceful "velvet revolution," young right-wing thugs have attacked and killed Roma with considerable approval from local townsfolk. In Romania, which has the largest Roma population of over 3 million, murderous pogroms against Roma have broken out. The ethnic hatreds and vicious scapegoating of the early years of post-communism have been most dangerous for this least-protected group.

In some areas of the former Soviet Union, new ethnic inequalities have sparked violent conflict: Uzbeks versus Tadzhiks; Russians versus Moldovans;

Ossetians versus Ingush; and Georgians versus Abzhaz. In other areas, ethnic conflict has not yet (as of 1994) erupted into violence but has become a major barrier to the establishment of free and democratic interethnic bargaining and establishment of a civil political competition that includes all residents.

Similarly, in post-Communist Eastern Europe, both real and perceived ethnic inequalities are fueling nationalist movements, In Czechoslovakia, it has pitted Czechs against Slovaks and Slovaks against Hungarians; in Hungary, it divides Hungarians and Jews; in Romania, it rouses animosities of Romanians against Hungarians; and in Bulgaria, anti-Turkish sentiment runs high. In Yugoslovakia, civil war between Croats and Serbs has erupted, and all ethnic groups, including Slovenes, Bosnians, Macedonians, and Albanians, feel that their group has been treated unfairly. (In this fever of ethnic nationalism, one's own group is perceived to have never done anything wrong to any other group; it is only the victim of others. Historical honesty is as much a victim of reactionary nationalism as it was of communism.)

An Equality Summary and Cautious Forecast

Communism produced important and basic shifts toward greater equality in income and wealth distribution, opened educational opportunities, widened the social basis for elite recruitment, and freed women from some of the restrictions of the pre-Communist social order. On the other hand, much of the egalitarian commitment of Communist regimes faded with the passage of time, and new inequalities arose associated with the Communist elite and its privileges. In addition, communism did not do much to alleviate some types of inequality (see Echols, 1981; Nelson, 1983). Regional inequality in Yugoslavia between the developed north and the underdeveloped south may have increased under communism, and racial inequality between blacks and whites in Cuba has not changed much. Communism, in its early years in power, did make a push for greater equality, but this was primarily concentrated on reducing class inequalities, necessary for building support among the working class. Other experiments with radically changing ethnic and family structures to achieve equality were abandoned.

As the Communist world enters a period of post-Communist transformation, the levels of inequality are increasing, often quite sharply. On the one hand, millions are losing their jobs, and more millions are finding their retirement or disability pensions destroyed by inflation; on the other hand, thousands of new business owners and traders are making new fortunes from legal, semi-legal, and criminal enterprises. Free markets should place no limits on income or wealth, and many of the new government ministers (including former Communists and former dissidents) are born-again believers in capitalist market theory, often of the nineteenth century variety. The wisdom of the moment at the beginning of the 1990s was that marked income and wealth differentials were required to build up a new capitalist class, and the threat of poverty and economic desperation was needed to "discipline" a slovenly, unmotivated working class.

With the collapse of the old economic structures and the disruptive drive to build up new market economies, desperation has added to the interethnic sense of "unjust" inequalities. The prospects for peacefully and democratically settling issues of ethnic and national inequalities under post-communism seem precariously balanced. If economic development, of whatever form, can show the value of interethnic cooperation, then clearly a happier outcome can be forecast. If the downward economic trend continues or accelerates, however, then the politics of ethnic inequality will become more abusive and less likely to remain within democratic bounds.

10

Post-Communist Gains
in Personal Freedom

The collapse of European communism, despite all of the problems of economic and social turmoil that have followed, has nevertheless produced the greatest gains in personal liberty since the defeat of European fascism at the end of World War II (see chapter 5). The dismantling of the extensive police controls and internal network of secret police informants and the ending of official censorship and of restrictions on travel have brought a new era of personal choice and individualism. This new era of personal freedom is still fragile, and the struggle to overcome past submissiveness to authoritarian command is

Table 10.1   Indicators of Liberty in the Communist and Post-Communist Nations

	Political Rights (scale of 1 to 7)		Civil Rights (scale of 1 to 7)		Human Rights Rating %
	1977	1992	1977	1992	1991
USSR[a]	7	3	6	4	54[b]
Czechoslovakia	7	2	6	2	97
Hungary	6	2	5	2	97
Poland	6	2	5	2	83
Yugoslavia[c]	6	6	5	5	55[d]
Cuba	6	7	6	7	30
China	6	7	6	7	21
Vietnam	7	7	7	7	27

Sources: Freedom House, *Freedom in the World: Political Rights and Civil Liberties* (New York: Freedom House, 1991), pp. 454–55; Charles Humana, *World Human Rights Guide* (New York: Oxford University Press 1992), pp. xvii–xix.

a. Russia, 1992
b. At dissolution of 1917 Union, August 1991
c. Serbia and Montenegro, 1992
d. At dissolution of 1945 Communist Republic, mid-1991
Note: The political rights and civil liberties indices are on a scale of 1 to 7, with 1 representing the most free and 7 the least free category. The Human Rights Rating is a percentage.

far from finished. There are already new attempts to limit, in old and new ways, personal choice and individual freedom in the post-Communist era. Yet the one area of most positive change in performance from Communist systems to the new post-Communist transition politics has been the increase in personal liberty.

In rankings on political rights, civil rights, and human rights scales, the post-Communist systems in 1991–92 showed great leaps forward for the USSR/Russia and the nations of Eastern Europe generally. In Czechoslovakia, Hungary and Poland, the post-Communist performance levels were close to Western democratic standards. In the post-Communist Yugoslavia of Slobodan Milosevic (Serbia and Montenegro), and still-Communist China of Deng Xiaoping, Castroite Cuba, and Vietnam, on the other hand, the performance on personal liberty was still poor, with no breakthrough to a new higher level of liberty.

Communist Systems—Failures in Personal Freedom

Communist systems have been noted for their heavy-handed and thorough suppression of personal liberty. This was a classic feature of these systems, and differentiated them from the liberal traditions of the Western democracies as well as from even the most authoritarian Third-World regimes (see chapter 15). Socialists committed to democracy have from the time of Lenin pointed out the contradictions between socialist goals of human emancipation and the systematic denial of liberty under communist regimes (see chapter 12, criticisms from Martov, Bernstein and Luxemburg). Communist suppression of personal liberty demonstrated for Western socialists the impossibility of achieving socialism through Leninist methods.

The contradictions between Leninist regimes and socialist ideals are clearly illustrated from Marx's writings. First, Marx and Engels (and other socialists) had clearly stated in the 1848 Manifesto that in a new classless society of the future, "the free development of each is the condition for the free development of all" (Marx and Engels, *Communist Manifesto*).

Second, Marx and Engels predicted that in the future classless society, the state (that is, a professional governing institution separate from the citizenry) would "wither away." In the *Communist Manifesto,* they specifically proclaimed that "the Communists do not form a separate party opposed to other working-class groups. They have no interests separate and apart from those of the proletariat as a whole. They do not set up any sectarian principles of their own, by which to shape and mould the proletarian movement." Marx did not advocate a Communist party-state that would rule over the proletariat or suppress liberty.

Communism has been a catastrophe for socialism, because it has associated socialist ideals with Communist practice. Democratic socialists predicted this from the beginning, even before Lenin's Bolsheviks had seized power in Russia. Instead of bringing greater liberty and worker freedoms, communist states have huge police and informer systems to suppress individual expression. Instead of the state "withering away" in favor of free political participation and expression by citizens, communist governments have grown huge and have developed into the new ruling classes of society. Whatever the rationale given, and from whatever standpoint, communist regimes failed in the area of personal liberty.

In all Communist systems, there was essentially no free choice in political elections at any level. Lists of officially supported candidates (part of the nomenklatura system) were presented to lower-level bodies for automatic approval. Non-Communist parties were either banned, as in the USSR, or, as in Poland, Czechoslovakia, and China, survived as docile vestiges of former opposition parties and groups. In Poland and Yugoslavia there was some choice of candidates for parliamentary elections, but only from among "approved" candidates. The same applied for Cuban trade unions and some other mass organization elections. The emergence of independent non-Communist candidates was a key criterion on which the Soviet leadership based its military intervention in Hungary in 1956 and in Czechoslovakia in 1968. The Soviet leaders tolerated an independent-minded Romanian regime and did not intervene in Poland in 1956 because in both cases it was more confident that the local Romanian and Polish Communist parties, despite some policy differences with Moscow, were firmly in control and would continue to suppress independent political groups.

In all Communist countries, censorship of press, radio, and television has been the rule, in some cases by a separate censorship office, in others through self-censorship within publication or broadcast facilities. Dissident publications, for example the so-called *samizdat* (self-publishing) network of typewritten journals and newsletters in the Soviet Union, occasionally appeared, but their authors were frequently arrested on charges of "slandering the state." In all Communist countries, there was a virtual ban on nonsponsored demonstrations, and violators were subject to arrest for "hooliganism" or "rowdyism."

In cultural affairs, there were limits on artistic freedom and religious practice in the Communist nations. To be sure, the Soviet government made its peace with a domesticated Russian Orthodox church, the Polish regime followed a relatively relaxed policy in its dealings with the Roman Catholic church, and other Communist parties gradually developed a kind of detente vis-à-vis the major organized religions in their countries. Yet activist or especially proselytizing behavior by Soviet Jews, Baptists, and Jehovah's Witnesses led to harassment and punishment, and obstacles were still placed in the way of normal religious observances. In art, sculpture, and music, a doctrine of "socialist realism" became the official guide to channel artistic

217

creation into the service of the party's goal of building communism. Poetry, novels, painting, and composition were supposed to encourage and support communism, never to oppose or question it, and defiant artists soon lost their jobs if they tried to express basic criticisms of the existing order.

In all Communist nations, the legal system was subservient to the party, and the right to a fair trial was not honored. Independent legal counsel was not permitted. In general, the outcome of political cases rested on political considerations rather than on evidence and legal statute. Psychiatric clinics and sanatoria were also used to imprison political dissidents without trial or benefit of any legal proceedings.

In Communist nations, although most workers were members of officially sponsored unions, there was no right to organize an independent trade union. Official trade unions, in practice, were subservient to the party and did not call for strikes. An exception was Yugoslavia, where strikes were sometimes called in the privately owned, small and medium-sized factories. Although it was claimed that there was no need for strike action since all major enterprises were publicly owned, worker support for the independent union Solidarity in Poland in 1980–81 and occasional slowdowns and mass resignations at some plants in the Soviet Union indicate that there was discontent with the official trade unions.

Finally, only in Yugoslavia were people free to emigrate from the country. In the USSR, during the era of detente in the 1970s, large numbers of Soviet Jews and lesser numbers of ethnic Germans and Armenians were allowed to immigrate to Israel or to the West, but this was an exception to the general rule. People who applied for emigration visas were harassed, especially if they joined in public protest or signed petitions about their desire to leave. In East Germany, Poland, and Czechoslovakia, thousands of ethnic Germans were allowed to emigrate after West Germany established normal diplomatic relations and trade relations with its Eastern neighbors, giving up its claim to the old borders of the Third Reich, but the Berlin Wall stood to prevent escape to the West by East German citizens. The Berlin Wall was for twenty-eight years the symbol of communism's denial of basic human liberty, and the fall of "the Wall" on November 9, 1989, was the single most graphic act in the collapse of East European communism and the transition to a post-Communist political era.

Stalinism, Destalinization, Post-Destalinization, and Glasnost

Although the level of personal liberty in the Communist systems was low compared with that in the liberal democracies, there had been change since the death of Stalin in 1953, and this change had been in the direction of greater relaxation and less coercion, even though this progress never led to a communist system that effectively guaranteed rights of speech, press, political and union activity, religious belief, due process of law, and emigration. The decline in terror gave rise to the rebirth of civil society, with its citizens expressing longing to have personal liberty and personal freedom of expression as a "normal" part of daily life. Once the Communist regime gave up its use of terror, the contradictions between regime authority and citizen demands for liberty gradually grew into unmanageable crises.

The worst years for personal liberty in the Communist systems came during the period of Stalin's rule in the Soviet Union (1928–53) and in the early postwar years of Eastern Europe (1945–53). During this period the power of the secret police agencies grew enormously, so that in the 1930s the Soviet NKVD controlled not only internal and external intelligence activities but also border and internal convoy troops, highway patrols, civilian registry bureaus, and the fire departments. The NKVD also oversaw a huge economic empire run by forced labor (the GULAG), which Stalin filled with his purge victims. The forced labor system may have included up to 20 million people, depending on who is considered a forced laborer and whose estimates are used (see Fainsod, 1963). Besides the perhaps 3 million who were put into labor camps, there were many millions more who were exiled to remote one-industry towns, who were forced to work at a particular job under constant secret police supervision, or whose wages were cut for political offenses. Those who served out their sentences or were released, often after the completion of some major GULAG project, frequently continued to suffer discrimination at the hands of the authorities. The NKVD operated whole mining towns, lumber camps, hydroelectric and canal construction projects. A few prominent purge victims, such as old Bolsheviks Zinoviev, Kamenev, Bukharin, and Rykov, went through elaborate "show trials" in which they confessed to crimes that they could not possibly have committed before they were sentenced to execution. Most of the people arrested simply disappeared from public view, their fates decided by secret courts run by the NKVD.

In the arts, the norm of "socialist realism" was dogmatically enforced by Stalin's associate Andrei Zhdanov. All thoughts of "art for art's sake" were denounced as bourgeois deviations, and avant-garde art was treated as a mental aberration. Even in science, the agricultural biologist T. D. Lysenko was able to use the political support of Stalin to purge Soviet biology of its most talented geneticists. At the same time he built up his own theory of "vernalization" (see Z. Medvedev, 1969) from falsified or incompetent research, which set Soviet biology back several decades.

Even within the party hierarchy, Stalin ruthlessly punished any dissent or suspected opposition. From 1939 to 1952 no Party congress was even held, and the Central Committee and Politburo, which in Lenin's time had been centers for debate and policymaking, were dormant. Stalin simply formed *ad hoc* groups of a few trusted people who carried out his directives. Between 1948 and 1952, after Tito's break with Stalin, new purges of suspected

"Titoists" were ordered throughout Eastern Europe, and it is thought that Stalin was about to launch a new massive purge in the Soviet Union shortly before his death. During Stalin's tyrannical rule, the Soviet system not only crushed opposition but also demanded rapid change of individual behavior, with obligatory displays of support and even enthusiasm for the goals of the regime.

Almost immediately after Stalin's death, a process of general relaxation of controls, a "thaw" in the frozen landscape of Stalinism, began to emerge. Without much fanfare, labor camp inmates were released, and the power of the secret police was dramatically downgraded. Stalin's last secret police chief, Lavrenti Beria, was executed. The military and economic functions of the secret police were turned over to other government ministries. In literature, books somewhat critical of the past and calling for a better future were published (e.g., Ehrenburg's *The Thaw*). This movement was accelerated in early 1956 when Nikita Khrushchev, first secretary of the CPSU, denounced Stalin for his crimes and his one-man dictatorship at the Twentieth Party Congress. Almost immediately, the release of millions from labor camps was ordered, and the process of their assimilation into Soviet society was aided by the Khrushchev regime (Medvedev, 1975). Khrushchev revealed the extent of Stalin's purges, his paranoia, and his mistakes as a leader that cost the Soviet people so much in World War II (see Khrushchev, Report to the Twentieth Congress of the CPSU, 1956), Khrushchev demolished the cult of Stalin as an infallible leader and launched a broad campaign to "destalinize" Soviet society.

Over the next six years, many purge victims were rehabilitated, reinstated in previous careers, and given some compensation for their losses. In the arts, critical voices like Solzhenitsyn and Yevtushenko were published; Khrushchev personally okayed the publication of *One Day in the Life of Ivan Denisovich*. In Soviet politics, a variety of interest groups began to lobby more openly and actively for influence over policy, without fear that Khrushchev would or could suppress such group participation as Stalin had (Skilling and Griffiths, 1971). Khrushchev never had the kind of one-man control that Stalin held, and several of his favorite reforms in education, fertilizer production, and party organization were defeated by his opponents. At one point in 1957 Khrushchev was faced with a hostile majority in the Politburo calling for his ouster. After a two-day debate in the larger Central Committee Khrushchev was sustained in his office, and his opponents were forced to resign. However, his defeated opponents, Malenkov, Molotov, Voroshilov, Bulganin, and Kaganovich, were not executed or imprisoned; some even continued as party members and government officials, though demoted several levels. Soviet government had returned in some ways to the Leninist norms of a collective leadership, and a higher level of tolerance for debate within party, state, military, trade union, educational, and cultural organizations had been re-established.

The limits of this initial destalinization were quickly demonstrated. In October 1956, Soviet troops marched into Budapest to arrest and later execute Imre Nagy, a liberal communist who had overstepped the bounds of acceptable destalinization by bringing non-Communists into high government posts and considering pulling Hungary out of the Warsaw Pact. In the Soviet Union, students rejected officially sponsored candidates for student offices in many universities in 1957 and wanted to put up their own candidates, but the party refused and simply appointed new officers. In literature, as writers demanded greater freedom and became more outspoken in their rejection of Soviet society, their works ceased being published. Even at the high point of Khrushchev's populist destalinization campaign, the basic commitment to achieve communism, the basic structures of the economy, and the right of the party to dominate the political life of the nation could not be questioned.

Khrushchev's removal from office in 1964, by majority vote of both the Politburo and the Central Committee, led to the formation of the Brezhnev-Kosygin collective leadership (see Tatu, 1969), in which from the start Brezhnev and Kosygin had to build Politburo majorities on various policy issues. We know that there were hawks and doves on detente, consumerists and "steel-eaters," decentralizers and central planning die-hards in the top ranks of leadership. In this post-Khrushchev period, a cautious pragmatism toward dissent and dissenters outside the party emerged. On the one hand, the reins were tightened in literature and the arts, and dissident writers Daniel, Sinyavsky, and Amalrik were brought to public trial for "slander." On the other hand, as part of detente with the West, the Brezhnev regime permitted large-scale emigration of Soviet Jews to Israel and Germans to West Germany. And in the social sciences, a new Soviet sociology emerged that was able to study such social ills as alcoholism, crime, delinquency, and discrimination against women in Soviet society. Rather than arresting or imprisoning many leading dissidents, the Brezhnev regime forced people like Solzhenitsyn, Medvedev, and human rights activist Chkaidze to leave the country.

Other dissidents, such as Jewish activist Sharansky and the physicist Sakharov, were either imprisoned or sent into internal exile. Still, Sakharov, from his exile in the city of Gorky, continued to protest against a variety of Soviet policies and went on hunger strikes to gain the right for his wife, Yelena Bonner, to travel to the West for medical treatment. Even in the worst years of the conservative Brezhnev era, dissidents were not terrorized into silence, as would have been the case under Stalin. Dissenters like Robert Haveman in East Germany and Vaclav Havel in Czechoslovakia continued their outspoken opposition. Ivan Szelenyi, commenting on dissent in Eastern Europe in the 1970s, wrote: "few political trials have been staged against intellectuals, and most of them get away with relatively mild, sometimes suspended, sentences. Nowadays, the lives of dissenting intellectuals are not threatened anymore and the worst that they can expect is a few years in jail or probably just a one-way ticket to West Germany or England'' (1979:189).

At the end of the Brezhnev era, there were, by CIA and U.S. State Department estimates, somewhere between 1 million and 2.5 million citizens in prisons and labor camps in the Soviet Union, of whom as many as 10,000 could be described as political prisoners (*New York Times*, Nov. 7, 1982). The CIA has stated that in the mid-1970s approximately 85 percent of those "confined" were in labor camps, with the remaining 15 percent in prisons. In the Gorbachev period further reductions in prison populations brought the number of prisoners down from the approximately one million estimated by Soviet emigre scholar Vadim Medish (1987:286) to about 750,000 at the end of 1990 (*New York Times*, Jan. 7, 1991, p. 14). According to private research done by the Sentencing Project, this means that the Soviet incarceration rate (268 per 100,000 population) had fallen below the level of both the United States (426) and South Africa (333), the other two nations with the highest levels of prison populations.

In 1985, after the deaths of Brezhnev and his short-term successors Andropov and Chernenko, a new leadership team under Mikhail Gorbachev began to steer the Soviet Union on a new course of openness and democratization, termed "*glasnost.*" The Soviet media were now reporting on such issues as drug abuse, official abuse of power, corruption, crime, and natural disasters, which were formerly out of bounds for normal reportage. Even subjects such as abuses of Soviet psychiatry and the war in Afghanistan were given more detailed and honest treatment in Soviet newspapers and journals; however, attempts to form nonofficial publishing cooperatives have been rejected, and this represents a clear barrier to still wider and more free press reporting. In early 1987, more than one hundred political prisoners were released, and Andrei Sakharov was allowed to return from exile in Gorky. Sakharov even became a cautious supporter of *glasnost,* though he continued to criticize Soviet policy in Afghanistan. In film and literature especially, formerly censored works were released, and new works were breaking down old barriers of censorship. There was an excitement again among Soviet intellectuals and reformers and a spirit of hope for greater freedom of expression.

In early 1989, the first relatively free and contested elections to a new Congress of People's Deputies gave opposition nationalist and radical democratic forces a voice in a parliament that was not just a rubber-stamp body. The four-month sessions of the Congress and the smaller Supreme Soviet were lively, uncensored, and televised. Quickly, in the course of 1989, everything became open to criticism, including the army, the KGB, and even Gorbachev himself. The new Soviet parliament refused to confirm several nominees for ministry posts, and Prime Minister Ryzhkov had to find new nominees who could get parliamentary support for confirmation. In 1989 and 1990, new elections in cities and republics gave new political groupings control of Leningrad and Moscow city governments, and control of several republic governments as well. The 28th Congress of the CPSU was more open than any since the early 1920s, and presented competing platforms. However, the more radical reformers, including Boris Yeltsin, walked out of the party, and Yeltsin was elected president of the Russian Republic of the USSR. New journals sprouted in 1990, representing all opinions from far-right nationalism and anti-Semitic Russian fascism to ultra-capitalist neo-liberalism, to greens environmentalism and an ultra-leftism outside the Communist party. New political parties, trade unions, and social organizations of all types began to organize freely and voice their grievances and politics. Public religious expression and involvement in social affairs grew rapidly. In general, 1989–90 saw a flowering of personal liberty in the USSR, despite the worsening economy and growing ethnic hostility. It was the freest period so far in Soviet history, and represented at least a temporary breakthrough in personal liberty. Gorbachev's policies of *glasnost* and democratization raised popular expectations about freedom of speech and press, freedom of political expression, and political participation for millions of Soviet citizens. Especially among the urban educated, the young, and those with strong ethnic, religious, or political ideals, the Gorbachev era of 1985–90 was a real breakthrough in the development of a free citizenry. It was in part this free citizenry's will to resist the August 1991 coup attempt by the reactionary "gang of eight" in the Soviet Union that made the difference in the outcome. Both by mass demonstrations in the largest cities and by widespread noncompliance with the decrees of the coup leaders, a large part of the Soviet populace showed that they would not support a return to the old order. The coup failed to generate the obedient response pattern of earlier times in both the Communist and tsarist eras.

Yugoslavia: From Liberal Communism to Ethnic Nationalism

Since its break with Stalin in 1948, Yugoslavia followed along a path different from that of the USSR and has been characterized as a more liberal type of communism. Its "market socialism" path was relevant to personal liberty in several respects. First of all, Yugoslavia was the only communist system that permitted citizens to emigrate. Second, through the development of workers' councils in the state-owned industries, about half the working population participated in an economic decision-making process that was unique. Yugoslav self-management, providing for election of workers' councils, gave blue-collar, white-collar, and managerial personnel opportunities to share in the running of the enterprise and its profits (or losses). Although this system had its setbacks over the more than three decades of its evolution, it represented an advance in the rights of ordinary citizens to express grievances, put forward their own ideas, and in general vote on issues that affect their daily lives. Bogdan Denitch (1976:273) in his extensive studies of this system in the 1970s concluded that "the norm of participation is now firmly rooted; and given the system of rotation which is used in electing representatives to self-managing bodies, this means that a major part of the working population at one point or another participates in running its own institutions."

Press censorship in Yugoslavia was also more liberal but remained censorship just the same. In general, critical articles appeared in print, but if they went too far, censorship was placed on further publications. This was a sort of after-the-fact censorship, as opposed to the pre-publication censorship that existed in most other Communist nations. Critics of Yugoslav socialism, from Djilas in the 1950s to Mihajlov in the 1960s and Stojanovic in the 1970s, were treated with relative leniency, yet they have been fired from their jobs and party positions and, in the cases of Djilas and Mihajlov, have been in and out of jail a number of times.

The Yugoslav parliament was a relatively active Communist legislature. Non-Communist candidates could run for office, and voters had some choice, but non-Communist candidates had to be acceptable to the Yugoslav League of Communists. Trade unions were also more active and occasionally capable of independent action. In early 1987, a wave of strikes swept across Yugoslavia to protest government austerity policies and to agitate for higher wages. And critical, even self-critical, debate among Yugoslav leaders was far more free-wheeling and public than elsewhere in Eastern Europe. In general, the League of Communists was a far less obtrusive fact of life than similar organizations in other Communist systems. Yet there are also numerous indications, including the party backlash in the early 1970s and the banning of the critical journal *Praxis*, that the party had the capacity and will to tighten controls a notch or two if it believed events were getting out of hand. Canadian political scientist Skilling nevertheless considered the Yugoslav system at that time as a "democratizing and pluralistic authoritarian" regime (1971:222–28).

As long as Tito ruled in Yugoslavia, ethnic conflict was kept under relative control. But after his death in 1980, the already decentralized Yugoslav Federation began to suffer from increasing conflicts among ethnic groups. The Serbian province of Kosovo had an ethnic Albanian majority, and in 1981 Albanian ethnic leaders rose up to demand greater autonomy and in some cases independence. They were suppressed, but continuing unrest in Kosovo gave rise to a new wave of Serbian nationalism led by Slobodan Milosevic, who rose from relative obscurity to become the new Serbian party leader.

Two-Line Struggle in China

By Western standards, freedom of speech, emigration, voting choice, protest, fair trial, political association, and privacy have been nonexistent in China. Many times the West has heard of examples of Chinese self-criticism, where citizens have been put under great social pressure to confess the error of their ways, to repent, and to humble themselves before the will of the party.

Yet there are also times when Chinese citizens have been mobilized for criticism and even punishment of high government officials. From 1966 to 1968, self-appointed Red Guards went through villages and cities to denounce government, educational, managerial, party, and even military leaders for their elitism, bureaucratism, and "betrayal" of socialism. Wall posters and impromptu Red Guard newspapers appeared to rally people against the "capitalist roaders" in positions of power. Liu Shaoqi, the president of the People's Republic, and Deng Xiaoping, deputy premier under Zhou Enlai, were among the most prominent targets. Intellectuals, educators, and state bureaucrats were often sent into the countryside to help the peasants with the harvest and learn from the daily life of the masses. Though the Great Proletarian Cultural Revolution was not the kind of blood purge that Stalin had conducted in the 1930s in Soviet Russia, it was indeed a rough time for many Chinese who had held top posts in many fields. In China's Communist history, competing factions within the ruling party have at various times mobilized segments of popular support for their own political purposes, until the mass movements threatened to get out of the regime's control and required a renewed crackdown or "rectification" campaign.

To understand some of the seemingly contradictory impressions, we must set the Chinese experience in the context of Mao and his opponents within the Chinese Communist party. Mao believed that even after the revolution had won political power, a class struggle would continue in China. There would be a tendency for the new governmental and highly educated strata to set themselves apart from the masses of workers and peasants and return to the "capitalist road" of development to become a new bourgeoisie. Mao believed that this had happened in the Soviet Union under Khrushchev and the destalinization was a betrayal of communism. In China there was no grand denunciation of Stalin, but rather a back and forth struggle between two major party factions, the Maoists (or radicals) and anti-Maoists (or moderates).

In the spring of 1957, Mao had invited the intellectuals to criticize the Communist system of the People's Republic—a "Hundred Flowers" to bloom and contend. When the criticisms turned out to be harsh and far reaching, Mao declared them to be weeds instead of flowers and launched his Great Leap Forward campaign. This decentralized the economy into self-reliant communes and put strong faith in local initiatives and efforts to build industries, including production facilities for machine tools, iron, and steel. The Great

Leap Forward reflected Mao's break with the Soviet pattern of urban-based, technocrat-managed industrialization. It also signalled his split with Liu Shaoqi and Zhou Enlai, who apparently wanted to follow the path of economic modernization that had already been introduced in the first Five Year Plan, 1952–56. The Maoists stressed the necessity for "politics in command," meaning the priority of anti-elitism and antibureaucratism, even at the price of slower industrial growth. The moderates stressed priority of economic modernization, with greater power for those technically trained and competent to build and manage the new factories and enterprises.

The Great Leap Forward achieved some early successes, but many failures as well, especially in the backyard iron and steel foundries. By the early 1960s Mao's power was in decline, with Liu Shaoqi, in particular, appearing to take over general responsibility for the course of government policy and a "normalization" of economic development. Mao seemed to go along with this arrangement, and it was widely assumed that the aging Mao would gradually fade from active political life. The Cultural Revolution, initiated by Mao's call for formation of Red Guard groups to attack Liu's policies, was a comeback attempt by the Maoist faction. Mao pinned his hopes on mass support, mobilized by the Red Guards, to oust his opponents from power. As Michael Oksenberg (1976) has noted, however, the Red Guard campaign rather quickly got out of hand, and even the People's Liberation Army (PLA) leadership, whom Mao counted on as allies, were by early 1968 calling for a return to normalcy and the reestablishment of control over China's rampant youth. By the early 1970s, Deng Xiaoping had been restored to his position, although Liu Shaoqi was still reported to be under house arrest. A group of Politburo radicals, including Mao's wife, Jiang Qing, continued to do battle with Deng and Zhou. After the death of Zhou in 1976, Deng was ousted from office in disgrace for a second time. After the death of Mao later in 1976, however, Deng made a remarkable second comeback, and the radical "Gang of Four" was purged and arrested.

At those times when the Maoist faction had the upper hand, a greater emphasis was put on political mass mobilization, including criticism of authority figures. When the moderates or anti-Maoists were in power, the better educated and technically trained were given more authority and greater freedom to pursue their specialized work. The question of personal liberty must always ask "for whom" in any system, and in China the swings of the political pendulum produced periods of alternating relaxation and pressure on different groups in the society. The trend has been more cyclical in nature, unlike the rather steady progression of change in the Soviet Union and Yugoslavia. The post-Mao leadership around Deng, after an early period of open and public contention of views through "wall newspapers" in Peking, once again tightened cultural and ideological controls for most citizens, while expanding the authority and autonomy of economic managers and educational and scientific specialists.

In late 1986, after a series of demonstrations by university students demanding more democracy and Western-style personal liberty, the Deng leadership, under pressure from more conservative elements still in the party, again tightened controls over public debate, and several more reformist leaders, including the top party secretary, Hu Yaobang, were criticized and demoted, although Hu still remained a member of the Politburo. On the other hand, at the Chinese Party Congress in 1987, the economic reformers made a modest comeback, and many aged party hardliners were retired from office, though not disgraced. Those Western observers who asserted that economic liberalization must also produce personal liberty at the same time or of economic necessity have been mistaken. The link between the two is far more problematic, as both the Chinese and Soviet experience have shown.

In 1989, beginning with small demonstrations of students from the elite People's University in Beijing to mark the anniversary of the death of Hu Yaobang, a reform communist, a mass movement for democracy and radical reform mushroomed into a month-long physical tug-of-war in Tienanmen Square. For a time, it appeared that the reform wing of the party, led by Zhao Ziyang, would be able to use this popular mobilization to press its reform policy agenda, but after much maneuvering for support within the top elite of the People's Liberation Army (PLA), the conservative faction won out, and ordered a crackdown on June 4, 1989, on the democracy movement in Beijing and across the country. Several hundred people were killed, thousands injured, tens of thousands arrested. Many student leaders escaped to the West for safety and formed an active democratic opposition abroad. For the moment, the aged conservative elite had restored order and had suppressed the popular protests for democracy, but at a severe price in further loss of legitimacy and alienation of a generation of educated youth. The Beijing crackdown was the only example in 1989–90 of a Communist regime successfully suppressing the democratic movement.

In the years following the Tienanmen crackdown on the democracy movement, the Deng leadership accelerated the economic liberalization of China, with spectacular results in terms of growth rates and a new consumerist culture. Some former dissidents complained that young Chinese were now less interested in democracy than in making money and that the communist regime had, for the time being, turned people's attention toward the new economic freedoms of business, finance, and consumption rather than political liberties. Although the Chinese Communist regime and the local police still kept individual secret files (called *dangan*) on each urban resident in the early 1990s, the effectiveness of this control system was declining with the new economic complexity and geographic mobility of Chinese society (*New York*

Times, March 16, 1992, p. 4). The new business class also seemed to value the stability of Deng's leadership, fearing that renewed political struggle would hurt economic development. Many observers speculated that only after the passing of the aged Chinese leadership would the democracy movement again reappear to press for greater political and civil liberties, as well as economic liberties.

Prognosis for Post-Communism: High Hopes, High Anxiety

The transition to post-Communist regimes in Eastern Europe and the former Soviet Union has raised hopes for a new era of personal freedoms in that region. Even the suppression of the democracy movement in China in 1989 seems likely to be temporary. The end of the Cold War and the end of classic communism has given personal liberty new life in many nations, both old and newly independent. Yet these tremendous gains in individual freedoms have not yet been consolidated or institutionalized. The new liberty in the short term has been more a gain from the new weakness of post-Communist political authority than a hard-won victory of a newly active citizenry.

Economic dislocation, political instability, and the legacies of old nationalist and Communist authoritarianism may still threaten newly achieved freedoms. In some successor states of the former Soviet Union, for example, Uzbekistan and Tajikistan, old ex-Communist elites still rule in pretty much the old fashion. In many post-Communist nations, ethnonationalism raises fears of new forms of intolerance and restrictions on liberties of minorities. The revolutions of 1989–90 had both liberal democratic and antiliberal nationalist tendencies, and the political struggle between these two interpretations is continuing. In some areas, for example Serbia and Georgia, nationalist intolerance had gotten the upper hand in the first phase of post-communism, and yet this sad outcome may be challenged, if authoritarian nationalist regimes bring suffering and isolation to their own people.

In order to balance the hopes for a stable gain in liberty against the anxiety of relapse into some new repressive regime, the events of the past few years should be placed in the longer term context of both Communist and pre-Communist periods. Most of the nations of Eastern Europe, including Russia and Yugoslavia, had little experience with democracy. East Germany is a special case, since its incorporation into unified Germany assures a more stable gain in liberty. The Czech Republic also can claim some special status, since the interwar Czechoslovak democracy was the only East European regime that did not slide into authoritarian dictatorship and that briefly reconstructed democracy after World War II as well. All of the other nations, however, have had little successful experience with regimes that supported personal liberty. This includes the Baltic states, which claim the greatest affinity to the West. In the interwar era, Lithuania, Latvia, and Estonia became right-wing nondemocratic regimes that engaged in mistreatment of minorities. The scale of historical experience with pluralism and tolerance ranges from fairly substantial to virtually nil. Yet postwar history shows that democracy has been able to expand its cultural geography. In other parts of East-Central Europe, for example, in Germany and Italy, as well as Austria and Finland, where interwar democracies deteriorated into right-wing or fascist dictatorships, democracy was able to revive and flourish in the postwar period. These stronger democracies are case studies of how history does not have to repeat itself, of how peoples and their political cultures can learn from bitter mistakes and try different paths.

In the Communist period itself, there were substantial differences among the various Communist regimes in terms of the use of coercion and violence, as well as some evolution in regime suppression of liberty after the death of Stalin. In general, the use of outright terror declined, and most regimes permitted a gradual "thaw" or "relaxation" of controls, though never a qualitative breakthrough to unfettered freedom of expression, travel, worship, or political organization. Studies of Communist system performance on human and political rights over time (White et al, 1990:312–18) indicated a general rise in levels of personal liberty from the 1960s to the mid-1980s, before the recent period of reform and revolution. Communist Albania and Ceaucescu's Romanian regime were the worst offenders against personal liberty. Charles Humana (1986), in his ranking of various nations on human rights performance, scored the Soviet Union as a 20 on a scale of 100; China, 23; East Germany, 33; Poland, 41; and Yugoslavia, 50. This compared with a rating for the United States of 90. These scores should not be given too precise an interpretation, but generally one can say that there was some general range, with Yugoslavia, Poland, and Hungary more "liberal," the Soviet Union and China notably lower on the scale, and Romania and Albania at the lowest levels. In some ways, the Communist systems were also an expression of the political culture of the society, with lesser or greater tolerance for personal liberty. It may be that those Communist regimes that compromised most with dissidents and opponents and that gave some leeway for expression and criticism have greater chances for a more pluralistic and tolerant future as well.

That the past is not a perfect guide to the future is illustrated by the Yugoslav example. Yugoslavia under Tito, and even after Tito, developed over the years into one of the more relaxed and "liberalized" Communist regimes, with greater freedom of travel, expression, religion, and property than most Communist regimes. It also had some achievements in ethnic tolerance, especially in view of the extreme Croat-Serb violence of World War II. The breakup of Yugoslavia and the violence that followed was a tragic demonstration of the negative potentials of post-communism, despite what might have seemed like a favorable starting point.

The need for some quick learning of the values of tolerance and support for freedom had already arrived in post-communism, which has suddenly opened the political arena to all kinds of demagogues, warlords, and fundamentalists. Already interstate, interethnic and civil wars have affected eight post-Communist states (Armenia, Azerbaijan, Georgia, Tajikistan, Croatia, Serbia, Bosnia-Herzegovina, Moldova), and the international community, including both the European Union and the United Nations, has been unable (for whatever reasons) to bring these conflicts to some political resolution. There are many more areas where lower-level ethnic violence (for example between Hungarians and Romanians) and skinhead or neofascist attacks on minorities (especially Gypsies) now poison the chances for a more free and tolerant civil culture.

Post-communism started with great gains for personal liberty. We have images of the Berlin Wall being broken apart and people being able to cross over to freedom, and of hundreds of thousands of people in Prague in 1989 and Moscow in August 1991 demonstrating for democracy and against Communist dictatorship. The establishment of a regime of liberty takes more than one symbolic act, no matter how moving. The difficult struggle to secure personal liberty, so that no new "walls" will be built and no new dictatorships established, is just one more feature of post-Communist transition.

11

Security and Alienation
in Communism and
Post-Communism

Communist systems provided a certain level of material security for the population, in terms of material consumption, education, health care, basic housing, and social services, and this physical security was fairly evenly distributed. The negative sides of the Communist security system were loss of personal liberty and individual economic opportunity. In the quality-of-life area as well, Communist systems provided basic security against crime, especially violent and organized crime, and also provided against loss of employment. On the other hand, Communist industrialization paid no attention to environmental destruction, and Communist policy on family life was filled with contradictions. While most Communist systems did not develop major drug abuse problems, many did experience growing alcoholism as a characteristic symptom of social alienation.

Post-communism in Eastern Europe and the former Soviet Union and marketization of the economy in China and Vietnam are changing the quality-of-life performance of these systems markedly. Common crime is on the rise throughout Eastern Europe, economic fraud is big-time and widespread, and organized crime "mafias" are a prominent feature of life in Moscow. Unemployment of varying proportions has returned as a normal feature of market economics, and due to a shredded social safety net, has already led to poverty and despair for whole towns and regions. Family life is under new economic pressure, but there is also some return to more traditional and religious family values. The worst environmental problems are at least now out in the open, and some of the worst polluters from heavy industry have been shut down, but there isn't much money for cleanup or introduction of newer and cleaner technologies. On the whole, post-communism suffers from many of the quality-of-life failings of both the developed liberal democracies (rising crime and family breakup) and many "Third World" developing nations (environmental disaster and mass joblessness with few public resources for improvement).

Criminality in Communist Systems

Under communism, special efforts were made to combat certain types of crime and to reshape human behavior to eliminate criminality. In the Soviet Union, this was part of the regime's ideological effort to create a "new Soviet man." The record of Communist systems prior to the collapse of communism in Eastern Europe and the dawning of post-Communist transformations in fighting crime was an important element in their claims to providing basic security for the working class.

During Stalin's reign, the Soviet Union claimed that Communist society was free from crime and that any criminal activity was the result of counterrevolutionary terrorists and economic saboteurs. In the post-Stalinist "thaw" and early destalinization period of the 1950s, Soviet authorities began to admit the persistence of common criminal behavior, although they claimed that such behavior was a cultural throwback to the tsarist society and would eventually die out as the socialization of the new Soviet citizen became more effective. Only in the mid-1960s did the newly born field of Soviet criminology introduce the idea that some criminal behavior was not a holdover from the prerevolutionary order, but was in fact produced by modern Soviet society. In the Brezhnev period, Soviet, East European, and some Western social scientists were producing more frank and reliable studies of both criminal and deviant behavior in Communist systems.

There was agreement among most observers that in fighting or preventing certain types of crime, Communist systems produced tangible results. Organized crime, violent crime, and the amassing of great wealth through corruption were markedly reduced in virtually all Communist systems. In these areas, communism was experienced by most citizens as an advance over prerevolutionary society, which was often notoriously crime-ridden, and typified by massive elite corruption.

With respect to organized crime, Communist systems were able largely to eliminate the type of crime syndicate that controlled much of the drug traffic, gambling, prostitution, and "protection" extortion from small businesses. Greater leeway for legal authorities, harsh penalties for ringleaders, the relative inability of organized crime to corrupt the regime, and mobilized popular support characterized the campaigns against organized crime by revolutionary Communist regimes. There were several outstanding examples that illustrate this success. The Cuban revolutionary regime drove the Mafia out of its once-lucrative Havana business in gambling, drugs, and prostitution. The Mafia (supported by the American CIA) tried to assassinate Fidel Castro several times because the Cuban revolution had effectively closed down its Havana operation. The People's Republic of China, in its first years in power, broke the back of drug trafficking to what was at that time the largest addict population in the world, ended prostitution and concubinage, and abolished the banditry and local warlordism that extracted "protection" tribute from villages and businesses.

This does not mean that there was no drug traffic, no illegal gambling, or no prostitution in the Communist nations (cf. Barry and Barner-Barry, 1978:263–64). There was some pot smoking, probably more in Cuba and Eastern Europe than in China or North Korea, but this was by Western standards small-scale and not part of a hard-drug subculture. In the Soviet Union, the glasnost policy revealed significant drug trafficking, associated in part with the Soviet occupation of Afghanistan. It was also clear that prostitution existed in Soviet cities.

Violent crime and especially street crime were also less common in the Communist countries than in many liberal democracies. Rates of homicide, serious assaults, and rape were far below American frequencies, though not so different from rates in Japan or Sweden. Effective gun control played a significant role, and the regime was able to mobilize people to aid police in crime prevention. In the Soviet Union, for example, the *druzhiny,* a nonpaid volunteer group sometimes derided for "vigilante" tendencies, helped to patrol parks, streets, and other public places and events; they took drunks to sobering-up stations, broke up fistfights, and generally added to public confidence in the safety of streets and parks. Donald Barry and Carole Barner-Barry, two thoroughgoing critics of the Soviet system who lived in the USSR for several years, concluded in the 1970s that "the Soviet people certainly seem to feel safer in their parks and on their streets than do Americans, though much of this atmosphere of security may be created by the failure of the media to report much in the way of crime news. But, given the efficiency with which news seems to spread by word of mouth, the safer feeling may also not entirely result from delusions on the part of the public" (1978:270).

In Cuba, the revolutionary regime inherited a society that had quite high rates of homicide and rape. Voluntary militia groups, called Committees for the Defense of the Revolution (CDR), were set up to patrol neighborhoods and look for crime and counterrevolutionary activity. The CDRs were instrumental in defeating the CIA-financed Bay of Pigs invasion in 1961, but they were also effective as a crime-fighting factor. Between 1959 and 1974, the murder rate dropped by more than 75 percent; the rate of violent crime fell by 77 percent between 1959 and 1968; and rape declined by 61 percent between 1960 and 1977 (Salas, 1979). Drug arrests declined from 1,464 in 1959 to 257 in 1968 (*Granma*, May 11, 1969), and common property crimes declined by 63 percent from 1959 to 1969. However, property crime rose again in the 1970s and by 1977 was 12 percent higher than in 1959; drug arrests also rose in the 1970s, though by 1977 they were still less than half the 1959 figure (Salas, 1979:52). In revolutionary Cuba, the gains made against organized crime, drug trafficking, elite corruption, and violent crime were maintained even though common criminal behavior gradually returned. After 1970, the

233

regime has generally taken a more modest view of the possibilities of reshaping citizen values and behavior. The sociology of Cuban criminals, mostly male, young, and poorly educated, has been similar to the prerevolutionary pattern and to most other nations.

Still a third crime area in which Communist regimes had success was that of high-level government or elite corruption. Especially in China, the Soviet Union, Vietnam, and Cuba, Communist systems replaced regimes infamous for the extent of corruption. In the late tsarist period, under the weak-willed Tsar Nicholas II, high political offices were commonly bought and sold, and the bureaucracy was noted not only for its inefficiency but also for its susceptibility to graft, bribery, and outright theft of public funds. The culmination of this was represented by the Siberian mystic Rasputin, who directed the most scandalous transactions from inside the circle of the imperial family until his assassination in 1916. While it was no secret that lower-level pilfering and nomenklatura middle-level corruption were quite common in the Soviet system, the Soviet system did not produce a Marcos, or a Duvalier, or a Mobutu, or top-level political elites that amassed great wealth from theft of public funds.

Communist revolutions in less-developed nations such as Cuba, China, and Vietnam have illustrated the ability of the new system to reform political cultures seemingly anchored in criminal corruption. In pre-Castro Cuba, Havana was the "sin capital" of the Caribbean, and massive corruption of the tax system enabled the wealthy to shift the burden of government onto the less fortunate (Groth, 1971:77). Maurice Zeitlin's public opinion surveys in Cuba in the early 1960s found that the Cuban revolution was given high marks for honesty, and Havana was no longer a crime capital or the seat of a government of thieves.

One analysis of political corruption in Vietnam in the 1960s noted the contrast between the American-supported Saigon regime and the communist N.L.F.:

> To take the most striking example, the cadre of the National Liberation Front of South Vietnam and the local officials of the Saigon regime are drawn from the same cultural milieu and operate within the same society. From all accounts, however, N.L.F. cadre administer the villages they control with scrupulous attention to N.L.F. regulations, whereas even Saigon's partisans concede that the South Vietnamese administration is generally characterized by dishonesty, malfeasance, and a rapacious attitude toward the local populace. (Scott, 1972:ix)

One might also note in this respect that those cities and states in India (Kerala, West Bengal) and in Italy (Bologna, Turin) where Communist governments were elected to office maintained a reputation for honesty and incorruptibility unusual for the political system as a whole. The uniformity of pattern is such that Communist government is at least partly a systemic alternative to political corruption. James Scott (1972) and Sam Huntington (1968) have argued that corruption is basically conservative and system-supportive, a way in which wealthy elites influence politics in the absence of legitimate and institutionalized channels. For those without financial resources, violence and ultimately revolution are major ways of influencing policy or changing the government priorities. For a generation or more, Communist leaders were able to resist the massive corruption that characterized the old elites, and generally earned popular recognition for regime honesty. Over time, however, younger generations of Communist leaders who were not self-sacrificing revolutionaries climbed their way up through the apparatus, the nomenklatura, and were not so resistent to corruption. Elite corruption and the use of privilege returned and spread through the bureaucracy. Even so, the longer-term record on elite corruption of Communist regimes was far better than that of most developing non-Communist nations.

Many non-Communist revolutions, such as those in Mexico (1910), Indonesia (1965), and Egypt (1952), while originally directed against the corruption of the previous regime, succumbed in a relatively short time to the development of new and widespread corrupt practices.

More important in keeping the levels of elite corruption low in Communist systems were: (1) the absence of great private wealth that could be used for high-level bribery; (2) the inability to enjoy the fruits of bribery and graft for conspicuous or luxury consumption: (3) a strong and disciplined party organization; and (4) Marxist-Leninist emphasis on collective well-being and effort rather than on individual self-seeking or egoism.

Since the rebirth of criminology in Eastern Europe as part of the post-Stalin evolution, research showed that many of the patterns and background factors associated with juvenile delinquency, theft, larceny, and more serious offenses were quite similar to those in the liberal democracies. As in the West, the convicted criminal was likely to be male, young, poorly educated, unskilled, and was often prone to excessive drinking. Juvenile delinquents were overwhelmingly male, poor students or dropouts, and often products of disturbed family environments. Soviet sociology pointed to problems in the family—alcohol abuse, fighting among family members, financial difficulties, negligence, physical abuse—as common correlates of delinquency, vandalism, and hooliganism.

Some statistics indicated greater success in the Soviet system in the 1970s in criminal rehabilitation. Both Connor and Chalidze estimated that fewer Soviet criminals became "repeaters," that is, returned to criminal behavior after serving their sentences, than in the United States. This lower rate of "recidivism" in the USSR was interpreted in different ways. Soviet authorities put greater effort into reassimilating young offenders into society, with the factory collective taking young parolees under watchful guidance. In

Soviet rehabilitative practice, there was a strong emphasis on work, education, and raised political consciousness; at least with respect to finding work for parolees, the Soviet system probably did a better job than in the West. Chalidze (1977:214) also suggested that both socially and geographically, crime in the USSR was less concentrated. The Communist systems had no urban ghettos where massive unemployment, segregation, and social despair made rehabilitation unlikely.

In China, the process of building a market-type economy under Deng Xiaoping's "four modernizations" program also brought increased crime, most significantly common theft, but also smuggling, gang violence, rape, murder, and even banditry. In 1983, the Deng leadership launched a major anticrime campaign that included several mass executions of criminals, perhaps a total of 1,000 to 2,000 (Schell, 1984:64). Chinese officials claimed that this campaign reduced the crime rate some 40 percent by the end of 1983, but it seems clear that the new consumerism in Chinese economic development and the abandonment of Maoist spartan ethics have continued to produce new growth of criminal behavior. Again in 1990, Chinese leaders cracked down on crime, especially murder, rape, and large-scale theft, with the execution of more than 1,000 convicts, three times the level of the previous years (*New York Times,* Jan. 15, 1991, p. 2). These law-and-order campaigns seemed to have broad popular support in China, since they address the new concerns and fears of crime that have grown during the economic marketization process. However, these crackdowns deal mostly with the symptoms of the new level of crime in China, which is more fundamentally related to the economic transformation process. After a short period, therefore, the effects of each new crackdown recede, and criminal behavior revives.

In the post-Communist era in Eastern Europe and the former Soviet Union, crime of virtually all varieties has taken a great leap forward. The sudden weakening of law and order, combined with new market opportunities, has produced rapid growth in street crime, organized crime, business fraud and embezzlement, big-time corruption, and violent crime throughout the region, with some important variations. The rise of violent organized crime has contributed to the public feeling of insecurity. In Moscow, ethnic "mafias" or organized crime syndicates have attached themselves to the growing proliferation of new shops and markets. A Russian political scientist in Moscow told me in October of 1993 that the great majority (he estimated 85 percent) of shops and market stalls must pay protection money to the "mafias" or face assault and execution by increasingly well-armed hit men. Russian businessman Konstantin Borovoi, chairman of the Party for Economic Freedom, estimates that only 2 percent of businessmen avoid some form of connection to organized crime (Schmidt-Häuer, 1993). Two-thirds of all so-called commercial institutions in Russia, including most banks and stock exchanges, are estimated to be tied into criminal operations. Alexei Grigoriev, a new entrepreneur shop owner in Moscow, explained that getting supplies meant taking goods stolen from state factories or imports stolen from warehouses and added: "Most of our customers are either businessmen, commodity traders, or Mafia. The Mafia are the ones who can afford to buy everything" (*Wall Street Journal*, March 25, 1992, p. 1).

Urban gangs are now able to get weapons without much problem, and there are fights over gang turf for prostitution, drug traffic, and smuggling operations in major Russian cities. Unemployed young men there, as in the U.S. ghettos, are drawn into the new crime operations at all levels and benefit from the new crime profits. Virtually every major hotel in Moscow has a thriving prostitution trade, controlled by a specific mafia (Chechen, Armenian, Azeri, Georgian, or Russian), which books blocks of rooms in the hotel. In some regions, organized gangs and informal militias have enough power to virtually control local government authority. The self-proclaimed independent Chechen Republic inside Russia was being run by a gang of thugs under "President" Djokar Dodayev, offering safe haven for criminals, for smuggling trade, and for arms trafficking.

More damaging for the Russian economy was the rise of large-scale elite corruption and corporate crime, however. The *Economist* of London, which tracks the problems of the new post-Communist economies, described the growing role of crime in the Russian economy:

> One of the many problems faced by the Russian government has been capital flight—the phenomenon has been closely linked with the rising corruption and mafia activities. The most common route for capital flight is the illegal export of easily saleable commodities such as oil, using forged export licenses. Another channel has been irregularities in invoicing. Corrupt company directors have reportedly been sending their foreign customers two invoices—part of the cash is sent back to Russia as required, while cash paid on the other invoice is kept in a private foreign account.

Estimates of the size of this illegal capital flight range from $12 billion by the Russian Commerce Bank to $26 billion by an unnamed senior official at the Ministry of Security (Economist Intelligence Unit, 1993:45). As pointed out earlier, this new upscale economic crime wave deprives Russia of badly needed investment capital. In 1992, illegal capital flow out of Russia was greater than the total flow of Western credits into Russia.

In Georgia, the largest militia, the Mkhedrioni, was run by the ageing former convict (not a dissident) Jaba Ioseliani, and its forces were both admired as fighters and feared for their atrocities against the people (*New York Times*, Nov. 16, 1993, p. 3). Yet in 1992–93 Georgian President Shevardnadze (the former foreign minister of the Soviet Union under Gorbachev) needed the support of these thuggish militias in his flight against Abkhaz separatists and the equally thuggish militias of ex-President Zviad Gamsakhurdia. In Georgia, as in many parts of the Caucasus, local warlordism of the crudest variety sprouted up in the vacuum of armed power after the collapse of communism. In Serbia, Croatia, and Bosnia, unofficial ethnic militias emerged in the civil and interethnic wars following the breakup of Yugoslavia to engage in some fighting and in lots of criminal extortion, mass rape, and looting often connected with "ethnic cleansing" but directed against their own ethnic group as well. In situations of weak post-Communist government and police authority, the new availability of guns and young recruits, and the chances for great profits from smuggling, pillage, and extortion, a new and vicious thuggery has emerged to blacken the reputation of post-Communist regimes, which have often been incapable of protecting and maintaining public order.

Changes and Problems in Family Life

The family underwent profound changes in the Communist nations, as did government policy toward the family. Some of these changes, such as the transition from the extended family structure to the smaller nuclear family (parents and minor children), the dropping of legal and religious barriers to divorce and abortion, the influx of women into the work force, and greater geographical and social mobility for the individual, were common to Western societies as well over the past half-century. These trends were greatly accelerated in many cases by the Communist revolution, with the result that the transformation of family life and child-rearing practices was compressed into a shorter time span and created greater generational change than the more gradual trend in the West.

Marx was very critical of the bourgeois model of marriage, especially the domination of husband over wife and the double standard of fidelity for men and women. In the earliest years of the Bolshevik Revolution, the family was seen as a holdover from the past order and a source of reactionary and religious values. The revolutionary Russian feminist Alexandra Kollontai called for a new communist family, "a union of affection and comradeship, a union of two equal members of the Communist society, both of them free, both of them independent, both of them workers. No more domestic servitude for the women. No more inequality within the family" (cited in Lane: 1971:375).

Kollontai also advocated extensive child-care services, to be provided by the state, to encourage a more communal style of raising children. In the early days of the Soviet experience and that of other Communist systems, the power of the family over private property was sharply reduced. Divorce and abortion were legalized and made readily available. Children born out of wedlock were given equal legal standing with children born in wedlock. The paralegal powers of the church over matters of marriage and divorce were curtailed. By the mid-1930s, however, in the midst of the industrialization drive in the USSR, and especially at the end of World War II, Soviet policy attempted to strengthen the family and encourage parenthood. This turnabout in family policy can be seen as a response to two factors. One was the recognition of the family in Communist society as a vehicle of support for the system. Most adults in the USSR after World War II were raised under communism, had assimilated its norms, and could be expected to pass them on to their children. That generation of parents who had been socialized under the tsarist regime had greatly declined in importance. What was once seen as an institution for preserving reactionary values could now be enlisted to preserve Communist values. Second was the need for public support of larger families to ensure a sufficient work force in an economy short of manpower especially after the loss of 20 million lives during the war.

The situation was rather different in China and Yugoslavia. China instituted programs for population control in the 1960s because of the strain of its more than one billion population on economic capacity; Yugoslavia had a severe unemployment problem since the scrapping of central planning.) But in the centrally planned economies of Eastern Europe there was a need for more workers, engineers, technicians, and office personnel. Every attempt was made to bring mothers and retired persons into the work force, and despite the continuing availability of abortion (except in Romania), government policy was pronatalist, in favor of childbearing.

But the same trends that produced higher rates of family breakup and declining birthrates in the West (see chapter 6) also affected Communist society in Eastern Europe. Since the 1950s, divorce rates climbed steadily in all these systems, and birthrates fell sharply.

Divorce became by the 1970s about as common in the USSR as in Britain or the United States; birthrates were as low in East as in West

Table 11.1 Divorce Rates in Communist and Post-Communist Countries

	1957	1967	1975	1984	1990
Bulgaria	0.9	1.16	1.27	1.48	1.26
Czechoslovakia	1.07	1.39	2.18	2.42	2.61
Hungary	1.81	2.06	2.46	2.69	2.4
Poland	0.55	0.85	1.21	1.43	1.11
USSR	1.27[a]	2.74	3.08	3.39	3.94[c]
Yugoslavia	1.14	1.05	1.18	0.92	0.81
Cuba	—	1.14[b]	2.45	2.89	3.51

Source: UN, *Demographic Yearbook*, 1976, 1982, 1986, 1991.
a. 1961
b. 1965
c. 1989, Russia

Germany. To be sure, the special problem of alcoholism in the USSR accelerated the divorce rate; according to Mandel (1975:247) about 40 percent of Soviet divorces are caused by alcoholism, almost always on the husband's part. The full-time careers of most Soviet women made them more economically independent of their husbands, making divorce less difficult financially. On the other hand, some evidence (Moses, 1987:400) indicated a growing poverty problem by the 1980s for single-parent female-headed households with minor children, as had occurred in the United States. This trend had crossed national borders and ideological system-types. In both Eastern and Western Europe, family breakup and declining birthrates posed new social problems. As in the West, the modern family was an institution in transition, without a clear image of its future.

Post-communism in some nations, particularly Catholic Poland, has brought a new struggle over social policies on abortion, divorce, and education that seek to revive the more traditional family structure. The Catholic church in Poland in the first years of the Solidarity government aggressively pushed a legislative agenda to encourage women to stay at home, to teach traditional Catholic values in the schools, and to outlaw abortion. However, this Catholic church campaign also produced a political backlash that was partly responsible for the return to power of two leftist parties (the urban Democratic Left Alliance and the Peasants party, both led by former communists) in the 1993 elections. Both church and Solidarity leaders had underestimated the resentment felt by Polish women toward the attempt to reregulate their lives by command. The struggle over family policies in post-communism will be far more complex and will not be settled by a simplistic return to pre-Communist traditional and religious norms.

Elimination of Mass Unemployment

One of the achievements of the Communist systems in the quality-of-life area was the ending of massive and chronic joblessness. Until the establishment of the strong central planning agency (GOSPLAN) in the first Five-Year Plan (1928–32), the Soviet Union during the NEP period experienced considerable unemployment (about 1.5 million registered unemployed persons in 1927). Planned economic growth, however, generated employment at a pace that kept up with the numbers of job seekers. The number of unemployed in the USSR declined to 1.1 million by 1930 and to only 200,000 by 1931. Canadian economist Alan Abouchar (1979:10–12), in a summary of Soviet performance, estimated that Soviet central planning since the late 1920s largely eliminated longer term secular unemployment and short-term cyclical unemployment associated in capitalist economies with the business cycle of expansion and contraction. The Communist economies (with the important exception of Yugoslavia) were able to eliminate mass joblessness through a program of extensive industrial growth. They provided a type of job security that, over time, undermined work discipline and failed to provide incentives for efficient and diligent work, and a job security that increasingly was unsupportable after a long period of extensive centrally planned industrialization. Yet this job security, from public opinion polls in the 1980s in these nations, was indeed perceived as a positive achievement of Communist politics, and cannot lightly be dismissed as a valued goal in post-Communist systems. Soviet economist Efim Manevich, summarizing how central planning provided for full employment, definitely viewed this as a quality of life achievement:

> The elimination of unemployment was a great attainment of the Soviet people. It meant, first and foremost, that each citizen's most important right—the right to work—had been put into practice. Doing away with unemployment gave working people confidence in the future and encouraged them to develop their abilities and talents. (Manevich, 1968:16–17)

Of course, there was still some unemployment in the USSR and Eastern Europe. There was frictional unemployment, people who are in the process of changing jobs. Abouchar (1979:11) estimated this frictional unemployment at less than 1 percent in the 1970s. There were a few "social parasites," adults who lived off their parents or friends or engaged in only occasional and sometimes shady work. There were cases of people who could not find the kind of employment they were trained for because of planning errors or geographical preferences. It was, for example, particularly difficult for Soviet planners to get highly trained people to accept employment in the frigid climate and barren landscape of the Far North, even with hardship pay incentives. Yet despite this minor unemployment, central planning for extensive growth eliminated mass chronic unemployment as a social problem. In the USSR and its East European neighbors there were no ghettos of the jobless, nothing comparable to Watts, Hough, the South Bronx, Belfast, Liverpool, London's East End, Amsterdam, Rome, and Naples, where, in the poor working-class districts, the jobless line the sidewalks, hanging out in winter and summer, in good years and bad, a constant feature of the social landscape.

A few of the liberal democracies—West Germany, Japan, and Sweden—have in their best boom years been able to reduce unemployment to levels comparable to those in the USSR, but none for such a prolonged period. Western analyst Keith Bush compared unemployment in the 1970s in four liberal democracies (the United States, Britain, West Germany, and France) with the situation in the Soviet Union:

> At the time of writing, over 10 million persons and their families in the four Western countries cited are undergoing the trauma and misery of unemployment; this is alleviated but not expiated by the various forms of unemployment

compensation. Others are on short time. In this respect, the Soviet citizen is, generally speaking, appreciably better off. (Bush, 1975:51)

One Communist system in which joblessness was a problem was Yugoslavia, which scrapped central planning of its economy in the 1950s. As Yugoslavia began to substitute market mechanisms for central planning, it experienced a ballooning of unemployment, from 2.3 percent in 1953 to 5 percent in 1963, and 10–15 percent in the 1970s and 1980s. This figure would have been even higher except for the migration of hundreds of thousands of Yugoslav workers to West Germany, Switzerland, and Sweden in search of jobs. And there was no doubt about which social strata and regions bore the brunt of joblessness in Yugoslavia. Parkin (1971:175) showed that it was overwhelmingly the unskilled working class (87 percent of all jobless) and the poorest regions that were most affected, increasing the inequalities among social strata and ethnic groups of the country. Supporters of marketization must consider that the return of large-scale unemployment is the negative cost for dropping central planning.

In the first years of privatization and marketization in post-Communist Eastern Europe, mass unemployment has returned as a regular feature of the social landscape. In Poland, which introduced "shock therapy" in early 1990, joblessness climbed to over 14 percent by 1993 (Economist Intelligence Unit, 1993b); in Hungary, which adopted a more gradual approach, unemployment was also over 12 percent in 1992. The Czech Republic, however, helped by a large-scale tourist boom in Prague and the attractive southern Bohemian and Moravian regions, held joblessness to under 3 percent (while in newly independent Slovakia, it was over 13 percent). In Russia, the Yeltsin reform team avoided large-scale unemployment in the first two years of economic marketization by continued subsidies to state industries. In mid-1993, the jobless rate was still less than 1 percent, or about 700,000 workers; on the other hand, "hidden unemployment" from production stoppages, unpaid leave, and shortened hours was estimated at between 10 and 12 million workers (Economist Intelligence Unit, 1993b). At some point, if state subsidies are cut, noncompetitive firms will face bankruptcy, and joblessness will soar in Russia as well.

In China, the rapid growth of the economy under Deng Xiaoping's leadership allowed the growing private sector to absorb workers from the countryside and from state industries, keeping the unemployment problem within manageable bounds. Yet, as the *Economist* reported in 1993, "the *China Daily* newspaper reported that the urban unemployment rate was expected to be about 2.3 percent this year—a fall from 2.8 percent last summer. The figures are misleading. They exclude the 50 million to 80 million migrant workers looking for employment in the cities, as well as young people—believed to number several million—waiting for their first jobs" (Economist Intelligence Unit, 1993a:21–22). Additionally, the Chinese government in 1993 began a program to reduce employment figures in several state-owned industries, especially in the coal and steel sector. Women workers were in many cases the most affected by the new layoffs.

Post-Communist governments have been hard-pressed by the International Monetary Fund (IMF) to keep their budget deficits as low as possible, and they have been unwilling or unable to provide much support for the new jobless. In independent Latvia, for example, in 1993, unemployment compensation was the equivalent of only $15 per month; clearly, the unemployed in post-communism could not survive on such low benefit levels. They had to seek alternative sources of illegal income or goods. Mass unemployment quickly became one of the main reasons for the resurgence of leftist parties in several post-Communist nations (Poland, Lithuania) and for a certain "nostalgia" for the job security of the Communist era.

Pollution and the Environment

Pollution and damage to the natural environment caused by rapid industrial growth and urban development characterized the communist systems. Indeed, the pollution of Lake Baikal in the USSR became in the 1970s an international environmental scandal. Large state-owned cellulose plants had for years dumped wastes into the world's largest freshwater lake. Pressure from a loose coalition of Soviet scientists, local residents, and international ecologists forced some government action to reduce the polluting activity, but it was not clear if this was sufficient to reverse the environmental decay. There were other reports in the Soviet press of oil spills in the Caspian Sea and of air and water pollution in different localities, without any corresponding vigorous response by the government to remedy the situation. Studies of Soviet environmental policies (Goldman, 1972; Enloe, 1975; Kelley, Stunkel, and Wescott, 1976) recognized that pollution was a systematic problem area in the Soviet Union and Eastern Europe.

The kinds of pollution that affected Soviet society differed from those that affected the Western democracies. Auto emissions were a smaller factor in urban air pollution, although this increased with the growing "auto-mobilization" of the USSR and Eastern Europe. Noise pollution was a greater urban problem, especially where industrial activity and residential units were in close proximity. Both in factory and in residential construction, noise considerations were not weighed very heavily in planning, and noise levels were considerably higher than in most Western factories and homes.

Goldman and Kelley argued that despite (1) public ownership of industrial plants; (2) central planning that should aid effective enforcement of environmental standards; and (3) the lack of a private profit motive antagonistic to ecological concerns, the Soviet record on pollution was no better than that of the United States or of any other industrial society. Soviet regulations concerning land development, public health, air emissions, and water purity were tightened in the late 1960s, and Enloe (1975:194) pointed out that environmentalism was given official backing in the ninth Five-Year Plan (1971–75), but it is clear that a number of factors hindered the fight against pollution.

Most important was the high priority given to increased production in heavy industry, consumer goods industries, and agricultural production. Within state-run factories, mills, and farms, those responsible for enforcing waste disposal and emissions regulations had less bureaucratic clout than those responsible for meeting production quotas. Second, although citizen complaints about pollution did appear in Soviet newspapers, there was little opportunity for independent citizen groups to intervene against polluters via court action or public hearings. Third, even when fines were imposed on polluters, they were often small and did not achieve the goal of reducing antienvironmental behavior. Cynthia Enloe summarized the dilemma of environmentalism in industrial communism as follows:

> The production ethic has elevated to top political posts men and women whose training and career aspirations bias them against policies that would restrict industrial output for the sake of public-health protection of nature. Likewise, those central ministries responsible for heavy industry have superior 'clout' in policy discussions and can frustrate the operations of agencies assigned to implement environmental laws. (1975:220)

Enloe concluded that the theoretical advantages that a centrally planned and state-owned economy should have in combating pollution and enforcing environmental conservation would not be realized unless and until industrial growth is lowered in priority. One benefit of glasnost in the Soviet Union, and of democratization generally in Eastern Europe, has been wider information and reporting on environmental problems in these nations. The late 1980s were a consciousness-raising experience, with the emergence of environmentalist movements and "green" parties throughout the region. Generally, this information confirmed and strengthened earlier suspicions that the Communist systems had almost totally neglected environmental issues until they became catastrophic, as the case of Chernobyl illustrates. Now it is apparent that there are environmental disasters caused by extensive industrial overgrowth throughout Eastern Europe and the Soviet Union, yet funds and material resources to remedy dangerous conditions in water purity, air pollution, and chemical waste dumps, and ecological damage to forests, rivers, and lakes are in short supply. In the short term, even though these issues can now be more freely discussed and debated, the prospect for quick action (no matter what political system emerges in post-communism) is not very high.

Perhaps the worst problems of environmental decay were found in East Germany, which was the most industrialized and urbanized communist society and which relied heavily on brown coal for heating and industry. Air pollution from brown coal was immediately noticeable in East German cities, as were the deterioration of building facades and the dying forests.

One exception to this general picture was the People's Republic of China in the 1960s and 1970s. William Ophuls (1977), in his discussion of ecology in the less-developed nations, singled out China for some praise. The Maoist strategy for development was far more favorable to the environment because of its emphasis on "decentralized, local self-sufficiency, 'appropriate technology' that is cheap and suitable for small-scale use, cadres with practical technical skills instead of highly specialized and expensive training, labor-intensive instead of capital-intensive modes of production, careful husbandry of resources and fanatical vigilance against waste, and some degree of ecological restoration (for example reforestation of mountains denuded since ancient times)" (207–8). While the Maoist strategy was probably less harsh on the environment, it was also less successful in modernizing the economy, although it may have helped build the basic infrastructure for development. In the 1980s, with Deng Xiaoping as leader of a new economic modernization drive, a shift in priorities occurred, to the detriment of environmentalism.

Alienation and Alcoholism

Chapter 6 discussed the rise in the affluent democracies of problems stemming from social alienation and loss of community morale. Sometimes these problems appeared in the forms of drug abuse, alcoholism, and the growth of cultism. Communist societies were more successful in preventing widespread drug abuse, and there was little evidence of the cultism found in the West. Clearly, Communist governments had greater power to prevent the free proselytizing and public appearances of sects like the Moonies, the People's Temple, or the Hari Krishna. The personal liberty of the individual to form or join a sect, even if ultimately harmful to the individual, is protected in the liberal democracies, but was not in the Communist nations, where the collective security of the society, for which the ruling Communist party claimed responsibility, had a higher priority.

A major social problem for the Soviet Union, as well as Poland, Hungary, and Czechoslovakia, was alcoholism and alcohol abuse. Alcoholism and drunkenness were recognized by Soviet authorities as the greatest factors in family breakup, criminality, home and automobile accidents, and production losses due to absenteeism or poor workmanship. Barry and Barner-Barry (1978:258) reported that in the Soviet Union about 90 percent of hooliganism, 84 percent of assaults with intent to rob, 82 percent of open stealing, and 60 percent of thefts were committed by people under the influence of alcohol. Nearly 30 percent of all intentional homicides were committed by intoxicated persons.

One might have expected that, since the Soviet government had direct control over state-owned distilleries, it could effectively dry up the source of alcoholism by turning off the vodka supply. However, there were several obstacles to this approach. First was the widespread practice of home brewing liquor (*samogon*), which was estimated to account for more than half of all vodka produced. Unless Soviet authorities took much stronger measures against this, a decrease in legal vodka production was simply offset by increased illegal samogon distilling. A second limiting factor was the tax revenue that the government got from legal liquor sales, which accounted, according to one estimate, for 10 to 12 percent of all government revenue (Treml, cited in Barry and Barner-Barry, 1978:261).

The Soviet government turned in the 1970s to public campaigns, peer group pressure, limits on hours of vodka sales, and price increases to try to moderate Soviet (and especially Russian) drinking habits. There were several problems with the government's antialcoholism effort (Walter Connor, 1972:1ff.). First, there was a long tradition in Russian culture of heavy drinking as a positive male attribute. Second, the campaign against alcoholism was often inconsistent, portraying alcohol abuse as a terrible evil but recommending only moderation in drinking. Third, problem drinkers were often those at the bottom of Soviet society, for whom alcoholism (and crime) were signs of a deeper alienation. We could also add a fourth factor, namely that alcoholism has been overwhelmingly a problem of a male macho subculture, and the political leadership in the USSR (and Eastern Europe as well) was a male-dominated elite. Only in the 1980s, first under Andropov in 1983 and under Gorbachev in 1985, did Soviet authorities launch antialcoholism programs with real muscle. Alcohol abusers were forced into treatment programs and face loss of jobs or severe demotion. Public intoxication was subject to stricter law enforcement, and raids on illegal brewers increased. Some initial gains were made; public drunkenness in Soviet cities decreased, and alcohol consumption dropped. After a short time, however, illegal vodka production increased to fill the demand, and Gorbachev's campaign fizzled out. Since the collapse of the Soviet Union, public drunkenness has become very visible in most cities and towns; in my own travels in Eastern Europe and the former Soviet Union in the first years of post-communism, alcoholism seemed to be on public display every night, in Moscow, Riga, Bratislava, or Budapest. Whether this indicates greater alcohol abuse or just the relaxation of police authority is an open question, but it does indicate that alcohol abuse remains a major social problem for these troubled times.

Marx had hoped that socialism would create a society without social alienation, a society in which people would be able to combine both mental and manual talents in their daily work. As Marx saw it, one of the most pressing problems of capitalism was its division of labor into segmented, tedious, and unchallenging occupational slots, which, combined with the exploitation of the worker's labor by the capitalist, produced alienation of the worker from his work. Soviet theorists and sociologists argued that since the elimination of the bourgeoisie, work in the USSR has ceased to be a source of alienation:

> Socialism, while possessing the same productive systems as capitalism, fundamentally changes the conditions of its utilization. The separation of labour from property is done away with. . . . That is why any labour, no matter how arduous and unpleasant, takes on a totally new quality under socialism, making it possible for the worker to work for himself. The alienation of man from the conditions of his existence is ended. For the first time in history work becomes a matter of honour, valour, and heroism. (Blyakman and Shkaratan, 1977:32)

This approach overlooked that Marx pinpointed the nature of the work process, the lack of creativity and autonomy allowed to the worker, as well as the capitalist exploitation of the work process, as a source of alienation. Assembly line work and unskilled manual labor in general was just as tedious, uninteresting, and alienating in Soviet factories as in the capitalist West. Soviet sociologists Zdravomyslov and Yadov (1966), in a survey of attitudes among young workers in Leningrad, traced highest job dissatisfaction to the unskilled manual occupations and to the elements of monotony and lack of opportunity to use ingenuity in other occupational roles as well. In practice, then, Soviet sociology did acknowledge the problem of providing satisfying work opportunities for Soviet citizens. The Soviet leadership placed great hope in automated systems to eliminate hard manual labor and job tedium: "As the current revolution in production develops it will eventually relieve the worker of various noncreative operations involved in the production process and of the need to spend a large part of his active life on the performance of monotonous, mechanical operations" (Blyakman and Shkaratan, 1977:35). Generally, the communist systems failed to provide opportunities for productive work that allowed for individual initiative, personal satisfaction, and a development of both mental and physical abilities, as Marx had hoped for a future Communist society. Instead, the worker was both secure in his or her job and alienated from the work process, as indicated by the lack of care and involvement in quality production.

The Struggle for Community in Post-Communism

Post-communism in Eastern Europe and the former Soviet Union has already brought significant changes in the areas of crime and joblessness. Societies, once organized to combat certain types of crime are now disorganized and weak compared to the power of criminal violence and corruption. Communist central planning, in its own clumsy manner, did provide basic job security, which workers came to expect as the norm; now jobs are insecure, and the competition for decent work is severe. Rising crime and joblessness impacts on the quality of family life as well. The feeling of community, that played an important role in building the challenge to Communist rule in the 1980s is now facing new threats. The question is whether the new wave of crime and breakdown of order and the new mass layoffs from industry are temporary painful symptoms of a transitional period, which will decrease to manageable proportions when the transition is completed, or whether these are now long-term features of the post-Communist future.

Optimists may see this as a short, painful period of adjustment, which will give way to a more stable and functioning market system and a renewed sense of law and order. After all, black markets and organized crime were not unknown in the West in the hard times of the Great Depression. But once those hard times had passed, and the postwar economic success formula took hold, these problems receded to manageable size. Why should this success formula not again be applied in post-Communist Eastern Europe and once again lead to prosperity and therefore to the shrinking of lawlessness and job insecurity?

But in many developing nations of Africa, Latin America, and South Asia with much longer experience in market-type economies, massive unemployment and underemployment, crime, and corruption at all levels of society have been characteristic features for a long time. And in the ghettos and ex-industrial slums of the once-great cities of the United States, Britain, Germany, Italy, and France, "Third World" conditions have emerged once again, along with mass criminality and job loss. Pessimists suggest that post-Communist conditions may come to resemble what exists in both the developing "Third World" and what is reappearing in the liberal democratic "First World," namely, areas of growth and affluence next to areas of decline and despair. The balance may vary from nation to nation, but post-communism will probably not be able to duplicate the post–World War II general prosperity of the Western democracies, and it will include many features of "Third World" development.

Perhaps the best hope for future improvement in quality of life may be greater openness and citizen opportunity for taking initiatives to address these issues, a sense of community empowerment rising out of the rejection of alienation and passivity of the past (and present). Post-Communist reform and turmoil have brought hardship and many new problems, yet citizens now have new chances to become active participants in shaping post-communism. The disillusionment of early post-communism led to the demobilization of public spirit in much of Eastern Europe and Russia in 1992 and 1993, yet the experience of people power from 1989–90, however brief, is still a valuable asset. The mobilization of a more active citizenry is ultimately the precondition for solving many social ills, reclaiming neighborhoods, demanding decent jobs, creating conditions for healthy family life, and fighting crime and corruption.

ESSAY: MANAGING CONFLICT AND CHANGE IN POST-COMMUNISM

With the fall of European communism and the economic marketization of Chinese and Vietnamese communism, there are only a few "classic" Leninist regimes left—Cuba and North Korea. There is now every expectation that these last relics of traditional Leninist party-states will also be transformed, probably after the death or retirement of the top leaders, Fidel Castro and Kim Il-sung.

Nevertheless, we know a lot more about the old Communist systems and their performance than we do about the still-changing politics of post-communism. A volatile period of economic disruption and decline associated with marketization and privatization, the rise and splintering of anti-Communist political coalitions, and the outbreak of ethnonationalist conflicts have complicated what in 1989–90 seemed to be an opening to liberal democracy and Western-type market economies. It now appears that post-communism may lead in many different directions, depending on the specific historical legacies of each country, the new problems and opportunities of economic transformation, and the wisdom or folly of post-Communist political leadership.

Some problems are common to most post-Communist regimes, however, and these problems will probably characterize the difficulties of managing "the great transition" for several years, and perhaps decades. In the area of economic performance, marketization and privatization will continue in some form and will also remain an arena of sharp policy conflict, for whoever controls the post-Communist governments also controls these processes, which can benefit clients and punish opponents (political, ethnic, regional). Because it will take time before market-type economies function efficiently in these nations, there will be substantial economic disorder and poverty, as well as new wealth and prosperity. The new economies offer fully stocked shops and fancy restaurants for those with money, but the basic material security of the old Communist system has vanished. Economic growth must return sometime, perhaps even in the next few years, but that will probably not mean that the majority will benefit in most post-Communist regimes. This is an era of building a new middle class of businessmen and shopkeepers, managers and accountants, not an era of satisfying economic aspirations of most workers and employees. If this succeeds, perhaps later the benefits will "trickle down" to the better-placed and more skilled workers.

One critical problem of managing "the great transition" will be the social backlash against the rising new inequalities of post-Communist economics. Without doubt, there is already some backlash developing, expressed in the latest rounds of elections; yet for the most part, the "losers" of post-communism are now passive, alienated from politics, convinced that no party or leader will change their fate. However, there are new nationalist-populist and some old ex-Communist leaders who offer an antiforeigner, antiminority, anti-elitist rhetoric, to mobilize protest and to place blame. There is also a renewal of a socialist or social democratic left alternative, which demands greater equity and a slower pace of economic change.

The immediate gain from post-communism has been the expansion of personal liberty. The old systems of institutional control, surveillance, and informer networks either have collapsed or have been much weakened, and citizens are in many ways learning to use their new liberty. New liberty has brought many antagonisms into full view, and it has been discouraging to see how much conflict has suddenly emerged. In some cases, post-Communist regimes have attempted to control television and radio and to intimidate the print media in the name of stability and order. But new regimes are also learning to live with some level of public criticism, and the print media in particular have been relatively brave in defending their new freedoms. In October of 1993, after Yeltsin's ban on over fifteen newspapers in the wake of the Moscow bloodbath, the print media protested, with Western support, and Yeltsin backed down in most cases.

With economic hardship and the new inequalities has come the growth of crime, corruption, violent crime, and especially organized crime as a prominent feature of the new insecurities of post-communism. Mass unemployment and greater pressures on family life also mark the new landscape. Regimes no longer are able to enforce full employment, and support for the jobless will be meager. Without strong economic growth combined with political commitment to social equity, these problems will persist. Authoritarian crackdowns on crime, which have been periodically tried by the reformist Deng regime in China, achieve only temporary results, and after a short while large-scale crime and corruption return. In periods of great economic transition and disruption, which may continue for a generation in both post-communism and reform communism, political regimes will be faced with tough policy choices for managing the effects of crime, corruption, and mass joblessness.

Managing great change in the 1990s is proving difficult even for the affluent and stable liberal democracies, but at least the Western democracies have a strong political legitimacy and institutionalization that can keep new political struggles within democratic bounds. Post-Communist regimes started out with some legitimacy through free elections and new cooperation from the West, but they are weakly institutionalized and are faced with much greater turmoil and conflict levels in managing their great transitions. It is much more likely, therefore, that ethnic conflicts and political struggles will threaten the new democracies and that nondemocratic traditions may reassert themselves in the attempt to reestablish some stability and order. Some nations, like the Czech Republic and Hungary, are better situated to consolidate liberal democratic and effective market institutions, whereas many Balkan and Central Asian nations are likely to consolidate authoritarian regimes. Exiting communism is also more filled with possibilities for repeated overthrow of institutions, continuing violence in political competition, and opportunities for radicalism of different varieties, without any guarantee of stability for a long time.

In every society, people's lives revolve mostly around their work, whether in formal jobs, informal trade and barter, or work in a home setting. In some societies, chronic large-scale unemployment and underemployment afford little opportunity for the full development of human skills and talents. In less-developed economies, work is often physically hard because of lack of machine power for transportation, fabrication of materials, field work, communication, and marketing of goods. The photos in this section focus on the ways people deal with their daily work in very different circumstances.

Top: Indian market women in Quito, Ecuador (photo by Ron McDonald).
Bottom: Commuters in Japan use the Bullet-Train to get to work in Tokyo (photo by Lou Kriesberg).

Above: A village bicycle mechanic in India.
Below: Working at a cook stove in rural India. (Photos by Sue Wadley.)

Left: Pedestrian shopping street in Tokyo (photo by Lou Kriesberg). *Below:* Making rope in a Tanzanian village (photo by Jim Newman).

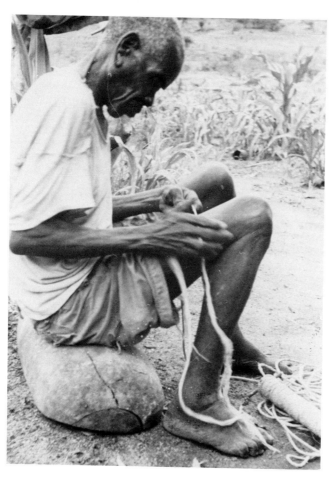

Top: A Kenyan village market (photo by Jim Newman). *Bottom:* An open-air market in Mexico (photo by Ron McDonald).

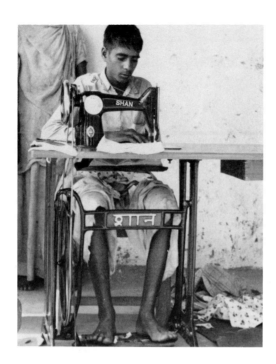

Left: A village tailor in India (photo by Sue Wadley). *Below:* Making rice flour at home in Luzon, Philippines (photo by John Tyo).

Above: Cairo market district in Egypt. **Below:** Market district in Damascus, Syria. (Photos by Lou Kriesberg)

Housing quality and availability for different classes and regions are strong indicators of material well-being, public health, sanitation, education, and other government services. In many developing nations, massive urban slums, homelessness, criminal and state-sponsored violence, and impoverished rural areas contrast with the luxurious city homes and spacious country estates of a tiny elite. Rapid population and urban growth added to great economic inequality degrade the environment for large parts of the population.

Top: Vigario Geral slum in Rio de Janeiro. In September 1993, police gunned down twenty residents in revenge killings (photo by Michael Farrar).
Bottom: Lower-class housing in Guayaquil, Ecuador (photo by Ron McDonald).

Top: Upper-class estate in Nairobi, Kenya. ***Bottom:*** Middle-class project housing in Nairobi, Kenya. (Photos by Jim Newman)

Top: Poor peasant housing in rural Mexico (photo by Ron McDonald).
Bottom: Street children sleeping on the steps of a government building
in downtown Rio de Janeiro (photo by Michael Farrar).

Top: Company-town housing for workers in Recife, Brazil. *Bottom:* Slums of Rio de Janeiro, Brazil. (Photos by Ron McDonald) *Facing page, top:* Middle-class housing in Ahmedabad, India (photo by Barbara Miller). *Facing page, bottom:* Mud, brick, and thatch rural housing in India (photo by Sue Wadley).

Post-Communist transformations in Eastern Europe and the successor states of the former Soviet Union have been filled with exciting new liberties and many disillusionments. New political conflicts and widespread poverty have quickly emerged. Democratization and marketization have given demagogues and organized crime new opportunities. In Communist China, on the other hand, reform policies have achieved rapid economic growth while the democratization movement was suppressed at Tienanmen in June 1989. China's economy is growing rapidly and is remaking Chinese society, but the political system is changing much more slowly.

Top: Conflicts in post-Communist Russia: the burned-out parliament building in Moscow after the tank shelling (photo by the author). *Bottom:* A mountain of garbage creates a serious health hazard for local residents of Jakarta, Indonesia (photo by John Tyo). *Facing page, top:* Fresh water supply in a Kenyan small town (photo by Jim Newman). *Facing page, middle:* Population control is a major issue in India and many poor nations (photo by Sue Wadley and Bruce Derr). *Facing page, bottom:* Homeless children in Bogotá, Colombia. An estimated 150,000 homeless children live in Bogotá alone (photo by Ron McDonald).

PRACTISE FAMILY PLANNING

Top: Impoverished old people selling their belongings in a Budapest street (photo by Jongwoo Han). ***Bottom left:*** A gay rights festival in former East Berlin (photo by Jongwoo Han). ***Right:*** Two young Russian fascists in Moscow during the October 1993 fighting (photo by Mark Suprun).

Top: Russian Communists march on Parliament in Moscow, October 1993.
Bottom: The Russian army supports Yeltsin in the shootout with Parliament in Moscow. (Photos by Mark Suprun)

Top: Open-air farm market in Canton, China. ***Bottom:*** Bicycle traffic in urban China. (Photos by John Hodgson)

12

Beyond the Third World
after the Cold War

The "Third World" is a concept that was born during the Cold War, and with the end of the Cold War, it has lost at least some of its usefulness. The concept of a Third World, as geopolitical analyst John Agnew (1993) has argued, really developed out of two basic ideas that only partially overlapped:

1. In the postwar era, the Third World was an arena for a competition between the United States (as leader of the First World) and the Soviet Union (leader of the Second World) for loyalty and adherence to either the Western capitalist or Soviet Communist development model. This arena included the large group of over one hundred nations that were mostly newly independent former colonies, although Latin America was also clearly an arena for East-West competition.
2. In the postwar era, the Third World represented the emergence of a group of mostly new nations that had suffered under Western imperialism and were searching for ways to break way from continuing Western domination and still avoid Soviet domination. The Third World in this sense focussed on the struggle to overcome its disadvantaged place in the world order.

Both ideas of a Third World played an important role in the Cold War era, and its history was closely tied to the framework of the East-West struggle. As Agnew argues, with the collapse of communism the first meaning of a Third World seems to have disappeared, but insofar as these nations may still be in a situation of structural disadvantage in the world order, the second meaning may still be valid. Indeed, the end of the Cold War by itself has not improved the position of Third World nations in the global economic or power structures. However, the gradual differentiation among Third World nations has made it more difficult to argue that these nations are all still disadvantaged or dependent on the developed West. At least some new nations, in particular

253

the East Asian NICs, seem to have overcome by their own efforts their earlier dependency status. New concepts are now being proposed to describe the ways in which some nations have exited the Third World status or may soon find another status that far better describes their current situation. The collapse of communism has created over twenty new states of the former Soviet Union and the former Yugoslavia, some of which may be on a track to Third World status, with only pockets of development through connections to Western MNCs. The definition of a neo–Third World is also in transition, from a perhaps flawed conception during the Cold War to competing new suggestions that attempt to reflect the changing geopolitical order and the changing geography of production.

The Third World in the Cold War Era

In the Cold War that followed World War II, most of the world's peoples belonged to neither the First World of affluent liberal democracies nor the Second World of Communist systems. With the breakup of the British, French, United States, Belgian, Dutch, and later Portuguese overseas empires, in a process called decolonization, nearly one hundred new nation-states were born. These newly independent nations embarked on a process of building a national political system, a state-building stage of political development, which had been blocked during their period of colonial rule from London, Paris, Washington, Brussels, Amsterdam, and Lisbon. The emerging politics of this new "world" of independent nations was one of the great themes of comparative politics in the postwar period, since they were by definition new and open to different possibilities.

These new nations immediately became an arena of contestation by the United States and the Soviet Union, the two superpowers of the Cold War period. The United States and its European NATO allies hoped that the new nations would remain allied with the West (as they had been as colonies), that they would attempt to develop their economies within the world trading guidelines set down by the Western powers and use free-market principles. The West hoped that the new nations would develop political systems that were, if not liberal democracies, at least friendly to the West and receptive to Western political influences. Conversely, the Soviet Union and its Warsaw Pact allies hoped that the new nations could be won over to communism, that they would imitate the Soviet model of industrialization, and that they would develop political systems that, if not explicitly communist, would be receptive to Soviet political influence. The United States and the Soviet Union, effectively deterred from direct military confrontation with each other, often intervened in Third World politics, and Third World politics was often used as an indirect or surrogate battlefield for the Cold War superpowers, as in Korea, Egypt, Vietnam, Angola, Nicaragua, Ethiopia, and Afghanistan (see especially chapter

15). Both superpowers feared that the other side would ''win over'' the new independent nations and both utilized a wide array of covert and overt tactics to manipulate the politics of the new nations.

Some of the new nations leaned toward the United States and its allies (although almost none became Western-style democracies), a few became client states of the Soviet Union (fewer still became Communist systems), but as the bipolar division of the world progressed, a large number of the new nations (and later, many of the Latin American states as well) began to develop their own image as a Third World of development, nonaligned in the struggle between East and West, and representing the interests of the poorer nations of the ''South,'' meaning the Southern Hemisphere (a gross symbolism, since some poor nations are in the Northern Hemisphere, and a few rich democracies are in the Southern Hemisphere). This reaction then became a trademark for the idea, the concept, of Third Worldism, a rejection of the logic of the Cold War, and the search for a uniting voice for the mostly poor developing nations.

What were the features of this Third World of political systems, and why is this concept eroding now in the 1990s?

Diversity in the Third World

In comparison to the geographically and institutionally rather well-defined affluent liberal democracies and the more diverse but still clearly identifiable one-party Communist systems of the Cold War years, the Third World category included Latin America, Africa, the Middle East, and South and Southeast Asia, with wide variations in culture, economic levels, political institutions, and nation-state origins.

In religious background, these nations range from Moslem (North Africa, the Middle East, Iran, Indonesia, Pakistan, Bangladesh), to Hindu (India), Buddhist (Burma, Thailand, South Korea, Taiwan), pagan-animist (much of sub-Saharan Africa), Christian (also much of sub-Saharan Africa) and Roman Catholic (Latin America, Philippines). Ethnic diversity is great, both across regions and within some nations, as in India, Nigeria, Iran, or Malaysia. In Latin America, where Catholicism and a Spanish/ Portuguese colonial heritage are common factors, individual nations have cleavages among Spanish, Creole, Mestizo, Mulatto, African American, and Indian groups as well as among groups of outside immigrants (Italian, German, Irish, Japanese, Slavic and Lebanese). Recently, Protestantism has made inroads into Latin America, changing the religious cast of Guatemala, Peru, and El Salvador. Moslem influence has been spreading southward through Africa over the past several decades.

Levels of economic development vary much more widely in the Third World than in the liberal democracies of Europe and North America, and these countries' postwar experiences in economic development are much more inconsistent. Some nations, such as Argentina, entered the postwar period as semi-industrialized and semi-urbanized societies, with great hopes of joining the affluent developed nations, only to experience a long period of decline and economic failure, under both civilian and military regimes. Other nations, such as Korea, Singapore, and Taiwan, began as poor societies and achieved rather spectacular economic success, becoming industrial and commercial leaders in international manufacturing and trading. Still other nations, including Brazil and Mexico, experienced periods of strong economic growth in the 1960s and 1970s, and were often called "economic miracles" of their regions, but in the 1980s saw these gains eroded by debt, inflation, and corruption. India (as well as Pakistan and Iraq) maintained a fairly steady if modest economic growth from a poor agrarian society to a still-poor society but with an emerging industrial and high-technology sector. A few states with small populations and great oil wealth (Kuwait, Saudi Arabia, the United Arab Emirates) have very high GNP/capita levels, and through OPEC generated great earnings by relatively simple exploitation of a single commodity. Other resource-poor nations with growing population pressures such as Chad, Somalia, Ethiopia, Haiti, Bangladesh, and Tanzania have experienced little sustained development, remaining at the bottom of the economic ladder.

Along with this great cultural, ethnic, and economic diversity, the Third World is notable for the diversity and relative instability of its political institutions. In most of these nations, the official description of the political system has changed. Since independence in South Asia and Southeast Asia in the 1940s, and in Africa since the 1960s, almost all these nations have experienced military takeovers, civilian coups, civil wars, or popular uprisings that have led to "new" institutional political arrangements. In Latin America, there was a relative return to civilian elected government during the 1950s (Venezuela, Columbia, Brazil, even Argentina and Guatemala for a while), followed by a resurgence of military regimes in the 1960s and 1970s (including Chile, Argentina, Brazil, Peru, Guatemala, Uruguay, Ecuador, and Panama), followed again in the 1980s by a return to elected civilian government. Yet even though the military officially returned to the barracks in the most recent period, they remain above the law, protected from criminal prosecution for torture, terror, and corruption, which they practiced while in charge of the government and continue to practice today (even though formally subject to civilian control). Thus in Brazil, El Salvador, Guatemala, Honduras, Uruguay, Chile, and, with a few exceptions, Argentina, the civilian regimes that replaced the military juntas have been too weak to bring to justice even the military officers who were responsible for the most gruesome human rights abuses only a few years ago. In 1987, the Argentine military refused to turn over accused officers to civilian courts and forced the Alfonsin government to pass a general amnesty for officers involved in the killings of some 20,000

Argentinians during the 1970s campaign against leftist "subversives." In El Salvador, the beneficiary of large-scale U.S. aid in the 1980s, virtually no military officers have been brought to justice for the deaths of innocent civilians by death squads, including the notorious 1989 murders of six Jesuit priests, their housekeeper, and her daughter. The United Nations Truth Commission in 1993 confirmed the Salvadoran military elite's direction of death squad murders and massacres.

As one of the best-organized and certainly the best-armed interest groups in the Third World, the military has become a natural and favored contender for political power, superseding in most cases the political movement, party, or leader who established the first independence governments. Even when the military has chosen to retreat from direct participation in governing, it remained a major power in national politics, and generally retained the option to reassert itself. In several nations, the most common cycle of government change was from civilian to military rule and back again.

In some nations, however, the party of the independence movement managed to entrench itself in government, usually as a one-party system. Jomo Kenyatta's KANU party in Kenya, Julius Nyerere's TANU party in Tanzania, Kenneth Kaunda's United party in Zambia, Habib Bourguiba's Neo-Destour in Tunisia, and Houphuët Boigny in Ivory Coast held their authority for a long period, and in some cases the top party leadership passed to a new generation's elite. The Mexican PRI belongs to this category as well, since it dominates the Mexican political system and has for more than sixty years maintained its civilian control of Mexican government. However, the PRI, while always winning presidential and almost all other important contests in rigged elections, has allowed opposition parties some role in political life.

Throughout much of the Third World, the strength of political parties has been difficult to judge. Kwame Nkrumah and his Congress People's party (CPP) in Ghana in the early 1960s appeared to have built up a considerable and powerful party apparatus, with organizations in most sectors of Ghanaian society, until he was suddenly dumped by the military in 1966. In many Third World political systems, external appearances of strength and stability were rather superficial. Organizations that seemed unchallengeable came apart in a short time, as with the Shah's regime in Iran, the Marcos dictatorship in the Philippines, or Emperor Haile Selassie's rule in Ethiopia.

A small but significant number of Third World systems are still governed by monarchies or feudal oligarchies (including Morocco, Saudi Arabia, Kuwait, Jordan, Yemen, the United Arab Emirates). Until the 1980s, this group also included Iran, Ethiopia, and Afghanistan. It would appear that feudal-monarchial regimes have become steadily less viable in the modern era, although the oil wealth of the Arabian states has heightened Western interest in the fate of these political dinosaurs.

More important, a number of Third World countries have multiparty systems that approximate political democracy, and that have provided significant liberty for opposition parties over a long period. India, Sri Lanka, Venezuela, Colombia, and Jamaica have for several decades been multi-party democracies, despite some crisis points and some periods of considerable political violence. Changes in government have been brought about by electoral competition among party elites. Jamaica and Colombia have basically two-party systems, Venezuela a three-party system, and India and Sri Lanka multiparty systems. The maintenance of this party electoral competition is all the more impressive considering the violence in Sri Lanka between minority Tamils and majority Sinhalese; in India between Moslems and Hindus, Sikhs and Hindus, and among various castes; in Colombia between government, leftist guerrillas, and drug cartels; and in Jamaica between political gangs affiliated with the competing main parties, the PNP and JLP. The difference between these Third World democracies and the liberal democracies of Western Europe, North America, and Japan lies not in their formal political institutions but in their pattern of political performance, which has more in common with the nondemocratic Third World systems. The limitation here of formal democratic institutions is most evident, faced with limited resources and severe social and economic problems.

The origins of the Third World nations are mixed. A few, such as Ethiopia, Iran, Turkey, and Thailand, are modern successors to ancient kingdoms or empires with histories of sovereignty going back thousands of years. These nations were never completely conquered and colonized (Ethiopia was briefly conquered by Mussolini's Italian fascist regime in the 1930s) as were most of Africa and Asia.

Most of the countries of the Third World, however, were for a considerable period colonial possessions of one of the nations of Europe or North America. Until the 1820s, all of Latin America was a colonial domain of Spain and Portugal. The British, French, and Dutch also held some colonial possessions in the Caribbean. Since the wars of independence (1810–26) against the Spanish crown and Brazil's secession from Portugal at about the same time, these nations have been independent, though their sovereignty often has been battered by the gunboat diplomacy of the Great Powers. Their boundaries as nations were in large measure determined by the economic, military, and diplomatic policies of the Spanish and Portuguese monarchies during the era of colonialism. This is also the case with the more recently decolonized areas of Africa, Asia, and the Middle East. Especially in black Africa, European imperial domains were carved out with little regard for tribal boundaries and even less regard for the requisites of a viable nation-state. Great tribes such as the Bakongo were split by the division of their land into the Belgian Congo and Portuguese Angola. The Somalis were divided five ways, into colonies of the French, Italians, British (two separate colonies), and parts of Ethiopia.

On the other hand, Western imperialism enclosed peoples of different religions, languages, and levels of development into colonies, which later became independent nations. The British colony of Nigeria, for example, included the Moslem Hausa-Fulani of the North, the paganist Yoruba in the West, the Christianized Ibo to the Southwest, and literally hundreds of smaller tribes in between, most with their own languages. Within the first years of independence, Nigeria fought a bloody civil war to prevent the Ibo, whose region held most of Nigeria's oil wealth, from breaking away to form an independent Biafra. In the liberal democracies we know that language, ethnic, and religious differences can cause tremendous problems for a political system, as with the French-English split in Canada, the Flemish-Walloon split in Belgium, or the Protestant-Catholic conflict in Northern Ireland. In Third World nations, the national governments generally have far fewer resources to try to reconcile antagonistic groups; thus these tribal/ethnic/linguistic/religious cleavages, often consciously used as part of a divide-and-rule strategy by the Western colonial powers, continue to plague the postindependence political systems. Such contradictions have led to: the secession of Bangladesh from Pakistan, of Eritrea from Ethiopia, and of Singapore from Malaysia; the attempted secession of Katanga (Shaba) from Zaire, the Tamils from Sri Lanka, the Sikhs from India, and the Kurds from Iraq, Turkey, and Iran; Moslem/black civil wars in the Sudan and Chad; and a series of wars between India and Pakistan over Kashmir.

History of a Concept

The concept of a Third World of nations developed through two broad but distinct stages: first, a foreign policy or strategic diplomacy period in the 1950s and 1960s; and second, an economic policy period begun in the 1960s and 1970s. Each stage contributed to the growth of a self-perception among Third World leaders and to a delineation of interests between the Third World and the industrialized capitalist systems of the West.

In the first stage, a group of prominent leaders of the emerging states, including Prime Minister Jawaharlal Nehru of India, President Achmed Sukarno of Indonesia, Marshal Tito of Yugoslavia, and President Kwame Nkrumah of Ghana, developed and elaborated a position of nonalignment with either the American-led capitalist West or the Soviet-led Communist nations. With the breakdown of the World War II U.S.-Soviet alliance in the latter 1940s, both the United States and the Soviet Union began to develop military alliances or blocs that, for example, partitioned Europe into the NATO nations of the West and the Warsaw Pact nations of the East. The United States in the 1950s, by far the stronger superpower, pressed for formation of additional regional military pacts in the Middle East (CENTO, now defunct, with Pakistan, Iran, Iraq, and Turkey as members), in Southeast Asia (SEATO, now defunct, with the Philippines, Thailand, and Malaysia originally as members), and in the

South Pacific (ANZUS—Australia and New Zealand). Separate defense arrangements were concluded between the United States and Japan, South Korea, and Taiwan. In Latin America, the Organization of American States (OAS), while not a military pact, became the key organizational forum for the policing of South America and Central America against communism. During this heightened Cold War diplomacy, U.S. Secretary of State John Foster Dulles considered nonalignment or neutralism to be both immoral and antagonistic to the interests of the free world.

The Bandung Conference, held in Indonesia in April 1955, represented a first attempt both to oppose pressures to join in Cold War military alliances and to develop a grouping of less-developed nations of Asia and Africa to represent their interests in the world community. Twenty-nine nations participated, including Communist China and capitalist Japan. While President Sukarno hosted the conference, the main speeches were delivered by India's Nehru and China's Zhou Enlai. No Latin American states were represented or even sent observers. The Bandung Conference did not set up any institutional structures, but did approve a set of principles, including:

1. support for national sovereignty;
2. noninterference in another state's internal affairs;
3. recognition of racial equality;
4. nonaggression;
5. recognition of equality of nations;
6. abstention from joining in military pacts headed by the major powers;
7. abstention from damaging the economic interests of other nations;
8. peaceful settlement of international disputes;
9. promotion of mutual interests;
10. respect for justice.

While these principles were quite general, they were clearly aimed at the attempts of the United States to force the emerging nations to accept anti-Communist military alliances. At the same time there was, despite China's presence at the conference, no attempt to forge ties with the Communist nations either. The Bandung principles were also directed against the colonialism of Britain, France, Portugal, Spain, and Belgium, which in the mid-1950s still held most of Africa and parts of Asia as colonial domains or semicolonies.

It is important to remember that, in the early 1950s, the independent nations of Africa and Asia were a distinct minority within the United Nations membership. In 1945, only a dozen of the original fifty-one U.N. member-states were Asian or African (not counting the Union of South Africa). By 1960, however, with the decolonization of much of British, French, and Belgian Africa, nearly half (forty-five out of ninety-nine) of the U.N. membership was composed of Afro-Asian states. By the 1970s, the Third World nations held a more than two-thirds majority on all U.N. bodies, except for the key Security Council, where the veto power of the United States, France, Britain, China, and the Soviet Union blocked majority rule. The Third World (even with its divisions) within the United Nations considerably changed U.N. policy and initiatives, as was evidenced by growing American dissatisfaction with U.N. performance, the growth of Western vetoes in the Security Council, the suspension of the United States share of payments for certain U.N. activities.

By the 1970s, we witnessed the culmination of the Bandung Conference trend, which sought to build a Third World of independent, less-developed states in international affairs, nonaligned with any of the great powers, avoiding and perhaps moderating, it was hoped, the East-West Cold War conflict. Though the main leaders (Nehru, Sukarno, Nkrumah, Nasser) of this first phase in the evolution of Third Worldism passed from the scene, the trend that they represented continued. And in the wake of America's defeat in Southeast Asia and the overthrow of the Shah of Iran in 1979, the SEATO and CENTO military alliances headed by the United States crumbled. In Latin America as well, the OAS was no longer the pliant tool of U.S. foreign policy that it once was.

With decolonization largely achieved and with neutralism internationally accepted by the mid-1960s, the second phase of development for the concept of a Third World focused on economic matters. One of the first organizational results of the Third World majority in the U.N. was the founding, in 1964, of the Conference on Trade and Development (UNCTAD), under the initial leadership of Latin American economist Raul Prebisch. At the first UNCTAD assembly at Geneva in March 1964, Prebisch put the international spotlight on a series of economic issues that came to be known as the North-South dialogue. The UNCTAD meetings (UNCTAD II was held in Delhi in 1968, UNCTAD III in Santiago in 1972, and UNCTAD IV in Nairobi in 1976) served to significantly shift U.N. activities and the debate from East-West tensions to the economic gap between the rich, developed nations of the Northern Hemisphere and the poorer, underdeveloped nations of Latin America, Africa, and Asia.

The United States opposed the foundation of UNCTAD, the first U.N. agency to be established against the wishes of the United States, whose policy towards UNCTAD has been highly negative. The birth of UNCTAD marks the start of the United States' displeasure with the United Nations generally, in sharp contrast to its support of U.N. activities in its first two decades of existence.

Prebisch and UNCTAD put on the U.N. agenda the problems that impede the economic development of the Third World: unfavorable terms of international trade, dependence on special commodity exports, trade barriers by the "have" nations against Third World manufactures, financial dependency on a Western-controlled international monetary system, and a mounting debt burden. The Third World nations pressed for the establishment of a New International Economic Order (NIEO), which would redress those problems in favor of the less-developed nations. It should be added that through UNCTAD the Latin American states became more closely identified with the concept of the Third World than in the 1950s, when Afro-Asian leaders took the initiative and Latin American leaders were reluctant to join their efforts.

With the foundation and development of UNCTAD came the evolution of two other centers for Third World activities, the Group of 77 and the Non-Aligned. The Non-Aligned grouping was a direct continuation of the Bandung Conference of 1955. Further conferences were held in Belgrade (1961), Cairo (1964), Lusaka (1970), and Algiers (1973), publicizing the mutual interests and desires of these nations to enhance their development without joining the military blocs of either superpower. With an enlarged membership of about eighty nations, the Non-Aligned greatly expanded its organization capacity over the previous two decades, including a Non-Aligned Coordinating Council, which under the chairmanship of Algerian President Boumedienne was particularly active from 1973 to 1976. The Group of 77 was originally made up of the seventy-seven states participating in UNCTAD I in Geneva and grew to about one hundred member-states, including many of the Latin American States not affiliated with the Non-Aligned. From the mid-1960s through the 1970s UNCTAD and the Group of 77 developed a sort of mutually reinforcing momentum for greater Third World unity and for the building of NIEO.

The Theory of Imperialism

Any attempt to study the political systems of the less-developed nations must recognize the realities of Western intervention in these societies. The industrialization of the West (and Japan) enabled these states both to raise their own productivity and to subjugate the nonindustrialized societies of Latin America, Africa, and Asia.

Modern imperialism was in part a continuation of the expansion of the West begun by the age of exploration and colonization. Already in the 1500s, Spain and Portugal, then England, the Netherlands, France, and Sweden were finding new trading routes to the New World and the Far East and implanting colonial rule over native populations in South America, North America, and some coastal parts of Africa and South and Southeast Asia. Much of the early exploitation of the Third World was through slave or semislave labor, used for the mining of gold and silver and on large plantations. The Spanish and Portuguese colonies represented a sort of feudal colonialism that transplanted a landed aristocracy to Latin America and parts of Africa. The British, Dutch, and French colonies represented expansive mercantile capitalist states that vied with each other for exclusive trading rights in the Caribbean, North America, South Asia, and on the China coast. By the early nineteenth century, these forms of Western colonial presence in the Third World were in decline. First in North America (1776–81) and then in Latin America (1810–26), British, Spanish, and Portuguese settlers rebelled against the mother country and won their independence. The greatest sea power of the nineteenth century, Britain, adopted a Little England policy of gradually granting self-rule to Canada, Australia, and New Zealand. The European powers seemed to have lost interest in conquering imperial domains, and former colonies were on the road to nationhood.

In the last quarter of the nineteenth century, a new imperialism was born. In a series of land-grabbing campaigns, loosely regulated among the great powers (as at the Berlin Conference of 1884–85 on Africa), the major industrial nations, including Germany, the United States, Italy, and Japan, as well as Britain and France, partitioned the Third World into colonies or semicolonies (protectorates or spheres of influence). The extent of this new industrial-power imperialism went much further than that of the previous colonialism. In Africa nearly every piece of land was gobbled up. Only tiny Liberia escaped conquest. The British expanded their holdings in Asia to include all of India, Pakistan, Bangladesh, Sri Lanka, Burma, and Malaysia, while the French took over Indochina Laos, Cambodia, and Vietnam). The United States, after achieving its continental "Manifest Destiny" at the expense of native Indians and Mexico, also laid claim to the Hawaiian Islands, and, in the Spanish-American War of 1898, seized Puerto Rico, Cuba, and the Philippines from Spain.

This land-grabbing by the industrial powers was not without bloodshed. The Dervishes in the Sudan against Lord Kitchener's campaign, various ethnic groups in India against British expansion, the Zulu in southern Africa against the British, the Hereros in southwest Africa against the Germans, and the Filipinos in the Philippines against the Americans all fought to defend their independence and avoid inclusion in Western imperial domains. But the industrial nations, with the aid of nineteenth-century technology, in particular the machine gun, the telegraph, and the railroad, were able to conquer and effectively administer huge empires at modest cost and with minimal personnel.

The practices of Western imperialism were justified by the Great Powers of Europe and the United States as part of their civilizing mission, and this "expansion of Europe," as it was often called, was associated at the time with Western domination over the non-Western world. Textbooks of that period often saw this Western domination in terms of racial and religious superiority. *Mitchell's School Geography*, a textbook of world geography published in the

United States in 1866 and adopted for use in twenty-six states, offered lessons not only in geography but also in government, religion, race, and stages of society. Under the "Races of Men" section, it contains the following assertion:

> The European or Caucasian is the most noble of the five races of men. It excels all others in learning and the arts, and includes the most powerful nations of ancient and modern times. The most valuable institutions of society, and the most important and useful inventions, have originated with the people of this race. (Mitchell, 1866:41)

This misinformed assertion, which was certainly untrue for ancient times and for many key inventions of human society, is combined with a religious justification of Western dominion. Mohammed is described as "a religious impostor" (p. 47), and Hindus and Buddhists are written off as worshippers of "false gods" or "idols" (p. 48). Mitchell concludes that:

> The Christian nations are much superior in knowledge and power to all others, and through the increase of their colonies, the influence of the press, and the exertions of missionaries, will no doubt, in the course of a few generations, spread their religion over the greater part of the earth. (P. 48)

Mitchell's text outlines five stages of society, from savage and barbarous to half-civilized, civilized, and enlightened. At the peak stand the enlightened nations, among which are the United States, Great Britain, France, Switzerland, and the German states. Among the half-civilized, on the other hand, are China, Japan, Persia, and the societies of South Asia. It was clear to S. Augustus Mitchell, and to those who adopted his textbook, that the Western cultures were justly spreading their rule and their domination to less civilized and less developed societies.

The British historian Ramsey Muir (1917) describes the expansion of Europe as the beneficial tutelage of European civilization over non-European cultures. Muir, writing during the first World War, is concerned mainly with the threat to this civilizing mission of the British Empire from what he called the "Evil Power," Imperial Germany, which for Muir represented a brutal and exploitative distortion of Western imperialism:

> The imperial expansion of the European nations has alone made possible the vision—nay, the certainty—of a future world-order. For these reasons we may rightly and without hesitation continue to employ these terms, provided that we remember always that the justification of any dominion imposed by a more advanced upon a backward or disorganised people is to be found, not in the extension of mere brute power, but in the enlargement and diffusion, under the shelter of power, of those vital elements in the life of Western civilisation which have been the secrets of its strength, and the greatest of its gifts to the world: the

sovereignty of a just and rational system of law, liberty of person, of thought, and of speech, and finally, where the conditions are favourable, the practice of self-government and the growth of that sentiment of common interest which we call the national spirit. These are the features of Western civilisation which have justified its conquest of the world." (1917:4)

Muir, who considered himself an advocate of a more progressive British Imperial mission, nevertheless is quite blunt in his support for "the just tutelage of the white man over the black, with a reasonable freedom for native custom" (p. 226), and clearly intends that India "may not for a long time become a fully self-governing state" (p. 285), and then only within the orbit of the Empire. "(T)he future towards which the Empire seems to be tending is not that of a highly centralised and unified state, but that of a brotherhood of free nations, united by community of ideas and institutions, co-operating for many common ends, and above all for the common defence in case of need" (p. 233).

Muir's eloquent description of Britain's civilizing mission in the world at times is simply imperial disinformation on the benevolence of British rule, and at other times ignorance of the achievements of local cultures conquered by superior British military power. Nonetheless, it is stark testimony to the European belief that the imperial division of the world was both justified and progressive, constructing a new world order of the modern era.

Many theories have been advanced to account for this burst of Western imperialism. Political theorist Hannah Arendt and historian Carleton Hayes blamed it on a new supernationalism of the West, fueled by the challenge of Germany to both Britain and France. Economist Joseph Schumpeter attributed it to a militaristic aristocracy that, in the capitalist societies of the West, still dominated the officer corps of Britain, France, and Germany. This aristocratic social throwback to feudalism (a social atavism) was pictured by Schumpeter as trying to regain its former glory through imperial conquest. Still others saw the new imperialism as an outgrowth of earlier explorations combined with new Western technology and a prolonged period of peace in Europe.

Lenin's 1916 work, *Imperialism: The Highest Stage of Capitalism*, has dominated the discussion of imperialism in this century, but Lenin was not by any means the only, or the first, to link industrial capitalism with Western imperialism in the Third World. British economist J. A. Hobson, a left-liberal publicist, had presented elaborate evidence in his 1902 book *Imperialism: A Study* for the thesis that modern finance and investor groups were the main beneficiaries of imperialism. Hobson, concentrating mainly on the British case, argued that these finance and investor groups were instrumental in pushing government policy in the direction of securing new Third World areas for their exploitation, and that even though imperialism did not bring much economic benefit to the average Englander (according to Hobson), it was increasingly profitable for the wealthy investor class. Hobson criticized the new imperialism as bad business for the nation, but did not outline a strategy for overcoming imperialism. Hobson's theory of imperialism is not based solely on economic interests, either, since he gives considerable attention to the forces of nationalism and racism in the conquest of nonwhite Third World peoples by the white Christian European powers.

Lenin included in his analysis the independent nations of Latin America as economic dependencies of the West, because their finances and their economies were so heavily penetrated and dominated by foreign (Western) capital. He also regarded tsarist Russia and imperial China as new targets of Western imperialism, despite the fact that in some areas (e.g., Korea, Tibet) these two systems themselves acted as imperial powers.

Lenin describes this new imperialism as the latest stage in the development of capitalism. This stage is quite different from Adam Smith's laissez faire model:

1. The concentration of production and capital developed to such a high stage that it created monopolies which play a decisive role in economic life.
2. The merging of bank capital with industrial capital, and the creation, on the basis of this "finance capital," of a "financial oligarchy."
3. The export of capital, which has become extremely important, as distinguished from the export of commodities.
4. The formation of international capitalist monopolies which share the world among themselves.
5. The territorial division of the whole world among the greatest capitalist powers is completed. (Lenin, 1916:89)

Lenin saw that imperialism was able, through the exploitation of Third World labor and natural resources, to generate higher profits for the large monopoly corporations (now generally called multinational corporations or MNCs). A part of these superprofits could be used to raise the standard of living of the most organized workers (usually the skilled union members) in the industrialized West. This "labor aristocracy," as Lenin called it, which had been quite militant in the nineteenth-century capitalist systems, could be bought off in this way and could even be enlisted in support of British, American, German, or French imperialism, since they too benefited from it. If this labor aristocracy could be bought off, then well-paid British workers would support British imperialism in India, American workers would support American seizure of Hawaii, Puerto Rico, and the Philippines, as they in fact often did, marching under the banner of patriotic nationalism. For the time being, Lenin predicted, imperialism would be able to defuse the class struggle in the already industrialized nations of the West, where Marx had predicted socialist revolution.

Lenin went beyond Hobson's analysis in predicting that monopoly finance capitalism, while staving off proletarian revolution in the West through imperialism, would rouse Third World peoples to struggle for liberation of their countries from the worldwide chain of imperialism. Lenin also predicted that imperialism would retard the progress of the less-developed nations and increase the gap between the rich and poor countries of the world. This uneven development among the world's nations would set the stage for the class struggle to be displaced from the industrially developed West to the less-developed nations of Asia, Africa, and Latin America; this struggle would for the first time take place on a worldwide scale.

The Special Role of the Multinational Corporation

The role of the multinational corporation (MNC) has assumed a special importance in the analysis of the Third World nations during the Cold War. For some, the multinational corporation was the best hope for economic progress in the new developing nations. They argued that only the MNCs had the capital resources, the productive technology resources, and the management and marketing resources for developing the poorer nations of the Third World within the world trading system based on the General Agreements on Tariffs and Trade (GATT). Western-based MNCs in general had the resources that were successfully developed in the rich nations and that were needed in the Third World. MNCs in this view were the most viable and dynamic mechanism for immediate investment and job creation in the less-developed countries (LDCs) and also for the longer term transfer of business skills and production know-how to Third World employees. What the large corporations made possible in the already developed nations they should be capable of providing for the LDCs, given sufficient freedom of operation and a favorable political climate for investment. Economics professor Harry Johnson, one of the enthusiasts of the MNCs, saw them as the most potent agent for economic transformation, the most efficient decision makers on a global scale, and indeed the best hope for overcoming national conflicts and narrow interests in the development of a single global system, integrated both politically and economically (Johnson, 1971:242–52). American political analyst Robert Wesson saw some of the problems that could arise from the activities of MNCs in the Third World, but on balance he was optimistic:

> Branch plants and joint enterprises transfer technology and ideas more effectively than does trade. They inject a new competitive impulse, increase employment, and stimulate new ideas of management. . . . The mobility of capital favors

market economies and gives an incentive for economic policies favorable to production. The exported enterprises, moreover, acquire a growing stake in the well-being of the countries where they become established. (Wesson, 1990:235).

In any case, the reliance on Western MNCs was unavoidable, a result of the great technological gap between the rich developed nations and the poorer nations.

The explosive expansion of technology makes it more difficult to narrow the gulf. Modern production techniques are out of reach of the poorer countries, except as introduced by foreign entities. . . . Nowadays advanced foreign technology and a leap of management and skills are necessary in order to produce even bicycles competitive on the world market, much less the sophisticated devices of the computer age. Only countries that work very closely with the United States or Japan (such as South Korea and Taiwan), that invite foreign corporations to do the job, or that can afford large expenditures and have a big protected market (such as Brazil and India) can make a start. (Wesson, 1990:243–44)

Critics of the MNCs, on the other hand, saw them as key agents of the West's continuing dominance over the Third World to be used in pressuring Third World regimes and to continue the colonial-era linkage between LDC economic development and Western business interests. James O'Connor argued further that "the multinational corporation has become the instrument for the creation and consolidation of an international ruling class, the only hope for reconciling the antagonisms between national and international interests" (1971:141). In this scenario, the multinationals (which in stock ownership and control were not multinational but overwhelmingly American, British, German, Japanese, Dutch, or French), driven by the overriding interest in maximizing profitability, would damage the long-term development of Third World nations and continue to undermine newly achieved national independence. American socialist critics Harry Magdoff and Paul Sweezy listed several real fears about the record of the MNCs:

1. Fear that the international corporation will take too much and leave too little. The fear is often expressed that the big foreign corporation will take away the national resources (oil, ore, foodstuffs, etc.), all the profits, the most able local people (hence the brain drain), and leave only the crumbs in the form of low wages, low compared to the wages the same corporations pay at home.
2. Fear that the international corporation will crush local competition and quickly achieve a monopolistic dominance of the local market if not the local economy. Who can compete with the enormous technical resources of a giant corporation whose annual sales are more than the French national budget?
3. Fear of becoming dependent on foreign sources of modern technology needed for national defense, and for being competitive in world markets.
4. Fear that the international corporation's local subsidiary will be used as an

instrument of foreign policy by the government of the parent company. For example, in the case of a U.S. subsidiary, fear that the U.S. government will prohibit sales to certain markets (Red China, Cuba, North Korea, North Vietnam, etc.); or that the U.S. government will prohibit the parent from sending certain technology to the subsidiary, which technology would be useful locally for national defense or other purposes; or fear that the U.S. government will prevent the U.S. parent from sending new capital to the local subsidiary, and will require the local subsidiary to remit virtually all of its earnings home, thus damaging the balance of payments of the local government.

5. Fear that the good jobs will be given to nationals of the parent company and not to local nationals.

6. Fear that decisions will be taken by the parent company in callous disregard for their impact on the local town, province, or even on the national economy. For example—a decision to close down a factory and put thousands of workers out of jobs. (Magdoff and Sweezy, 1971:109)

James Petras and Harry Magdoff highlighted a number of cases in the Cold War where U.S. foreign and military policy was intimately linked to the interests of U.S. multinationals in developing nations. The case of U.S. intervention against the elected Chilean government of President Salvador Allende from 1970 to 1973 is only one well-documented example of the use of privileged MNC links to the State Department, the CIA, and the Pentagon to undermine a regime deemed hostile to U.S.-based multinationals.

Other observers agreed that MNCs might be able to abuse their economic power in the Third World but that over time the governments of Third World nations were learning how to better negotiate with MNCs and make their investments more favorable to overall development goals. James Howe of the Overseas Development Council, a U.S. think tank for global development issues, gave the following reasons for this trend:

> First and foremost are the rapidly increasing knowledge, skill, and determination of most developing-country governments in the negotiation process. Second is the continuing competition for both raw materials and world markets among MNCs; together with the more frequent presence of generally greater flexibility of Japanese and some European investors, this trend offers host countries a viable alternative to American investment and a greater opportunity to play off foreign firms against one another. (Howe, 1976:22)

On the other hand, Howe also realized that MNCs could play off one Third World nation against another, seeking to find the most "friendly" or least demanding nation to which to locate its activities. The unanswered question here is which actor, the multinational firm or the Third World nation, would have the stronger hand?

The decentralized distribution of production on a global basis by the MNCs has also created new networks of economic growth and material benefits that increase inequality within nations, with pockets of growing affluence coexisting with deepening poverty. As John Agnew (1993) has noted, the geography of development is increasingly divorced from the boundaries of the nation-state. With the crisis of Western welfare state democracies, some areas of Europe and North America are on a track to "Third Worldism," and on the other hand some areas of East Asia (Singapore, Hong Kong) have surpassed the affluence of their former colonial masters.

Development or Dependency in the Third World

The key point of this debate during the Cold War was whether the MNCs would in the long run benefit the economic modernization of the Third World, or whether the benefits of MNC investment and production would go primarily to a small Third World elite and their Western MNC partners. Was the Third World experiencing a healthy process of economic development or was its development leading to new forms of dependency that would leave most of its people in poverty? The MNC question was part of a broader conceptual debate on the appropriate model of modernization for the Third World.

A first conception, offered in the 1950s by Western economists like Walt W. Rostow and Simon Kuznets, was that the model of modernization, or development, had already been sketched out by the experience of the affluent Western democracies in the nineteenth and early twentieth centuries, and the now-independent "new nations" of Africa, Asia, the Middle East, and the long-independent but still less developed nations of Latin America should duplicate, within their special and unique characteristics, this basic formula. This conception of modernization was often termed "westernization," an expression of the notion that the Western model was suitable for all. This perspective views the world economic system established after World War II, through the creation of the International Monetary Fund, the World Bank, the General Agreements on Tariffs and Trade, and the Bretton Woods agreement on major currency exchange rates, as an open framework within which any nation, with the correct policies to foster business enterprise and market capitalism, can achieve success. This development theory, applied to political systems, assumes that liberal democracy is the political system-type best suited to this modernization process, and that economic modernization also reinforces political democracy. From this perspective, attempts to modernize through socialist or Communist methods were harmful to both democracy and economic progress, and traditional political forms led by a monarchy or landed oligarchy were also not desirable, though not as dangerous.

An example of this perspective applied to U.S. foreign policy was the Alliance for Progress in the 1960s. Scared by the Cuban Revolution's turn to communism, the Kennedy administration put together a wide-ranging program of economic and military aid to Latin American states, to help them achieve economic modernization according to the Rostow "stages of growth" plan, and to develop democratic political structures that could break down the rule by the military and landed oligarchs. The star pupils in this exercise were Chile, Brazil, Peru, Uruguay, Venezuela, Argentina, and Colombia, all with multiparty systems and elected governments in the early 1960s. But by the end of the decade, most of these nations had reverted to military dictatorships of various types, and Chile had elected a socialist, Salvador Allende, as president (see chapter 15). Economic development under the more democratic systems had not made any breakthroughs, and to many U.S. policymakers it seemed that authoritarian military regimes could better safeguard Latin America against the threat of more "Cubas," that is, more socialist revolutions. This period of failure to duplicate the Western experience in the most promising Latin American nations was a considerable setback for Western modernization theories, although this conception is still well represented in theories on Third World development. Thus, Sorman (1990) sees the Western pattern of economic development described by Adam Smith in his *Wealth of Nations* as still appropriate to the problems of the Third World; in this view the wisdom of the West is universal, and can be repeated by any society anywhere at any time.

In response to the perceived failures of the Alliance for Progress, a group of Latin American social scientists (Presbisch, Dos Santos, Sunkel, Cardoso, Faletto) developed a critique of Western modernization theory, which came to be known as dependency theory. This critique was then expanded by analysts like Andre Gunder Frank, Samir Amin, and Arrighi Emmanuel to apply to the Third World generally. They argued that the world economic system had been established by the rich liberal democracies (the core of the system) for their own benefit, and the less developed nations of Latin America, Africa, the Middle East, and Asia (the periphery and semi-periphery) were not able to develop in ways that would provide general well-being for the great majority, not the other correlates of economic growth such as decent education, health care, housing, and social services. This form of misdevelopment they called "dependent development" or even "under-development."

The ruling elites of the Third World, according to this perspective, were not able or interested in economic development that would benefit the masses. Their interests were tied to important international financial and corporate elites from the core nations, and their positions as ruling elites were bolstered by Western political and, if necessary, military intervention. An important conclusion of dependency theory was that the world economic system is structured unfairly, and perpetuates an "unequal exchange" process between core and periphery, so that until the world trading system is changed, the Third World nations may grow economically, but their people will not prosper. Dependency theorists have been divided on what alternative strategies Third World governments might pursue to overcome dependency, but they agreed that dependent development is not and cannot duplicate the success of the early industrializing Western nations. Only a process of radical struggle and change, both in the political systems of the Third World and eventually of the Western designed and dominated world trading system, could bring about a healthy and sustainable pattern of development. Egyptian-born economist Samir Amin (1990), one of the most steady proponents of dependency theory, has argued that only a delinking of the Third World nations from the current global trading system can redirect their economic development toward meeting domestic human needs in the Third World.

In the 1970s, dependency theory attracted considerable support, and modernization theory was on the defensive in academic debate over development prospects for the Third World. But in the 1980s, dependency theory suffered from several counter-arguments. First and foremost, some of the Third World nations, especially the "four tigers" of East Asia (South Korea, Taiwan, Singapore, and Hong Kong) were doing so well economically within the world trading system that their GNP/capita was rising to levels of considerable affluence, and was bringing higher education, health care, housing, and even social services to broader groups in the population. In somewhat less dramatic fashion, several other nations of ASEAN (Thailand, Malaysia, and Indonesia, though not the Philippines), and Chile in Latin America were pursuing international trade policies that seemed to be working well. In other words, a number of Third World nations, operating within the rules of the world economic system, were seen as successful new entrants into the global trading system.

Second, several of the suggested strategies for overcoming dependency, by "delinking" from the world trading and finance system and/or by attempting to pursue either nationalist protection or socialist welfare paths to independent development, ended in failure. Burma's and Tanzania's delinking strategies were judged as complete failures. The Mexicanization strategy of the ruling PRI, similar to the import substitution industrialization (ISI) policies of many Latin American and other Third World regimes, was also judged to have reached an impasse (Szentes, 1988: 69–74). Inefficient industry and regime corruption were seen by many observers as the results of unwise challenges to the established trading system, and this perspective was strengthened by the collapse of communism in Eastern Europe and the desire of new governments there to join the world trading system.

A new globalist/interdependency perspective is now emerging that sees the necessity for individual nation-states in the Third World to open wide their economies to international investment and to pursue aggressive trade policies. Within this perspective, regional integration is seen as playing an important role in developing larger markets and pooling local capital. Also, the rise of the "global corporation" has made national strategies for both labor and business increasingly less viable, although it appears that capital has the upper hand over labor in the globalization process (Ross and Trachte, 1990). Both workers and businesses must face up to international competition in prices, products, wages, and benefits. Neither the Western development model of the nineteenth century nor the core-periphery dependency model is an adequate construct for this emerging global interdependency (Jenkins, 1987). Those Third World nations willing to join in the globalization process (Wesson, 1990:9) may be able to prosper; those resisting will suffer. This successful commitment may not come from democratic regimes, however, as the examples of South Korea and Taiwan have shown, but from authoritarian, one-party-dominant or military-backed governments with little resemblance to Western parliamentary democracies. In this view, Third World political development may not follow the Western democratic path, but may still break through the legacy of colonial-era dependency.

Each of these perspectives has some validity. It is possible that some Third World nations may yet follow the path blazed by the Western democracies in the previous century. This possibility should not be ruled out in principle, and the attraction of the Western model, in the wake of the collapse of communism, will be increased in the 1990s. Yet it is also clear that the Third World success stories over the past several decades have not been liberal democracies, but rather a small number of authoritarian regimes.

Likewise, dependency theories overgeneralized the situation of Third World nations within the world trading system. There were more opportunities for national economic development within the GATT/IMF/ World Bank system than just continued economic and technological dependency. Furthermore, the strategies for single-nation ''delinking'' from the world trading system have simply not worked, and will probably not be copied by other nations in the 1990s.

Yet, after taking these criticisms into account and giving them due weight (Szentes 1988:98–102), dependency theories still have the value of pointing out the weaker position of the Third World within a world trading system that they did not establish, to which they did not consent, and that is still largely the same as when it was established by the major Western powers at the end of World War II. Within that system, growth still has not produced broadly based benefits for the whole population, nor has it given workers' organizations an equitable share of political influence. Third World governing elites, of various official descriptions, continue to pursue policies that benefit largely themselves and that continue the basic underrepresentation of human needs within the global trading system.

However, telling arguments can be made against the generalized dependency perspective. First, there are several nations, including South Korea, Taiwan, and Singapore, with mainly human but few natural resources, that have done very well competing within the world trading system. Starting from low levels of economic development in the 1950s, they have become strong and relatively wealthy societies, while several better endowed Latin American nations, notably Argentina, Mexico, Peru, and Brazil have seen earlier economic projects collapse. While the economic ''tigers'' of East Asia have not achieved these successes as political democracies but rather as military or civilian authoritarian regimes, they have nevertheless shown that either dependency is not universal in the Third World, or that under certain conditions it can be overcome, and at least some Third World nations can join the world trading system as first-class members.

In the late 1980s, many Third World debtor nations began privatizing state-owned industries and assets to service their foreign debts, and the buyers for these industries were primarily Western multinational corporations. Privatization and asset swapping for debt reduction became patent neo-liberal formulas for reducing debt and placing production facilities, at reasonable prices, in the hands of Western MNCs with, presumably, management skills and investment resources superior to either the Third World government or the Third World business class. The sale of the public telephone company in Mexico and the national airline in Argentina, of parts of the oil industry in Venezuela, Nigeria, and Mexico to private foreign corporations indicate that the processes of dependent development continue into the 1990s, and have perhaps accelerated for many Third World nations squeezed by the debt crisis.

Third World Politics in the Cold War

Much of the Cold War era politics of the newly independent nations (and later, Latin America as well) were a reflection of the dilemmas described above in conceptual terms. The political instability of the Third World nations in the Cold War expressed the general failure to find a political ''success formula'' that could meet the needs of the people in material well-being, social equity, personal liberty, and most quality-of-life issues. Political instability, as Robert Gamer nicely expressed it, was also tied to the instability of the environments of the majority of citizens:

> A healthy political system will provide a great many of its citizens with a basic human need—a stable personal environment. Developing nations once contained healthy political systems; since the introduction of extensive commerce they no longer do. This is because political systems once emerged from the societies in which indigenous people lived. Today, political systems are actually quite separate from indigenous social systems, and they will remain so until the structure of international trade changes. (1976:viii)

During the Cold War and continuing today in most countries of the Third World, the political system does not provide for basic human needs for many or most of its citizens. One might well expect that such a system would breed discontent, revolt, and revolution. Indeed, most readers of this text, on first thought, would surely find the standard of living and social inequities of most developing nations totally unacceptable and would fight, rebel, or struggle to improve matters. Or would they? The failures of these political systems produce not only discontent, anger, and frustration but also ignorance, despair, hopelessness, and fatalism (see chapter 16), which lead people (not only in the poorer nations, to be sure) to try to solve or avoid their problems through alcohol, drugs, gambling, crime, random violence, and otherworldly mysticism. Migration to another, more affluent land is always more practical than fighting to radically change one's own native country, so millions of dissatisfied or desperate Third Worlders chose emigration over political struggle.

Still, although mass political struggle was relatively infrequent, there was enough dissatisfaction within most Third World systems to cause frequent changes in government institutions, structures, and official programs. There were several regular and recurring political responses to the dilemmas that faced Third World regimes. These regular or modal response patterns corresponded to competing elites or would-be leaders within the society, and each pattern in some way attempted to reestablish the legitimacy of the political system. These patterns may be identified as: (1) nationalism, (2) Third World socialism, (3) authoritarian capitalism, (4) democracy, and (5) communism.

Nationalist regimes, very often in the form of military or military-backed dictatorships or juntas, have emphasized the unity of the people across all classes in the defense of the national interest, national honor, or national sovereignty. Real and concocted threats and "alien" ethnic groups or foreign ideologies provide fertile soil for a nationalist elite to assume power. For societies whose independence was only a recent achievement or whose practical independence is degraded by dependency or indebtedness, nationalism is a powerful political response. The Peruvian military junta under General Bermudez rallied nationalist support behind territorial claims to parts of Chile, and the Argentine military regime tried to rally the populace behind claims to the Malvinas/Falkland islands. Idi Amin aroused nationalist sentiment against "foreign" Indian and Pakistani merchants in Uganda, and the Suharto military-backed regime in Indonesia utilized nationalism against an "alien" Chinese Communist ideology. The Nigerian junta stressed national unity in the fight against the secessionist Ibo movement in the Biafran war. Dictator Saddam Hussein relied heavily on Iraqi nationalism in his war with Iran from 1980 to 1988 and his invasion of Kuwait in 1990.

Nationalists may call for tighter control over foreign-owned companies, the sale of foreign firms to local businessmen, or even nationalization. The right-wing Chilean Nationalist party, despite its hatred for Socialist President Allende, nevertheless supported the nationalization of the U.S.-owned copper companies in Chile in the early 1970s. Nationalist regimes try to stimulate the local business class to greater activity and may give them support against foreign firms. Nationalism seeks its legitimacy through a restoration of patriotic pride in systems where loss of national control over economic development, or "excessive" foreign cultural influences, have damaged local self-esteem.

Third World socialism built upon an image of a more just society, a new path to socialism that was neither Western nor Communist. Generally, Third World socialism had no central planning or total state ownership of the means of production, but its foreign policy was often marked by militant anti-imperialism and support of Third Worldism in the North-South confrontation. These non-Marxist socialisms sought their legitimacy in the priority they gave to popular welfare, education, and local development. Presidents Julius Nyerere of Tanzania and Kwame Nkrumah of Ghana pictured an African socialism based on the asserted classlessness of African society. Tanzania's program, embodied in the Arusha Declaration, stressed economic self-reliance, village development, and limitations on Western imports. Colonel Quadaffi's regime in Libya, the ruling Baath parties of Syria and Iraq, and the National Front regimes in Algeria based their legitimacy on concepts of an Arab socialism that attempted to combine pan-Arabist sentiment, some elements of Islamic social justice, and some elements of popular welfare. In Latin America, both within the Catholic church and outside it, Christian socialist movements and parties have used the "liberation theology" and the "option for the poor" to develop a new program for social justice, although no regime during the Cold War years tried to implement this type of program. The legitimacy of Third World socialism rested on its association with social justice and welfare, while stressing anti-imperialism in its foreign policy.

Authoritarian capitalism in the Third World represented an acceptance of the world capitalist trading system and attempted to carve out a profitable space within that system, usually through government sponsored support for export industries and maintenance of strict controls on worker demands. In East Asia, especially, this type of authoritarian developmentalism was quite successful—in Singapore under the leadership of Premier Lee, in Taiwan under the Nationalist party, and in South Korea under successive military-backed regimes in the Cold War era. In all cases, a strong, nondemocratic state efficiently managed an economic development project that has raised these nations to important players in international trade, based on aggressive export trade, domestic development of technical know-how, increased productivity, strong disciplining of labor and business, and government support for selected business sectors.

In other Third World nations, regimes fostered a more dependent authoritarian capitalism through junior partnerships with foreign investors. These regimes relied on foreign MNCs to develop export industries to serve Western consumer markets and followed policies that favor foreign investment even to the detriment of local businessmen. Foreign investment was warmly courted, even given extra tax breaks. Labor unions were suppressed or tamed. Local businessmen in this strategy played secondary or middleman roles for the MNCs, often in catering to the needs of Western personnel. Franz Fanon, in the late 1950s, castigated this role of the national bourgeoisie in his *Wretched of the Earth* description of "comprador capitalism":

> The national bourgeoisie organizes centers of rest and relaxation and pleasure resorts to meet the wishes of the Western bourgeoisie. Such activity is given the name of tourism, and for the occasion will be built up as a national industry. If proof is needed of the eventual transformation of certain elements of the ex-native bourgeoisie into the organizers of parties for their Western opposite numbers, it is worthwhile having a look at what has happened in Latin America. The casinos of Havana and of Mexico, the beaches of Rio, the little Brazilian girls, the half-breed thirteen-year-olds, the ports of Acapulco and Copacabana—all these are the stigma of this depravation of the national middle class. Because it is bereft of ideas, because it lives to itself and cuts itself off from the people, undermined by its hereditary incapacity to think in terms of all the problems of the nation as seen from the point of view of the whole of that nation, the national middle class will have nothing better to do than to take on the role of manager for Western enterprise, and it will in practice set up its country as the brothel of Europe. (1971:306)

Cuba under the Batista regime, Nicaragua under the Somoza family dictatorship, Ivory Coast under President Houphuët-Boigny, Kenya under the KANU regime, Zaire under the Mobutu dictatorship, Iran under the Shah, and Mexico under the presidency of Miguel Aleman best characterized this strategy of dependent authoritarian capitalism. These regimes were most often pro-Western in foreign policy and relied on the United States, Britain, and France for economic and military aid, and sometimes covert or overt Western intervention, to bolster their positions (see chapter 15). Their claim to legitimacy lay in economic growth and a Western-style level of consumption for a small but influential urban middle class.

Democracy deserves to be included as an important Third World pattern of political response to the dilemmas of the new developing nations, especially since India is the world's most populous democracy. Other Third World democracies include Sri Lanka, Venezuela, Turkey, Colombia, and Jamaica. Chile, before the 1973 military coup and again since 1989, has had extensive periods of democratic rule. The Philippines, before the Marcos dictatorship of 1972 and since the fall of Marcos' regime in 1986, has been a multiparty system with an elected civilian regime. Many other Third World nations have had shorter or longer periods of government by elected civilian regimes, cut short by personal dictatorships, party dictatorships, or military takeovers. The list of casualties among Third World democracies in the Cold War era indicates how difficult it has been for this system-type to survive over an extended period. Yet the example of India over the past forty-six years since independence shows that even in a poor nation, with many ethnic, religious, caste, and language conflicts, basic rules of democracy have maintained considerable strength. In 1975–76, during the period of limited dictatorship by Prime Minister Indira Gandhi, it seemed as though Indian democracy was about to crumble. Yet Mrs. Gandhi did not, by most accounts, try to establish a full dictatorship; rather, she called for new elections, which she lost, and peacefully handed over power to her opponents. Whatever damage had been done to the personal liberty of citizens during the eighteen-month emergency rule period, the whole structure of Indian democracy had not collapsed like a house of cards, as had been the case in so many other Third World nations. For many newly independent nations, where under colonial rule the people had no right to vote, no right to free speech or a local free press, free trade unions, or other democratic political rights, the Cold War era was the first chance for popularly elected government. The "democracy trend" of the 1980s—which saw a revival of elected civilian government in most of Latin America; in South Korea, Thailand, Pakistan, Turkey, and the Philippines in Asia; and in Zambia, Zimbabwe, Ghana, and Senegal in Africa—demonstrated the continuing legitimizing power of democracy in the Third World.

A systemic alternative for the Third World nations during the Cold War was, of course, communism, as discussed previously. We have already noted that a number of less-developed nations (China, North Korea, Cuba, Vietnam, Angola, Mozambique) experienced Communist revolutions leading to the establishment of more-or-less classic Communist systems, though with increasingly different strategies for development. Third World Communist regimes suppressed opposition, nationalized both MNC holdings and businesses of local elites, and dramatically reshaped foreign policy along anti-Western, anti-imperialist lines. Third World communism had an appeal based on its goals, and in some cases its record, of economic development, greater social equality, and successes in dealing with crime, joblessness, corruption, and homelessness. Third World communism also had an image of being part of a long-term power shift away from the former Western colonial masters to an anti-imperialist coalition headed by the Soviet Union. Third World communism often blended both nationalist and internationalist appeals in order to gain legitimacy.

With the collapse of European communism and transitions to market economies in China (and Vietnam), Third World communism would seem to have been discredited or to have lost its bearings. Yet the political crises that gave rise to Communist insurgencies in parts of the Third World over the past four decades have not disappeared, and there is still the potential for developing new variants of social revolution. The new revolutionaries will not, however, be able to count on aid from a Communist Soviet Union or from China and will be isolated in the world order. For the short term, without a model to emulate or even deviate from, rebellions such as the Maoist Shining Path in Peru or the

New Peoples Army in the Philippines are very much on their own, ideologically and materially.

We could also mention monarchy, populism, and fascism as Third World patterns that attempt to solve the riddle of political legitimacy. Monarchy, where it still exists, rests on a traditional aristocracy, often with religious underpinnings ("divine right") for its legitimacy, as in Saudi Arabia and some other small Gulf states. Populism, as in Argentina under Juan Peron or in Mexico under Cardenas in the 1930s, is somewhat akin to Third World socialism but generally lacks longer-term vision and has been mostly tied to the personal legitimacy of a particular charismatic leader. Third World fascism stresses an ultranationalist, violently antileftist and antidemocratic rhetoric, glorifies the role of the military, and often utilizes racist slogans against minorities or neighboring states. The Fatherland and Liberty Front in Chile, the Greek EOKA-B movement on the island of Cyprus, and more recently the Afrikaner Resistance Movement (AWB) of Eugene Terre Blanche in South Africa and the National Salvation party in Turkey have been examples of this tendency.

Many Third World regimes, of course, are mixtures of these competing but sometimes overlapping response patterns. Democratic India developed a strong nationalist tendency in its border wars with Pakistan and its annexation of Goa, and had a strong secular socialist orientation under Nehru. Thailand's politics mixed a still-vital monarchy with frequent nationalistic military takeovers and a more halting evolution of a democratic parliament. In Ethiopia in 1974, the military-led Derg toppled the monarchy of Emperor Haile Selassie, a traditional feudal regime closely tied with the United States. The Derg under Colonel Haile Mengistu Miriam combined elements of communism (but without any communist party), new alliances with Moscow, and strong nationalist appeals against secession of Eritrean and Somali provinces. The overthrow of the Mengistu regime in 1991 by Eritrean and Tigrean rebels signalled the independence of Eritrea and a search for a new political legitimacy to avoid the further breakup of Ethiopia.

We should note finally that the instability of many Third World systems has been a reflection of the failure to provide what Robert Gamer called a "healthy" political system. Often the seemingly dramatic shifts in regime legitimizating ideology among nationalist, socialist, authoritarian capitalist, democratic, or even Communist symbols were manipulated by political elites and would-be elites struggling to stay in power or to come to power. Political reality did not necessarily match regime rhetoric, either old or new.

Exiting the Cold War, Exiting the Third World

In the latter 1980s, as the Cold War began to wind down, the concept of the Third World itself came into question. The Third World as a concept had been closely related to the Cold War, and if that era was ending, and if the Second World of communism was eroding, was the concept of a Third World still useful? On the other hand, if the concept of the Third World was no longer as useful as before, was there some other concept (or concepts) that could be more insightful? In thinking about what comes after the Third World in the post–Cold War era now launched, there are several basic points of reference. An elaboration of these basic points may give some clues as to what it means to "exit" the Third World.

The End of Decolonization

After forty years of postwar efforts, the last remnants of Western colonial empires finally achieved independence. After the dismantling of the British, French, Dutch, and Belgian empires from the 1940s through the 1960s, the Portuguese regime of Antonio Salazar attempted to hold on to its colonial domains. But in 1974, the Portuguese military itself staged a coup that overthrew the authoritarian regime in Lisbon and granted independence to Angola and Mozambique, Guinea-Bissau, and East Timor (which was brutally seized by Indonesia). In the late 1980s, Namibia, the former German Southwest Africa, illegally controlled by South Africa's apartheid regime, was given independence and elected Sam Nujoma and his SWAPO party as its first government. The end of the era of decolonization was at hand; virtually all of the colonial domains of European empires in the Third World had been granted freedom or had fought their way to independence. One of the driving forces of Third Worldism, namely, anti-imperialism, had reached its goal. Especially for the new nations of the postwar era that had experienced independence for more than a generation, the focus of attention was shifting from dealing with the colonial legacy, though still important, to dealing with the legacy of a generation of independence governments and the record of their leadership. Less blame for failure could be allocated to the colonial past, especially since some former colonies had done much better than others. The generation of independence movement leadership was now old or had passed from the scene, and younger leaders were beginning to shape new agendas. It was only natural that, with the passage of time, the Third World nations could usefully be differentiated by their post-colonial development, and their commonalities as former Western colonies would become less salient and have less explanatory power.

NICism—The Newly Industrialized Countries

The spectacular growth of the trade-oriented economies of East Asia, in particular, the success of South Korea, Taiwan, Singapore, and Hong Kong (the so-called "four tigers"), gave rise to the concept of successful newly industrialized countries or NICs. The NICs of East Asia represented a break with both Western modernization theory and dependency theory. They were economically successful but politically authoritarian, and so they did not follow the expected modernization theory path of the West. But they did seem to be able to break through dependency barriers and become new major players in the international economy designed by the West. The successful developmentalist strategy of South Korea from 1960 through the 1980s, for example, included strong government intervention in economic planning, price-fixing, restriction of competition, protection of favored industries, suppression of wage pressures, and an authoritarian politics led by a military elite. As Alice Amdsen (1990) pointed out, this was hardly what the IMF and the World Bank recommended as the standard Western formula for economic growth.

Other non-Asian NICs, such as Mexico and Brazil, have also made their mark in the world trading system and have developed an industrial capacity that puts them into a new category, though again this has been achieved largely under authoritarian regimes, the PRI in Mexico since 1929 and the military junta from 1964 to 1985 in Brazil. The continuing success of the ASEAN nations, especially Malaysia, Thailand, and Indonesia, makes possible the emergence of further NICs as important manufacturing and trading nations.

In the post–Cold War years, more attention will be paid to new success formulas as nations exit from Third World status to new and varied positions as industrial and trading nations in the increasingly competitive global marketplace. The issues that these nations face will likely be of a different type from the problems of the Third World period, and their political evolution will be shaped by this new agenda. The new and still unfolding development path of the NICs is one exit from the Third World.

Democracy Trend

The reappearance in the 1980s of elected civilian regimes in most of Latin America, the return to democratically elected government in the Philippines in 1986, in South Korea in 1989, and in Pakistan in 1988, and the gradual broadening of electoral competition in Taiwan, Ivory Coast, Jordan, Morocco, Kenya, and Zambia, combined with the collapse of communism in Europe in 1989–91, gave rise to the idea that a tide of democracy was sweeping the planet. This may have been an overstatement, since in several other cases, most notably Thailand, Burma, Algeria, Haiti, and Nigeria, election results were ignored by military leaders, who were determined to remain in power. Teri Lynn Karl (1992) has pointed out that, in Latin America, the return to elected civilian rule does not equate with liberal democracy, since the human and political rights that underpin democracy in the Western sense are still absent or insecure. Her comment is even more applicable to most of the non–Latin American examples of the "democracy trend," since in Kenya, Morocco, or the Philippines individual rights are violated regularly by local police, military, economic, and political elites. In fact, it may well be that in the Philippines, more human rights abuses were committed under the elected President Coryzon Aquino than under the dictator Ferdinand Marcos.

Even with some cautionary notes, however, and the near certainty that some of these newly established elected civilian governments will fall victim to political crises that may end up with military juntas or personal dictators in control, the spread of basic democratic practices in the former Third World is a significant development, which has established some new ground rules for political legitimacy in the post–Cold War era. A democratic politics has increased in value as a legitimizing force in the world, and one exit from the Third World involves a qualitatively new consolidation of a democratic political life of the nation.

The Failure of Nations

At the other end of the spectrum of Third World development, there is a group of nations whose Cold War history has been nothing short of disastrous (Kaplan, 1994), to the point where some observers have raised the question of a new international trusteeship status, which would take over from the failed national government for some period. Liberia, for example, as a result of totally incompetant military rule under Samuel Doe and then a brutal civil and tribal war, was virtually without any functioning national government by the early 1990s. A group of West African nations provided an international military force to intervene and to try to arrange for a new political system, and this effort dragged on for several years while Liberia essentially ceased to exist as a nation-state. In Somalia, likewise, the disastrous dictatorship of Siad Barre followed by intense clan warfare divided the nation, destroyed any remnant of national government, and pushed Somalia into famine. Beginning with a humanitarian rescue mission, the United Nations and the international community increasingly were drawn into the process of administering various social services in the absence of a functioning government. The situations in Afghanistan, beset by bloody mujahedeen conflict after the withdrawal of Soviet forces in 1989, and in Haiti after the ouster of freely elected President Jean-Bertrand Aristide by military thugs, are additional possible cases of the failure of nations, the bankruptcy of the nation-state as a sovereign political unit.

In Cambodia, after twenty years of warfare and devastation, both internally and externally fueled, the United Nations began, in 1991, the mission of negotiating a cease-fire, organizing and overseeing the disarmament of military forces on all sides, and organizing and monitoring the first free and fair elections in Cambodian history. The U.N. role, which led to elections in 1993 and the establishment of an internationally recognized government in Pnom Penh, demonstrated the new activism of the international community in the post–Cold War era in intervening in rebuilding national political systems along internationally acceptable lines where the process of state building has failed. These considerations of renewed international trusteeship for failed nation-states would have been virtually unthinkable in the era of decolonization, since they would have inevitably raised memories of Western domination and would, in addition, have become part of the East-West competition in the Third World. But now, it appears that the loss, at least temporarily, of national sovereignty and relapse into formal dependency status under international mandate is a possible exit from the Third World.

The End of Nonalignment?

If there is no longer an East-West conflict at the end of the Cold War, then the Third World concept of nonalignment between the contending superpowers is also outdated. Beside the support for decolonization, the position of neutrality in the East-West conflict was the second great pillar of Third World political identity. Without the U.S.-Soviet competition for military allies and military bases around the world and with only one superpower left standing, the concept of a Third World nonalignment has lost its rationale. The organizations of Third World neutralism, primarily the Nonaligned and the Group of 77, are now searching for a new role, but they cannot continue to rally the less-developed nations around the old issues. With the breakup of the Soviet Union, there is no longer leverage for the Third World to play off East and West.

It remains to be seen whether some grouping of former Third World nations may be able to formulate a new North-South dialogue that would aim at reworking the international trading system along lines more favorable to the poorer nations. This new grouping could not count on help from several of the already successful NICs, however, nor could it gain much from the support of the poorest, "failed" nation-states, which have lost virtually all influence in the international community. A new North-South divide could provide a new political identity for a significant number of less developed nations, but it would face a global trading order already quite different from that of the Cold War era.

13

Economic Growth Strategies for the Developing Nations

The nations of Latin America, Asia, the Middle East and Africa that were for a long time colonial possessions of the European powers have faced many problems in their search for economic modernization strategies. Their search for a success formula contrasts sharply with the strategies of the Western capitalist systems and the classic Communist systems. In some ways, they have faced and for the most part still face severe obstacles to discovering their own success formulas for economic development. In this sense, I will refer to these nations as a "Third World" of development from which a few nations are now exiting in the post–Cold War era.

In the Western capitalist nations—the earliest industrializers—the leading forces of modernization were the enterprising native business class and locally developed and controlled machine technologies serving, initially, a domestic market. The early modernizers gained and have maintained a leading role in the international trade field as well. The role of the national government in this process was limited, though still important, but became more visible for late-capitalist nation-states like Germany and Japan. The role of the state further increased as a stabilizer and regulator of the national economy.

In the classic Soviet model of communism, the state undertook a rapid and forced industrialization from above, using military-like mobilization techniques and concentrating on heavy and defense industries to the neglect of consumer goods and services. Here the strong centralized state monopolized the leading role and suppressed opposing market-type mechanisms. This extensive type of industrialization required full control of the national economy and virtual delinking from the international world of commerce. Only in the post-Communist era are these economies again becoming a part of the global economy, with considerable difficulty. In this sense, post-communism shares some features of "Third World" economic problems. (Communist China and Vietnam are exceptions; they seem to have learned from the non-Communist East Asian experience.)

Most developing nations are still part of a "Third World" in regard to the search for economic success in the global economy. Although the Cold War is over, most of these nations are confronted with problems of economic development but have neither the native business class and locally developed technology of classic capitalism nor a strong state with the mobilization and control capacities of classic communism. As Joel Migdal (1988) has argued, most Third World regimes are weak states that can be heavily influenced by strong economic elites, both domestic and international. Robert Gamer (1976) has emphasized that the economic elites (and their patron-client networks) that influence the state do not look or behave like the Western entrepreneurial business class of the nineteenth century in their leading role in the overall development of the economy.

Most Third World regimes have been caught on the horns of a late-development dilemma. In the modern era of government responsibility for economic development, which no regime can seemingly avoid, the government must adopt some development strategy. Most regimes of the newly decolonized nations lack the skills and resources to implement an overall or comprehensive development project. There have been a few exceptions, primarily the East Asian "four tigers" (Taiwan, Korea, Singapore, and Hong Kong); these exceptions have gained great attention in recent years and offer lessons for other Asian and perhaps post-Communist societies as well.

Many Third World regimes have been too weak to survive failure or mistakes, which are inevitable in any complex and lengthy development process. They have often been overthrown by military coups or civilian uprisings and replaced by new regimes that must start the learning process all over again. Some of the highly praised "economic miracles," such as Brazil and Mexico from the 1950s to the 1970s, or Ivory Coast and Kenya in the 1970s, went sour in the 1980s, with resultant turmoil and challenge to once-stable (but in all cases nondemocratic) regimes. Only the state-driven authoritarian "developmentalism" of South Korea and Taiwan continued their healthy growth through the debt crises of the 1980s (see Cumings, 1989; Amsden, 1990) and have in the 1990s begun gradual political democratization.

In Brazil, Mexico, and Argentina authoritarian corporatist projects for industrialization have characterized one type of development strategy, based on state investment in a wide variety of industries and economic activities, and coupled with protective barriers for national industry against foreign competition. In Burma and Tanzania, the state attempted a development strategy of international isolation and self-reliance on domestic technologies and resources. In South Korea, Taiwan, and Singapore, the state developed an international export and commercial strategy for competing within the world trading system, working closely with an enterprising and innovative domestic business class. In India, the state developed a policy of limited economic planning, with a large role for the state sector in certain key industries and in the sponsorship of domestic technology. The Third World state has been actively involved in trying to promote a primarily private market economy, but with heavy state sector involvement and privileges. In this sense, the Third World strategies, both the more successful and the dismal failures, have been more "statist" than was the experience of the earlier Western economic modernization, but have not reached the level of comprehensive and total state planning of the classic Communist model. The learning process of building institutions that can promote successful economic modernization is still ongoing, and even the few success stories are not following Western liberal models. Economist Alice Amsden concludes that "the East Asian model is far from ideal. Labour is repressed, women in particular are exploited, business and government are in league, and pollution is extreme. More to the point, that process is the only one that has achieved industrialization in the underdeveloped world" (1990:19).

Criticism of this Third World state-centered or "statist" approach to economic development has arisen from a new school of thought, developed most cogently by Hernando de Soto (1989) of the Peruvian Institute for Liberty and Democracy. This critique comes from a synthesis of both new left and economic libertarian views, which reject the privileges of the traditional right and the state planning of the orthodox left. In their view, the real hope for meeting human needs in the Third World rests with the emancipation of innovative workers and small business owners in what is now the "informal" sector of the economy, neglected and harrassed by the economic elites who have privileged access to state power. De Soto describes "the other path" of development as based on the promise of human capital, "of people who know how to seize opportunities by managing available resources, including their own labor, relatively efficiently" (1989:243). The World Bank has also praised the efficiency and productivity gains from grassroots community "informal finance" associations in sub-Saharan Africa and South Asia (World Bank, 1990:67–68). This synthesis, represented in Peru by President Alberto Fujimori and in Colombia by ex-guerrilla Antonio Navarro Wolff and the now-legal M-19 movement, aims at promoting a locally based market-type path of development from the bottom up, with much greater local self-reliance and freedom of initiative. This approach depends in large measure, however, on the assumption that democratic politics can work, and will be able to eliminate elite privileges peacefully, without suffering a military coup or destabilization by powerful internal and external economic interests.

Economic Growth and Population Growth

An initial point to be stressed in any discussion of Third World economic development is the rapid population growth that has complicated all attempts to raise standards of living for the people of these nations. A second point is that despite the tremendous increases in population, economic output (the total value of goods and services produced) has still managed some modest gains in GNP/capita for most, though not all, Third World nations. Unfortunately, the record is worst for the poorest of the poor, nations like Bangladesh, Somalia, Chad, Niger, and Afghanistan. Especially in comparison with both the liberal democracies and the Communist systems, annual rates of population growth (about 2.9 percent in Latin America, 2.5 percent in Africa, and 2.7 percent in Asia from 1950 to 1970) have been dramatically higher, which puts greater pressure on resources and requires higher levels of growth just to remain at the present standard of living. On the other hand, Third World nations have done fairly well (on average) in increasing national economic production (GNP), providing a real increase per person of over 2 percent per year. This is no small achievement, and aggregate economic development should be regarded as the most favorable area of system performance.

The rapid population growth in Third World areas is a phenomenon of the post-World War II period and is unprecedented in human history. Prior to World War I, world population growth was about 0.6 percent per year. Population growth was somewhat higher in the more developed nations of Europe and North America than in the less developed regions. In the latter

Table 13.1   Third World Population and Economic Growth

	Population (millions)	Annual Population Growth Rate		GNP/Capita Growth Rate
	1988	1965–80	1980–88	1965–88
Mexico	83.7	3.1	2.2	2.3
Brazil	144.4	2.4	2.2	3.6
Nigeria	110.1	2.5	3.3	0.9
Kenya	22.4	3.6	3.8	1.9
Egypt	50.2	2.1	2.6	3.6
India	815.6	2.3	2.2	1.8
Indonesia	174.8	2.4	2.1	4.3
South Korea	42.0	2.0	1.2	6.8
Third World averages:				
Low-Income[a]		2.6	2.8	1.5
Middle-income		2.4	2.2	2.3
For comparison:				
Rich liberal democracies		0.8	0.6	2.3

Sources: World Bank, *World Development Report*, 1986, 1990.
a. excluding India.
b. years for communist data are 1965–73, 1973–84, and 1965–84.

stages of Western colonialism, however, the more advanced medical practices of the West spread noticeably throughout the colonies and semi-colonies, producing a rapid drop in mortality (death) rates, while birthrates remained high. Between the 1940s and the 1960s, annual population growth rates doubled for the Third World, from about 1.2 percent to 2.4 percent. Although the increase in population growth rates peaked in the 1970s at about 2.7–2.8 percent, this is a high figure for poor nations struggling to modernize their economies and raise the level of general welfare, in many cases now at bare subsistence.

French economist Paul Bairoch has noted that when the Western nations began their industrial revolutions in the eighteenth and nineteenth centuries, they too experienced an increase in population growth rates, but only a modest increase from about 0.5 percent to 0.7 percent (Bairoch, 1975:7–8). Even as of 1986, Lester Brown (1987:22) reports that population growth rates in the less developed nations (not including China) still averaged 2.5 percent. Though there was some significant variation from Africa and the Middle East (2.8 percent) to Latin America (2.3 percent) and South Asia (2.4 percent), all were still quite high in historical perspective. The Third World nations are in this respect, as in so many others, faced with an entirely different situation and are not likely to be able to duplicate or tolerate the pattern of development that typified the Western world over the past two centuries.

Even if population planning were to make unexpected and radical advances toward lowering the birthrate, the effects of the population inflation of the past generation would continue to affect Third World prospects for development in the future, since the absolute number of women of childbearing age has increased so dramatically. In the present situation, the high rate of population growth, along with considerably shorter life expectancy, has created a youthful age distribution in most Third World nations. Whereas in the developed countries only about 27 percent of the population is under fifteen years of age and 10 percent is over sixty-five, in the Third World 41 percent is under fifteen and only 3 percent is over sixty-five. This means that a smaller proportion of the Third World population (56 percent compared with 63 percent) is of working age (fifteen to sixty-five). The disparity is even greater when we take into account the greater proportion of people (mainly women) tied to child care and the higher proportion of physical infirmity and invalidism among working-age people in the Third World (Uri, 1976:28–29). This means that a smaller segment of the total population is working (or seeking work) to support dependents (children, the aged, or invalids). For every 100 people active in the workforce in the Third World, there are 162 dependents to support; the comparable number of dependents for the developed nations is 123. The Third World working population has to increase productivity more to achieve a real per capita gain than is true for the developed nations. Once again, the Third World must run harder just to stay at current levels, run

Table 13.2   Growth Rates of Agricultural Production in the Third World

	1961 to 1985		1985 to 2000*	
	Total	Per Capita	Total	Per Capita
Africa (sub-Saharan)	2.0	−0.9	3.4	0.1
Near East/North Africa	2.9	0.2	3.1	0.5
Asia	3.5	1.3	3.0	1.5
Latin America	3.0	0.5	2.7	0.6

Source: Nikos Alexandratos, Ed., *World Agriculture: Toward 2000* (New York: New York University Press, 1988), p. 75.
*projection

harder to keep from falling further behind, let alone close the gap with the rich nations.

Agriculture and Food Security

Still, it would seem that in general the Third World has made some progress in raising per capita output (2.9 percent per year between 1965 and 1984), even with the population inflation. This is comparable to the historical rates of per capita growth achieved in the period 1865–1950 by developed nations like the United States (2 percent), Sweden (2.5 percent), and Japan (2.4 percent), and better than nations like Germany (1.4 percent), France (1.3 percent), and Britain (1.2 percent) (Weiskopf et al., 1972:365). But this aggregate-level comparison is misleading, for it masks many crucial differences between what was taking place in the Western nations in the past century and what has been happening to the Third World.

At the time of the industrial revolution in the West, agriculture had already achieved a level of productivity capable of supporting a growing non-farm population without constant threat of famine or need for large-scale import of foodstuffs.

Paul Bairoch (1975:17–19) has shown that the rates of growth for total agricultural production in most Third World nations have been quite good and compare favorably with those of most developed nations during their earlier period of industrialization. Only in the United States and Russia during the latter part of the nineteenth century were even higher rates of growth achieved, in large part due to the opening up of new frontiers to settlement and cultivation. This possibility is largely absent in the Third World today, especially in Asia and Saharan Africa, where the food supply is most precarious. The unprecedented population growth in the Third World has eaten up the gains in production and in some cases caused a net decline in per capita food production. The introduction of Western medicine and the rapid fall-off in

289

death rates occurred before the Third World countries had achieved an agricultural revolution. In the West the development of modern medicine was part of an indigenous technology and one of the fruits of industrial modernity itself. By the time medical technology became available to further lower death rates in the West, birthrates had already begun to decline as families began to plan that more children would survive to adulthood. This demographic transition from high birthrates and high death rates to (first) lower death rates and (later) lower birthrates is now taking place in the Third World nations as well. A decline in birthrates has now begun. But the timing of this transition, introduced from outside the Third World societies, has brought with it a population explosion before the economic transition to modernity and especially before agricultural development has advanced enough to sustain both population growth and provide for real improvement in the standard of nutrition.

In the late 1960s and early 1970s there was a burst of optimism that a "Green Revolution" would quickly transform agricultural production in the Third World. For many years, the Rockefeller Foundation had sponsored research to develop new wheat varieties (and later, in cooperation with the Ford Foundation, rice varieties) that were both high yielding and resistant to stem rust (blight). A research team headed by Nobel Prize winner Dr. Norman Borlaug did develop several wheat types that were initially tested in Mexico, then in the Middle East, India, and Pakistan. In the small test cases, impressive increases in wheat yields per hectare (one hectare = 10,000 square meters = 2.471 acres) were recorded. A new rice strain (called IR-8) developed in the Philippines also gave much-improved yields and was named the "miracle rice." Introduced on a larger scale in the latter 1960s, these new advances in Western agricultural technology seemed to indicate that a Green Revolution in Third World agriculture was at hand, a revolution that would turn famine-prone nations into cash crop exporters. Lester Brown, in his 1973 book *Seeds of Change: The Green Revolution and International Development in the 1970s*, stated his belief that this agricultural revolution would in turn bolster investment in other sectors of the economy, provide rural employment, and counter the massive migration from countryside to the cities. In a 1970 international conference sponsored by Columbia University, Brown summarized his findings:

> Countries traditionally in food deficit are now using the new seeds and becoming self-sufficient, some actually generating exportable surpluses. The Philippines, the first country to use the new rices on a commercial basis, has ended half a century of dependence on rice imports, becoming a net exporter. Pakistan, as recently as 1968 the second-ranking recipient of United States food aid, has sharply reduced its dependence on food imports and is expected to be self-sufficient in both wheat and rice in 1970. Food imports into India are now less than one-half those of the food crisis years of 1966 and 1967.
>
> Gains in cereal production in countries where the new seeds have been

successfully introduced are without precedent. Pakistan increased its wheat harvest 60% between 1967 and 1969. India upped its wheat harvest by one-half from 1965 to 1969. Ceylon's rice harvest increased 34% in two years. (Ward, Runnels, and D'Anjou, 1971:128)

Over the next decade, the Green Revolution did in fact increase grain production in India and Pakistan to the point where they no longer had to import basic cereals; rice production in the Philippines also expanded to the point where rice became an export commodity. But, while the new "miracle" seeds have made a sizeable impact in selected nations, the Green Revolution has not yet spread more generally through the Third World and has been notably absent in Africa.

Further, in order to produce higher yields, the new seed varieties require larger inputs of fertilizer and pesticides and better-controlled irrigation than the traditional varieties they replace. Pesticides and fertilizers are petroleum-based products, and the costs of these inputs have risen rapidly as the price of crude oil and its derivatives has escalated. Soviet analyst V. G. Rastyannikov, also a participant at the 1970 Columbia University conference, pointed out that only a small minority of big landowners in the poorer nations can afford to adopt the new grains. The poor peasantry are generally precluded from sharing in the potential gains of the Green Revolution, and their economic position may even deteriorate in relation to that of the rich farmers (Ward et al., 1971:127–31; also Bairoch, 1975:47; see also chapter 14). This social polarization in the countryside between a small minority of increasingly productive and wealthier farmers and a majority of poorer and less productive peasants who cannot afford the new agricultural technology erupted into violence in India in the latter 1970s. Unless there is a strong government program to assure equitable participation by poorer peasants, or adequate compensation for their deteriorating position, one unintended consequence of the Green Revolution could be class polarization and violence (as Lester Brown also admits; see Ward et al., 1971:134–35). Transplantation of Western technology and Western expertise may not produce the kind of development that can satisfy basic human needs in the Third World, even though it may seem promising (a technological "quick fix") on the basis of previous Western experience.

In the decade of the 1980s, food production per capita in the Third World grew at a pace of 0.2 percent per year (Statistical Abstract of the United States, 1990:854), with notably higher growth in India (1.9 percent), overall stagnation in Latin America and the Caribbean (0.1 percent), and more decline in Africa (− 0.8 percent) and the Middle East (− 0.2 percent). Twenty years of the Green Revolution have not brought the kind of breakthrough in food production in the developing nations that was initially envisioned, but it has permitted the Third World to keep pace with its historically high population growth rate. The agricultural development of the Third World in the postwar period is still in a race between food production and population growth.

In an evaluation of Third World agriculture after twenty years of the Green Revolution, Edward Wolf (1987:139–40, 154) notes that the adoption of the new grains had reached 36 percent of grain area in Asia and the Middle East, 22 percent in Latin America, but only 1 percent in Africa, and that the spread had slowed in all areas. The main reasons have been, as were predicted by the early critics, the cost factor for poorer farmers, the lack of attention to new agricultural research and financial support for poorer farmers, and the domination of private-sector commercial interests in setting priorities for agricultural research. In nations such as India and Mexico, grain harvests leveled off in the 1980s, as the Green Revolution reached its limits as a result of overworking the soil and even a reversal of short-term gains (Fornos, 1991:45). Wolf calls for new approaches, which "are needed to reach farmers who could not afford to follow this path, as well as to correct inequities in the distribution of resources and to confront widespread environmental problems" (p. 156). Norman Borlaug now says that the Green Revolution only "bought us some time" but was not a long-term solution to agricultural production in relation to population growth (Fornos, 1991:45). A future agricultural strategy that does not take into account social equity, and relies only on technological advances that are controlled by export-oriented commercial interests, is not likely to produce basic food security for the whole population.

Dependent Development: Extractive Industry

The growth of extractive industry (mining, petroleum) in the Third World during the twentieth century has provided the classic illustration for dependent development, an economic growth sector that was closely tied to the needs of the already industrialized Western nations and that did not produce a broader modernization of the Third World domestic economy.

The rapid growth in output from extractive industry in the Third World began in the early 1900s, when most of these nations were still colonies or semicolonies of the Western powers. Between 1900 and 1940, output of fuel and minerals grew at an annual rate of about 6 percent, quite high by historical standards. In the post–World War II period, however, annual rate of growth in Third World extractive industry averaged an even higher 9 percent (1948–70), with production of fuels increasing nearly seven-fold and that of minerals more than three-fold (Bairoch, 1975:52). These rates were much higher than the rates of population growth. In the Western nations, the growth of extractive industry went hand in hand with the early growth of the manufacturing sector; mining and drilling activities fed raw materials into local iron and steel mills, processing plants, and factories. In the Third World nations, fuel and mineral production did not go hand in hand with an overall pattern of economic development:

> It must be emphasized that the enormous increase in the output of the extractive industries in the developing countries was in no way due to the demands of local industry. Indeed local industry absorbed only a fraction of production. For proof of this it is only necessary to compare—either globally or country by country—output with exports of the products of mining and extraction. Thus, for countries like Brazil, Chile, Liberia, and Malaysia, exports of iron ore vary from 80 to 100 per cent of production. Further, while in 1970 the under-developed countries produced 39 per cent of world output of iron ore (excluding China and the USSR), the same countries produced slightly less than 5 per cent of the world's steel. Thus, some 90 per cent of the iron ore mined in the under-developed countries goes to feed the blast furnaces of the developed countries. (Bairoch, 1975:54)

The rapid growth of oil and mineral exploitations has been directed toward export to the West (and Japan), and has been financed and managed by Western-owned MNCs. The interests of the multinationals, such as Anaconda Copper, Union Miniere, Reynolds Aluminum, and the great oil corporations, are not connected to the overall development of Third World economies, but to returns for shareholders who live in the rich, developed nations. Economist Charles Rollins has illustrated the impact of MNC investment in extractive industries:

> The Bolivian tin-mining operations provide an excellent example of the importance that such a negative influence can attain. The tin mines were established in an economy very largely dominated by feudal agriculture. Within this economy they created a monetary sector (the cities and mines of the *altiplano*) whose chief interests were oriented toward the advanced Western nations where the tin was sold, and which remained to an extraordinary degree separated from the bulk of the populace, who continued in their old ways. (Rhodes, 1970:196)

Rollins argued that in some "new" countries, such as Canada and Australia, large-scale and rapid development of mineral resources has aided overall economic development. Here the institutional structures, including a strong and capable national government, plus the cultural, social, and economic prerequisites to capitalist development were present. This is to some degree also true for the nation of South Africa, where strong economic growth aided by gold and diamond mining has taken place, dominated by the European white minority. For the great majority of Third World nations that are not settler spin-offs from Europe (as Canada, Australia, and white South Africa are), these conditions were lacking. Most Third World governments were neither strong nor very capable. They were what Gunnar Myrdal (1968) called "soft states," easily penetrated by stronger outside or internal elite interests. Furthermore, the weakness of Third World governments may be one reason for investment interest by Western mining and oil companies:

> If, prior to the consideration of a raw-material-exploitation possibility, there were in power a government willing and able to take the necessary measures to promote development, it is unlikely that large-scale investments would be made, for the country would be regarded as one in which a "hostile" investment climate prevailed. If such a government came to power after the scheme had begun, the companies involved could be expected to oppose the adoption of the necessary measures. (Rhodes, 1970:203)

Unless and until Third World governments were able to bargain effectively with the giant mining and petroleum MNCs and to improve the terms of trade for their nations' natural resources, as well as survive hostile actions by MNCs and their Western political backers (military coups, CIA covert actions, and political bribery), the growth of extractive industry would continue a pattern of dependent development.

The OPEC experience since the 1970s has been a shocking anomaly to the West, primarily because of this unprecedented ability of a group of Third World nations to demand higher oil prices, to stick together as a group, and to resist being overthrown through overt or covert Western intervention.

In most Third World nations, the post–World War II growth of extractive industry has had few benefits, largely because these industries serve the needs of foreign developed markets, not local economies:

1. Machinery and equipment necessary for mining and drilling operations come almost exclusively from the developed countries, seldom from local producers.
2. Because Western "high" technology, which is capital-intensive and labor-saving, is employed, a relatively small workforce of skilled and unskilled workers is created, although these workers are often, by local standards, quite well paid. This tends to build small pockets of "labor aristocracy" among a much broader mass of poor and unemployed workers.
3. Management and technical employees are mainly drawn from the MNC home country, not from the local population. Modern technology is not being transferred socially to control by the host nation, but is only geographically present in the host nation. From the viewpoint of the MNC, it is to its best interest to retain control over technology, the better to avoid nationalization or expropriation. The few local managers allowed to rise within the MNC structure must prove their loyalty to the company

over country. Foreign management and technical personnel form small islands of conspicuous Western-style consumption in the midst of poverty (for example, the Belgian-French personnel in Kolwezi, Zaire, or the American personnel in Isfahan, Iran, before the overthrow of the Shah).

4. Profits from foreign-owned extractive industries (as well as from other MNC investments) are repatriated (taken out of the Third World nation) to the MNC home office to pay stockholder dividends. Only repatriation of a high proportion of profits will make foreign investment attractive, and repatriated profits are in general not reinvested in the host country but either consumed by the stockholder or reinvested elsewhere. Major diversification of MNC investment to manufacturing industries within one country, as part of an overall development plan, is in general not favored, since this might in fact force up local wages and might also make nationalization more practical in a company-government conflict. If the MNC spreads its facilities among many nations, nationalization of assets by one Third World government leaves the total operation still relatively intact and the nationalized assets useless without the extended network of manufacturing, transport, and marketing.

5. There is the final danger, recognized by OPEC and now by UNCTAD, that the MNCs may exhaust irreplaceable natural resources so that when such resources are needed for domestic industry, they will no longer be available from local mines and wells. Indeed, with the postwar growing demand for raw materials from the rich nations, there is the danger that certain materials will either be too depleted to sustain new manufacturing development or too expensive for the poor nations (cf. Tanzer, 1980).

Export-Oriented Manufacturing

Manufacturing industry has grown more slowly than extractive industry, but has made progress in the postwar period. For the years 1950 to 1970, total output grew by 6.6 percent per year; if population growth is considered, the per capita gain was still a decent 4.1 percent annual average. According to Paul Bairoch (1975:66–69), this compared favorably with per capita rates of manufacturing growth in the West during the last two centuries, although it fell short of the postwar achievements by the capitalist economies of Japan (14.8 percent) and Italy (7.3 percent).

The World Bank Development Report (World Bank, 1990:180–81) indicates that manufacturing growth in the Third World continued at a strong pace in the 1965–80 period, but slowed generally in the 1980s, with some important exceptions. Overall, the low-income developing nations increased manufacturing output by 9.1 percent per year in the earlier period, but this declined to 5.9 percent in the latter period, with sharp declines in Kenya and negative growth recorded in the 1980s in Nigeria, Tanzania, and several other

African nations. India was an exception to this trend, since its manufacturing growth rate accelerated from 4.5 to 8.3 percent over the two time periods, and it is important to note India's less spectacular but steady industrialization under long-range state involvement and planning. Likewise, for the middle-income developing nations, manufacturing rates of growth declined on average from 8.2 percent to 3.8 percent annually, and nations like Argentina, Mexico, Brazil, Venezuela, the Philippines, and Thailand suffered sharp declines in growth of manufacturing output. The severely indebted Third World nations and the regions of Latin America and sub-Saharan Africa were hardest hit.

In a number of developing nations, including South Korea, Taiwan, Singapore, Hong Kong, and Israel, strong governments supported and nurtured the growth of export-oriented industry as a way out of economic dependency and into a modern economy. These first Newly Industrialized Countries (or NICs) were not typical of the Third World generally. Hong Kong and Singapore were city-states with special relationships and access to the British market; Taiwan and South Korea were firm military allies of the United States, recipients of extensive U.S. aid and granted favored treatment for their products. Israel by many standards beyond geography did not belong to the Third World category at all. In 1968, these nations represented only 3 percent of the population of the developing world, yet they accounted for 42 percent of Third World manufacturing exports. In the East Asian NICs, manufacturing growth was sponsored and subsidized by authoritarian regimes, with labor costs held low and labor protests suppressed. Over the course of a generation this East Asian developmentalist strategy radically transformed these economies. South Korea had manufacturing growth of nearly 17 percent annually over the 1965–88 period. In 1965, Korea's exports were 40 percent raw materials and other primary goods, 27 percent textiles, and only 3 percent machinery. By 1988, Korea's exports were 39 percent machinery and transportation equipment, 22 percent textiles, and only 7 percent primary products. Taiwan and Singapore showed similar patterns of great change; together, these nations pioneered what has become known as the ''East Asian model'' of development, which includes strong and competent authoritarian regimes, an enterprising business class, locally developed technical know-how, and government protection of domestic markets. This model has been adopted, with some variations, by ASEAN (Association of Southeast Asian Nations), including Thailand, Malaysia, and Indonesia, all with authoritarian regimes. Undoubtedly this Asian development model, in some form, was also adopted by the Chinese communist regime after 1978 and by Communist Vietnam after the mid-1980s. Asian authoritarian developmentalism has been the new success story of the developing world. It has been quite different from the textbook free market model advocated (not always practiced) by the West. In the increasingly tough global trade competition of the 1990s, this Asian success model was coming into conflict with Western demands for ''fair trade,'' opening up of domestic markets to Western products, and cutting government subsidies to export industries.

In Latin America, by comparison, Mexico and Brazil, which were considered NICs and "economic miracles" under authoritarian corporatist regimes up to the 1980s, suffered severe setbacks from the debt crisis of the 1980s. In 1988, Mexico's exports were still 45 percent raw materials and 33 percent machinery, and Brazil's exports were 51 percent raw materials and 19 percent machinery (World Bank, 1990:209). Their state-sponsored modernization projects deteriorated and reached a dead end. Chile, on the other hand, under the military dictatorship of General Pinochet, followed a free-market reform outlined by several U.S. economists of the "Chicago school" and showed strong export growth in the 1980s. By the latter 1980s, new regimes of President Collor in Brazil, President Salinas in Mexico, and President Menem in Argentina were working to attract new international capital in order to restart economic growth. The North American Free Trade Agreement (NAFTA) among Mexico, Canada, and the United States was one part of that strategy. Other measures of both the Brazilian and Mexican regimes included selling off state-owned industries and lowering tariff barriers for imports, allowing more competition into the domestic economy. In Peru, under President Alberto Fujimori, new initiatives for small business and grass-roots entrepreneurship among the poor were part of his "Other Path" for capitalist development from the bottom up.

In summary, the former elite corporatist strategy for state-sponsored development in Latin America, once seen as that region's own authentic success formula, was in decline, and new experiments of various types were promoted. Most of these new experiments involved less government control and planning, more open domestic markets, and greater efforts to compete in international markets. In some cases, these new experiments were part of the "democracy trend," which replaced military dictatorships with elected civilian governments (Brazil, Argentina); in other cases they were associated with policy change of authoritarian regimes (Mexico's PRI), and in still others they were brought about by new "outsider" leadership (Fujimori in Peru).

Control of Trade, Finance, and Technology

Despite the achievements of economic growth in the Third World, which has outpaced population growth rates, the position of the Third World in the global economy is still largely dependent on Western sources of finance and technology. Through their continued control of finance and technology in the international trading system, the Western democracies continue to dominate the international trading system and its rules. Attempts by the developing nations, working through UNCTAD, to challenge the rules of the GATT and the IMF in favor of the Third World have met with failure.

Most Third World trade with the major blocs of nations (liberal democracies, Communist systems, and the Third World) takes place between the Third World and the rich Western nations. In the 1970s, only 5 to 10 percent of all Third World import and export trade was with the Communist world, despite a steady expansion of Communist trade since Stalin's death. And less than 25 percent of Third World trade was with other Third World nations. Between 70 and 75 percent of Third World trade was, therefore, with the developed Western nations (Bairoch, 1975:102; Sewell, 1978:206–7). The liberal democracies (70–75 percent) and the Communist nations (55–60 percent) did most of their trading with other members of their own blocs. Until recently, no Communist or post-Communist nation played a major role in trade with the Third World or international trade generally. Only in the latter 1980s did Communist China begin to play a significant role in international trade with the West, running up large trade surpluses with the United States ($20 million in 1993) and Germany (about $5 billion).

The Third World entered the postwar international trading system with mainly raw materials and fuels for export, while they had to import mainly manufactured goods and high-technology equipment from the West. Through the 1960s, between 80 and 85 percent of Third World exports were primary products, while 65 to 70 percent of Third World imports were manufactured goods. The terms of trade in the Western-established economic order have generally favored nations that export manufactured goods rather than primary goods (The OPEC oil exporters in the 1970s were an exception to this rule). Over the postwar period, the globalization of production by Western MNCs has transferred considerable manufacturing to the Third World, and some East Asian NICs have joined in the international trade in manufactured goods; these nations have prospered. In 1988, the exports of rich Western nations were overwhelmingly industrial goods, with over 40 percent machinery and transportation equipment, and only 19 percent primary goods and fuels. For the low- and middle-income Third World nations, exports in 1988 were still 43 percent primary goods and fuels, and only 16 percent in the more profitable machinery category (World Bank, 1990:209).

The United States, despite its own extensive mineral wealth, still relies, like Japan and Germany, on access to Third World suppliers for raw materials at the "right" price (see table 13.3). These figures might indicate that the Third World nations should be able to demand favorable terms of trade for their raw materials so clearly in demand in the West. And yet the terms of trade between primary goods of the Third World and the manufactured goods of the industrial Western nations have actually deteriorated since the early 1950s. Bairoch (1975) calculated that, except for the brief rise in prices for most minerals in 1951, which was fed by the Korean War, there was a deterioration in the terms of trade for primary products versus manufactured goods of about 18 percent between 1952 and 1970. Export trade is a matter of

Table 13.3   Western Imports of Raw Materials

	United States	West Germany	Japan
	Imports from Third World (as percent of total imports)	Imports from Third World (as percent of total imports)	Imports from Third World (as percent of total imports)
Aluminum	16	18	35
Copper	43	26	67
Iron and Steel	22	6	70
Lead	26	2	66
Nickel	9	4	14
Tin	74	75	97
Tungsten	5	8	8
Zinc	19	4	67
Petroleum	83	62	99

Sources: UN, *Commodity Trade Statistics: United States*, 1989, Series D, Vol. 39, No.1–11, 1991; UN, *Commodity Trade Statistics: Federal Republic of Germany*, Rev. 3, 1990, Series D, Vol. 40, 1991; UN, *Commodity Trade Statistics: Japan*, Rev. 3, 1991, Series D, Vol. 41, No. 1–3, 1992.
Note: Figures for the United States are for 1989; for Germany, 1990; and for Japan, 1991.

life or death for most Third World nations, since without sufficient exports to the West they cannot pay for Western imports of machinery and manufactured goods. Most Third World nations (with the exception of some OPEC states) are in fact not able to pay for imports with export earnings and are forced to borrow money from Western governments, Western banks, and Western-dominated international funds. Even supposed success stories of Third World development, like Mexico and Brazil, are deeply in debt (see Hansen, 1974, and Hellman, 1983, for an excellent summary of Mexican development).

Since the early 1970s, the foreign debt (public and private) of Third World nations has grown in alarming proportions (see figure 13.1). In the 1980s, it became clear that many of the most indebted Third World countries were unable to keep up with their debt servicing, payments of interest and principal, to their Western creditors. Increasingly, more repayments were going just for interest and less for reducing the outstanding principal of the debt. For Latin America, in 1976, 21 percent of foreign debt servicing went to interest payments, but by 1983 this had risen to 79 percent. In this situation, debtor nations would remain permanently in debt, never able to repay the loan principal. The extent of the debt crisis was heightened in August of 1982 when Mexico announced that it was bankrupt and unable to continue its debt servicing without major new financial aid. While this situation had occurred before for smaller debtor nations, and periodically occurs in the troubled financial life of many Third World nations, Mexico was one of the largest

Figure 13.1: Debt burden of non-OPEC developing nations.

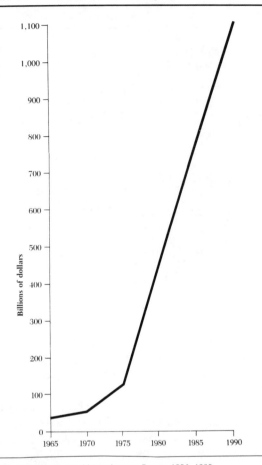

Sources: Sewell, 1977; World Bank, *World Development Report*, 1986, 1990.

debtor nations. Western banks had a large stake in Mexico's foreign debt, which in the latter 1980s stood at about $110 billion. When a Third World debtor nation finds itself unable to keep up its debt repayment schedule, it has generally sought additional loans and a rescheduling of existing loans over a longer payback period. In the 1950s and 1960s, these debt reschedulings were handled by a variety of international financial groupings of the wealthy Western powers, such as the so-called Paris Club, the Hague Club, and the OECD Donor Consortium (cf. Payer, 1985). In more recent times, the Western democracies have designated the International Monetary Fund (IMF) to handle the bulk of international debt problems for Third World nations and to discipline the debtor nations (Payer, 1974, 1982).

In the 1980s, Mexico, Argentina, Brazil, Peru, Chile, the Philippines, Egypt, Nigeria, Zaire, Sudan, Jamaica, and many other Third World debtor nations have had to submit to IMF "austerity plans" drawn up by IMF officials in order to receive debt relief and to avoid complete default. The IMF austerity plans include an array of measures to increase exports, reduce imports, and in general to increase the ability of the debtor nation to generate a foreign trade surplus to be used to satisfy its Western creditors. Such measures often include: cuts in government spending (on health, education and social services); cuts in government subsidies on basic essentials like bread or flour, cooking oil, and bus fares; devaluation of the local currency to make exports cheaper and imports more expensive; an opening of the country to more Western investment and abolition of controls on profits from operations in the debtor nation; and monetary and banking controls monitored by the IMF. In short, many Third World debtors are faced with either default or giving up control (sovereignty) over substantial economic and social policy areas to an international agency, which is funded by the affluent Western democracies and widely perceived as their agent in maintaining Third World debtor discipline. IMF officials are seen as the real governors, or imperial "proconsuls," of the economic fate of the peoples of the debtor nations.

Perhaps no other agency or institution is as widely hated in the Third World as the IMF, because the burden of IMF austerity plans is borne by the poor in those nations. Agreements to IMF austerity plans have sparked food riots, looting of stores, strikes, and spontaneous uprisings in Brazil, Sudan, Morocco, and Tunisia. Third World leaders are caught between the prospects of social unrest if they agree to IMF controls and default if they resist. Some individual nations, notably Peru under President Garcia, have resisted the IMF and placed limitations on the rate of debt servicing. This policy by Garcia alone ended in dismal failure, for himself, his party, and Peru. Most Third World leaders, after denouncing the IMF loudly for its policies, still eventually submit to IMF requirements to remain credit worthy.

A 1992 IMF assessment project report by an independent panel of economists concluded that IMF austerity plans have generally hurt the poor and helped the rich. The report found that in IMF programs from 1986 to 1990, 92 percent of the forty-eight nations involved cut spending in public housing, health care, and food subsidies. In twenty nations with IMF programs, the average top tax rate was cut from 59 percent to 39 percent between 1982 and 1990 (*New York Times,* March 10, 1992, D2).

The OPEC nations, on the other hand, have since 1973 been able to build up their export earnings by changing the terms of trade for oil dramatically. They were able in 1973 to quadruple the price of oil because: (1) they organized the oil-producing nations into a common bloc (cartel), which the West, despite its obvious dissatisfaction, has not yet been able to undermine; and (2) they took the price-setting power for oil away from the Western-owned oil MNCs. Oil is, of course, a special commodity; it is by no means clear that Third World producers could do so well with OPEC-type organizations for other raw materials. Nor is it clear that the OPEC nations had invented a path of self-sustained development merely because of their financial gains. In many areas they are still just as dependent on Western manufacturers, technology, and investment outlets for their newly acquired wealth, and for military supplies as well.

A major weakness of the OPEC strategy, taken in isolation from a whole array of transformations, is that control of technology still remains in Western hands. Indeed, this weakness may be one reason that the West's response to OPEC has not been more hostile or overtly military. One of the main characteristics of economic growth in the Third World has been the lack of local control over technology and its applications. Many observers of the Third World have asserted that without the independent development of technologies adapted to local conditions and needs, economic growth that would benefit the great majority, the masses of the poor, is exceedingly unlikely. Despite the increasing penetration of Third World economies by the MNCs, despite the drawing in of their resources to the world market, it cannot be said that the Third World is now in control of Western technology, but rather the reverse is true:

> No caricature is involved in describing modern science as a European invention which enabled the white nations to achieve military, economic and cultural domination over the rest of the world, and to make themselves prosperous while leaving the natives of the poor countries to progress very much more slowly. No injustice is done to say that most research workers and technologists have unthinkingly connived in these uses of science which are, at bottom, racist. Declarations about using science to feed the world's hungry have not stopped the prosperity gap growing wider; nor can they alter the fact that the intellectual interests of the great majority of research workers are far removed from any such program and that the preoccupation of technologists is with machines that enrich the rich. (Calder, 1970:252)

Calder's harsh judgment has been shared also by Sutcliffe (1971), Sachs (1978), Bairoch (1975), and, in far more diplomatic language, the 1976 ILO report. Sachs, a keen observer of the Third World for many years, states in fact that, in terms of practical application, the Third World still has no "indigenous science" (Sachs, 1978:84). Research and development (R&D) represents only 0.2 percent of GNP for the Third World nations, less than 1 percent of the R&D (per capita) spent by the rich Western nations. Further, less than 1 percent of Western R&D is for adaptation of Western science and technology to Third World problems. Even the MNCs with considerable investment and profit stakes in the Third World spend less than 5 percent of their large R&D funds in the Third World (Apter and Goodman, 1976:109). For example, U.S.-owned multinationals in 1966 spent 97 percent of their global research and development funds in the United States (Erb and Kallab, 1975:87).

This Western dominance over production technology is mirrored by underemphasis on science and technology within higher education in the Third World itself. According to Bairoch's figures for 101 Third World nations, in 1966–68 only 36 percent of students were in the fields of science, engineering, medicine, and agronomy, compared with 45 percent in Western Europe and 65 percent in Communist Eastern Europe. Even worse is the "brain drain" of Third World specialists to the rich nations caused by lack of demand in the local economies and, by comparison, the glittering opportunities for the highly trained in the West (see chapter 15). As a result, "technology transfer" to the Third World from the West represents mostly the continuation of the Western monopoly through patent and licensing rights. By the early 1960s, over 90 percent of new patents granted in most Third World nations were granted to (and therefore controlled by) foreigners, overwhelmingly Westerners. Foreign-controlled patents for the years 1957–61 made up 89 percent of all new patents in India, 92 percent in Turkey, 93 percent in Egypt, 96 percent in Pakistan, and 91 percent in Chile (Wilbur, 1973:127). Indian political scientist Jyoti Singh (1977:79) reports that, according to UNCTAD estimates, the cost to the Third World for the use of Western patents, licenses, and trademarks was nearing $10 billion annually by the latter 1970s.

The Western dominance over new technology development continued and even strengthened with the collapse of European Communist systems. From 1980 to 1990, in total world research and development spending, the rich Western democracies actually increased their dominance from 74.6 percent to 81.1 percent, while the Third World share declined from 6 percent to 4 percent (see table 13.4). With the collapse of communism, their share of global R&D spending went into a tailspin, and the post-Communist nations are now rapidly becoming dependent on Western R&D for future technological development.

One heavily advertised strategy for industrialization in the Third World, and especially in Latin America, was called import-substitution. This called for gradual replacement of imported Western manufactures with locally produced manufactured goods. While import-substitution seemed earlier to be making some progress in Latin America, it has faltered in more recent years. Now import-substitution strategies have come under criticism for their failure to come to grips with the need to develop an independent technological foundation for growth that would reach out beyond a few modern industries. Sutcliffe points out that the late industrializers like Japan and the Soviet Union were able to develop technical capacities adapted to society-wide conditions.

> By contrast, most underdeveloped countries, partly through government policy, partly because of the role of foreign industrial capital in those countries, have

Table 13.4   World Distribution of Research and Development Expenditures

	Total R&D Expenditures (billions of US dollars) 1980	Percent of World R&D Expenditures 1980	Total R&D Expenditures (billions of US dollars) 1990*	Percent of World R&D Expenditures 1990*
Developed countries with market economies	155.5	74.6	367.0	81.1
Developed Eastern countries (including USSR)	40.3	19.3	67.3	14.9
Developing countries	12.6	6.0	18.3	4.0

Source: UNESCO, *Estimation of World Resources Devoted to Research and Experimental Development*, 1980, 1985, 1991.
*Projection

followed a pattern of more wholesale adoption of the more advanced Western industrial techniques. The result has been that, as import substitution possibilities come to an end, industrial progress has tended to grind to a premature halt; and one of the major reasons for this has been not the failure to assimilate technology but the absence of the technological dynamism which further industrial growth would need. (Sutcliffe, 1971:336; see also ILO, 1976:164 and Sachs, 1978:ch. 2.)

While this characterization is a valid generalization, several Third World nations have made great strides in developing new locally controlled and locally applied technologies. India, Brazil, Taiwan, South Korea, Pakistan, and Iraq, to name a few, have developed high-technology programs in the fields of nuclear energy, computers, electronics, missiles, communication satellites, and aircraft design. India has launched its own space satellites. Brazil has a very advanced methanol fuel program. Korea is at the forefront of video recorder equipment technology, and Taiwan has made impressive developments in computer and communications equipment. For these nations, control over modern technology has given them opportunities for economic development not possible for most of the Third World. In some cases, notably in Pakistan and Iraq, these developments of local technology have been aimed at potential military applications, which explains the extent of government effort and determination. Yet overall, Third World resources spent on research and development remain a tiny percentage of the levels spent by both the rich liberal democracies and the industrial Communist/post-Communist states. Most new technologies continue to emerge from research and development projects undertaken outside the Third World and in all likelihood controlled by Western governments and by Western multinational corporations.

Correlates of Economic Development

Within the grouping of developing nations, the range of material levels of consumption runs from the very poorest nations (Somalia, Haiti, Zaire, Bangladesh) to some oil-rich OPEC states with small populations and very high GNP/capita (Kuwait, United Arab Emirates, Libya, Saudi Arabia). In recent years, the calculation of purchasing power parities (PPP) per capita has shown considerably greater economic progress for nations like India, Indonesia, Mexico, and Brazil than the more mechanical comparisons of GNP/capita (see table 13.5). The gaps between these developing nations and the United States, for example, appear much smaller according to these more recently devised measures of actual purchasing power.

Among the regions of the "Third World," Latin America started out in the postwar era with the highest levels of development in GNP/capita, but in the 1990s several formerly poor East Asian nations (Taiwan, South Korea, Singapore) have surpassed even the middle-income Latin American NICs (Mexico, Brazil). In general, the economic dynamism of East and Southeast Asia has raised that region above the Latin American level. The nations of sub-Saharan Africa are now the poorest region in the Third World, having virtually no success stories or durable economic miracles among them. In

Table 13.5   Levels of Consumption in Selected Third World Nations

	GNP/Capita 1990	PPP 1990	TVs/1,000 Population 1990	Radios/1,000 Population 1990	Autos/1,000 Population 1985–89
Mexico	2,490	5,918	139	243	65
Brazil	2,680	4,718	213	379	104
Nigeria	290	1,215	32	172	4
Kenya	370	1,058	9	125	6[b]
Egypt	610	1,988	109	324	20
India	360	1,072	32	79	2
Indonesia	560	2,181	60	147	7
South Korea	5,450	6,733	210	1006	27
Kuwait	16,150[a]	15,178	285	343	227
For Comparison:					
United States	21,810	21,449	815	2123	748
Russia	3,430	7,968	323[c]	685[c]	45[d]

Sources: UNDP, *Human Development Report*, 1993; U.N. Economic Commission for Africa, *African Social and Economic Indicators*, 1989, 1992.
a. 1989
b. 1985
c. USSR, 1988–89
d. USSR, 1986–88

South Asia, India has continued to make gradual progress, as have several North African nations (Egypt, Morocco, Tunisia), raising general living standards modestly. In neither region has there emerged a new "success formula" or "miracle economy" for other nations to emulate.

Educational opportunities in the Third World have grown considerably since World War II. Bairoch (1975:137–41) estimates that illiteracy in the Third World was about 80 percent at the turn of the century and was still about 74 percent in 1950. This figure was reduced by 1970 to 56 percent, ranging from 76 percent in Africa to 50 percent in Asia and 24 percent in Latin America. In secondary education and college-level (higher) education as well, considerable gains in enrollments were achieved between 1950 and 1970. In fact, by 1970 secondary-school enrollments had reached levels (in per capita terms) attained by the developed nations in the 1930–50 period, well after industrialization and economic modernization had taken place. In 1970, there were some 5.6 million college-level students in the Third World, compared with only nine hundred thousand in 1950, and compared with 5.4 million college-level students in the developed nations as of 1950.

These impressive gains, however, have had limited impact on economic development in the Third World for several reasons. First, the facilities and staffing of educational institutions is in general quite inadequate, and most Third World nations spend a smaller portion of GNP on education than do the liberal democracies or the Communist nations. Mexico and Brazil, often

Table 13.6   Educational Attainment in the Third World

	Illiteracy (percent) 1990	Percent GNP Spent on Education		Students per 100,000 Population	
		1970	1986–90[a]	1970	1985–90[a]
Mexico	12	2.6	4.1	492	1,480
Brazil	19	2.7	3.9	452	1,064
Nigeria	49	2.5	1.7	28	282
Kenya	31	4.1	6.4	69	135
Egypt	52	4.8	6.7	700	1,698
India	52	2.8	3.2	702	581
Indonesia	18	2.5	0.9	208	600
South Korea	3	3.7	3.7	642	3,953
Kuwait	27	4.2	5.0	353	1,384
For comparison:					
United States		6.4[b]	5.3	4,148	5,608
USSR		6.8	7.9	1,895	1,820

Sources: UNDP, *Human Development Report*, 1993; *Unesco Statistical Yearbook*, 1978–79, 1980, 1992.
a. Most recent available figure from this period.
b. Includes private expenditures on education.

referred to as showplaces of capitalist-style development in the 1950s and 1960s, were among the less generous in educational financing. Thus, even though more children were going to school, the schools were often overcrowded and poorly equipped. Many Third World governments have allowed university enrollments to soar, while funding levels for building, libraries, laboratories, and faculty have stagnated or, as a consequence of the debt crisis in the 1980s, shrunk. The University of Cairo in Egypt and the National Autonomous University of Mexico have official enrollments of several hundred thousand students, but it is doubtful that, except for some sheltered elite programs, most students are getting a real chance at a college education. Many Third World regimes are afraid of reducing enrollments, however, because that would destroy the illusion of possible advancement through higher education. So many Third World universities turn out huge numbers of new graduates, for whom there are few jobs and whose education is inadequate for professional employment. A third factor is the migration of highly educated citizens from the Third World where their talents are most needed to the developed West, where the financial rewards and secure consumer life-style are most attractive. This is in many respects the natural outcome of higher education in the Third World, since in many ways it is dominated by Western standards and therefore trains people for positions and careers that exist (in sufficiently large numbers) only in the developed West. Educational growth is out of synchronization with overall economic opportunities, ensuring that many college-educated will be able to pursue stable and financially rewarding careers only outside their homelands. In the Third World, educational growth has outpaced job creation for the highly educated.

As indicated in the beginning of this chapter, a rapidly declining death rate, beginning in the 1930–50 period, has produced a rapid population growth in the Third World that has helped to increase life expectancy even in very poor nations like India and Egypt. Infant mortality rates, while still much higher than in the liberal democracies or Communist systems, have declined from pre-World War II levels. Life expectancy, while still considerably lower than in the developed nations, has also increased, with relatively higher levels in Asia and Latin America and lower levels in Africa. This does not mean that the overall health and nutrition levels have also risen. Medical care, especially in rural areas and for the urban poor, remains at low levels, and medical personnel, both inadequate and unequally distributed in most Third World countries, are unable to meet basic health needs of the population. Nutritional standards may even have declined (Gamer, 1975) in many Third World nations, despite officially recorded increases in the value of agricultural production per capita. In some nations, where agriculture has converted from growing basic diet foods to growing commercial crops for export or for middle-class consumption, nutritional levels of the average citizen's diet have suffered. Agriculture in northern Mexico, now specializing in tomatoes and lettuce for the U.S. market rather than in beans and maize for basic local needs, is an example. In many Third World countries, average daily calorie intake is well below the 2,750 calories recommended by the World Health Organization (WHO). Protein intake often falls below the minimum eighty grams a day necessary to support normal mental and physical development. Under conditions of constant undernourishment, life may be sustained, but with marked mental and physical retardation. Past a certain age in children, this retardation becomes irreversible, even with later improved diet. In the West, population growth and increased life expectancy corresponded to an improved diet with higher nutritional content (see chapter 3) and to the improved physical and mental development of a large portion of the population. The impaired health of a large portion of the Third World population, on the other hand, creates a further hindrance to economic development, reducing the numbers of capable, able-bodied workers and increasing the ratio of dependents to workers.

One of the main features of economic development in the West was the growth of cities as centers of manufacturing and trade. The housing conditions of early capitalist societies have already been described. Third World urbanization differs from the Western pattern in several fundamentals. First, the growth of cities in the Third World has not been closely related to the growth of industry and industrial employment in the cities (Weitz, 1973:5; Sinclair, 1978; Goldthorpe, 1975:112–27), for reasons cited above. Although possibilities for employment in urban culture yearly attracts millions of peasants to the cities, many are driven from the land by the decline of employment and subsistence agriculture.

Table 13.7   Health Care and Nutrition in the Third World

	Life Expectancy	Infant Mortality Rate		Population per Physician	Daily Calorie Supply per Capita	
	1990	1965	1991	1984–89	1965	1989
Mexico	69.7	82	37	1,240	2,570	3,052
Brazil	54.6	104	59	1,080	2,417	2,751
Nigeria	51.5	177	99	6,420	2,185	2,312
Kenya	59.7	112	68	10,130	2,208	2,163
Ethiopia	45.5	165	125	78,780	1,853	1,667
Egypt	60.3	172	59	770	2,399	3,336
India	59.1	150	90	2,520	2,021	2,229
Indonesia	61.5	128	68	9,410	1,791	2,750
South Korea	70.1	64	22	1,160	2,178	2,852
For comparison:						
OECD countries	76.4	24	8	440	3,097	3,423

Source: UNDP, *Human Development Report*, 1993.

The uncontrolled growth of the Third World cities has been a combination, well described by Stuart Sinclair (1978), of "push" and "pull" factors. Second, urbanization proceeded at a much faster pace than was the case in the West, overwhelming the capacities of relatively weak and inexperienced municipal governments to supply essential water, sewage, garbage, power, and health services. By 1980, nearly one-fourth of the Third World population lived in cities of over twenty thousand, compared with less than 10 percent in 1940. Much of this urban growth has taken the form of slum and squatter settlements around the periphery of the core city. By recent estimates, one-third to two-thirds of the urban population live in slum and squatter (self-built) housing (see table 13.8).

Lagos, with a population of perhaps 3.3 million in the early 1970s, is the capital of Nigeria and Africa's fastest-growing city. By some accounts it is the best example of the ills of Third World urbanization: "It now chokes on bad housing, traffic jams, and cement pile-ups. Whole streets are littered with compost, broken bottles, pieces of furniture, empty cans. The stench is intolerable during the dry season and worse when it rains. Then, over half the streets are flooded." The results are that "85 percent of Lagos school children have either hook-worm or round-worm; and that 10 percent of deaths are attributable to dysentery or diarrhea" (Sinclair, 1978:20).

On the other hand, Mexican economist Eduardo Flores offered the following commentary from a visit to Calcutta, India:

> Calcutta affords the opportunity to see large-scale misery in its full harshness. At night its broad sidewalks become public dormitories, heaped with more than 600,000 emaciated men, women, old people, and children. . . . The poor of Calcutta lack the most elementary belongings, owning neither pillow, mattress, nor blanket; their bodies stink and are covered by soiled rags. At dawn, before the city awakens, carts collect the corpses of those who have died in the night.
>
> I, at once, realized that the misery of Calcutta was quite familiar to me. Hungry, ragged human beings were no novelty, since they are a standard part of the rural and urban landscape in Mexico, Bolivia, Peru and Brazil, countries I know well. What moved me in Calcutta was the overwhelming proportions of its misery. (Weitz, 1973:95)

The case of Calcutta is interesting for another reason: since electing a government in West Bengal State led by the Communist party (Marxist), Calcutta has managed to clean up its streets considerably and to build a modern new subway system that has instilled pride in city residents. This is an indication that with competent and motivated government leadership, improvements can be made, even in very poor societies, using the level of local resources at hand. The problem is the development of a responsible government (local, state, or national) that in fact does have a commitment to improving the lives of poorer citizens and providing adequate social services.

Table 13.8   Slum and Informal Settlement Populations

City	Percentage of Population Living in Slums and Informal Housing	
	1970s	1980s
Latin America		
Mexico City	46	40
Rio de Janeiro	30	32
Lima	60	33
Bogota	—	59
Caracas	40	34
Asia		
Bombay	45	57
Ankara	—	51
Seoul	30	12
Manila	35	40
Karachi	—	37
Delhi	—	50
Africa		
Tunis	—	45
Lagos	—	58
Addis Abada	90	85
Luanda	—	70
Lusaka	—	50
Nairobi	33	34

Sources: Barbara Ward, *The Home of Man* (New York: Norton, 1976), p. 193; Stuart Sinclair, *Urbanization and Labor Markets in Developing Countries* (New York: St. Martin's Press, 1978), p. 16; U.N. Center for Human Development (HABITAT), *Global Report on Human Settlement*, 1986; EC, *The Courier: Africa-Caribbean-Pacific-European Community* 131 (Jan./Feb. 1992) 64.

Without such organized social commitment, however, the problems of Third World homelessness are unlikely to be solved.

Hernando de Soto, using the case of Peru, shows also how many illegal urban housing settlements over the years have improved their status and the quality of housing they provide for 47 percent of Lima's now huge population (1989:13). With minimal starting resources, but with ingenuity and hard work, illegal squatters continue to build new shelter for their families far more efficiently than either the legal private housing market or the state-subsidized public housing sector. The success stories of Third World housing are sometimes overlooked, because they are often outside the formal economy and defy both the economic and political power centers in their efforts at local self-improvement.

Another effect of Third World urbanization combined with desperate conditions for the poorest strata is the growing numbers of homeless children, thrown out of their families or fleeing abuse from their parents. These children, often grouping together in gangs for protection, survive on the streets through peddling, washing cars or windshields, shining shoes, picking pockets, pimping, running numbers and sometimes drugs, and child prostitution. In Brazil, the state-run Foundation for the Welfare of Minors (FUNABEM) estimates that there are some 7 million homeless children in that nation, mostly in big cities like Rio de Janeiro and Sao Paulo. They attribute the disintegration of poor families to inadequate housing and massive unemployment among the urban lower classes. One consequence of this family disintegration is that 47 percent of Brazilian children never go beyond the first grade, because they must either work to support a single parent or must fend for themselves outside the family. This problem of homeless children and the disintegration of family life among the poor is not peculiar to Brazil. Any visitor to a big city in the Third World can see the large numbers of small children engaged in the wide range of activities, legal and illegal, made necessary by desperate circumstances.

Both the liberal democracies and the European communist nations expanded government welfare systems and spending levels in the postwar years to the point where a national welfare system of social security, old age and disability benefits, unemployment compensation, health care, public housing, and family assistance characterizes most of the advanced industrial nations. In the case of the liberal democracies, the development of the welfare system was an explicit commitment to basic human needs and an implicit guarantee that the suffering of the Great Depression will not return. In the Communist systems, it represented the fulfillment of regime ideology. In the Third World, basic human needs are not met for the average citizen, either through the private market or through governmentally sponsored programs. As a percentage of Gross Domestic Product (GDP), welfare spending remains quite low, welfare programs generally cover only a small fraction of the population (often privileged government and skilled workers in pro-regime unions), and welfare payments are generally insufficient to provide economic security.

In many Third World nations, corrupt dictatorships have pillaged government funds, leaving their people with tiny allocations for social security (see also chapter 16). In the Philippines, President Marcos' regime cut welfare spending while looting the country for over twenty years. In Nigeria, both civilian and military regimes have failed to use the nation's oil wealth to improve social welfare services for Africa's most populous nation. Kenya, once touted by Western economists as an "economic miracle" story of Africa, cut its already minimal social spending to virtually zero, while the regime of President Daniel Arap Moi enriched itself from government contracts and bribe taking. In Malaysia, one of the new Asian success stories, social welfare spending actually declined during years of rapid growth. Middle-income Mexico and Brazil, which had strong economic growth in the 1950s and 1960s, still had low allocations for social security programs, and under the IMF austerity programs for debtor nations in the 1980s, both nations cut their welfare budgets. What table 13.9 demonstrates is the unwillingness of almost all Third World regimes to devote the necessary resources to provide some basic sense of security for its citizens, even while ruling elites and their allies enrich themselves from control of government budgets.

Summary

Economic growth in the Third World has been impressive in its overall ability to keep pace with rapid population growth. Yet the pattern of economic growth in the Third World generally has not made the kind of transformation in jobs, health, education, housing, and social welfare that would give its citizens the prospect of a fairly healthy and fairly secure family life.

Although a few nations (in East Asia mainly) have been able to prosper within the Western-dominated world trading system, most Third World nations have not, and the dependency syndrome outlined in this chapter still characterizes most of the developing nations. Some nations that seemed to be on the road to economic success in the 1960s and 1970s have fallen into the "debt trap," which has severely set back their development prospects. Of thirty-two Third World nations designated as "success stories" (5.5 percent annual growth in

Table 13.9   Social Security Expenditure in the Third World as Percentage of Gross Domestic Product (GDP), 1960–1986

	1960	1970	1980	1986
Mexico	1.6	3.0	2.6	2.7
Venezuela	2.5	3.1	1.3	1.1
Brazil	4.7	5.7	5.3	5.0
Colombia	1.5	2.6	2.8	2.0
Kenya	—	1.9	0.06[a]	0.2
Nigeria	0.7	0.8	0.02[b]	0.02
India	1.4	1.9	1.6	1.5[c]
Philippines	1.1	1.1	0.6	0.7
Malaysia	3.0	2.9	1.0	2.2
For comparison:				
United States	6.8	9.6	12.7	12.5
Soviet Union	10.2	11.9	14.1	15.5

Sources: ILO, *Cost of Social Security*, 1975–77, 1978–80, 1984–86.
a. 1981
b. 1979
c. 1985

GDP) in the 1970s, only fourteen retained growth rates of 4.5 percent or better in the 1980s, out of eighty nations surveyed (United Nations, 1987:156). No Latin American nations and only two small African (Congo and Cameroon) nations were still on the "success" list.

Considerable change has occurred in the Third World economic situation, bringing virtually all these nations into the global economy in a more serious fashion, so that they are increasingly affected by the existing system of trade and finance. Some number of East Asian NICs, as outlined above, may be exiting the Third World through their own export-driven success formulas, which are quite different from the established Western democratic pattern. Some other Third World nations, including Liberia, Haiti, and Somalia (and soon perhaps Zaire), are such dismal failures that they are becoming totally dependent, losing even their formal sovereignty through the venality and incompetence of their political elites. Most Third World nations have experienced some economic modernization within the global trading system, but this has not yet produced a pattern of broad-based benefits and sustained material achievements for the great majority of citizens.

14

Inequality—Failures in Social Justice

The dimension of social inequality in the developing nations includes the various inequalities between these Third World nations and the rich, developed nations and multinational corporations. The end of the Cold War and the collapse of communism in Europe did not change these international inequalities, which continue to define relations between the Third World and the affluent Western democracies in the global economy. These international dimensions of inequality in wealth, power, and control over both human and material resources are intimately linked to the development of internal inequalities within individual Third World nations. Indeed, the dependency syndrome arises from a combination of transnational inequalities that create the preconditions for dependency and is at the same time a process that adds to both international and internal inequalities. Dependency cannot be understood without reference to both types of inequality. Of course, no single nation is completely self-sufficient, and every nation is therefore somewhat limited in its relations with other nations whose products and services it wants to use. Yet, for most of the Third World, relationships with the rich nations of the West are on such an unequal basis of wealth, power, and resource control that they are the basis for a system of dominance rather than bargaining among relative equals.

Most governing elites in the Third World have accepted this unequal relationship, since cooperation within the international trading system can also benefit elite interests, although it does not provide for the basic human needs of the poor. Should a Third World government try to challenge the existing relationship to the international trading system, it faces tremendous pressures and various forms of intervention to remove it (see chapter 15).

Transnational Inequality—Income

While it is difficult to measure the extent of world income inequality for years prior to 1900, Dutch economist L. J. Zimmerman (1965) estimated income levels for the developed and underdeveloped areas of the world for the years 1860, 1913, and 1960. To these figures we have added estimates for income levels for the year 2000 developed by Indian economist Jagdish Bhagwati (1972) and develop a time-series of Lorenz curves for world income inequality from 1960 to 2000.

While we may dispute some figures in these global estimates, the major trend over the past two centuries has been toward greater global income inequality. In 1860, the richest 25 percent of the world's population received nearly 58 percent of world income. In 1913, this top 25 percent got 69 percent; in 1960, it controlled 72 percent. Meanwhile, the share of world income going to the poorest half declined from less than 27 percent in 1860 to about 14 percent in 1913 and only 10 percent in 1960 (Zimmerman, 1965:38). The gap between the rich and poor nations had increased from about a 2 to 1 ratio in the early 1800s to 20 to 1 by the 1960s (Hansen, 1975).

Over the last thirty years, the gap in GDP per person between the developing nations of the Third World and the rich industrial nations has grown in most regions (see table 14.1). Only the regions of East and Southeast Asia, where the "four tigers," the ASEAN nations, and more recently Communist China have shown very strong export-driven growth, and the Arab states that benefited from the OPEC oil revenues windfall after 1973, have held their own or closed the gap. But Latin America, sub-Saharan Africa, and South Asia have lost ground relative to the affluent Western democracies, and overall, the least-developed countries fell from 9 percent of Western GDP/capita in 1960 to just 5 percent by 1990. The GDP/capita figures for this most recent time period, after independence had been achieved by almost all former colonial states, shows an increasing differentiation in performance by region but with a still-widening gap between the rich and poor nations of the global economy.

Table 14.1   Widening Gaps in GDP per Capita by Region, 1960–1990
(regional figures as percent of rich nations GDP per capita)

Real GDP/ capita	Sub-Saharan Africa	Arab States	South Asia	East Asia
1960	14	21	12	15
1990	8	23	9	15

	Southeast Asia	Latin America	Least Developed Countries	All Developing Countries
1960	13	37	9	17
1990	18	31	5	15

Source: UNDP, *Human Development Report*, 1993.

The United Nations has undertaken a more intensive International Comparison Program, which in 1985 estimated that Ethiopia's GDP/ capita was only 1.6 percent of the United States' level, with Tanzania at 2.6 percent, Bangladesh 5 percent, India 4.5 percent, Philippines 10.8 percent, Egypt 15.8 percent, Thailand 16 percent, Tunisia 19.8 percent, and South Korea 24.1 percent (World Bank, 1990:236–37). While these figures may seem rather bleak, they point out a considerable range, a fact that should not be neglected in any analysis. Additionally, a study by the United Nations indicates that because of very high growth rates in China and relatively good results in India between 1980 and 1987 (United Nations, 1989:107), world income disparity (as measured from the Lorenz curve) actually decreased slightly during this period. Continued strong growth just in these two most populated and poor nations would by itself reverse the two-century trend toward greater global inequality.

If we use purchasing power parities (PPP) instead of GDP/capita, the gap between the Third World nations and the affluent Western democracies appears smaller. Since the beginning of the century (1913) to 1985, some nations, such as Japan, closed the gap between themselves and the early industrializers such as the United States and Great Britain (see table 14.2). Japan is one of the few nations (one must include also Hong Kong, Singapore, and Taiwan) that have accomplished this. Other nations, such as India, lost considerable ground. In 1913, Indian PPP stood at $409, or 11 percent of the U.S. level; by 1985, Indian PPP was $639, which was only 5 percent of the U.S. level. Argentina, which in 1913 had purchasing power parity nearly 47

Table 14.2   Estimated Real per Capita GDP for Selected Nations, 1913–1985 (purchasing power parities in 1980 dollars)

	1913	1950	1985
Argentina	1,711	2,325	3,177
Brazil	349	918	3,299
Chile	1,106	2,053	3,301
Colombia	836	1,374	2,833
India	409	366	639
Mexico	714	1,010	2,591
Peru	603	1,410	2,265
For comparison:			
Japan	826	1,157	9,839
Britain	3,185	4,334	8,948
United States	3,653	6,485	12,290

Source: Inter-American Development Bank, *Long-Term Trends in Latin American Economic Development*, 1991.

Figure 14.1 World distribution of income, 1860–2000: Inequality is becoming more pronounced over time.

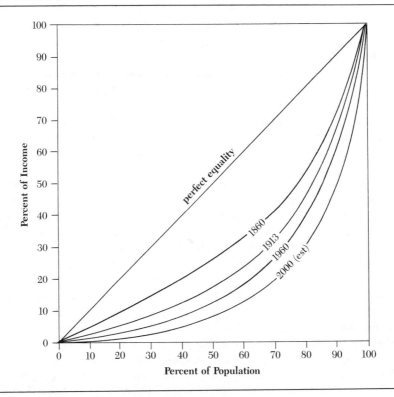

Sources: Adapted from Zimmerman, 1965:34–40, and Bhagwati, 1972:28.

percent of the United States level, had by 1985 declined to less than 26 percent. In Latin American nations covered in the U.S. study, only Brazil made significant progress in closing the gap, going from less than 10 percent of U.S. purchasing power parity in 1913 to almost 27 percent by the mid-1980s.

In the comparison between the rich and poor nations, "equal pay for equal work" does not exist. Barnett and Muller (1974), in their analysis of MNC penetration of the Third World, compared industrial wage rates for comparable jobs and skill levels between the United States and several developing nations. Not surprisingly, workers in the United States were paid generally five to ten times as much per hour for the same work that a Third World worker performed. Twenty years later, their conclusions are still valid. While wages in Europe and Japan caught up to those of the United States by 1990 and European hourly wages were at 125 percent and Japanese wages at

100 percent of U.S. wages in 1992 (*Statistical Abstract,* 1993:862), wage differentials in the developing nations generally remained very large. Wage rates for manufacturing work in Sri Lanka are in fact only 2 percent of U.S. wage rates, and workers in Mexico and Brazil have actually lost ground over the past decade. Only the East Asian "four tigers" (Hong Kong, Singapore, Taiwan, and South Korea) have experienced wage increases relative to American wage rates, so that in these East Asian growth economies, industrial workers may now get hourly pay that ranges from one-quarter to one-third of American wage rates.

As part of an adequate education in comparative politics, American students should go to Sears, J.C. Penney, Montgomery Ward, or nearly any apparel, appliance, sporting goods, or toy shop, and look at the labels that tell where the product was made (or assembled or sewn). Why are all these electronic calculators, digital games, Winnie-the-Pooh dolls, tennis racquets, running shoes, jackets, hardware items, and so much else being produced by Third World labor? What would they cost to American consumers if "equal pay for equal work" applied on a global scale? Why don't the highly productive workers in Taiwan, South Korea, Mexico, Costa Rica, India, Pakistan, or Haiti receive higher wages? In some countries, like South Korea before 1988, the Philippines, Guatemala, and Chile under the Pinochet dictatorship, labor union organizations are violently suppressed. Union organizers are periodically butchered by the regime and its assassination squads. Those unions that are permitted are led by docile and uncomplaining collaborators with the companies and the political system. In countries like India, Sri Lanka, and Venezuela, real unions do exist, often under quite militant leadership. But here the MNC has the option of pulling up stakes and setting up its operations elsewhere, where the investment climate is more favorable. As long as there are enough countries with repressive regimes, and workers are unable to organize effectively on an international scale, this tactic remains a powerful hindrance to Third World workers' movements. A docile and disciplined labor force is a vital ingredient of a favorable investment climate, and this factor explains why so much Western investment has gone to the worst dictatorships, rather than to the most democratic or progressive nations in the Third World. Thus, while U.S. foreign policy may verbally disagree with racist apartheid in South Africa, the atrocities of the Shah's SAVAK, the "disappearance" and murder of labor leaders in Chile, Argentina, and Brazil, and the suppression of human rights in South Korea, Taiwan, the Philippines, and Indonesia, U.S. and other Western MNCs are eager to exploit a tamed and defenseless workforce in these nations. U.S. presidents may proclaim their support for human rights, but MNCs owned and operated by American citizens both benefit from oppressive Third World regimes and provide international acceptance (and often financial aid) for repressive regimes and local collaborators with Western corporate interests.

The debate in the U.S. House of Representatives in fall 1993 over passage of the North American Free Trade Agreement (NAFTA) pointed out that U.S. workers were already in competition with low-wage, low-benefit workers in Mexico, where workers are not free to form real unions, where labor laws are not enforced, and where elections are fraudulent, rigged by the long-ruling (over sixty-five years) Party of Revolutionary Institutions (PRI). But Mexico is not unusual in this regard, and increasingly the well-paid jobs with good benefits in all the affluent liberal democracies are in competition with low-wage and low-benefit Third World nations.

An increasingly important aspect of this unequal international division of labor is the growth of "sex tourism," involving tourist packages for wealthy European, North American, and Japanese men to buy the services of prostitutes in Bangkok, Manila, Rio de Janeiro, Tijuana, Nairobi, Seoul, and Goa. There are several hundred thousand prostitutes in Bangkok alone servicing the booming tourist industry, which in 1986 earned more foreign currency for Thailand than any other industry. Cynthia Enloe, who has studied gender inequality within the international division of labor, has stated, "To succeed, sex tourism requires Third World women to be economically desperate enough to enter prostitution; having done so it is made difficult to leave. The other side of the equation requires men from affluent societies to imagine certain women, usually women of color, to be more available and submissive than the women in their own countries. Finally, the industry depends on an alliance between local governments in search of foreign currency and local and foreign businessmen willing to invest in sexualized travel" (1989:36–37). Added to this are the brothels and barroom prostitutes, male and female, adult and children, whose services are bought by U.S. military personnel stationed at military bases around the world. It is estimated, for example, that between 5,000 to 10,000 prostitutes provided their services to the recently closed U.S. naval base at Subic Bay in the Philippines (Enloe, 1989:86–87).

Table 14.3 Wage Rates for Production Workers in Manufacturing, 1980–1992, for Selected Developing Nations (as percent of U.S. wage rates)

Country	1980	1992
Brazil[a]	14	11
Hong Kong	15	24
Mexico	22	15
Singapore	15	31
South Korea	10	30
Sri Lanka	2	2
Taiwan	10	32

Source: *Statistical Abstract of the United States*, 1990, 1993.
a. Years for Brazil are 1975 and 1988.

Transnational Inequality—Power

Inequalities in power between rich and poor nations are apparent in military terms. Even after formal decolonization in Africa and Asia, the Western powers have intervened militarily with some regularity in the Third World. The Soviet Union intervened with military forces in places like Angola and Ethiopia as well, much to the dismay of the Western powers. But it was Britain and France (and Israel) that invaded Egypt in 1956, the United States that sent troops to Lebanon in 1958, to Vietnam from 1958 to 1973, to the Dominican Republic in 1965, to Grenada in 1983 and Panama in 1989. It was France and Belgium that sent paratroopers to prop up the corrupt Mobutu regime in Zaire in 1977, and France that sent troops to aid its client regimes in Chad and the Central African Republic. (More will be said of this with respect to political liberty in the Third World in chapter 15.)

The military and police forces of many Third World nations have been dependent on the developed nations for their armaments, training, and leadership. The United States for years trained several thousand Latin American officers in antiguerrilla warfare at Fort Gulick in the Panama Canal Zone. Somoza's national guard in Nicaragua was organized, equipped, and trained by the U.S. Marines. The Shah's SAVAK was organized and equipped by the CIA and the Israelis. Over twenty thousand U.S. military advisors were stationed in Iran during the Shah's reign to outfit, train, and even lead the army and air force. (Britain played a similar role for the Shah's navy.) The CIA and the Office of Public Safety (OPS) gave extensive training in interrogation techniques to national guard, secret police, and military forces in many nations. The OPS gave special aid to the Uruguayan military, which used torture and assassination in its battle against the Tupamaros in the late 1960s and early 1970s (Langguth, 1979). More recently, the CIA, along with Argentine and Chilean trainers, helped the Honduran military in kidnapping, torture, interrogation, and "elimination" techniques (LeMoyne, 1987). While it is claimed that American advisors do not actually participate in the use of torture and assassination, evidence indicates that they have been aware of torture and murder of political prisoners and have still continued to provide their expertise.

The USSR and its Warsaw Pact allies (East Germany, Poland, and Czechoslovakia) also played an active role in arming, advising, and leading certain Third World military forces (Angola, Ethiopia, South Yemen, Syria, Iraq, Afghanistan, and Nicaragua). While such military aid ties have on occasion backfired (Iran kicked out U.S. advisors in 1979, Egypt kicked out Soviet advisors in 1972), developing nations remain the "arms junkies" of the developed world. The United States and the Soviet Union each played major roles in the militarization of the Third World. From 1963 to 1983, arms exports to the Third World totaled some $223 billion, about half coming from NATO countries and 36 percent from Warsaw Pact nations. The United States alone accounted for 28 percent of the total and the Soviet Union for 33 percent (Sivard, 1986:12). In just the decade from 1972 to 1981, Third World expenditures on military armaments increased from 7.9 percent of world armament expenditures to 15.6 percent (Castro, 1983:202), despite the desperate financial squeeze being put on social and welfare expenditures in many of these nations. This Third World arms race has been a direct and growing channel of influence for both the industrial democracies and the industrial Communist states in the affairs of the less developed nations.

With the collapse of communism in Europe, and the crisis of the Soviet economy, it appears now that only the West will have the capacity to continue this arms linkage dependency. Whether the end of the Cold War has a "peace dividend" for the Third World depends in great part on the West's continued interest in supporting unpopular and repressive Third World client regimes in the name of U.S. national security interests (van Evera, 1990).

Still another aspect of the transnational power inequalities was illustrated by Lester Brown (1972:214–15) in a simple listing of gross national products for nations and annual sales for the largest MNCs. In the top one hundred on his list, there were fifty-nine nations and forty-one MNCs. In the top twenty, there were no corporations, but ten liberal democracies, six Communist nations, plus India, Brazil, Mexico, and Spain. Of the bottom eighty, a majority (forty-one out of eighty) were not nations but MNCs, including twenty-five that are American in stock ownership, six West German, four British, two Japanese, one Italian, one Dutch, and two British-Dutch.

In the financial sector, the picture is also one of continued dominance by the rich nations of the West and Japan. Of the world's largest fifty banks in 1989, as measured by assets, there were nineteen Japanese (including all the top seven), eight German, seven French, four British, three Dutch, three United States, and two Swiss and two Italian banks (Wright, 1990:121). Bank assets ranged from $100 to $300 billion, greater for each bank than the total Gross National Product of nations like Nigeria, Egypt, or Indonesia, and in the same league as the GNPs of Mexico, Brazil, and India. Only two banks, one in the Peoples Republic of China and one in Hong Kong, were outside the developed Western and Japanese bloc. As economic concentrations, each large MNC or large Western bank has more clout than most individual Third World nations and can direct that economic power far more freely and rapidly than most Third World governments. In trying to regulate or discipline the behavior of MNCs with investments in its territory or to negotiate with a major international bank, a Third World government is, even without considering the possibility of retaliation by Western government or the possibility of military intervention, challenging an economic power larger than itself. It should not be surprising that Third World governments, those that desire and attempt to challenge the multinationals (Allende in Chile, Manley in Jamaica, Velasco in Peru, Arbenz in Guatemala, Mossadegh in Iran) for control of the nation's resources, have found great hindrances requiring a strong government and strong, organized popular support, and even this may not be enough. It will probably be necessary for Third World governments to form effective coalitions as the OPEC oil cartel did, to combine their strengths, in order to shift the balance of power in negotiations with the MNCs.

Transnational Inequality—Resource Consumption

Global natural resources are not infinite in supply; several key resources may in fact be largely depleted within a few decades. The Club of Rome (an association of prominent Western business and intellectual leaders) sponsored two reports in the 1970s, *The Limits to Growth* (1972) and *Mankind at the Turning Point* (1974), that made the public aware of a future resource crunch. Both reports utilized complex computer simulations of the global economy to predict the consequences of current patterns of growth and of various alternatives to the present pattern.

The developed nations, and especially the most affluent consumer societies of the West, use a disproportionately large share of global natural resources, and this has now reached such high levels that through Western consumption these resources may not be available for development of Third World nations. Oil is, of course, the single resource that has attracted most attention. According to estimates made by the U.S. Bureau of Mines and Geological Survey and used by Dennis Meadows et al. in the *Dynamics of Growth in a Finite World* (1974), world petroleum supplies could be exhausted in the next two to four decades if present patterns of growth in demand continue.

On a per capita basis, the United States was already leading in energy consumption in the early 1950s; by the early 1970s oil consumption had increased in all regions of the world, and the economies of Japan, the USSR, and Eastern Europe had especially increased their levels of per capita consumption. The Third World, on the other hand, which in 1952 averaged only 5 to 6 percent of U.S. per capita consumption, had fallen to about 4 percent of U.S. per capita levels twenty years later. By 1990, energy consumption of most Western capitalist and industrial Communist nations had closed the gap with the United States even more, and the Third World had just barely moved up to 6–7 percent of U.S. energy consumption per person. Thus, the inequality worldwide in petroleum use has remained huge over the postwar years, while in Western and industrial Communist nations consumption has reached levels that could exhaust petroleum reserves within our lifetime.

Since the OPEC-instituted oil price rise in 1973, U.S. and Western consumption of Third World oil has increased rather than decreased at the same time that Western technology is feverishly pursuing nuclear, solar, fusion, geothermal, and other alternative energy sources. Mesarovic and Pestel, in the second Club of Rome report, pointed out the tragic irony of this situation for the underdeveloped countries: "The industrialized world is thus granted the time to develop alternative energy sources only by using nearly the entire world oil reserves and by that action preempting the supply of the most efficient and convenient energy source precisely when the developing nations need it most" (1974:68–69).

Oil is a leading illustration of resource consumption by the developed nations at the possible risk of resource exhaustion and resulting damage to even the potential of the less developed countries (LDCs) for growth. But petroleum is not the only resource whose transnational inequality of consumption poses this danger. Geological Survey figures for a list of major industrial minerals indicate that at current rates of growth in consumption, reserves will be depleted in the next several decades. William Ophuls (1978), in his thoughtful study of the emerging global politics of scarcity, presents a pessimistic but perhaps realistic overview:

> Alas, the emergence of ecological scarcity appears to have sounded the death knell for the aspirations of the LDCs. . . . In short, the current model of development, which assumes that all countries will eventually become heavily industrialized mass-consumption societies, is doomed to failure. Naturally, this conclusion is totally unacceptable to the modernizing elites of the Third World; their political power is generally founded on the promise of development. Even more important, simply halting growth would freeze the current pattern of inequality, leaving the "have nots" as the peasants of the world community in perpetuity. Thus an end

Table 14.4   Ratios of Per Capita Energy Consumption, 1952–1990
(United States = 100)

Country/Region	1952	1972	1990
United States	100	100	100
Canada	76	93	128
United Kingdom	59	46	47
West Germany	41	46	45
France	30	36	49
Japan	11	28	46
USSR	26	41	69[a]
Communist Eastern Europe	21	39	60[b]
Third World	5–6	4	6–7

Sources: Adapted from D. Chirot, *Social Change in the Twentieth Century* (New York: Harcourt Brace Jovanovich, 1977), pp. 160–61; World Bank, *World Development Report*, 1984, 1986, 1988; UNDP, *Human Development Report*, 1993.
a. 1986
b. 1984

of growth and development would be acceptable to the Third World only in combination with a radical redistribution of the world's wealth and a total restructuring of the world's economy to guarantee the maintenance of economic justice. Yet it seems absolutely clear that the rich have not the slightest intention of alleviating the plight of the poor if it entails the sacrifice of their own living standards. Ecological scarcity thus greatly increases the probability of naked confrontation between rich and poor. (P. 211)

If Third World governments are in fact (as well as in rhetoric) interested in economic justice, they must in the near future bring this resource drain under their own control, for the first time since the imposition of Western colonial dominance. However, it is questionable that ruling elites in many if not most Third World systems are committed to economic justice, either globally or within their own countries. Elites in the Third World, in business, government, and the military, are not generally concerned as long as they continue to live in their sealed-off and well-guarded neighborhoods of luxury. It cannot be assumed that any government will act in favor of, or fight for, economic justice.

Transnational Inequality—Capital Drain

It is sometimes assumed that because Western-owned corporations are expanding investments in mining, manufacturing, or commercial agriculture in the Third World, or because foreign aid is given by Western governments, there is a net flow of capital funds from the developed West to aid development in the poor nations. This would be true if the amounts of Western capital and foreign aid transferred annually to the Third World economies were not exceeded by the amounts of profit being "repatriated," taken out of the Third World for stockholders in the West. In fact, the amount of profits taken out of the Third World each year by Western MNCs greatly exceeds the amount of Western capital newly invested to build up productive facilities. According to the U.S. Department of Commerce, between 1950 and 1965 new U.S. investments in the underdeveloped nations totaled some $9 billion, while repatriated profits (and other returns, such as Third World debt repayment, royalties for patents, licenses, and payments for technical services) took $25.6 billion out of the underdeveloped world. Hungarian economist Tamas Szentes (1973:198–99) has summarized official data from a variety of sources on the extent of capital drain from the Third World. For French and British investment in former colonies in Western Africa, for British investment in India, for American, British, French, and Dutch oil investments in the Middle East, and for total Western investment in Latin America, the story is the same. It is clear that at least up to the mid-1970s the Third World as a whole was sending development

Table 14.5 The Brain Drain from Developing Countries to the United States, Canada, and the United Kingdom, 1961 to 1983

	Number of skilled migrants from developing countries to:			Share of developing countries in total skilled immigration (%)		
	United States	Canada	United Kingdom	United States	Canada	United Kingdom
1961–65	9,655[a]	2,049[b]	10,205[c]	37	20	26
1975	29,830	6,362	8,833[e]	77	25	14
1983	30,212	3,273[d]	—	77	38[d]	—

Source: J. d'Oliveira e Sousa, "The Brain Drain in International Negotiations," in *Impact of International Migration on Developing Countries* (OECD, 1989).
a. average for 1961–65
b. average for 1963–65
c. average for 1964–65
d. 1979
e. 1972

capital to the rich nations of the West, mainly through the activity of Western-owned MNCs. The effects of the OPEC oil price actions since 1973 changed this picture for some OPEC member states, although this is difficult to determine, since whenever the Shah invested Iran's oil revenues in the West (i.e., in Krupp industries) or whenever the Saudis invest in U.S. properties or simply deposit their funds in Western banks, this also returns capital funds to the West. Szentes (1973:199) estimated the official capital drain from the Third World at between $3.5 billion and $4 billion annually. This is probably an underestimate, since it excludes indirect capital drains through the entire inequitable structure of exchange rates. To put the matter another way, for every dollar of U.S. investment in the Third World between 1946 and 1959, about 2.5 dollars of profit were drained from the Third World. Dos Santos (1971:232) has calculated that for every U.S. dollar invested in Latin America between 1946 and 1967, 2.73 dollars left Latin America as repatriated profits (see also Chaliand, 1976:12).

Another, perhaps even more serious, source of capital drain from the Third World to the rich Western nations is "capital flight," the transfer, whether legal or illegal, of massive amounts of wealth by the rich elites of Third World societies to banks and investments in North America and Western Europe. Some spectacular cases that have come to light include the stashing of stolen public funds and ill-gotten riches in Swiss bank accounts and Miami bank accounts and the purchase of real estate in Europe and the United States by the Shah's family in Iran, the Marcos family in the Philippines, the Duvalier family in Haiti, Mobutu in Zaire and the Somoza family in Nicaragua.

But these cases are just the best-publicized tip of the iceberg. Capital flight by the rich is a daily large-scale drain on the investment resources of most Third World societies. It indicates a lack of confidence, ability, or loyalty by the Third World economic elite in the future of their own nations and a failure to invest their fortunes in their own societies' development. It has been estimated that $180 billion has been drained from Latin America by the rich elite of that region, which would be about half of that region's foreign debt (Magdoff, 1986). In just the three years from 1980 to 1982, Third World elites transferred an estimated $71 billion from seven of the largest debtor nations (Mexico, Argentina, Venezuela, Indonesia, Egypt, the Philippines, and Nigeria) at the same time that their nations' foreign debt was rising by some $102 billion (Payer, 1985). It is common practice for wealthy families in developing nations to keep a good portion of their assets in the rich developed nations, to do much of their luxury item shopping in the West, and to make arrangements for transferring additional wealth in case of domestic unrest or political upheaval. But this practice, while understandable from the perspective of protecting elite family wealth, is a critical failure in terms of maintaining and utilizing these resources for national development. Instead, these resources are turned over to Western banks and corporations for their use as productive investment capital.

Thus, elite insecurity in an unstable and inequitable society leads to capital flight, which only diminishes further any possibility for more equity and stability in that society; this is a devastating, vicious cycle throughout most of the Third World. In the absence of any broad-based and durable social contract between elites and masses, Third World elites, despite any nationalist sentiment, will protect their wealth by exporting it to safe havens.

Foreign aid to the Third World, which might seem an example of unblemished Western generosity, in fact adds almost nothing in the way of transferred investment funds. Between 75 and 90 percent of the development aid is tied, either by law or by practice, to purchases of goods and services from the donor nation. That is, U.S. aid to poor nations requires them in large measure to spend that money on products made by U.S. corporations. It is no paradox that the U.S. corporate community is one of the firm backers of U.S. development aid, since it means increased sales to Third World nations of their products and services. This then forms a new dependency on U.S. firms for resupply, repair, and related services, while providing little or no new investment in productive facilities in the recipient nation (see Bairoch, 1975; Sachs, 1978; Sutcliffe, 1971, for more extensive commentary).

In the latter 1980s, as a result of the debt crisis, Third World nations were draining capital to repay interest and principal on their enormous $1.1 trillion debt. Net transfer of wealth from the developing nations to the rich creditor nations was estimated at $45 billion in 1988, $51 billion in 1989, and $33 billion in 1990 (World Bank, 1990:1).

Transnational Inequality—The Brain and Skill Drain

Certainly one of the most disheartening results of transnational inequality is the strong incentive for the highly educated and highly motivated to migrate from the Third World to the rich, developed nations of the West. The reasons are not difficult to understand, and at the individual level, they make perfectly good sense. Third World doctors, engineers, and scientists find more stable and secure careers and consumer life-styles in the West than in their homelands. Social unrest, violence directed against the well-to-do, and the danger that one's property and wealth may be confiscated either by an arbitrary regime or by revolution all predispose the well-educated to migrate to the West. Additionally, nations like the United States and Australia give immigration preference to the highly educated professionals, assuring them of relatively easy entry. These professionals, however, have the skills necessary and perhaps most vital to the development of their homelands, and their loss hampers development prospects. As already mentioned in the previous chapter, the Third World has scarce resources in highly trained professionals; because of the dependent under-development of many Third World economies, opportunities for those who are highly educated lie not so much within their home country as in the developed Western nations.

The extent of the Third World brain drain has apparently been increasing over the postwar period. Between 1947 and 1961, some 43,000 engineers emigrated from all over the world to the United States, and of this number, 60 percent came from the Third World (Castro, in Fann and Hodges, 1971:194). Between 1951 and 1963, over 5,000 qualified engineers emigrated from Argentina alone to the United States. In a more recent study on this brain drain, the ILO reported that from 1962 to 1972 over 170,000 scientists, engineers, doctors, and teachers emigrated from the underdeveloped nations to the United States, Great Britain, and Canada. The estimate rises to 250,000 if immigration to other rich nations of the West is also included.

India alone lost 13,000 scientists and engineers to the United States. The Philippines lost 11,000 scientists, engineers, and doctors to the United States. In 1970, emigration of physicians, surgeons, and dentists from the Philippines amounted to more than half of new graduations of doctors (ILO, 1976:129). Asia, and especially India and Pakistan, where health care is lacking for the average citizen, lost 36,000 doctors to the United States, Canada, and Great Britain. Africa, where highly educated personnel are most scarce among the regions of the Third World, lost nearly 15,000 professionals to these three rich nations in just ten years. Particularly for "brain drain" to the United States and Canada (see table 14.5), the percentages of Third World highly educated among all skilled immigrants increased sharply from the 1960s to the 1980s. Already by the 1970s, over three-quarters of all skilled immigrants to the United States were from the developing nations, and of

327

skilled immigration to Canada in the 1980s, nearly two-fifths came from the Third World. Furthermore, the annual numbers of skilled immigrants to the United States tripled from the 1960s to the 1980s.

In addition, millions of workers, often with valuable skills and high economic motivation, migrate to the wealthy Western democracies in search of decent jobs and good pay. Workers from Mexico, Central America, and Latin America make their way into the United States and Canada (see Cockcroft, 1986). North African, Turkish, and South Asian workers move into the European Community nations; Pakistanis, Filipinos, Koreans, and Palestinians perform most of the labor in the small oil-rich sheikdoms of the Gulf region. A United Nations study notes that through labor migration the developing nations "lose their most skilled and motivated people. The host countries receive immigrant workers whom they have not had to rear and train" (UN, 1989:87). Often these workers send home considerable remittances (perhaps as much as $19 billion in 1985 [p. 89]) to support their families. This is an important offset to the capital flight from the Third World mentioned above, but it does not match the amount of capital flight, nor do family remittances generate much in the way of new capital investment and new jobs, although some savings of migrant laborers return home for starting new small businesses. This loss of able and dedicated workers is another aspect of the loss of human capital that could, under different circumstances, be used more directly in building decent living conditions in the Third World.

Internal Inequality—Income Distribution and Development

In addition to the tremendous gap between the rich and poor nations the dependent capitalist development of the Third World nations since World War II has produced a huge gap between the rich and poor within the under-developed nations as well. In the early 1950s, Harvard economist Simon Kuznets, on the basis of some studies of Western capitalist development, put forward the theory that income distribution becomes more unequal in the early stages of industrialization and only later decreases at more advanced levels of modernization. This thesis has been partially refuted by evidence from several Communist nations (China, Cuba, parts of Eastern Europe) where early industrial growth went hand-in-hand with stable or lower levels of income inequality (see Cromwell, 1977:291-308). But for Third World nations, the pattern of dependent development has so far mainly enlarged internal income inequality. Conventional (i.e., diffusionist) wisdom in development economics of the 1950s asserted that the benefits of growth, while going initially and heavily to the wealth strata of businessmen and landowners, would then be plowed back into the economy as new investment. By raising the rate of savings and investment, new productive facilities would be built, creating new jobs and raising total production levels. Through new employment opportunities and great productivity of the economy, benefits would "trickle down" to the lower classes. Paul Baran, Irma Adelman, Cynthia Taft Morris, and Roger Hansen, among others, have shown that the "trickle down" strategy has produced few benefits for the lower classes, and in fact has led to a deterioration of conditions for large proportions of the population, what Hansen has called the "forgotten 40 percent." In Brazil, the percentage of income received by the poorest 40 percent of the population fell from 10 percent of national income in 1960 to only 8 percent in 1970; the share going to the richest 5 percent grew from 29 percent to 38 percent over the same period. And during these years Brazil's GNP per capita was growing by a healthy-looking 2.5 percent annually (Adelman and Morris, 1973:1). Henry Bienen reports that in Nigeria economic growth, in particular the rapid growth of the oil industry as a mainstay of Nigerian growth, has produced a sharp increase in income inequality, with the Gini index rising from around 0.5 in 1960 to around 0.6 in 1979 (Bienen and Diejomaoh, 1981:7). In Mexico, the poorest 40 percent of the population received 14.3 percent of national income in 1950, but only 11 percent in 1963; the share going to the richest 20 percent went from 59.8 percent to 59 percent (Hansen, 1974:75). Mexico, during this period, averaged a per capita GNP gain of nearly 3 percent annually. Similarly, a study of the Philippines between 1971 and 1975 shows that the percentage of income going to the top 20 percent increased in just those four years from 53.9 to 55.5 percent, while the income of the poorest 40 percent of the population declined from 11.9 to 11.2 percent (Third World Studies Staff, 1982). Adelman and Morris correlated wide-ranging cross-national data on the rela-

Table 14.6   Income Distribution in the Third World

		Percentage of National Income Going to:	
	Year	Top 10%	Bottom 40%
Mexico	1977	40.6	9.9
Brazil	1983	46.2	8.1
Kenya	1976	45.8	8.9
Ivory Coast	1986	36.3	13.0
India	1983	26.7	20.4
Indonesia	1987	26.5	21.2
Egypt	1976	33.2	16.5
South Korea	1976	27.5	16.9
Philippines	1985	32.1	15.2
For comparison:			
United States	1985	25.0	15.7
Hungary	1982	20.5	20.5

Source: *World Development Report,* 1986, 1990.

tionship between development and income inequality (in the non-Communist nations) and related the increase in income inequality to penetration of the Third World economy by foreign (in their terms, "expatriate") corporations:

> When economic growth begins in a subsistence agrarian economy through the expansion of a narrow modern sector, inequality in the distribution of income typically increases greatly, particularly where expatriate exploitation of rich natural resources provides the motivating force for growth. The income share of the poorest 60 percent declines significantly, as does that of the middle 20 percent, and the income share of the top 5 percent increases strikingly. (1973:178)

Economist Gary Fields, from a wide-ranging evaluation of evidence on inequality and growth rates, questions whether there is any clear relationship between the two, but concludes that: "in the absence of a firm commitment to developing for the poor and the courage to act on that commitment, it seems only natural that economic systems will perpetuate the flow of resources to the haves with at least some trickle-down to the have-nots" (1980:242).

A recent study of changes in income distribution in the developing nations between the 1970s and 1980s found that in five (Indonesia, South Korea, Dominican Republic, Guatemala, and Colombia) of fourteen nations for which data was available, income inequality did in fact decrease. In three nations there was virtually no change, but in six nations (Argentina, Bangladesh, Chile, Pakistan, and Sri Lanka) inequality increased further (United Nations, 1989:39). It might be added that in Guatemala, Colombia, and the Dominican Republic, while there was some decline in the share of national income going to the top 20 percent, it still remained at very high levels (56, 50, and 53 percent, respectively), well above levels found in the rich liberal democracies. There is still no general trend seen toward a more equitable distribution pattern, and in the 1980s, especially in the most debt-plagued nations, the trend has most often been toward even greater inequality.

The reasons for the failure of the "trickle down" approach are now fairly clear. First of all, it is now apparent that in most Third World nations the fruits of growth are monopolized to an extraordinary degree by a small class of wealthy landowners and businessmen, and also by a small stratum of well-paid workers in the "modern" sector of the economy. This coalition is backed by the power, both military and economic, of the rich Western democracies. Any attempt to shift income distribution in favor of the lower classes must figure on resistance from this internal-external coalition of vested interests. Thus, when the democratically elected socialist government of Salvador Allende introduced reforms that began to shift income distribution, it was overthrown by the rightwing coalition of military, landowning, and business elites, with the aid of several U.S.-owned MNCs, the Western-dominated international finance banks, and the CIA.

Second, the fruits of growth do not necessarily go into new savings or new investment that would aid overall economic development. The upper classes of the Third World have developed consumer desires no less opulent than those of the upper classes in the developed West. Therefore, much of the excessive income of Third World elites is not saved or invested in new productive facilities, but spent lavishly on Western-style overconsumption. French political scientist Gerard Chaliand (1976:30) has calculated that for fourteen African nations, nearly twice as much was spent on imports of liquor, private cars, gasoline for cars, and various cosmetics as for machinery and equipment necessary for raising production. The parasitic nature of many Third World elites has been most vividly described by authors Frantz Fanon for Africa, in *The Wretched of the Earth,* and Eduardo Galeano for Latin America, in *The Open Veins of Latin America.* In Africa and in much of Latin America, the elite does not emulate the frugality and efficiency in production of the nineteenth-century Western entrepreneur, even if it possessed the technical skills and inventiveness, which it generally does not (see Chaliand, 1976; Sutcliffe, 1971). Chaliand has argued that the main goal of the Third World bourgeoisie has become control of government as the means to sharing in the fruits of dependent development in collaboration with the much more powerful Western MNCs.

Third, the use of Western labor-saving technology in the modern industrial and commercial agricultural sectors has created little new employment, which means that for both urban and rural poor, unemployment and underemployment have grown. A deterioration of conditions for the poorest strata is the result of such dependent development, even when impressive gains in GNP growth are recorded for individual nations:

> Regional income inequality typically increases as the concentration of rapidly growing, technologically advanced enterprises in cities widens the gap between rural and urban per capita income. Income inequality also intensifies in the urban sector with the accumulation of assets in the hands of a relatively small number of owners (usually expatriate) of modern enterprises. The concentration is accelerated by the spread of capital-intensive industrial technology through at least three factors—the case with which owners of modern enterprises obtain capital abroad, the inability of small-scale enterprises to obtain financing, and a growing preference of medium and large entrepreneurs for advanced modern technologies. This labor-saving bias of technological advance, the rapidity of urban population growth, the migration to the cities of unemployed rural workers, and lack of social mobility all tend to swell the numbers of urban impoverished and to decrease the income share of the poorest segments of the urban population. (Adelman and Morris, 1973:182)

A few Third World nations, such as Taiwan and South Korea, with an enterprising business class, a highly disciplined and hardworking labor force, special access to Western (especially U.S.) consumer markets, and high levels of U.S. aid, have developed export industries at a rapid pace without such extremes of income inequality. So there are also capitalist exceptions to the rule of growing inequality. The governments of Chiang Kai-shek and Chiang Ching-kuo in Taiwan or Park Chung Hee and Chun Doo Hwan in South Korea were hardly examples of democracy, so these "showpieces" of Western-aided and export-oriented development do not demonstrate any connection between democratic politics and greater income equality.

Internal Inequality—Patron-Client Networks

In terms of social elites, dependent development has shifted power as well as wealth to new elements of the Third World bourgeoisie, whose current interests and future prospects rest on collaboration with Western MNCs and Western finance institutions. Within the Third World we can identify several groups of elites. These are found in differing power elite coalitions in individual nations: (1) traditional elites, (2) landowning elites, (3) national bourgeoisie, (4) comprador bourgeoisie, (5) government bourgeoisie, and (6) military elites.

Traditional elites played major roles in many Third World societies during the colonial period. In many colonies, Western authorities would exercise their rule through tribal or religious leaders, village elders, or local notables, who agreed to collaborate in return for official recognition by the colonial power of their status and sometimes for material payoffs for themselves and their following (or clientele). Robert Gamer (1976) has described this earlier penetration of Third World societies as the development of a system of patron-client relationships wherein the client, in return for recognition of and obedience to the patron, receives some recognition and/or reward. Patron-client relationships, of course, were common to Third World societies before the advent of Western colonial-imperial dominance and were often quite complex networks just at the local level. Western penetration added several new elements to the system, which gradually transformed the basic nature of social evolution and continues to shape that evolution today. First, the chain of patron-client relations was stretched beyond the traditional village or small town or region, beyond the boundaries of the native society. The top patrons were now Western elites who had no family, kinship, or cultural ties to local society. Top patrons were now foreign (in nearly every sense of the word) to local Third World society. Second, the former traditional elites, by collaborating with the colonial authorities, lost much of their independence and responsibility for the well-being and development of local society. Traditional elites and their peoples who resisted collaboration, like the Herrero in German South West Africa, the Filipinos in the American seizure of the Philippines in 1899,

Marathas, Gurkhas, and others in the British domination in India, the Dervishes in the British Sudan, and the many Indian groups in the United States itself, were brutally crushed, often to the point of ethnic or racial genocide. Third, the new and more complex patron-client chain meant that more goods from the local economy were being siphoned off for Western elites as well as for traditional elites, leaving generally less for those at the bottom of the ladder. In some cases, colonial authorities favored certain ethnic or religious minorities, who acted as native policemen for the Western power, as with the South Moluccans in the Dutch East Indies (Indonesia). This meant better payoffs for these monorities, but also later hostility from nationalist independence movements.

In several postindependence political systems, especially in neocolonial states like Rhodesia (now Zimbabwe) and South Africa but also in more conservative regimes like those in Liberia, the Ivory Coast, and Kenya, traditional elites continued to serve important intermediary roles. In general, however, the influence of those traditional elites has declined with the continuing decline in traditional rural society, with the privatization of land ownership, the migration to the cities, the growth of a money-based economy, and the rise of other, stronger elites. The political power of Chief Mangosuthu Buthelezi and his Zulu-based Inkatha Freedom Party in South Africa and the continuing role of traditional clan leaders in Somalia and Afghanistan show that traditional elites may still play important political roles in some Third World nations. Indeed, with the massive failure of some regimes, as in Somalia, Liberia, and Ethiopia, traditional leaders may reemerge to pick up the pieces; in sub-Saharan Africa, after more than a generation of central government mismanagement and corruption, tribal leadership systems may appear as more responsive and more accountable to local wishes.

One elite with considerable power in many Third World nations is the large landowning class (*hacendados, latifundistas, zamindaris*). Latin America and large parts of South Asia and the Middle East have a longer tradition of private ownership of land than most of Africa. Often a tiny minority of aristocratic families control not only most of the agricultural land but the best farmlands as well. In the early 1950s this landowning elite was a formidable force in both the economy and the political system. In Chile, for example, the richest 4.4 percent of landowners owned over 80 percent of total farmland. In Peru, a mere 1.5 percent of big landlords controlled 63 percent of the land; 189 rich families owned 60 percent of agricultural lands, and the 920 largest *latifundia* took in about 80 percent of total land. In Iran, a few families owned about 70 percent of fertile farmlands. In Egypt, 6 percent of landlords owned 65 percent of arable land (Gamer, 1976:ch. 7). The Gini index for inequality in land tenure, which ranges from 0 at perfect equality to 1.0 at maximum possible inequality, stood at .87 for Argentina, .85 for Brazil, .87 for Colombia, .95 for Peru, .94 for Venezuela, .61 for Turkey, .61 for India, .61 for

Pakistan, .58 for the Philippines, and .62 for Iran (World Bank Group, 1975). By comparison, in Communist Poland and Yugoslavia, which carried out a redistribution of land without creating a collective agriculture, the Gini indices of land tenure inequality were .47 and .44 respectively. In a few Third World nations, notably Taiwan and South Korea, with Gini indices of .46 and .39, thoroughgoing land reform significantly reduced the power of large landowning elites. In other nations, such as Iran, Egypt, Mexico, and more recently Peru and Ethiopia, land reforms also reduced the power of landowners as an economic and political elite, to a greater (Ethiopia) or lesser (Mexico) extent. In many cases, however, land reforms have either been a farce or so minimal as to make no great impact on landholding inequality and the power of the big landowners. What has made an impact on the power of the landowning elite in many nations has been the expansion of commercial agriculture for export and the rising power of urban bourgeois elements, both native and foreign. On the whole, the power of the landowners, insofar as this class has not itself turned to commercial export agriculture or investment in industry, has been on the decline, but is still a force, often nationalistic or fascist in orientation, to be reckoned with in the politics of many Third World systems.

The national bourgeoisie corresponds to the entrepreneurial class, which was instrumental in the industrialization of the West in the previous century. Very weak and embryonic in most of black Africa, stronger in some of the Latin American nations with the longest history of national independence (Argentina, Chile, Brazil, Mexico) and most dynamic in the East Asian NICs, the national bourgeoisie is the class of investors and business leaders who would have to lead capitalist development if the previous history of the West were to be repeated. André Gunder Frank (1970) studied the attempts of the national bourgeoisie in Latin America to foster a self-sustaining capitalist development since independence and found that the most promising periods of industrial progress were achieved during World War I, the Great Depression, and World War II, when the great Western powers were either embroiled in major war efforts or crippled by economic disaster, so that their dominance over the path of economic development in Latin America was temporarily disrupted or diminished. Certainly nations like Argentina, Uruguay, and Chile, by the end of World War II, were close to joining the community of advanced capitalist systems. And yet the performance in the postwar era of these systems has been one of stagnation and growing dependence of the national bourgeoisie on foreign capital, foreign technology, foreign markets, and Western intervention in suppressing revolutionary forces. Cockcroft, Frank, and Johnson concluded that, after the disruptions of two world wars and a major depression, Latin America had been reassimilated into the international capitalist system as a periphery region dominated by the core capitalist powers and their MNC extensions:

The Latin American middle classes, strengthened by industrialization at one time, played vaguely nationalist and progressive roles as classes in ascendance. Now they engage in what Claudio Veliz terms "the politics of conformity" and have developed a close ideological affinity with the precepts of the political and social thought promoted by established interests within the international system and national oligarchies. (1972:105–6)

In only a few Third World nations has the national bourgeoisie been capable of competing with Western investors and leading the industrialization of the nation economy. The national business class of Taiwan and South Korea in East Asia has clearly been able to take such a leading role. Peter Evans (1979) makes a good case for the existence of a still-important national bourgeoisie in Brazil, which is part of a triple alliance of MNCs, state-owned industry, and top private industrialists that controls the Brazilian economy. While Evans admits the inability of the national bourgeoisie to develop the economy or a political system on its own, he argues that the top national industrialists have more bargaining power within the top elite than some dependency theories assume. There are a few other nations such as Mexico where this triple alliance includes a national industrialist class of comparable stature. On the other hand, the national bourgeoisie, within the context of its own nation, still acts as an important political elite, vying for control of the government.

A fourth elite element, and a growing one in the Third World since World War II, is the comprador middle class, the relatively pure and straightforward product of the economic dependence of these societies on the core capitalist systems. The main role of the comprador middle class is that of the intermediary for foreign interests, the supplier of local services and minor products to foreign-owned corporations and their Western personnel. In some Third World regions, especially in Africa, where the national bourgeoisie was weakest, the comprador middle class has grown up as an integral part of the postindependence era. In Latin America, where the national bourgeoisie was stronger, the inability to compete with Western capital progressively transformed an existing nationally oriented entrepreneurial class into a comprador middleman for foreign capital.

The governmental middle class consists of the higher civil service and the top staffs of government ministries. In almost all Third World nations, the size of the government bureaucracy has grown considerably as governments have taken on greater responsibility for economic growth. Chaliand (1976) noted that in Africa especially, given the weakness of other bourgeoisie elements (except for white settler minorities in certain states), control of government by an administrative middle class has become the basic means of accumulating wealth. That is to say, governmental corruption has become a basic feature, not an aberration, in those regimes where the main service of the local bourgeoisie is to provide and safeguard the avenues of foreign exploitation through maintenance of government power. Suzanne Bodenheimer, with reference to Latin America, summarized the position and function of this elite:

> The state bureaucracy and other sectors of the middle class—for example, the technical, managerial, professional or intellectual elites—become clientele when their interests, actions, and privileged positions are derived from their ties to foreign interests. Particularly with the expanded role of the state in the national economy, the state bureaucracy (including the military in many countries) has been viewed by some as the key to national autonomy. Nevertheless, when the primary function of the state is to stimulate private enterprise, when the private sector is largely controlled by foreign interests, and when the state bureaucracy itself relies on material and ideological support from abroad (as in Brazil today), the "autonomy" of the state bureaucracy must be illusory. (Cited in Fann and Hodges, 1971:163)

The Third World military leadership has been one of the main contenders for power, since it is usually the best-organized and the heaviest armed force in the society. Often the officer corps may be recruited from one of the other elites, such as the landowners or traditional elites, in which case it may be tied to these interests. In systems with long-term military regimes, on the other hand, military men may blend in with the administrative bourgeoisie. Most military elites in the Third World are dependent on foreign sources for weapons, without which their ability to provide ultimate safeguards for private property, both national and foreign-owned, would be endangered. Several Third World military elites during the Cold War were able to switch their main sources of military hardware (and thus their dependence) from the West to the Soviet Union (Egypt in the latter 1950s, later Syria and Iraq, and still later Ethiopia). More important, however, the military elite is able to use its muscle, whether directly controlling the government or just providing its services in policing the political arena, to accumulate substantial fortunes through smuggling, drug trafficking, or theft from military budgets. The Brazilian generals who ran that country for more than twenty years became rich in the process. Honduran, Bolivian, Pakistani, and Panamanian military officers have used military transport and freedom of international travel to enrich themselves in the drug trade. Nigerian generals got rich from kickbacks in phony "cement" contracts with Western MNCs. Control of the military is an important source for corrupt accumulation of wealth in most Third World systems (see also chapter 16).

Politics in Third World nations, except for the rare occurrence of an authentic social revolution (as in China, Vietnam, and Cuba), are characterized by shifting coalitions and conflicts within these elite groupings. Each elite grouping has its own clients, or followers, who benefit when their patrons are able to increase their utility to maintaining the current economic order. The great majority of the population does not belong to any patron-client network and are thus outside the "normal" politics of the nation. They are also outside the reward systems that make up the political system. Gamer likened Third World political systems to the systematic looting of the society by a pirate ship anchored offshore:

> It is as though governance of these nations took place from ships moored off the shore. On these ships are government leaders, all those involved with major financial transactions, the bureaucracy, and the military. Contact is kept with those needed to extract resources for export and intercept profits from the internal distribution of goods and with those needed to enforce coercive measures. These shore dwellers are paid for their services, but their percentage of the populace is small. When these indivuduals do not perform their jobs well, or spies report they are engaged in malfeasance, they can be replaced with others. . . .
>
> Basic political activities take place aboard ship. The military are capable of terrorizing the ship, but do not know how to keep it supplied with consumer goods, or how to build the roads, electrical power, and other basic services on which they depend when they occasionally go ashore to quell civil disturbances. The bureaucracy plays a key role in keeping those services (which also create profits) flowing, and hence cannot be ignored. The businessmen are the only ones capable of generating the profits that keep the ship prosperous. (1976:166–67)

The institutional or symbolic format of government may change, and quite rapidly, with shifting coalitions and power struggles among the elite groupings. Whether the government is a military junta, a one-party system, a multiparty democracy, or some sort of monarchy at the moment is less important than the system of dependency within the global economic order. The power struggles among elites matter a great deal in terms of the division of spoils among these patron-client minorities. But for the masses of the population, these changes are basically cosmetic and matter little, for they do not alter the basic system that is maintaining the gross inequalities of dependent development.

Women and Development in the Third World

Women play a major role in the economic development of the Third World but have in general been among the least rewarded for their efforts. In much of sub-Saharan Africa and South Asia, women perform some of the hardest work in agriculture and carry heavy loads of water and firewood for cooking. In Latin America, the Caribbean, Africa, and Southeast Asia, market women play a leading role in the distribution network, and throughout the NICs of Latin America and East and Southeast Asia, they bear the brunt of the new industrialization for world exports. In Mexico's U.S.-owned *maquiladora* sweatshops, often over 90 percent of workers are young women. Similar figures and situations exist in the free enterprise zone industries of Manila, Singapore, Santo Domingo, and Bangkok. Women have been drawn into the modern sector of economic development of the Third World as the most vulnerable and exploitable, for whom the political system offers few protections and little concern.

Women have shown themselves to be among the most reliable and able of small entrepreneurs in many Third World nations. The Grameen Bank in Bangladesh, which makes small (very small) business loans to poor people (83 percent of them women), has a repayment rate of 95 percent. The Working Women's Forum in Madras, India, which also makes small business loans, has achieved repayment rates of 90 to 95 percent, well above the national average for commercial banks. The World Bank (World Bank, 1990: 67-68) experience with loans to micro-enterprises run mostly by women in India, Bangladesh, Zimbabwe, Ghana, Indonesia, Nepal, the Philippines, and the Dominican Republic has demonstrated how much can be done through working with businesswomen at the grass roots level, bypassing the hopelessly corrupt and inefficient state structures dominated by the established elites. Despite this proven track record of success, most international lending agencies and development banks still choose to deal overwhelmingly with established elites and official bureaucracies.

Women are barely represented in the political elites of the Third World, including both the success stories and the dismal failures (see table 14.7). In parliaments and more importantly in executive offices women are almost invisible. Despite some exceptional cases, such as Prime Minister Indira Gandhi of India, President Cory Aquino of the Philippines, and more recently Prime Minister Tansu Ciller of Turkey, women are regularly shut out of political life. In some Islamic regimes, women have even lost ground. In Pakistan, in the mid-1980s, a new law stated that in court trials the testimony of two women would equal the testimony of one man. Islamic regimes in Iran and Sudan have likewise restricted women's roles even more than before. Certainly one of the greatest inequalities in Third World development is the almost complete exclusion of women from political representation at the same time that their labor and work skills are most in demand for the growing export manufacturing sector of the economy.

Table 14.7 Women Decision Makers in Government, 1987

	Parliamentary Seats Occupied by Women (percentage)		Year of Women's Suffrage	Executive Offices: Economic, Political and Legal Affairs (%)	Social Affairs (%)	All Ministries (%)	Ministerial Level (%)
	1975	1991					
Mexico	5	12	1953	0	7	1	0
Brazil	0	6	1934	5	0	4	3
Nigeria	—	—	—	6	7	4	0
Kenya	4	1	1963[a]	0	0	0	0
Egypt	2	2	1956	0	0	0	0
India	4	7	1950	4	6	4	0
Indonesia	7	12	1945[b]	0	4	1	5
South Korea	6	2	1948	—	—	—	—
Kuwait	—	—	—	2	7	3	0

Source: UN, *The World's Women: Trends and Statistics, 1970–1990*; UNDP, *Human Development Report*, 1993.

a. The right to vote was given to European women in 1919; in 1956 it was given to African men and to women under certain conditions, education level or property; in 1963, all Kenyans were given the right to vote.

b. The right to vote was given earlier under certain conditions. Details not provided.

15

Liberty—A Difficult History

The performance of Third World systems in the area of personal liberty is not generally encouraging, and the reasons for this are often misunderstood in the West. The Freedom House political rights ranking of India, which has a democratically elected civilian government, is much higher than Egypt, which has a nondemocratic, authoritarian regime backed by the military, but Charles Humana's human rights rating for both nations is about the same. Brazil's rankings on political and civil rights rose in its transition from a military dictatorship after 1985, but its human rights rating still remains qualitatively lower than any of the Western liberal democracies. On the other hand, Algeria, which had a one-party dictatorship and no free elections, had just as high a rating on its overall human rights as Brazil in 1991. In general, the political system type in the Third World does not by itself determine the general level of personal liberty for its citizens. Whether a Third World regime is, at any given moment, a military dictatorship, a one-party system, a personal dictatorship, or a multi-party elected civilian government may make little difference for most of the citizens of that society in terms of personal liberty. At the most local level, even in democratic Brazil in the latter 1980s, for example, the local landlords can and do hire gunslingers to intimidate and, if necessary, kill campesino organizers or those who support them, including teachers and priests. In the Philippines, after the overthrow of the Marcos dictatorship and the return to democracy under President Aquino, vigilante groups financed by local plantation owners continue to attack Catholic clergy who side with the peasants in their grievances (Mydans, 1987). The protection of personal liberty, even in those Third World nations which have elected civilian governments, may be pitifully weak in practice for people at the local level. On the other hand, for the minority with some resources, financial and organizational, and with some links to the elite patron-client networks that participate in the system of benefits, the state of personal liberty may vary considerably and quite suddenly with changes in the nature of the regime. But

Table 15.1   Indicators of Liberty in the Third World

	Political Rights (scale of 1 to 7)*		Civil Rights (scale of 1 to 7)*		Human Rights Rating (%)
	1977	1992	1977	1992	1991
India	2	3	2	4	54
Indonesia	5	6	5	5	34
Brazil	4	2	5	3	69
Mexico	4	4	3	3	64
Egypt	5	5	4	6	50
Algeria	6	7	6	6	66
Tanzania	6	6	6	5	41
Kenya	5	4	5	5	46
Iran	6	6	5	6	22

Sources: Freedom House, *Freedom in the World: Political Rights and Civil Liberties* (New York: Freedom House, 1993), pp. 620–21; Raymond Gastil, *Freedom in the World: Political Rights and Civil Liberties 1978* (New York: Freedom House, 1978), pp. 10–13; Charles Humana, *World Human Rights Guide* (New York: Oxford University Press, 1992), pp. xvii–xix.
*The political rights and civil liberties indices are on a scale of 1 to 7, with 1 representing the most free and 7 the least free category.
Note: The findings of The Comparative Survey of Freedom by Freedom House are through December 1992. The World Human Rights Guide covers the period to November 1, 1991.

even for this minority, as for the majority, the penetration of strong outside forces, predominantly from the rich Western nations, into these dependent systems has placed limitations, explicit and implicit, on the exercise of political and civil freedoms, even where the local political system permits it or attempts to permit it. The realization of personal liberty in the Third World, as with other performance areas, is tied to both transnational and domestic factors. Those liberties which are most frequently permitted are the rights of emigration and property ownership, which support the continuation of the dependency syndrome. Those most often suppressed, under a variety of regimes, are the rights of free trade unions, worker political organizations, free speech and press, and peasant activist movements, which are most likely to challenge both local power structures and international dependency relations.

Western Imperialism and Liberty

When the exercise of political liberty has gotten "out of hand" in an individual Third World nation, Western interests (i.e., governmental, corporate, and international finance) have attempted to reimpose "acceptable" limits or, if necessary, to suppress political liberty generally. Empirical investigations of what is acceptable and what is unacceptable to Western interests reveal that almost any government is minimally acceptable so long as it does not threaten either (1) the freedom of Western-owned MNCs to invest and repatriate profits or (2) the social existence of the local propertied elites. Dictatorships such as those of General Park in South Korea, Suharto in Indonesia, Kitikachorn in Thailand, the Shah in Iran, Selassie in Ethiopia, Pinochet in Chile, Somoza in Nicaragua, Duvalier in Haiti, and the white apartheid regime in South Africa have been acceptable. They will receive trade, investment financing, and military aid from Western sources. The list of undemocratic regimes supported by the West or installed by the West could be extended considerably.

Third World nations that accepted economic and/or military aid from the Soviet Union have been also minimally acceptable (though not welcomed, naturally) as long as they were not engaged in socialist revolutions in their own countries. Thus, while the West did not appreciate Nasser's acceptance of aid from the USSR for the Aswan high dam and of large-scale military aid as well, it did not generally fear a socialist transformation of Egypt as a result (though Sir Anthony Eden, who ordered the 1956 British-French invasion of Egypt, apparently did). Much the same can be said for the West's attitude toward Soviet economic and military aid to India, Algeria, Guinea, Iraq, Syria, and Afghanistan (until the 1978 takeover by the Afghan Communist party). In Nicaragua, the Sandinista revolution was initially judged minimally acceptable by the Carter administration, but totally unacceptable by the Reagan administration, which sought to overthrow that regime by all means available.

Third World governments that nationalize Western assets with compensation agreeable to the corporation are also minimally acceptable, though also not encouraged. Only when nationalization of MNC holdings is not, in the view of the corporation, sufficiently compensated does this behavior signify an unacceptable regime. There is a ladder of escalation in the forms of Western intervention utilized to remove "unacceptable" political choices from the Third World, even when, and perhaps especially when, these governments represent the popular choice of the society.

Tactics of Western Intervention

The most blatant form of Western intervention is, of course, direct military invasion. Because it is so blatant a limitation on political freedom, direct military action is generally used only after other more limited tactics are judged to be ineffective or insufficient. Especially after formal decolonization, the adverse reaction to direct armed intervention in the Third World made this option even less palatable. Still, the United States has used direct military intervention on occasion, as in the Dominican Republic in 1965 and in Vietnam, Laos, and Cambodia in the 1960s and 1970s, and in Lebanon, Grenada, and Panama in the 1980s. The French and Belgian rescues of the

Mobutu regime in Zaire in 1977 indicate that direct military action is not completely ruled out by other Western powers.

Covert intervention, which does not involve the open and direct use of regular Western armed forces, covers a broad array of tactics. The American CIA was successful, through the use of paid mob actions and economic sabotage, in overthrowing the nationalist Mossadegh government in Iran in 1953 and restoring the Shah to his throne. The CIA arranged for hired mercenaries to oust the agrarian reform Arbenz regime in Guatemala in 1954 after it had expropriated some (unused) United Fruit Company landholdings. It arranged for the minor civil war that toppled neutralist Prince Souvanna Phouma in Laos in 1960 and replaced his regime with the pro-Western regime of Prince Boun Oum. The CIA was active in "destabilizing" the elected Marxist regime of Salvador Allende in Chile between 1970 and 1973. Of course, the CIA failed in its Bay of Pigs invasion of Cuba in 1961 and in its many attempted assassinations of Fidel Castro. It failed in its support for the FNLA of Holden Roberto in the 1975 Angola civil war. The CIA attempted for many years to engineer the overthrow of the Sandinista regime in Nicaragua through the contra forces, which were organized, financed, trained, and armed by the CIA. In general, the CIA has found it increasingly difficult to repeat its successes of the 1950s and 1960s (Ranelagh, 1986).

The CIA is not as powerful as it is sometimes portrayed in conspiracy theories of world politics, but it has considerable resources. The CIA budget, while secret, was estimated at several billion dollars annually in the mid-1970s, and it openly employed some fifteen thousand personnel in the 1960s (Wolfe, 1973:193). The CIA has at times been responsible for running mercenary armies, such as General Vang Pao's Meo tribesmen in Laos and the Cuban exiles in the Bay of Pigs operation. The CIA set up "dummy" companies as a channel for supplying heavy weapons and bombers to the Portuguese dictatorship of Antonio Salazar for its war against national liberation movements in Mozambique, Angola, and Guinea-Bissau, when it was deemed inappropriate for the U.S. government to aid the Salazar dictatorship openly. The CIA was, along with the Israelis, responsible for setting up and training the Shah's SAVAK (secret police) in Iran. On a regular basis, the CIA offered its expertise and assistance to military and police forces for suppression of dissent and insurgencies in the Third World. The CIA, according to revelations by a former CIA regional director, Philip Agee, also infiltrated labor unions, student organizations, and U.S. AID programs in the Third World. Former dictator Manuel Noriega began his political career as a paid CIA informer on student radicals in Panama. And when the occasion has called for it, the CIA has arranged for the assassinations of unwanted political figures, sometimes in large numbers, as with the infamous Operation Phoenix, which may have killed twenty thousand Vietnamese suspected of aiding the Vietcong (Prados,

1986:309), but who were often the victims of family feuds and racketeering in Vietnamese society.

One of the ways in which Western imperialism limits political freedom in the Third World is through the training and arming of military and police forces in nondemocratic systems or for use in suppressing democracy, as in Chile. One instrument for United States training of police forces in the Third World was the Office of Public Safety (OPS), a division of AID concerned with carrying out "aid" missions to the underdeveloped world. Third World police were trained both in the United States and in the home countries. In the United States, police training is carried out at the International Police Academy (IPA) in Washington, D.C. As of 1970, IPA had graduated some thirty-five hundred police officers (NACLA, in Leggett, 1973:380–81). Other Third World police have received training at American universities, at the John F. Kennedy Special Warfare Center at Fort Bragg, and in special schools for counterinsurgency in the Panama Canal Zone and in Puerto Rico. The School of the Americas at Fort Benning, Georgia, informally called the "School for Dictators," has trained more than 56,000 Latin American military men since 1946. Some of its graduates include Roberto d'Aubuisson, the Salvadoran death squad leader (also a graduate of the IPA in Washington), dictator Manuel Noriega of Panama, Argentine junta leader General Leopoldo Galtieri, Bolivian dictator General Hugo Banzer, and the Honduran chief of staff, General Humberto Regalado, linked to the Colombian drug cartel (Waller, 1993). The U.N. Truth Commission report on human rights abuses in El Salvador implicated twenty-seven Salvadoran military officers in the murders of six Jesuit priests and their housekeeper and her daughter in November 1989. Of those twenty-seven, nineteen were graduates of the School of the Americas at Fort Benning. Although the school was officially supposed to "professionalize" Latin American armies and promote democracy, the graduates of this training have turned up regularly among those accused of the worst massacres and tortures in their countries.

In the home countries, U.S. OPS agents known as "public safety advisors" trained police and provided expertise for local operations. Many of these advisors have been FBI and CIA personnel. OPS advisors were especially active in the Dominican Republic after the U.S. invasion of 1965, reorganizing police forces and working to suppress leftist political support for popular leader Juan Bosch. In Uruguay, OPS agent Dan Mitrione, who had earlier been an advisor to the Brazilian police, was special advisor to the secret police in the suppression of the Tupamaro urban guerrilla movement (for a particularly unpleasant account of the Mitrione story, in terms of what American taxpayer money paid for, see Langguth [1979]). Mitrione was eventually kidnapped and executed by the Tupamaros, and several other OPS agents were killed in the line of duty (see also Klare, in Leggett, 1973: Tobis, 1971). OPS developed an elaborate national identification (ID) system in South Vietnam, with fingerprints, political and biographical data, and photos on 12 million people for a computer data bank to be used for more efficient police control of the Vietnamese population. This system has been introduced into various Latin American police systems.

After the fall of the Argentine military junta following the Falklands War debacle, an official investigation by the Argentine National Commission on the Disappeared (CONADEP, 1985: part 5) of the state terror from 1976–83 revealed a doctrine of national security in which Argentine officers were schooled in counterinsurgency methods by United States personnel both in Argentina and the United States. This support for the Argentine military was used to legitimize state terror as part of the struggle against Communist subversion, and is typical of how United States' military and police aid is tied to political repression in developing nations. It is clear that protection of U.S. interests, through suppression of dissent, is a major goal of police aid to repressive regimes. General Maxwell Taylor, speaking at the 1965 graduation ceremony of the International Police Academy, admitted this goal openly:

> The outstanding lesson [of Vietnam] is that we should never let another Vietnam-type situation arise again. We were too late in recognizing the extent of the subversive threat. We appreciate now that every young, emerging country must be constantly on the alert, watching for those symptoms, which, if allowed to develop unrestrained, may eventually grow into a disastrous situation such as that in South Vietnam. We have learned the need for a strong police force and strong police intelligence organization to assist in identifying early the symptoms of an incipient subversive situation. (Quoted in Leggett, 1973:380)

As Alan Wolfe has pointed out in his study of repressive tactics used in U.S. policy, much of U.S. foreign aid is spent in a systematic and global effort to "police" the Third World against political developments perceived as harmful to U.S. investment or other economic and strategic interests, regardless of the interference in the internal politics of these nations:

> Aid funds seem to have been used to repress anti-government riots in South Korea, help anti-communists win elections in Colombia and the Dominican Republic, supply Venezuelan police with up-to-date police equipment, suppress labor agitation at Goodyear and Gulf and Western plantations in the Dominican Republic, and pay for the training of Firestone Rubber's security police in Liberia. Here is the internationalization of police repression in its most blatant form. When it is supplemented by the presence of American soldiers around the globe—in at least sixty-four countries in the early 1970s—the result is a most extensive apparatus for violent repression. (Wolfe, 1973:202)

This police aid to Third World nations has been symptomatic of the dependency of these regimes on the advanced Western democracies. The power relationship has been clearly one of domination, not equal partnership, although Third World elites clearly "use" U.S. fears for their own purposes. United States security policy has been charged with responsibility for keeping these nations within the boundaries acceptable to the West, and it was common in U.S. domestic politics for aspiring candidates to charge that certain administrations were responsible for "losing" Cuba or China or Angola, Mozambique, Vietnam, Iran, or Nicaragua, as though these nations were "owned" in some sense by the United States prior to the overthrow of a certain regime. It should also be noted that the West reserved the option to drop previous allies in the Third World when they seem to become liabilities in the protection of Western interests. The United States arranged for the assassination of South Vietnamese President Diem in 1963 after it was clear that his government was losing the struggle against the NLF. The assassination of Dominican dictator Trujillo in 1961 and the French-planned and aided overthrow of "emperor" Jean Bokassa of the Central African Republic in 1979 are other examples of right-wing regimes toppled by Western covert action in order to install more effective pro-Western regimes.

Economic sanctions and threats of economic reprisals are common weapons used to affect the politics of Third World nations. Thus, in 1961, when it dawned on the United States that the Castro government was serious about social revolution in Cuba and intended to expropriate U.S. holdings, the United States declared an economic blockade against trade with Cuba and pressured other Western and Latin American governments to break all ties with Cuba as well. The idea was to strangle the Cuban economy, which was dependent on the U.S. sugar market for selling its largest export commodity. Most Cuban transport and industrial equipment and in general all technology of the modern sector of the economy was dependent on Western corporations for service and spare parts. A CIA-managed campaign of economic sabotage aimed at further crippling Cuban sugar production, machinery, and transportation facilities (Kwitny, 1984:242–51). The reliance on Western technology by Third World nations can always be used by the West to blackmail Third World systems. In the case of Cuba, the Soviet Union agreed to buy up the sugar crop for an extended period at prices above the world market average, and the Soviet Union and other industrialized East European Communist states have provided technological and financial aid to partially offset the Western economic blockade. But the costs of the transition have been high, and only a strongly motivated regime with firm and organized popular support could attempt to defy a complete cutoff from its traditional sources of trade, finance, and technology. With the end of Soviet aid to Cuba, which had been estimated at $4 to $5 billion annually, Cuba faces U.S. economic and military threats alone. Third World regimes know that in the 1990s, there is no longer any Soviet counterbalancing force to Western intimidation. This is another important effect of the end of the East-West conflict—a freer hand for the victorious West in disciplining the developing nations.

The major international finance organizations, including the International Monetary Fund (IMF), the World Bank, the Inter-American Development Bank, and the United States Export-Import Bank, are also useful for disciplining Third World governments that get out of line (see chapter 14). While these banking agencies are either private or multinational, their capital for financing Third World development projects and programs comes largely from Western sources and is therefore aligned with Western interests. In the 1980s, some OPEC funds for Third World development were beginning to become available, and Western news media were quick to point out how this money was used to buy political influence for the Arab point of view vis-à-vis the Palestinian issue. It should come as no surprise, although it is not well covered in the Western press, that Western finance capital has been used for generations to peddle influence in the Third World and to shape Third World politics to meet Western interests. Most (non-OPEC) Third World nations are debtor states (i.e., in debt to foreign and international banks and governments), and must repay interest and principal on these debts annually (called debt "servicing"). They must often come to these sources of financing for further loans and credits in order to pay for imports for both consumption and production. If they cannot secure further credits, they will not have the hard currency necessary to pay for imported food, machinery, spare parts, and fuels. Decreased food imports will mean higher prices for available foodstuffs, and decreased fuel and production equipment supplies will mean slowdowns in industry and agriculture. It is extremely difficult to quickly break these ties of financial dependence and embark on an independent course of internally directed and self-sustained development. Therefore, even progressive governments, such as Michael Manley's democratic socialism in Jamaica or Juan Velasco's radical military regime in Peru, had to compromise their policies, even scrap whole reform programs, to meet conditions for "stabilization" (enforced austerity) set down by the IMF. There is no pretense about the IMF dictating political conditions for the continued extension of credits, and there is little doubt that the IMF, even if it wanted to support social reform in the Third World, could not long oppose the interests of its major capital contributors (although see below for the relative neutrality of the IMF, compared to other banking agencies, in the Chilean case).

The Example of Chile

The tactics used by Western imperialism to limit political liberty in the Third World when that liberty begins to threaten Western interests were illustrated by the events in Chile in the early 1970s. In the postwar period, and in the

347

twentieth century generally, Chile had the best record for constitutional government and free elections anywhere in Latin America. In many ways, Chilean society was closer to some of the societies of Western Europe in its social, cultural, and political traditions than it was to many of the less stable and less developed nations of Latin America. In 1970, a Popular Unity coalition of leftist parties led by socialist Salvador Allende won the presidency in a three-way race. Allende received 36 percent of the vote, the Christian Democratic candidate Tomic got 28 percent, and the National party candidate Allesandri got 35 percent. The United States and several U.S. MNCs had pinned their hopes and several hundred thousand dollars of campaign contributions on the right-wing Allesandri. Nevertheless, Allende received a plurality and was confirmed by the Chilean Congress as the new president. U.S. Ambassador Edward Korry, in a secret statement to outgoing President Eduardo Frei, promised that "once Allende comes to power we shall do all within our power to condemn Chile and the Chileans to utmost deprivation and poverty" (revealed in *U.S. Senate Report on CIA Assassination Plots* in November 1975 and quoted in Roxborough, O'Brien, and Roddick, 1977:277).

The Popular Unity government was then attacked along two fronts: first, an informal economic blockade was established by the United States to strangle the Chilean economy and punish the Chilean people, as Ambassador Korry had promised; second, aid and encouragement were given to internal opponents of Allende and increasingly to those groups intent upon a military overthrow of the government. Like most Third World economies, Chile's was open to attack from the United States for several reasons. Even before Allende took office, Chile was in debt to Western banks and governments to the tune of $2.6 billion, a very high debt for a nation of only 8 million people. Chile's ability to pay off its debts and to continue paying for imports from the West was closely tied to its ability to export copper, its most abundant natural resource, to the West. Additionally, Western and mainly U.S. interests in Chile were extensive across the economy, so that many production, transport, and communications facilities were dependent on the West (the United States in particular) for replacement and spare parts.

The economic blockade against Chile tightened by steps as it became clear that Allende was serious about nationalizing, by legal statute, U.S. corporate holdings in Chile, including those of Kennecott Copper, Anaconda Copper, Cerro Copper, and ITT, on terms that these MNCs deemed "unacceptable." Almost immediately, U.S. aid projects were halted and loan money granted through signed agreements with the previous Christian Democratic Frei government was withheld. Private U.S. bank credit dried up quickly, declining from a level of about $220 million annually to only $35 million in 1972. Under U.S. pressure, the multilateral Inter-American Development Bank and Robert McNamara's World Bank stopped their loans. The United States Export-Import Bank, which had given a $25 million loan to the state-owned Chilean Steel Corporation in 1969 for expansion, refused to disburse the final $13 million after Allende took office. Only the IMF, despite obvious pressure from the United States, took a relatively neutral position and granted some credits ($148 million) in the first year of Allende's government. Additionally, $90 million in aid and credits were given by the Communist nations, $32 million came from Brazil, and $100 million from Argentina. Even so, these were not sufficient to keep Chile's international debt situation from deteriorating markedly between 1970 and 1973.

In the transport sector, the denial of spare parts had a debilitating effect on the Chilean economy. By 1972, some 30 percent of privately owned microbuses, 21 percent of taxibuses, and 33 percent of public buses were inoperative because of lack of spare parts and tires. Similar effects were visible in the trucking industry. United States multinationals also added their weight to the economic blockade. Kennecott Copper, expropriated from its huge El Teniente mining complex, took legal action to block payments to Chile for exports of copper to other nations. By 1973, Chile's copper sales, its main source of export earnings, were falling, and its foreign customers were being scared off by threats of court suits if they continued to do business with Chile.

The second broad avenue of attack was through support for Chile's internal enemies. While economic aid, trade, and financing were being cut off, military aid to the Chilean armed forces was continued, clearly to maintain support for the United States among the Chilean military. In 1971, $5 million in credits were granted for military purchases and $10 million in 1972, despite the fact that U.S. policy is, by law, to cut off aid to governments that nationalize U.S. corporate properties without satisfactory compensation (Petras and Morley, 1975:127). In May of 1973, five months before the military coup, President Nixon, through presidential waiver power, approved the sale of F-5E fighter aircraft to the Chilean air force, with the rationale that this was "important to the national security of the United States" (Petras and Morley, 1975:128). Clearly the Chilean military, many of whose officers had received training in the United States, was the trump card of U.S. strategy and was afforded favored treatment in preparation for the coup of September 11, 1973. Additional aid went to nonmilitary opponents of the Allende government. The Inter-American Development Bank made two exceptions to its blockade policy, a $7 million loan to Catholic University and a $4.6 million loan to Austral University, both conservative strongholds. And in 1972–73, when Chilean truck owners organized a strike in an attempt to paralyze the economy, the CIA funnelled tens of millions of dollars to aid the truck owners' action to compensate for lost business and income.

After the September military coup, which killed Allende and overthrew Chilean democracy, the economic blockade was immediately lifted and the Pinochet dictatorship was extended financial aid. In the first month of military rule, U.S. banks offered nearly $200 million in new credits. The Inter-American Development Bank approved $8.5 million for the junta before its own project study was even complete. The World Bank added $13.5 million, and in February 1974, the IMF approved $95 million in "standby" credits, which was later increased to $158 million. In just the first six months after the military seizure of power and the suppression of democracy in Chile, some $468 million in financial aid was given to the military regime (Petras and Morley, 1975:144). For its part, the Pinochet dictatorship agreed to pay $253 million to Anaconda Copper and $68 million to Kennecott Copper for their nationalized property.

The Chilean military, in overthrowing Allende's government, also destroyed the liberties upon which Western democracies are built. All political parties, including the Christian Democrats and the Nationalists as well as the Socialists and Communists, were suppressed. Freedom of the press and free speech were destroyed. Leftist political and union leaders were hunted down by the new secret police, the DINA, which appeared quickly on the scene as a major element of the military rule. Political dissidents by the thousands were dragged off in the night to unknown fates (several unmarked mass graves were publicly reported in the Western media). Thus United States policy, which verbally supports human rights throughout the world, actively and vigorously promoted and encouraged the brutal suppression of personal liberty in one of the few successful democracies in Latin America.

> The United States long ago gave up the idea that a parliamentary facade is a necessary accompaniment of capitalist development in Latin America. The incapacity of parliamentary regimes to offer guarantees against radicalism and nationalism and their inability to create favorable conditions for foreign investment have for some time provoked U.S. policy-makers and economic influentials into rethinking the "best" political formula to serve their interests in Latin America. (Petras and Morley, 1975:157)

Allende's Popular Unity program would certainly have run into fierce internal opposition even without U.S. intervention, but it is useless to try to separate out internal and external components. The ties between the Chilean bourgeoisie and U.S. corporate interests were so strong that Popular Unity was inevitably struggling to maintain a democratic system against an internal/external coalition. In the view of many observers, the national bourgeoisie will utilize Western external aid against the domestic left to save capitalism, even if this means sacrificing its own democratic liberty. A progressive government, however democratically elected, must reckon with a political onslaught by the bourgeoisie that utilizes tactics both legal and illegal and both peaceful and violent, an onslaught that can draw on Western resources for tipping the balance of power in its favor. The extent of democratic liberty in the Third World is not an internal matter alone and must be placed in the largest context of Western economic interests. In the 1960s, the United States officially promoted democracy as part of its Alliance for Progress in Latin America; by the 1970s, it had decided that the Brazilian military junta was a more appropriate model for Chile to follow.

Regime Strategies for Limiting Personal Liberty

Democracy remains a possibility in Third World nations, and even without effective parliamentary democracy, certain civil liberties are not inconsistent with dependency and Western interests. Indeed, there are occasions when the United States and its allies have used their influence to try to "humanize" or "liberalize" certain Third World governments. This often occurs when the U.S. government perceives that excessive regime violence is leading to a truly revolutionary situation, one that might endanger not only the present government but the entire social order and its ties to international capital. The United States in 1977 did put some pressure on the Somoza regime in Nicaragua to liberalize its practices in the hope of preventing a Sandinista guerrilla victory (which occurred anyway). The United States encouraged a moderation of the vicious Thai military junta in 1977 when it appeared that widespread attacks on students and intellectuals were forcing them into an underground alliance with the Communist insurgents in the northeast provinces. The British began to put pressure on the white minority regime in Rhodesia to include blacks when the ZAPU and ZANU (Patriotic Front) insurgency began to have some success in its armed struggle. Other Western efforts to promote liberalization as a means of forestalling revolution were undertaken in Iran in 1978 and El Salvador in 1979. Western pressure on South Africa to end apartheid and to bring blacks, colored, and Indians into political participation has been based on the fear that eventually an armed black insurgency will threaten long-term Western interests there.

It is also possible that certain liberties may be tolerated within the dependency system, so long as they are either (1) limited to members of the ruling elite grouping or (2) not effectively used by nonelites to demand greater social equity or economic benefits. In the first case, a degree of liberty among elites helps to keep the elite coalition together and may be institutionalized as part of the bargaining process over economic policy. Thus, for example, even while the Somoza family ruled in Nicaragua for over forty years, it did permit some competition to its Liberal party base from the Conservative party, and moderate opposition newspapers were permitted to publish. It was only in the 1970s, and especially after the 1972 earthquake that destroyed Managua, the capital city, that the middle class began to oppose Somoza's rulership more vigorously. This was a result of Somoza's land speculation in the rebuilding of the city of Managua. Somoza forced the rebuilding of the city on Somoza-owned land and reaped huge windfall profits, while denying similar opportunities to other bourgeois groups. In other words, he hogged the whole thing for himself and in the process alienated much middle-class support. With the assassination of Conservative party leader and newspaper publisher Joaquin Chamorro in 1978, presumably by Somoza henchmen, the split between Somoza's Liberal party and the moderate middle-class opposition forced the abandonment of the interelite tolerance and relative liberty for bourgeois groups that had characterized much of the forty-year Somoza dynasty.

Another example of the coexistence of liberty and coercion is the Mexican political system, one of the most stable in Latin America (and the Third World generally) since the 1930s. Formally, Mexico has a federal structure, with a multiparty system of competing parties at local, state, and federal levels. However, the system has been dominated for sixty years by one party, the Institutional Revolutionary party (PRI), which has manipulated the nominal opposition parties, the more conservative PAN and the moderate left PPS. On occasion, when the PRI has lost a local election that it wanted to win, the counting of the votes has been simply rigged, or the election has been annulled by a higher authority (R. Hansen, 1974:122). The PRI is organized into three sectors, representing agrarian, popular, and labor groups affiliated with the party. These sectors act as patron-client networks and include campesino, state bureaucracy, and trade union organizations that have agreed to work within the PRI framework and abide by its rules. These groups are then granted some rewards; in turn they help to maintain the social peace, the "peace of the PRI," by not making militant demands on the government on behalf of peasants and workers. Of course, new and more militant groups arise under the conditions of extreme inequality, landlessness, and poverty that afflict great numbers of Mexican citizens who do not benefit from its economic growth.

Bo Anderson and James Cockcroft (in Cockcroft, Frank, and Johnson, 1972:219–69), Roger Hansen (1974: especially ch. 5), and Pablo Gonzalez Casanova (1970) have described the PRI's methods for dealing with independent political groups that fall outside its definition of acceptable behavior. If possible, the PRI leadership attempts to coopt the leaders of independent unions, student groups, and campesino organizations. Offers of money or political office are common, as are threats of violence if cooptation is refused. If the PRI can coopt militant leaders, it can defuse the demands of their followers. This is a common tactic, of course, and one not peculiar to the Mexican system, except that it is so highly refined and so institutionalized in that system. For those groups whose leaders refuse cooptation, the PRI has not been hesitant to employ assassination squads, to arrest or deport militant leaders, and to employ government troops to shoot strikers and rebellious students. The goal of this dual strategy of cooptation and coercion is to exclude the great majority of the populace from making any effective demand on the political system. The PRI system attempts to maintain the majority of the citizenry in an unorganized, politically passive condition. It is a demobilization system that it sets up threats and punishments against independent groups that want to exercise political liberties. In the late 1970s and 1980s, with the growing debt crisis and the collapse of the Mexican economy, the PRI regime turned more often to violence and corruption to reinforce its political hegemony (Hellman, 1983). In the 1988 elections, the PRI was faced with a strong challenge from PAN candidate Manuel Clouthier on the right and from a coalition of leftist-populist groups united behind the candidacy of Cuauhtémoc Cárdenas, a popular former PRI leader and son of Lázáro Cárdenas, the populist president of Mexico from 1934 to 1940. The PRI candidate, Carlos Salinas de Gortari, a colorless Harvard-educated economist, officially won with 50 percent of the vote (Cárdenas 31 percent, Clouthier 17 percent), but only through massive vote fraud and intimidation by the PRI political machinery.

Hansen (1974:120–21) identified "manifest" and "latent" aspects of Mexican politics. At the manifest (official) level, the PRI provides representation of popular needs and grievances arising from the workers and peasants. At the latent (practical) level, the PRI sectors serve to repress and demobilize, through cooptation and coercion, popular demands for social reform. (In this respect, it is appropriate that the U.S. attempt to break the Vietnamese peasantry's support for the NLF was called a "pacification" program, aimed at demobilizing peasant demands for land reform, honest government, and attention to local health and education needs.)

Mexico and Nicaragua are only two examples and differ from many other Third World systems in that the PRI and the Somoza family provided a "stable" political order for over forty years in each nation. In many Third World nations, of course, the ruling elites have not been able to provide an enduring organizational structure for government. The Mexican PRI is exemplary in that it has maintained an effective elite consensus and a passive populace without serious interelite violence and without a military coup for over half a century. Most Third World elites have not been able to accomplish this nearly as well and have invited military intervention into the political arena (Sumberg, 1975:28–29).

Robert Gamer (1976) has provided a description of common techniques used to limit the practical expression of liberty while at the same time retaining the facade of a constitutional or democratic order. These include:

1. Limitations on potentially challenging groups such as unions, teachers' organizations, and the press. Techniques such as antistrike laws, security or loyalty clearances for teachers and students, purges of suspect educators, restrictions on importation of newsprint, and government ownership or secret sponsorship of certain news media are common.
2. Limitations on independent political groups. Techniques here include

police permission for political gatherings, outlawing of selected parties or ideologies, cooptation or coercion of opposition candidates, and rigged vote counting.
3. Intimidation of selected politically active individuals. Methods often employed are loss of employment, threats to family members, arbitrary harassment, arrest, torture, and deportation.
4. Extraordinary extension of government powers, presumably of limited duration. Measures include temporary suspension of part or all of the constitution, declaration of a state of emergency or martial law, and postponement of certain elections.

While these measures can be found in various mixtures at different times in most Third World systems, some greater attention should be placed on the use of torture and death squads, particularly against radical leaders of political, student, peasant, and worker groups. These terrorist squads, similar in function to the earlier Ku Klux Klan in the United States political system, are a basic deterrent to the effective organization of lower-class interests that would threaten the major elite networks of dependency relations. Death squads are closely affiliated with official police and military forces, although the government in power disowns their activities and pleads ignorance. A brief Third World survey of more prominent death squads would include: the Argentine Anticommunist Alliance (AAA) in Argentina; *Orden* (Order) and the White Warriors Union in El Salvador: *Mano Blanco* (White Hand) and *Ojo por Ojo* (An Eye for an Eye) in Guatemala; the *Red Gaurs* in Thailand; the infamous Tontons Macoute (and more recently the ''attachés'') in Haiti; the ''death squad'' in Brazil; the House of Israel in Guyana; the so-called Lost Command and, at an earlier period, the *Ilagas* (now officially recognized as the Civilian Home Defense Forces) in the Philippines; ''Battalion 316'' in Honduras; and *la Banda* in the Dominican Republic. The continued formation and functioning of these thinly disguised, government-sanctioned death squads, even in situations where there is widespread international criticism of this aspect of the regime (as in the case of El Salvador), is an indication of the important need, periodic but systematic, for the regime to prevent at all costs the emergence of organized peasant, labor, or leftist political interests. If other tactics (cooptation, bribery, and so on) should fail, application of officially disowned terror is the systematic pattern of regime response to demobilize various groups in the population.

It should be noted that the brutal killing of six Jesuit priests, their housekeeper, and the housekeeper's daughter in late 1989 by members of the Salvadoran armed forces, at first denied and even attributed to the FMLN rebels in a blatant disinformation campaign, did not change the Bush administration's commitment to military and economic aid to the Salvadoran government. Human rights are only conditionally supported by U.S. policy in the developing nations; when other interests are at stake, even the most terroristic regime may be supported.

Still, the symbolism of democracy and personal liberty has its uses in Third World systems, since they give the impression of free choice and participation. Liberalizations and humanizations continue to appear in the Third World in attempts to restore or build up legitimacy for governing elites; but these liberalizations disappear whenever the actual use of liberty threatens major patron-client networks.

Theodore Sumberg, writing for the conservative Center for Strategic and International Studies, concluded in his survey of freedom in the Third World that the lack of personal liberty was related to some natural incapacities for self-rule:

> Originating in Europe, freedom has also settled among peoples of unequal capacity for self-government. We must be careful here because contemporary xenophobia does not like raising a question about the political capacity of different peoples. It is perhaps our bad conscience on racial matters that shuts off such a discussion. So we will merely state without emphasis that the political arts seem to be no more universal than the arts of dance or sculpture, and that the first in particular seem to be sparse in most areas of the world for hundreds, even thousands, of years, and are not to be acquired on the quick. The political incapacity of some peoples will naturally show up soon after they are free to govern themselves. (1975:65–66)

Sumberg's argument was that the lack of freedom in the Third World and its dim future are a result of the gradual recession of Western influence. According to Sumberg, the West took the ideas of liberty and democracy to the Third World during the colonial period, but the inherent native incapacity of Third World peoples for self-government is now apparent. (It should be remembered that Freedom House, whose definitions of freedom Sumberg relied on, recognized the *Transkei bantustan* set up by the racist South African regime as not only an independent state, but a ''partly free'' one as well.) This argumentation runs counter to the logic of dependency represented here, which sees freedom or lack of freedom as not purely a local matter, but rather in some measure a function of an international system of dependency in which Western interests and collaborating local elites may find liberty sometimes of use to the dependency system, but more often threatening.

Indian Democracy and Personal Liberty

India, the largest political democracy, illustrates on a huge scale the possibility of combining basic political rights with the continuing limitations on personal liberty from a variety of nonofficial sources. The experience of Indian democracy in its performance on personal liberty shows much about the trials and tribulations of personal liberty in the developing nations. Along with a very few developing nations like Sri Lanka and Costa Rica, India has maintained a democratic system with the greatest tenacity in the Third World since independence in 1947 and has maintained broad personal liberty in an environment seemingly hostile to democracy. India is a huge multilingual, multiethnic society, divided also along religious (mainly Hindu and Moslem) and caste lines. India is still a poor nation that has made slow progress in raising the standard of living and building a modern economy. Despite extensive government programs for family planning, India's population growth has continued to nullify much of the economic growth that has been achieved. India was born in a spasm of rioting and communal violence centered on the issue of the border that separated Pakistan from India, and India has fought several border wars with Pakistan and one with China since 1947. India has been beset by secessionist movements in Kashmir, Assam, Punjab, and Gurkaland; by continued communal violence between Hindus and Moslems and Hindus and Sikhs; and by violence among castes and between language, ethnic, and social class groups. Between 1948 and 1967, there were 558 large-scale riots in India and over seventeen hundred armed attacks by political groups on either the government or other organized groups in India (Taylor and Hudson, 1972: 94, 102).

In the early 1950s, many Western observers looked to India as a democratic Western-oriented model for development that competed with the Communist model being applied then in China. Few would now put India forward as a model for other Third World nations to emulate or to claim it as a "test case" of successful Western-style development. A. H. Hansen and Janet Douglas, in an assessment of Indian democracy in the early 1970s, reflected the pessimism over India's failure to combine economic development and social justice with parliamentary democracy:

> That India's experiment in combining political democracy with economic development may conceivably be running into the sands is a tragedy, on any showing. It is not only sad for the Indian people, who have had more than their measure of sadness, but of deep concern for the Third World as a whole, and particularly for the Asiatic part of it. There was a time, hardly more than ten years ago, when India was the hope of the well-informed and progressive people throughout the world. It seemed that, contrary to ideas that had gained wide currency, there was at least one underdeveloped country—and a very large and important one—that was making a go of social-democracy. This was the period when India was identified with Nehru, and when Nehru himself was making a bid for Third World leadership, based not on military power but on moral persuasion and practical example. That period came to an end with the Chinese border conflict, Indian rearmament, and the virtual collapse of the Third Five Year Plan. Today India looks much more like a sick man than a pioneer; and, in

the manner of sick men directs attention inwards rather than outwards. (1972:216–17)

How, then, has democracy managed to survive in India despite low performance in economic development and social justice? In many ways this is one of the great surprises, but perhaps some factors can be noted. At the time of independence, the new Indian state possessed a competent and coherent civil service system, which was able to provide a basis for both governing and uniting the multitude of Indian groups. The Indian Civil Service already had a long organizational integrity absent in many other Third World nations. Additionally, the independence movement was headed by the Congress party, an umbrella organization founded in 1885.

The Congress party was much more than a political party through its history, and by the time of independence it had enormous political authority and prestige, which were lacking in so many other new nations. The Congress party had built up an elite consensus going far beyond the borders of the party itself; even members of the major opposition parties often got their start in political life through the Congress party and still considered it the legitimate leader of the new nation. In many other new nations, the political organizations of even strong leaders like Nkrumah in Ghana, Nasser in Egypt, or Sukarno in Indonesia crumbled after the death or overthrow of the top personality. In India, the Congress party could withstand the assassination of Gandhi, even in its early years of self-government, because the Congress organization was not tied to the charisma or fortune of any one personality. The Congress party, however, dominated the Indian system while getting only about 45 percent of the vote in national elections through the 1950s and 1960s. This was largely because the opposition was greatly divided among the panorama of parties of the left and of the right, and regional and local parties, with whom Congress often made temporary or localized coalitions. On the right were the traditionalist Jana Sangh and the pro-business Swatantra; on the left the moderate Socialists, the pro-Moscow Communist party of India (CPI), later also the more militant CPI-Marxist (CPI-M) and the pro-Peking CPI-Marxist-Leninist (CPI-ML). Thus, while the Congress party was not able to mobilize overwhelming popular support for its policies, the extremely divided nature of Indian society and the anti-Congress opposition made stable government possible until the early 1970s. This stability in government, backed by a loyal army and coherent civil service, was sufficient to ward off localized and sporadic uprisings without the necessity of suppressing oppositional activity across the board. Finally, the very failure of the government in promoting development meant that large segments of Indian society remained rooted in traditional village life, immobile, nonparticipant, and passive toward central government authority. As long as local society remained largely intact for tens of millions of Indians, it was difficult for antisystem groups to organize on a broad basis, although this was certainly attempted, most notably by the pro-Peking Naxalites in the later 1960s and early 1970s.

Even so, Indian democracy in the 1970s began to show serious strains. The Congress party had been split several times and was torn into competing factions. The first split came in the late 1960s, when Indira Gandhi challenged the most conservative old-guard elite, producing a New Congress around Mrs. Gandhi and a rump Old Congress, which did poorly in the 1971 elections. In June of 1975, under mounting pressure from opposition parties and the press to resign, Prime Minister Gandhi declared Emergency Rule, under which press freedom was curtailed and many opposition party and union leaders were jailed. The "Indira dictatorship," as the twenty-one month Emergency is sometimes called, was the most serious breach of parliamentary democracy since independence. The Emergency Rule period signalled the end of the elite consensus against throwing political opponents into jail for nonviolent dissent. Nevertheless, in a surprise move in January of 1977, Mrs. Gandhi called for new elections, in which free political debate was again permitted. Various opposition groups, including the traditionalist Jana Sangh, the Old Congress, the pro-business Swatantra, and the moderate Socialist party formed a new coalition party, the Janata, specifically for the purpose of defeating Mrs. Gandhi. In mid-campaign, Jagjivan Ram, a prominent leader of the untouchables, broke away from Mrs. Gandhi's New Congress and founded the Congress for Democracy, which supported the Janata party in the elections. For the first time since 1947, a non-Congress majority was elected to the Indian parliament (the Lok Sabha), with Janata getting about 43 percent of the vote and Mrs. Gandhi's New Congress falling to 34 percent of the national vote. In a style uncharacteristic of most Third World authoritarian leaders, Mrs. Gandhi accepted the defeat and resigned her office. Press, party, and union freedoms were quickly restored. Indian democracy had made a strong comeback.

This resurgence of democracy was hailed at the time as an historic event and even as the beginning of a more stable two-party system (Janata and Congress) within India (see Weiner, 1978:95–97; Park and Bueno de Mesquita, 1979:172–74). Yet, even the enthusiastic appraisals of the 1977 elections and of Janata, insofar as they were not simply partisan rhetoric, contained some reservations as to the solidity of the Janata coalition and skepticism of its ability to govern effectively (Weiner, 1978:106–10).

In less than two years, the Janata party had broken up into its original component parts, its coherence as a majority government collapsed, and Mrs. Gandhi was triumphantly returned to power in national elections. However, the Congress party in the 1980s continued to lose its legitimacy as a national governing party and appeared more as the extension of patronage and corruption controlled at the top by the Gandhi family, under Indira Gandhi until her assassination in 1984, and then under the leadership of her son, Rajiv Gandhi, prime minister from 1984 to 1989. In 1987, after a period of great popularity of Rajiv Gandhi, who introduced bold initiatives in the Punjab and Sri Lankan crises, and who seemed to steer the Indian economy towards a more unregulated market-oriented path of development, a series of scandals, expulsions of dissident leaders, and splits in the Congress party again threatened its legitimacy and governing capability. In 1989, at the height of several scandals involving the Gandhi family and kickbacks from Swedish multinational weapons-maker Bofors, new elections brought to power an anti-Congress left-right coalition, headed by V.P. Singh, which lasted only eleven months in office, did very little to reform the political system, and was replaced by a new government dependent on Congress party support to stay in office. Growing violence in India in recent years, from a wide variety of areas and causes, challenged the very integrity of the Indian state. The assassination of former Prime Minister Rajiv Gandhi during his political comeback attempt in the spring 1991 national elections in India is another example of this trend, although it did not prevent the elections, which resulted in a new Congress-led government.

Thus, on the national level, the Indian government has been mostly dominated by a single party, the Congress party, with the Gandhi family at the top, while at the state level, regional, ideological, ethnic, and caste-based parties have done quite well. Personal liberty in the area of political choice, freedom of press, assembly, and speech survived because of lack of capacity and will by Congress, as demonstrated in 1975–77, to suppress its opponents effectively. Yet the Congress party, even in decline, has been able, due to the fragmented nature of the opposition, to dominate national politics.

At the local level, Indian citizens are subject to a series of unofficial but pervasive restraints which limit their personal liberty. Caste restrictions, while formally abolished, remain in force through caste-based violence, in which poor lower castes, sometimes organized into peasant guerrilla bands, are pitted against armed vigilantes hired by higher castes. Communal violence between Hindus and Moslems, between Hindus and Kashmiris, between Hindus and Sikhs, between Gurkhas and Bengalis, between Assamese and Bangladesh immigrants also limits personal freedoms, including freedom of travel, job opportunities, education, interest group organization, and even marriage and personal friendship. The organized violence used to restrict these personal freedoms is no less real because of its unofficial or traditional social basis. Nevertheless, the future of Indian democracy is of tremendous importance for the viability of political democracy and its proven *potential* for expanding personal liberty.

The irony of this situation is that Indian development in the 1980s has been relatively healthy, both in agriculture and in some high-tech industries. More people have begun to feel the effects of modernization, and this has progressively weakened the traditional order of village society. At the same time, growth and social mobility have increased, not decreased, social tensions among the myriad ethnic, caste, regional, and class divisions in India, raising the level of violence at a time when Congress is weaker than ever and no nationwide political alternative has yet emerged.

The rise in the early 1990s of the Bharatiya Janata party (BJP), a militant Hindu nationalist party, has exacerbated once again the tensions between Hindus and Moslems in India. The BJP had called for the removal of a Moslem mosque at Ayodhya and construction there of a temple to the Hindu god Ram. The destruction of the Ayodhya mosque by Hindu mobs in December 1992 set off several waves of communal violence, some of the worst India has seen since independence. The Congress party has historically been committed to secularism, with a clear separation of state from religion, but the challenge from the Hindu right-wing BJP has challenged this commitment. The secular and democratic program of development led by the Congress party was under siege, says Indian fiction writer Marian Budhos, because

> India sees itself as a country under siege—perhaps by the West's tempting consumer pressures; an affirmative action system for lower castes and untouchables crowding out high-castes from schools and political jobs; a political system cracking under the weight of corruption; or even the shocks of modernization, which means women bobbing their hair, divorce, and unheard-of fissures in the Indian family. (1993:721)

In state elections in November 1992, both the BJP and the Congress party did poorly, while parties representing the lower castes gained ground. The main question is whether the Congress party, organizationally weakened and disgraced by internal corruption, is capable of renewal. In the absence of a democratic alternative to the Congress party, the caste, class, and religious conflicts dividing India may indeed destroy its democracy and lead to a much less tolerant and more repressive regime.

Democracy Trend and Post–Cold War Prospects

In the 1980s, the return of elected civilian governments in most of Latin America (Argentina, Brazil, Chile, Uruguay, Ecuador, Bolivia, and even Paraguay) led some observers to talk about a "democracy trend" that promised greater respect for individual rights and protection of liberty in that region. The overthrow of the Marcos dictatorship in the Philippines, the end of military rule in South Korea and Pakistan, the gradual democratization in Taiwan, and freely elected regimes in Namibia and Zambia gave further evidence that democracy was gaining ground in much of the Third World.

The collapse of communism in Eastern Europe and the breakup of the Soviet Union meant that classic communism was no longer a viable alternative for Third World political development, and with the end of the Cold War, perhaps the West would not need to support right-wing dictatorships in the global struggle against communism. Stephen Van Evera (1990) argued that after the Cold War, with the Soviet challenge gone, the Third World didn't count for much in the larger strategic interests of the United States (or Europe). The United States didn't need to support the murderous ARENA regime in El Salvador, the mujahideen "freedom fighters" of the fanatic Golbuddin Hekmatyar in Afghanistan, or the butchery of Jonas Savimbi's UNITA in Angola. American intervention in the Third World had mainly aided repressive regimes and had not helped to build democracy or protect human rights. A more noninterventionist U.S. policy was now both possible and desirable.

It remains to be seen whether the end of the Cold War and the "democracy trend" will make a significant difference in the achievements of personal liberty for the citizens of the developing nations. In some cases, holding elections for a new government, as in the Philippines or Brazil, has not stopped either police brutality or death squad activity. There is much more to building a tolerant and free society than holding a "demonstration election" every once in a while (as valuable as that experience might be). The end of the Cold War did not suddenly produce a new crop of tolerant and democratic elites in the Third World nor did it change the basic mechanism of Third World development. In fact, the economic dynamism of the East Asian NICs under authoritarian regimes has provided a new success formula for other developing nations (and for post-communism too), one that puts off personal liberty to some distant future, after economic modernization has been completed.

The wealthy elites of Third World societies (and their international investors) will still be fearful of popular movements for social justice, and these hopelessly unfair systems will continue to generate new demands for social justice. Liberty will still be uncertain under these circumstances, for the protection of liberty requires some minimum of social trust and mutual security for all classes, elites and masses.

16
Quality of Life— Dilemmas of Third World Modernization

Ever since the "discovery" of the non-Western world over five hundred years ago, and the conquest of huge empires by the great powers of Europe, Western influences have penetrated the societies of the Third World not only through military domination, colonization, and economic investment but also through the extension of Western communication media, consumer styles, and educational values. These factors are sometimes tied together under the concept of "Westernization," which is often equated with modernization. But Westernization carries with it some heavy baggage from the experience of Western imperialism, and for many citizens of the developing nations, it continues a pattern of unequal relationships within the global economic order. Marina Budhos, an Indian expatriate writer, describes the mixture of attitudes toward the modern and the West on her passage back to India:

> Phones don't work; the poor are not getting any relief; rural areas are stripped waste-lands of red dirt and clay; and cable TV zapped in from Hong Kong is promising a life style this country can't deliver. And the recent demise of Communism has sent a fresh wave of jitters through this country, leading some to turn to an age-old identity—Hinduism—however opportunistic its uses.
>
> By February I am living in Madras, at the house of an old friend of my father's from his consulate days. In many ways, his is a typical middle-class family: both children overseas, sending dollars each month since inflation has eaten away at their rupee-based pension. Uncle—as he's properly called by me—harps back to the "good old days" in the States, believing everything in the West is better, while Auntie wakes up before sunrise to perform her morning *puja* (ritual). (1993:722)

During the Cold War, Soviet-style communism, also a product of European thinking and culture, provided one alternative image of modernization for Third World societies, and radical political elites in at least some developing nations (Cuba, Vietnam, Angola, Afghanistan, Mozambique) attempted to break with the Western capitalist model. With the collapse of the Soviet Union and the restoration of capitalism in Eastern Europe, this model now has lost its attraction and its Soviet sponsorship, and this has put even greater pressure on Third World societies to adopt the Western model and its values for modernization. The leading Western powers now claim that there is no other path to modernity, and all deviations from the Western path are dead ends.

However, the dynamism of East Asian NICs has produced a highly competitive model of development that has deviated from both Western liberal democracy and free-market orthodoxy and has maintained its own cultural identity. This model was advanced with increasing self-confidence by leaders of these nations and was offered as a different path for rapid growth and competitive entry into the global economy. The East Asian developmentalist model may in the 1990s offer proof of the continued openness to variations in modernization, especially for the nations of Southeast and South Asia, and for several Central Asian successor states of the former Soviet Union.

For most Third World nations, however, the ingredients for duplicating either the Western liberal market model or the East Asian authoritarian developmentalist model are still missing. The pressures for finding a success formula, and the frustrations of continued failure, continue to mark a specific Third World syndrome that permeates the quality of life in these societies. This chapter deals with a range of issues related to this dilemma, namely, the question of how to modernize without losing one's cultural identity and independence once again to the West.

Cultural Imperialism—"Westernization"

Cultural imperialism involves so many factors that we will be able to concentrate on only a selected number for purposes of illustration. In the colonial period, cultural imperialism was expressed through the spread of Western languages as *the* languages of government, science, the professions—of higher education in general (or even middle-level education). English in India, the Philippines, Nigeria, Malaysia; French in Indochina, Senegal, Algeria, Madagascar, Djibouti; Dutch and English in South Africa; and Belgian-French in the Congo became the languages of rulership. This penetration of Western languages did not evaporate with the end of colonialism, and in the postcolonial period the West has continued to heavily influence the mass media of Third World nations. Aside from the continued use of the languages of the former colonial powers by educated elites, Third World newspapers, magazines, and radio and television are dependent on the developed nations for news of international events, since they lack their own organization of reporters and news "stringers" stationed around the world. From the developed West, UPI (United Press International), AP (Associated Press), Reuters, and Agence-France Presse are the major sources of events coverage; from the Communist world TASS is the major source. These are the interpreters of important happenings for the Third World media, and they are organized from the perspective of the liberal democracies and the industrialized Communist nations. Moreover, "most of the news that circulates in the world is news about rich countries distributed to the people of rich countries. Apart from local news, the media in poor countries are filled with news from rich countries, hardly at all with news from other poor countries" (Goldthorpe, 1975:205–6). Even when the local language of communication is used, the information, values, and orientation of Third World media may be thoroughly "Westernized." With the spread of satellite television in the 1980s, and the emergence of worldwide cable news networks such as CNN, based in Atlanta, it appears that Western technology now dominates this medium of international news coverage as well.

Some examples drawn from Mexico, relatively advanced in GNP/ capita and industrialization, may be useful. Magazines with the largest circulation in the 1960s were *Life en Español* (the Spanish edition of *Life*) and *Selecciones* (the Spanish edition of *Reader's Digest*). The three largest U.S. magazines published in Spanish and sold in Mexico had a total circulation (546,000) greater than that of the largest ten Mexican magazines (338,000). In terms of international news coverage by the major newspapers (*Excelsior, El Universal, Novedades, El Sol de Puebla*), from 60 to 80 percent was provided by the two U.S. news agencies, UPI and AP. Some additional stories were drawn from APF and Reuters; only an occasional international report came from sources beyond these four. Along with the predominance of Western (and mainly United States) news agencies as sources of international news information, there was also a predominance of stories about the rich Western nations. Newspaper space devoted to news about the United States in *Novedades* and *Excelsior*, two large Mexican dailies, in one single month was as great as the space devoted by the *New York Times* to all foreign countries (Gonzalez Casanova, 1970:59–64, 216). Films are another avenue for both entertainment and communication, particularly through the "demonstration effect" —showing what consumer life-styles look like in other nations or cultures. Between 1950 and 1964, fully 52 percent of films shown in Mexico were U.S.-made. Among the Third World nations, only India had a well-established and vigorous motion picture industry, able to compete with United States, British, Soviet, French, and Japanese films. With the demise of the Soviet Union and the shrinking of both the British and French film industries, movie theaters around the world show predominantly American "Hollywood" films; distribution of videos is dominated by U.S. firms and U.S. products.

Mexico might seem to be a special case because of its geographic proximity to the United States and the extensive economic and tourist trade between the two nations. But, in fact, this pattern exists for other Third World nations as well. Wilbur Schramm (1964), in a study of mass media and development, reports that for three large daily newspapers in Pakistan, 33 percent of all foreign news was about the United States, 17 percent about Great Britain, 16 percent about France, 13 percent about the Soviet Union, and only 13 percent about India, Pakistan's immediate neighbor and adversary. In the case of Argentina, only 6 percent of international coverage was about Brazil, while 43 percent was about the United States, an additional 15 percent about France, 11 percent about Great Britain, and 12 percent about the Soviet Union.

In the colonial period, Western standards of education were introduced into Third World societies, displacing or competing with traditional and local religious educational practices. The language of middle and higher education was generally that of the colonial power, the language of success, material affluence, Western domination, and of the white man. The double connection between Western science and "modernization" and between native ways and impoverished ignorance created and continues to create feelings of alienation for Third World peoples in their own countries, perhaps most acutely for those interested in progress and development for their nations. Frantz Fanon, the black Algerian psychoanalyst, has probably described these feelings in their full fury in his *Wretched of the Earth*. Novelists like V. S. Naipaul and N'gugi na Thion'go have described from other perspectives these feelings of alienation from society and from self. Political scientist Elbaki Hermasi has observed that "against what they consider cultural imperialism . . . Third World writers try to take national culture in its authenticity as a reference point and to express in the realm of culture the ongoing political and social struggles of emancipation from imperialism" (1980:147).

The economic, political, and military successes of Western values over native ways on the one hand lead to feelings of insecurity and inferiority, reinforced by colonial authorities and by the pattern of dependent development beyond the colonial period. On the other hand, those who assimilate Western ideas, including language, dress, science, and life-style, become isolated from their own people; they become "Westernized," even though their goal may be to free their nations from the domination of Western interests. "Modern" education and "modern" science, in part because it is Western and foreign, unadapted to local environment and social history, contains within it both the hope for development (personal and societal) and a continuing demonstration of the "backwardness" of the local culture:

> Among the critical shortages in educational development in poor countries is often that of textbooks and other educational materials related to the local environment. There are many "horror stories" about the importation of unsuitable material and inappropriate methods into the schools of the Third World—of African pupils being taught about the coalfields of England or the dissolution of the monasteries, of Algerian Muslim children taught to refer to "nos ancetres les Galles," of the 300-acre demonstration farms attached to agricultural colleges

in countries where the average peasant holding is less than 10 acres, and of the teaching of science by means of the Bunsen burner in countries with no indigenous source of gas. Many such stories are told about the colonial period, and are cited as examples of "cultural imperialism," the foisting of an alien culture on a subject people. But not all the "horrors" came at once to an end with political independence, and there were reasons for them more substantial than the cultural arrogance of white missionaries and colonial officials. (Goldthorpe, 1975:202–3)

What types of reaction are generated by the systematic and largely successful challenge to local control of social values? With the failures of these systems to provide for basic economic needs, social equity, and political liberty, why haven't there been more social revolutions in the Third World? There are clearly other responses to the dependency syndrome besides revolution. These responses may be at various levels: individual, small group, or mass. They may be peaceful or violent, but only rarely do they threaten to overthrow the entire social order. These reactions to the pattern of Third World development may be characterized generally as: (1) elite corruption, (2) fatalistic resignation, (3) emigration or deflected rebellion, and (4) counterorganization and revolution.

Corruption in Third World Systems

High levels of corruption and crime are characteristic of dependent political systems. Widespread political corruption is a typical feature of the systems we have been describing and as such can be seen as an integral part of the dependency syndrome.

Definitions of corruption can be problematic, especially so in comparative analysis (see Scott, 1972: ch. 1). James Scott, in a thoughtful study of comparative political corruption, opts for a basically legalistic working definition that defines corruption as behavior that violates formal legal norms set down for public officials, regardless of whether such behavior is widely practiced or publicly accepted or in the public interest.

Although there is by nature a general lack of comprehensive and accurate data as to the extent of corruption in any political system, most observers agree that corruption has been far more prevalent in the Third World than in either the liberal democracies or the Communist systems. (Post-Communist societies, however, have experienced a rapid rise in elite corruption, which in some cases now is similar to the situation in many developing nations. Some have concluded from this evidence that post-communism may lead to Third World, not First World, status for several nations.) Individual visitors to Indonesia, Brazil, Nigeria, or India can document the extensive demands for bribes by lower-level bureaucrats for various services (getting a ticket on a plane flight, getting on the flight, getting baggage through customs, getting money changed in a bank). For the Third World citizen, gifts and bribes for officials to overlook tax evasion or to grant a business permit, government license, or health service are commonplace, though not universal to all systems at all times. The variety of such practices across cultures defies short description. Some are related to long traditions of gifts to social or caste superiors or to kinship relations (nepotism), and in that sense are not necessarily new or locally perceived as corrupt. British sociologist J. E. Goldthorpe warned, however:

> Cultural relativity on this topic can be exaggerated, however. New situations arising as a result of modern economic activity create new opportunities for, and new forms of, corruption, in ways for which there may be little or no traditional sanction, such as bribing a tax inspector to accept a low return of one's income, or an airport official to overlook excess baggage. It is simply not the case that corruption is condemned only by the codes of modern Western democracies. On the contrary, it is condemned everywhere. Indeed, whenever there is a military coup in one of the new states of Asia or Africa, one of the justifications that are invariably advanced is the corruption of the former regime. (1975:105)

Other evidence of Third World corruption comes from high-level scandals, sometimes in the wake of a military coup or revolution or from revelations about the behavior of MNCs in these nations. After the Sandinista victory in Nicaragua, the extent of the Somoza family's looting of that country became officially documented. After the Iranian revolution, at least some of the corrupt elite enrichment under the Shah made international news in the West. After the rebellion in Shaba province in Zaire, the media noted that President Mobutu became a billionaire through straightforward pilfering of government funds. The military coup in Ghana by Flight Captain Jerry Rawlings revealed the blatant self-enrichment of General Akufo and General Acheampong, leaders of earlier military regimes. The fall of the American puppet regime in South Vietnam brought to light some details of high-level corruption by President Thieu and other top aides. The overthrow in 1986 of the Marcos dictatorship in the Philippines revealed that Ferdinand and Imelda Marcos had amassed over $10 billion in personal wealth, much of it stashed abroad in New York real estate and Swiss bank accounts. Similarly, the ouster of President Jean-Claude (Baby Doc) Duvalier in Haiti brought media attention to the personal wealth built by the Duvalier family at the expense of one of the world's poorest peoples. Rare is the case of a Third World dictator who has not used control of government to enrich himself, but in recent years the amounts of corrupt wealth have reached new heights. The personal gain of Marcos accounts alone for nearly half the foreign debt of the Philippines, the fortune of Zaire's Mobutu for most of that nation's foreign obligations. This is just the tip of the iceberg—the most egregious cases that were already widely suspected by competent observers of these systems. In Mexico, the ruling PRI long ago institutionalized a pattern of elite corruption. Frank Brandenburg, in his description of graft in the upper levels of the Mexican system, reported in the early 1960s:

> The precise amount a cabinet minister or state-industry manager finally accumulated . . . largely depends on himself, although when grafting becomes excessive and injurious to his rule, the President of Mexico may step in and close some sources of a subordinate's income. The average minister or director finishes his term with two or three houses, a good library, two or three automobiles, a ranch, and $100,000 cash; about 25 directors and ministers hold posts from which they can leave office with fifty times that amount in cash. (1964:162)

In India there is some information from official investigations (the Kripilani Report, the Santhanam Committee Report) on the relatively stable patterns of corruption at lower levels of the government civil service. John Monteiro (in Heidenheimer, 1970:223) cited one documented example of corruption in the administration of government contracts:

> One sub-contractor on the Railways was candid enough to admit that the Railway contractors (including himself) made regular payments to the engineering officials on a percentage basis. The following percentage breakdown on the amount of their bills was indicated by him:

Executive Engineer	5%
Assistant Engineer	5
PWD Supervisor	5
Accounts section	2
District pay clerk	¼
Head clerk in XEN	1
Ministry/work-in-charge	1
Miscellaneous	¼
Total	20%

> It may not be so meticulously systematic as represented here, but the fact of the percentages was mentioned by many witnesses, and is popularly known.

Another well-documented case is the famous "cement racket" in Nigeria. In 1975–76, the Nigerian government ordered approximately ten times the amount of cement it needed for its development plans from foreign suppliers at approximately twice the international market price. Roughly $2 billion of Nigeria's oil earnings were siphoned off through this scheme, which represented a pure loss for Nigerian development, but a windfall profit for top-level

Nigerian officials and the Western MNCs who supplied the cement (see Evans, 1979:313). Further accounts of political corruption in the Third World are provided by Scott (1972), Heidenheimer (1970), Goldthorpe (1975), and Chaliand (1978); despite the great cultural diversity, the underlying patterns become clear. Political corruption has, of course, been denounced within the Third World by nearly every government upon taking power. Yet even military coups that initially were dedicated to the suppression of corruption have fallen into much the same routine of behavior. Thus the record of the Nasser regime, which ousted the corrupt King Farouk in Egypt, or the Suharto regime, which replaced the graft-ridden regime of President Sukarno, or the Mexican PRI, successor to the classic corrupt machine politics of Porfirio Diaz, demonstrates the extreme difficulty of combating corruption in the developing nations.

Robert Kaplan (1994) has argued that the line between regime corruption and ordinary theft is becoming increasingly blurred in a number of "failed" nations, especially in sub-Saharan Africa, where both fragile regimes and organized gangs of various origins vie for pillage of the helpless and weak. Crime at Nigeria's Murtala Muhammad Airport, both from official and unofficial sources, has become so bad that the United States, in 1993, banned direct flights into that airport. The State Department report cited as a reason "extortion by law-enforcement and immigration officials" (Kaplan, 1994:45). Kaplan expands on Gunnar Myrdal's earlier notion of the "soft state," which was always susceptible to corrupt manipulation by stronger outside forces, to argue that the sharp rise of criminality in political life in Africa, South Asia, and much of the Arab world is a final phase of collapse of political order in the wake of more than a generation of ineffectual rule by the post-independence political elites, and he predicts a lengthy period of anarchy and civil wars for much of the Third World.

It is often forgotten that some Third World dictators, like Ferdinand Marcos and François (Papa Doc) Duvalier, achieved national leadership with the reputation of reformers or populists. Marcos was first elected president in the Philippines in 1964 with a program of honesty in government and was reelected in 1968 before declaring martial law in 1972 and ruling as a dictator thereafter. François Duvalier was elected president of Haiti in 1957 as a populist representative of poor blacks running against the interests of the mulatto elite of the island. This might suggest that these leaders, whose reform credentials once seemed so strong, at some point turned cynical about the prospects for improving their nations' fortunes and opted instead for changing their personal fortunes through the use of political power. The frustrations of progressive reform are high and the possibilities of financial corruption so tempting that it takes a truly remarkable leader or organization to keep faith and resist the offers to sell out.

Some amount of this elite corruption is clearly linked to the activities of the Western MNCs. In the 1970s, the era of Watergate revelations, a number of bribery payoffs by MNCs to high government officials were revealed. While some payoffs went to high-level officials of nations like Italy and Japan, many others were made to Third World government leaders. The common excuses given by the MNCs are: (1) such corruption is standard operating procedure and (2) any MNC not paying bribe money would lose out to competing MNCs who do make payoffs. Recently the U.S. Justice Department reported that McDonnell Douglas, producer of the DC-10 aircraft, was involved in payoffs to business and government leaders in Pakistan, the Philippines, South Korea, Venezuela, and Zaire. In the case of Pakistan, McDonnell Douglas is also charged with defrauding Pakistan International Airlines of a total of $1.6 million on the sale of four DC-10 aircraft, a sum that was pocketed by the McDonnell Douglas sales team. The U.S.-based firm is charged with paying $3.3 million to two owners of Korean Airlines, $2.1 million to three businessmen for sales to the government-owned Venezuelan airline, $625,000 to Zaire's minister of transportation and the governor of Zaire's National bank, and $400,000 to two officials of Philippine Airlines (*Guardian*, December 19, 1979:2). In Zaire, under the Mobutu regime, one of the most corrupt in the developing world, it is estimated that only 40 percent of aid money (some say only 10 percent) reaches specified projects (Greenhouse, 1988:8). Most money is stolen. From top to bottom, one must pay bribes or ''metabeesh'' for governmental services, from mail delivery to phone repair. Government officials are also heavily involved in diamond and ivory smuggling.

Scholarly analysis of political corruption in Third World systems has gone through a number of changing emphases since the early 1950s. Sociologist Daniel Bell, in a 1953 article entitled ''Crime as an American Way of Life,'' denounced the moral indignation of affluent Americans and academics over behavior that was, in America's own history, part of its economic development and immigration socialization:

> The pioneers of American capitalism were not graduated from Harvard's School of Business Administration. The early settlers and founding fathers, as well as those who ''won the west'' and built up the cattle, mining and other fortunes, often did so by shady speculations and a not inconsiderable amount of violence. They ignored, circumvented or stretched the law when it stood in the way of America's destiny, and their own—or, were themselves the law when it served their purposes. This has not prevented them and their descendants from feeling proper moral outrage when under the changed circumstances of the crowded urban environments later comers pursued equally ruthless tactics. (Bell, in Heidenheimer, 1970:164–65)

Bell's analysis, while limited to the American experience, related corruption and organized crime to the process of economic development and the widening of economic opportunity to newer immigrant groups within American society.

Bell concluded that organized crime and political corruption played positive roles in making room within the system for "latecomer" ethnic groups. He asserted that both organized crime and political corruption decline after these latecomers have achieved higher economic status, so that economic success can be had through legitimate business activities and when respectability and social status become more pressing goals. Crime and corruption, in other words, were useful vehicles for some ethnics to achieve the good life, but the very success of that behavior leads to its later decline, since it becomes both unnecessary and counterproductive to other goals.

Following on this general train of thought, which was less ethnocentric and less moralizing than much of the earlier commentary on corruption, a number of observers began to perceive positive functions of corruption in the development process of Third World "latecomers" (Ley, Leff, Veloso Abueva, and Greenstone, in Heidenheimer, 1970). These studies, while not trying to justify all forms of corruption as useful to development, nevertheless assert that political corruption served in many cases to: (1) aid in capital formation through the building of individual fortunes, which could then be invested in the economy; (2) sustain and promote entrepreneurial activity, especially among certain minority groups, who are ethnic "pariahs" or socially marginal within the dominant culture (Chinese in Indonesia, Lebanese in West Africa and Brazil, Indians in East Africa); (3) avoid delays and inefficiencies associated with government bureaucracy and avoid public disclosures that, in view of public hostility to the wealthy business class, could retard investment; and (4) promote nation building through the ability of different groups, using money-power to buy influence, to achieve benefits within the system. It was also stressed, especially by American political scientist Samuel Huntington (1968), that corruption in the Third World was a major mechanism for preventing basic social reform and avoiding social revolution. In political systems with weak legitimacy and low levels of institutionalization, Huntington saw corruption as a conservative force for stability:

> Like machine politics or clientalistic politics in general, corruption provides immediate, specific, and concrete benefits to groups which might otherwise be thoroughly alienated from society. Corruption may thus be functional to the maintenance of a political system in the same way that reform is. Corruption itself may be a substitute for reform, and both corruption and reform may be substitutes for revolution. (1968:61)

For Huntington, "he who corrupts a system's police officers is more likely to identify with the system than he who storms the system's police stations" (1968:61). Huntington's analysis was one of the most supportive of political corruption's positive role in the Third World, but with the primarily negative goal of avoiding revolution, rather than promoting development. Huntington believed that social revolution, and particularly Communist revolution, was the main alternative to systemic corruption.

A turning point in the debate over the effects of corruption in the Third World came in the latter 1960s, when observers began to argue that the human costs outweigh any benefits that might arise from the widespread corruption in Third World systems. Myrdal's *Asian Drama* (1968) pointed out the extensive delegitimization of the government through graft and pocket lining by officials, generating a tendency toward military coups and political cynicism. Myrdal further asserted that bureaucracies riddled by corruption were likely to become even more inefficient and ineffective to keep the price of bribery high. They grew, in parasitic behavior, in response to the money-making potential from graft and bribery. Myrdal also mentioned the extensive role of Western MNCs:

> Among the Western nations, French, American, and especially West German companies are usually said to have the least inhibitions about bribing their way through. Japanese firms are said to be even more willing to pay up. On the other hand, the writer has never heard it alleged that bribes are offered or paid by the commercial agencies of Communist countries. (Cited in Heidenheimer, 1970:236)

Although investment capital may be accumulated through corruption, wealth is often deposited in Swiss or American banks (as Haile Selassie and the Shah of Iran did) or in Miami real estate (as Somoza of Nicaragua did), in which case it constitutes an absolute drain of the resources of the Third World nation. Further, much of the wealth of the corrupt elite may be spent on luxury consumption or invested in luxury goods, import businesses, or speculative real estate, which does little to foster development to meet basic human needs for the poor and jobless. Corruption also wastes valuable government skills and provokes social unrest and military takeovers. James Scott concluded that it is less likely to hinder economic growth when:

1. National rulers are either uninterested or hostile to economic growth.
2. The government lacks the skills, capacity, or resources to effectively promote economic growth.
3. Corruption is "market" corruption where all the "buyers" of influence have equal access to bureaucrats and politicians. (The assumption here is that if parochial considerations are weak, only the ability to pay will count and efficient producers will have more of an advantage.)
4. Corruption benefits groups with a high marginal propensity to save (e.g., wealthy elites) more than groups with a low marginal propensity to save (voters).
   —this situation is, in turn, more likely in a noncompetitive political system than in a competitive one where votes can be traded for influence.

5. The cost of a unit of influence is not so high as to discourage many otherwise profitable undertakings.
    —this situation is more likely when there is price competition among the bureaucrats who sell influence.
6. There is greater certainty as to the price of a unit of influence and a high probability of receiving the paid-for "decision." This is more likely when:
    a. The political and bureaucratic elites are strong and cohesive.
    b. Corruption has become "regularized"—even institutionalized after a fashion—by long practice.
7. Corruption serves to increase competition in the private sector rather than to secure a special advantage or monopolistic position for any one competitor. (Scott, 1972:90–91)

Even if these conditions were met, it is uncertain whether economic growth within the dependency syndrome would bring significant benefits to any but the well-connected members of the dominant patron-client groupings. But it was clear to Scott, in any case, that most of these conditions are not fulfilled, in part because of pervasive political corruption itself. Most citizens do not have equal access to government officials nor do they have equal resources with which to buy influence. The benefits of corruption are heavily weighted in favor of the wealthy, the top bureaucratic bourgeoisie with control over government purchases, franchises, and operations, and the large corporations (both locally and Western owned).

Resignation: Fatalism, Alcoholism, Machismo, Violence

For the great majority of Third World citizens, there is little opportunity to participate in the networks of political rewards (legal and illegal). Yet, despite widespread disaffection and discontent among those outside the major patron-client networks, organization for social revolution is still an unusual response to the political system. Given the riskiness of open political dissent and the ability of ruling elites to coopt or coerce leaders of potentially challenging groups, it should not be surprising that many people are deterred from any organized political challenge to the system.

One type of response to great social inequality, poverty, joblessness, disease, and oppression is fatalistic resignation. Fatalism reflects a feeling of powerlessness to struggle for change and a passive, even passionate, acceptance of the status quo. Social fatalism may be found in traditional village society where the forces of nature (monsoon, drought, disease) are still viewed (worshipped) as more powerful than human effort—as beyond human control. This is the fatalist coexistence with nature that existed before the rise of modern science and industry, the spread of education, and increasing human mobility. But social fatalism clearly persists even in the most modern urban environments. In many areas, organized religion preaches passive acceptance of the social order and opposes social change. The Catholic church as an institution has historically acted as a powerful force for acceptance of the existing system in exchange for consolation and hope for eternal salvation.

Only since the 1960s, in the wake of Vatican II, which affirmed the "option for the poor" as a goal of the Catholic church's work, has "liberation theology" gained a foothold within many Latin American and Philippine parishes. This new path has emphasized church efforts to help the poor to organize, to break out of poverty and repression, conditions no longer seen as their inevitable fate but as the unacceptable degradation of the individual. The "option for the poor" has made many priests and nuns targets of right-wing death squads, but this partial break with the church's traditional acceptance of existing injustices is of great importance and has engaged many local Catholic organizations in activist politics and community organizing among the poor. In Latin America especially, the politics of religion is no longer dominated by fatalistic acceptance of poverty and social injustice. However, the church hierarchy is split over "liberation theology," and Pope John Paul II has appointed bishops and cardinals generally opposed to this path, while at the same time calling on political leaders to build a more just economic and social order.

In a rather more decentralized fashion, Hinduism in India and Buddhism in much of Southeast Asia tend toward acceptance of the social order (or caste system) and downplay the need to organize and struggle for social change. The role of Islam in the Middle East, Africa, and South Asia is more difficult to characterize. Certainly the mullahs in Iran and Afghanistan provided a rallying point for popular uprisings, in the one case against the American-supported Shah and in the other against the Soviet-supported Afghan Marxist regime, although not with the goal of revolutionizing the social order, but rather in the spirit of national independence from the great powers.

Fatalism may also be expressed in pervasive gambling or playing the numbers or the lottery; here the individual hopes to escape from poverty, through luck or fortune or some magical charm. Alcoholism and drug addiction are forms of individual-level escapism, attempts to drown out problems of daily life, to achieve, temporarily, a state of euphoria. These expressions of social fatalism are found in the developed industrial nations, and it should not be surprising that many people in the Third World also turn to drink and drugs rather than social or political organizing for solutions to their problems. In some cases, dominant elites may utilize alcoholism as a social weapon to try to defuse or sidetrack worker and peasant anger. In the Republic of South Africa, the apartheid regime supplied cheap "bantu beer" to black industrial workers, even though white Afrikaner society was fairly puritanical in its attitude toward drinking. In the huge black township of Soweto outside white Johannesburg, Saturday night was an occasion for widespread drinking, gambling, and individual-level violence among the local population. This catharsis, or release of pent-up emotion, can be seen in local sporting events; for example, soccer matches in some Latin American countries, where heavy drinking, gambling, fist- and knife-fighting often explode into full-blown riots, costing the lives of scores of people. Within the family setting, urban working-class males are able to vent their frustrations on wives and children. Oscar Lewis (1959) and Wayne Cornelius (1975) noted the high frequency of physical force in arguments, of wife- and child-beating, and of alcoholism among the urban poor in Latin America. While the "machismo complex" of male domination within the family is also found in more traditional rural society, the greater mobility, diversity, and anonymity of urban society weaken the force of local opinion and traditions in restraining family violence. Robert Gamer (1976), Eric Wolf and Edward Hansen (1972), and Oscar Lewis (1959) described the great variety of means for cathartic release that does not challenge the social or political system, yet provides temporary outlets for anger and frustration. There is no doubt that feelings of alienation (of not being able to cope, of powerlessness, of physical and social insecurity) are widespread in Third World societies. Gamer in particular emphasizes that repression of organized protest, combined with opportunities for deflecting hostility from the social and political spheres onto localized objects, may be a significant stabilizing force for the dominant elites. Gamer (1976:187–88) explores the possibility that through the effective use, or simply the availability, of liquor, gambling, fighting, sports, and other distractions from class-based grievances, Third World regimes may avoid systemic change indefinitely.

Deflection from Revolution: Emigration, Ethnic and Generational Conflict, Criminality

Even when individuals are bitterly dissatisfied with their government or desperate for greater economic opportunities to hold themselves and their families together, it does not follow that they will organize to challenge the current regime or to join a movement for economic and political change. At the individual and family level, the course of wisdom and highest probability for success is emigration—leaving the social and political system which has failed them and migrating to a country with greater opportunities. This has always been preferable to facing repression by the police and military or struggling for years in a seemingly hopeless union, peasant, populist, or socialist effort to change the basic social and political system. Emigration is not a fatalistic alternative; it has a high success ratio for those with the enterprise and possibility to attempt it. After all, emigration by individuals and families to the United States from Europe and later from Asia and Latin America has been a success story for millions of American citizens. Not just higher wages but greater security and avoidance of turmoil lead many families to join the international migration to the more stable and affluent democracies. Sociologist Douglas Massey sees this as eminently rational strategy:

> Although a large wage differential is clearly an incentive to movement, it is neither a necessary nor a sufficient condition. . . . Migration decisions in developing countries are typically made by families, not individuals, and . . . families migrate not only to maximize earnings but also to minimize risks. Economic conditions in developing countries are volatile, and families face serious risks to their well-being from many sources—natural disasters, political upheavals, economic recessions. Sending different family members to geographically distant labor markets represents a strategy to diversify and reduce risks to household income. (1992:14)

Furthermore, the supply of new industrial jobs in the modernization process in the late-developing nations is different from the early Western industrial revolution:

> At the same time, the technology of production has become increasingly capital intensive. During the nineteenth century, gains in productivity were achieved largely through the reorganization of production and the division of labor; the machines themselves were crude by modern standards. . . . Over the course of the twentieth century, however, technology has become increasingly capital intensive. Agricultural mechanization now has the potential to displace far more people from rural employment, while factories need fewer workers to produce the same output. Technological improvements have also reduced substantially the time and money required to travel internationally, and modern mass communications have made inhabitants of the Third World more aware of opportunities and conditions abroad than were European peasants of the past. (1992:16)

The continuing instability in the Third World and its rapid population growth, along with the changes in production technology, communications, and travel, make international worker migration a generally safer and more immediately rewarding option at the individual and family level, deflecting dissatisfaction with regime performance from organized political challenge. So, while there were in 1987 perhaps 6,000 to 8,000 guerrillas fighting to overthrow the regime in El Salvador, it is estimated that between 250,000 and 300,000 Salvadorans migrated to the United States, some legally but most illegally, rather than fight on either side in the Salvadoran civil war. More than 200,000 Nicaraguans have left that country for the United States since the overthrow of Somoza, most of them hostile to the Sandinista regime, but less than 20,000 were fighting with the contras to overthrow the Managua government. Literally millions of Mexicans, lesser numbers of Filipinos, Koreans, Taiwanese, Haitians, Guatemalans, and Guyanese have migrated to the United States in search of a better life, rather than organize to try to change the political or social order in their own country. It is not necessary that the nation to which one migrates be a free or democratic society, as long as it provides opportunities or physical safety unavailable in one's home country. More than a million Ghanaians migrated to find work in oil-rich Nigeria in the 1970s (before being expelled when oil revenues shrank); hundreds of thousands of Egyptians, Koreans, and Pakistanis have found work in the oil-rich Gulf states of the Arabian peninsula despite severe restrictions on personal and political liberty there. In Europe, Turks, Yugoslavs, North Africans, Pakistanis, Indians, Caribbean blacks, and in most recent times Tamil refugees from Sri Lanka, boat people from Southeast Asia, and Sikhs from India have made their way to lands where better opportunities and physical safety are available.

The United Nations Report on the World Social Situation (1989:87–88) estimates that some 20 million people are working outside their own countries, with about 6 million in North America, 3 million in West Asia, and 3 million in Latin America. Several million, mostly from Turkey, North Africa, and South Asia, also work within the European Union. Even these large and increasing numbers account for only a tiny fraction of those in the Third World seeking greater opportunity and physical safety.

Several additional factors may deflect lower-class alienation away from social revolution. One is the cultural diversity of many Third World societies that makes organization of a broad popular movement difficult and offers ruling elites opportunities to play off ethnic, religious, racial, caste, or regional groups against each other. In some cases, popular anger may be shifted from the regime or the economic system onto "outcast" minorities. Overseas Chinese minorities, concentrated in the cities and prominent in trade and commerce, are often the subjects of racial distrust and open hostility (as in Malaysia, Indonesia, Vietnam, and Thailand). Lebanese communities in Ghana, Nigeria, and Brazil, Indians and Pakistanis in Uganda and elsewhere in East Africa, Jews in Iran and Argentina occupy similar positions as potential scapegoats.

In other cases, ethnic hostility among major population groupings may produce competition for political power, but along ethnic lines rather than class lines. Shifts in regimes may signal changes in fortune for ethnic patron-client networks, but do not challenge the basic dependency system, since cross-ethnic organization of workers and peasants is so difficult. In Guyana, there has been political competition between Cheddi Jagan's PPP (People's Progressive party) representing the East Indian population and former leader Forbes Burnham's PNC (People's National Congress) representing the black population. In Nigeria, divisions among the major (Hausa-Fulani, Yoruba, and Ibo) and minor tribal groupings have contributed to political instability and several military coups. Much the same could be said for Malaysia, where Malay, Chinese, and Indian patron-client networks have built a three-sector coalition party, the Alliance party, which has tried to maintain an ethnic balance over patronage and at the same time maintains an ethnic "division of labor" within the economy. Demands of the lower class find little opportunity for organized expression and the lower class lacks the strength to challenge the system in this environment.

Many examples of cultural cleavages overriding and hindering the expression of worker-peasant demands can be cited: Moslems and Christians in the Philippines; Indians and Europeans and mestizos and blacks, in varying mixtures, in Latin America; Persians, Azerbaijanis, Arabs, Baluchis, and Kurds in Iran; a welter of ethnic, linguistic, caste, and religious groups in India. In most circumstances, ethnic politics, even when racial, caste, or religious rioting and bloodshed result, may lend support to the maintenance of the dependency syndrome by deflecting class issues and making multiethnic worker-peasant movements unlikely. Ultimately, ethnic conflict tends to support existing patron-client networks and facilitates control of the system by dominant elites.

An exception to this notion may be found in societies where the ethnic dividing lines are also the social class divisions. In the white settler regimes in Rhodesia and South Africa, for example, the white European minority was both an ethnic group and the dominant bourgeoisie, while the black population, divided along tribal lines, was almost totally excluded from elite status. Cynthia Enloe (1973), in a study of ethnic conflict in the Third World, suggested that, in this situation, an ethnic confrontation with the dominant group might become a revolutionary challenge to the entire social order. Some Caribbean societies like Jamaica may fit into this category; the revolutionary overthrow of the Portuguese colonial regimes in Mozambique and Angola offered partial support for this thesis.

Another hindrance to broad-based class organization is the generational cleavage that is often found among the poor, especially within the urban working class. Wayne Cornelius (1975) has shown that, among the urban poor in Latin America, first-generation migrants from the countryside are less likely to engage in political protest or rebellion. Continuing links of kinship to the countryside, seasonal or occasional migration back to the village, general lack of urban social and political skills, and optimism about future prospects in the city all tend to diminish the likelihood that the first generational wave of urban migrants will revolt in any organized and sustained fashion against the system. Stuart Sinclair (1978) has also noted the optimism that pervades certain squatter developments on the edges of large Third World cities, and Lisa Redfield Peattie (1968) has described the pride in material progress that characterized one Venezuelan working-class barrio. For first-generation urban migrants, the basic orientation may be one of optimism and general support for an urban environment of apparent broad opportunities, particularly compared with the rural village. Mounting disappointments and frustrations of the first urban migrant generation may not change this basic orientation, at least not enough to produce a radical rejection of the entire system. Rejection of the system as a whole is far more likely within succeeding urban generations born and raised in the barrios, favelas, Sowetos, and bidonvilles of the Third World, who are wise in the ways and skills needed in the big city, are less likely to be optimistic about chances for personal success, and perhaps most important, do not compare their life-styles with an even poorer village life, but with the Western-style affluence of the urban elite, within sight but beyond reach.

One more outlet that may deflect mass alienation from revolutionary activity is criminal behavior. Crime in many societies, not only in the Third World, represents a mixed rejection and acceptance of the existing system. It represents personal rejection of the existing law and order, since the criminal seeks to attain goals through illegal means. Yet, this is a low-level rejection of the system and even at the level of large-scale urban looting, well-organized rural banditry, or urban crime syndicates, criminality does not threaten basic social and political structures. No social system has been overthrown by massive criminality. Occasionally rural bandits like Pancho Villa in Mexico and bandit insurgents in Colombia and India have become politicized, but these are the exceptions. It is the armed politicization, not the banditry, that represents a challenge (which is still ineffective). Professional crime may connect to and support the political system through routine corruption of government officials. Government corruption is a component of drug trafficking, smuggling, piracy, large-scale prostitution, and slave trade in various parts of the Third World. Mass prostitution for Western tourists was once one of the main attractions and a source of hard Western currency in prerevolutionary Havana. It is now a major tourist attraction in Manila, Bangkok, Nairobi, and Rio de Janeiro. It is estimated that drugs have replaced coffee beans as Colombia's leading export to the United States. These activities, although formally illegal and occasionally risky for the individuals involved, are a normal part of economic activity within the dependency syndrome, and therefore do not represent a challenge to, or even a deviation from, the pattern of dependent development.

At the local and most decentralized level, criminality may represent an acceptance of the system. Given the levels of unemployment and under-employment, criminality may represent a job placement decision to try to achieve a better material life through the use of personal skills and available opportunities. As in the developed nations, poverty in the Third World does not itself cause criminal behavior. Indeed, although there has been a general rise of rural crime (rustling, smuggling) in many Third World areas, the great growth in crime has been in the urban areas, which are economically better off than the villages. As in Sweden, Germany, and the United States, economic growth in Brazil, Mexico, and Nigeria has not reduced crime, but has been

Table 16.1   Percentage of the Labor Force Unemployed and Underemployed
in the Third World, 1975

	1975 Total	1975 Urban Only
Africa	45.0	35.9
Asia	40.3	30.1
Latin America	34.0	29.3
Third World	40.4	31.3

Sources: Adapted from *UN Handbook of the Social Situation*, 1979, and Sewell, 1977.

associated with large increases in crime. Criminologists Marshall Clinard and
David Abbott (1973), in a wide-ranging account of crime in the Third World,
point to the raised expectations and wider opportunities for criminal behavior
in the cities as reasons for the dramatic growth of crime. Urban areas, with
their glittering array of consumer goods, which change ideas of what is
"needed," offer greater anonymity, social disorganization, and heterogeneity.
The political system is both corrupt and institutionally less interested in
fighting crime than in repressing radical dissent and potential rebellion.

If it is correct that social revolution is one alternative to widespread
crime and political corruption, as we have argued, then it is probable that
widespread crime will continue to characterize the growing urban environments
of the Third World. One of the basic features of fighting crime and corruption
in Communist systems (see chapter 11) was thorough mobilization and coherent
organization of the population, combined with effective limitations on the
ability to accumulate great wealth. In post-communism, sudden social
disorganization and growing government corruption have led to growing
criminality, similar to the pattern in many Third World nations. Dependent
political systems are uninterested in organizing and mobilizing the population,
but are actively trying to prevent lower-class organizations from emerging.
They attempt to disarm or repress efforts by workers and peasants to politicize
their needs.

Rebellion, Counterorganization, and Revolution

Despite all barriers to an organized challenge, there are opportunities and
possibilities for organized resistance to imperialism and dependency. The
Japanese nationalist response to Western encroachments in the mid-nineteenth
century and the Russian, Chinese, Vietnamese, and Cuban revolutions in the
current century indicate that such challenges do arise, are difficult to defeat

once they become organized, and are able to overthrow entrenched Western-supported regimes.

The purpose of this chapter is to put into perspective the struggle against imperialism and dependency. In one fashion or another, this struggle has been going on for centuries in certain regions (India, South Africa, China). We noted (in chapter 12) that the division of the underdeveloped world into colonies and semicolonies during the latter part of the nineteenth century was not unopposed. The Filipino uprisings against American occupation, the Chinese Boxer Rebellion against all Western influences, the national liberation movement of Augusto Sandino in Nicaragua in the 1930s, and the MauMau rebellion in Kenya in the 1950s show that organized struggle for national independence and freedom from external domination has been constant though not continuous. Many of these earlier challenges have been forgotten or relatively undocumented by Western historians. The unsuccessful challenges tend to be relegated to historical oblivion, just as Indian and black slave revolts tended to be written out of American history.

Three types of organized response to imperialism and dependency outlined here have been: (1) traditionalism/fundamentalism; (2) nationalist counter-organization; and (3) socialist revolution. All three elements may be present, may form partial coalitions, may be synthesized within single organizations, or may compete for leadership of the anti-imperialist struggle, so that different orientations of the struggle may emerge in a single society.

Cultural or religious fundamentalism attacks the secularism and materialism of Westernization, the loss of ethical norms, and the intrusion of foreign life-styles by advocating a return to traditional ways, even to a rural peasant society. A recent example of the fundamentalist struggle is the Islamic movement in Iran, led by the organized mullahs and the Ayatollah Khomeini against the Shah and the American influence in Iranian society. The Ayatollah Khomeini regarded virtually all forms of modernization as signs of erosion in ethical values and of elements of foreign (mostly American) dominance within Iran, a dominance symbolized by the monarchy of the Pahlevi family. The overthrow of the pro-American Shah after several months of bloody confrontations between largely unarmed masses and the Shah's well-equipped army gives testimony to the potential strength of this reaction, at least in some areas. In Algeria, the Islamic Front would probably have won the first free elections there in 1991 after thirty years of one-party rule by the corrupted secular nationalist FLN, but the Algerian military cancelled the elections and started a campaign of repression that has led to violence against foreigners and mass executions of Islamic militants. In Egypt, the militant Moslem Brotherhood played a role in the opposition to former President Sadat's ''opening to the West,'' though without the success of the Ayatollah. In Afghanistan, local mullahs and village chiefs led an Islamic resistance movement to both the Marxist government in Kabul and the Soviet military occupation. In this

Islamic resurgence, Soviet hegemonism as well as Western imperialism were regarded as dangers, since both represented expansionist secular and materialist worldviews.

Outside the Moslem world, however, the strength of the traditionalist challenge to dependency seems to be in decline. The feudal Ethiopian monarchy has crumbled, and the Latin Catholic nationalist landowning oligarchies are in decline. At the local village level, traditionalism is now simply no match for the forces of development. Barring another worldwide depression, which would halt the expansion of the world market system, even the most remote regions will probably be reached by the international money-based economy, by mass communications, and by modern transportation by the end of the century.

A second response to dependency has been Third World counterorganization for defense of its interests against the core capitalist powers. A counter-organizational approach seeks to generate a self-sustained economic development through more effective bargaining between periphery and core capitalist nations (the post-Communist world is still relatively marginal to this strategy). The staff of the U.N. Economic Commission on Latin America (ECLA) and the thinking of Raul Prebisch was one center of this counterorganizational strategy and the inspiration for the birth of UNCTAD (see chapter 12), a forum for the North-South dialogue. One school of Latin American dependency theory hoped to foster national state-supported efforts to change the terms of trade between the periphery and core nations. This could be the result of more nationalist government orientations toward development by individual states, which would encourage the growth and support demands of a modern national business class able eventually to compete and bargain as equals with Western MNCs. It could also include formation of Third World bargaining coalitions or cartels with increased leverage to bargain with Western consumer nations or Western MNCs. Finally, counterorganization sometimes involved a conscious effort to "delink" the local economy from Western markets, not to improve the terms of trade, but rather to re-establish autonomous and internally directed development, with reliance on local skills, materials, and technology.

The first variety of counterorganizational response was tried by some nationalist regimes in Latin America, including the military government in Brazil, the Perón regime in Argentina, and through the policies of Mexicanization under the PRI in Mexico. Part of this strategy involved "import substitution," the gradual replacement of Western manufactured imports with domestically produced manufactures, sponsored and protected by the government through tariff barriers, quotas, or direct and indirect subsidies. Through this process, the national bourgeoisie was supposed to grow in strength and industrial competence and eventually to take the lead in a self-sustaining development. This strategy had much more appeal in the 1950s than it has today. Brazil, with its large population and natural resources, continued this import substitution industrialization (ISI) strategy under both civilian and military regimes from the 1940s to the 1980s; but under the recent regime of President Collor, Brazil has turned toward a more liberal trade and deregulation policy (which continued even after Collor was removed from office for corruption). In Mexico as well, the debt crisis of the 1980s forced the long-ruling PRI regime to abandon its Mexicanization program, and President Salinas' sponsorship of NAFTA now represents Mexico's new free trade and investment strategy.

A second type of counterorganization is illustrated by OPEC (Organization of Petroleum Exporting Countries). Although OPEC became widely known in the 1970s, it was originally founded in 1960 by Venezuela, Iran, Iraq, Kuwait, and Saudi Arabia for the purpose of checking the decline in oil prices, which were then set unilaterally by the Western oil multinationals. The price of crude oil had fallen from $2.17 per barrel in 1948 to only $1.80 per barrel in 1960. It was not until 1971 that OPEC succeeded in restoring oil prices to their 1940 level (Singh, 1977:4,6–7). Over this period from 1960 to 1971, however, OPEC was able to wrest basic control over price setting from the MNCs, and the Arab oil-producing nations were able, during the 1973 Yom Kippur War between Israel and Egypt, to institute an oil embargo against selected Western consumer nations and to immediately quadruple the price of OPEC-produced oil. OPEC has been the leading example of what a coalition of Third World nations, encompassing the major producers of a key commodity required by Western consumer nations, can achieve in shifting the terms of trade in favor of an organization of developing nations.

OPEC now includes a variety of nations from Latin America (Venezuela, Ecuador), black Africa (Nigeria, Gabon), and Asia (Indonesia, Iran), as well as the Arab world. Western governments have vacillated between hopes that OPEC would quickly disintegrate (from internal divisions, from Western covert or overt intervention, or from Western consumer cartelization) and fears that OPEC would become a model for Third World producer cartels. Neither fondest hopes nor darkest fears have proved accurate. OPEC became a relatively stable organization with three decades of experience, in which time it has effectively removed Western corporate control from the pricing system for crude oil. Oil, however, is a "special" commodity, vital in the short run to the economies of the West and unable to be replaced quickly by other energy sources or by conservation. Some efforts were made to repeat the OPEC counterorganization formula for bauxite (source for aluminum), with Jamaica's government taking the lead. Some possibilities existed for copper and tin; just four Third World nations accounted for at least half of all exports (52 percent in copper, 75 percent in tin) (Fishlow et al., 1978:35–36). But in these areas, alternative sources, both proven and potential, including recycling of scrap and greater possibilities for substitution of other metals, decreased the prospects for OPEC-like success.

OPEC has been an elite cartel, which has successfully challenged

Western oil companies' control of pricing. It did not attempt to build a broad popular movement or to provide new strategies for independent technological growth, military self-reliance, or democratic political institutions needed for a decisive break with the dependency syndrome. OPEC has certainly been far more successful than the broader counterorganizations, such as the Group of 77 working through UNCTAD and the fifty-eight Third World nations that negotiated the LOME I and LOME II trade agreements with the European Community. Even if OPEC were the only case of Third World counterorganization leading to a decisive break with dependency, it would still be an important strategy for a sizeable group of nations.

A third type of counterorganizational response was represented by the Tanzanian system, which has attempted to selectively "delink" itself from the world market system. President Julius Nyerere and the TANU party sponsored a development program, outlined in the Arusha Declaration, of both abstention from expensive consumer imports and local village self-development (Ujamaa). Here the state acted to restrict dependency on Western technology and manufactures and to promote development of an adapted, self-controlled technology appropriate for overall development at the village level. The Tanzanian program reduced social inequalities between city and village, and TANU allowed within its one-party system for considerable local feedback through multicandidate competition in parliamentary elections. Yet, by most accounts economic progress was slight, and the system did not achieve self-reliant development. The "delinking" strategy was also tried, to some extent, by the Burmese regime of General Ne Win and his Burmese Socialist Program party (BSPP); evaluations of the Burmese experience are even less favorable than those of the Tanzanian. It is doubtful that small and poor Third World nations can develop in isolation, since they lack material resource riches, a large labor pool, and a sizeable internal market for domestic products.

A relatively rare response to imperialism and dependency is socialist revolution. The aim is the overthrow of capitalism, which includes the overthrow of the local bourgeoisie's political and economic power and the power of the Western multinationals. This has included armed struggle against the bourgeoisie, the military, Western suppliers and advisors, and potentially against the soldiers of the Western powers. The tactics, intensity, and duration of armed struggle have been quite varied. In China, huge peasant-based forces of the People's Liberation Army (PLA) fought a bitter civil war against Chiang Kai-shek's Nationalist armies (backed by the United States) for two decades before final victory in 1949. In Cuba, on the other hand, Fidel Castro's Rebel Army of at most three thousand was able, in a few years of hit-and-run raids, to demoralize Batista's military and to convince Batista and his army associates to flee the country, leaving the rebels victorious largely by default. In Vietnam, the Vietminh of Ho Chi Minh fought against the Japanese occupation in World War II, against the French attempt to recolonize the country from 1945 to 1954, and against the American intervention in the 1960s and 1970s. Some of this epic struggle took the form of guerrilla warfare, some was a more conventional battlefield campaign. The main adversary of the Vietnamese communist (Lao Dong) party was the foreign occupier of the country, and once the Japanese, or the French, or the Americans withdrew, the outcome of the internal struggle was clear. The puppet regimes supported by the French and the Americans in Vietnam had little support and crumbled quickly once their foreign sponsorship weakened.

Broad-based revolutionary movements in the Third World had some success in virtually every region during the Cold War, from Cuba and Nicaragua in the Latin America/Caribbean realm, China and Vietnam in Asia, to Angola and Mozambique in Africa. But these were still exceptions, since many more revolutionary movements were defeated or stalemated in long inconclusive struggles. The Tupamaros in Uruguay and the Montoneros and the Trotskyite ERP in Argentina were defeated in the so-called "dirty wars" of military and police repression. Fretelin in East Timor was starved to death by the Indonesian military dictatorship. The Communist party of Thailand and the New People's Army of the Philippines were unable to duplicate the victory of the Vietnamese Communists, just as leftist guerrilla fronts were stalemated in El Salvador and Guatemala, despite the example of the Sandinistas in neighboring Nicaragua. Democratic openings led other Third World revolutionary movements to adopt more moderate reform politics. SWAPO in Namiba came to power through free elections, not through revolution, and the African National Congress abandoned its armed struggle after the white elite announced its intention to abandon the racist apartheid system in South Africa.

Revolutionary victories during the Cold War produced both encouragement and support (the "domino effect") for other radical movements and also increased support from the United States and its allies for counterinsurgency measures and support for threatened Third World countries. The general tricontinental (Asia, Africa, Latin America) wave of popular insurgency called for by Che Guevara ("one, two, many revolutions") never even remotely materialized. Social revolution is a traumatic and exceptional event in the history of any society, one which the people do not risk without great provocation and some hope of success.

Soviet support or military intervention for some Marxist regimes—in Afghanistan, in Cambodia, in Ethiopia, and in Angola—provoked Western-backed anti-Communist guerrilla resistance but kept these regimes in power as increasingly Soviet-dependent client states. With the collapse of the Soviet Union, all of these regimes were critically weakened; the Dergue regime in Ethiopia collapsed in 1991, the Hun Sen regime reached a power-sharing coalition with royalist forces after elections in 1993, remnants of the Communist Kabul military still contest for power with mujahideen factions in Afghanistan, and the Angolan civil war resumed after UNITA's Jonas Savimbi refused to accept his defeat in free elections by the ruling MPLA. The end of the Cold War has not yet (in 1994) led to a full peace in any of these nations, but has opened some new prospects for negotiated settlements.

The social and economic conditions that produced revolutionary uprisings with some regularity in the Third World have not been transformed by the end of the Cold War. It is likely that the miserable performance of some Third World regimes will continue on occasion to provoke a radical challenge to established elites. Revolutionary organizations may, after the demise of the Soviet Union, prefer to work for democratic change, especially if the West is willing to drop its support for its most corrupt or brutal former clients (Mobutu in Zaire, the military in El Salvador, Guatemala, Honduras, or the Suharto regime in Indonesia). However, if the "democracy trend" falters, or if U.S. policy continues to back right-wing authoritarian regimes in support of U.S. investments and "favorable" trade relations, then revolutionary situations will reappear under new guises and with new strategies for greater equity and social justice.

ESSAY: FINALLY EXITING THE THIRD WORLD?

With the end of the Cold War, the Second World of Communist party-states is gradually disappearing, and the conception of a Third World of political systems comes ever more into question. One concept of the Third World—as an arena of East-West superpower competition—has vanished, but another conception, that of a disadvantaged group of mostly "new" ex-colonial states, remains. In the post–Cold War era, more attention will be directed to the successes and failures of the developing nations in overcoming and therefore "exiting" this remaining Third World definition. There is reason to think that pressures on Third World regimes to perform better for the majority of citizens, rather than for foreign patrons, tiny privileged elites, or narrow-based middle classes, will grow.

Three interconnected themes mark the growing pressures on political systems of the developing nations. The severe disconnection between aggregate economic growth and a fair distribution of its benefits is all the more glaring in the aftermath of the Cold War. The Western success model promised both growth and some measure of social justice, a combination that helped build solid popular support against communism, which also promised both but could not sustain the promise. With communism defeated, but with inequalities in Third World regimes still enormous, the rising question must be: When does social equity show up at long last? Especially in the more successful Newly Industrialized Countries (NICs) of East Asia, Latin America, and Southeast Asia, economic modernization has long ago passed Kuznets' early stage of increasing inequality, and now the benefits of economic transformation should be broadly shared by the whole people. The growing urban working class, which produces wealth from export-oriented industries, is less fatalistic than the traditional peasantry and increasingly compares its standard of living to that of workers in the Western democracies (just as East German, Soviet, and Chinese citizens have done). Equity cannot be forever sacrificed on the altar of growth in the Third World, any more than growth could forever be held back by statist egalitarianism in the Communist world.

Authoritarian dictatorship in the Third World, now that communism is disappearing, has become significantly more unacceptable. The democracy trend in Latin America and Asia was seen in the 1980s as an argument against communism, which by comparison looked even more dictatorial and outmoded (the "dinosaur" imagery). But with the collapse of most Communist regimes, now the "dinosaurs" of authoritarianism are the long-running dictatorships of Mobutu in Zaire, the PRI one-party state in Mexico, the military-backed regime in Indonesia, the feudal monarchies of the Persian Gulf, and the military juntas of Nigeria. Of course, even with the decline in economic power of the older landowning and traditional elites, and the opening of the Catholic church to an "option for the poor," the military and state bureaucratic elites have considerable power to repress, to divide, and to divert popular discontent. Still, with the historic failure of Communist dictatorship, there is ever less legitimacy for other types of dictatorship (and little reason for the United States to continue to support murderous or hopelessly corrupt thugs as it did during the Cold War).

The collapse of one system of dependency, the 1989–90 largely peaceful overthrow of Moscow-dependent regimes in Eastern Europe, and the restoration of national sovereignty and self-determination in that region, may also provide hope for Third World nations overcoming their dependency relations. The restoration of self-confidence and pride in independent achievement, which can be seen also in East Asia, makes it less possible to blame outside forces for political failures and makes political corruption, incompetance, and venality all the more intolerable. If dependency relations can be overcome by some success formulas, and they may be varied, then the "failure of nations" becomes less excusable. The first generation of postindependence leaders or regimes are now departing. To take one illustrative case, Felix Houphoet-Boigny, who ruled Ivory Coast for thirty-three years after independence from France, died in December 1993, leaving his potentially rich land, once considered a budding success story in West Africa, in an economic tailspin and with a totally looted treasury. For better or for worse, a new generation of leaders faces the challenge of picking up the pieces, learning from experience, and managing the political life of the nation more effectively.

New leaders and new regimes, however, may not be able to

govern effectively, especially if there is no sense of nationhood or popular solidarity after years of elite misrule and corruption. Some Third World nations may face long-term turmoil and division along ethnic, clan, religious, or tribal lines in an attempt to find some new basis for a common political life. Exiting the Third World after the Cold War may mean the death of some failed states; there is no guarantee or blanket optimism that a success formula will emerge for each nation. But the pressure on regimes to do better will likely increase.

Although the end of the Cold War did not directly change any regimes in the Third World and did not improve the bargaining position of the developing nations in the world trading (GATT) and financial (IMF, World Bank) order, the new era will contrast even more the social situation of the developing nations with that of the affluent democracies. Political regimes, now deprived of easy Cold War leverage with Washington or Moscow, will have to perform better, hopefully with less external patronage, to gain some minimal loyalty of their own people. In an era of great change in all regions of the globe, the developing nations have a new challenge, and their people have new expectations, of a more responsible and effective political leadership.

References

Chapter 1: Learning from Comparison—Today More Than Ever

Bell, Daniel. *The Coming of Post-Industrial Society.* New York: Basic Books, 1974.
Huntington, Samuel. ''The Clash of Civilizations?'' *Foreign Affairs* (Summer 1993), 74(3).
Jowitt, Kenneth. *The New World Disorder.* Berkeley: Univ. of California Press, 1993.
McClelland, J.S., ed. *The French Right from de Maistre to Maurras.* New York: Harper, 1970.
Laidler, Harry. *The History of Socialism.* New York: Crowell, 1968.
Rejai, Mostafa. *Comparative Political Ideologies.* New York: St. Martin's, 1984.
Ross, Robert, and Kent Trachte. *Global Capitalism: The New Leviathan.* Albany: State Univ. of New York Press, 1990.
Sigmund, Paul. *The Ideologies of the Developing Nations.* New York: Praeger, 1967.

Chapter 2: From the Liberal Welfare State to a Post-Industrial Democracy

Adams, John Clarke. *The Quest for Democratic Law.* New York: Crowell, 1970.
Bracher, Karl-Dietrich. *The German Dictatorship.* New York: Praeger, 1970.
Brogan, D. W., and Douglas Verney. *Political Patterns in Today's World.* New York: Harcourt, Brace and World, 1968.
Giddens, Anthony. *The Class Structure of the Advanced Societies.* New York: Barnes and Noble, 1973.
Hancock, M. Donald. *Sweden: The Politics of Post-Industrial Change.* Hinsdale, Ill.: Dryden Press, 1972.
Hartz, Louis. *The Liberal Tradition in America.* New York: Harcourt Brace, 1955.
Heidenheimer, Arnold. *The Governments of Germany.* New York: Crowell, 1971.
Heidenheimer, Arnold, Hugh Heclo, and Carolyn Adams, *Comparative Public Policy: The Politics of Social Change in America, Europe and Japan.* New York: St. Martin's, 1990.
Herlitz, Nils. *Sweden: A Modern Democracy on Ancient Foundations.* Minneapolis: Univ. of Minnesota Press, 1939.
Hobbes, Thomas. *Leviathan.* New York: Collier Books, 1962. Originally published in 1651.
Ike, Nobutaka. ''Economic Growth and Intergenerational Change in Japan.'' *American Political Science Review* (Dec. 1973), 67:1194–1203.
Johnson, Chalmers. *MITI and the Japanese Miracle.* Berkeley: Univ. of California Press, 1982.
Kennedy, Paul. *The Rise and Fall of the Great Powers.* New York: Random House, 1987.

Knauerhase, Ramon. *An Introduction to National Socialism 1920–1939*. Columbus, Ohio: Merrill, 1972.

Krieger, Leonard. *The German Idea of Freedom*. Chicago: Univ. of Chicago Press, 1972.

Leicht, Robert. "Wenn die alten Lehren wanken." *die Zeit*, Oct. 22, 1993, p.3.

Linz, Juan. "The Perils of Presidentialism." *Journal of Democracy* (Winter 1990), 1(1).

Lipset, S. Martin. *Political Man*. New York: Doubleday, 1963.

Locke, John. *The Second Treatise of Government*. New York: Bobbs-Merrill, 1952. Originally published 1690.

Mann, Golo. *History of Germany Since 1789*. London: Chatte and Windus, 1968.

Nagle, John. *The National Democratic Party: Right Radicalism in the Federal Republic of Germany*. Berkeley: Univ. of California Press, 1970.

Neumann, Franz. *Behemoth*. New York: Harper and Row, 1942.

Nolte, Ernest. *Three Faces of Fascism*. New York: Mentor, 1966.

Pempel, T. J. *Policy and Politics in Japan: Creative Conservatism*. Philadelphia, Penn.: Temple Univ. Press, 1982.

Prestowitz, Clyde. *Trading Places: How We Allowed Japan to Take the Lead*. New York: Basic Books, 1988.

Reischauer, Edwin. *The Japanese Today: Change and Continuity*. Cambridge: Harvard Univ. Press, 1988.

Riding, Alan. "In a Time of Shared Hardship, the Young Embrace Europe." *New York Times*, Aug. 12, 1993, p.1.

Rustow, Dankwart. *The Politics of Compromise*. Princeton, N.J.: Princeton Univ. Press, 1955.

Scalapino, Robert, and Junnosuke Masumi. *Parties and Politics in Contemporary Japan*. Berkeley: Univ. of California Press, 1962.

Schweitzer, Arthur. *Big Business in the Third Reich*. Bloomington: Univ. of Indiana Press, 1964.

Smith, Adam. *An Inquiry into the Nature and Causes of the Wealth of Nations*. New York: Modern Library, 1939.

Tucker, Robert, ed. *Marx-Engels Reader*. New York: Norton, 1972.

Vermeil, Edmond. *Germany's Three Reichs*. New York: H. Fertig, 1969.

Verney, Douglas. *Parliamentary Reform in Sweden, 1866–1921*. Oxford: Clarendon Press, 1957.

Chapter 3: Affluent Consumerism—Now in Danger?

Anderson, Odin. *Health Care: Can There Be Equity?* New York: Wiley, 1972.

Ashton, T. S. *The Industrial Revolution 1760–1830*. London: Oxford Univ. Press, 1948.

Groth, Alexander. *Comparative Politics: A Distributive Approach*. New York: Macmillan, 1971.

Heidenheimer, Arnold, Hugh Heclo, and Carolyn Adams. *Comparative Public Policy*. New York: St. Martin's, 1975.

Heidenheimer, Arnold, Hugh Heclo, and Carolyn Adams, *Comparative Public Policy: The Politics of Social Change in America, Europe and Japan*. New York: St. Martin's, 1990.

Jackman, Robert. *Politics and Social Equality: A Comparative Analysis*. New York: Wiley, 1975.

Parkin, Frank. *Class Inequality and Political Order*. New York: Praeger, 1971.

Pryor, Frederic. *Public Expenditures in Communist and Capitalist Nations*. London: Allen and Unwin, 1968.

Rosenstein-Rodan, Paul N. "The Haves and Have-Nots Around the Year 2000." In J. N. Bhagwati, ed., *Economics and World Order*. London: Macmillan, 1972.

Schmid, Klaus-Peter. "Modell mit Mängeln." *die Zeit*, June 29, 1990.

Tomasson, Richard F. "From Elitism to Egalitarianism in Swedish Education." *Sociology of Education* (Spring 1965).

Tucker, Robert, ed. *Marx-Engels Reader*. New York: Norton, 1972.

Wilensky, Harold. *The Welfare State and Equality*. Berkeley: Univ. of California Press, 1975.

Chapter 4: Social Equality—An Eroding Commitment

Aburdene, Patricia, and John Naisbitt. *Megatrends for Women*. New York: Villard, 1992.

Bacon, John, and J. B. Mays. *Crime and Its Treatment*. London: Longman, 1970.

Bell, Daniel. "Meritocracy and Equality." *Public Interest* (Fall 1972).

Bell, Daniel. *The Coming of Post-Industrial Society*. New York: Basic Books, 1974.

Bernard, Jesse. *Women and the Public Interest*. Chicago: Aldine, 1971.

Blondel, Jean. *Comparative Legislatures*. Englewood Cliffs, N.J.: Prentice-Hall, 1973.

Bottomore, Thomas B. *Elites and Society*. London: Penguin, 1966.

Clinard, Marshall, and Peter Yeager. *Corporate Crime*. New York: Free Press, 1980.

Cohen, David. "Does IQ Matter?" *Commentary* (April 1972).

Coleman, James, et al. *Equality of Educational Opportunities*. Washington, D.C.: U.S. Government Printing Office, 1966.

Coons, John, et al. *Private Wealth and Public Education*. Cambridge, Mass.: Belknap Press, 1970.

Cressey, Donald. *Delinquency, Crime, and Differential Association*. The Hague: M. Nijhoff, 1974.

Cromwell, Jerry. "The Size Distribution of Income." In *Review of Income and Wealth*. New Haven, Conn.: International Association for Research in Income and Wealth, 1977.

Geis, Gilbert. "White Collar Crime." In M. Clinard and R. Quinney, eds., *Criminal Behavior Systems*. New York: Holt, Rinehart and Winston, 1967.

Giddens, Anthony. *Class Structure of the Advanced Societies*. New York: Barnes and Noble, 1973.

Giele, Janet. *Women: Roles and Status in Eight Countries*. New York: Wiley, 1977.

Gordon, David. "Class and the Economics of Crime." In D. Gordon, ed., *Problems in Political Economy*, 2d ed. Lexington, Mass.: D. C. Heath, 1977.

Gurr, Theodore, Peter Grabosky, and Richard Hula. *Politics of Crime and Conflict*. Beverly Hills, Calif.: Sage, 1977.

Harrington, Michael. *The Twilight of Capitalism*. New York: Simon and Schuster, 1976.

Heidenheimer, Arnold, Hugh Heclo, and Carolyn T. Adams. *Comparative Public Policy*. New York: St. Martin's, 1975.

Henle, Peter. "Exploring the Distribution of National Income." *Monthly Labor Review* (Dec. 1972), 95 (12).

Hewlett, Sylvia. *A Lesser Life: The Myth of Women's Liberation in America*. New York: Morrow, 1986.

Howe, James. *United States and World Development: Agenda for Action 1975*. New York: Praeger, 1975.

Iglitzin, Lynn, and R. Ross. *Women in the World*. Santa Barbara, Calif.: CLIO Books, 1976.

Jencks, Christopher. *Inequality*. New York: Basic Books, 1972.

Kessler, Denis, and Andre Masson, "Personal Wealth Distribution in France." In E. Wolff, ed., *International Comparisons of the Distribution of Household Wealth*. Oxford: Clarendon, 1987.

Kloby, Jerry. "The Growing Divide: Class Polarization in the 1980's." *Monthly Review* (Sept. 1987), 39(4).

Kolko, Gabriel. *Wealth and Power in America*. New York: Praeger, 1962.

Kubota, Akira. *Higher Civil Servants in Postwar Japan*. Princeton, N.J.: Princeton Univ. Press, 1969.

Lampman, Robert. *Changes in the Share of Wealth*. New York: National Bureau of Economic Research, 1960.

Little, Alan, and John Westergaard. "The Trend of Class Differentials." *British Journal of Sociology* (1964), 15.

Mandel, William. *Soviet Women*. Garden City, N.Y.: Anchor, 1975.

Matthews, Donald. *The Social Background of Political Decision-Makers*. New York: Random House, 1954.

Mayer, Lawrence. *Politics in Industrial Societies*. New York: Wiley, 1977.

Meade, James. *Efficiency, Equality and the Ownership of Property*. London: Allen and Unwin, 1964.

Means, Ingunn N. "Scandinavian Women." In L. Iglitzin and R. Ross, eds., *Women in the World*. Santa Barbara, Calif.: CLIO Books, 1976.

Miliband, Ralph. *The State in Capitalist Society*. New York: Basic Books, 1969.

Miller, S.M. "Comparative Social Mobility." *Current Sociology* (1969), 1.

Mills, C. Wright. *The Power Elite*. New York: Oxford Univ. Press, 1956.

Musgrove, Richard. *Fiscal Systems*. New Haven, Conn.: Yale Univ. Press, 1969.

Nagle, John. *System and Succession*. Austin: Univ. of Texas Press, 1977.

Nagle, John. "In Banks We Trust." In H. See and D. Schenck, eds., *Wirtschaftsverbrechen*. Cologne: Kiepenheuer and Witsch, 1992.

Nasar, Sylvia. "Those Born Wealthy or Poor Usually Stay So, Studies Say." *New York Times*, May 18, 1992, p.1.

Parkin, Frank. *Class Inequality and Political Order*. New York: Praeger, 1971.

Peters, Guy. *The Politics of Bureaucracy*. New York: Longman, 1978.

Pizzo, Stephen, Mary Fricker, and Paul Muolo. *Inside Job: The Looting of America's Savings & Loans*. New York: HarperCollins, 1991.

Putnam, Robert. *Comparative Study of Political Elites*. Englewood Cliffs, N.J.: Prentice-Hall, 1976.

Quinney, Richard. *Social Reality of Crime*. Boston, Mass.: Little, Brown, 1970.

Rimlinger, Gaston. *Welfare Policy and Industrialization in Europe*. New York: Wiley, 1971.

Schafer, Stephen, ed. *Readings in Contemporary Criminology*. Reston, Va.: Reston, 1976.

Schnitzer, Martin. *Income Distribution*. New York: Praeger, 1974.

See, Hans. *Kapitalverbrechen*. Düsseldorf: Claassen, 1990.

Smeeding, Timothy. "Why the U.S. Antipoverty System Doesn't Work Very Well." *Challenge*, Jan.–Feb. 1992.

Smeeding, Timothy, and John Coder. "Income Inequality in Rich Countries during the 1980s." *Journal of Income Distribution*, June 1993.

Smith, James. "Recent Trends in the Distribution of Wealth in the U.S." In Wolff, *International Comparisons*, 1987.

Spant, Roland. "Wealth Distribution in Sweden, 1920–1983." In Wolff, *International Comparisons*, 1987.

Stern, Philip. *The Rape of the Taxpayer*. New York: Random House, 1973.

Sullerot, E. *Women, Society, and Change*. New York: McGraw-Hill, 1971.

Sutherland, Edwin. *Criminology*, 9th ed. Philadelphia, Pa.: Lippincott, 1974.

Tanzi, Vito. *Individual Income Tax and Economic Growth*. Baltimore, Md.: Johns Hopkins Univ. Press, 1969.

Westergaard, John. "The Withering Away of Class: A Contemporary Myth." In P. Anderson and R. Blackburn, eds., *Toward Socialism*. Ithaca, N.Y.: Cornell Univ. Press, 1965.

Wilensky, Harold. *The Welfare State and Equality*. Berkeley: Univ. of California Press, 1975.

Williamson, Jeffrey, and Peter Lindert. "Three Centuries of American Inequality." In P. Uselding, ed., *Research in Economic History*. Greenwich, Conn.: JAI Press, 1976.

Wolff, Edward. "Introduction and Overview." In Wolff, *International Comparisons*, 1987.

Wolff, Edward, and Marcia Marley. "Long-term Trends in U.S. Wealth Inequality." In R. Lipsey and H. Tice, eds., *The Measurement of Saving, Investment, and Wealth*. Chicago: Univ. of Chicago Press, 1989.

REFERENCES

Chapter 5: Liberty—Historic Gains Need to Be Defended

Darnton, John. "Western Europe Is Ending Its Welcome to Immigrants." *New York Times*, Aug. 10, 1993, p.1.

Gans, Herbert. *More Equality*. New York: Pantheon, 1973.

Gastil, Raymond. "Survey." *Freedom at Issue* (Jan.-Feb. 1976).

Gastil, Raymond. *Freedom in the World: Political Rights and Civil Liberties 1978*. New York: Freedom House, 1978.

Jones, Mary. *The Autobiography of Mother Jones*. Chicago, Ill.: C. H. Kerr, 1925.

Nagle, John. *The National Democratic Party: Right Radicalism in the Federal Republic of Germany*. Berkeley: Univ. of California Press, 1970.

Parenti, Michael. *Democracy for the Few*. New York: St. Martin's, 1974.

Smothers, Ronald. "Memorial Honors the Victims of Racial Violence." *New York Times*, Nov. 4, 1989.

Stouffer, Samuel. *Communism, Conformity and Civil Liberties*. Garden City, N.Y.: Doubleday, 1954.

Wolfe, Alan. *The Seamy Side of Democracy*. New York: McKay, 1973.

Chapter 6: Quality of Life—The Disillusionment of Modernity

Bakalar, James, and Lester Grinspoon. *Drug Control in a Free Society*. New York: Cambridge Univ. Press, 1984.

Bejerot, Nils. *Addiction and Society*. Springfield, Ill.: Charles C. Thomas, 1970.

Bell, Daniel. "Crime as a Way of Life." *Antioch Review* (Summer 1953), 13(2).

Bell, Daniel. *The Cultural Crisis of Capitalism*. New York: Basic Books, 1976.

Bohm, Peter, and Allan Kneese, eds. *The Economics of Environment*. London: Macmillan, 1971.

Cantril, Hadley. *The Pattern of Human Concern*. New Brunswick, N.J.: Rutgers Univ. Press, 1965.

Commoner, Barry. "The Environment." *New Yorker*, June 15, 1987.

Daniels, Arne. "Blockade in der Job-Maschine." *die Zeit* July 23, 1993, pp. 9–10.

Enloe, Cynthia. *The Politics of Pollution in a Comparative Perspective*. New York: McKay, 1975.

Erlanger, Stephen. "Japan's Urban Underside Erupts." *New York Times*, Oct. 11, 1990.

Fromm, Erich. *The Sane Society*. New York: Holt, Rinehart and Winston, 1955.

Goodwin, Richard. *The American Condition*. Garden City, N.Y.: Doubleday, 1974.

Gordon, David, ed. *Problems in Political Economy*, 2d ed. Lexington, Mass.: D.C. Heath, 1977.

Gurr, Theodore R., Peter Grabosky, and Richard Hula. *The Politics of Crime and Conflict*. Beverly Hills, Calif.: Sage, 1977.

Holahan, John F. "The Economics of Heroin." In P. Wald and P. Hutt, eds., *Dealing with Drug Abuse*. New York: Praeger, 1972.

John Paul II. 1991 "Centesimus Annus." Reprinted in *Origins* (May 16, 1991), 2(1).

Lewis, Paul. "For the World Economy, Even the Best Signs are None Too Good." *New York Times* Briefing Papers for Public Affairs, 1978.

Loraine, John A. *The Death of Tomorrow*. Philadelphia, Penn.: Lippincott. 1972.

Marcuse, Herbert. *One Dimensional Man*. Boston, Mass.: Beacon Press, 1967.

May, Edgar. "Narcotics Addiction and Control in Great Britain." In P. Wald and P. Hutt, eds., *Dealing with Drug Abuse*. New York: Praeger, 1972.

Nettler, Groyan. *Explaining Crime*. New York: McGraw-Hill, 1974:

Quinney, Richard. *The Social Reality of Crime*. Boston, Mass.: Little, Brown, 1969.

Quinney, Richard. *Class, State and Crime*. New York: McKay, 1977.

Reisman, David, Nathan Glazer, and Reuel Denny. *The Lonely Crowd*. Garden City, N.Y.: Doubleday, 1950.

Rhinestein, Max. *Marriage Stability, Divorce, and the Law*. Chicago, Ill.: Univ. of Chicago Press, 1972.

Schneider, Hans Joachim. "Crime and Criminal Policy in Some Western European and North American Countries." In *International Review of Criminal Policy*. New York: United Nations, 1980.

Schnitzer, Martin. *The Economy of Sweden*. New York: Praeger, 1970.

See, Hans. *Kapitalverbrechen*. Düsseldorf: Claassen, 1990.

Sussman, Marvin. "Family, Kinship and Bureaucracy." In A. Campbell and P. Converse, eds., *The Human Meaning of Social Change*. New York: Russell Sage, 1972.

United Nations. *1989 Report on the World Social Situation*. New York: United Nations, 1989.

Wald, Patricia, and Peter Hutt. *Dealing with Drug Abuse*. New York: Praeger, 1972.

Ward, Barbara. *The Home of Man*. New York: Norton, 1976.

Ziegler, Jean. *In der Schweiz wird weisser gewaschen*. 1990.

Chapter 7: The Rise and Fall of Communism

Bernstein, Eduard. *Evolutionary Socialism*. New York: Schocken, 1975.

Bertsch, Gary, and Thomas Ganschow, eds. *Comparative Communism: The Soviet, Chinese, and Yugoslav Models*. San Francisco, Calif.: W. H. Freeman, 1976.

Harcave, Sidney. *Russia: A History*. Chicago, Ill.: Lippincott, 1959.

Moore, Barrington. *Terror and Progress*. New York: Harper and Row, 1966.

Tucker, Robert, ed. *The Lenin Anthology*. New York: Norton, 1975.

Tucker, Robert. *The Marx-Engels Reader*. New York: Norton, 1978.

Westoby, Adam. *The Evolution of Communism*. New York, Free Press, 1989.

Chapter 8: Two Historic Transitions in Economic Development

Abouchar, Alan. *Economic Evaluation of Soviet Socialism*. New York: Pergamon Press, 1979.

Beyme, Klaus von. *Reformpolitik und sozialer Wandel in der Sowjetunion, 1970–1988*, Baden-Baden: Nomos, 1988.

Bush, Keith. "Soviet Living Standards: Some Salient Data." In *Economic Aspects of Life in the USSR*. Brussels: NATO Directorate of Economic Affairs, 1975.

Campbell, Robert. *Soviet Economic Power: Its Organization, Growth, and Challenge*. Boston, Mass.: Houghton-Mifflin, 1960.

Economist Intelligence Unit. "Country Report—Russia—3rd Quarter, 1993." London: Economist, 1993.

Feldmesser, Robert. "Social Status and Access to Higher Education." *Harvard Educational Review* (1957), 27 (2).

Gaaster, Michael. *China's Struggle to Modernize*. New York: Knopf, 1972.

Gripp, Richard C. *The Political System of Communism*. New York: Dodd, Mead, 1973.

Groth, Alexander. *Comparative Politics: A Distributional Approach*. New York: Macmillan, 1971.

Hinton, William H. "China's New Family Concept." *Monthly Review* (Nov. 1983), 36 (6):1–28.

Horvat, Branko. *An Essay on Yugoslav Society*. White Plains, N.Y.: International Arts and Sciences Press, 1969.

Jacobs, Everett. "Urban Housing in the Soviet Union." In *Economic Aspects of Life in the USSR*. Brussels: NATO Directorate of Economic Affairs, 1975.

Lane, David. *The End of Inequality?* Middlesex, England: Penguin, 1971.

Mayer, Lawrence. *Politics in Industrial Societies*. New York: Wiley, 1977.

Milenkovitch, Deborah. *Planning and Market in Yugoslav Economic Thought*. New Haven, Conn.: Yale Univ. Press, 1971.

Millar, James, ed. *Politics, Work, and Daily Life in the USSR*. New York: Cambridge Univ. Press, 1987.

Oksenberg, Michael. *China's Developmental Experience*. New York: Praeger, 1973.

Osborn, Robert. *Soviet Social Policies: Welfare, Equality and Community*. Homewood, Ill.: Dorsey Press, 1970.

Pryor, Frederic. *Public Expenditures in Communist and Capitalist Nations*. London: Allen and Unwin, 1968.

Rose, Richard. "Contradictions between Micro- and Macro-Economic Goals in Post-Communist Societies." *Europe-Asia Studies* (1993) 45(3):419–44.

Schell, Orville. "A Reporter at Large (China)." *New Yorker*, Jan. 23, 1984, pp. 43–85.

Segbers, Klaus. *Der sowjetische Systemwandel*, Frankfurt: Suhrkamp, 1989.

Sewell, James. *United States and World Development: Agenda for Action 1977*. New York: Praeger, 1977.

Sherman, Howard. *The Soviet Economy*. Boston: Little, Brown, 1969.

U.S. Department of Commerce. *Statistical Abstract of the United States 1990*. Washington, D.C.: U.S. Government Printing Office, 1990.

Wilensky, Harold. *The Welfare State and Equality*. Berkeley: Univ. of California Press, 1975.

Chapter 9: Social Equality—From State Egalitarianism to the New Inequalities

Aspaturian, V. V. "The Non-Russian Nationalities." In A. Kassof, ed., *Prospects for Soviet Society*. London: Pall Mall Press, 1968.

Chapman, Janet. "Are Earnings More Equal Under Socialism?" In John Moroney, ed., *Income Inequality*. Lexington, Mass.: Lexington Books, 1979.

Cromwell, Jerry. "The Size Distribution of Income: An International Comparison." *Review of Income and Wealth* (Sept. 1977), 23 (3): 291–308.

Djilas, Milovan. *The New Class*. New York: Holt, Rinehart and Winston, 1957.

Dodge, Norton. "Women in the Professions." In D. Atkinson, A. Dallin, and G. Lapidus, eds., *Women in Russia*. Stanford, Calif.: Stanford Univ. Press, 1977.

Echols, John M. "Does Socialism Mean Greater Equality?" *American Journal of Political Science* (Feb. 1981), 25 (1).

Fischer, George. *The Soviet System and Modern Society*. New York: Atherton, 1968.

Funk, Nanette, and Magda Mueller, eds. *Gender Politics and Post-Communism*. London: Routledge, 1993.

Giddens, Anthony. *Class Structure in the Advanced Societies*. New York: Harper, 1973.

Gordon, Leonid, and E. Klopov. *Man after Work*. Moscow: Progress Pub., 1975.

Hoffmann, Erik. *The Politics of Economic Modernization in the Soviet Union*. Ithaca, N.Y.: Cornell Univ. Press, 1982.

Howe, James. *United States and World Development: Agenda for Action 1975*. New York: Praeger, 1975.

Huntington, Samuel, and Zbigniew Brzezinski. *Political Power: USA/USSR*. New York: Viking, 1973.

Kamm, Henry. "End of Communism Worsens Anti-Gypsy Racism." *New York Times*, Nov. 17, 1993, p.12.

Kirschen, E.S. *Economic Policies Compared*. Amsterdam: North Holland-Elsevier, 1974.

Lane, David. *Politics and Society in the USSR*. New York: Random House, 1971(a).

Lane, David. *The End of Inequality?* Manchester: Penguin, 1971(b).

Mandel, William. *Soviet Women*. New York: Anchor, 1975.

Matthews, Mervyn. "Top Incomes in the USSR." In *Economic Aspects of Life in the USSR.* Brussels: NATO Directorate of Economic Affairs, 1975.

Moses, Joel. "The Soviet Union in the Women's Decade 1975–1985." In L. Iglitzin and R. Ross, eds., *Women in the World.* Santa Barbara, Calif.: Clio Press, 1986.

Nadle, Marlene. "For Men Only? NO!" *World Monitor*, May 1992.

Nagle, John. *System and Succession: The Social Bases of Political Elite Recruitment.* Austin: Univ. of Texas Press, 1977.

Nelson, Daniel, ed. *Communism and the Politics of Inequalities.* Lexington, Mass.: Lexington Books, 1983.

Parkin, Frank. *Class Inequality and Political Order.* New York: Praeger, 1971.

Rai, Shirin, Hilary Pilkington, and Annie Phizacklea, eds. *Women in the Face of Change: The Soviet Union, Eastern Europe, and China.* London: Routledge, 1992.

Sacks, Michael P. "Women in the Industrial Labor Force." In *Women in Russia.* Stanford, Calif.: Stanford Univ. Press, 1977.

Scott, Hilda. *Does Socialism Liberate Women?* Boston, Mass.: Beacon, 1974.

Szczepanski, Jan. *Empirical Sociology in Poland.* Warsaw: Polish Scientific Pub., 1966.

Szczepanski, Jan. *Systems of Higher Education: Poland.* New York: International Council for Educational Development, 1978.

Vinocur, Aaron, and Gur Ofer. "Inequality of Earnings, Household Income, and Wealth in the Soviet Union in the 1970s." In James Millar, ed., *Politics, Work, and Daily Life in the USSR.* New York: Cambridge Univ. Press, 1987.

Wiles, Peter. "Recent Data on Soviet Income Distribution." In *Economic Aspects of Life in the USSR.* Brussels: NATO Directorate of Economic Affairs, 1975.

Chapter 10: Post-Communist Gains in Personal Freedom

Brown, Archie, and Jack Gray, eds. *Political Culture and Political Change in Communist Systems.* New York: Holmes and Meier, 1977.

Conquest, Robert. *The Great Terror.* New York: Macmillan, 1968.

Denitch, Bogdan. "The Relevance of Yugoslav Self-Management." In G. Bertsch and T. Ganschow, eds., *Comparative Communism.* San Francisco, Calif.: W. H. Freeman, 1976.

Fainsod, Merle. *How Russia Is Ruled.* Cambridge, Mass.: Harvard Univ. Press, 1963. Especially ch. 13.

Hough, Jerry. *The Soviet Union and Social Science Theory.* Cambridge, Mass.: Harvard Univ. Press, 1977.

Humana, Charles, ed. *The Economist World Human Rights Guide.* London: Hodder and Stoughton, 1986.

Khrushchev, Nikita. *Report to the Twentieth Congress of the CPSU.* New York: Columbia Univ. Press, 1956.

Lane, David. *Politics and Society in the USSR.* New York: Random House, 1971. Especially ch. 8.

Marx, Karl, and Friedrich Engels. "The Manifesto of the Communist Party." In Robert Tucker, ed., *Marx-Engels Reader.* New York: Norton, 1972.

Medish, Vadim. *The Soviet Union.* Englewood Cliffs, N.J.: Prentice-Hall, 1987.

Medvedev, Roy. *On Socialist Democracy.* New York: Knopf, 1975.

Medvedev, Zhores. *The Rise and Fall of T. D. Lysenko.* New York: Columbia Univ. Press, 1969.

Oksenberg, Michael. "Occupational Groups and the Chinese Cultural Revolution." In Bertsch and Ganschow, eds., *Comparative Communism.* San Francisco, Calif.: W. H. Freeman, 1976.

Skilling, Gordon, and Franklyn Griffiths, eds. *Interest Groups in Soviet Politics*. Princeton, N.J.: Princeton Univ. Press, 1971.
Szelenyi, Ivan. "Socialist Opposition in Eastern Europe." In Rudolf Tökes, ed. *Opposition in Eastern Europe*. Baltimore, Md.: Johns Hopkins Univ. Press, 1979.
Tatu, Michel. *Power in the Kremlin: From Khrushchev to Kosygin*. New York: Viking, 1969.
Tokes, Rudolf, ed. *Dissent in the USSR*. Baltimore, Md.: Johns Hopkins Univ. Press, 1975.
White, Stephen, John Gardner, George Schöpflin, and Tony Saitch. *Communist and Postcommunist Political Systems*. New York: St. Martin's, 1990.

Chapter 11: Security and Alienation in Communism and Post-Communism

Abouchar, Alan. *Economic Evaluation of Soviet Socialism*. New York: Pergamon Press, 1979.
Barry, Donald, and Carole Barner-Barry. *Contemporary Soviet Politics*. Englewood Cliffs, N.J.: Prentice-Hall, 1978.
Blyakman, L., and O. Shkaratan. *Man at Work*. Moscow: Progress, 1977.
Bush, Keith. "Soviet Living Standards: Some Salient Data." In *Economic Aspects of Life in the USSR*. Brussels: NATO Directorate of Economic Affairs, 1975.
Chalidze, Valery. *Criminal Russia: Essays on Crime in the Soviet Union*. New York: Random House, 1977.
Connor, Walter. *Deviance in Soviet Society*. New York: Columbia Univ. Press, 1972.
Economist Intelligence Unit. "Country Report—China—Report No. 1, 1993." London: Economist, 1993(a).
Economist Intelligence Unit. "Country Report—Russia—2nd Quarter, 1993." London: Economist, 1993(b).
Enloe, Cynthia. *The Politics of Pollution in a Comparative Perspective*. New York: McKay, 1975.
Goldman, Marshal. *The Spoils of Progress*. Cambridge, Mass.: MIT Press, 1972.
Groth, Alexander. *Comparative Politics: A Distributional Approach*. New York: Macmillan, 1971.
Hinton, William H. "China's New Family Concept." *Monthly Review* (Nov. 1983) 35 (6): 1–28.
Huntington, Samuel. *Political Order in Changing Societies*. New Haven, Conn.: Yale Univ. Press, 1968.
Juvilier, Peter. "Crime and Its Study." In H. Morton and R. Tokes, eds., *Soviet Society in the 1970s*. New York: Free Press, 1974.
Kelley, Donald, Kenneth Stunkel, and Richard Wescott. *The Economic Superpowers and the Environment: The United States, the Soviet Union, and Japan*. San Francisco, Calif.: Freeman, 1976.
Kollontai, Alexandra. "The New Morality and the Working Classes." In Lane, *Politics and Society in the USSR*. New York: Random House, 1971. Pp. 374–77.
Lane, David. *Politics and Society in the USSR*. New York: Random House, 1971.
Mandel, William. *Soviet Women*. Garden City, N.Y.: Anchor, 1975.
Manevich, Efim. *USSR: Full Employment?* Moscow: Novosti, 1968.
Moses, Joel. "The Soviet Union in the Women's Decade." In L. Iglitzin and R. Ross, eds., *Women in the World*. Santa Barbara, Calif.: Clio Press, 1986.
Ophuls, William. *Ecology and the Politics of Scarcity*. San Francisco, Calif.: Freeman, 1977.
Parkin, Frank. *Class Inequality and Political Order*. New York: Praeger, 1971.
Salas, Luis. *Social Control and Deviance in Cuba*. New York: Praeger, 1979.
Schell, Orville. "A Reporter at Large (China)." *New Yorker*, Jan. 23, 1984, pp. 43–85.
Schmidt-Häuer, Christian. "Die verlorene Idee von der Ordnung der Dinge." *die Zeit*, Oct. 15, 1993, p.7.
Scott, James. *Comparative Political Corruption*. Englewood Cliffs, N.J.: Prentice-Hall, 1972.

Zdravomyslov, A. G., and V.A. Yadov. "Effect of Vocational Distinctions on the Attitude to Work." In G. V. Osipov, ed., *Industry and Labour in the USSR*. London: Tavistock, 1966.

Zeitlin, Maurice. *Revolutionary Politics and the Cuban Working Class*. Princeton, N.J.: Princeton Univ. Press, 1970.

Chapter 12: Beyond the Third World after the Cold War

Agnew, John. "What Is the Third World after the Cold War?" Occasional paper No. 93-03. Milwaukee, Wis.: Center for International Studies of the Univ. of Wisconsin and Marquette Univ.

Amsden, Alice. "Third World Industrialization: 'Global Fordis' or a New Model?" *New Left Review*, Oct. 1990.

Amin, Samir. *Delinking: Towards a Polycentric World*. London: Zed Books, 1990.

Baran, Paul, and Paul Sweezy. "Notes on the Theory of Imperialism." In K. T. Fann and Donald Hodges, eds., *Readings In U.S. Imperialism*. Boston, Mass.: Porter Sargent, 1971.

Bodenheimer, Suzanne. "Dependency and Imperialism: The Roots of Latin American Underdevelopment." In Fann and Hodges, *Readings*, 1971.

Chilcote, Ronald, and Joel Edelstein, eds. *Latin America: The Struggle with Dependency and Beyond*. Cambridge, Mass.: Schenckman, 1974.

Cockcroft, James, Andre Gunder Frank, and Dale Johnson. *Dependence and Underdevelopment*. Garden City, N.Y.: Anchor, 1972.

Dos Santos, Theotonio. "The Structure of Dependence." In Fann and Hodges, *Readings*, 1971.

Erb, Guy, and Valerian Kallab. *Beyond Dependency: The Developing World Speaks Out*. New York: Praeger, 1975.

Fanon, Frantz. "The Pitfalls of National Consciousness—Africa." In Fann and Hodges, *Readings*, 1971.

Fishlow, Albert, et al. *Rich and Poor Nations in the World Economy*. New York: McGraw-Hill, 1978.

Gamer, Robert. *The Developing Nations: A Comparative Perspective*. Boston, Mass.: Allyn and Bacon, 1976.

Howe, James. *The U.S. and World Development*. New York: Praeger, 1976.

Jenkins, Rhys. *Transnational Corporations and Uneven Development: The Internationalization of Capital and the Third World*. London: Methuen, 1987.

Johnson, Harry. *Trade Strategy for Rich and Poor Nations*. Toronto: Univ. of Toronto Press, 1971.

Kaplan, Robert. "The Coming Anarchy." *Atlantic Monthly*, Feb. 1994, pp. 44–76.

Karl, Terry Lynn. "Dilemmas of Democratization in Latin America." In D. Rustow and K. Erickson, eds., *Comparative Political Dynamics*. New York: HarperCollins, 1991.

Lenin, V. I. *Imperialism: The Highest Stage of Capitalism*. New York: International Pub., 1969. Originally published in 1916.

Magdoff, Harry, and Paul Sweezy. "Notes on the Multinational Corporation." In Fann and Hodges, *Readings*, 1971.

Mitchell, S. Augustus. *Mitchell's School Geography: A System of Modern Geography*. Philadelphia, Penn.: Butler & Co., 1866.

Muir, Ramsey. *The Expansion of Europe*. Boston, Mass.: Hougton Mifflin, 1917.

O'Connor, James. "The Meaning of U.S. Imperialism." In Fann and Hodges, *Readings* 1971.

Oxaal, Ivar, Tony Barnett, and David Booth, eds. *Beyond the Sociology of Development*. London: Routledge and Kegan Paul, 1975.

Payer, Cheryl. *The Debt Trap: The IMF and the Third World*. New York: Monthly Review Press, 1976.

Ross, Robert, and Kent Trachte. *Global Capitalism: the New Leviathan*. Albany: State Univ. of New York Press, 1990.

Singh, Jyoti Shankar. *A New International Economic Order: Toward a Fair Redistribution of the World's Resources*. New York: Praeger, 1977.

Sorman, Guy. *The New Wealth of Nations*. Stanford, Calif.: Hoover Institution Press, 1990.

Soto, Hernando de. *The Other Path*. New York: Harper, 1989.

Szentes, Tamas. *The Transformation of the World Economy*. London: Zed Books, 1988.

Wesson, Robert. *International Relations in Transition*. Englewood Cliffs, N.J.: Prentice-Hall, 1990.

Wriggens, W. Howard, and Gunnar Adler-Karlsson. *Reducing Global Inequalities*. New York: McGraw-Hill, 1978.

Chapter 13: Economic Growth Strategies for the Developing Nations

Amsden, Alice. "Third World Industrialization: 'Global Fordism' or a New Model?" *New Left Review*, Oct. 1990.

Apter, David, and D. Goodman. *The MNC and Social Change*. New York: Praeger, 1976.

Bairoch, Paul. *Economic Development in the Third World Since 1900*. Berkeley: Univ. of California Press, 1975.

Brown, Lester. *Seeds of Change: The Green Revolution and International Development in the 1970s*. New York: Praeger, 1973.

Brown, Lester. "Analyzing the Demographic Trap." In L. Brown, ed., *State of the World 1987*. New York: Norton, 1987.

Calder, Nigel. *Technopolis: Social Control of the Uses of Science*. New York: Simon and Schuster, 1970.

Chaliand, Gerard. *Revolution in the Third World*. New York: Viking, 1978.

Chirot, Daniel. *Social Change in the Twentieth Century*. New York: Harcourt Brace Jovanovich, 1977.

Cockcroft, James, A. G. Frank, and Dale Johnson. *Dependence and Underdevelopment*. Garden City, N.Y.: Anchor, 1972.

Cumings, Bruce. "The Abortive Abertura: South Korea in the Light of Latin American Experience." *New Left Review* (Jan.-Feb. 1989).

Erb, Guy, and Valerian Kallab. *Beyond Dependency: The Developing World Speaks Out*. New York: Praeger, 1975.

Fornos, Werner. "Population Politics." *Technology Review* (Feb.-March 1991), 94(2):42–51.

Gamer, Robert. *The Developing Nations*. Boston, Mass.: Allyn and Bacon, 1976.

Goldthorpe, J. E. *Sociology of the Third World*. Cambridge: Cambridge Univ. Press, 1975.

Hansen, Roger, ed. *The United States and World Development: Agenda for Action 1976*. New York: Praeger, 1976.

Howe, James, ed. *The United States and World Development: Agenda for Action 1975*. New York: Praeger, 1975.

International Labor Office (ILO). *Cost of Social Security (1967–1971)*. Geneva: ILO, 1976.

Migdal, Joel. *Weak States and Strong Societies*. Princeton, N.J.: Princeton Univ. Press, 1988.

Payer, Cheryl, *The Debt Trap*. New York: Monthly Review Press, 1974.

Payer, Cheryl. *The World Bank: A Critical Analysis*. New York: Monthly Review Press, 1982.

Payer, Cheryl. "Repudiating the Past." *NACLA Report* (March-April 1985), 19(2).

Rhodes, Robert I. *Imperialism and Underdevelopment*. New York: Monthly Review Press, 1970.

Rollins, Charles. "Mineral Development and Economic Growth." In Robert Rhodes, ed., *Imperialism and Underdevelopment*. New York: Monthly Review Press, 1970.

Sachs, Ignacy. *Discovery of the Third World*. Cambridge, Mass.: MIT Press, 1978.

Sewell, James, ed. *The United States and World Development: Agenda for Action 1977.* New York: Praeger, 1977.

Sinclair, Stuart. *Urbanization and Labor Markets in Developing Countries.* New York: St. Martin's, 1978.

Singh, Jyoti Shankar. *A New International Economic Order: Toward a Fair Redistribution of the World's Resources.* New York: Praeger, 1977.

Soto, Hernando de. *The Other Path.* New York: Harper, 1989.

Tanzer, Michael. *The Race for Resources.* New York: Monthly Review Press, 1980.

"Two Faces of Third World Debt." *Monthly Review* (Jan. 1984), 35(8).

Uri, Pierre. *Development without Dependency.* New York: Praeger, 1976.

Ward, Barbara. *The Home of Man.* New York: Norton, 1976.

Ward, Barbara, J. D. Runnels, and Lenore D'Anjou, eds. *The Widening Gap: Development in the 1970s.* New York: Columbia Univ. Press, 1971.

Weiskopf, Thomas, C. Edwards, and M. Reich, eds. *The Capitalist System.* Englewood Cliffs, N.J.: Prentice-Hall, 1972.

Weitz, Raanon, ed. *Urbanization and the Developing Countries.* New York: Praeger, 1973.

Wilbur, Charles, ed. *The Political Economy of Development and Underdevelopment.* New York: Random House, 1973.

Wolf, Edward. "Raising Agricultural Productivity." In L. Brown, ed., *State of the World 1987.* New York: Norton, 1987.

World Bank. *World Development Report 1990.* Oxford: Oxford Univ. Press, 1990.

United Nations. *World Economic Survey 1987.* New York, United Nations, 1987.

Chapter 14: Inequality—Failures in Social Justice

Adelman, Irma, and Cynthia T. Morris. *Economic Growth and Social Equity in Developing Countries.* Stanford, Calif.: Stanford Univ. Press, 1973.

Bairoch, Paul. *The Economic Development of the Third World since 1900.* Berkeley: Univ. of California Press, 1975.

Baran, Paul. *Political Economy of Growth.* New York: Monthly Review Press, 1957.

Barnett, Richard, and Ronald Muller. *Global Reach.* New York: Simon and Schuster, 1974.

Bhagwati, Jagdish, ed. *Economics and World Order from the 1970s to the 1990s.* London: Macmillan, 1972.

Bienen, Henry, and V. P. Diejomaoh, eds. *The Political Economy of Income Distribution in Nigeria.* New York: Holmes and Meier, 1981.

Bodenheimer, Suzanne. "Dependency and Imperialism." In K. T. Fann and D. Hodges, eds., *Readings in U.S. Imperialism.* Boston, Mass.: Porter Sargent, 1971.

Brown, Lester. *World without Borders.* New York: Random House, 1972.

Castro, Fidel. *The World Economic and Social Crisis.* Havana: Council of State Publishing Office, 1983.

Chaliand, Gerard. *Revolution in the Third World.* New York: Viking, 1976.

Clifford, Juliet, and Gavin Osmond. *World Development Handbook.* London: Charles Knight, 1971.

Cockcroft, James. *Outlaws in the Promised Land.* New York: Grove Press, 1986.

Cockcroft, James, A. G. Frank, and Dale Johnson. *Dependency and Underdevelopment.* Garden City, N.Y.: Anchor, 1972.

Cromwell, Jerry. "The Size Distribution of Income." In *Review of Income and Wealth.* New Haven, Conn.: International Association for Research in Income and Wealth, 1977.

Dos Santos, Theotonio. "The Structure of Dependency." In K. T. Fann and D. Hodges, eds., *Readings in U.S. Imperialism.* Boston, Mass.: Porter Sargent, 1971.

Enloe, Cynthia. *Bananas, Beaches, and Bases: Making Feminist Sense of International Politics.* Berkeley: Univ. of California Press, 1989.

Evans, Peter. *Dependent Development: The Alliance of Multinational, State, and Local Capital in Brazil.* Princeton, N.J.: Princeton Univ. Press, 1979.

Fann, K. T., and Donald Hodges, eds. *Readings in U.S. Imperialism.* Boston, Mass.: Porter Sargent, 1971.

Fanon, Frantz. *The Wretched of the Earth.* New York: Grove Press, 1968.

Fields, Gary S. *Poverty, Inequality and Development.* Cambridge: Cambridge Univ. Press, 1980.

Frank, André Gunder. *Latin America: Underdevelopment or Revolution?* New York: Monthly Review Press, 1970.

Galeano, Eduardo. *Open Veins of Latin America.* New York: Monthly Review Press, 1973.

Gamer, Robert. *The Developing Nations.* Boston, Mass.: Allyn and Bacon, 1976.

Hansen, Roger. *The Politics of Mexican Development.* Baltimore, Md.: Johns Hopkins Univ. Press, 1974.

Hansen, Roger. "The Emerging Challenge: Global Distribution of Income and Economic Opportunity." In J. Howe, ed., *The United States and World Development.* New York: Praeger, 1975.

International Labor Office. *Employment, Growth, and Basic Needs.* Geneva: International Labor Office, 1976.

Langguth, A. J. *Hidden Terrors: The Truth about U.S. Police Operations in Latin America.* New York: Pantheon, 1979.

LeMoyne, James. "Honduran Army Linked to Death of 200 Leftists." *New York Times*, May 2, 1987.

Magdoff, Harry. "Third World Debt" *Monthly Review* (Feb. 1986), 37 (9).

Meadows, Dennis, et al. *Dynamics of Growth in a Finite World.* Cambridge, Mass.: Wright-Allen, 1974.

Meadows, Dennis, et al. *The Limits of Growth.* New York: Universe, 1972.

Mesarovic, Mihailo, and Eduard Pestel. *Mankind at the Turning Point.* New York: Dutton, 1974.

Ophuls, William. *Ecology and the Politics of Scarcity.* San Francisco, Calif.: W. H. Freeman, 1978.

Payer, Cheryl. "Repudiating the Past." *NACLA Report* (March-April 1985), 19(2).

Sachs, Ignacy. *Discovery of the Third World.* Cambridge, Mass.: MIT Press, 1978.

Sivard, Ruth L. *World Military and Social Expenditures 1986.* Washington, D.C.: World Priorities, 1986.

Soto, Hernando de. *The Other Path.* New York: Harper, 1989.

Sutcliffe, Robert. *Industrialization and Underdevelopment.* Reading, Mass.: Addison-Wesley, 1971.

Szentes, Tamas. *The Political Economy of Underdevelopment.* Budapest:Akamemiai Kiado, 1973.

Third World Studies Staff. "The Philippines: Growth of Poverty." Unpublished paper, Univ. of the Philippines, 1982.

United Nations. *Report on the World Social Situation 1989.* New York: United Nations, 1989.

U.S. Department of Commerce. *Statistical Abstract of the United States.* Washington, D.C.: U.S. Government Printing Office, 1990, 1993.

van Evera, Stephen. "The Case against Intervention." *Atlantic Monthly*, July 1990, pp. 72–80.

World Bank. *World Debt Tables 1989–90.* Washington, D.C.: World Bank, 1990(a).

World Bank. *World Development Report 1990.* Oxford: Oxford Univ. Press, 1990(b).

World Bank Group. *Assault on World Poverty.* Baltimore, Md.: Johns Hopkins Univ. Press, 1975.

Wright, John. *The Universal Almanac.* Kansas City, Kans.: Andrews and McMeel, 1990.

Zimmerman, L. J. *Poor Lands, Rich Lands.* New York: Random House, 1965.

Chapter 15: Liberty—A Difficult History

Agee, Philip. *Inside the Company: CIA Diary*. New York: Stonehill, 1975.

Birns, Lawrence, ed. *The End of Chilean Democracy*. New York: Seabury Press, 1974.

Budhos, Marina. "India—A Hard Passage Back." *Nation*, Dec. 13, 1993, pp. 721–25.

Cockcroft, James, A. G. Frank, and Dale Johnson. *Dependence and Underdevelopment*. Garden City, N.Y.: Anchor, 1972.

CONADEP. *Nunca Mas* (Never Again). New York: Farrar Straus Giroux, 1985.

Gamer, Robert. *The Developing Nations*. Boston, Mass.: Allyn and Bacon, 1976.

Gonzalez Casanova, Pablo. *Democracy in Mexico*. London: Oxford Univ. Press, 1970.

Hansen, Albert H., and Janet Douglas. *India's Democracy*. New York: Norton, 1972.

Hansen, Roger. *The Politics of Mexican Democracy*. Baltimore, Md.: Johns Hopkins Univ. Press, 1974.

Hellman, Judith. *Mexico in Crisis*. New York: Holmes and Meier, 1983.

Humana, Charles. *World Human Rights Guide*. New York: Oxford Univ. Press, 1992.

Klare, Michael. "The Military Research Network." In J. Leggett, ed., *Taking State Power*. New York: Harper and Row, 1973.

Kwitny, Jonathan. *Endless Enemies*. New York: Congdon and Weed, 1984.

Langguth, A. J. *Hidden Terrors: The Truth about U.S. Police Operations in Latin America*. New York: Pantheon, 1979.

Leggett, John, ed. *Taking State Power*. New York: Harper and Row, 1973.

Mydans, Seth. "Grenades and Shrapnel for the Priests Who Dare." *New York Times*, May 23, 1987.

Park, Richard, and Bruce Bueno de Mesquita. *India's Political System*. Englewood Cliffs, N.J.: Prentice-Hall, 1979.

Petras, James, and Morris Morley. *The United States and Chile*. New York: Monthly Review Press, 1975.

Prados, John. *Presidents' Secret Wars*. New York: Morrow, 1986.

Ranelagh, John. *The Agency: The Rise and Decline of the CIA*. New York: Simon and Schuster, 1986.

Roxborough, Ian, Philip O'Brien, and Jackie Roddick. *Chile: The State and Revolution*. New York: Holmes and Meier, 1977.

Sethi, J. D. *India in Crisis*. Delhi: Vikas Publishing House, 1974.

Sumberg, Theodore. "Freedom in the World." Monograph. Washington, D.C.: Center for Strategic and International Studies, 1975.

Taylor, Charles L. and Michael Hudson. *World Handbook of Political and Social Indicators*. 2d ed. New Haven, Conn.: Yale Univ. Press, 1972.

Tobis, David. "Foreign Aid: The Case of Guatemala." In K. T. Fann and D. Hodges, eds., *Readings in U.S. Imperialism*. Boston, Mass.: Porter Sargent, 1971.

Van Evera, Stephen. "Why Europe Matters, Why the Third World Doesn't: American Grand Strategy after the Cold War." *Journal of Strategic Studies* (June 1990), 13(2): 1–51.

Waller, Douglas. "Running a School for Dictators." *Newsweek*, Aug. 9, 1993.

Weiner, Myron. *India at the Polls*. Washington, D.C.: American Enterprise Institute, 1978.

Wolfe, Alan. *The Seamy Side of Democracy*. New York: McKay, 1973.

Chapter 16: Quality of Life—Dilemmas of Third World Modernization

Achebe, Chinua. *Things Fall Apart*. London: Heinemann, 1958.

Achebe, Chinua. *Morning Yet on Creation Day*. London: Heinemann, 1975.

Bell, Daniel. "Crime as an American Way of Life." *Antioch Review* (Summer 1953), 13:2.

Brandenburg, Frank. *The Making of Modern Mexico*. Englewood Cliffs, N.J.: Prentice-Hall, 1964.

Budhos, Marina. "India—A Hard Passage Back." *Nation*, Dec. 13, 1993, pp. 721–25.

Chaliand, Gerard. *Revolution in the Third World*. New York: Viking Press, 1978.

Clinard, Marshall, and David Abbott. *Crime in the Developing Countries*. New York: Wiley-Interscience, 1973.

Cornelius, Wayne. *Politics and the Migrant Poor in Mexico City*. Stanford, Calif.: Stanford Univ. Press, 1975.

Enloe, Cynthia. *Ethnic Conflict and Political Development*. Boston, Mass.: Little, Brown, 1973.

Evans, Peter. *Dependent Development: The Alliance of Multinational, State and Local Capital*. Princeton, N.J.: Princeton Univ. Press, 1979.

Fanon, Frantz. *The Wretched of the Earth*. New York: Grove, 1968.

Fishlow, Albert, et al. *Rich and Poor Nations in the World Economy*. New York: McGraw-Hill, 1978.

Gamer, Robert. *The Developing Nations*. Boston, Mass.: Allyn and Bacon, 1976.

Goldthorpe, J.E. *Sociology of the Third World*. Cambridge: Cambridge Univ. Press, 1975.

Gonzalez Casanova, Pablo. *Democracy in Mexico*. New York: Oxford Univ. Press, 1970.

Greenhouse, Steven. "Zaire, the Manager's Nightmare." *New York Times*, May 23, 1988.

Heidenheimer, Arnold, ed. *Political Corruption*. New York: Holt, Rinehart and Winston, 1970.

Hermasi, Elbaki. *The Third World Reconsidered*. Berkeley: Univ. of California Press, 1980.

Huntington, Samuel. *Political Order in Changing Societies*. New Haven, Conn.: Yale Univ. Press, 1968.

Kaplan, Robert. "The Coming Anarchy" *Atlantic Monthly*, Feb. 1994, pp. 44–76.

Lewis, Oscar. *Five Families: Mexican Case Studies in the Culture of Poverty*. New York: Basic Books, 1959.

Masey, Douglas. "The Economic Foundations of Immigration." *The CASID Connection* (June 1992), 7(4):14–16.

Myrdal, Gunnar. *Asian Drama*. New York: Twentieth Century Fund, 1968.

Nagle, John. *System and Succession: The Social Bases of Political Elite Recruitment*. Austin: Univ. of Texas Press, 1977.

Naipaul, Vidiadhar S. *A Bend in the River*. New York: Knopf, 1979.

N'gugi Wa Thiog'o. *Petals of Blood*. London: Heinemann, 1977.

Peattie, Lisa R. *View from the Barrio*. Ann Arbor: Univ. of Michigan Press, 1968.

Schramm, Wilbur. *Mass Media and National Development*. Stanford, Calif.: Stanford Univ. Press, 1964.

Scott, James. *Comparative Political Corruption*. Englewood Cliffs, N.J.: Prentice-Hall, 1972.

Sewell, James. *The United States and World Development: Agenda for Action 1977*. New York: Praeger, 1977.

Sinclair, Stuart. *Urbanization and Labor Markets in Developing Countries*. New York: St. Martin's, 1978.

Singh, Jyoti Shankar. *A New International Econmic Order*. New York: Praeger, 1977.

United Nations. *Report on the World Social Situation 1989*. New York: United Nations, 1989.

Wolf, Eric, and Edward Hansen. *The Human Condition in Latin America*. New York: Oxford Univ. Press, 1972.

Index

Marcuse, Herbert, 115
Marx, Karl. *See* Marxism
Marxism, 148–51, 208, 216, 238, 246–47
Massey, Douglas, 376
Matthews, Mervyn, 202
Mayer, Lawrence, 76–77, 187–88
Mays, J. B., 97
Meadows, Dennis, 322
Medish, Vadim, 222
Mesarovic, Mihailo, 322
Mexico: corruption in, 368; economy of,
    297; PRI system in, 319, 352–53
Migdal, Joel, 285
Mishkin, Alexander, 168
Mitchell, S. Augustus, 263–64
Montesquieu, Baron de, 20, 21
Morris, Cynthia Taft, 329
Muir, Ramsey, 264–65
Muller, Ronald, 317
MNCs (multinational corporations): and
    Chile, 347–49; and corruption, 369–70;
    debt crisis, 299–300; 386; extractive
    industry and, 292–95; roles of, 267–70,
    382; size of, 321–22
Myrdal, Gunnar, 294, 372

Nehru, Jawaharlal, 260, 261, 356
Nettler, Groyan, 127
Nicaragua, 351, 352
NICs (Newly Industrialized Countries),
    280–81, 285–86, 296–97, 363, 387
Niemoller, Martin, 106
Nigeria: corruption in, 368–69; income
    distribution in, 329
Nomenklatura, 161, 207, 217

OPEC (Organization of Petroleum Exporting
    Countries), 301–2, 383–84
Ophuls, William, 245, 323
Owen, Robert, 147

Parkin, Frank, 59, 60, 85, 87, 242
Parliament. *See* Liberal democracy.
Peattie, Lisa Redfield, 378
Pestel, Eduard, 322
Peters, Guy, 92–93
Petras, James, 269
Poland: church politics, 240; and Solidarity,
    165
Population growth rates, 286–89
Post-communism. *See* Communism

Prague Spring, 161
Pryor, Frederic, 72
Putnam, Robert, 90, 94

Quinney, Richard, 126

Rastyannikov, V. G., 291
Reagan, Ronald, 52, 53
Religion: and feudalism, 19, 23; fatalism
    and, 373–74; fundamentalism and,
    381–82
Rheinstein, Max, 129
Rimlinger, Gaston, 77
Rollins, Charles, 293, 294
Roma (gypsies), 212
Romania, 163–64
Rose, Richard, 193
Russia. *See* Soviet Union
Russian Revolution, 153–56

Sachs, Ignacy, 302
Sakharov, Andrei, 221, 222
Schnitzer, Martin, 78, 82, 84, 85
Schramm, Wilbur, 364
Schweitzer, Arthur, 36
Scott, James, 235, 366, 372, 373
See, Hans, 96, 126
Serbia, 164
Sinclair, Stuart, 309, 378
Singh, Jyoti, 303
Smith, Adam, 20–21
Social contract theory, 19–21
Socialism, 149–51. *See also* Communism
Solidarity (Poland), 160
Solzhenitsyn, Alexander, 220
Sorman, Guy, 271
Soto, Hernando de, 286, 310
Soviet Union (and Russia): alcoholism in,
    245–46; and crime, 235–37; dissidents
    in, 220–22; education in, 185–87,
    204–5; elite recruitment in, 206–7;
    employment in, 240–42; environment
    and pollution in, 243–45; family life
    in, 238–40; health care in, 187–89;
    housing in, 190–91; income distribution
    in, 200–202; nationality issues, 211–13;
    nomenklatura in, 207, 217; planned
    economy of, 172–74; and Russian
    Revolution, 153–56; and Stalinism,
    156, 218–20; women in, 208–10
Spiegel affair, 114–15

411